Photo No. 1
The last word in independent buses. Pro Bono Publico's Leyland Titan of April 1932 pauses to change crews at the Bakers Arms, Leyton. The busy route 511 was inspired and developed by the independents.

Diagram of the area covered by this volume as arranged in chapters.

LONDON'S BUSES

VOLUME ONE

THE INDEPENDENT ERA
1922—1934

by

K. C. BLACKER
R. S. LUNN
R. G. WESTGATE

H. J. PUBLICATIONS

ISBN 0 9502035 2 1

Printed in Great Britain by W. J. Ray & Co. Ltd., at Warewell Street, Walsall, Staffs. for H. J. Publications, 6 Ardentinny, Grosvenor Road, St. Albans, AL1 3BZ, Herts.

LONDON'S BUSES

VOLUME ONE

CONTENTS

LIST OF ILLUSTRATIONS

vii

INTRODUCTION
by
KEN BLACKER

Buses have played a vital and vigorous role in the capital for over a century. Passing through good times and bad they have adjusted to, kept pace with, and sometimes even led the ever-changing development of one of the world's greatest cities. Comparatively little has been documented about London's buses in their earlier years, about the services they provided to the public or about the men who owned or worked upon them. And generally, even where these aspects have in the past been written about, they have seldom been dealt with in depth. Public transportation in all its forms is an essential ingredient of modern living, and it seemed to the authors of this volume only right that we should discover as much as possible about London's bus history before it is too late.

Eighteen years ago, back in 1958, my fellow researchers and I decided to make a determined effort to obtain, collate and eventually publish for the benefit of others as much information as possible on London's buses. This book is the first tangible result of our years of research. We three co-authors have basically each specialised in various aspects of the subject, although so complex is bus operation that inevitably there has been a considerable amount of overlapping. Ron Lunn has concentrated mainly on research and documentation relating to vehicles, Reg Westgate has specialised on routes and garages, and I have endeavoured to cover the remaining aspects including the legal and financial background and such items of human interest as can still be unearthed at this late stage. To me has also fallen the task of bringing together the many thousands of facts and figures, combining them into what we sincerely hope is an interesting and informative volume.

In choosing the independent operators of the between-war years for our first volume we unwittingly took on a more formidable task than we had anticipated. There were over two hundred such operators, and obtaining more than the sketchiest details on many of them proved extremely difficult. Countless hours of research have been spent at Companies House, the Public Record Office, the British Museum and Guildhall libraries, local libraries, the muniments section of London Transport, British Railways archives, newspaper offices, local taxation offices, and elsewhere. Many rewarding hours have been spent "in the field", tracking down former bus proprietors, their relatives and their former staff, resulting in fascinating interviews with many of them as they reminisced over days long past. Such, alas, are the ravages of time that several of the people whose recollections proved invaluable in the completion of this work are with us no longer.

Though it is impossible to record by name each and every one of the many people to whom we are indebted for their help, there are certain names which simply cannot be omitted because of the great assistance they have given. One-time bus proprietors who deserve special mention are the late A. T. Bennett and Messrs. J. M. Birch, V. Boorer, M. Cravitz, A. Gannon, G. Harnett, F. Hart, E. L. Lewington, H. F.

Matthews, L. Perkins, J. Pike, J. M. Potter and F. Sainsbury, and the widows of the late R. de Casagrande and E. Tatnall. We have also had help from several garage proprietors in whose premises the independent buses were once based, and particularly from members of the Toler family. Historians and others who have kindly assisted in one way or another to augment our knowledge have included Messrs. John Cummings, E. Gaffney, David Gray, Charles E. Lee, Alan Nightingale, W. J. Noel Jackson, C. Newman, S. A. Newman, J. Purton and G. J. Robbins. Mr. Jack Purton kindly wrote appendix 2 dealing with tickets, towards which Mr. R. J. Durrant also made a valuable contribution. Mr. C. Preece kindly gave permission to quote from his book "Wheels to the West" and Mr. Peter Birch gave access to many of his family's records relating to their years of bus operation. We have called on the assistance of many people in our quest for interesting and, as far as possible, previously unpublished photographs with which to bring the text to life, and in this context we must acknowledge particularly the name of the late Mr. J. F. Higham whose deep interest in the independent London operators led him to photograph many of their vehicles. I must sadly mention Peter Aldridge, who was originally a fourth member of our research team but whose untimely death robbed him of the chance of seeing any of our work come to fruition. And lastly, on a happier note, I would like to thank my wife Jill for patiently deciphering my handwriting and typing the text for us.

With a multitude of small operators to cover in one volume, the problem arose as to how best to deal with them. We could have arranged them alphabetically or in chronological order of starting or ceasing business, but we finally rejected both in favour of working geographically around London starting at Plumstead in the south-east and working clockwise back round to Romford. We have taken, in their geographical sequence, the garages which the independent proprietors used, describing the operators that were based in each in their order of arrival. Many worked from more than one garage during their life span as bus owners, and where this was the case each individual operator concerned is described fully under one garage heading linked with a brief mention under other garages where appropriate. The only exception to this is the largest of the independents, Cambrian Coaching & Goods Transport Ltd., which had garages in various parts of London simultaneously and has been given a chapter of its own.

As its title indicates, this volume deals with independent (or "pirate") operators, in other words those who were unconnected in any way with the giant Underground group which controlled most of London's bus operations through its subsidiary, the London General Omnibus Co. Ltd., and two smaller concerns. The operators covered in this volume are, generally speaking, those who ran within the area which nowadays forms London Transport's territory. The great majority of these were inside the Metropolitan Police area and were governed by the stringent licensing and construction & use regulations imposed by that body. With only a few exceptions every one of the operators working short stage services within the Metropolitan Police area at the time of the formation of the London Passenger Transport Board on July 1st 1933 is included, as are all those whose operations ceased or were acquired by others prior to this date. The omissions are Thomas Tilling Ltd. and Tilling & British Automobile Traction Ltd. (fleet name "British") who, though nominally independent of the Underground group, ran in conjunction with it; the London Public Omnibus Co. Ltd. and Overground Ltd. (from January 1st 1928 onwards) which were subsidiaries of the LGOC; and three small operators on the fringe of the area who will be dealt with in a subsequent volume on country operators, namely Filkins & Ainsworth Ltd. of Harefield, F. Steer (trading as Colne Services) of London Colney, and St. Albans & District Motor Services Ltd. of St. Albans. On the other hand a few operators in and around Romford, which was outside the Metropolitan Police area, are included as this is now London Transport territory. Many independent concerns were purchased by the LGOC in 1926/27 but for legal reasons contrived to operate for a while as separate entities. For the sake of completeness we have traced those once-independent concerns through their spell of LGOC ownership to their final demise which, in nearly all cases, came on January 1st 1928.

A word of explanation is needed in regard to the many takeover dates quoted throughout the text giving the dates of transfer of businesses from one ownership to another. Unless it is specifically stated otherwise, the date given for a take-over is the first one on which the new operator has control, the old owner having ceased at midnight marking the close of the previous day. Similarly dates of withdrawal of services or vehicles represent the first day the service or vehicle concerned was non-operational, it having ceased to function actively when the previous day came to its close. Slight date discrepancies may appear to exist in regard to new vehicles, particularly in comparing the text with dates quoted in the vehicle lists (Appendix 6). This is because the text variously refers to dates of delivery, of passing the police test, or of entry into service whereas the "date new" column in Appendix 6 relates solely to the day the vehicle was first licensed for road use and a registration number issued to it. Sometimes buses were submitted to the police before they were taxed for road use and sometimes afterwards; some were even approved and licensed on the same day. Throughout the text, where specific dates are quoted these have been verified as far as possible by the authors. In cases where there is doubt about dates or any other facts contained in the text we have endeavoured to indicate that such doubts exist. Our aim has been to be as accurate as possible in the knowledge that information given in this book may be quoted and re-quoted in other works in years to come, and we have no desire to make errors that may be perpetuated in this manner. Even so we must regretfully acknowledge that, however careful we have tried to be, occasional errors may have crept in. For even official records can sometimes unwittingly be wrong and people's memories can play tricks with them as the years pass by. We are hopeful, and indeed are reasonably confident that such errors are few and far between, and we trust that we may be forgiven for any there may be.

As a sequel to describing the many operators at the time they were in business, we have—where the facts are known to us—followed the stories of the men concerned up to the present day. This also applies to the garages in which they were based, several of which are still in existence and in some cases largely unaltered despite the passage of up to half a century. Where matters are quoted concerning the present day these are accurate as at December 1975, the date which the text of this book was finally completed ready to go to the printers.

In many instances we have quoted sums of money, usually in relation to the cost of vehicles or the price for which businesses changed hands. Inflation has played havoc with our monetary system since the days forty to fifty years ago with which our story deals, and to understand the true value of the amounts quoted it is useful to remember that prices in the early nineteen-twenties were only approximately one tenth of what they would be today. £1 in 1934—the last year of independent bus operation—had diminished in real terms to a mere 14p in 1975.

We have found enormous interest in compiling this story of one of London's most colourful chapters in its bus history. It has been hard work, for most of it covers entirely new ground. But if, as we sincerely hope, you the reader find it interesting and also valuable as a source of reference, then we shall be content.

K. C. BLACKER
LONDON
OCTOBER 1976

THE CASE FOR
THE NON-COMBINE OMNIBUS.

The Principle of wholesome competition, as applied to London's road traffic has been in sharp conflict with the forces of Monopoly since 1922.

Monopoly, in its application to transport in the streets of the Metropolis, implies the strangulation of improvement in the means of travel for London's millions.

It is Three Years since the now familiar practice of attempting to crush legitimate competition was started, by the harassing and hounding of the first non-combine omnibus, the " Express," on the part of L.G.O.C. vehicles, until the police had to intervene to put an end to the abuse.

But the Public Imagination was stirred, and it began to sit up and take notice, so to speak. And one of the most noticeable developments it perceived was the remarkable improvement that almost immediately set in. Bus queues began to dwindle and disappear ; more numerous and better equipped 'buses were serving the routes that had previously been indifferently catered for.

Competition was responsible for this ; but Monopoly is the enemy of Competition. And Monopoly said : "We must crush these newcomers !"

So, the First Step was to place 1,500 more Combine omnibuses on the streets. Then the engineering of an artificial agitation against congestion of omnibus traffic on the roads of the Metropolis—a congestion for which the L.G.O.C. were themselves responsible—paved the way for the passage of the Traffic Act.

This Act, by an order of February 20th, gave retrospective force to a provision which prohibited any more 'buses from plying for hire on certain streets after December 31st, 1924.

The Effect of this was to invalidate the use of vehicles that were delivered by the makers between those two dates ; thus, at one stroke, ruining the business of some of the " smaller " owners, and depriving the public of extra means of commodious transport.

A Second Order under the Act, proposed on April 17th, by the Minister of Transport will further restrict the number of streets by 660. As the majority of these are between five and fifteen miles from Charing Cross, a much-needed development of transport between many residential suburbs and the more important business and shopping centres has been arrested — again to the public inconvenience. It is significant that these streets include every street on which trams are running.

What is this but an utterly unnecessary mandate, designed to create or maintain a passenger-carrying monopoly?

The Cure is in Your Hands. Keep the Non-Combine Omnibuses running by your continuous support. They are **Your Safeguard** against monopoly.

To-day the 'Bus Waits for You. But if healthy competition be allowed to disappear, it is the Public who will suffer, and the time will come when **You will be forced to wait for the 'Bus again.**

Issued by the Association of London Omnibus Proprietors Ltd.
Further information on this subject will be gladly given to anyone interested who applies to the Association Offices, 7 Great St. Andrews Street, Bloomsbury, W.C.2.

TAYLOR & READ, 31 Churchfield Road, Acton, W. 3.

Facsimile of a pamphlet issued on behalf of the independent bus operators in 1925.

CHAPTER ONE
THE "PIRATES"—THEIR RISE AND DECLINE

London of the nineteen-twenties is far behind us. In the half century that spans the gap between the start of our story and the present day, much has changed. The ravages of time, of war, of property developers, all have played their part in altering the outward face of London. The sounds and smells have changed too under the pressures of a society made cosmopolitan by immigration and tourism. Gracious living has given way to brashness, accepted moral standards have given way to lower ethics. Slums have been bulldozed in favour of housing estates and high rise blocks, where neighbourliness finds survival more difficult than ever before. All around there has been change, some good, some bad. But one feature for which London has long been famed still remains; its fleet of red double-deck buses is still to be found everywhere. Of course the units that comprise this fleet come and go according to their age and to the ever present blight of obsolescence. But the overall service which they provide remains, despite its myriad critics, as world famous today as it was in the nineteen-twenties.

This is not to say that London's bus services have been without their ups and downs. At the time of writing they are trying to emerge from a trough of depression which might be ascribed to years of unfortunate policy decisions and indifferent management. Sadly there has been a failure to respond to and cope with outside pressures like television and the immense increase in car ownership which, between them, have vastly altered travel patterns, particularly for pleasure purposes. Early in the nineteen-twenties the bus services in London were similarly going through a bad spell. They had failed to keep pace with travel requirements which had increased enormously once the war ended, and complaints of inadequacies and of indifference on the part of crews were bitter and widespread. A single large company, the London General Omnibus Co. Ltd. (better known by its fleetname General) effectively had complete control over London's bus services. There were four other operators besides General, but all four worked on a "pooling" arrangement with General whereby each operated an agreed proportion of the total London bus mileage, and on agreed routes. Road supervision for all of them was provided by General. Two of the companies were financially controlled by the vast organisation known as the Underground Electric Railways Company of London Ltd. as, indeed, was General, who operated these buses as an integral part of its own fleet. These were the Tramways (MET) Omnibus Co. Ltd. whose vehicles, numbering about 330. carried the fleetname Metropolitan, and the small ten-bus Southern fleet operated for the South Metropolitan Electric Tramways & Lighting Co. Ltd. The two operators not financially aligned to the Combine (a term often loosely applied to the Underground company and its subsidiaries) were Thomas Tilling Ltd., whose London fleet of petrol-electrics ran services based in garages in the south and south-east suburbs, and the London branch of Tilling & British Automobile Traction Ltd. whose 33 green Daimlers were to be found on routes 24 and 63 proudly carrying the fleetname British. There

1

was, of course, competition from trams, but in many instances these were still suffering from the aftermath of war and, in any case, as far as the company-owned systems were concerned, were connected with General through their parent company, the London & Suburban Traction Co. Ltd. This, like General, was in the Underground group, and also in the same camp were all the underground railways except the Metropolitan and the Waterloo & City. At the head of this massive organisation was the famous British-born but American-educated Lord Ashfield (formerly Albert Stanley), who enjoyed almost universal respect as a shrewd administrator and a fair employer. Also in the top echelon at Electric Railway House—now better known as 55 Broadway—was Frank Pick, the Assistant Managing Director of the Underground company and Managing Director of the LGOC. Pick's name, like that of Ashfield, has become legendary in the history of London's transport. He was a man who set high standards which he expected others to follow, and he is a prominent figure in our story because of his bitter opposition to the small private bus owners who began to come on to the London scene in the summer of 1922.

In that fateful summer the corridors of Electric Railway House were buzzing with rumours. A new bus had been seen; a chocolate and cream vehicle with the name Express. It was going to run in London. Inter-departmental memos were circulated requesting information on the new bus. Frank Pick wrote to George Shave, the LGOC's Operating Manager & Chief Engineer. Shave wrote to Harry Lansdown, the Traffic Superintendent, who passed the message on down the line to his Divisional organisations. "I was told that buses have been seen in London recently with the word "Express" upon their panels. Have you any information as to this Express 'Bus Company?" Inspectors made discreet enquiries at Dodson's coachbuilding factory at Willesden on a Saturday late in July, and elicited the information that the bus was a Leyland which was being bought by a man called Partridge for £1,600 at a third cash down (£530) and the balance, plus 5%, by twelve monthly instalments of £93 12s. 0d. Equally discreet enquiries at Scotland Yard revealed that the bus had been inspected and had passed their stringent driving tests with twenty points to the good. Certain minor modifications had to be made to the bodywork before it could be finally 'plated' but, despite this, it was unofficially reckoned to be the finest bus yet presented to Scotland Yard. Harry Webb, of Tilling's, tracked the actual vehicle down to Leyland's depot near the Elephant & Castle. Finally, there came the information that the Express was to be plated on Saturday, August 5th, at Battersea Bridge Road police station, where it was down in the diary to appear at 8.30 in the morning. Rumour had it that the bus was going to run between Liverpool Street and Shepherds Bush and, working on the assumption that this was correct, General made arrangements for buses manned by hand-picked crews to work fore and aft of it wherever it went.

The man 'Partridge', whose name was linked with the new Express bus, was Arthur George Partridge. In 1922 he was a completely unknown quantity, a man whose business ability was so far untried. He soon turned out to be a man of great determination in the face of relentless

2

opposition by the LGOC, aimed at driving him out of business. Later, as his business skill became apparent, he became accepted as the unofficial leader of, and spokesman for, the many men who were to follow his example in becoming London bus proprietors. Even Frank Pick, who had little time for most of the private bus owners, held Partridge in high esteem.

Partridge got the idea of buying a bus through travelling around London in his capacity as a taxi driver, where he could not help noticing the inability of the bus services to cope with passengers, especially at rush hours. It seemed to him that General and its associates were doing little, if anything, to meet the demand, as the inadequacies in the bus services persisted month after month, the months extending into years. He felt sure that there was room for private enterprise which, wisely operated, would help to fulfil an urgent public need and, at the same time, show a reasonable margin of profit. With two former war-time colleagues to back him up in providing capital and working as crew members, he ordered a bus.

The inadequacy of the bus services provided by General and its associates had become so bad that a large section of the travelling public had lost confidence in their ability, or even their desire, to provide a truly public service. Of course the LGOC saw matters in a different light, and it was labouring under difficulties to which the ordinary man in the street was oblivious. The war had seen the commandeering by the military authorities of large numbers of buses, and this had left the LGOC with a heavily depleted fleet which could not be brought up to the desired number of units overnight. According to figures provided by the Home Office, there were 3,522 buses licensed in London in 1913. In 1920 there were 3,182, a decrease of 9.6% despite the huge increase in passenger demand. The general public, who were naturally quick to criticise what they regarded as glaring inadequacies, really had little or no conception of the economics of bus operation. The same, of course, applies today. From its inception, motor bus operation had seldom made stable profits, and in 1920 the Common Fund administered by the Underground group had been required to provide £286,942 to make good the loss on the year's bus operations. 1921 saw an upswing in results and the LGOC traded profitably in that year, but at the same time no less than £1½m. had to be expended on new vehicles and on the construction of an overhauling and coachbuilding factory at Chiswick. The LGOC was by no means completely insensitive to its inadequacies, but equally it was determined to retain its complete grip on London's bus services and not to let its trading results drop back into the red. It did not intend to tolerate opposition under any circumstances, and it saw its task of bankrupting Partridge and his colleagues as one of great urgency for, if they were seen to succeed, the flood-gates could well open to let in a large number of private bus owners from which chaos could ensue.

At about midday on Saturday August 5th 1922 the Express bus entered service on the LGOC's route 11, and from the very outset the opposition it encountered was remorseless. In its early days it was seldom to be seen without LGOC chasers in front and behind. Inspectors charted its movements and officials in plain clothes even travelled on it to observe its workings. A typical day in its early career was August 8th, its first Tuesday in service, when it started work at 12.5 p.m. from the "Worlds End" at Chelsea, travelling via route 11 to Liverpool Street. Two LGOC chasers picked it up there, and accompanied it when it departed at 1.3 p.m. bound for Shepherds Bush carrying two passengers. Only six more people boarded en route, and when the bus arrived at Victoria at 1.30 p.m. Partridge took it out of service. He parked it outside the "Spread Eagle" in Grosvenor Road, where he perhaps went for a conference of war over a pint. At 2.20 p.m. the bus proceeded to Parliament Square where Partridge held a demonstration before about 100 people, calling attention to the "persecution" he was suffering. The policeman on point duty finally moved the bus on, and it then toured around the Charing Cross area with Partridge on the back platform drawing the attention of passers-by to the two LGOC buses which were now both closely following behind it. As it appeared that there was no likelihood of the Express bus going back on to service for a while, the two chasers were withdrawn, and Partridge did not, in fact, sally forth into service again until 6.15 p.m. at Charing Cross Station. The chasers picked him up at Munster Road, but this time Partridge was obviously determined to carry on, chasers or not, and for the rest of the evening the convoy of three, two LGOC's and the Express, ran up and down between Hammersmith and Victoria. The Express would have made three complete round trips, but one journey was cut short at Walham Green coming from Shepherds Bush because the chasers were so close that it was picking-up no customers at all. By the time the Express finally went off service for the day at 9.58 p.m., its sum total of passengers had been a mere 106.

On the face of it the low number of passengers carried spelt out a recipe for disaster. But, though he often became discouraged, Partridge resisted the temptation to give in, though he later admitted that he got close to doing so at times. The tide was turned after an interview reluctantly given to a young reporter from the Daily Herald. This reporter's sympathetic story of the ex-servicemen, striving to obtain an honest living but being persecuted at every turn by the heartless monopoly, quickly caught the public imagination. The story was taken up by other sections of the national press and within a week people from John O'Groats to Lands End knew about the trials and tribulations of the Chocolate Express, as it became popularly known. The LGOC felt obliged to bow to the pressure of the press, and after the end of the day's operation on August 12th it withdrew the chasers. Officials in plain clothes still kept close observations on the Express bus, particularly on its passenger loadings, and they were told to report any LGOC crews who, through reasons of sympathy, held back or speeded up to give the Express bus a clear road.

Partridge and his colleagues had successfully crossed their first and most difficult hurdle. Conversely, the LGOC had lost a battle it could not afford to lose. At Electric Railway House they knew that it would now be only a matter of time before further private buses came on to the roads of London, followed by more, and more. For the Express was seen to prosper, and inevitably others would wish to join in the apparent prosperity. The trouble, from the LGOC's point of view, was that there

4

were no regulations to control the number of buses on London's streets, or their movements. The LGOC and its associates ran a network of regular scheduled services, each bus having its own timecard showing its appointed journeys. In other words, though no licensing procedure, as we nowadays know it, then existed, the LGOC and its associates had voluntarily adopted their own system of regulations which they were able to maintain through their position of monopoly. Indeed the LGOC ran many services, particularly in suburban districts, at a loss, relying on the principle of cross-subsidization from the better-paying routes to achieve an overall trading surplus. The only regulations to which motor buses were subject were in relation to the type of vehicle operated and the routes over which each type could run. Under powers of the Cab and Stage Carriage Order 1917 (Statutory Rules and Orders 1917 No. 426), article 4(3)(a), the Commissioner of Police of the Metropolis was empowered to require bus owners to submit any new type of vehicle for police examination. They also had to specify the route or routes upon which they intended to ply. The Commissioners specified the wording for route and destination boards, and additional or extended routes could not be operated until after due notice had been given to the Commissioner, and approval received. Nothing in the regulations prevented a bus owner from changing from route to route as often as he liked provided the routes were ones upon which he had approval to operate. The powers of the police extended as far as specifying the type of vehicle which could work along any particular road, but they had no jurisdiction over the number of vehicles on a road.

Just as the LGOC had feared, the Express Leyland paved the way for other independent buses. On September 7th 1922 the large Samuelson coach concern put into service three double-deckers converted from charabancs. On November 12th Percy Frost-Smith started up in business with a pair of petrol-electrics of his own design, and a few days later George Adams' Straker Squire called Primrose took the road. After him came Bernard Cosgrove with a pair of buses named Admiral. At the end of 1922 there were five independent operators running thirteen vehicles, the largest fleet being that of Frost-Smith which now totalled six. From February 1923 onwards new independent operators came on the scene every month, bringing with them a variety of colour schemes and a whole host of fleetnames. From a mere trickle of new operators at the end of 1922, there developed a steady stream in 1923. In 1924 the stream became a flood. The LGOC was clearly perturbed at the situation, and justifiably so. They tried at first to reintroduce the chaser system. This inspired A. T. Bennett, the proprietor of some of the Admiral buses, to display on the back panels the conundrum—"Why is an Admiral like a troopship? Because it always has its escort." Before long the sheer number of new independent buses being introduced ruled chasing out of the question, and the LGOC then retaliated in the only other way they knew how, by flooding the roads with large numbers of extra buses of their own irrespective of cost. Thus, in 1923, on Lord Ashfield's own admission, the LGOC placed 1,060 additional buses in service. At the end of that year the Home Office figures showed a total of 5,117 buses licensed in London (of all ownerships) compared with the 1920 figure of 3,182. The position with regard to the actual number of independent operators and

5

vehicles was difficult at that time to ascertain as some operators lasted only a short time, but the LGOC estimated that on January 31st 1924 there were 208 private buses in 74 ownerships. At the end of that year these figures had increased to 501 and 180 respectively.

At first the independent buses were welcomed by the travelling public, who were frustrated by the seeming indifference of the LGOC and its crews. Painted in a variety of colours, these made a great impact, and people began to look to see what new fleetnames they might see passing by. They found the fleetnames of great interest, especially some of the more humorous or bizarre of them. People even wrote to the newspapers to say how many new names they had seen. But in time the independents made things bad for themselves in their scramble for business. They were nicknamed "pirates" by the press, and by Lord Ashfield, who remembered that the same term had been applied before the war to horse-bus proprietors who worked outside the established associations. And some revelled in being regarded as "pirates" and behaved accordingly. Almost without exception they went where passenger pick-ups were likely to be heaviest, with the result that some of the most lucrative routes were flooded-out with independent buses. Incredible as it now seems, over sixty operators ran at times on routes 11 and 73, whilst the 27 and 29 were almost as popular with over fifty independents recorded on each. Like sheep, they followed each other on to the best routes which, naturally enough, quickly ceased to be the best routes. Local authorities began to be apprehensive about the independents' activities within their areas, particularly about their lack of concern for public service and even about the danger to the public which some of their methods of working involved. Instead of complaining, as they had in the past, about the insufficiency of buses, some local authorities began to feel that there were too many buses around. In July 1923, for example, the Council at Southgate was complaining about the effect the excessive number of buses on route 29 was having on road surfaces, which were beginning to break up. Chronic overbussing led to fare cutting, which started in June 1923 with route 29. Not only did some of the independents offer return and workmen tickets, but soon most of them were offering the most ridiculous of low rates. General had no option but to follow suit, and the net result was that little extra traffic was generated per bus, but overall receipts were falling lower than ever. The folly of this action soon became apparent to all, and in 1924 the 'Fares War' abated, though on May 18th 1925 nearly all independents cut their fares once again.

As a rule the earliest independents did not display route numbers on their vehicles, though there were a few exceptions to this, such as Frost-Smith, who unsuccessfully tried to establish numbers of their own. From the spring of 1923 the fashion quickly caught on whereby independents displayed the LGOC route number applicable to the route, or section of route, over which they were travelling. The LGOC had no copyright over its route numbers. Sometimes, if they were following a combination of LGOC routes, independents would display the route number applicable to the longest section of the journey, and in some cases they used a number which was vacant in the LGOC series. Details

6

of where this is known to have happened are outlined in the history of the operators concerned and also in appendix 1.

Some bus owners applied to run over large numbers of lengthy stretches of road, applying, in effect, for any conceivably profitable bit of route that they may forseeably have wished to ply along. The huge British Empire Exhibition held at Wembley in 1924 only increased the number of route applications, Wembley acting like a magnet to many operators for a few, short, profitable months. Though, as a result of public demand, the Exhibition re-opened for a further season in 1925, the independents could no longer run there (except on Sundays) as schedules had become regulated, as we shall see later. Here is an example of the vast range of route approvals granted to a single bus, the Regent. Storage of all the appropriate route boards must have been a headache as they had to cover:-

Cricklewood	— Victoria	East Acton	— Liverpool Street
Shepherds Bush	— Dulwich	Shepherds Bush	— Liverpool Street
Cricklewood	— Dulwich	Cricklewood	— Old Ford
Stanmore	— Liverpool Street	Wembley Park	— Stoke Newington
Roehampton	— Camden Town	Wembley Park	— East Ham
Hampton Court	— Hornsey Rise	Wembley Park	— Liverpool Street
Hendon	— Liverpool Street	Wembley Park	— Liverpool St. (via Victoria)
Ladbroke Grove	— East Ham	Hampton Court	— East Ham
Hampton Court	— Highgate	Richmond	— Stoke Newington
Golders Green	— Wandsworth Bridge	Hampton Court	— Strand
Raynes Park	— Upton Park	Camden Town	— Reigate
Kings Cross	— Tooting		

Inevitably racing occurred between competing buses, and some hair-raising exploits were recorded. And it didn't always stop short at racing, for sometimes one driver might try to ram another into an obelisk, or at least force him on to the pavement. The LGOC was as guilty in this respect as the independents, a favourite practice amongst LGOC crews being that of 'pushing an odd-un along'. (To LGOC staff, the independents were usually known as "odd-uns".) Lord Ashfield, addressing the Acton Chamber of Commerce on March 5th 1924, had something to say about racing and also about his use of the term 'pirate', over which he had, he said, received some very offensive letters. He had never intended to use the word in the offensive sense (he said). "They are just as much entitled to put omnibuses on the road as we are. They operate within the law—sometimes—just as we do (laughter). I do not believe their buses engage in racing; neither do ours—all the time (laughter)." Tempers often ran high, and when they did the poor passenger was the last to be considered. By 1924 racing and other malpractices had become so rife that the press, local councils, trades associations and, of course, the police, were all expressing concern at the situation which was rapidly deteriorating. The LGOC and its associates tried to maintain the established order of things, but the sheer weight of independent competition on the best paying services meant that the combine's efforts to maintain regulated services were inevitably eroded.

Police court cases for speeding and other associated offences were commonplace, and the situation got so serious in mid-1923 that questions were asked about it in the House of Commons. The more lurid cases frequently received coverage in the newspapers, and they did no good to either side. On balance the independents began to suffer the heaviest as public opinion turned against them. Already many had found it expedient to repaint their vehicles in colours resembling those of the LGOC, in place of the variety of greens, yellows, blues and browns with which many of them had started, simply because the public was beginning to show reluctance to board odd-coloured buses. This reluctance was largely caused by the independent owners themselves who made a common practice of switching routes or curtailing their journey if they saw the opportunity of grasping greater custom other than where they were going. Time after time passengers found themselves with the balance of their fares refunded, ejected on to the pavement so that their independent bus could change its route. Sometimes crews would feign mechanical trouble or shortage of petrol to get rid of passengers. The even more unscrupulous would put the passengers off, telling them to retain their tickets and wait for the next bus of the same name to come along. Sometimes it never did. Activities such as these helped to make the name of 'pirate' stick.

Naturally there were those among the independents who abhorred the practices of their colleagues, just as they resented the stigma attached to being called a 'pirate'. They genuinely wanted to provide a public service and to earn a fair living in so doing, and they saw only ruin lying ahead if the chaotic state of working was to continue. The many owners varied widely as to their backgrounds and their business abilities. A few of the independent companies, such as Central, were subsidiaries of larger business concerns, and several others (twenty-two in all) were existing coach operators to whom the operation of stage carriages was a natural follow-through. Some also had garage and haulage interests and, in fact, the total number of independent bus companies known to have motor industry connections of one sort or another totals forty-two. At least twelve companies were started-up by LGOC drivers and conductors and a further fifteen were run by men who owned, or had previously owned taxis. Other budding bus owners came from a wide variety of trades unconnected with transport, including no less than five publicans. Many who bought buses had little or no experience of the intricacies of buswork; even more had no grounding in business and accountancy methods, or in the control of staff. A feature common to very many of the independent bus proprietors was that they had been servicemen who had left the forces after the armistice and were unsettled in their post-war employment. They had their gratuities from the forces, and it seemed to them a good idea to invest these in the down-payment on a bus. Many were owner-drivers or conductors who worked very hard indeed to secure a living. Others, though they did not drive or conduct, found the bus business very demanding. John Pike of the Claremont once recalled that there were many occasions when he was at functions in the West End or City, which he had to leave prematurely after a phone call from the fitters to say they had too much to do to get the buses out in time next morning. There was nothing for it but to lend a hand all-night in the garage.

Inevitably the trade attracted the worst elements too, including disreputable company promoters. The Henslowe Bus Co. Ltd. was a glaring example of a glowing prospectus being issued to attract unwary investors to put money into a business that could not hope to prosper, and hence into the promoters' pockets. Sidney Moreton, whose prime objective right from the start was fraud, ultimately found himself in deep water over his London and New London buses, but not until after he had successfully relieved others of their savings.

There were a few people who, for one reason or another, made all the necessary arrangements to run a bus, but backed down from doing so at the last moment. W. H. Lawrence of Pasley Road, Walworth intended to run a Straker Squire on routes 11 and 73 from June 1923, and J. E. Maurice obtained approval for a Daimler with the fleetname Metrobus to run on the 11 in May 1924. Neither operated. Perhaps they got cold feet when they thought of the enormity of the task ahead of them, or perhaps they had last-minute money difficulties. We shall probably never know. The Federal Omnibus Company of 23A Napier Road, West Ham, was formed early in 1925 with the intention of running a Daimler in London service. It never did so, probably because it was unable to obtain satisfactory in-town schedules owing to the London Traffic Act having come into force. This was definitely the reason why J. W. C. Tatler of 19 Ridley Mews, Kensington gave up his plans to run a bus. He had—misguidedly as things turned out—delayed entering the bus business until the Act was placed on the statute book in the belief that the passing of the Act, with its attendant compulsory timetables, etc., would make things much easier. So sure was he of making an easy entry into the industry that he even joined ALOP.[1] He could not have been more wrong. Another recruit to ALOP at about the same time as Tatler and whose ambitions were likewise thwarted, was a potential operator with the curious trading name of G-Speed. Doubtless there were other prospective operators whose schemes also, for one reason or another, fell short of fruition.

Where did the independents get their staff from? Many worked the buses themselves, of course, but to crew just one bus for a day needed four men so there were very few cases where proprietors did not have to seek employees. Very many of these employees came from the LGOC. Most were attracted by the higher rates of pay which the independents offered plus, in many cases, bonuses on takings. Some simply preferred the prospect of working for a small concern to the claustrophobic atmosphere of the LGOC who lost many good staff to the opposition. But some bus owners were less than careful when selecting staff and were happy to take men who had previously been discharged from the LGOC for dishonesty or other malpractices. Not surprisingly some of the independent companies suffered badly from pilfering of cash, and some soon began to experience a rapid turnover of staff to the detriment of the business as a whole.

Busmen worked long hours and the only days they had off, apart from their summer holidays, were Sundays once a fortnight. But, though the job was a demanding one, it also had its lighter side, for busmen generally developed a racy sense of humour. Mark Cravitz of the Grafton recalls, for instance, the harmless tricks busmen from opposing companies would play on each other in a good-humoured way. A

1 The Association of London Omnibus Proprietors. See page 11.

9

favourite place for crews on the 511 to play practical jokes was at the Royal Forest Hotel, Chingford, during the long Sunday layovers. A kipper tied to the exhaust pipe was a popular trick. On one occasion a crew retaliated by placing a child's enamel potty, found discarded amongst the undergrowth in Epping Forest, surreptitiously under an upstairs seat. It rolled and rattled all over the place each time the bus went round a corner.

A key factor to success or failure was each owner's business acumen and his ability to obtain the loyalty and confidence of his staff. Men like Arthur Gannon of the Prince who were regarded as harsh but fair, had few staff problems. Nor did organisations with the family touch, like Wellington, where one of the Reeves family would always have tea and hot toast and dripping available for staff when they arrived at their railway arch office in Cambridge Heath. Chocolate Express, the original independent, introduced a pension scheme for staff, which was something even the LGOC's employees did not enjoy. A feature of buswork in those days was that each vehicle had to be taken off service for roughly a fortnight once a year for a complete overhaul. On these occasions, and also when a bus was receiving routine maintenance or being repaired after a break-down, the better employers would pay the crews at a reduced rate although they did not work. Less generous employers worked on a basis of no bus, no pay. Thus, staff faced with a fortnight out of work during a major overhaul, sometimes sought temporary employment on someone else's buses otherwise they and their families would be without food. Even the four Perkins brothers, who were self-employed on their own bus, would go to work on A. T. Bennett's Admiral buses for the two weeks when their own was away being overhauled.

There was no form of standardisation between employers as far as rates of pay were concerned, and some paid much more generously than others as these few examples from the year 1926 show.

	Basic Pay Per Day Drivers		Basic Pay Per Day Conductors		Bonus
	Mon.-Sat.	Sun.	Mon.-Sat.	Sun.	
A1	15/-	22/6	15/-	22/6	1/- in £1 over £3. 2/- in £1 over £4.
Alberta	14/7	18/3	14/7	18/3	10% over £4. 12½% over £5.
Celtic	14/6	25/-	13/6	25/-	1/6 in £1 over £20 per week early turn and 1/6 in £1 over £24 per week late turn.
Central	14/6	18/1½	14/-	17/6	2/6 in £1 over £4 Mon.-Sat. 2/6 in £1 over £5 Sun.
Direct	15/-	15/-	14/2	14/2	Nil
E.P.	13/4	20/-	12/11	17/6	3d. in £1 Mon.-Sat. 6d. in £1 Sun.
Fleet	15/-	20/-	14/-	18/-	Nil
Horseshoe	14/7	18/-	13/7	18/-	2/6 in £1 over £5
Royal Blue	15/-	22/6	13/-	19/6	Mon.-Fri. Nil 10% over £5 Sat. 10% over £7 Sun.
Uneedus—					
Route 29	14/8	30/-	13/4	28/-	Nil
Route 551	13/4	13/4	12/-	12/-	

Quite early in 1923 the realization came upon the independent proprietors that they would benefit from the formation of a mutual self-defence organisation. On June 23rd F. W. Prowse, the owner of the Fleet buses, announced that a meeting had taken place attended by forty bus proprietors at which it was agreed to form an association. A committee of seven was appointed to go into the whole matter. The result was the formation, on November 1st 1923, of the Association of London Omnibus Proprietors Ltd. ALOP was a company limited by guarantee, and its principal objects were to promote, safeguard and protect the interests of members in relation to their respective businesses of motor omnibus proprietors, and to provide and procure concessions and facilities for them. There was to be co-ordination to promote economy and efficiency between members, and also co-ordination over fares. It built up a library of route and fare boards which it supplied at a moderate cost; it secured advantageous insurance terms, and gave advice on suitable garage accommodation. The Association also functioned as an arbitrator in disputes between members. There was an entrance fee of £2 per member, and each member contributed the sum of 5/- per week to the Association in respect of each vehicle he owned. Only one vote was granted to each member irrespective of his fleet size. There was a Management Council which could not exceed fifteen, and the original Council consisted of W. J. Dangerfield, Percy Frost-Smith, A. G. Partridge, J. B. Parrington, H. O. Parmenter, W. F. Mallender and F. W. Prowse. The Association secured an office at 19 Woodstock Street, W.1., and appointed Sir Charles Cleveland as Secretary. The solicitor to the association was James Richard Cort Bathurst, for whose expert advice and tireless efforts on their behalf many of the proprietors had reason to be deeply indebted over the years to come.

The formation of ALOP did not come a moment too soon. Opposition to the independents was mounting, not just at public opinion level but in high quarters. The Metropolitan Police made it quite clear that they were opposed to the continuance of the traffic free-for-all in London, and in December 1923 Supt. Bassom was appointed to act as Director of Traffic Services to deal with London's increasing traffic problems and to advise upon them. He was bestowed with the temporary rank of Chief Constable, and he soon made it obvious that he had little or no sympathy for the independents. Then, of course, there was Lord Ashfield. His opinion of the independents was summed up in his report for 1923 when he said that "their intention appears to be to snatch a doubtful gain by snatching at the cream of the traffic without a thought of what is to be done for the thin milk and without a care for what is meant by public service." Ashfield had been placed in a predicament which he did not like. The independents had overrun many of the Underground group's tram services, especially the London United Tramways' service along the Uxbridge Road, and in consequence the LGOC had not been able to restrain any longer its own operations in tramway areas. The tramway companies' joint income was down by £57,000 compared with 1922 and no dividends could be paid. It was a serious situation. Ashfield was preaching that there must in future be a halt to the free-for-all, and when Ashfield preached people listened. Moreover he had a powerful if unlikely ally in the Transport & General Workers Union which had secured a satisfactory arrangement in relation to the LGOC but had few members in the independent companies, and did not appear interested in getting more. The TGWU openly stated that it saw no place in London for small bus proprietors, whose businesses should be closed down. Lastly, there emerged from County Hall the most dangerous opponent of all, Herbert Morrison, the leader of the Labour Party in the London County Council. In 1923 he already had his dream for the future of London's transport, and this dream did not include capitalism in any form. Though, at this stage, his power had not reached the zenith that lay a few years hence, his voice was nonetheless one that was heeded. In their dealings with him, the independents found his attitude to be not far short of hatred.

Through Parliament, during 1924, passed the London Traffic Bill which received Royal Assent on August 7th. Regulation and restriction lay ahead. The appointed day for the London Traffic Act 1924 to come into force was October 1st. It was a far-reaching Act designed to facilitate and improve the regulation of traffic in and near London, and it ensured a far greater personal intervention in traffic matters by the police than had ever before been envisaged. Much of the Act, such as its provisions for dealing with the development and improvement of the existing system of road communications, and the co-ordination of street works by the public utilities, lies outside the scope of this book. We are here concerned with the sections of the Act dealing with bus operation. Section 6 of the Act was of particular significance, for it required each proprietor to deposit schedules of routes and times. The schedules applied only to Mondays to Saturdays, on which days each bus had to adhere strictly to the schedule deposited for it. Schedules could not be changed to another route, or even re-timed on the existing route or routes, without police approval. As far as Sundays were concerned, the previous arrangement still held good whereby the operator was free to work where he wished provided due notification had been given to police and provided also, of course, that the vehicle concerned was an approved type for the route or routes concerned. Section 7 of the Act was of equal significance in that it empowered the Minister of Transport, on the advice of the London & Home Counties Traffic Advisory Committee, to designate streets as 'Restricted' and, on Mondays to Saturdays, to limit the number of buses passing along these streets. The London & Home Counties Traffic Advisory Committee was a body set up under the Act to advise the Minister on a wide range of matters connected with traffic. Many organisations were represented on the Committee including the police and local authorities. The independent bus operators had a spokesman at first, F. W. Prowse of the Fleet, but he resigned in May 1925 as a protest against the way the Act was being implemented which, he alleged, brought the independent proprietor face to face with ruin. Under the Act, the police were made responsible for authorising fares and for allocating route numbers. In November 1924 a list of approved routes with their appropriate numbers was issued by the police. It was a massive document and was based on routes that were operating in the summer of 1924, showing the terminals, the streets traversed, the types of bus suitable, and the route number under the new system of numbering which was popularly known as the 'Bassom' system. In addition the police had added a number of routes which they judged, from replies received to a draft published earlier, might be introduced later. Generally speaking LGOC routes retained their existing numbers, though suffix letters to denote branches off the main route were done away with and a number 100 higher was allocated instead, or sometimes even a completely unrelated number. Letter suffixes were in future used to denote each short working, making the system unnecessarily complicated and resulting in buses displaying numbers like 29F and 295E which meant little or nothing to the travelling public. A second list of routes, twice as large, was published in April 1925. It contained some routes which had run since December 1st 1924 but were not on the old list. In 1926 many defunct routes were deleted from the approved list.

The ALOP fought hard against the London Traffic Act even though many of its members saw that order had to be brought out of the prevailing chaos. In fact its members were divided in their views. Some thought legally enforceable schedules would bring them the financial stability they needed through elimination of competition. Others thought that they would go to the wall if they were no longer allowed to seek without restriction the maximum passenger traffic. A lot depended on how astutely the proprietors chose their scheduled routes and timed their buses. Unfortunately there were many operators who had no idea how to compile schedules and the police found themselves having to accept temporary schedules rather than have nothing at all, while the operators concerned struggled to overcome the complexities of it all. In an effort to clear up the confusion once and for all, Chief Constable Bassom convened a meeting at Scotland Yard early in December, to which all operators were invited, where he explained to them exactly what was required under the Act. The dead-line for implementation of the scheduling procedure, which had twice had to be deferred because of the unreadiness of many of the independents, was finally fixed for January 1st 1925.

The independent proprietors, having got over this first hurdle, were soon confronted with the next one when, on January 13th, the Minister of Transport notified his intention to declare as 'Restricted' certain streets in the central area. On February 17th the first Restricted Streets Order was published and it included most of the roads served by buses in inner London, including the City. Operators were horrified to find that the Order was retrospective from January 1st, as this meant that many of them who had placed buses in service since that date, after correctly depositing schedules and fare charts, would have to withdraw them and find routes which were not restricted. This effectively meant that any of the main, good-paying routes were now out of the question. Chief Constable Bassom again convened a meeting at Scotland Yard, this time for March 2nd, to explain to operators exactly what the Order meant. He admitted that "some of the private owners will be a little hit by the new Order, chiefly those who have put on new buses since the New Year and others who are endeavouring to augment their existing services." ALOP protested strongly about the unfairness of the Order and circulated a statement in the House of Commons in support of its annulment.

Considerable sympathy was evoked amongst MP's and several questions were asked in the House. To these questions, the Minister replied on March 12th, "there may be cases of real hardship and I understand the (London & Home Counties Traffic Advisory) Committee are going into these cases and I hope they will be able to recommend the fullest sympathy it is possible to give to this class of people. I do not think there are a great number, but I will do everything in my power to avoid injustice to them." Meanwhile, Chief Constable Bassom produced for distribution a list of "Suggestions for Routes in Unrestricted Streets." These included the 526, which had originally been suggested by Cornwall, and which—as we shall see later—became the famous West London Association service. On April 17th the Minister declared his intention of making a second Restricted Streets Order, this one to include nearly every tram route, and on June 5th he announced that the Order had taken effect from June 3rd. He also gave a warning that he intended to impose cuts on bus services running over tram routes, though several more months were to elapse before he took any further steps in this direction. The London & Home Counties Traffic Advisory Committee set up a "Hard Cases" Committee to deal with the effect of the Restricted Streets Orders, and, though occasionally operators managed to obtain the Committee's approval (through the Minister) to change services—Westminster were particularly successful in this respect—on grounds of hardship, most failed to get a sympathetic hearing. This was probably because the London & Home Counties Traffic Advisory Committee was to a great degree judge and jury. After all it was they who, in the first place, had advised the Minister and who had selected the streets and suggested the introduction date for each Order. One good thing which happened was that, on June 18th, the Minister re-dated the first Order to February 17th. This enabled several operators who had been badly hit by the retrospective nature of the Order, to return their buses to their original operations, and it saved a few from early financial collapse.

Though highly unpopular with the faction amongst bus owners who wished to 'pirate' without any consideration for public service, the London Traffic Act was, overall, a good piece of legislation for it brought stability at last to the London bus scene although many suspected that it was operated with a bias towards the LGOC, as in the case of Birch's route 214 (see chapter 7). Admittedly some of the small operators quickly went to the wall after the Act was implemented, but they may well have done so anyway. A lack of capital, or of business acumen, or both, was bound to defeat them in the end. The fact that quite a number of independents were able to develop very profitable businesses which most sold out either to the London Public Omnibus Co. Ltd. in 1927/8, or compulsorily to the London Passenger Transport Board in 1933/4, at extremely favourable rates, illustrates that the Act was not to the detriment of the independents at all provided they were capable of adjusting themselves to work within it. Indeed, once the Restricted Streets Order had begun to become operative, each schedule became a valuable possession.

The Act had a most interesting side effect. It produced a number of

14

important services upon which independents worked in co-ordination and in a fair degree of harmony. The idea of independents working their own services on a regular headway basis was not completely new. Timpson's had developed a successful operation along these lines in south-east London, and City had contemplated such an operation for some while, from which developed the famous route 536 which they operated in conjunction with United and Birch. The other major independent services to develop as a result of the introduction of the Act were 511, 525 and 526, upon which a maximum of 16, 12, and 16 operators worked respectively. They were selected from the police list of suggested routes by operators whose buses were made redundant by the retrospective first Restricted Streets Order, or by operators who bought new buses after Orders had come into effect, prohibiting them from main LGOC routes. There were a few cases of other routes from the same list being similarly tried-out but proving unprofitable, of which the 527 is probably the best example. Most of the seven operators on this subsequently transferred to the 526. Though the influx of new independent buses eased-off considerably from 1925 onwards because of the Act, there were naturally some operators enterprising enough to wish to expand further. Many of them looked to the rapidly-expanding northern suburbs, and a number of useful routes were developed, notably the 551. The bus-owners in the far east of London were even more fortunate as they were ideally situated to expand in line with the L.C.C.'s massive programme of house construction in and around Dagenham, and their efforts culminated in the very profitable route 293.

A number of operators' associations were set up to bring together the bus owners on routes where several were working. They were mostly very loosely-conducted affairs whose main aims were to co-ordinate schedules and fares. Several died a natural death because of petty jealousies between members, and in the absence of anyone strong enough or with sufficient time to devote to the association. Thus, after the East London Association's secretary, Mark Cravitz of the Grafton, got tired of the antics of some of his fellow proprietors on the 511, the association broke up. The North London Association of proprietors on the 284A fell apart as the smaller concerns began to get suspicious of the motives of W. J. Dangerfield of the Overground, who dominated it. This association was of interest in that some of its members' buses carried the association's name on the route number stencil above the number. There was an attempt to form the North East London Association for operators on the single-deck route 263. H. H. Clench was the prime mover in this, and for a short while his tickets bore, on their backs, the inscription "NORTH EAST LONDON ASSOCIATION. These first class saloons for hire." As with the East and North London Associations, the scheme proved a failure. On the other hand, the West London Association, which covered route 526, was very successful and in a class of its own. It formally adopted its title on August 31st 1925, and regular meetings were held and a minute book kept. Birch Bros. Ltd. did the administration, including scheduling, and provided two inspectors towards whose salary each member contributed. The West London Association even adopted a common livery for all members of red and white with a gold star insignia, and a free combined map and timetable was issued. Each bus on the route was allocated a running number, and each proprietor kept to his allocated number which meant that he always retained his same position on the schedule, there being no weekly variations to even out the proportion of good and bad journeys. In April 1927 the running numbers were allocated as follows: A1—4 Robert Thackray Ltd., A5 J. D. Thackray, A6 Favourite, A7—11 Cornwall, A12 Glandfield, A13 Paragon, A14 The Royal, A15 Tally Ho!, A16 Clarence, A17 Alma, A18 Varsity, A19—21 Birch. This association ceased after most of its members sold out to the London Public Omnibus Co. Ltd. during 1927.

The Metropolitan Police were very vigilant in making sure that buses kept to their schedules, and both uniformed and plain clothes men kept a particularly careful eye on the independents. The independent owners rightly claimed that the amount of attention paid to their operations by the police was out of all proportion to that given to General and its associates. The reason for this was obvious; independent buses were individualistic and comparatively small in number, so it was easy to keep trace of their activities. General had so many buses on so many routes that no-one was really able to check whether an individual vehicle was complying with its schedule or not. Thomas Tilling Ltd., who were in a similar position, ran unscheduled buses illegally on numbers of occasions and there is no reason to suppose that General did not do likewise. The attention paid by the police to the independent buses was well justified judging by the number of cases which were brought to court in 1925 and early 1926 for failing to maintain a regular service and using a bus on a 'restricted' street otherwise than in accordance with the schedule. Magistrates were treated to a wide variety of excuses for the schedules having been ignored though they must have suspected that, in almost every instance, the real truth of the matter lay in the fact that the bus had departed from schedule because the crew thought it would be more profitable to do so. Take, for example, the time when H. O. Parmenter appeared before the West London magistrate. On November 14th 1925 his New Times bus on route 11 had run from Liverpool Street as far as Hammersmith Broadway, where it halted instead of going on to Wembley as scheduled. Then, without route number stencils or service boards, it proceeded to Fulham football ground. The crew disputed that they had gone to the football match and claimed that they had taken the bus to its garage in Fulham Palace Road because the engine kept breaking down. It was coincidental that the garage was near the football ground. The conductor admitted that there were passengers on board, but they were persons who knew him and he took no fares. He was certainly not carrying them to the football match. The magistrate concluded that the police were correct in their evidence, but in this case he held that Parmenter, as licensee, was not to blame for the misdeeds of his crew, and he was dismissed on the payment of five guineas costs.

At the same court T. E. Greenwood stood in the dock because, on January 9th 1926, one of his Enterprise buses on route 14 was seen in Fulham High Street by PC Watts showing 'Putney High Street' as its destination. About ten minutes later it returned en route for Kings Cross, so it was safe to assume that it had, in fact, gone to Putney. It should have gone to Hampton Court. The driver and conductor stated that there

16

was nothing about Hampton Court on the timecard, and it was produced in evidence to prove that this was so. Greenwood admitted that the timecard did not accord to the schedule. He said, "It's not much good running to Hampton Court. We tried it once and took sevenpence." As he had two previous convictions, he was fined £5. H. E. Briskham used a novel defence when he appeared at North London Magistrate's Court on March 25th 1926 for an offence committed earlier that month. His Hav-a-ride bus should have run from its garage at Wood Green direct to Hadley Highstone to pick up its first scheduled journey of the day at 8.00 a.m. to Victoria, but at 7.20 a.m. it was seen plying for hire in Highgate. Briskham's defence was that he was committing no offence in working outside the hours specified in his schedule; that, outside these hours, he could work as he wished. The Magistrate's interpretation of the Act did not co-incide with Briskham's, and he was fined ten shillings with three guineas costs.

Throughout London, police court cases also continued unabated on a variety of other topics of which speeding came top of the list. Overloading was another all too frequent offence, and on one occasion in May 1925 Admiral was convicted at Enfield Police Court because one of its 26-seaters arrived at Enfield Town with no less than 46 passengers on board. Despite the London Traffic Act, a certain amount of racing continued to take place between independent buses and those of the combine companies. At 11.20 p.m. on the evening of December 23rd 1925 a "thrilling episode in the bus war" (as it was later described in a newspaper) took place between an Admiral and a General on a northbound run from Wood Green. They first clashed while climbing Jolly Butcher's Hill when the Admiral, which was on the outside, edged inwards and forced the General's front nearside wheel to mount the pavement. Battle then commenced and they cut and weaved, irrespective of oncoming traffic, until after about half a mile the General forced the Admiral on to the pavement and considered matters all square. Four General passengers got off in preference to completing their nightmare journey although they had paid to go further, and a lady passenger from the Admiral was so scared that she took refuge in Wood Green police station. There she made the complaint that resulted in both drivers being fined £5.

Perhaps we should interrupt our narrative here to take stock of the different types of vehicle the independents were running. As we have already seen, the police had old-established powers to inspect and approve every type of stage carriage used in the metropolis. Before any new model from a bus manufacturer could enter service in London it had to conform to the extremely rigid standards set by the police. They were conservative almost to a fault in the interests of public safety and this conservatism had the effect, for a few years, of stinting bus development. Covered tops on double-deckers, for example, were strictly taboo and so were four-wheel braking systems. Each bus had to pass a police inspection once a year, prior to which it had to be completely overhauled and repainted. This generally meant that the body had to be removed from the chassis and returned to its builders, or to firms specialising in body overhaul, of which the principal exponent in London was Birch

Bros. Ltd. The chassis was normally overhauled by the maker or an agent, though a few of the larger independents such as Admiral dealt with their own. Most of the smaller businesses lacked the equipment to carry out major repair work, which meant that their overhauls were relatively more expensive that those of, say, General, because of the need to employ outside contractors. The annual overhaul was, indeed, one of the independent bus owner's principal expenses. After overhaul, each bus was subject to rigid inspection before it could go back on the road.

Between overhauls buses were subject to the scrutiny of police officials from the public carriage office who had the power to call at garages in the night to inspect the condition of the buses, and who could also order buses to be taken out of service during the day if they thought there were defects present which warranted such drastic action. Buses with a minor fault could be issued with a '24-hour stop', which meant that the vehicle could go out again next day provided the fault was rectified. More major defects received a 'full stop', and this meant that the vehicle could not re-enter service until it had been submitted for examination at the local branch of the public carriage office (which was normally the local police station) with the fault or faults rectified. One of the most common reasons for a vehicle to be 'stopped' whilst on service was excessive noise, and it was of course well known in the trade that a judicious application of sawdust in the gearbox would often cure this, at least temporarily. Rattling windows and boards were always a problem, but it was sometimes found that a half-crown tip to the right examiner could ease the situation. On one occasion Red Rose unwisely put a bus back into service after a police 'stop' without repairing it, but the police found out and taught Red Rose a salutory lesson by suspending all their licences for a day.

We have already seen that overhauls worked out proportionately more costly for the independents than for the LGOC. This also applied to routine maintenance costs, because the indpendents did not have the same advantage of buying their supplies in bulk at discount rates. Some kept a very minimum of spares so that nearly every breakdown meant a panic journey to the dealers for replacements. Othèrs went to the opposite extreme and tied up large amounts of capital in parts sufficient to cover any possible emergency. Similarly standards of maintenance varied from one extreme to the other and, whilst some independent buses were markedly superior in turn-out to anything the LGOC had to offer, others tried to get away with running vehicles in an appalling condition.

Except for minor examples in the outer suburbs, all the independent buses up to 1925 were double-deckers. Here again, though there were a few exceptions to the rule such as the petrol-electrics of Cambrian Landray and Percy Frost-Smith, they were nearly all of standard, police-approved types of five makes, Leyland, Straker Squire, Thornycroft, Dennis and Daimler, to quote them in order of appearance.

The first independent bus was, of course, the famous Chocolate Express Leyland. It marked the start of the LB series (LB standing, it is thought, for 'London Bus') of which the best-known models were the

18

LB2 and the LB5. The model was based on the standard Leyland lorry chassis, but the frame was widened behind the dash to give greater steadiness as a double-deck bus. A large steel reinforcement plate was fitted where the chassis bent. The only real departure from Leyland practice was the constant mesh gearbox on which, according to a contemporary report, "the gearwheels are provided with herring-bone teeth which are always in mesh . . . it is very silent." Quiet running was something the police were very insistent upon, and it proved a difficult problem for engineers as there was no equipment then available for recording noise levels, which remained very much a matter of personal opinion. Anyway the Leylands, with their highly efficient four-cylinder side-valve engines, ran fairly silently and extremely efficiently. Like any other machine they had their faults, such as the tendency for rear wheels to crack (Birch recorded seven failures at one time on their fleet of nine), but by and large they were superb vehicles. An early design deficiency, which gave them a wider turning circle than their competitors and thus got them banned by the police from certain tight spots, including popular termini such as The Swan, Sudbury and Hampton Court, was rectified with the LB5. Possibly the biggest drawback with the Leyland, certainly up to the end of 1923, was the manufacturer's inability to quote an early delivery date. Even when a date had been agreed upon, there was always doubt as to whether the machine would turn up on time or not.

Straker Squire, on the other hand, could deliver almost immediately, and were also able to construct their own bodywork to comply with police requirements. In fact there was almost nothing on a vehicle Straker Squire could not construct; their factory at Edmonton was extremely well-equipped. In 1919 they had decided to standardise on a single commercial vehicle model and brought out their well-known A-type with its unusual semi-forward control driving position. Their London bus was a modification of this, the main difference from the standard model being in the gearbox which was given a cast iron shell instead of aluminium to make it less resonant and thus quieter running. "To possess an 'A' type machine is to become a supremely satisfied owner" said Straker Squire's publicity. And to be sure the A-type was a splendid design—on paper. It had an overhead valve engine, built entirely at Edmonton, which developed 54 bhp at 1,000 rpm and drove through a single-disc clutch. When it was on form it was fast, very fast. In fact a Straker Squire in good condition was unsurpassed in London for speed. But the o.h.v. engines embodied push rods which could become loose and very noisy, and sometimes even fell out. The chassis design did away with torque rods or radius rods and there was a unique springing system, sliding at the rear, which did the duty of the torque rods and had the effect of softening the starting jerk. This had the side-effect of causing the body to roll, and the Strakers soon got a bad reputation for skidding. Sometimes, if they got right into the kerb on a slippery-wet day, it was almost impossible for the driver to get them out again until the next road junction was reached. Because of the design the propeller shaft was unduly long and there was a tendency for it to develop a skipping-rope action. In 1923 an A-type chassis cost approximately £800 compared with £1,050 for a Leyland so, with its quicker delivery, it could hardly fail to sell well to independents. During

19

1923 83 Strakers entered service compared with 66 Leylands. But the Straker's infamous performance soon became legendary, and once the Dennis came on the scene at much the same price, Straker's sales began to tail off. They ceased altogether in October 1924.

The Straker Squire company was subjected to a number of damaging rumours which did little to help its reputation. One was that it was buying back secondhand chassis, reconditioning them, and selling them off as new vehicles. The fact that it was making a heavy trading loss gave credence to such rumours in some people's minds, and did not help it in its strenuous efforts to make a financial recovery. Its money troubles came to a head in 1925, and it was purchased by the Aurora Trust (formed by Joynson-Hicks, the well-known solicitors to the LGOC). Thereafter the supply of spare parts to the London independents dried up, and this hastened the demise of the Straker Squire on London streets.

The Basingstoke firm of Thornycroft introduced the first completely forward-control bus which independents could buy. By the time Pioneer put the first J-type into London service in July 1923 the LGOC had large numbers of forward-control vehicles of the K and S types in daily use. But these were built by AEC who, being a member of the Underground group, was expressly prohibited from selling its vehicles to London independents. In any case the LGOC designs, though modern in their forward-control configuration, lacked the finesse or speed, or both, of the Leyland, Straker Squire and Dennis. So did the Thornycroft, which was little changed from the standard reliable, but slow-moving, J-type lorry chassis except for the revised driving position and special rear springing to give the requisite flexibility for passenger work. At 50, the seating capacity was the highest an independent could buy, but these were ponderous buses and only thirty-four of them saw service in London. Most ended their working lives with Thames Valley whose rural operations were better suited to their characteristics than was the hustle and bustle of London.

Following hot on the heels of the Thornycrofts came, in August 1923, the first Dennis, destined for A1. These were similar to and every bit as good as the Leylands. A Dennis, once its engine was near boiling point, would purr along happily for hours and it had a good turn of speed when required. In terms of the number of vehicles produced, this was the most successful of the first generation independent buses. It says much for the high standard of Dennis design in those days that no single modification of any importance was required to the standard commercial chassis design. It may be of interest to record such minor details as the police insisted should be altered, which in themselves were trivialities compared with the many difficulties which the other manufacturers encountered in this respect. The front wheels had to be 850 mm instead of Dennis's customary 720 mm, the hubs had to be modified so as not to project beyond the body line, a tray had to be fitted under the engine to catch drips of oil and petrol, and the ordinary steering wheel had to be replaced by one of non-flammable type. The engine was a side valve unit built at Dennis's White & Poppe factory.

A Daimler entered London service in the same month as the A1 Dennis; it was called the BBP. It was not a new vehicle, but was a reconstruction

20

by Josiah Morris Roberts of the Cathnor Motor Works, Shepherds Bush, of a war surplus chassis. Roberts specialised in rebuilding and selling Daimler vehicles, but to get one into a condition where it would pass the eagle eyes of the Metropolitan Police marked the culmination of many months of trial and error, sweat and tears. Eventually, after the official tests on Putney Heath, the police had to concede that there was no doubt about the vehicle's suitability for public service. Some major structural alterations had taken place, including the lowering of the frame by 6 inches by reducing the bend of the front dumb irons and the use of shorter spring brackets. The wheelbase was lengthened by 1ft. 3ins. Deeper channels were required for the frame and the front wheels had to be repositioned to correspond with the track of the rear wheels. The cylinders of the 40 hp engine were fitted with new sleeves and the crankshaft reground and set in new bearings. The gearbox had new wheels and shafts in the original casing and the differential gearing was renewed and so were the anchor brackets for the springs. Ball and roller bearings were renewed throughout the vehicle, and other new items included a longer propeller shaft, universal joints, Zenith carburetter and Simms magneto. Production of a batch of vehicles based on the original began in November 1923 and an average of two a month was completed up to March 1925. The motor taxation authorities regarded each as a new vehicle to which they issued a new registration number, and each application for a log book bore the inscription by Roberts, 'This is to certify that this vehicle has never before been licensed and same has been assembled by me at Cathnor Motor Works, Shepherds Bush of 95% new parts and 5% used ex Govt. Parts.''

The performance of the Daimlers can fairly be described as variable. The sleeve-valve engines, by their very nature, needed more care and attention than normal types. A few of the Roberts Daimlers ran reasonably well, but many soon proved highly unreliable. Some, indeed, were atrocious, and brought their owners close to ruin because they were off the road so frequently. No fewer than ten of them failed to see two years service and some, such as the Daisy, Cosmopolitan and Fairlop, were sent back to Roberts by dissatisfied clients after less than a year, never to run again. A number of legal wrangles ensued, but Roberts remained unperturbed by these and by the widespread dissatisfaction at the exorbitant price he was charging for repair work and spare parts. His buses were not particularly cheap to start with. For instance a standard vehicle with new Hickman bodywork cost £1,450 in December 1923 whereas a Dodson-bodied Dennis retailed for only about £1,414 (there were slight variations according to specification). The reason Roberts managed to dispose of over thirty of his machines probably lay in the fact that he was able to entice customers with the easiest of hire purchase terms. It is interesting to note that the original BBP Daimler lasted longer than many. This might perhaps indicate that it was rebuilt to a higher standard than many of those that followed.

Amongst bodybuilders, Christopher Dodson Ltd. was prominent throughout the independent era. If ever the independent busmen had an angel in disguise watching over them it was Christopher Dodson, whose death at his Jersey home in 1959 at the age of 85 marked the passing of a very kind man. He detested monopolies and in his later years as a coachbuilder would not carry out any work for the LGOC for this reason. The bus bodies turned out from his Cobbold Road, Willesden, factory were of the highest quality. More than this, he was always ready to help and advise his customers on bus operation, on financial matters and, indeed on almost anything else, and even today some of the survivors still recall his kindnesses. He even suggested fleetnames for some of the less imaginative of his customers as J. M. Potter of the Cardinal is pleased to admit. He arranged hire purchase terms at reasonable rates by means of his own extensive private capital, and if any of his customers were unable to pay in a particular month due to illness or for some other good reason, he was willing to defer payment until they could.

The Dodson design of body was later copied almost identically, and without permission, by the Wilton Carriage Co. Ltd. Christopher Dodson threatened taking action against Wilton for infringement of his company's registered design, which may account for the fact that no Wilton bodies were built for London service after 1925. In April 1924 a Wilton body cost approximately £395 compared with £442 for the equivalent Dodson version, but there is evidence that the Wilton was somewhat less sturdily constructed. Birch built bodies which externally were also very similar to the Dodsons, the majority being for their own use plus a sprinkling for outsiders. They could be distinguished from the Dodson and Wilton products by the absence of the second line of waist-rail mouldings below the windows.

Another major supplier was Strachan & Brown Ltd. which was then one of the country's leading coachbuilding concerns. Its gentle decline did not set in until the nineteen-thirties. Though similar to, and somewhat more expensive than the Dodson, the Strachan & Brown version was distinguishable in having slightly shallower windows and, in profile, the side panels were slightly curved. Dodson and Strachan & Brown bodies appeared on Leyland, Dennis and Thornycroft chassis. Strachan & Brown also bodied some of the Daimlers, and Dodson supplied the bodies for the Frost-Smiths and for some of the Straker Squires, though the great majority of the latter carried the chassis maker's own well-built body which was easily distinguishable in having five even-length bays. Birch and Wilton bodies appeared only on Leylands and Dennises. The Hickman Bodybuilding Co. Ltd. produced a design which was easy to identify by its short central bay and, in most cases, by its deep driver's canopy. Most of these went on to Daimler chassis but two examples were bought for Dennises and five were ordered by Cambrian Landray for reconditioned Tilling Stevens.

Buying a bus was one thing. Finding somewhere to house it was a different matter entirely. As readers will see in the narrative that follows, many of the independents had trouble finding suitable accommodation and a large proportion of them changed garage at least once in their career. Generally they sought accommodation where the garage owner provided, as part of the weekly all-in terms, someone to wash and refuel the buses and to check the water and oil levels. Many of the garage owners also carried out running repairs, a very necessary function since,

22

in some cases, the bus owners were far from mechanically minded. There were rare instances where the garage owner also attended to licence renewals, received the daily cash takings, paid out wages at the end of the week, and generally controlled the day to day running, leaving the bus owner with only one regular commitment, that of providing tickets and waybills. Arthur Bell Hewitt of the B.B. Motor Works, St. John's Wood and William Christmas of the Commercial Motor Garage & Repair Co. Ltd. at Clapham were such men. There were a few isolated cases where independents went to the extent of having their own garage built, and there were also a couple of notable cases where they built garages large enough to provide accommodation for other companies' vehicles as well as their own. These were Empress (of Wood Green) and Gray. People being what they are, garage proprietors and their busmen tenants did not always get on well together, and this accounted for some of the changes from garage to garage that bus owners made. Sometimes moves came about because cheaper facilities had been offered elsewhere by a garage proprietor anxious to increase his trade in this respect. Equally, some bus owners found themselves kicked out by garage owners exasperated by continuous arrears in rents. Some busmen worked on such a shoestring that their indebtedness to the garage owner came well down on their list of financial priorities.

An event that was later to convince many bus owners that the Minister of Transport and the police were biased against them in favour of the Combine occurred in June 1925 when the Minister announced his intention of cutting the number of buses running over tram routes. It soon became known that his first target was to be the Uxbridge Road. On June 18th he wrote to all proprietors whose buses were scheduled along the Uxbridge Road saying that he was considering that a variation might be desirable in frequency either on sections of the road or throughout. He was going to take a census. In January 1926 the real bombshell occurred when the Minister announced the extent of the cuts. On route 526, for instance, the headway was to be reduced from 9 mins. to 30 mins. which—as every operator on it realized—would almost completely kill it off. It meant that fourteen out of the twenty-one buses on the route would have to be withdrawn. A similar position occurred on the 17 and other routes using the Uxbridge Road and, as the majority of bus owners concerned were independents, their indignation at this seemingly unfair treatment was tremendous. There was immense public condemnation too, and spurred on by this, the bus owners quickly began to get signatures for a petition to Parliament. On March 6th the Minister wrote to the operators telling them to confer amongst themselves over how the cuts were to be apportioned. The operators on the 526, represented by the West London Association, decided to make no cuts, and a prominent member of the Association, Birch, wrote to the Minister protesting that this was a gross breach of faith in view of a statement in April 1925 by Chief Constable Bassom that bus operators would be secure on their schedules provided they were deposited quickly. This gentleman had died in January 1926 so was unable to defend his honour in this matter. To rub salt into the wound the London & Home Counties Traffic Advisory Committee wrote, with the approval of the Minister, to suggest that the bus operators concerned should set up a voluntary fund

23

for compensating those persons whose services may be withdrawn as a result of the regulations, since the Act made no provision for compensation out of public funds. The crux of the matter was that operators with only one bus, and there were several of these on the Uxbridge Road, could not reduce the service level without putting themselves out of business. The Minister remained aloof, and refused to meet a deputation from the West London Association. Instead he wrote to Birch indicating that, as operators would not confer amongst themselves to produce a reduced schedule, he would schedule the service himself. Birch's share of route 526 would thus be reduced from fifteen journeys a day each way to five. Inevitably the matter became one of debate in the House of Commons where, on April 1st, the Minister in reply to a question from Capt. Ian Fraser, the Member for North St. Pancras, stated, "The Honourable Members will find that in the end very little injustice will really be done." This injudicious remark brought the inevitable protests that the Minister should not condone any injustice, however little, to anybody.

The operators on the 526 steadfastly refused to comply with the Minister's Order, and no action was ever taken against them. A test case was, however, taken against Cornelius Beattie, one of the operators on other Uxbridge Road services who was designated to surrender his schedule. After a prolonged battle in the courts Beattie won the day. But the whole episode had been extremely damaging to the morale of bus owners, who were dismayed that everyone of importance was against them. In fact two of the Uxbridge Road operators, Dominion and T & W, who were designated to withdraw, actually did so. They were told that they may be found an equivalent mileage elsewhere, but as this was likely to prove inconvenient or unremunerative they sold their businesses to the LGOC, who were anxious to acquire schedules, even ones held in abeyance.

May 1926 was the month of the still-remembered General Strike, when industrial dissatisfaction and unrest reached a climax in bitter conflict. Public transport, along with all the other essential services, ground to a virtual halt leaving London almost paralysed. Volunteers endeavoured to keep skeleton services going and were regarded as public-spirited heroes or industrial blacklegs according to one's point of view. The LGOC, being strongly union-associated, came almost to a halt, but not so the independents who had very few union members amongst their ranks. Almost to a man they kept running, though in some areas they encountered hostile mobs of strikers intent on bringing them to a halt through intimidation or by breaking windows or causing other damage. Tempers ran high because both sides were convinced of the rightness of their views; the strikers saw their action as the only means to fight repression and other evils, the non-strikers saw it as their democratic right to continue to work if they so wished. In some areas the situation got really nasty. Despite police escorts, Redburn's reluctantly decided on May 4th to run no more buses through Tottenham, Stoke Newington or Kingsland Road because of the extreme danger involved in doing so. Nevertheless, they were back two days later. On May 6th no Admiral buses ran on route 29 because, on the previous day, such a vast number of stones had been thrown at drivers at Camden Town and at 'The Brecknock' junction. Next day they returned and, like all the others, carried capacity loads wherever they went. Strikers soon realised that the easiest place to sabotage buses was in their garages at night, so after a few days the police decided to centralise the overnight parking of buses in Regents Park where they would be safe under an army guard. The crews camped there with their buses, and many of them were away from their homes for several days. Schedules were suspended for the duration of the Strike and J. M. Roberts, the Shepherds Bush vehicle builder, took advantage of this to run a few buses which he had in stock in his capacity as a dealer, under the title of J. M. Roberts Motor Service. He started to run on May 6th and withdrew on about the 12th as the Strike drew to a close.

The Strike over, tempers still ran high for a long time afterwards. Walter Dangerfield of the Overground sacked everyone who was a union member; A. T. Bennett of Admiral was slightly less harsh. He sacked only those who had joined the TGWU during the Strike; those who had been members beforehand he retained. Old hostilities between Combine and independent crews, which had been on the wane, flared up again. A Universal driver, fined for exceeding the 12 mph speed limit by driving at 20 mph, claimed that he was being pushed along by a General, whose drivers had been very hostile to the independents since the Strike. A driver from General's Palmers Green garage was fined £2 or 28 days imprisonment for striking a Clarendon driver with whom he had clashed verbally during the Strike. They met on the bus stand at the Cherry Tree, Southgate, where the General driver said to the Clarendon, "You dirty blacklegging bastard", immediately hitting him in the face and knocking him to the ground. At the trial the defence solicitor remarked that the independent drivers who continued to work were always put up as the angels from heaven, and the LGOC drivers castigated as the men who went on strike.

The years 1926 to 1928 saw a mass exodus from the industry. No fewer than 54 businesses passed to the LGOC in 1926/7. Generally speaking these were the operators whose finances were slender and who would, in time, have capitulated anyway. Some, indeed, were only just saved from ruin in the nick of time by selling out. Those who remained were the stronger ones. Many of them were depressed by the large odds that appeared to be stacked-up against them and would be pleased to leave the industry, but would never consider selling out to their arch-enemy, the LGOC. Their dissatisfaction was well known in many quarters, but it came as a surprise to many of them when they received handwritten postcards dated 19/3/26 which said, "You do not stand a dog's chance under the present Capitalist system. When Ashley & Ashfield have finished you off we will welcome you into the ranks of the Communist Party." A most unlikely way to get recruits! The reference to Ashley indicates Colonel Wilfrid Ashley (later Lord Mount Temple), the Minister of Transport. General was well aware that many of the independents whose schedules it so badly required, would not consider a direct sale even on the most favourable of terms. On July 2nd 1927 a new organisation, the London Public Omnibus Co. Ltd. was formed, its stated aims being to purchase, combine and co-ordinate in strength and as an independent undertaking the businesses of the many small operators. The new company was found to be offering approximately £3,000 for each scheduled bus—about double what the LGOC normally offered—and shares could be purchased in it if desired. At the head of the business were the Marquis of Winchester and Alfred Temple Bennett, the wealthy owner of the Admiral fleet. From July 1927 to the May of 1928 Public acquired 77 bus companies holding 219 weekday schedules. Not unnaturally, some were suspicious of the new Company and how its capital was obtained; there were even rumours that Winchester and Bennett were front men for the LGOC. This, alas, proved to be the case, and though some later regretted having sold out to Public for this reason, there is no doubt that the payments they received for their businesses were, judged by the values then prevailing, generous in the extreme. In other words General had been prepared to acquire schedules at almost any price.

The prospect of being taken over by General was by no means always a bright one for independent bus employees. For a start, it nearly always meant a drop in earnings and a restriction of personal freedom. But, more important, it often heralded dismissal, and it was no joke to be on the dole queues of the nineteen-twenties. Anyone over the age of fity was automatically sacked by General and so, normally, was anyone who had previously been employed by them. Many employees of the independent bus companies fell into this category. Twenty-six was the minimum age limit, and anyone under this age was out. Many others found themselves mysteriously declared medically unfit for such things as flat feet or for being too thin. Some independents sold out in completely hush-hush conditions without even their staff being in the know. When General's officials went to take over the Lonsdale buses at their Shepherds Bush garage the staff refused to hand the buses over, suspecting a trick. Their ex-employer, Charles Hall, could not be found, and it was late in the day before the new owners finally gained control of their property. The Uneedus staff were surprised to be told by a fitter when reporting for duty at their Palmers Green garage, "You sign on over there today"—indicating the LGOC garage across the road. They had never suspected a thing.

Buying and selling of businesses was not as easy as it might seem, for with the introduction of the London Traffic Act the police steadfastly refused to sanction the transfer of licences from one operator to another. However they could not, in all justice, prevent an owner from turning his business into a limited company (though they insisted that the vehicles owned had to be submitted for a fresh inspection if this was done), and this proved to be a loophole through which licences could change hands. If one operator wished to acquire another, it was necessary for the vendor to first turn his business into a limited company. He could then dispose of his shareholding to the purchaser, and the police had no powers to stop him from doing so. General bought out many small companies by this means in 1926, though it meant, of course, that the old companies' trading identities had to be retained. The LGOC thus finished up with a large number of tiny subsidiary companies. In January

1927 the police relaxed slightly by allowing acquired buses to be painted in the livery of the parent company, although they had to retain the name of the subsidiary company in white lettering on the rocker panels. A. T. Bennett managed, in 1927, to persuade the police to abandon their opposition to the transferring of licences, indeed his scheme for the formation of the London Public Omnibus Co. Ltd. was only possible provided businesses could be bought and sold in a normal commercial way. General took advantage of this complete relaxation on January 1st 1928 when all but one of its subsidiaries were absorbed either by General or by the Tramways (MET) Omnibus Co. Ltd., the General associate. They were wound up on August 27th of the same year.

After the period of mass acquisitions, there remained 64 independent operators with 169 schedules. This figure excludes operators on the fringe of the area such as Romford which was, in any case, outside the Metropolitan Police Area and not subject to the London Traffic Act. A few more sold out later to other independents or to General but fifty remained in business until the London Passenger Transport Act of 1933 came into force, under which their businesses were compulsorily acquired to allow monopoly to be restored. Their last few years were worked in an atmosphere of security, almost tranquility, compared with earlier days. The deep financial depression of the early 'thirties hit everyone to an extent, but in spite of this some of the firms even managed to increase their schedules slightly.

Which brings us back to the buses the independents used. The early part of 1928 saw the entry into service of the very last of what might be regarded as the old "standard" London buses. Thereafter their numbers were to dwindle rapidly just as the number of unusual fleetnames had gone so quickly from the London scene in 1926-8. Pneumatic tyres had come on the scene in May 1925 when Admiral put the first of its little Dennis 2½ tonners into use in the outer suburbs. In fact Barnet Motor Services had beaten Admiral for the honour of getting approval for the use of pneumatics within the Metropolitan police area, but their little Fiats only penetrated just inside the area and the main honour for the break-through must go to Admiral. This enterprising organisation also persuaded the police to permit four wheel braking after exhaustive tests with an E-type Dennis. Thereafter it was only a matter of time before both features became standard, as did covered tops on double-deckers from 1928. The police even withdrew their objection to windscreens and enclosed staircases, both of which they once regarded with great suspicion as potential danger hazards. So, in time, the 'modern' type of bus emerged, to remain basically unchanged as far as London was concerned for the next four decades.

Two highly reliable Dennis models have already been mentioned; the 2½ tonner for up to 26 seats, and the E-type, a forward-control model normally seating 30. These both found limited favour, the first mainly on outer suburban use, and the other more usually on central area operation. For a while there was a minor craze, fostered by Admiral, for replacing solid-tyred, open-toppers with pneumatic-tyred E-type single-deckers, but the low seating capacity soon proved this idea to be a loser. Several operators bought E-types and then disposed of them prematurely to return to double-deckers. A contemporary of the E-type was the Leyland PLSC, better known as the Lion. Examples appeared in London but, though this was in most respects a classic machine which thoroughly justified its country-wide popularity, its transmission brake proved hopelessly troublesome on London's stop/start operations. Brakes that had to be adjusted daily and relined fortnightly were just not good enough. The LB's had also had a transmission brake, but it was never as troublesome.

The second generation of independent double-deckers was never as standardised as the first. It began with a pair of Guy six-wheelers, one for City and the other for Pickup, the City vehicle being the first independent bus with a covered top. The double-deck six-wheeler was becoming popular in many parts of the country because of its potentially high seating capacity, so it was inevitable that London operators would be attracted by its merits. The City and Pickup vehicles had been preceded in London service by a small fleet of Guys for Public and a few unimpressive ADC's for the LGOC. General later went on to order a huge fleet of AEC Renowns, but independent six-wheelers stayed small in number. In July 1927 Field Marshal considered buying a Karrier WL6/2 68-seater, which would have been the largest bus in London had it been built, and in January 1928 Birch ordered an experimental Leyland six-wheeler which never materialised. The ailing Sunbeam company, anxious to break into the heavy vehicle market, tried hard to sell its products in London and in 1930 delivered one of its SMC Sikhs to Ambassador. It was rejected by them, and afterwards also by Westminster, before returning to its makers for a chequered career in the provinces.

The double-deck four-wheeler remained the most popular specification. The new era of these began with a few Dennises of the H, HS and HV types, the last two being six-cylinder models. But Dennis was now starting its decline as a front-line bus manufacturer, and it was the Leyland Titan which really caught the busmen's imagination and secured their orders. This was a beautifully-designed, low-slung chassis with a six-cylinder engine that purred along but could respond to almost any demand put on it. The LGOC had brought out its drop-frame NS model as early as May 1923 but it was a mediocre machine at the best of times and bore no comparison with the Titan. The Underground group's reply to the Titan was the AEC Regent which was a very similar model, not surprisingly since both had been designed by G. J. Rackham. Perhaps on the basis of "if you can't beat 'em, join 'em." AEC was permitted to sell the Regent to the London independents, who bought ten. Too late, Dennis introduced its Lance late in 1930. The performance of its sweet-running engine was up to modern standards even if the gear-change layout was not, and it was an economical user of petrol. But its sales to independents only notched the eight mark. A pair of Daimler CF6's (for Eagle and Red Line) proved too light for London work, and the later, better CH6 found only one independent customer despite its preselective gearbox. Further novelties were a lone Maudslay ML7 for Gordon and a whole batch of City double-deckers based on the single-deck Leyland Tiger chassis. The only six-wheelers to enter independent service in the 'thirties were some reconstructions by City of old Leyland four-wheelers, a trio of new Leyland Titanics for the same operator, and an SMC Sikh for Westminster. Undoubtedly the Titan was king. Independents bought 118 of them in double-deck form plus a few as single-deckers. Crews loved them and so did the passengers, proof of this being that, wherever they were put into service in replacement of older vehicles, receipts rose immediately.

After 1930 the number of older-type double-deckers in regular all-day service showed a steady decline. Most of those that remained were converted to pneumatic tyres, but towards the end there were several of these which saw service only on Sundays and in the event of breakdowns or overhauls. The last operator of this type of vehicle on regular schedules was, rather surprisingly, City, the firm that had done much pioneering work to improve bus design and performance and who, apart from a solitary Birch Leyland, had the only independently-owned diesel-engined buses in service in London.

Two coachbuilders figured prominently in the later era. Dodson continued to hold its position as major supplier to the independents, and evolved a distinctive style of double-deck bodywork which soon became well-known throughout London. The familiar outline of the Dodson body remained basically unchanged from the summer of 1929, when the first two Titans were delivered to Triumph and Chocolate Express, through to November 1931 though minor structural alterations took place meanwhile. First the quarter-light windows were eliminated from the lower deck in November 1929 after fourteen Titans had been produced, and in August 1930 the five bay configuration gave way to six bays to provide the bodywork with greater strength. As the police were no longer as rigid as hitherto in the standards they laid down, many minor variations from the standard pattern were to be found such as would never have been tolerated in the 'twenties. Some operators favoured windscreens but many did not. Some went in for closed staircases, though open stairs were still favoured by some as late as 1933, by which time London had become, without doubt, the last bastion of this legacy from a bygone era. Some buses had roller blind indicators, others had boards, and occasional ones had both. A few copied the LGOC idea of placing the front route number in the roof dome; one or two even put the destination there. At the Commercial Motor exhibition of 1931 a new style of Dodson body was unveiled, the chassis in this case being Gordon's Maudslay. This was developed as an enclosed staircase body with a front which was almost upright as far as the top deck waist rail, above which there was a ledge from which the front windows raked back sharply. Though perhaps not handsome by modern standards, these were impressive, solid-looking bodies of which thirteen were supplied on Titan and Lance chassis. A few bodies of the older style appeared after the new model had been introduced, and indeed the last vehicle of all to be delivered to a London independent, Renown's HV 2822 of April 1933, was of this style. In addition to their own distinctive types, Dodson also built bodies to City's design for that operator's use. With their three front upper-deck windows, and their high skirt lines, these were less in keeping with modern trends than were Dodson's own designs, and would have been altogether less satisfactory in appearance had it not been for the very fine City livery with which they were embellished.

Birch was the other major supplier of double-deck bodies, though their output was considerably lower than Dodson's and a large proportion was for their own use anyway. They had a fairly standard product, generally similar to Dodson's, but with shallower windows resulting in a higher waistline and a less satisfactory overall appearance externally. Inside the saloons, the smaller windows gave a more cosy effect than on Dodson bodies, and this effect was heightened by the rich polished mahogany window surrounds and the thick-cushioned seats with their coverings of grained leather or moquette. A few open cab examples appeared on which the curved cab roofs had been given a pronounced downward droop. Ostensibly to provide greater weather protection for the driver, this was a brave endeavour to introduce a new trend in styling, and it must have held a certain appeal at the time for it induced at least one customer, Ambassador, to order a Birch body on grounds of styling where normally a Dodson would have been preferred. With the London Passenger Transport Bill going through Parliament, orders for new buses declined greatly in 1932, the year in which Birch's last three double-deck bodies were built for London service. These three, of which Birch themselves ran two and Red Rover the other, had flat, sloping fronts, of the style which was just beginning to come generally into vogue. Without doubt they were the most 'modern' looking double-deckers ever run by London independents.

Thirteen vehicles were supplied by Duple, who were not noted at the time for their activity in the double-deck sphere. They were all bought by Premier, and were almost identical in outward appearance to the first style of Titan body built by Dodson. They were such a close copy of Dodson's design that it would be charitable to assume that they were built under licence from Dodson. It is, of course, possible that Duple simply examined, measured and copied the Dodson body carried by Premier's first Titan.

A few double-deck bodies came to London independents from other suppliers. Hickman provided four rather ugly enclosed staircase bodies on Dennis H-type chassis for Martin, Pickup bought five open-top bodies from Park Royal for AEC Regent chassis, and City went to Ransomes, Sims & Jefferies for five bodies for Leyland chassis rebuilt by City as six-wheelers. The absence of Strachan & Brown will be noted. Strachan's (now without the Brown on their name) had opted out of the independent market and preferred to fulfil orders from the LGOC for bodies for their ST and LT types. Christopher Dodson, on the other hand, maintained his steadfast refusal to accept work from large, monopolistic operators of any sort, (though, illogically, he built many of the ST-type bodies for Thomas Tilling Ltd. who, though theoretically independent, worked hand in glove with General, at least in London), and with the demise of the London independents in sight he decided, in 1933, to close his works down.

In the single-deck sphere, Dodson had a standard type of body which was suitably modified to fit varying chassis. Birch also gained a number of single-deck orders, and developed a design of one-man operated bus for Bean chassis which obtained Metropolitan Police approval. There was never much real standardisation of any sort amongst the independents' single-deckers in the early 'thirties; the demand for such vehicles was fairly small anyway. In the Romford area, which, though outside the Metropolitan Police area, lies within the scope of our book because it falls inside the present London Transport boundaries, single-deckers reigned almost supreme as far as independents were concerned, but they followed provincial rather than London practice in their variety. Diminutive Ford model-T's gave way to slightly larger Chevrolets which, in turn, were displaced by bigger and more robust Dennises. Many of the vehicles in and around Romford had bodywork by Metcalfe whose factory lay on the outskirts of the town.

Starting in 1927, there was a minor craze amongst London bus proprietors to enter into the wider sphere of coaching, and many who sold out to General or Public re-invested their money in this way. Coastal coach excursions were booming and so were race course outings and private hire. Then there was the massive break-through into the sphere of medium and long-distance coach services on a regular timetabled basis, in which many bus owners participated and which ultimately cost many of them dearly. For, until the Road Traffic Act of 1930 came into force, competition on this type of operation was cut-throat to say the least, and on some services, like those on the Great North Road to the West Riding towns, Newcastle and Edinburgh, the London bus scene of 1923/4 was recaptured all over again and revived some of its worst features like racing and mindless fare-slashing. Two of the London bus companies, Premier and Westminster, built up large fleets of coaches on express services, the former on runs within the home counties to destinations such as Windsor and Aylesbury, the latter on rather longer runs to towns in East Anglia. In both cases the size of the coach fleet, which soon outnumbered the buses, ultimately justified the formation of a separate company to control it. Some other operators, of whom Prince is a good example, favoured the more seasonal but less rigid type of coach operation centred around day excursion trips and private hire, and generally fared better from it.

In its 1929 session, Parliament once again became the arena for the power struggle over who should provide London's transport. The Tory-led London County Council and the Underground group had put their heads together and produced a scheme for the co-ordination of traffic facilities in the London area. Based on what was said to be the outcome of recommendations from the London & Home Counties Traffic Advisory Committee, twin Bills were steered through Parliament entitled The London County Council (Co-ordination of Passenger Traffic) Bill and the London Electric Railway Companies (Co-ordination of Passenger Traffic) Bill. The effect of the Bills, if they were successful, would be to set up a common management embracing the Underground subsidiary companies and the LCC tramways, with a common fund into which the traffic takings on each would be paid and from which operating and other expenses would be met, the balance to be shared as profit. This would, in effect, be an enlargement of the common fund

31

which the Underground organisation had operated since 1915. The Bills gave provision for the inclusion in the co-ordination scheme on a voluntary basis of all the other providers of public transport in London. The promoters clearly expected the municipal tramways to join in, and stated that Tilling and the independent bus companies would be invited to participate also.

The Bills met opposition from the Labour and Liberal parties. In particular the London Labour Party, led by Herbert Morrison, was vociferous in its condemnation. They saw the Bills as part of a capitalist counter-offensive against public property; the vested interests behind the Tory Government and the LCC wished to dispossess the council of any effective control over its tramways. Such powers as it had formerly had over fares and alterations to services would be transferred to the tender mercies of a Board of Directors consisting almost exclusively of nominees of Lord Ashfield's companies, on which the voice of the LCC would be inadequate. How, in all conscience, asked the Labour Party, could control of the LCC's tramways be placed in the hands of people who had made such a mess of running their own tramways? Lord Ashfield himself had admitted, when reviewing the tram companies' results at the annual meeting of the Underground group in March 1928, that their fortunes since 1922 had been little short of disastrous. "If the Combine manages LCC tramways as 'brilliantly' as it has handled its own", wrote Herbert Morrison, "the outlook is black indeed." Labour made its position abundantly clear. If Parliament should be so unwise as to pass these Bills, the Party held itself perfectly free—indeed it would consider it a duty—to promote amending legislation at the earliest possible moment.

At the opposite end of the political scale was the loose fraternity which Labour saw as the worst example of capitalism, at least as far as it applied to transport in London, namely the independent busmen represented by the Association of London Omnibus Proprietors. These gentlemen were equally worried about the twin Bills which they naturally viewed as a further step towards monopoly, a further turning of the screw to put them eventually out of business. 'Monopoly' was the spectre which loomed most darkly on their horizon. They lost no opportunity to criticize the LGOC and its associates, and over the years ALOP published many tirades against the Combine and the monopolists similar to the abbreviated extract which follows. "Most of you will probably recollect how you were served by transport of the combine prior to the introduction of the independent buses and of the inadequate and obsolete facilties offered to you. The old conditions were not to your advantage. You were probably the sufferers who had to wait a considerable time for a bus or tram and when it arrived usually full, you would still have to wait with a hope of getting accommodation in the next and so the merry game of the 'Combine' went on . . . It was hardly in the interest of the 'Combine' to ascertain and provide for the Public convenience—it was your extra fares they were after." Or to quote another independent offering, "Londoners should realize the growing danger of Monopolies, which in the past 25 years have been developing rapidly in every branch of industry, particularly in that branch dealing with London's Passenger Transport . . . Monopolies are not even modern, because history tells us that they were rife 250 years ago and that the Monopolists' goods of those days were bad in quality and high in price. The Monopolists' ideas have not changed since then. Once in the power of a Combine, the Consumer (or Passenger) pays more and receives less. Competition is the Soul of Business. Ride with the Competitors of the Tram-Omnibus-Tube Combine and remember that YOUR INDEPENDENCE DEPENDS ON LONDON'S INDEPEN-DENTS.''

A peculiar feature of much of the anti-Combine criticism, no matter which side it came from, was that it sometimes leaned favourably towards Lord Ashfield as an individual, tacitly admitting that he was genuinely a public spirited man wishing only the best for the travelling public, despite being head of a great commercial Combine, and director (in 1928) of fifteen companies outside the Underground group in the spheres of transport, cinemas, banking and chemicals. But, as the London Labour Party stated in a pamphlet of 1929, "Lord Ashfield will not live for ever." He was, on his own admission, much too busy, to the extent of having to shed certain directorates. Whosoever may one day take his place, may well not be so public spirited, and what then? Looking back, it would seem that Ashfield did, indeed, care about London and Londoners. Despite their critics, and despite their administrative and other shortcomings, his companies basically operated for the public good despite the absence of any commercial obligation to do so. If this were not the case, they would not have provided unremunerative suburban services to the extent which they did, nor would they have developed the principle of cross-subsidisation (as it later became known) between loss-making and profitable services. Lord Ashfield admitted he was puzzled by the prejudice that existed against the Underground Group just because it was private enterprise engaged in public work.

The twin Bills made their faltering way through Parliament, but a new Labour Government had come into power and, at the third reading on July 17th 1929, they were thrown out on the advice of Herbert Morrison, who was now Minister of Transport. Morrison saw public ownership as the only answer to the London transport problem, and before long the civil service solicitors were drawing up a Bill for a statutory Public Utility Undertaking to take over the passenger transport facilities within an approximate 25-mile radius of Charing Cross except for the suburban services of the main line railways, which would be co-ordinated. Within the new authority's boundaries would be an area of complete monopoly of road services approximating roughly to the area covered by the 1924 Act. The Bill was introduced into Parliament in December 1930 and was heralded as "Socialism in Our Time."

Herbert Morrison treated the London independents with disdain. His dealings with Birch, for example, are outlined in chapter 7 and are an illustration of the depressing situation with which they were faced. It says much for their stamina and determination that only two of them (Martin and St. George) are known to have considered selling out to General in the early 'thirties. This was the time when Britain was going off the gold standard, when the economy was at a desperately low ebb and when, because of all this, traffic receipts were falling. Luckily these began to show an upward swing from 1933 onwards as the country struggled back on to its feet, and though the independents didn't last long to enjoy the renewed prosperity, they benefited to the extent that it was reflected in the compensation payments they received for their undertakings.

Herbert Morrison's London Passenger Transport Bill was at first subjected to determined opposition from almost every quarter, including the Underground group (whose end it would mark) and the LCC. But one by one the opposition was converted, sometimes, it would seem, after it found out the extent to which it might expect to benefit through generous compensation arrangements. On May 12th 1931 Counsel for the promoters was able to announce that agreement had been reached with the Underground group. The independent busmen, through ALOP, protested as vehemently as they could, but they knew at heart that their cause was lost. Even when it began to appear likely that each and every independent owner would finish up a wealthy man, hardly any of them viewed the prospect with relish. For most of those whose businesses survived into the nineteen-thirties were men dedicated to their profession. They wanted no other. A. G. Partridge summed up the feelings of many of them when, at the ALOP's ninth annual dinner at the Holborn Restaurant on November 7th 1932, he emphasised the despair with which he viewed the prospect of losing touch with the business for which he existed. Despite the demise of the Labour administration, the Bill continued its way through the Parliamentary process, having the support of the new National Government of August 1931. Debate on the Bill was heated and lengthy, but finally the Royal Assent was given on April 13th 1933 and the 'Appointed Day' for the London Passenger Transport Board to begin operations was fixed for Saturday, July 1st 1933. On that date the companies within the Underground group, the municipal tramways, the Metropolitan Railway and the British buses of Tilling & British Automobile Traction Ltd., were transferred to the Board.

Under section 5 of the Act, all the independent stage carriage operators within the Metropolitan Police area were listed for compulsory acquisition by the Board with the exception of H. F. Phillips of Dagenham, who had started his service after the Bill was drafted. The section 5 operators comprise all those described in these pages who were still in existence in 1933 with the exception of two Romford-based concerns, Imperial and Romford District, plus, of course, Phillips. The Romford concerns operated entirely outside the Metropolitan Police area but were within the area designated under the Act as the London Passenger Transport Area. Operators between these two boundaries could be acquired if the Board so wished under section 16, and where the Board decided to exercise its option those operators concerned were entitled to the same compensation arrangements as the section 5 cases. The Board lost no time in implementing section 5. On July 14th a letter was sent to all operators requesting copies of their profit and loss accounts for the years 1930 to 1932, the mileage on each service, lists of vehicles stating types, dates of purchase and hire purchase arrangements, details of garages, plant and fittings, notification of all continuous obligations including leases, contracts and agreements transferable to the Board, together with lists of staff. The acquisition of independent buses began on November 1st 1933. No final agreement over valuation had proved possible, so the former owners were paid an amount on account that appeared to the Board's accountants to be well within the final probable valuation of the business. By arrangement with their owners, nearly all those acquired up to December 20th 1933 remained at their former garages and, usually, under their old managements (though, of course, all money transactions were through the LPTB) until such time as a general reorganisation came about on Wednesday, January 17th 1934 under which they could be absorbed into the Central Omnibuses Department as a whole. Up to January 16th the principals of the acquired independent undertakings were paid nominal weekly salaries by the Board ranging from £2 10s. 0d. to £7 10s. 0d. per person. All companies acquired subsequent to January 1934 were directly absorbed into the LPTB organisation.

Not unnaturally, the affairs of the various operating departments of the LPTB came under officers and staff from the largest of the acquired component organisations. Thus, the Central Omnibuses Department looked like an enlarged LGOC, whilst the acquired tramways tended to become LCC orientated in administration and outlook. It was perhaps unfortunate that the former LGOC colour scheme was adopted as standard, but it was absolute folly that the name General was perpetuated and applied to the sides of acquired buses. To say the least, this practice proved unpopular, and deservedly so, for it began to look as though the London Passenger Transport Act had been a device to give General the monopoly which it had not been able to achieve by conventional business means. Imagine the ire with which bus owners, who had been forced to hand over their businesses against their will, viewed the sight of their former vehicles carrying the livery and the name of the enemy to whom they would never willingly have acquiesced under any circumstances. The fleetname London Transport did not come into general use until the later part of 1934.

With no hope whatever of saving their businesses, the independents turned their attentions to the task of extracting every possible penny from the LPTB in compensation. On September 19th 1933 ALOP announced that it had advised its members to refuse an offer to acquire all of them on a standard basis of three times their average net profits over the three years before the passing of the Act, plus the value of all acquired assets. There were two very important and justified objections to the Board's proposal. First it was clearly inadequate to take such a short period of years as three as the basis on which to compute the goodwill value, for every firm was trading profitably and could under normal circumstances have been expected to do so for well in excess of three years. Secondly, it was unfair to take as a base for calculation the average net profits over the three years prior to the passing of the Act, i.e. 1930 to 1932 inclusive, as these had been depressed years. 1932 had been the worst year of all because it had also seen a rise in petrol prices. Every bus operator knew that 1933 was showing a great improvement in results, which were steadily rising month by month. ALOP considered that 1931 to 1933 should be taken as the base years for calculating average annual profits. They advised each of their members that, if they could not conclude satisfactory negotiations with the Board, they should take their individual cases to the Arbitration Tribunal, an independent body set up under the Act, to deal with matters of contention arising from it. The ALOP's solicitor, J. R. Cort Bathurst, handled all the cases except those for Birch, C.C., City, Eagle, Pembroke and Premier who employed their own solicitors, and entered into a voluminous correspondence over each case.

Cort Bathurst and his staff worked astutely on behalf of the independents and ultimately achieved extremely good results on their behalf. After the rejection by ALOP in September 1933 of the Board's proposed basis for the calculation of compensation, the two parties found themselves in a state of impasse. Certain of the independents not represented by Cort Bathurst, such as Birch, put forward their own schemes for compensation which the Board immediately rejected as excessive, but Cort Bathurst refused to put forward schemes on behalf of his clients within the time permitted under the Act. This put the onus on the Board to submit schemes of purchase which, when they did so, revealed that they were now prepared to offer more generous terms based on five (instead of three) years' purchase of the average annual profits, plus assets, and in most cases it included at least part of 1933 in calculating average profits. The independents considered the Board's schemes inadequate and rejected them en bloc. As it was still proving impossible to find a common basis of compensation acceptable to both sides, Cort Bathurst and the LPTB agreed to submit two test cases to the Arbitration Tribunal to see if any formula would emerge from the Tribunal's findings on which compensation in all the other outstanding cases could be based. Renown and Ryan were selected as being fairly typical, and their cases were heard by the Tribunal in February and March 1935. Birch, City and Premier also took their claims before the Tribunal and, in each case, the result was unfavourable to the Board who was also faced, under the terms of the Act, with paying the independents' legal costs. These could be extremely high, for example the cost to the LPTB of the five-day Birch hearing was £6,500. To make matters worse it became apparent, on reviewing the Tribunal's awards, that it had not worked to a set formula in dealing with each of them. It had clearly not attempted to take a specific number of years' profits into account as the Board had sought to do. As a result of this, in May 1935, Cort Bathurst suggested to the Board that their searchings for a formula were in vain and that, like the Arbitration Tribunal, they should take each case on its merits. He offered to provide schemes for discussion on each of the forty-three cases still outstanding with him, provided the Board would refrain from the many deep, technical accountancy points which had helped to bog things down previously. Reluctantly the Board acquiesced, with the result that most cases were cleared by October 1935. The former owners were then paid the balance of the purchase price which carried an interest rate at 5%. The dispossessed owners could, if they wished, take all or part of their payment in the form of LPTB 'A', 'B' or 'C' Stock. Only City and Red Rover are known to have done so.

Several of the independent operators delayed for as long as they could the handing-over of their businesses, partly for sentimental reasons and partly to benefit for as long as possible from the growing passenger traffic figures which sent receipts rising steadily higher as 1933 went on, and higher still in 1934. Those who had businesses involving possible severance claims were able to delay takeover more easily than those without because of disputes over the extent of the business to be transferred. They were people who had other business activities in addition to buses which the Board was not empowered to continue. These were sometimes coaching operations which went outside the boundaries allowed for the LPTB, or, more usually, garage businesses. Such cases as these involved the Board in complicated and expensive claims for severance payment, which they were obliged to make by law, otherwise they had to acquire the business and attempt to find purchasers for the activities they were not permitted to conduct themselves. The very last independent of all, Prince, lasted as long as it did largely because of severance complications.

A particular bone of contention, and one which led to several appeals to the Arbitration Tribunal, was the extent of property to be transferred to the LPTB. The Act specified that no property acquired by the absorbed undertakings after July 1st 1933 was transferable to the Board. Notwithstanding this, ALOP advised its members to transfer property in which they were tenants into the ownership of the bus company wherever possible, and several deeds of sale to this effect were signed in late 1933. In almost every case they were almost subsequently held by the Arbitration Tribunal to be not binding upon the LPTB.

Though bus owners benefited handsomely, in money terms, from being taken over, the same did not always apply to their staff, many of whom found themselves working for lower wages in a more impersonal organisation. The Board's standard weekly rate of pay was £4 6s. 6d. for a driver and £3 19s. 6d. for a conductor. These were high in relation to most other forms of employment, and, combined with the security which the job offered, made employment on the buses highly attractive. But it was less than nearly all the independents paid. Here, as a comparison, are four typical examples:

	Drivers	Conductors
Chocolate Express	£5. 1s. 0d.	£4 16s. 9d.
Pickup	£4 12s. 2d.	£4 5s. 3d.
Renown	£5 0s. 0d.	£4 5s. 0d. (plus commission of 1/- in £1 on takings over £75 per fortnight on 15A and £60 on 293).
City	£4 12s. 1d.	£4 4s. 9d.

The Act gave provision for employees to claim compensation for worsening of conditions of service, which many of them did. The compensation took the form of a lump sum payment which, of course, varied from firm to firm. As an example, crews from the Reliance concern eligible for compensation were each awarded £17. For a man with many years still to work at a lower rate of pay, this sort of sum was but small compensation. On the other hand some of the inspectorate and administrative grades from the independent companies did well because, by virtue of their high salary levels, they found themselves placed well up

37

in the LPTB organisation (which was based on that of the LGOC) sometimes with jobs much increased in their level of responsibility over what they had been used to.

An unfortunate episode occurred while the Tribunal was sitting in 1934. At a meeting at the London School of Economics, Frank Pick, speaking on behalf of the LPTB, read a paper which conveyed the impression that the independent companies had carried on their businesses with unmoderated and undisguised selfishness and with the intention of making an exaggerated claim for compensation before the Tribunal. The independents naturally resented this deeply, especially as their cases before the Tribunal were still pending, and a series of libel actions was brought against Frank Pick and the LPTB by forty of them. Fortunately common sense later prevailed on all sides, and in the Kings Bench Division of the High Court on November 2nd 1934 it was announced that a settlement had been arranged out of court following the receipt of a suitable letter of explanation and apology from Mr. Pick.

The last independent bus, a Prince Leyland Titan, ran into its Ponders End garage in the early hours of December 5th 1934, seventeen months after the formation of the LPTB. A state of monopoly was restored; London Transport reigned supreme. The last few vehicles quickly disappeared into Chiswick for repainting, and all traces of the independents were gone from London streets. It took another year before all their Arbitration cases were settled. In February 1936 the bus owners got together for the last time for the ALOP's farewell dinner at the Holborn Restaurant. Representatives of the Ministry of Transport and the police attended, and even Frank Pick was there. The after-dinner dancing was to the famous band of Billy Cotton, who was a friend of Joseph Ryan, one of the former bus owners. The evening came to an end, and they all went their separate ways, most to new careers, some into retirement.

The independent buses may have gone from the streets but they did not disappear from memory. Even now, after forty years have elapsed, those who were young them and are old now are sometimes heard to say that it would shake things up a bit if we had the 'pirates' back again. But, in the final analysis, what did they really achieve? Admittedly they provided a stimulus to the LGOC in the mid-twenties, but there was ample evidence that the LGOC was already well on the way to setting its own house in order when the independents came along. To an extent they must even have slowed down the LGOC's service developments in outer areas, for the money which could have been spent on this went instead on bolstering up inner London routes badly hit by unregulated competition. The independents developed relatively few truly useful services of their own, though of course the famous 536 stood out as a wonderful example of private enterprise at its very best. The operators on it provided the public with a service that in its efficiency, reliability, standards of comfort, and economy was second to none. If more private operators had co-operated in harmony in this way to create something worthwhile, those who wished to cast doubts on their usefulness and sincerity would have had much less to work on. As it is, there are today only rare cases of routes which survive that were created by the independents. Of those that do, the best examples are probably the 551 (which is now part of route 34), the 263 (now 236) and 231 (now 187). This very paucity of surviving ex-independent routes speaks for itself.

On the vehicle side, the independents undoubtedly gave the establishment a jolt, for their standard vehicles, both in the first and second generations, were usually better finished, more lively and marginally more comfortable than those of the General. Almost certainly the fear of adverse comparisons led the LGOC to attain its highest standards ever when designing its famous LT and ST classes. Perhaps even more noticeable was the Underground Group's reaction on its tramways, on which almost every route was subject to heavy bus competition, where instead of bowing to this competition the companies produced the magnificent "Feltham" tramcars which remain one of the most inspired passenger vehicle designs in the history of London's transport. It is perhaps significant that in 1931, with competition at last perceptibly on its way out, the LGOC felt itself safe in reducing the standards of comfort on its "Bluebird"-type LT's and on the STL's that followed. Even so, London bus design continued on a high plane until the early nineteen-sixties, but here again it is most difficult to determine whether this would have been any less high had there never been any independents.

The 'pirates' provided employment for those who may otherwise have had none. Despite the rogues amongst them, they gained a following, a regular clientele, because they could give the personal service which a large undertaking cannot do. With the 1933 Act the last vestiges of personal service were submerged in the sea of anonymity which is the consequence of centralisation, of monopoly. True, there is no room whatever in London, or any other city or town, for unregulated competition. But by 1933 there was little competition left, the London Traffic Act of 1924 had seen to that. Regrettably, neither was there any co-ordination between the Combine and the independents. The 1933 Act brought about co-ordination all right. In fact it created a situation very much like the Passenger Transport Authorities which are favoured today as the answer to the transport evils in all the large conurbations. Could it be, though, that the 1933 Act went too far? Is the monolith organisation the answer in a business as personalised as public transport? Would the survival of a few of the best independents, under strictly controlled conditions, have provided the spur to maintain standards, the yardstick for comparison which might have kept London Transport's standards in every sphere at least a little higher than they are now? The politicians, in their wisdom forfeited our chance to know.

CHAPTER TWO

SOUTH-EAST LONDON

Our story now takes us on a clockwise tour of London, seeking out the garages used by the independents and outlining the history of the operators who were based in each of them. Unfortunately details of some operators are comparatively sparse, and this applies to the first one we meet, Mr. A. J. Paterson.

Lakedale Road, Plumstead

PAT

The most easterly-based of the independents south of the Thames was Pat, alias Arthur John Paterson. He lived at 42 Lee Street, Woolwich and when he bought his first and only bus he arranged for it to be garaged in Lakedale Road, Plumstead. Paterson's bus was XX 1896, a Daimler whose date of first registration was February 28th 1925. In its early days the Pat bus operated a variety of routes and was one of the pioneers in April 1925 of the 527. In 1926 Paterson moved his home from Woolwich to Ilford and his bus accompanied him to his new location north of the Thames. On April 19th 1926 he was given approval to operate the then unrestricted services 101E and 256 (with its various short workings lettered from 256A to D) and in time he obtained permission to move on to the 23E, 86 and 186 which were more profitable propositions. In November 1926 he arranged with A. H. Martin, who owned the Martin buses, to buy him out. The circumstances in which he did so, and the formation of the Paterson Omnibus Co. Ltd., are described in chapter 8.

The garage at 14 Lakedale Road where Paterson first garaged was once a tram depot and had been opened in 1881 by the Woolwich & South East London Tramways Co. for the operation of its narrow gauge horse cars. Ownership later passed to the LCC who ran electric trams from there until its new Abbey Wood premises became available in 1910. Today a sign with plastic letters still proclaims "TRAM YARD" as a reminder of times gone by. It is not known where Paterson garaged after his move to Ilford.

175 Rushey Green, Catford

TIMPSON'S

One of the larger and more distinctive fleets of independent buses was that run by Alexander Timpson & Son whose head office, garage and workshops were at 175 Rushey Green, Catford. The twenty buses that formed the fleet could be easily distinguished by their silver livery which, especially when it glistened in the sun, made the red Tillings which abounded in the Lewisham area look decidedly drab in comparison. The Timpson buses were only a small part of a much larger enterprise. Alexander Timpson had, in years past, run horse brakes and by about 1912 had become a well-established travel agent in Plumstead. From there he successfully developed a coach and car hire business, and also branched profitably into general cartage and furniture removals. The coaches, which Timpson began to purchase just after the close of the Great War, became the firm's main activity. By 1925 the fleet had grown to almost sixty and had carried twelve million passengers without an accident, mainly on coastal runs which included a twice-daily service to Hastings pioneered by Timpson's. Timpson's flair for publicising its "Silver" service of charabancs, and its reputation for the reliability of its modern silver vehicles, ensured success in a business which quickly became highly competitive. A natural follow-up to this success was the purchase of a fleet of buses.

Between March 1923 and April 1924 Timpson took delivery of eighteen new double deckers from Straker Squire. The first three were submitted to the police on March 20th and by April 17th six were in service. In the early days the buses ran without route numbers over various LGOC routes, notably 47, 53 and 75. Before long Timpson secured police approval to operate a comprehensive series of routes, mostly based on south-east London, as follows:-

A   Plumstead Common to Green Street Green
B   Lewisham Obelisk to Westerham Hill
C   Hither Green to Lewisham
D   Plumstead Common to Charing Cross (via route 53)
F   Plumstead Common to Bromley Station
G   Lewisham Obelisk to Green Street Green
H   Plumstead Common to Bromley Common (Crown)

Route E, which is omitted from the list, was probably intended to have been Hither Green to Victoria via Dulwich which was turned down by the police on the grounds that Dog Kennel Hill was too steep for motor buses. The grandiose scheme of seven lettered routes was soon abandoned and Timpson decided instead to concentrate on and develop just one important service of his own between Plumstead Common and Bromley (Southlands Road) via Woolwich, Blackheath, Lewisham and Catford. Several main centres of commerce which had hitherto been accessible from each other only by changing buses were now linked by a direct service, and as the headway became more frequent with the arrival of additional vehicles, so the service grew in popularity. After a while a southwards extension was introduced to Green Street Green with a branch westwards from this to Westerham Hill. No route number was carried initially but under the Bassom system the Green Street Green service became 289 and Westerham Hill became 213. Timpson buses also worked on route 47F which was more or less a short working of the 213/289 and ran direct from Rennell Street, Lewisham to Bromley Common. Green Street Green was later abandoned as a regular operation and the pattern of service became 47F and 289A (Plumstead Common to Bromley Common) operated daily augmented by a summer Sundays only 213 (Plumstead Common to Westerham Hill).

The success of Timpson's "Silver Queens"—as they became nicknamed—soon proved a source of concern to General who replied to the challenge in May 1923 by increasing the number of buses on their route 54, and in July 1923 route 2A was increased from 31 to 44 buses and extended from Lewisham to Plumstead. Meanwhile Timpson, after placing in service the last of its eighteen Straker Squires in April 1924 went on to purchase six further double deckers in March 1925. These were the interesting and ill-fated F.S. petrol electrics built and operated by Percy Frost-Smith and now being sold off by his executors (see chapter 3). Though the whole Frost-Smith fleet passed to Timpson only two of them (XM 2057/5761) were placed in service in their original form as double deckers. Three others were converted to charabancs and the sixth (XM 2056), though it remained as a double decker, stood disused in the Timpson garage.

Timpson's garage at 175 Rushey Green, Catford, merits special mention because of its transport connections dating back long before Timpson days. In the last quarter of the nineteenth century it was a horse tram depot of the South Eastern Metropolitan Tramways Company, from whom ownership passed to the London County Council on April 1st 1902 as part of the Council's policy of taking over the tramways within its area. Timpson bought the premises for conversion into a charabanc garage in 1920. Since May 1974 it has been the headquarters of National Travel (South East) Ltd.

Despite its policy of intensifying its own services along "Timpson" roads, the LGOC failed to drive the Timpson bus service out of business. Indeed it flourished, aided from the end of 1924 onwards by the stability provided by the London Traffic Act. General could only remove this thorn in its side by purchasing the Timpson buses, which it offered to do. A mutually acceptable purchase price was eventually agreed upon and on Tuesday March 23rd 1926 Timpson's Omnibus Services Ltd. was registered at 175 Rushey Green to which the assets of the bus section were immediately transferred. Two days later, on March 25th, ownership passed to General who, on the same day, re-sold the company to Thomas Tilling Ltd. as part of a balancing-up of Tilling's agreed proportion of the overall mileage worked by the "pool" companies. In fact the sale of the Timpson bus assets to Tilling overbalanced the proportion of buses on the road in favour of Tilling and to counteract this five units of the twenty strong Timpson fleet remained General property though operated by Tilling. These were Straker Squires XN 2557, XO 3947-9/51. Inevitably the Company's head office was transferred to the Tilling headquarters at Peckham on takeover and the buses were transferred to Tilling's Bromley (TB) garage for operation. On May 31st 1926 the coaching and other interests retained by the Timpson family were reorganised under the title of A. Timpson & Sons Ltd., a title which has remained unchanged to recent times. These "other·interests" included bus services based on Hastings which the company retained until 1934 when they were sold to the local Tilling & B.A.T. operators, Maidstone & District and East Kent. Coach operations based on Hastings, Ramsgate and Torquay were also disposed of at this time, and a considerable reduction was effected in the coach fleet which, at the start of the 'thirties, had reached about 250 units. The business was sold to the B.E.T. (who took 60% of the shares) and Thomas Tilling (40%) in 1944, following the death of Alexander Timpson. It is now a unit of the National Bus Company.

Tilling kept the Straker Squire fleet in service for a surprisingly long while after takeover and did not make a serious start in replacing it until February 1927. Not so the two FS petrol-electrics whose performance Tilling described as "very bad". They came to an arrangement with Timpsons to acquire two Straker Squire chassis, which had formerly been charabancs, on which to mount the Dodson bodies from the FS's. XK 6806 was one of the two acquired for this purpose; the other is believed to have been MC 9827. The body swop was completed in time for the two Straker Squires to enter service in July 1926, bringing the Tilling-owned Timpson bus fleet to one hundred per cent Straker Squire. The two FS chassis went back to Timpson as part of the same deal, the latter having found a Deptford motor dealer, Mr. E. Ash, prepared to purchase all six.

Replacement of the Straker Squires started off in February 1927 when a batch of six Tilling Stevens petrol electrics became available. These were from the former Cambrian Landray fleet which General had recently acquired, and which Tillings agreed to take from General to replace a like number of Straker Squires. They included four with the unusual IT-registration numbers, and all but one of the six had Hickman bodies and were unique amongst London Tilling Stevens in being thus equipped. The ex-Cambrian Landrays were then followed by a miscellany of fourteen Tilling Stevens chassis which varied from two to six years old and had formerly carried lorry or charabanc bodies. They were overhauled at Peckham and fitted with bodies taken from the Timpson Straker Squire chassis and upseated to carry 48. The last of the conversions was carried out on September 23rd 1927 and completed the replacement of the original Timpson vehicles. The later Tilling Stevens were painted in Tilling's red livery though they carried the Timpson fleetname. At an unknown date, as part of the balancing up of pool vehicles, the five units of the Timpson bus fleet on General's books were transferred to Tilling ownership. On January 1st 1928, the date on which General absorbed most of its acquired companies, Tilling did likewise with the Timpson fleet.

Eureka Garage, Mason's Hill, Bromley

GLEN

Walter Robert Crockett of 3 Loxton Road, Forest Hill (altered to 91 Lewisham High Road from July 1925 onwards) selected a pleasant livery of peach with brown upper parts, dash and bonnet for his new Straker Squire in August 1923. For its garage he chose the Eureka Garage (now a factory) at Prospect Place on Mason's Hill, Bromley, deep in the heart of Tilling territory. XO 8835 carried its name Glen in bold red block capitals.

Crockett had been in business for just under a year when, in July 1924, he left the Eureka Garage and moved into Charles White's premises in Porson Street, Lewisham, a base also favoured by several other independents. One of Glen's fellow operators, Julius & Lockwood, later bought the Porson Street garage and, when they disposed of their own bus interests in March 1928, Crockett moved to a garage nearer London at 97 Peckham Road. A final move came about in November 1931 to the Shardeloes Garage owned by Sidney Stotesbury at 2A Shardeloes Road, New Cross, on which Crockett obtained a lease expiring on December 1st 1933. He had a lock-up garage built to house the Glen buses, of which there were now two. Nowadays the Shardeloes Garage still survives, and though many old lock-up buildings continue to exist there, Glen's one-time bus garage in lock-up no. 78 has long since been demolished.

XO 8835 had been repainted red and white by December 1924 and in October 1926 its replacement arrived in the form of YR 2258, a Dodson-bodied Leyland. This vehicle later received pneumatics and stayed until LPTB days although its place as first-line vehicle was taken from June 1930 by a new covered-top Titan, GJ 8489. This vehicle perpetuated the block-capital style of fleet name of its predecessor, with a full stop both before and after the fleet name, and it sported a silver mascot on its filler cap. A 1925 Chrysler car, XX 3114, was also owned by the company.

Crockett's list of routes for which approval was sought in his early days is impressive and includes 11, 33, 36, 42, 47, 49, 69, 75 and 289. In addition he operated route 70 on Epsom race days during 1924 and later in the same year reached the Wembley Exhibition on a northwards extension of route 49. When schedules were required to be deposited under the London Traffic Act Crockett settled down on the 36 and 173E on Mondays to Fridays and on the 36 alone on Saturdays. On Sundays the Glen could often be found on the 69A or, in summer months, the 146.

On March 17th 1931 Crockett formed the Glen Omnibus Co. (London) Ltd. with a share capital of £300 and registered office at 24 Wickham Road, Brockley. Ownership of the business passed on November 1st 1933 to the LPTB for whom it posed something of a problem. All the omnibuses acquired in the autumn of 1933 were retained, by agreement, in the control of their former operators who ran them as agents for the LPTB pending absorption into the main fleet. Apart from the change of wording on the legal owner panel they were expected to retain their independent livery for the time being. But the LPTB was unhappy about the continued existence of the Glen because it charged a lower scale of fares than the LPTB and other operators acquired by them. Within a few days of takeover notices appeared in its windows stating that it was to be withdrawn within seven days. It then went to be prematurely repainted in General red livery, after which it returned to its old base at Shardeloes Road. Crockett was duly awarded £7,800 compensation in November 1935 for the loss of his business.

Porson Street, Lewisham
[also 57 Victoria Road, Peckham
and 100 Queens Road Arches, Peckham]

JL
J.S. & S.R.

Flats now cover the site in Porson Street, Lewisham, where C. A. White, a firm of transport contractors and charabanc owners, had once owned a substantial garage. In the period 1924-6 this garage became a favourite base for independent operators in South East London. Percy Frost-Smith, whose small fleet of specially-constructed petrol electric buses became well-known in London during their short career, was the first independent operator to garage in Porson Street. But his stay was only of short duration, and as he spent longer at Waterworks Road, Brixton, we shall recount his story in greater depth when we reach there. Frost-Smith had already departed by the time a small band of other bus operators arrived. The most important of these were Julius & Lockwood for it was they who, in 1926, bought the garage from White's.

Though the green Julius coaches have now been gone from the London scene for more than twenty years their memory lingers on and the names of Julius & Lockwood are still familiar to many, especially in the south-eastern suburbs. In the nineteen-twenties the two partners had a flourishing coach fleet which was based mainly in railway arches at 57 Victoria Road (now Bellenden Road) Peckham and at 100 Queens Road Arches nearby. Their rising fortunes dictated the need for further garage space and saw them renting accommodation in Porson Street in the garage which, after they bought it, became known as the J & L Garage. Like several other established excursion and hire operators Julius & Lockwood tried their hand at bus operation. Their charabanc fleet consisted primarily of Daimlers and it was natural that, when they bought their first double-deck bus in October 1923, this too was a Daimler. Hickman provided the body for XP 4810. Another Daimler bus now enters the story. XR 8933, a Strachan & Brown specimen, was bought in April 1924 by John Bertie Statham and Stanley Hugh Roberts of 247 Lordship Lane, East Dulwich, who ran it on the 12 and 36 as the J.S. & S.R. It appears to have run in conjunction with the Julius & Lockwood fleet from their depot at 57 Victoria Road and was soon merged with them when Statham & Roberts joined Julius & Lockwood in an enlarged partnership. After six months in service it was sold—in October 1924—to Venture upon the arrival of a new Strachan & Brown-bodied Dennis, XU 9098, in Julius & Lockwood livery and with the JL monogram.

The two JL buses appear to have operated out of all three JL addresses (Victoria Road, Queens Road Arches and Porson Street) though latterly Porson Street was the main base. They could be found mainly on routes 11B, 21D and 36A. An August 1925 application for a Sundays-only Victoria to Farnborough (Kent) service was allocated the number 215, but it is now known if it ever ran. In September 1926 a third bus—YR 1662—joined the fleet, adding still further variety to the chassis operated in being a Leyland. It was quite a rarity in having a Birch-built body and it is interesting to recall that the complete vehicle, which was ordered from Birch in July 1926 for £1,210, was in service only two months later. This feat would be considered miraculous by most operators if it could be achieved today. The Daimler was probably relegated to spare on the arrival of the new bus.

During the latter part of 1927 most of the independent operators who rented space at Porson Street sold out to Public and on March 8th 1928 Julius & Lockwood followed suit. Bus operation had, in any case, only been a very minor part of their business compared with their more richly rewarding coastal and race-course coach operations. At the same time the last remaining privately-owned bus at Porson Street, the Glen, moved to accommodation elsewhere.

Lockwood and Statham had been departed for two decades and Roberts had also been gone from the business for several years when, in January 1952, a limited company was formed called Julius & Lockwood Ltd. with registered office at the Porson Street garage and entirely owned by Julius and his wife Rosetta. Ten coaches were in stock at this time. On November 12th 1953, after the death of Bill Julius, ownership of the business passed to Charles W. Banfield Ltd. The company remained in existence but in name only as no vehicles were latterly owned. In 1973 the Banfield organisation came under the control of Bee-Line Roadways, the Middlesbrough-based operating subsidiary of the Gold Case Travel Group. Long since gone are the days when the Julius coaches vied with their many competitors for day trippers to the coast. In the balmy days of coaching just after World War II the Julius coaches always struck a note of pity in at least one heart because they seemed to be just a little slower and a good deal older than the Grey Greens, Oranges, Timpsons, Valliants and others that passed them on the road. But they got there in the end, and in doing so brought pleasure to many.

LEWIS/ESSENTIAL

The other Porson Street operators are now described starting with Lewis Myers who was unusual amongst London busmen in that he tried to run a bus business in the capital and a coach service on the Kent coast at the same time. He lived at 47 Fitzroy Avenue, Margate, and was doing quite well with a small fleet of Unic charabancs when he decided to buy a London bus. XR 4694 was a pale blue Thornycroft which was licensed on March 6th 1924 and entered service soon after passing its police inspection on the 11th. The fleet name, which was first of all Lewis, was soon changed to Essential. Myers' bus was garaged at Porson Street for the whole time it was in his ownership, which was not very long. When the bus was new he took lodgings in London with the intention of driving it himself. But he soon found himself in difficulties, for when he was in London he would receive telegrams telling him of troubles with his coaches in Margate. When he went to Margate things would go wrong in London. It did not take long for him to realise that he would be better off enlarging his Margate business and, on January 31st 1925, he sold the Thornycroft to an east London garage and hire car proprietor, W. T. Lacey. During its spell under Myers' control XR 4694 is thought to have run mainly on the 36 and 73 and probably also on route 11.

OVERLAND

Henry Stephen Hooker and William John Irvine were the owners of XU 551, a Dennis with Strachan & Brown bodywork in red & white livery and carrying the name Overland. It was licensed on July 2nd 1924 and ran thereafter mainly on south-east London routes such as 1, 21 and 36 although it was also seen on occasions further afield on such routes as 25, 33, 37 and 192. The introduction of fixed schedules at the end of 1924 saw the Overland working an odd combination of Monday-Friday routes—21D, 25A and 36A. Saturdays were spent on 21D and 36A only and its Sunday workings from 1925 onwards are not known. On March 29th 1926 the partners formed a limited company entitled Hooker & Irvine Ltd. with a share capital of £1,000. The former trading address of 71 Fawcett Road, Rotherhithe—Hooker's home—became the company's new registered office. Hooker, who had hitherto been the senior partner, was appointed secretary. On August 31st 1927 the company's share capital was acquired for £3,000 by Public who transferred its registered office to 54 Coleman Street, E.C.2, prior to winding it up on March 8th 1928.

CERTAINTY/CBC

The Certainty Bus Company was owned by Fred Henry John Hewish of 46 Springrice Road, Lewisham. Its one and only vehicle was XU 5469, a red & white Dennis bodied by Strachan & Brown and first taxed for road use on August 11th 1924. In the first place Hewish used the fleet name Certainty though by March 1927 he had changed it to CBC. XU 5469 could be found on weekdays on the 36, with additional journeys on the 173E on Mondays to Fridays. Sunday operation was probably also largely on the 36 though it could, of course, have varied at the whim of the proprietors. Early in his career Hewish even applied to operate Arkley to Hampton Court on Sundays, a route as far removed from his home base as it was possible to be, though it is not known whether he ever in fact ran it. On August 3rd 1927 the CBC bus was taken over by Public for £3,000 and a month later Hewish entered the coach business by taking delivery of YT 9150, a new 32-seater Dennis E. His coach career, during which he traded for at least part of the time as Blue Line Coaches, ceased in about March 1940.

ELMS

Elms Longman Motor Services' only bus was a Dodson-bodied Leyland, XU 8238, which entered service in September 1924. It was all-red and it carried as its fleet name the company's initials which formed the word ELMS. The 36 was always a popular route with James Elms and Alfred Longman and they also operated on the 47 for a while. Under the London Traffic Act schedules were deposited to operate routes 21D and 36 on Mondays to Fridays and 36 only on Saturdays from the end of 1924. The 527 was added to the Monday to Friday roster from August 1925 onwards.

James Elms and Alfred Longman had been acquainted for several years prior to going into partnership together. Longman was a trained motor mechanic and was thus an ideal man to drive and maintain the bus. The partners employed a second driver and the two conductors were Elms' sons. It was probably more than a happy coincidence that the company's name—Elms Longman Motor Services—was contrived so that its initial letters spelt ELMS which was, of course, the name of the senior partner. It served as a very appropriate fleet name.

August 17th 1925 saw the formation of Elms Longman Motor Services Ltd. with a nominal share capital of £2,000 and with its registered office

47

at Elms' home address, 277 Lewisham High Road. Two years later the owners, convinced that a brighter future lay in coastal coaching and private hire, sold the bus to Public on August 3rd 1927 (the same day as CBC) for £3,000 as a preliminary to the start of a successful new career. In October 1931 James Elms bought Longman's share of the business. Two years later he died and the company's management thereafter was in the capable hands of Montague Frank Hole, who duly acquired a half share in the business, though he was assisted part-time by the elder Elms son, Ernest Thomas Elms, who preferred to retain as his full-time employment his job as a bus driver with London Transport. In February 1960 ownership of Elms Longman Motor Services Ltd. passed to C. W. Banfield Ltd. together with one coach, a Duple-bodied Tilling Stevens.

REGINA

James Hartley of 46 Ewart Road, Forest Hill, was another bus proprietor to start from Porson Street. Hartley had formerly been a naval Chief Petty Officer and he commuted his pension to raise the capital for the initial deposit on the bus. He named the bus Regina after the ship of that name on which he reckoned the happiest years of his life had been spent. Hartley's remained a one bus business, the bus in question being XU 50, a red & white Strachan & Brown-bodied Dennis, which was licensed on October 8th 1924. Regina worked on more or less the same pattern of services as the other Porson Street buses in its early days, its wanderings taking it on to routes 11, 12, 36, 37, 47, 53 and 75. During its last two years or so the Regina concentrated on routes 21 and 36, but it is possible that the 21 was a Sundays-only operation. Like most other Porson Street bus proprietors Hartley sold his bus to Public and was, indeed, the first of them to do so. XU 50 passed to Public on July 29th 1927 for £3,000. He afterwards opened a successful garage and filling station in Stanstead Road, Forest Hill.

THE ROGUE

One of the more unusual titles chosen for a London bus was The Rogue. This was the name selected by Harold Smith of 24 Linden Grove, Nunhead, for XW 1157, a Dodson-bodied Dennis which was about two weeks junior to Regina and which spent its whole career at Porson Street. XW 1157 was red & cream and carried its name in gold script on the side panels. Before he started operating, Harold Smith obtained approval for routes 12, 36, 37 and 47. From the implementation of the London Traffic Act at the start of 1925 Smith concentrated on the 33 (Sundays only) and 36. On December 4th 1926 a limited company was formed entitled Harold Smith Co. Ltd. On August 4th 1927 The Rogue was taken over by Public for the sum of £3,000 which was the standard amount paid by them for all the one-bus concerns at Porson Street.

The only other operator at Porson Street, and the only one who continued to run buses into LPTB days, was W. R. Crockett, owner of the Glen. As we have already seen earlier in this chapter, Crockett arrived at Porson Street in July 1924 and he left when Julius & Lockwood ceased their own bus operations in 1928.

Tye Garage, Forest Hill

WAVERLEY

There were once two operators in Forest Hill. One, Edward Paul Ltd., was, by independent standards, a substantial business and it had other important interests besides the operation of buses. The other was, in contrast, a one-man one-bus concern run by Robert Scott Conacher of 8 Park Road, Forest Hill. For a fleetname, Conacher delved into the realms of literature from his native Scotland, and the title he selected was Waverley. XN 5203 was the vehicle concerned, and its Dodson body sported a colour scheme of violet & putty. Licensed on April 16th 1923, it ran as Waverley for about two years. It was withdrawn and put into store at an unknown date when Conacher decided to quit bus operation, and in July 1925 it was bought by Henslowe as a spare.

Conacher's original operations appear to have been on routes 12 (Forest Hill to Shepherds Bush section) and 16 with the 37 added about a month after operations first started. He later also received permission for route 36 but two further applications were turned down by the police because his bus, being one of the earlier type of Leylands, had an unsatisfactory turning lock. The two routes he was refused were Oxford Circus to South Croydon and Lewisham to Wembley.

During its period of ownership by Conacher XN 5203 operated from one of the garages then owned by Tye Brothers in the Forest Hill area. It is thought that the one in question was in Forest Hill Station yard, but this is only a deduction based on the fact that Conacher's "when working" journeys commenced at Forest Hill Station, to which this particular Tye garage was the nearest.

127 Stanstead Road, Forest Hill

EP

Long before the erection of a modern building on the site, 127 Stanstead Road, Forest Hill, was the address of a thriving business known as Edward Paul Ltd. The limited company had been formed on November 10th 1922 but the business went back much earlier than this to the year 1880. Before the operation of buses was ever considered, Edward Paul had developed a healthy trade as a coal and coke merchant and also as a general haulier. He had for many years specialised in furniture removals and house furnishing and had his own depository at 127 Stanstead Road. Charabancs probably first came on the scene just after the end of the 1914-18 war, and a lucrative trade was created in services from London to the coast. His son, Edward Henry Paul, was in charge of the business at the time the limited company was formed and he was also principal shareholder. The remaining shares were held jointly by the late Edward Paul's widow, Edith, and John Oswald Murgatroyd who was a colliery representative by profession.

The firm tested out the potentialities of bus ownership with a pair of Straker Squires which were bought in April 1923 (XN 6182/3). Their livery was crimson & grey with yellow lining-out, and they bore the letters EP in gold on a white circle. Results were encouraging and four similar vehicles were purchased between August 1923 and the following March (XO 8747, XR 3506/7 and XR 5274). Further expansion of the bus operations was then envisaged, but in an endeavour to keep costs as low as possible Paul shopped around for low-priced second-hand vehicles. Other operators were already beginning to tire of the troublesome Straker Squires and Paul, who apparently did not mind their idiosyncracies as much as did some of his contemporaries, looked around for suitable second-hand ones. In October and November 1924 XN 513, XM 9888 and XM 9995 joined the fleet. XM 9888/9995 had been the original vehicles owned by Premier and XN 513 was the former Regent bus owned by Schiffer and Harsant which had been worked in conjunction with the Premiers. These three differed from the other Strakers in the Paul fleet in having Dodson bodies as distinct from those made by the chassis manufacturer. In January 1925 Paul discovered two ex-Admiral vehicles which their owner, G. J. Heast, had put up for sale and duly bought them. These were MF 1020/9171 and at least one of them, possibly both, ran for a while in their former Admiral livery of navy blue & white, though with the EP fleet name.

Further expansion of the bus fleet to its maximum of thirteen vehicles took place in October 1925 with the arrival of YL 8115 and in January 1926 when YM 6664 was received. These broke previous tradition in being Leylands with Dodson bodies, and they were both bought new. By this time the entire EP fleet was operating on various sections of route 12, upon which eleven buses were licensed to run on Mondays to Fridays and twelve on Saturdays. On Sundays the firm could, of course, operate up to its maximum of thirteen vehicles provided all were serviceable. To run the bus fleet the firm employed in 1925 a staff of over fifty including twenty-five drivers and the same number of conductors. Their operation was supervised on the road by a uniformed inspector, Mr. Emblin, and the traffic office was run by Mr. H. Metcher, who also attended to the discipline of the bus staff when needed.

The second of the two new Leylands had not long arrived when it was decided to sell the bus section to General. It was arranged that General would purchase the whole of the assets of Edward Paul Ltd. and that a new company, called E. H. Paul & Co. Ltd., would be formed to buy back all those assets not connected with the buses. Meanwhile, pending the formation of the new company, the assets in question were purchased from the LGOC by E. H. Paul as an individual. The arrangements for the transfer of the buses having been agreed beforehand, the official change of ownership took place on March 5th 1926 at No. 1 Bush Lane, E.C.4.

Because of garaging problems it was agreed that the EP fleet should continue to run from 127 Stanstead Road for a short while until its new owners could find accommodation elsewhere. When, after a month had expired and there appeared to be no move in the offing, Mr. Paul urged the LGOC to expedite matters. They did so on April 28th when the whole EP fleet was transferred into Nunhead (AH) garage as a temporary measure. When General took over EP, one of the Straker Squires, XM 9995, was away being overhauled, and a further vehicle was due to be dealt with likewise on March 20th when its police plates expired. This was

XN 6183, one of the two original EP buses of April 1923. Its temporary replacement while it was away for overhaul was a standard K-type, K329, which arrived at Stanstead Road on March 20th in Cambrian green livery with EP fleetname. This vehicle stayed only a few weeks before being transferred to Cambrian on the return of the Straker. The bodies on some of EP's Straker Squires had been allowed to get into a bad condition and two of them, those on XO 8747 and XR 3507, were replaced in March 1926 with overhauled bodies from Cambrian Strakers which had been out of use for some months prior to General's takeover of the Cambrian concern.

August 18th 1926 saw the transfer of the EP buses from Nunhead to 81A Page Street, Westminster, a garage owned by S. H. Hole, the proprietor of the Samuelson coach fleet. Under an agreement made between Hole and the LGOC, the former took complete control of the EP's including the servicing and overhaul of the buses, the appointment of staff, and collection and banking of cash. The arrangements made between the two parties are outlined more fully in chapter 4. It was further decided to standardise the EP fleet on Straker Squires for the length of time that it remained at Page Street. XN 5243/4 became EP buses in August 1926, having formerly operated for Fleet. They displaced the Leylands which, after overhaul, went north of the river to join Tottenham Hotspur. Their departure rendered EP one hundred per cent Straker Squire. When the Leylands arrived at Tottenham Hotspur they made a couple of Strakers surplus, and these two—MH 295/1095—were overhauled and joined EP on October 22nd. They, in turn, enabled XM 9888/9995, whose lives as buses had expired, to be disposed of. Two further Strakers received ex-Cambrian bodies in the latter part of 1926; these were XN 513 and MF 1020.

Hole's control of the EP fleet was not a great success. In particular the standard of maintenance on the buses deteriorated causing many journeys to be lost through breakdowns, and in February 1927 Hole was notified that the agreement for operating them would be terminated. Between the 8th and the 15th of that month the whole Straker Squire fleet had been replaced by K's in General livery except for the legal ownership lettering so that when, on March 16th, the fleet was transferred back to Nunhead, this garage received an allocation of completely standard LGOC vehicles.

On January 1st 1928 the EP fleet was absorbed by General, and in March 1929 E. H. Paul & Co. Ltd. was renamed Edward Paul Ltd. under which title it continued to trade from Stanstead Road for many years (although coach operating ceased to be part of its activities in May 1949).

70/72 Perry Vale, Forest Hill

ENTERPRISE
The Enterprise Transport Co. Ltd. occupied the Parkfield Garage at 70/72 Perry Vale, Forest Hill, during their last six years of existence. Prior to that they had had five different homes in as many years, starting in April 1923 with a railway arch (it is not known which) at Astbury

Road, Peckham. By December 1923 the vehicle—there was still only one at this time—ran from Samuelson's garage at 81A Page Street, Westminster. In May 1924, when the fleet grew to three vehicles, the garage was Smith & Kempton's at Salamanca Place, Lambeth, and by March 1926 the company had moved from there to Peraeque's garage at 6A Neville Street, Upper Kennington Lane. There remained one further move in August 1926 to 97 Peckham Road before the final one to Perry Vale on September 21st 1927. After five years of constant upheaval the company was fortunate in securing a 21-year lease on the site from its owner, Miss E. Torr Smith. The wanderings of the Enterprise buses serve as a good example of the difficulties independent bus owners faced in finding suitable permanent accommodation. Enterprise built their own garage on the site which also included a house. This was sub-let into five flats and brought in £214 10s. 0d. a year against a ground rent of £130.

Enterprise was very much a family concern. The idea of buying a bus originated with Thomas Edward Greenwood who became the bus manager and whose home address at 8 Coldharbour Lane, Brixton, was used as the first business office, changing later to 94 Underhill Road, East Dulwich. Greenwood was brother-in-law to seven Hart brothers the eldest of whom, James Tovey Hart, joined him in the purchase of the first bus along with another brother-in-law, Edward Chapman. Under the title of the Enterprise Omnibus Company they bought a chocolate & primrose Leyland, XN 4292, which began work on route 12 on Saturday April 14th 1923, having been licensed five days previously. Greenwood had meanwhile submitted boards for the 9, 11, 12, 19, 33, 35 and 47 and later, before the London Traffic Act took effect, added routes 3, 5, 15, 21, 29, 30, 34, 37 and 59. In other words he worked in the worst pirate tradition on most of the profitable central area routes before the London Traffic Act forced him to settle down. When weekday operations became restricted at the start of 1925 schedules were obtained for three buses on routes 14A/B (Mondays to Fridays) and 14/A/B/D on Saturdays. Stabilisation of Sunday workings took longer to achieve and the variety of mid-twenties operations included the summer 535 to Green Street Green. Later route 14 became the sole Sunday service as it already was on weekdays. A growth in the fleet strength had taken place in May 1924 with the arrival of a pair of new Dennises (XT 2173/4825) which, like all double deckers ever operated by Enterprise, carried Dodson-built bodies. These were licensed to Greenwood and not to the Company but finance for them had been obtained by the simple method of the whole family—the seven Hart brothers, Greenwood and Chapman—each contributing a little. The Hart family had many business ramifications of which the buses came to occupy a place of importance. In this they replaced a once-thriving football coupon business which had suffered from taxation and had to be sold. About a quarter of a century separated the Hart brothers in age but all but one took an active interest in the buses at one time or another though it was Charles, Thomas, Edward and Ernest who stayed actively to the end in 1933. Edward Chapman, who was an elderly man, conducted for about a year whereafter he spent a period pottering about in the garage until his retirement.

The Enterprise buses prospered handsomely, and towards the end of 1926 finances were such that they were in a position to put a

52

further new vehicle into service. An order was placed with Leyland, and YE 1753 was duly licensed on January 4th 1927. At first it served as a spare but this was uneconomical and Greenwood found an unrestricted service on which to operate it. Thus, later in 1927, Enterprise began to be seen on 26D/E in the eastern suburbs except on Sundays when restrictions did not apply and the whole fleet of four vehicles could run on route 14. In October 1928 a fifth new vehicle was purchased in order to allow one of the older vehicles to become a spare. XV 1354 was a Leyland Lion, and was the first single decker in the fleet, the first vehicle with forward control, and the first on pneumatic tyres. It probably operated mainly on the 26, but could also be found on route 14 on occasions.

James Hart and Greenwood wanted to expand further, but suitable bus routes within London became impossible to find as the number of roads officially listed as 'restricted' grew. They decided to enter the field of long distance coach operation and in April and May 1929 took delivery of three 24-seater Dodson-bodied Maudslay ML3B's (GU 6714, UU 820/1). Throughout the summer of 1929 the Enterprise Omnibus Company ran an express service from London to Ilfracombe. Towards the end of the season Greenwood and J. T. Hart obtained an interest in Bucks garage at 67 High Street, Watford, and on September 26th the three Maudslays were transferred to a new limited stop service from London, Oxford Circus, to Watford. In November 1929 a limited company was incorporated entitled Bucks Expresses (Watford) Ltd. with Greenwood and S. F. St. George (owner of the Bucks garage) as directors. The Bucks Express Maudslay fleet was augmented by the arrival of five new Gilfords and later by a pair of new AEC Regals. St. George left and was replaced as a director by J. T. Hart, and on February 19th 1932 the business was sold to the LGOC who operated the company as a subsidiary from the following day.

Meanwhile, back in London, the Enterprise Transport Co. Ltd. had been formed on April 6th 1929 to take over the bus fleet. The word "Transport" was chosen in preference to "Omnibus" in order to embrace the company's other activity, chauffeur-driven car hire. In 1931 three cars were owned; two Wolseleys and a Rolls Royce. The bus fleet was vastly modernised in 1930 when four out of the five Enterprises were replaced by new Leyland Titans. GJ 3435 arrived in May followed by GH 1100/1 and GK 8925. These displaced the original Leyland, both the Dennises and the Lion single decker. The low seating capacity of the latter probably contributed to its early demise. The only remaining open-topper, YE 1753 of 1927 vintage, departed in May 1931 when a fifth new vehicle, GO 8472, arrived on the scene making the Enterprise a hundred per cent Titan fleet.

In about 1930 Greenwood severed his connection with the Enterprise business and with the Bucks Express coaches. It is thought that a family disagreement precipitated his decision to take a grocer's shop in Acton. James Tovey Hart had meanwhile gone into semi-retirement though not yet aged fifty. Management of the buses was taken over by Thomas Hart who, along with his six brothers, owned the entire share capital of the Enterprise Transport Co. Ltd.

Compulsory acquisition by the LPTB took place on December 5th 1933. The Board became the possessors of a pair of miscellaneous vehicles used in connection with the Enterprise buses, though they did not acquire any hire cars. GJ 4572 was an unlicensed 1930 Morris van and UL 1143 was a 1929 car of the same make. The lease on the Perry Vale property passed to London Transport, who quickly found someone willing to take an underlease on it. The whole property was demolished in the late 'thirties to make way for a block of flats, Vale Lodge. The compensation paid by London Transport to the Enterprise Transport Co. Ltd. was fixed by the Arbitration Tribunal at £45,000.

2A Shardeloes Road, New Cross

Shardeloes Road is nowadays a comparatively quiet suburban thoroughfare, but it was not always so. It was once a one-way street for electric trams, but it ceased to resound to their rumblings two decades ago. At no. 2A are the premises where, years ago, S. Stotesbury once ran a garage business. From 1931 to 1933 lock-up no. 78 at Stotesbury's Garage was let out to Walter Crockett for his Glen buses, as we have seen earlier in this chapter.

9 St. Mary's Road, Peckham

GENIAL/BUCK/ST. GEORGE

Peckham was a favourite gathering point for independents who managed to find several garages in S.E.15. One such operator was the St. George Omnibus Co. Ltd. who had premises at St. Mary's Road, Peckham for its last five years.

The St. George business was started in December 1923 by George Frederick Buck who was himself proudly at the wheel. Buck first of all had trouble getting hold of a bus as new ones were in short supply at the time. But he had contacts in the trade, and James Rickard of United helped him to procure a Leyland chassis whilst friends in the City company suggested that he might try Wilton for a body, as City had themselves done. Buck's Leyland was painted in a livery similar to that of General and it carried the fleetname Genial, an inspired choice as it helped to keep General drivers at bay, thinking the vehicle was one of their own, and it drew custom from travellers who mistrusted the antics of the independents and thought they were boarding a General. Buck issued return tickets which passengers, mistakenly thinking they were bought on a General, duly presented to General conductors on their return journey. The LGOC honoured the tickets to save passengers inconvenience but, following an incident on a 25 at Stratford, retaliated by taking out a successful injunction against Buck to restrain him from using the fleetname Genial. In March 1924 XP 8535 was renamed Buck.

Buck's bus was widely travelled in its youth. In true "pirate" fashion he applied for many of the best paying routes; 9, 11, 12, 18, 22, 25, 28, 29, 33, 34, 36, 37, 40, 53, 68 and 73. During the 1924 season of the Wembley exhibition he reached it by means of route 93 (Putney High Street—Wembley). Business was good and Buck decided to buy another bus. He approached Dodson who advised him to get his second bus on the road as soon as possible in view of the London Traffic Act. Buck had wanted another Leyland but none was available at the time so he settled for a Dennis. At Christopher Dodson's suggestion it was named St. George, the inspiration for this being Buck's own first name. The new bus, XX 9806, came on the road in April 1925 but by this time it was too late to get onto the choice routes and Buck had to be contented with the 527 though he later moved to the 70. At this time he was garaging at Toler's Garage in Lothian Road, Camberwell, a popular base with independents throughout the period 1924-34.

On February 4th 1926 a limited company called the St. George Omnibus Co. Ltd. was registered with head office at 22 Carden Road, Peckham, Buck's home address. He held all the shares with the exception of a few which were in the name of his wife, Mrs. E. M. K. Buck, who was company secretary. October 1927 saw the departure of the Leyland to City in exchange for XW 910, a Dennis which City had recently acquired when it took over the Veleta business. The transaction was a straight swop and no cash was involved. Buck was so pleased with the performance of his Dennis that he approached City with the proposal for the exchange of vehicles when he heard that they were taking the Veleta business over. The St. George weekday operations at this time comprised one bus working routes 12C, 37B and 173E, with the second bus concentrating on route 70 on which it was scheduled to work six journeys a day each way. By 1931, when the fleet had grown to three buses, all three were scheduled to run on Sundays, two on the 70 and one on the 37B, though in later days all three tended to be on the 37B in the morning, transferring on to the 70 in the early afternoon.

In about August 1928 Buck was fortunate in securing the premises at no. 9 St. Mary's Road which he converted into a garage for his buses and for other private vehicles. Part of the money to pay for this was borrowed from the bank, and the remainder was partly from Buck's personal account and partly from the Company's. In November 1933 the property was transferred to the ownership of the Company for £4,500. It included a dwelling house, part of which he let at 15s. a week and part of which he himself occupied. Apart from the bus garage there were nine lock-up garages, three of which were let at £1 2s. 6d. a week. A haulage business, which Buck started for his son, also ran from the premises at 9 St. Mary's Road, all of which have since been demolished.

In 1932 the LGOC seriously considered the purchase of the St. George business, largely because of the possibility of enlarging the St. Mary's Road garage to enable it to become the principal one in the Peckham area, thus allowing those at Old Kent Road (P) and Nunhead (AH) to be closed. However in view of the pending reorganisation of transport in London nothing materialised and the St. George fleet continued in business as usual until absorbed by London Transport on July 18th 1934. The LPTB acquired only one St. George open-topper, XX 9806, and this was now on pneumatics. Two Leyland Titans had been bought in May 1931 (GO 5448) and January 1933 (JJ 1269) respectively to cover normal weekday workings. The first of these had the standard open staircase Dodson body and the other was a very late example of the same type and very outdated when it appeared. St. George had a six months old

Chrysler car, ALW 79, which was also taken over but a former Alberta Dennis, XX 7606, which St. George had used as a lorry since September 1928 was disposed of before the LPTB took over. The freehold premises in St. Mary's Road passed to London Transport after the latter had resisted having to take them over at the Arbitration Tribunal. They had inherited the Bull Yard, Peckham, site with the Tilling business and did not regard the St. Mary's Road premises as desirable for their future garage requirements as the LGOC had done.

Astbury Road, Peckham (Queens Road Arches)

CITY
DISPATCH
VELETA
FW

The handsome brown Leylands of the City Motor Omnibus Co. Ltd. were a splendid advertisement for independent enterprise at its best, and were a living answer to Lord Ashfield and his colleagues at 55 Broadway who held that only operators within the "pool" could be relied upon to provide bus services in a responsible manner. The success of City came as a result of the skills and capabilities of its joint Managing Directors, Walter Crook and William Frederick Mallender. These two men had known each other in pre-war days through their connection with the old London Central Motor Omnibus Co. Ltd. Crook had worked for the company at its headquarters in Penrose Street, Walworth, until it became an Underground subsidiary in 1913, when he transferred to Leyland's employment in preference to working for the LGOC. Mallender's association with the old London Central Motor Omnibus Co. Ltd. had been as an employee of Leyland Motors Ltd. and his job was the maintenance of the Central fleet. He had been with Leyland since the beginning of the century when it was then known as the Lancashire Steam Motor Co. Shortly before the war Crook decided to start an independent bus service of his own using Leyland vehicles similar to those which had operated very successfully for Central. On July 1st 1914 the Alliance Motor Omnibus Co. Ltd. was incorporated with office at 411 Finsbury Square, E.C., and a small fleet of buses was ordered from Leyland. War came along and prevented the delivery of the vehicles, and almost a decade was to pass before he was able to make further plans to re-enter the bus industry.

The early post-war years found Crook employed as Works Manager at Leyland's Kingston-upon-Thames plant and Mallender as the firm's London Manager. Crook still nursed plans for running buses in the metropolis, and a run-down in reconditioning work at Leylands spurred him into putting his plans into fulfilment. Mallender, who also felt it was time to sever his connection with Leyland, agreed to join him in the project. The Alliance company was not used for the post-war operations; instead a new company was incorporated on January 13th 1923 with a capital of £15,000 in £1 shares, all of which were held jointly by Crook and Mallender and Mallender's brother, Basil Arthur, who lived in Derby and did not take an active part in the management of the business.

These three were also the company's sole directors throughout its career. Its head office was at the arches under the railway at Astbury Road, Peckham, on which Mallender had taken out a tenancy agreement with the London, Brighton & South Coast Railway Company in December 1922.

City's Peckham headquarters were already full of transport history before City moved in. From at least 1871 until September 1904 the arches provided a depot and stables for the London Tramways Company. Though there was road access from Astbury Road, the trams entered the arches from a service road on the opposite side of the railway, leaving the main Queens Road on a spur which ran under the up platform of Queens Road railway station. This service road still exists today though the tracks are now covered over with tarmacadam. Several traces of tram track can still be seen inside arches 110 and 111 where the horse-cars were repaired, and in the yard facing Astbury Road, and the stables for sick horses are also still in evidence. City occupied arches 106 to 111, and were fortunate that in two of them were pits. Arch 109 accommodated the company's offices and was where the bus crews reported for work and paid in. Though the official address of these arches was 106-111 Queens Road Arches, City always used the name of Astbury Road, from which their buses entered the premises. Besides the arches, City also had use of a substantial building immediately behind the high brick wall fronting Astbury Road, and used it as their running shed. In fact this garage, plus its offices and arches 108 and 109, formed the subject of City's first lease which was signed with the LB & SCR on December 18th 1922. Expansion of the business dictated the acquisition of arches 106/7 in March 1925 followed by arch 110 and part of 111 in June 1928. At various times City had other bus operators as neighbours. Julius & Lockwod and F. H. Raper (Standard) both used arch 100, though they probably entered it from the opposite side of the railway as access to this arch from the Astbury Road end is not easy. Enterprise also used one of the Queens Road arches in 1923, but we do not know which.

Credit for much of the success of the City company must go to its two senior employees. William Courteney, as Traffic Manager, was one of the most able of men and, like Walter Crook, was a former Central employee and had never really been happy working for the Combine. He alone of those intimately connected with the development of the City Motor Omnibus Co. Ltd. did not live to see his efforts absorbed overnight into London Transport, for he died late in September 1932 after having suffered ill health in latter years which left him in much pain at times. Frank Grinyer joined the company on March 9th 1923, the day before the first bus entered service, and became its very competent Mechanical Superintendent. Under his skilled direction City was able to carry out considerable pioneering work and even to construct its own chassis, an endeavour which even the most wealthy and highly developed bus operator would hesitate to do today.

In view of their loyalties towards the products of the Lancashire factory, it is no surprise that Crook and Mallender ordered Leylands, starting with an initial order for ten. Construction of the bodies was entrusted to Dodson. The first was delivered in January 1923 and was examined by the police at New Scotland Yard on the 30th of that month. It was not, however, licensed until March 6th when it received the number XN 732. City allocated to it the fleet number A1, and used class letter A for all subsequent LB-type Leylands taken into stock. The remaining nine vehicles in the first batch were licensed between March 9th and June 1st, and the whole initial fleet of ten vehicles was in operation on June 2nd.

In its early days City operated very much on "pirate" lines, and it was not until the London Traffic Act of 1924 stabilised the position and prevented operators from pirating at will, that City was able to achieve its aim of establishing a service of its own. On the first day of operation, March 10th 1923, the two buses then licensed were used on routes 33, 37 and 73. On one day alone, June 2nd, the fleet of ten buses ran on 2, 3, 6, 7, 9, 11, 12, 13, 16, 25, 27, 32, 34, 35, 36, 37, 38, 40, 53, 73 and 88; a total of twenty-one routes. During the intervening three months City buses had also worked on the 5, 8, 10, 15, 17, 22 and 47. 'New' services served subsequent to June 2nd were 14, 21, 29, 49, 50, 59 and 78. In the early part of 1924 City tried to establish its own service between Oxford Circus and Putney via Bayswater Road, Kensington Church Street and Hammersmith Broadway using route number 65 which was vacant in the LGOC series at the time. It was worked jointly with James Rickard (United), and though not a success was a foretaste of things to come.

Spurred on by the necessity to submit schedules under the London Traffic Act, City decided to try once again to establish a service of its own, route 517 between Highgate and Peckham Rye via Oxford Circus, Marble Arch, Victoria, Vauxhall and Camberwell. It commenced to run daily from December 5th 1924 and was operated by sixteen City buses augmented by four of James Rickard's Uniteds except on Saturdays when the City allocation was increased by one. Henceforth City and United ran in close co-operation with each other, both companies combining their entire fleets to provide the maximum service possible on a single route. The 517 was shortlived and on January 21st 1925 the twenty-one City and United vehicles were transferred on to 536A, Highgate Station to Brockley Cross, Coulgate Street. This bore a good deal of similarity to the 517 but operated through the central area via Euston Road, Great Portland Street and Oxford Circus as against the routeing of the 517 which went along Tottenham Court Road and Oxford Street. The introduction of the 536A called for two extra vehicles which were provided from the Archway fleet of Birch Bros. Ltd. On Saturday afternoons and Sundays buses operated through to the Chandos, Brockley Rise as route 536. All three operators on the 536 adhered strictly to a mutually agreed schedule, and the vehicles carried running numbers in similar manner to those of the LGOC. At this stage Birch operated running numbers C1/2; United were allocated C5/10/15/20 and City the remainder. April 15th 1925 saw route 536A extended to run daily from Highgate Station to Southend Village (Tigers Head) on a regular 7½ minute headway. Twenty-eight vehicles were now required, an increase of six over the former schedule. Five of the additional buses were supplied by City (C23/4/6-8) and the other by United (C25). Birch withdrew from the 536 on April 11th because of retrospective Restricted

Streets regulations but resumed again on August 1st after the starting date of the restrictions had been amended. A short-lived summer only extension in 1925 to Farnborough on Sundays starting on April 15th required a running time from end to end in the region of two hours, but the Sunday service was cut back to Southend Pond on October 18th. The basic operation remained unchanged for two years until, on April 14th 1927, daily operation was extended from Southend Village to Beckenham, Elmers End, as route 536. This further development meant that another eight buses were needed, of which Birch and United provided one each and City six. City owned some vacant land at the Elmers End terminus and it was rumoured at one time that they were to build houses for their employees there. With the extension to Elmers End the route reached its maximum of weekday development and employed no fewer than thirty-six buses. Birch's three vehicles were now C1-3, United's six were C11, 16, 21, 26, 31 and 36, and City's twenty-seven occupied running numbers C4-10, 12-15, 17-20, 22-25, 27-30 and 32-5. Peak hour shorts, or "swingers", which ran from time to time were usually numbered S1-3 (City) and US 1 (United). It has been reported that at Christmas times Birch operated two all-day short-working extras as X1/2.

Route 536 became a supreme example of the type of public service that could be operated through independent enterprise and co-operation. City's directors estimate that it operated at a loss for the first six months, at one time to the huge tune of about £200 a week, but once it became known by the travelling public it developed into one of the best-paying services in London. Probably the handsome and distinctive common livery used by all three operators helped to establish the individuality of the service. Birch, who at one time kept a few buses in red & white livery for the West London Association route 526, found to their cost that the public were reluctant to board one of these vehicles if ever they were called upon to help out on the 536. City provided inspectors for the route, towards whose salaries the other two operators paid a proportion of the total, and these officials ensured that a frequent service could always be relied upon. Return fares were in operation throughout the route.

We now return to City's fleet of immaculate Leylands. The original ten vehicles were soon augmented by A11-23 which were ordered in five batches and entered service between December 15th 1923 and August 2nd 1925. It is interesting to recall the various purchase prices of the successive batches of new vehicles which, until the latter part of 1925, showed a steady decline. A1-10 cost £1,295 apiece, A11/12 £1,136, A13/14 £1,134, A15-17 £1,126, A18-22 £1,086 and A23 £1,098. A11 to A17 were bodied by Wilton and A18 onwards by Dodson, though there was little external difference in body styles between the two. In April 1924 a new Dennis was purchased and numbered D1. This may have been obtained to test its performance against the Leylands, but it was disposed of in February 1926 when the opportunity arose for it to be exchanged with the Liberty Leyland owned by P. H. R. Harris. This new arrival, the first second-hand vehicle to be taken into the fleet, was numbered A24. On April 2nd 1926 another second-hand Leyland entered service as A25.

It was only a little over a year old when purchased and had previously been run by Arthur Daniel of 4 Dunton Road, Leyton as the red & white Dispatch bus. It is not known where Daniel garaged; indeed little is known about him at all. He bought his bus after the London Traffic Act came into force and in all probability had been unable to find a profitable service and had returned the vehicle to its makers. A26-31 were further new Dodson-bodied Leylands which entered service between April 14th and September 1st 1927 and were the last solid-tyre, open-top double deckers to be bought new by City.

As time went on and more and more Restricted Streets Orders came into effect covering a great variety of suburban as well as central London thoroughfares, it became clear that the only means of further profitable expansion would be by purchasing existing businesses. City embarked on a policy of acquisition which, between August 1927 and January 1929, brought five valuable additional schedules into the fleet from four operators. This new development in the Company's activities meant that City buses could once again be found on a variety of routes other than the 536. The first two operators to be taken over were Frederick Willson, whose one bus ran under the fleet name FW, and Thomas Frederick Ambridge who had two buses called Veleta.

Willson, of 75 Beckwith Road, Herne Hill, purchased XW 9346, a red Dodson-bodied Leyland, on January 27th 1925 and applied for a schedule on route 3B. It first operated on January 31st but, on April 14th, was forced to transfer to an "unrestricted" route because of the retrospective Restricted Streets regulation. Willson chose route 527 but this soon proved to be a loser and on May 27th the FW bus started a short-lived career on the West London Association route 526D. Willson was subsequently permitted to return to the 3B which he duly did as and from June 19th 1925. On Sundays the FW ran at varying times on routes 3, 527, 526, 37A, 2D and 37B in that order. XW 9346 was garaged at Toler's in Lothian Road, Camberwell, which was conveniently situated for the 3B. When, in August 1927, City wished to assume control a limited company was formed on the 8th of the month under the title FW Omnibus Co. Ltd. City took over on the 15th and the registered office then became Astbury Road, to which garage the FW bus was transferred. Relaxation by the police of their restriction on the transfer of licences enabled City to absorb the FW operations on November 11th 1927, the FW bus having operated under its old title for the last time on the previous day.

Following the purchase of the FW Leyland came the take-over of the two Veletas owned by T. F. Ambridge. Ambridge was a licensed victualler by trade and had kept the Gun Tavern at 75 High Street, Wapping for some years. In March 1924 his first bus, a red & white Leyland XR 6498, was licensed ready for service. It was presented to the police on March 21st by Chris Wolff of 43A Daneville Road, Camberwell, who, along with a Mr. Rogers, was a junior partner in the business. In all probability Rogers and Wolff worked the bus and Ambridge was a sleeping partner who provided the bulk of the capital. A second bus, this time a Dennis, joined the Leyland in October 1924 and was registered XW 910.

Many different routes were applied for at first but by December 1924 those mainly operated were 12, 36 & 37 and schedules were submitted for these on the 9th in accordance with the London Traffic Act. According to the schedules both buses worked route 12C in the morning peak after which they parted company. One finished the day out on the 36 and the other worked on the 37B. On January 5th 1925 the a.m. peak operation was transferred to the 21D but otherwise weekday operations remained unchanged thereafter. On Sundays routes 12C, 36 and 37B were operated until July 1925 when the 36 was abandoned. In September 1927 the 12C was also abandoned, and both buses then spent all day on the 37B.

Ambridge's buses were kept, like Willson's, at Toler's in Lothian Road. Again, like Willson, Ambridge arranged with City for the latter to take over his business in August 1927, and on the 8th of that month the Veleta Omnibus Co. Ltd. was registered with its office at 14 Queen Victoria Street, E.C.4. On August 15th the registered office was transferred to Astbury Road when City took control. The two Veleta workings were absorbed by City on December 11th 1927.

The Veleta Leyland passed into the City fleet, but the Dennis did not last long enough to do so. In October 1927 it was sold to St. George who in return let City have their Leyland, XP 8535. This did not enter service until after Veleta had ceased to operate, having been fitted meanwhile with a Dodson body in place of the Wilton one which it had carried before. Ambridge meanwhile continued in charge of his first love, his Gun Tavern, where he remained until 1937.

City's next acquisition was that of Webber Brothers' Empires Best service on March 2nd 1928 which added a further Leyland (MH 2484) to the City fleet. On January 31st 1929 B.D.L. Burton's Fairlop Dennis (PU 8660) was acquired, but it stayed only until April when a replacement vehicle became available, and may never have carried City colours. These two undertakings are described in greater detail in later chapters. Their acquisition meant that City inherited licences on routes 294 (ex Empires Best) and 511 (ex Fairlop). On Sundays the Empires Best bus worked route 69 and this was retained by City until April 1st 1928 when the vehicle was transferred to the 536. The ex FW and Veleta buses had always worked on the 536 on Sundays right from the time City took control. The Fairlop Sunday working on the 511 was retained until February 16th 1930 when it too was transferred to the 536. One City vehicle operated route 34 on Sundays from February 19th 1928, but was withdrawn very quickly afterwards on March 18th, and a vehicle ran on route 37B for a rather longer period (May 27th 1928 to October 27th 1929) before it, too, was withdrawn. Thereafter all Sunday operation was confined to route 536 which, at its maximum, employed 38 City buses.

On weekdays the acquired workings on routes 3B, 21D, 36, 37B, 294 and 511A/B, were, of course, retained right up to the end, though City would probably have liked to transfer them to the 536 had the opportunity arisen. One further extension to route 536 remains to be recorded. On Sundays starting from May 25th 1930, an extension was introduced southwards from Elmers End to West Wickham, The Wheatsheaf. The weekday operation was henceforth renumbered 536C.

An event of the greatest significance in the light of things to come was the purchase by City of a controlling interest in New Empress Saloons Ltd. who operated a coach service from Wood Green to Southend. The New Empress service had been inaugurated on May 27th 1927 by A. H. Young who had formerly been one of the proprietors of the Wood Green-based Empress Omnibus Co. Ltd. which had sold its business to General in the previous year. On July 3rd 1928 the business was incorporated as a limited company as New Empress Saloons Ltd. and formally took over operation on July 10th. Young was joined by two more former independent bus owners, H. J. Barnett who had run the Clarendon buses and S. F. G. Collier of the Varsity. A fleet of nine coaches was built up comprised of seven Dennis E's and a pair of ex-London Public Maudslays which had originated with Fallowfield & Knight. They operated from the Regent Garage at Palmers Green once used by Mason Brothers' Uneedus fleet. City purchased 1,000 of the 1,500 issued £1 shares on October 25th of the same year, and Barnett and Collier then left the board, though Young stayed on for a little longer. The business became completely City-owned during the financial year ended March 31st 1932.

City lost no time in supplementing the fleet with new and second hand Leyland Lions, and the Dennises were subsequently sold. Beginning in November 1928 the buff City livery was applied to the whole fleet and so was the City fleet name. As soon as City gained control the London terminus became Camden Town, and a further extension was made in 1929 to a new garage opened by City at Leighton Road, Kentish Town. The Southend-based Westcliff-on-Sea Motor Services Ltd. competed with City over the bulk of the New Empress route, but on January 1st 1929 competition was eliminated with the introduction of a joint timetable. Though no further joint timetables were issued after this, efforts were made to ensure that the scheduled times of each operator did not clash. The route, which ran by way of Tottenham, Gants Hill, Romford, Brentwood, Billericay, Wickford and Rayleigh became extremely popular and duplicate coaches were frequently operated. New Empress's original hourly service had become two buses per hour by the latter part of 1930; departures from Southend were at 10 and 55 mins. past each hour; intermediate journeys being worked by Westcliff vehicles. A similar arrangement applied in the reverse direction. The Westcliff journeys terminated at Wood Green but the London terminus for all the New Empress workings was Kentish Town, which meant that an uneven headway was worked over the Wood Green-Kentish Town section.

The success of its New Empress route convinced City of the desirability of having a garage in the Kentish Town area which would serve a dual purpose of being the London base for the Southend service and a northern garage for part of the 536 fleet. Five of City's 536's were scheduled to start and finish in the north and since May 8th 1925 five vehicles had been kept in Birch's garage in Cathcart Street, Kentish Town at a weekly charge of £2 10s. 0d. per bus. City employed its own fitter at Birch's and contributed 1,000 gallons of petrol to Birch's tank whenever its buses were estimated to have used this amount. In December 1928 an area of freehold land in Leighton Road, Kentish Town, was purchased from the London County Council and construction of a garage and main workshops began almost immediately. It was completed at an overall cost of £26,308 in time to open for traffic on December 8th 1929. Henceforth all major engineering work was carried out at Kentish Town where the Company had extensive and enviable workshop and store facilities. Normally only six buses were garaged at Kentish Town, the rest of the vehicles there being New Empress coaches.

A second freehold garage was purchased in 1930 for £3,626. This was in Tylers Avenue, Southend-on-Sea, and was used as a day time coach station and night time garage for the New Empress coaches. Many a homeward bound Londoner will long remember the lengthy but good humoured queues which used to wind themselves around the now-vanished garage, particularly on bank holidays and fine summer Sundays, waiting to be borne away by a constant stream of scheduled coaches augmented by many duplicates. The Tylers Avenue garage was owned officially by the City Motor Omnibus Company Ltd. who made a charge to its New Empress subsidiary for use of it. A similar arrangement existed in regard to certain of the New Empress vehicles, although we do not know which, and the whole of the New Empress fleet was maintained by City and charged at cost price.

The year 1928 was noteworthy not only for the purchase of the New Empress business and the garage land at Kentish Town. It also marked the purchase of City's first modern double decker and saw the first major rebuilding job to be carried out by City on an older vehicle. City was probably influenced by the success of Public when it ordered a six-wheeled, covered-top double decker from Guy Motors Ltd. No doubt City would have ordered from Leyland had they included a comparable model in their range of products at the time. G1, a Guy FCX, was licensed on February 2nd 1928 and carried a Dodson-built body seating 62, fourteen passengers more than any previous City vehicle. G1 entered service on February 26th on the ex-Veleta working on route 36 and won the distinction of being the first independent covered top bus in the metropolis. On Sundays it initially operated on route 34. By all accounts the new Guy ran quite successfully but its usefulness was limited because at the time the police would not sanction its use on the 536 because of the sharp turn from Oxford Street into Great Portland Street, a restriction on which they later relented.

October 1928 saw the completion of C1 (C standing, presumably, for City). This vehicle was a very extensive rebuild of A18, a standard Leyland LB of March 1925 vintage. City's experiments with new clutches and gearboxes to improve economy were well known, and the whole fleet of Leyland LB's had already been fitted with these features and with Ricardo cylinder heads. But C1 represented the first attempt by a London independent to produce a vehicle to suit its own requirements. It emerged from the workshops as a forward-control vehicle with pneumatics, to which much of the City fleet was then being converted, and with other refinements such as ball bearing axles, it turned out to be a speedy machine. Dodson had provided a new body which seated 55 and, somewhat surprisingly, had an open top. Indeed, after the arrival of

63

the Guy FCX in February 1928, two years were to elapse before City bought any more covered-top vehicles. No further rebuilds like C1 were carried out, but the experience gained from this experiment was no doubt widely called upon in the later and much more substantial rebuilds carried out by City in 1930/31.

The years 1929 and 1930 saw the construction of two very different vehicles. In April 1929 A36 was completed, and was to all intents and purposes a normal Leyland LB. It was built from parts which City had held in their workshops and was required as a replacement for the previous A36, the Dennis acquired with the Fairlop business. The new A36 had a Dodson body which probably came from A18 when the latter was rebuilt as C1. May 1930 marked the completion of a truly remarkable vehicle, CS1, to the designs of Walter Crook. It was nothing less than a covered-top, double-deck, six-wheeler which, though comprised mostly of new units, made use of the engine—with bores enlarged to give more power—and radiator from a withdrawn Leyland LB, A22. It was only the second covered-top bus to join the fleet and, like its predecessor G1, seated 62 in a Dodson-built body. In service its petrol consumption averaged 6.5 mpg compared with the 6 mpg of the Guy, but with its small Leyland 4-cylinder engine it was decidedly more sluggish. A great feature in favour of CS1 was that its total cost of construction came out at only £1,519, a saving of £254 over the cost of G1. The experiment proved so successful that in 1931 arrangements were put in hand for the construction of five more City Sixes.

By 1931 the time had come for the wholesale replacement of the original fleet to begin. With only two covered-top buses to its credit, City was lagging behind other operators in the provision of modern vehicles. Six new four-wheeled Leylands (T1-6), classified by Leyland as TD1 Special, arrived in March 1931 and were based, for an unknown reason, not on the standard Titan double-deck chassis but on the Tiger TS3 version normally used for single deckers. 56-seat Dodson bodies were fitted, and they were easily distinguishable from their contemporaries employed by other operators on Titan chassis by their higher skirt line Like the body on C1 and all subsequent new City Buses these were designed by Walter Crook and were unlike standard Dodson designs particularly in their front upper deck window layout with curved corner glasses. Enclosed cabs were fitted but the staircases were open. Six more apparently identical vehicles (T7-12) arrived in 1932. Between March and August 1931 CS2-6 entered service. They differed little from the prototype except that brakes were fitted on the rear bogie only and the wheelbase was extended by ½ inch. They were re-registered, unlike CS1 which kept its original number. Perhaps Dodson were too busy to construct the bodies, for City gave the contract to Ransomes, Sims & Jefferies Ltd., of Ipswich, who produced bodywork for CS2-6 which was almost identical in appearance to that on CS1.

The fleet additions of 1932, T7-12, have already been mentioned. City's stock of covered-top buses was brought to a total of 28 in that year by the arrival of no fewer than nine second-hand Guy six-wheelers. All had once been the property of the London Public Omnibus Co. Ltd., but General, who took them over from Public, had disposed of them and they had run for various operators in the meantime. They were thoroughly overhauled by City before entering service, and thereafter proved very useful additions to the fleet, with their high seating capacity of 62. A couple of them were discovered by Mr. Mallender on Canvey Island with their wheels jacked-up and in use as tea rooms. Their last owner, the Canvey & District Motor Transport Co. Ltd., had apparently found them too troublesome to continue in service. The remainder came via a firm of motor dealers, the Waterloo Motor Company. At a cost of between £510 and £650 apiece these four to five year old Guys seemed to City to be a bargain too good to resist.

T12, which was licensed on May 1st 1932, was a very special bus; it was the first diesel engined vehicle to be operated by a London independent. In fact, apart from one solitary vehicle owned by Birch, City was the only independent to run diesel vehicles. T12 made its smoky way around London at an average of 11.5 mpg; a very satisfactory result indeed. Due to the extra weight of the engine, compared with a comparable petrol unit, T12 had to be fitted with two seats fewer than the other members of its class to bring it within the weight regulations. A lesser-known but much more significant experiment carried out by City was the fitting of diesel engines to its complete fleet of eighteen New Empress Leyland Lion coaches. Some of these, it will be recalled, were owned at one stage by City and leased to New Empress but were later sold to New Empress. On November 25th 1932 the whole fleet of Leyland Lions was transferred to City ownership along with M2, the only Maudslay still left. The reason for this was that City, aware that it was only a matter of time before their buses were compulsorily taken away from them under the London Passenger Transport Act, wished to keep alive the name of the City Motor Omnibus Co. Ltd. by acquiring the entire New Empress assets, including the licences. This scheme was thwarted by the Traffic Commissioner who refused to transfer the road service licence and on March 31st 1934 the whole coach fleet was transferred back to New Empress ownership.

The eighteen Leyland Lions which received diesel engines were all of the then-obsolete PLSC type. The new engines fitted to them were Dorman-Ricardo 4HW Units made at Stafford by W. H. Dorman & Co. Ltd., and the results obtained from them were very encouraging. The PLSC Lion, itself a very good bus when equipped with the petrol engine designed for it, could achieve 9.5 mpg in its normal form. With the four-cylinder Dorman diesel it averaged no less than 14 mpg and gave the firm a saving in the region of £100 a week. In about 1933 the bodies on some of the Lions were modernised by Birch who lowered the roofs. This was done by eliminating the 'standee' windows. In some cases the front dome was rebuilt squarer than usual to incorporate the destination indicator, making the general appearance more modern still.

City's last new vehicles of all were a trio of diesel-powered Leyland Titanics, TS1-3, which were licensed on March 24th 1933. At £2,152 apiece they were among the most expensive vehicles ever bought by a London independent. Their engines were Leyland 8 litre direct injection units and their bodies were 62-seater Dodsons. What a pity they were spoilt by antiquated City-style open-stair bodies which compared ill with

Dodson's own contemporary style as applied to Westminster's six-wheeled Sunbeam which preceded the City Titanics by a month. Their arrival reduced the number of weekday workings regularly carried out by Leyland LB's to six. The acquired schedules on routes 3B, 21C and 294 continued to be exclusively LB-worked, and one LB was scheduled to work on route 36 and another on 536C right up to the end. Other duties were worked by LB's when the regular vehicles were away for overhaul, and all could be found on the 536 on Sundays. In March 1933 ten complete LB's were in stock, of which A20/25/31-6 were in use and A28/30 were unlicensed. A16 was an orange & black coloured petrol tank lorry, to which it had been converted in September 1932, and the chassis of A9/13/14/29 and XN 8524 were still owned but had no bodies on them. The last had been acquired from Triumph in November 1931 in exchange for A23, but was never used by City. As far as is known the T and TS classes worked nothing but the 536. C1 was often to be found on route 37B, and the CS's and G's could be found on 37B and 511A as well as 536.

With acquisition by the LPTB looming on the horizon, City began to repaint its vehicles in its future owner's red & white livery from December 1933 onwards, though the City fleet name was of course retained. T1 appears to have been the first vehicle to be done, but several others followed suit, even old A35.

On November 7th 1934 the axe fell. Thirty-nine buses passed to the Board comprised of seven A's (25/31-6), C1, T1-12, CS1-6, G1-10 and TS1-3. With them went the petrol tank lorry and a 1929 Morris van, GU 9017. The LB's had the honour of being the last of their type to operate on regular London service. All were on pneumatic tyres, and of the covered-top double deckers, all but CS1-6 had windscreens. 292 staff passed to their new employer, and the garage at Kentish Town also became London Transport property. City arranged to lease the garage for the continued use of the New Empress coaches, and retained the use of most of the plant and machinery that was there. Compensation of £366,213 was paid in London Transport Stock, and the City Motor Omnibus Co. Ltd. passed into oblivion, but luckily the enterprise that had built it into one of the most profitable of all London bus companies was free to unleash its attention to developing the Southend coach route to the full. City had never at any time bought a vehicle on hire purchase, and even the Kentish Town and Southend garages had been bought out of revenue.

In the same month that City surrendered its London bus services, its directors were negotiating with Westcliff for the purchase of its Southend-Wood Green service. This came into New Empress ownership in January 1935 and thereafter the brown New Empress coaches with their City fleet names maintained a 15-minute service over the bulk of the route. The fleet was replaced by the famous fleet of 36 six-wheeled Leyland Tiger 43-seaters, which were the backbone of the route for over fifteen years. In time the Kentish Town garage was vacated when a new, more convenient base was obtained in Lordship Lane, Wood Green, and in March 1936 the New Empress title was finally disposed of and the company was renamed the City Coach Co. Ltd. Expansion took place by the acquisition of small stage carriage operators in the Brentwood area, five of whom had been taken over by City by February 1945. Double deckers were introduced in 1947 and, like the vehicles first bought by Crook and Mallender over twenty years earlier, were Leylands. Though Leylands always predominated in the City coach fleet, other makes were bought from time to time from acquired companies; for special types of service or because of vehicle availability. In post 1939-45 war years the Leyland fleet was augmented by Daimler double deckers and Bedford, Commer and Seddon single deckers. The service from Wood Green to Kentish Town, discontinued temporarily during the war, was resumed on February 1st 1946 but was permanently withdrawn on October 1st 1947.

The saddest moment of all came on the midnight of February 16th/17th 1952 when the business was sold to the British Transport Commission and placed under the control of its old rival, Westcliff-on-Sea Motor Services Ltd., then a Tilling-group company. As far as the Wood Green to Southend route was concerned, the wheel had now turned a full circle. Twelve services passed to Westcliff together with the garages at Southend, Wood Green and Brentwood. The last had formerly been used by the Brentwood Engineering Co. Ltd., a City associate, who in turn took over City's more modern premises in the town. On the last night a Leyland Titan, LD16, worked City's last journey from Wood Green at 9.25 p.m. and a similar bus, LD4, operated the 9.28 p.m. from Southend. On arrival at Brentwood both were decorated and completed their journeys with streamers flying. The staff were all given mementos to mark the occasion.

Today Eastern National, as successor to the Westcliff company, still maintains a frequent daily service from Wood Green to Southend via the old City route. The Bristol FLF 70-seaters which are used almost exclusively are bigger vehicles by far than Crook and Mallender were ever able to run. It says much for those pioneers of forty years ago that their route, of over forty miles in length, is still a highly successful proposition in these days of declining bus travel. The only pity is that the old City garage in Tylers Avenue, which was so full of character, now lies but a memory under the flat expanse of a municipal car park.

Harders Road, Peckham

R. HAWKINS/RH/ASTORIA/NIL DESPERANDUM

Harders Road, Peckham, is our next port of call. Two operators occupied premises in Harders Road: Robert Hawkins was at number 39 and Wolvett & Carswell were at number 47.

Robert Hawkins was, like several other bus owners, steeped in taxicab tradition and had been in the cab business since 1902. He forsook horse transport with the coming of motors and developed a general motor engineering and tyre merchant's business alongside the cabs at the long-defunct premises which he then occupied at 101 Camberwell Road, S.E.5. The post-war era saw Hawkins branching out into charabanc

67

operation and in December 1922 he interested himself in buses for the first time when he became a founder member of the New Times Omnibus Co. Ltd. He left this in about October 1924 along with W. J. Loveland. The latter started in the bus business on his own account at Highbury whilst Hawkins ordered a bus of his own to run from his home territory at Camberwell. Members of the Toler family have recollections that it ran from their garage in Lothian Road and it is very possible that it did so although returns made by Hawkins at the time show it as being kept in his own premises at 101 Camberwell Road. It seems that Hawkins and Loveland intended initially to run in co-operation with each other as both issued tickets bearing the name Hawklove which was never, however, applied to any vehicles. Hawkins' bus was licensed on the first day of 1925 as XW 6925 and was a Wilton-bodied Dennis. It was replaced in January 1927 by YE 3678, an identical chassis on to which the Wilton body from XW 6925 was placed. The older vehicle then received a 32-seat body and joined Hawkins' coach fleet.

Hawkins did not expand his bus interests to more than one unit until September 1928, nearly three years after he first commenced operation. Central London services were no longer available to him, so he ordered a new Leyland PLSC-type Lion single decker for operation in North London on route 551. This materialised as YX 9732 and bore a crimson lake livery and an unexpected choice of fleet name. Instead of carrying the RH monogram (which replaced R. Hawkins as a fleetname) in line with the double decker, it received the title Astoria. In April 1930 a similar vehicle was bought second-hand from Pembroke. YX 7703 received yet another unexpected title; Nil Desperandum.

Meanwhile, on January 15th 1927, a limited company had been incorporated under the title Robert Hawkins & Co. Ltd., the directors of which were Robert Hawkins and his wife Gertrude. On February 15th 1930 the registered office was changed from 101 Camberwell Road to 39 Harders Road, Peckham, when the company bought the house, garage and petrol station at this address. The house fronted the roadway, the garage being at the rear of the house with a drive-way beside the house to give access. The premises cost £3,100 of which £500 was paid out of the Company's money. The remainder was obtained as a bank loan to Robert Hawkins on the security of a mortgage on the premises. The buses henceforth ran out of the Harders Road garage though Hawkins continued to carry on some of his other interests at 101 Camberwell Road. At the time of writing the old Harders Road premises were still in commercial use although all the indications were that their demise could not be far away.

The operation of YX 9732 on the 551 lasted only for about a fortnight. Thereafter it was worked on route 202, a service much nearer home which had been pioneered in July 1929 by G. H. Allitt & Sons Ltd. The second-hand Lion joined it on the 202 when it arrived. The double decker meanwhile ran on the 3A and 59A on Mondays to Fridays, the 59A on Saturdays and the 42A on Sundays. On Bank Holiday Mondays it ran from Strand, Aldwych to Richmond on the 33. Sunday proved to be a poor day on the 202 so the single deckers could usually be found on the 42A once a week.

Three new Leylands were bought in the 'thirties and some further body-swopping also took place. August 1930 saw the arrival of the company's first covered-top double decker, GH7079. Its arrival witnessed the departure of YE 3678 (which had collected a set of pneumatic tyres by this time), rendering the bus fleet all-Leyland. In February 1932 GH 7079 was returned to its body-builders, Birch, for the open staircase to be enclosed at a cost of £95. It could not have run long in this form, for in April 1932 the body was removed altogether and placed on to a new TD1 chassis which was duly licensed on May 1st as GX 1955. GH 7079 then received a new single-deck Birch body and became a Nil Desperandum bus in May 1932. Prior to this the Nil Desperandum fleet had been doubled in size in March 1931 by the purchase of a new Birch-bodied Leyland LT2 Lion, GN 7512.

At midnight on June 12th/13th 1934 the London Passenger Transport Board took over, six days later than originally planned. They inherited not only the buses but also the Harders Road garage and taxi business which Hawkins no longer wished to retain; the coaches had gone by this time. The five buses passed to the new owner together with a pair of Unic taxis, XC 6901 of 1921 and XN 450 of 1923, plus a 1933 Chrysler 19.8 hp saloon car. This was one of the cases where London Transport objected to having to take over the freehold premises, their grounds for objection being that they were held individually and not by the Company. A lease from Mr. Hawkins to the Company dated December 19th 1933 was claimed to be non-effective as it was made after the LPT Act came into force. The Arbitration Tribunal gave judgement against London Transport after learning that the Company's money had been used to make weekly payments of £10 to reduce the loan and to allow improvement of the premises. It was held that Hawkins had purchased the premises as an agent of the Company. The Hawkins, who received £19,250 for their business, later retired to Gravesend where Robert Hawkins took on greyhound training up to the time of his death in February 1962. R. H. Hawkins & Co. Ltd. remained in existence, though no longer connected with the transport industry in any way, until it was dissolved on May 26th 1967.

CARSWOOL

Just along Harders Road from the Hawkins garage was a lock-up (demolished in 1974) used to house the Carswool bus. Owned by Fred George Woolvett and William Robert Carswell, this vehicle started life in February 1924 in much the usual way, but it lived to be something of a curiosity. XR 2120 was the only vehicle ever owned, and it was an all-red Leyland with Strachan & Brown bodywork which was notable in its earlier days for carrying its coachbuilder's advertisements. Woolvett was the licensee of the bus and his home address at 36 Cooks Road, Walworth, was used as the firm's business headquarters. As far as we know, the vehicle was always housed in the lock-up at the rear of no. 47 Harders Road, for which the partners paid 12/- a week rent. The fleetname, Carswool, was obviously derived from the surnames of the vehicle's owners, and in the early days was written in squashed-up block capitals on a white panel background. Later the white panel was eliminated and the name was written in "General" fashion. In the early days application was made to run on many routes including most of the favourites such as 12, 13, 21, 29, 36 and 73, but its wanderings were short-lived and for most of its life Carswool could be found on the 21. On Mondays to Fridays it ran only in peak hours, but it could usually be seen running all day on Saturdays, Sundays and Bank Holidays.

The Carswool bus led an entirely uneventful history, and therein lay its interest. It survived the large-scale sale of independent buses to General and Public; it remained faithful to solid tyres when all others were favouring pneumatics; and it even remained on first-line duties when new Dennis Lances, Leyland Titans and suchlike were replacing what remained of its fellows. In 1932 it received a particularly thorough and extensive overhaul which kept it off the road for forty-seven days, but even then the opportunity was not taken to fit pneumatic tyres. Even as late as 1933 the Carswool Leyland could be found each day travelling up and down the lengthy route 21 on its solid tyres, the only solid-tyred independent bus still in daily service. Many of its regular passengers remained faithful to the very end, which came on November 24th 1933.

Woolvett & Carswell were unique among London bus proprietors in being unrepresented by any solicitor. This streak of independence worked to their distinct disadvantage when it came to getting compensation for their business. Being divorced from the mainstream of bus activity, they were possibly unaware that all their fellow central area bus proprietors had, through their solicitors (in most cases the redoubtable J. Cort Bathurst), rejected the Board's formula for compensation. The partners dealt with the Board direct on this very important matter, settled for a lowly sum of £2,400, and in doing so achieved the doubtful distinction of being the first independent operator to agree on terms of settlement. London Transport must have viewed the Carswool bus with some disdain, for it was moved straight into Chiswick Works and never ran again. After a month's holiday W. R. Carswell became a conductor with London Transport and enjoyed, for the first time in his bus conducting career, the benefits of enclosed stairs, covered tops and pneumatics. The entire stock of spare parts which the Carswool business possessed was delivered by hand by Mr. Carswell to Chiswick Works; it consisted of one magneto! Carswell was one of the few independent proprietors to accept employment with the Board. His partner, F. G. Woolvett, who was over fifty years of age and therefore ineligible for employment under the rules of the LPTB, received compensation in the normal way.

East Dulwich Road
(also Victoria Road Arches)

NEWLANDS DISTRICT

F. H. Bruce's struggle to establish his Newlands District buses is one of the most unusual of all stories connected with the London independents. Bruce's battle against the Authorities was doomed to failure from the start; he was fighting against overwhelming odds.

Frederick Henry Bruce, who lived at 246 Peckham Rye, had already been associated with an unsuccessful bus concern, the London Circular Omnibus Co. Ltd. Before that he had held a position with the LGOC as an official, and after his ill-fated London Circular Omnibus Company venture he was taken on by Thomas Tilling Ltd. as a bus driver. The hankering to run his own buses must have remained for early in 1926 he unsuccessfully applied to operate a service from Nunhead to Leicester Square. When this was turned down on the grounds that it was over restricted streets he applied to operate Brockley to Peckham High Street via Ivydale Road. He was convinced that the area of Nunhead known as Newlands held great potential for the bus operator, but he was not at that stage given the chance to prove his point as this application was also refused on the same grounds as the other. He tried again in March 1927, this time for a short Peckham Rye—Peckham High Street route, but this met failure also. So, too, did a series of applications in March 1928 for the following: Hither Green (Verdant Lane) to Camberwell Green via Nunhead, Hither Green to Rye Lane via Lewisham, Brockley to Rye Lane via Nunhead, and Newlands Hotel to Peckham High Street.

It was during Bruce's fortnight summer holiday in April 1928 that folk in Peckham Rye and thereabouts became aware of his existence. A petition for a new bus service was being promoted in Stuarts Road, Peckham Rye, with Bruce himself in charge of the proceedings. His proposed route would be between Verdant Lane, Catford—at the entrance to the big Downham L.C.C. estate—via the estate, Bromley Road, Catford Road, Ravensbourne Park, Manwood Road, Marnock Road, Brockley Road, Beecroft Road, Howson Road, Harcourt Road, Brockley Cross, Endwell Road, Mantle Road, Brockley Station, St. Asaph Road, Ivydale Road, Hall Road, and Peckham Rye to Peckham High Street. Though sections of the proposed route were over restricted streets Bruce hoped that the Minister of Transport would be sufficiently impressed by the quantity of signatures on his petition to make an exception in this case. He stated publicly that he had collected 14,000 signatures by the end of his first week's holiday; many of them obtained as a result of door to door canvassing. In case the Minister remained unsympathetic, Bruce had alternative plans up his sleeve. These were to run a peak hour service from Downham to Piccadilly Circus or Oxford Circus via Peckham Rye on a booked seat principle. In either case, he intended to run pneumatic-tyred Maudslay 32-seaters.

Though there was some antipathy towards Bruce's proposal to operate through parts of Lewisham, his scheme to serve the Newlands area of Nunhead was well-received. This heavily-populated area was badly served by public transport and clearly justified better facilities than those provided by the Southern Railway and the L.C.C. trams; it especially needed a direct local service to Peckham. Certain public bodies, including the influential Camberwell Chamber of Commerce, gave their support to Bruce's proposed Downham-Peckham service, which he said would operate on a five minute headway.

After Bruce's initial burst of activity and publicity in April 1928 almost six months were to elapse before his scheme came to the public's attention again. Meanwhile, predictably, Bruce had been called before

Reginald Tilling, as a result of which interview he and his employer parted company. Then, on September 29th, a notice appeared in the window of the "Waverley Arms" in Ivydale Road announcing the inauguration on October 1st of a service of twenty-seaters from there to Peckham Rye Station. The route was quoted and the duration of operation given as 7.45 a.m. to 8 p.m. A fare chart accompanied the notice, and introduced the title Newlands District Motor Service Company. The through fare was to be 2d. single or 3d. return, with a minimum fare on the service of ½d. between the Heaton Arms, Rye Lane, and Peckham Rye Station. All this marked a considerable reduction on Bruce's original plans, both in the length of route to be operated, in the headway, and in the size of vehicle.

Bruce's petition to the Minister of Transport took time to be dealt with and Bruce was impatient to start work. In order to overcome the law, as he thought, Bruce arranged for tickets to be sold by five shops en route. However, even before the service commenced the Police had visited all the proposed booking agents and warned them that the sale of tickets for the Newlands service was illegal. Despite this serious setback Bruce began operation as planned on Monday October 1st, using a Bean twenty-seater which he himself drove all day, maintaining a headway of about 25 mins. At the Peckham end he turned in the forecourt which the station had in those days, with access from Blenheim Grove. Officially no fares were charged, but certain shops were selling 2d. tickets in defiance of the police's warning. At the Waverley Arms end of the route only people holding these tickets were picked up. When the day ended, Bruce had carried 807 passengers. The police lost no time in warning the offending ticket sellers that they were liable to a £5 fine for aiding and abetting Bruce, and no further tickets were sold after the first day. On Tuesday, October 2nd, Bruce had to attend at the Ministry of Transport in connection with his petition, so the bus did not run. Nor did it appear for the next few days. Its reappearance came on Monday, October 15th, and it now carried a notice "Free to Adults", and had its Newlands fleet name painted out. By the side of the driver was a tin box with the words "tickets only" painted on it into which grateful passengers tended to drop gratuities as they alighted. Certainly it was not tickets they dropped, for they usually made a metallic sound as they landed in the tin! Later the tin was replaced by a piece of canvas lying on the floor beside Bruce who, when asked the amount to be paid, usually replied "pay what you like" and sometimes added "we all have to live".

Bruce had a flair for publicity, and before long his efforts to establish his bus service became national news. On October 19th a letter was received from the Minister refusing to make the necessary amendment regulations to the London Traffic Act to allow Bruce to run, and three days later the Daily Mirror sent a reporter hot foot from Fleet Street to find out what was going on. "I shall run this service until the General Election if it costs me £1,000", Bruce told the paper. He also informed them that his petition of the previous May to the House of Commons had been signed by 4,500 householders (a more conservative figure than the 14,000 he quoted at the time, and probably nearer the truth) and had been supported by the Camberwell Borough Council, the Lewisham Camber of Commerce, and nine M.P.'s. He told the same newspaper that "Our local M.P., Mr. Dalton, is resigning, and if no-one else puts up who will support the bus service, I will stand myself." There is no doubt that Bruce's bus was carrying good loads, and when Bruce boasted that on Friday the 19th he carried over 1,000 passengers he was probably not exaggerating. He announced that he intended to have a second bus in service by Friday, October 26th.

Three days late, on October 29th, Bruce's second Bean entered service. At the same time the route was extended from the Waverley Arms via Ivydale Road to Queens Road Station, except after 7.30 p.m. when it continued to turn at the Waverley Arms; the resultant route being somewhat in the shape of a horseshoe. The same fare collection methods were used on this bus as on its predecessor, though it was still ostensibly free. The service worked almost daily from October 15th until Friday, November 23rd. On that day Bruce appeared in court on eleven charges of plying for hire with an unlicensed vehicle and was fined £7 10s. 0d. plus £9 9s. 0d. costs. The service did not run again.

The court case must have come as a bitter blow to Bruce. He must have wondered time after time how the Minister could refuse him permission to operate when he had proved that there was a tremendous demand for his service, and when he had such strong support from so many influential people. Looking at it from the Minister's viewpoint, he clearly could not condone Bruce's illegal working, as to do so would encourage similar services to spring up on restricted streets all over London. Bruce clearly had not expected to be found guilty. Only eight days before he appeared in Court he had addressed a public meeting of over three hundred people at St. Silas' Church Hall, Nunhead, where he outlined his future plans. Soon he would have six more buses ready for service, and he was going to run every 2½ minutes during the peaks—5 in the slack—on the Waverley Arms—Peckham Rye section. A new route was to begin shortly to Hither Green, Verdant Lane, and would be extended in summer to Sevenoaks. The Southern Railway had already given permission for the use of Catford Bridge Station forecourt. Bruce also announced to a very enthusiastic meeting that he hoped soon to run routes in Balham, Epsom, Sutton, Sunbury and Knockholt. Furthermore a limited company was to be formed and would issue 5,000 shares at 5/- apiece to Newlands residents.

A further public meeting took place at the same hall on November 30th. Bruce's service had been withdrawn by this time, and the result of his appearance in court was well known. Compared with a fortnight earlier, the meeting was a very sober one indeed. Bruce proposed the formation of a social club whose members would hold cards and could ride on a special peak hour service from Nunhead to St. Pauls, Moorgate or Victoria via London Bridge. The scheme did not meet with the approval of the audience, who felt that the local service was all that was required.

Bruce's two Beans were disposed of as soon as the service ceased. It is possible that Bruce never in fact owned the vehicles, but hired them from H. Lane & Co. Ltd. of 71 Uverdale Road, Chelsea. The earlier of the two was YX 7518; it was first licensed on August 31st 1928. This was a smaller and less powerful vehicle than XV 5218, which was licensed on October 26th, three days before it entered service. Both bore a livery of chocolate up to the waist line with dark cream above. The fleet name, Newlands District Motor Service Company, was carried along the waist rail, and though painted out on YX 7518 for a while, was later restored. YX 7518 carried eighteen passengers in its Holbrook body and XV 5218 was a Birch-bodied twenty-seater. The earlier bus carried the name A. M. V. Bruce as legal owner (Agnes Maud Victoria; F. H.'s wife), and the other carried "Frederick Henry Bruce, Managing Director, 246 Peckham Rye." Boards at the bottom of the left hand front window on each carried the destinations. YX 7518 passed from Bruce to C. M. Hever's Darenth service at Eynsford, Kent, whilst XV 5218 finished its working life in June 1933, far from home, with the Highland Transport Co. Ltd., at Inverness.

Bruce was down for the count, but not beaten. On March 6th 1929 a yellowish-brown single decker appeared in the East Dulwich Road garage which Bruce used. UC 4840 was a 30-seater Dennis E coach which was not built to Metropolitan Police requirements for a London bus. It had formerly been owned by Red Line until it was traded in to Arlingtons on January 11th. Nothing happened for a few days and then, on March 15th, the report came that Bruce intended to run on Sundays, starting from the 17th, between Elephant & Castle and Honor Oak as route 563. The southern terminus of the route was to be by the gates of Camberwell cemetery, near the Forest Hill Tavern. It did not start on the 17th as planned, as the vehicle did not go for its police plate until Tuesday, March 26th. Meanwhile, on Sunday 24th, it operated an excursion from Barry Road, Dulwich to Windsor for 2/- return.

March 15th saw the formation of the Newlands & District Motor Services Ltd. with a share capital of £2,500 in £1 shares. 36 Peckham Rye, S.E.15. was its registered office. The directors were Bruce and his wife, together with Charles Jonas Meeson and John Frederick Meeson. The Meeson brothers had founded the well-known Arlington Motor Company at Ponders End in 1920 and were now prepared to back Bruce and to provide the vehicles he required. A second ex-Red Line Dennis, UC 3013, this time with bus body, arrived soon after the first and three brand new vehicles were subsequently delivered. MT 2992 was licensed on March 28th, 1929, and was a 32-seater Leyland PLSC-type Lion; MT 3232/3 were a pair of Dennis E's licensed on April 11th and with a similar seating capacity to that of the Lion. All bore the livery introduced by UC 4840, and their arrival brought the Newlands fleet up to its maximum of five vehicles. Good Friday, March 29th, saw the two vehicles then licensed, UC 4840 and MT 2992, running an excursion from Barry Road to Virginia Water and the next day they did a private hire trip to Windsor. Sunday March 31st saw the start of route 563 with one vehicle working the service, MT 2992.

Though Bruce had an expanding fleet of vehicles, he still had no weekday service on which to operate them at this stage. He could only run the 563 on Sundays and Bank Holidays when the Restricted Streets regulation did not apply. He still wanted to link Newlands with Peckham on weekdays but the regulations prevented him from taking his obvious

74

route from the Newlands area along Peckham Rye and Rye Lane to Peckham Rye Station. He made plans to link the Peckham Rye tram terminus with the Heaton Arms, Peckham—the nearest he could get to the Peckham shopping centre, via Cheltenham Road (then called Hall Road), Ivydale Road, Linden Grove, Gibbon Road, Hollydale Road, Evelina Road, Consort Road (then Albert Road) and Heaton Road—all unrestricted streets—to the Heaton Arms. The service, which was numbered 221, began operation on Friday, April 12th with two buses. It was doomed to failure from the start, because two days earlier the LGOC had introduced its "frying-pan" service, 621A/B from Lord Hill, Peckham Rye and Nunhead via Newlands, covering the route that Bruce had tried so hard to pioneer. The service operates almost unchanged to this day, and is now worked by one-man-operated single deckers as the P3. LGOC had commenced the service after approaches from the Camberwell Council, who also asked the London Public and City to consider operating it. At one stage the Council had promised to support only Bruce as the future operator, but changed its mind at the last moment and decided to support anyone who was willing to run the service. The Minister of Transport had insisted that whoever ran it would have to withdraw an equivalent number of buses from services on restricted streets elsewhere, and the Council realised that this excluded Bruce once and for all.

Despite this latest setback, Bruce had more plans for the future, and he still had great faith in the power of public meetings. On Saturday, April 20th, he organised a further meeting at St. Silas's Church Hall with the vicar, the Rev. W. H. Browning in the chair. It got off to a bad start as the main speakers arrived late, and business did not begin until 9.0 p.m., half an hour after the publicised time. The mood of those present was pessimistic, and a suggestion by Bruce that there should be a deputation to the Minister to allow Newlands to run one way round and the LGOC the other met with little enthusiasm. Nominations to form the deputation could not be obtained, so the matter was dropped. Bruce outlined his future hopes. He wanted to extend the 221 from the Heaton Arms to Peckham Rye Station, running free from the Heaton Arms; and on Sundays he would run from Nunhead Station to Peckham Rye Station via Ivydale Road and Hall Road. This would be subject to his ability to find drivers. In the last few days he had sent about a dozen to Scotland Yard but only one had passed out. Finally, Douglas Cooper, the Conservative candidate for Peckham, agreed to support Bruce, who agreed to stand down as Independent candidate at the next General election.

April 24th saw Bruce canvassing in Bellingham Road, Catford, in an abortive attempt to start a service there. On May 30th six sandwichmen were to be seen parading up and down Rye Lane protesting about unfair treatment by the government. After preparing the Newlands buses for three years the route was given to the LGOC, not Bruce. "Why should the large syndicate be favoured against the small trader?" asked the sandwich boards.

In April and May 1929 one or two buses normally ran the 221 on weekdays; occasionally three. On Sundays one and sometimes two were to be found on the 563. The majority of the fleet of five could normally be found in the garage—which was now at the railway arches in Victoria Road (now Bellenden Road), Peckham—because of Bruce's inability to get drivers. It is possible that Bruce never used UC 3013 at all because of this. Friday, May 24th, saw the extension of the 221 for a short distance beyond the Heaton Arms terminus along Rye Lane to Bournemouth Road, close to Peckham Rye Station, by permission of the police. It turned in Holdrons Yard and brought the service nearer to the main centre of Peckham, but it came too late. The LGOC's 621A/B were running Bruce off the road. Even now he tried desperately to hang on, despite a further proposed new route from Brockley Cross to Peckham Rye via Nunhead Lane being rejected in April 1929. In May he tried, probably in desperation, to obtain "when working" journeys from Arlington's premises in Ponders End to Camberwell Green via route 69, right through the heart of the City. Had this scheme worked Bruce would have at least ensured a few busy journeys a day but it did not; the police turned it down and Bruce continued to garage his buses in Peckham. At the same time they rejected a proposal to operate Hither Green Station to Catford Station via the Downham estate. On June 29th Bruce's luck changed momentarily when police approval was given to a new route 202 between New Cross and Rotherhithe, but Bruce no longer had the resources to operate it. A few days later the two new Dennises, MT 3232/3, were seized by Arlingtons for debt. On July 8th a notice appeared on the windows of the 221's proposing the formation of a public company to run the Newlands business; £2,000 had been subscribed—it said—and a further £5,000 in 5/- shares was required. It was too late. On July 12th, two months after it began, 221 ran for the last time. On August 20th Bruce surrendered his licences; beaten at last.

According to a friend, Bruce had lost £3,700 on the project. He moved away from the area and was fortunate in being given a job by the LGOC as a driver at their Turnham Green garage. In April 1932 he became an inspector; a poor substitute for the high ambitions he had once held. Newlands & District Motor Services Ltd. was formally wound up on December 1st 1931.

80 Henslowe Road, East Dulwich
32 Bonar Road, Peckham

HENSLOWE
SWIFT

Henslowe was one of the stock market gambles aimed at making a quick financial killing at the expense of those who could be persuaded that investment in buses would secure a quick and certain profit. The company originated as the brainchild of Henry Alfred Amos of 180 Oakhurst Grove, Dulwich, and Robert Ernest Munn of 5 Scylla Road, Peckham. Amos was described as a merchant and traded from an office in Down Street, Piccadilly, and Munn was quoted as an engineer. On September 1st 1924 they formed the Henslowe Bus Co. Ltd. with an authorised share capital of £5,000 divided into 4,000 10% cumulative

Photo No. 2

The bus that began it all. The original Chocolate Express Leyland is seen in its early days heading, lightly loaded, through Victoria towards Liverpool Street.

Photo No. 3

A Knightsbridge scene of years gone by. Featuring prominently is XN 5761, the newest of Percy Frost Smith's six unsuccessful petrol electrics making its way towards Hammersmith Broadway on the busy route 9.

Photo No. 4

Arthur Ansell's first Skylark bus, Straker Squire XN 555, edges its way through Ewell en route to the Derby with an LGOC B-type following closely behind.
Like many others of its type, its life in London was short, and early in 1926 the body was transferred to a new Dennis.

Photo No. 5
Wintry conditions make driving a hazardous business on an icy road surface where the thin solid
tyres can break into a skid at the slightest opportunity. The driver of an Archway Leyland battles
against the cold in his exposed position behind the wheel on the quiet route 26, one of the comparatively few rural services to interest the independent operators.

preference shares of £1 each and 20,000 ordinaries at 1/-. The company's title was derived from Henslowe Road, East Dulwich, where Amos and Munn had already secured the lease on a former Camberwell Borough Council yard at no. 80, and this location was used as the Company's registered office. A pair of Dennis buses had been ordered prior to the formation of the company and were delivered in August and September 1924 respectively as XU 6730/8234. Their bodies were by Strachan & Brown and were in an attractive colour scheme of green with white windows and upper deck panels and brown bonnet.

Three gentlemen of repute were found willing to lend their names to the Henslowe company by becoming directors although their shareholdings were nominal. On January 14th 1925 Bridgeman Rochfort Mordaunt-Smith, an insurance broker, and William Joseph Coplestone, proprietor of the Pennycomequck Hotel in Plymouth, were elected permanent directors. As company chairman the name of the Rt. Hon. Lord Rotherham lent an air of solidarity. This member of the nobility had latterly been connected with a number of companies none of which had been notably successful. A score of purchasers was quickly found for Henslowe shares apart from the foregoing and these included, as may well have been anticipated, a number of ex-servicemen unable to obtain employment elsewhere and with savings to invest. Thus the company found itself with three drivers and six conductors who were shareholders. The shares were, however, taken up by no means as quickly and eagerly as had been hoped and, after five months, less than £2,000 had been subscribed. Amos and Munn, it should be pointed out, themselves purchased only one preference and 200 ordinary shares (total value £11) each.

In December 1924 the Industrial Issuing Corporation Ltd. had been set up under the auspices of Sir Robert Grierson Bt. to peddle shares and in March 1925 this organisation issued a glowing prospectus written by Amos and aimed at disposing of 2,000 10 per cent profit-sharing and convertible Henslowe bonds. The company already had some buses on the road, said the prospectus, although it did not say how many (there were actually three by this time), and it was estimated that when the number of buses was increased to twenty these would bring in something like £60,000 a year with a gross profit of over £20,000. These figures were said to be based on the actual weekly takings of the existing buses which were nearly £60; with twenty buses this could be raised to over £1,100 per week. The fallacy of the argument was, of course, that there could be no certainty of such results being arrived at, indeed it was almost ludicrous to suggest as a certainty that an enlarged Henslowe company could trade at a profit margin of over 32 per cent. Amos told prospective investors that, as all business was on a cash basis and free of hire purchase, there should be no bad debts, thus the certain amount of trading risk which other companies had to bear was eliminated. This was true of course. The prospectus went on to say that the company hoped to increase its nominal capital to £75,000, omitting to state how little was so far subscribed. The restrictions of the London Traffic Act, then coming very much into force, were carefully omitted from the mug-hunting prospectus.

The low level of issued share capital was clearly a drawback for Amos, Munn and their cronies when seeking bond holders, who would obviously check with the Registrar of Companies as to how much capital was issued. The position improved in March 1925 when a finance company, the E.B.H. Syndicate Ltd., took up 1,600 preference and 2,000 ordinary shares. E.B.H. had been incorporated on December 14th 1922 but had lain dormant until it was activated late in 1924, presumably for the sole purpose of taking shares in Henslowe. Its directors and shareholders were Amos, Munn and their nominees. Having taken out a substantial shareholding in Henslowe in March 1925 E.B.H. went into liquidation five months later upon a resolution that, by virtue of its liabilities, it could no longer continue. Its purpose had presumably been served. Despite warnings in "John Bull", the popular weekly of the time, two gentlemen had unwisely been tempted to invest heavily in Henslowe as bondholders. Many more small shareholders were also induced to invest sums generally between £50 and £150.

Between them, Vice Admiral Sir Cecil Foley Lambert K.C.B. and Lieut. Colonel S. Hickstall-Smith F.R.Ae.S. invested no less than £30,000 in profit sharing bonds plus a premium of ten per cent, their only security being the leasehold premises at Henslowe Road and four buses. They had presumably hoped to make a quick financial killing but this privilege had doubtless gone to the initiators of the Company. Instead a worrying time lay ahead of them as their investments steadily disappeared in the face of Henslowe's trading loss. Sure enough, additional buses continued to be purchase so that, by the end of 1925 the fleet stood at seven. But there were only four schedules on which to run them, so for the greater part of each week almost half the fleet stood idle. Control of an eighth bus, the Swift, was purchased in November 1925 at about which time the company surrendered its lease on the Henslowe Road yard and moved to larger leased premises at 32 Bonar Road, Peckham, which became the registered office on January 1st 1926. This was another former council yard where the outline of the old garage buildings can still be seen in surviving brickwork to the present day.

Details of the first two Henslowe buses have already been noted. The five subsequent arrivals started off in November 1924 with XW 3809 and March 1925 with XX 4194. These were identical to XU 6730/8234. XX 9918, which dated from April 1925, was also a Dennis but differed from the others in being bodied by Wilton. Then came two second hand vehicles. XN 5203 was Henslowe's only Leyland and entered the fleet in July 1925 having previously run for R. S. Conacher as the Waverley. Towards the end of 1925 came MH 2480 ex Edwards & Perkins who had traded for a short time as The Leader. It carried the same combination of Dennis chassis and Strachan & Brown body as the first four Henslowes. The original attractive colour scheme was modified on later deliveries by the elimination of the brown and by the upper parts being painted green. The fleet name was carried in large capital letters on the panel below the lower deck windows, which was painted white. From about the time of its first overhaul each bus was repainted red & cream with the fleet name in "General" fashion. Henslowe's scheduled weekday operations were on 11E, 12C, 37B, 73A, 112B and 535D; Saturdays were the same but with the addition of the 173D. Their operation on the 535 and its various short workings is of note. During summer Sundays the route operated to its full extent as 535 (with no suffix) starting in about April 1925 between Peckham and Green Street Green. For the 1927 season it was extended to run Oxford Circus to Green Street Green.

The Swift business, which has already received brief mention, was an older-established concern than Henslowe. It had been started in May 1923 by John Jacomb of 14 Second Avenue, Mortlake, as the Swift Omnibus Company. On May 18th Jacomb took a chocolate-coloured Dodson-bodied Leyland to Scotland Yard for police examination, and it was duly registered in the following month as PD 5976. It ran principally on routes 37 and 73, though approval was also obtained for the 14 and 88. Not so the 22, which was turned down by the police because of the wide turning circle of Swift's early type Leyland. Under Jacomb's ownership, PD 5976 was garaged at Craig's Garage, 224 Fulham Palace Road but, after a little over two years, he agreed to sell out to Henslowe. On November 18th 1925 a limited company was incorporated with a nominal capital of £1,100 in £1 shares of which 1,095 were held initially by Jacomb and Frederick William Herbert Curtis, a motor engineer of 85 Disraeli Road, Putney, with whom Jacomb appears latterly to have been in partnership. Jacomb and Curtis sold the entire share capital to the Henslowe Bus Co. Ltd. who transferred the registered office to Room 23C, 82 Victoria Street, Westminster. This address was that of E. G. Davison, the proprietor of the Chariot bus, who appears from at least March 1925 to have been in charge of the operational mangement of the Henslowe company. It is assumed, but not confirmed, that the Swift bus operated from Bonar Road along with the Henslowes after its acquisition.

It is doubtful if Henslowe ever ran at a profit except, perhaps, in its first few months. By the Spring of 1926 it had run into serious financial difficulties which led the worried bondholders to apply for the appointment of a Receiver. Charles Sidney Gazzard of 315 Euston Road, N.W.1. was appointed to this position on May 31st 1926 and immediately set about reorganising the business to make it a saleable proposition. Almost immediately he sold one of the surplus buses, MH 2480, to Varsity. Then he separated the Swift concern, which was trading profitably, from its parent company and placed it under the control of Charles H. Pickup who had indicated his readiness to purchase it in due course. Firstly its share capital was transferred on July 24th from Henslowe's name to that of Coplestone and Mordaunt-Smith before passing to Pickup between January and March 1927. The registered office of the Swift Omnibus Co. Ltd. was transferred in July 1926 to 97 Peckham Road whence Pickup's own buses were at that time operating and in January 1927 it moved to Pickup's operational headquarters at 25 Dulwich Village. On June 18th 1928 the company was formally wound up, its licences having been transferred to Pickup about three months previously. At the end the Swift's scheduled weekday operations were 37B, 73A & 173E on Mondays to Fridays and 37B/73D on Saturdays.

In February 1927 Gazzard sold another of the surplus Henslowe buses. This time it was the turn of XN 5203 to be sold, the new owner being

Rapid. A substantial capital reorganisation was now clearly needed if profitable trading was ever to be achieved and on March 30th 1927 a special resolution was passed by the board of directors to reduce the company's share capital from £5,000 to £199 17s. 0d. made up of 2,997 preference shares of 1/- each and 1,000 ordinaries of the same value. Sanction was given for this to be done in the Chancery Division of the High Court on May 17th, and as a result the Receiver was able to withdraw on June 13th and hand over the assets to the Company. A winding-up petition which had been entered by the Avon India Rubber Co. Ltd. on December 8th 1926 was withdrawn. The bondholders, Vice Admiral Lambert and Lieut. Colonel Hickstall-Smith, had lost a great amount of money, but at least there was now the prospect that something could be saved out of the ruins and that the Company could be sold as a going concern. They now took over as the Company's sole directors and appointed John Alfred Dowty as secretary and licensee. Also showing a loss on their investments due to the capital restructuring were 240 small shareholders including the City Motor Omnibus Co. Ltd. who held five preference and twelve ordinary shares.

The Henslowe registered office, which had been moved to Gazzard's Euston Road address when he took over as Receiver, remained there until the business was sold to Public on February 17th 1928 for £9,700 plus £2,300 for the leasehold property. Negotiations for the sale had been in progress since about November 1927 and Public began to operate the vehicles on December 19th in anticipation of completion of the sale. They continued to use the Bonar Road garage until May 19th 1928 when all the Public operations in south London were transferred to the LGOC. Henslowe's demise meant that another operator, A. H. Raper, who had rented space at Bonar Road for his Standard buses, had to look elsewhere for accommodation. The luckless Henslowe Bus Co. Ltd. was wound up on April 7th 1930.

97 Peckham Road, Peckham

At no. 97 Peckham Road, opposite the Walmer Castle public house, was a branch of Tankard & Smith Ltd., a garage chain whose various premises figure prominently throughout this history of the independent operators. The extensive garage buildings still exist though they have long since been converted for another use and are not, when viewed from Peckham Road, immediately recognisable as having once been a garage. The earliest recorded operator in the garage is Pickup who had arrived before July 1926 when Swift moved in. The Pickup concern was the biggest and longest-lived bus business at 97 Peckham Road, remaining there until April 1931, in which month they moved to Toler's Garage in Camberwell whence they had come originally. Another tenant was Enterprise from 1926 to 1928 followed by Glen from March 1928 to 1931. The histories of all these four companies are outlined elsewhere in this chapter.

Toler's Garage, Lothian Road, Camberwell

At no. 5 Lothian Road, Camberwell, is Toler's Garage Ltd. whose main occupation is nowadays the garaging and operation of three fleets of newspaper vans together with vehicles of W. H. Smith & Sons Ltd. The business is still in the hands of the Toler family, though control now rests with a younger generation than that which bought the Lothian Road site from a jobmaster during the first world war.

In terms of the number of operators using it, Toler's was the most important of all the garages used by independents. Sixteen are known to have garaged there between 1923 and 1933. Pickup arrived first in March 1923; the others were Belgravia, British Lion, Clarence, F.W., Genial, Independent, Pembroke, Peraeque, Phoenix, Shamrock, Tally Ho!, Trinity, United, Veleta and Wilton. Some stayed only a short time before moving elsewhere or selling out, and the Tolers recall the difficulty they had in getting some of them to pay their rents which were frequently in arrears.

UNITED

Toler's best customer among the bus-owning fraternity was the United Omnibus Company which started in June 1923 with two buses. The man best remembered in connection with United was James Rickard of 75 Clayton Road, Peckham in whose name the licences were held. He was designated Manager though he also took his turn at driving or conducting as did his co-partners, Frank Sainsbury and Edward John Bradford. In addition to garaging the United buses, Tolers also rented United a workshop inside their garage building where they carried out engine overhauls including, at one time, City's.

Inspiration for forming the bus business came from Frank Sainsbury. Back in January 1908 he had started his working life as a Leyland apprentice at Penrose Street, Walworth. The main work of the depot was maintaining buses and mail vans on a mileage contract, and when the London Central Omnibus Co., who were also at Penrose Street, took over much of this work Sainsbury transferred to their employment, passing to the LGOC in due course. After army service, from which he was invalided out after being gassed at Ypres, he worked briefly for Waring & Gillow before returning to the LGOC late in 1916 as a fitter at Old Kent Road garage. It was then that he met James Rickard who ran a taxi business from nearby premises, and before long he was servicing the cabs for him in the evenings and at weekends. In 1919 he returned to Leyland's, becoming foreman of the unit shop at Kingston. Here he renewed old acquaintances, with Crook and Mallender who later formed the City Motor Omnibus Co. Ltd. and with Edward Bradford, another Leyland employee from Penrose Street days who was now an Assistant Manager at Kingston. When, early in 1923, Sainsbury made up his mind to enter the bus business, Bradford readily agreed to join him. The major problem was that neither had any money but, very kindly, Rickard agreed to loan £600 to Sainsbury and a similar amount to Bradford—whom he did not know personally—on the promise of it being repaid as soon as profits allowed. Rickard himself joined in the business, contributing £1,200. Two Leyland buses were ordered by Bradford and, upon delivery in June 1923 as XO 1390/2962, the United Omnibus Company was in business. The fleetname which was suggested by Sainsbury expressed the sentiment "united we stand, divided we fall."

Early days found the United buses on a number of services, usually 12, 25, 29, 37 and 47. Sundays were enlivened with journeys into the country at Lower Kingswood. The close co-operation with City, which marked most of United's successful career, began tentatively in the early part of 1924 on the unsuccessful and short-lived 65. The United partners kept in touch with Crook and Mallender, the proprietors of City and their former colleagues from Leyland days, and joined them operationally once again in December 1924 on service 517. This time the link between the two proved permanent, and although the 517 ran at a heavy loss, the switch to the 536 a month later ultimately brought wealth and prosperity to United. The two fleets looked similar as United adopted a brown livery like that of City.

From December 1923 to June 1927 five Leyland LB's were purchased (XP 8732, XW 4090, XX 9059, YL 6337 and YT 346) to augment the original two. All except one were bodied by Dodson, the odd man out—XO 2962—having a Wilton body which the partners soon regretted buying as it turned out to have been built of unseasoned timber. The whole fleet of Leyland LBs with the exception of XX 9059 was replaced by seven new Dodson-bodied Titans in 1930/1 (GC 1679/4321, GK 607/608, GP 168/2512, GW 738). These all had open staircase bodies of the standard Dodson style and also had open drivers' cabins. XX 9059, which was now on pneumatic tyres, served as the spare bus.

Back in 1926, on March 8th, a limited company had been formed to take over the business, Rickard, Sainsbury and Bradford being the sole directors. Rickard at this time increased his share of the business to a three-fifths interest, the others holding one fifth of the equity each. Later in the same year the company's registered office moved from Peckham to 83 Avondale Road, Bromley, when Rickard moved house to this more select part of the southern suburbs.

Take over date was fixed by the LPTB as November 1st 1933. After continuing to run their former buses as agents of the LPTB until these were completely absorbed on January 17th 1934, the three partners went their separate ways. Only Sainsbury accepted employment with the Board, becoming a depot engineer until 1937 when—at the age of 42—he decided to retire and to move to Worthing to enjoy the pursuit of golf. Compensation had been fixed at £65,000 and Rickard's three-fifths share of this enabled him to give up work immediately at an even earlier age. Enterprise and hard work had paid handsome dividends.

C.H.P./PICKUP

C.H.P. was the monogram originally used by Charles Henry Pickup for his London buses though this was later replaced by the word Pickup written in a variety of styles. Pickup had been in the motor trade since long before the 1914-8 war and had a successful garage and Daimler hire business at 25 Dulwich Village. This was used as the address for the bus undertaking though Pickup's buses were never garaged there. They were at Toler's Garage to start with but in about 1926 they moved to 97 Peckham Road. Their return to Toler's took place at the end of the day's operations on Friday April 24th 1931 and they remained there until the end. Prior to buying the buses Pickup ran charabancs and two Unics (XF

7628/XH 4004) have been traced to him though there were probably others. These were only small and were probably housed at Pickup's own garage in Dulwich Village. They were regularly used for race outings and made frequent visits to most of the race courses around London starting from Charing Cross, popular destinations being Ascot, Epsom, Gatwick, Hurst Park, Kempton Park, Lingfield, Newmarket and Sandown Park. Popular country destinations such as Windsor, Virginia Water and Dorking were also served from Charing Cross. Coaching would appear to have been discontinued in 1925.

Pickup did not occupy much of his time on the bus business. He lived in Eastbourne where he had cinema and laundry interests and he only visited London two, or at the most three, times a week. His son-in-law, Augustus East, managed his London interests for him.

The first Pickup bus, XN 2799, was a Dodson-bodied Leyland LB which was licensed on March 26th 1923. An identical vehicle, XN 4194, joined it the following month. These two were in an attractive but short-lived colour scheme of pale blue with off-white window frames and black lining-out. A third bus, XP 4668, was licensed on November 1st of the same year and was in the City brown livery into which the first two were repainted in March 1924. XR 8753 arrived in April 1924 and was in a livery officially described as red & straw; but these colours may not have pleased their owner very much as XU 9118 of September 1924 introduced yet another colour scheme of red & off-white which was henceforth adopted as standard for all vehicles. Standardisation on Dodson-bodied Leylands was maintained with the ordering in October 1924 of a further similar pair of vehicles due for delivery in April 1925. This order was later reduced to one, which materialised in the form of XX 9738, but a seventh Leyland eventually came on the scene in January 1926 registered YM 4735.

The seven vehicles were scheduled to work weekdays on routes 21D, 37B and 70. On fine summer Sundays the whole fleet could often be found on the 70 in contrast to the one weekday operation; and all could be fully laden from Clapham Common for a fast afternoon run to the Surrey countryside. On Sundays in 1926 route 261 was an interesting operation which appears not to have been perpetuated in later years.

As we have already seen, the only vehicle in the fleet of the Swift Omnibus Co. Ltd. was placed under Pickup's control in July 1926. PD 5976 was a Dodson-bodied Leyland, just like Pickup's own fleet, and it operated in common with the Pickups on route 37B, with additional journeys on the 73A/173E on Mondays to Fridays and the 73D Saturdays. Pickup purchased the Swift business early in 1927 and in March 1928 the Swift schedules were transferred to Pickup's name and PD 5976 was absorbed into the Pickup fleet as its no. 8.

Up to 1928 the bus fleet had been standarised entirely on the Leyland/Dodson combination. The first break in this standardisation came in June 1928 with the arrival of YW 7829, a 62-seater Guy FCX. This was a unique vehicle, in being the only six-wheeler in London ever to carry an open top body. Its performance was not entirely satisfactory and, when a new bus was placed on order in September 1929, Pickup

83

reverted to Leyland who were asked to supply a Titan. This vehicle, UW 1478, also emerged from the Dodson workshops as an open-topper. Pickup was clearly not as convinced as his contemporaries of the benefits of covered tops. Perhaps the popularity of the open decks on Summer runs on route 70 to Epsom influenced his judgement.

Two more new Titans arrived in April 1931. GO 4367/5424 at last acknowledged that covered tops had come to stay. They had an unusual indicator layout using roller blinds with destination mounted in the roof dome. Then, in January 1932, there arrived the greatest surprise of all. GW 1224 was a long-wheelbase AEC Regent with bodywork supplied by Park Royal, a firm not normally associated with the London independents. This was the forerunner of a fleet of no fewer than five such vehicles (GW 1224/1744/1785, GX 167, GY 839) and was the largest fleet of independent Regents in London excepting, of course, Tillings. All five carried bodies with enclosed stairs and cabs and were thoroughly modern except that they had open top decks, the wooden seats on which were in marked contrast to the moquette-covered cushions of the lower saloon. The engines on the Pickup Regents were bored out to oversize with enlarged pistons to match. This, plus the reduction in body weight resulting from the absence of an upper deck roof, meant that the vehicles were capable of remarkable acceleration and could attain a thrilling turn of speed. Three of them (GW 1744/1785, GX 167) started life in an unusual livery of red relieved by pale green window surrounds, but they later reverted to the standard red & off-white. The arrival of the five Regents between January and June 1932 meant that Pickup had a fleet of seven modern type buses with open tops, plus the two covered-top Titans and an old LB5, XU 9118, which lasted through to LPTB days though by now it had pneumatic tyres. While the Regents were being built at Park Royal the Guy six-wheeler was also dispatched there for a windscreen to be fitted plus lower skirt panels to modernise its appearance.

Pickup's fleet passed to London Transport on November 10th 1933, and he later received £46,000 in compensation. The new owners lost little time in putting upper saloons of the standard STL-type on the Regents, most of which lasted in this form well into the post-war period and were the last ex-central area independent double deckers to run in London.

WILTON

Two new operators began running from Toler's in May 1924; Wilton and British Lion. The proprietors of the Wilton bus were Harry Francis Jolly, who was the licensee, and William Albert Wells. They used Jolly's address of 89 Curtain Road, Shoreditch, as their office. Their new Dennis, XT 5708, was licensed on May 30th 1924 and was examined by the police two days later. It carried the fleet name Wilton and it was probably no mere coincidence that this was also the name of its coachbuilders. As far as is known its main sphere of operation was route 14. In May 1926 the partnership between Jolly and Wells ceased and Wells joined forces with H. Allen. The bus moved to Barrett's garage in Claremont Street, Edmonton at this time and was renamed W.A. (see chapter 7).

BRITISH LION

British Lion was the patriotic name chosen by George Albert Wright for XT 2645, a red & cream Leyland/Dodson. Wright lived at 155 Central Street, Islington, but the bus was garaged at Tolers. The fleet name was carried in a handsome arrangement of black letters around a gold, buckled strap. A second bus, XU 7545, arrived in September 1924 and was a Dennis. The earliest operations appear to have been largely on the 14, and perhaps the 17, though police approval was also obtained for many others. The London Traffic Act led to schedules being deposited for 59A, 73A, 173E Mondays to Fridays and 59A, 73A Saturdays. The first regulated schedules also included route 520 which was also operated by Gray, but this was probably short lived. The British Lion buses were recorded on routes 37B, 49A and 535 but these were Sunday operations.

A limited company was formed on August 22nd 1925 to purchase the business for £150 plus the discharge of all liabilities. Registered office of the British Lion Omnibus Co. Ltd. was Toler's garage at 5 Lothian Road at first, but in February 1926 it became 69 Peckham Street, S.E. On April 6th 1926, it was changed to 33 Effra Road, Brixton, S.W. and on December 13th 1926 it moved yet again to the Stockwell Service Station at 189 Clapham Road, S.W.9. where the buses would also by this time have been housed. The sole shareholders and directors were G. A. Wright and his wife, Mary Anne. On September 2nd 1927 the buses were sold to Public for £6,000 but the company remained active as a garage business. After G. A. Wright died on December 29th 1930 his daughter Cissie became a director in his place. Less than a year after his death, on December 3rd 1931, the company was formally wound up, its proprietors each receiving £2 4s. 3d. for each £1 share held. It had proved a profitable venture for the Wright family.

INDEPENDENT

A man with a most impressive string of christian names was Marcus Aurelius Giovanni Salvatore Forno. He chose for his bus the most appropriate title of all; Independent. Forno lived at 40 Bellefields Road, Brixton, and chose Toler's garage as the base for his bus operation which began in August 1924 with XU 4662, a red & white Daimler. With the introduction of schedules in December 1924 Forno deposited schedules for weekday operation on routes 59A/173E; on Sundays he generally operated on route 69. A second bus was purchased at some time in 1926 or 7, and was also a Daimler. XT 5611 was the vehicle in question, and it had previously run for Peraeque until it and another like it were returned to Roberts by a dissatisfied Mrs. Pinch upon the arrival of a pair of new Leylands in February 1926. Its acquisition meant that Forno could run two Independent buses on Sundays, and it provided a spare vehicle for the other days of the week.

Forno got into money troubles and in May 1928 control of his bus business passed to Sydney Francis Rattenbury of 84 Chancery Lane, W.2., the Receiver in Hedges v Forno. Rattenbury arranged the transfer of XU 4662 and Forno's schedules to Public on May 15th 1928. The other Independent Daimler, XT 5611, was excluded from the sale and reverted to Forno's control. Public, and no doubt other operators too, were dumbfounded when Forno resumed operation with XT 5611 which he now worked daily on route 69, despite having been well-paid by Public for his business. Public lost no time in making a formal complaint to the police who were equally quick to investigate Forno's latest activities. They were singularly unimpressed by his contention that he had only sold his bus to Public and not his times, and duly made the necessary arrangements for him to appear in court on several counts of operating without a licence. He was found guilty, fined £19, and subjected to the withdrawal of his Sunday schedule which had remained in his name. The last recorded date on which Forno's Independent bus operated was Tuesday, November 20th 1928, six months after he had sold out to Public. XT 5611 passed to Cleveland who kept it as a spare until July 1930 when its public service career came to an end.

PEMBROKE

George Frith and Edgar Gilchrist Hope went into partnership as bus owners in September 1924 with the purchase of XU 7474, a Strachan & Brown-bodied Dennis; the Pembroke. Frith was licensee in the early years but he later left the business which was then run solely by Hope. The partners' office address was at 72 (later 143) Railton Road, Herne Hill, and their garage was Toler's. According to the "Motor Transport Year Book" the Pembroke entered service on September 6th 1924 on 59 extending southwards on Sundays from Croydon to Coulsdon. The services always most popular with Frith & Hope were 3 and 59, and schedules were deposited for 3A/59A late in 1924. For Sunday operation they chose, in later years at least, the 184.

In September 1928 the fleet grew temporarily to two when a new bus was purchased. YX 7703 was a single-deck 32-seater supplied by Birch on a Leyland Lion chassis, and upon arrival it normally operated Pembroke's only weekday schedule relegating XU 7474 to a spare. In March 1929 the partners applied, jointly with Robert Hawkins, for a schedule to operate a service from Thornton Heath to Kingston via Carshalton and Worcester Park. This would have provided suitable work for the Leyland Lion but unfortunately the application was refused. Like several others who bought single deckers for central London operation at about this time, Frith & Hope soon decided that a return to the use of a double decker would be a wise proposition. After considering the merits and obtaining quotations for the Leyland Titan and Daimler CF6 the purchase of an A.E.C. Regent was decided upon and Birch were commissioned to supply the body. Before GJ 3020 was delivered in May 1930 Frith had left the partnership, Hope becoming sole proprietor. The original Dennis and the Leyland Lion were both disposed of in 1930, reducing the fleet back to one.

In about July 1929 the Pembroke buses were moved to new headquarters at Wise's garage, 43 Effra Parade, Brixton. Life thereafter was uneventful until the "appointed day" arrived on November 10th 1933 when the Pembroke A.E.C. Regent passed to the LPTB. An award of £6,000 was made to Hope in November 1935.

PHOENIX

Unlike most others at Toler's garage, Phoenix did not start off in business there. George William Glascock, the proprietor of the Phoenix Motor & Omnibus Company, originally garaged at the Brixton Motor Works at 289A Brixton Road, but moved to Toler's in January or February 1925. The one and only Phoenix bus, XL 5250, was first licensed on January 31st 1924 and was the only Thornycroft double decker ever to operate out of Toler's garage. August 10th 1925 saw the incorporation of the Phoenix Omnibus Co. Ltd. of 20 Waterloo Road, Sutton, Surrey; Glascock's home address. The authorised share capital of 500 7½% cumulative preference shares of £1 and 2,000 £1 ordinaries was held entirely by Glascock and his wife, Mrs. C. M. Glascock, who were the sole directors. Glascock's operations prior to 1925 were widespread and he was one of several operators to favour the Camden Town-Reigate run on fine summer Sundays. From 1925 the red & white Phoenix bus worked on routes 3A/17B/59F/170B until November 9th 1927 when it was sold to Public for £2,500 plus £600 which was paid to Glascock for loss of office as Managing Director.

Newton's Garage, Verney Road, Rotherhithe

STANDARD

Arthur Herbert Raper of 72 Waller Road, New Cross, was the proprietor of the Standard buses. Raper bought his first bus, XN 5401, in April 1923 at the age of thirty-six, and built his fleet up to four by November 1926. XT 2565 was the second to arrive, in May 1924, followed by XW 2012 in November 1924, and finally came YR 9020. All were Dodson-bodied Leylands in a brown & cream livery. Under the London Traffic Act three schedules were obtained by Raper who held the fourth bus as a spare. Weekday operation was on routes 12C, 21D and 112B. Sunday operation varied over the years. A notable route worked in the mid-twenties was 535 but by 1933 the Sunday allocation was confined to 12C and 37B.

When he first started in bus work Raper housed his vehicles in the Astbury Road arches at an address officially known as 100 Queens Road Arches. At some time in 1926 they joined the Henslowe fleet at 32 Bonar Road. Fortunately for Raper his buses were much more financially successful than were the Henslowes, but the latters' sale to Public in January 1928 brought a problem for Raper in that he now had to find another garage. Public had purchased 32 Bonar Road and wished to use it for vehicles acquired from other fleets besides Henslowe. Raper was fortunate in being able to rent alternative accommodation at £6 a week in Newton's garage in Verney Road, Rotherhithe, which still stands opposite the present premises of John Newton & Co. Ltd.

On November 29th 1929 Raper licensed his first covered top bus, UW 6777. True to his tradition of maintaining an all Leyland/Dodson fleet, this new Titan was built by the same combination of chassis and body makers. A further similar TD1, GN 4832, arrived in February 1931 and, like its predecessor, ousted one of the earlier open-toppers. GW 550, another new Titan, but this time of the new TD2 variety, arrived in

December 1931 and in July 1932 the process of replacing the original fleet was completed with the purchase of GY 2042. These two splendid, all enclosed vehicles bore the last and most striking of the bodies designed by Dodson for service in London. On November 1st 1933 the Standard fleet, looking the worse for neglect, passed to London Transport who also acquired from Raper a 1930 15.7 hp Crossley car, GH 8874, which he had used in connection with the business. The price paid was £20,500.

72/74 Silwood Street, Rotherhithe
42 Raymouth Road, Rotherhithe

G. H. ALLITT & SONS LTD.

G. H. Allitt & Sons Ltd. of 121 St. James' Road, Bermondsey was one of several road transport contractors who became interested in bus operation in the peak years of 1923/4. Allitts had run charabancs in a small way since at least 1920, but this was a very minor side of their activities compared with their business as carriers, forwarding agents, warehousemen and general motor engineers. Bus operation began in July 1924 with the arrival of XU 3915, a Wilton-bodied Leyland. It was in a red & white livery and bore the title G. H. Allitt & Sons in full. Its first operations appear to have been on the 12, 29 & 36, augmented soon after by the 78, then 11 & 37 before settling down to work regularly on the 47. A further Wilton-bodied Leyland double decker, XW 3199, was licensed in November 1924 and joined its predecessor on route 47. The two double deckers ran alongside the Allitt coach and haulage fleet from very large railway arches at two locations in Rotherhithe; 72/74 Silwood Street, and 42 Raymouth Road.

On March 22nd 1926 a limited company entitled G. H. Allitt & Sons Ltd. was incorporated with registered office at 42 Raymouth Road to take over the existing activities. The four original directors were all Allitts; George Henry was also a cabinet maker, Frank was principally a dairyman, Emile Maurice ran the Rotherhithe business and John had no specified occupation. The authorised share capital was £5,000 of which £4,088 was issued and was held entirely by these four. Under the Managing Directorship of E. M. Allitt the company prospered, particuarly in the field of passenger transport. The firm became well-known for the fleet of Karrier buses and coaches which it built up between 1927 and 1929. This make, which was always rare amongst London operators, was not a successful one when compared with the more reliable products of a comparable nature from other factories such as Dennis, Leyland and Maudslay. Amongst their Karrier fleet Allitt's had a pair of WL6-type six-wheeled coaches. This model was notorious and Allitt's two were returned to their makers en route for the scrap yard after little more than two years in service.

Amongst the Allitt Karrier fleet were two JKL-type four wheelers bought specifically for bus work. UL 4686 and GU 2533 were red-coloured 30-seaters purchased in February and March 1929 respectively. Two more single-deck buses were bought in July 1929; UC 3013, a Dennis E, and MT 2992, a Leyland Lion. These were almost new vehicles bought from Arlington's, the dealers, who had taken possession of them from Newlands & District Motor Services Ltd. On July 23rd these four single deckers commenced a new route, 202, over unrestricted roads from New Cross to the Red Lion, Rotherhithe, with police approval but against the wishes of the Deptford Borough Council. This route, though inaugurated by Allitt's, was the one obtained by F. H. Bruce for his Newlands buses but which he was unable to operate for financial reasons. It prospered and Allitt was joined by Robert Hawkins & Co. Ltd. (Astoria & Nil Desperandum) and E. Puttergill Ltd. (Golden Arrow). The Renown Traction Co. Ltd. also ran a bus on the 202 for a while, but did not resume the operation after the bus concerned caught fire and burnt out in May 1931. Allitt's were obviously impressed by the Dennis E's and purchased two further specimens. UW 1417 was new in September 1929 and UU 1907 came second-hand from Eagle in June 1932. The company then had a maximum of seven single deckers available for the 202, four Dennises, two Karriers and a Leyland.

In 1930 it was considered that the time had arrived for the renewal of the two double deckers, and a pair of Birch-bodied Leyland Titans was ordered as their replacements on route 47. GK 6337 was available for service in December 1930 and GN 3185 in the following month. Both carried a predominantly-red livery with a cream band below the windows on each deck; they had enclosed cabs and open stairs. Upon the arrival of the Titans the Leyland LB's were withdrawn and sold.

With the passing of the London Passenger Transport Act the company decided to dispose of all its passenger transport interests and to invest the capital received therefrom into the development of its other activities. The coach fleet was sold in about June 1933 to Wiggs & Sons Ltd. of Peckham, who traded as Grey Coaches. Allitt's express licences passed to Wiggs together with a small fleet of Karrier and Commer coaches. The buses went to London Transport on December 5th 1933 and the company was subsequently awarded £36,000 compensation by the Arbitration Tribunal. The departure of the buses meant that Allitt's lost a very useful means of free advertisement for its removals business.

It will be recalled from chapter 1 that companies acquired by the LPTB in November and December 1933 remained at their old garages, working under the management of their former owners, until January 17th 1934. The Allitt fleet was an exception to this as the Allitts wanted the buses out of their garages as soon as possible. The LPTB found that A. H. Raper, former owner of the Standard fleet, was prepared to take charge of them temporarily, so from December 5th the ex-Allitt buses ran from the Newton garage in Verney Road for the six weeks up to the date of absorption into the main fleet on January 17th.

G. H. Allitt & Sons Ltd. continued in the hands of the Allitt family until November 1959 when it became a subsidiary of Wells & Son (London) Ltd., based at Cumberland Wharf, Rotherhithe Street, S.E.16. The various haulage and warehousing activities of the Wells family, who had been in business through five generations over a span of 180 years, were put into liquidation in September and October 1974 having latterly been a victim of the Union versus Employer confrontation which has bedevilled and injured London's dockland so gravely in post-war years.

CHAPTER THREE

SOUTH-WEST LONDON

Hercules Road, Lambeth
Fitzalan Street, Lambeth
Salamanca Street, Lambeth

The Southern Railway arches on the west side of Hercules Road, Lambeth, provided homes for three independents. Holiday, Bangs & Dengate ran as Imperial out of arch 192 from August 1924 until 1926 or 7. Percy Frost-Smith rented arch 194 for a while in 1924 and R. S. Quickett ran as the Liberty from March 1923 until July 1925 from an arch whose number has remained unidentified. Also in Hercules Road, but not in a railway arch, was F. H. Hort's Belgravia bus which was garaged at 147 from the time it was bought new in September 1924 until it moved to Toler's at an unknown date. In nearby Fitzalan Street, at nos. 1-5, Shamrock garaged for a few months in 1925. These premises, which were demolished in 1970 to make way for new housing, had for some years prior to 1925 been connected with the motor trade and were at the time occupied by Bee Gee Transport Ltd., a firm of motor engineers. Smith & Kempton's in Salamanca Place, just off the Albert Embankment and on the corner of Salamanca Street, was another railway arch garage and was one of the several homes used by the Enterprise buses which were there from about May 1924 to March 1926. This site is still a motor garage today. When Enterprise left Salamanca Place they spent a few months at the A.B. Garage at 6A Neville Street, Upper Kennington Lane, which was better known as one of the Peraeque garages. Neville Street has now disappeared entirely beneath an estate of LCC flats. All these Lambeth-based operators are dealt with in greater detail elsewhere.

1-3 Brixton Road, Kennington

At the northern end of Brixton Road, at its major junction with Camberwell New Road, is no. 1-3, which in 1972 housed a complex of businesses. It was much the same in the early 'twenties when part of it was a motor cab garage and had been since the earliest days of motorised cabs. This part of the premises was controlled for many years by the British Motor Cab Co. who provided garage space for cabs belonging to private owners as well as their own. One of these private owners was P. H. R. Harris who, when he branched out into buswork in 1924, kept his buses there until he obtained his own premises in Paradise Road, Stockwell, about a year later.

Fleet Garage, Hackford Road, Brixton

Running parallel to the Brixton Road is Hackford Road. The garage at its southern end, no. 96, was once the Fleet Garage & Engineering Works which housed several independents during the period 1923-8. Before this the premises had for many years been a Pickfords depot after which they had housed for about a year the lorries of Express Hauliers Ltd. A short period followed in about 1922 when it was known as the Lansdowne

Garage after which it adopted the Fleet title which it retained up to the war. In 1975 the premises, though used by a firm of wood chips and sawdust contractors, are little changed and the collection of old buildings, the cobbled yard, and the fuel tank lying horizontally on its old brick base still seem to echo a reminder of the A-type Strakers and the Leyland LBs of years gone by.

FLEET

The first bus operator at Hackford Road was the Fleet Omnibus Co. Ltd. This was the brain-child of a vociferous gentleman by the name of Frederick William Prowse of 13 Elsie Road, East Dulwich. Prowse was a taxicab proprietor by profession until he turned his attentions to buswork. He was permanent Managing Director of the company, which was incorporated with a share capital of £1,000 on March 7th 1923 and had its registered office at Prowse's home address until April 5th 1924 when it was transferred to the Fleet garage. His co-directors were a trio of taxi drivers; Frederick Charles Wright, Henry Reuben Chapman and James Alfred Balderson. The four directors held only seventy £1 shares between them, and they endeavoured to raise capital by finding takers for the remainder. There were finally thirty-six shareholders including several relatives of the four directors. The investors, in what appeared to be an undertaking with a bright future ahead of it, came from a variety of trades and included a printer, an inspector of naval ordnance, a newsagent, a tobacco packer, a soldier, a typist, a book folder, two civil servants and four leather dressers. The highest share holdings, 100 each, were by a porter in Walworth and a mechanic in Rio de Janeiro!

Business began with the licensing of a pair of Straker Squires (XN 5243/4) on April 17th. These were painted dark green & white with gold lining. During 1923 the Fleet buses were recorded on a great variety of routes: 3, 11, 12, 14, 27, 33, 35, 53, 59, 73, 78; there may well have been others. At about the time operation began Prowse applied to the police to run a service from Liverpool Street to Twickenham, but permission was refused because Richmond Bridge was considered unsuitable for buses. A. L. Balderson, a relative of one of the directors, was put on the road for a month from August 20th to recommend a system of operation for the future. The result is not known, except that his services were dispensed with in 1924 after it became known that he had become connected with an opposition company. On March 31st 1924 the fleet reached its maximum of four when a pair of Dodson-bodied Dennises, XR7776/8, were licensed.

The Fleet Omnibus Co. Ltd. appears never to have prospered. After less than a year the Board of Directors found it necessary to transfer 10/- a week from the wages of every employee into a suspense account to strengthen the company's finances. Wages were reduced in January 1924 and again from June 1st 1924 making the Fleet crews, who received no bonuses on their takings, some of the lowest paid independent busmen in London and no doubt some of the most discontented! The London Traffic Act saw the company concentrating all its efforts on the 12 group of routes but, deprived of its ability to switch from route to route, it soon found that receipts were diminishing.

At a board meeting on March 2nd 1926 Prowse was empowered by his co-directors to negotiate the sale of the Fleet buses to the LGOC and, three days later on Friday March 5th, ownership of the Fleet Omnibus Co. Ltd. changed hands. It was arranged that the Fleet buses would stay at Hackford Road for the time being under Prowse's supervision, until suitable arrangements could be made to put them into an LGOC garage. Two of the former directors, F. C. Wright and J. A. Balderson, joined the LGOC as a driver and conductor respectively. At the time of acquisition the pattern of operation was: 12 weekdays, 12A/C daily, 12E Sundays. Only three Fleet buses were operated for a while as the police plate on XN 5243 expired on the day of the takeover and the vehicle had to depart to Chiswick for overhaul. On March 26th a temporary replacement was drafted in. It was K163 which, like K329 that went to the EP Fleet on the same date, had been overhauled in green livery with the intention that it should join the Cambrian fleet. K163 was lettered Fleet and ran from Hackford Road until April 15th when it finally went to Cambrian.

On April 28th 1926 the Fleet buses left Hackford Road for the LGOC's Nunhead (AH) garage, and in the following August the two Straker Squires were sent to the EP fleet upon the arrival of a pair of K's, 712/787. These were in a red livery with creamish-grey windows and bore the Fleet fleetname. Two further K's, 722/986, replaced the Dennises, which went to Redburns, between November 1926 and January 1927. The Fleet Omnibus Co. Ltd. was absorbed into the LGOC on January 1st 1928.

PIRATE/H.L.

The Pirate Motor Omnibus Company came into existence in December 1923 as a partnership between Henri Leon, Edward Larthe and Walter Warren Holness. The partners' first and only bus, XP 7724, was licensed on December 13th and approved for service by the police five days later. It was a dark red & white Thornycroft which had a lighter red flag painted on each side sporting the word Pirate. Leon, of 35 Brixton Road, S.W.2., ran the business and held its licences in his name. He is recorded as being previously the owner of a Daimler charabanc XA 9312 which he bought in February 1920. He was described by "Commercial Motor" as courageous in calling his bus Pirate, a sentiment with which many of his fellow independent operators, anxious to live down the stigma of piracy, heartily disagreed.

The Pirate bus operated from the Fleet Garage on a variety of routes before settling down to a regular routine on the 59A. After a while Edward Larthe left the business, and on November 25th 1927 a limited company was formed to take it over. Long before this, at its second overhaul in November 1925, the Pirate bus had been repainted red & white and renamed H.L.; perhaps Pirate had not proved to be such a happy choice of name after all. The new Company was the H.L. Omnibus Co. Ltd. of 35 Brixton Hill, and it had a nominal capital of £600 which was held in equal proportions of 200 shares by Leon, Holness, and Leon's wife Christine Ada, a milliner by trade. The limited company was not long in business, for on March 2nd 1928 its assets were

92

sold to Public, XP 7724 being one of the few Thornycrofts acquired by them. At an extraordinary general meeting on May 2nd it was decided to wind the company up voluntarily, February 28th 1929 duly becoming its last day of existence.

CLARENCE/B & V

Cecil Clarence Brackin of 51 Solon Road, Brixton, joined forces in July 1924 with Reuben Leyton Vandy of 203 High Street South, East Ham, to work on the Clarence bus, whose none-too attractive title may have been inspired by Brackin's middle name. Armed with a hire purchase agreement from the British Motor Trust Co. Ltd. they ordered a new Dennis from Strachan & Brown. XU 3027 was licensed on July 18th 1924 and was garaged initially at Toler's. XU 3027 was obtained for a down-payment of £400 by the partners, who had to repay the balance at a rate of £15 1s. 4d. a week for 78 weeks beginning on July 28th.

The partners had the ambition of obtaining a second bus but had no money with which to do so until they found Mrs. Elizabeth Kipps, a Stockwell widow, willing to put £450 into the business. First of all a limited company had to be formed; this was Brackin & Vandy Ltd. which was incorporated on January 7th 1925 with registered office at 51 Solon Road. A sale agreement was drawn-up to be completed on January 24th, under which Brackin & Vandy Ltd. took over the purchase of XU 3027 (on which £813 8s. 0d. was then outstanding) and bought for £950 the goodwill and stock in trade. Brackin was appointed Managing Director and Mrs. Kipps was Chairman. Vandy, who was also a director, continued as one of the company's drivers, and Mrs. Kipps' sons, Henry and William, were employed as conductors. The only other shareholder was George J. Webster who gave up his job as a cinema manager to become a conductor for the company; he was not a director. The second Dennis was ordered on hire purchase from Strachan & Brown on January 14th 1925 with a down-payment of £100. A further £300 was paid in the February, in which month the bus was licensed, on the 10th as XX 772.

In December 1924 Brackin & Vandy moved from Toler's garage to the Fleet Garage, where they stayed until the business was sold to the LGOC. They were unfortunate in that their second bus entered service after the first retrospective Restricted Streets Order had come into force. They had placed the vehicle on to route 127, where it ran very profitably, but were not allowed to keep it on there despite an appeal to the Minister of Transport. For the same reason it could not join bus no. 1 on the 25 and 59. On April 10th 1925 XX 772 became one of the vehicles initiating the unsuccessful route 527, and shortly afterwards it was switched to the 526, Brackin & Vandy Ltd. becoming a member of the West London Association in due course. On Sundays in 1925 one, and sometimes both, buses operated on route 70 with a maximum of three full journeys to Dorking plus a short to Epsom. The 70 was very much a fair weather service and the company looked around for a more dependable one for its Sunday work. They had inaugurated the 542 (East Acton—Keston) early in the 1925 season and apparently found it none too successful. The 15, 15A, 47 and 78 were all investigated, resulting in the 70 being abandoned in favour of one bus on the 15A and one on the 526. The pattern of operation from 1926 onwards thus became: Bus no. 1 25/59A Mon.-Fri.; 59A Sat.; 15A Sun: Bus no. 2 526D daily. At an unknown date bus no. 1 was renamed B & V, no. 2 having already lost its Clarence fleet name in favour of the diamond insignia of the West London Association.

Early in 1926 the proprietors of Brackin & Vandy Ltd. decided to dispose of the business to the LGOC and negotiated its sale for £3,000. On the afternoon of Thursday, March 18th, the sale was completed at 55 Broadway to take effect from the next day, the 19th. Vandy, the two Kipps sons and Webster stayed with the buses as employees of the LGOC. At the time of takeover one of the buses was away at Birch's being overhauled and was not returned until the 23rd. For just over a month Brackin & Vandy Ltd. continued to run from the Fleet Garage until on Wednesday April 28th the two Dennises were transferred into the LGOC's garage at Nunhead (AH). In November and December 1926 XX 772 and XU 3027 respectively departed for Chiswick Works for repainting en route to join the Redburn fleet. Their replacements, K754/200, maintained the B & V workings until the company was absorbed into the LGOC on January 1st 1928. The only variations in the workings during the period of LGOC control were the addition of route 25A to the operations of bus no. 1 on Saturdays, and the reallocation of bus no. 2 to Battersea (B) garage on January 19th 1927, this being considerably closer to route 526D than Nunhead.

★　　★　　★　　★

Three other operators also ran from the Fleet Garage for varying lengths of time. A1, who had the distinction of running the first standard Dennis 4-tonner, stayed from August 1923 until some time in the following year. The Regent Straker Squire was a tenant from December 1923 until it ceased trading in October 1924, and Mrs. F. V. Brailey's two buses, Magnet and Felix, stayed for a few months in the latter part of 1924. A1 and Regent are described in more detail in chapters 4 and 5 respectively, whilst Mrs. Brailey's bus career is summarised fully later in this chapter.

297A Brixton Road
SHANGHAI/GOLDEN ARROW

For over thirty years the name of Maskell's was connected with the motor car premises at 297A Brixton Road, which at the time of writing had recently been closed for demolition under a wide-ranging redevelopment scheme. One of Maskell's predecessors on this site was the firm of E. Puttergill Ltd. who ran buses under the titles of Shanghai and Golden Arrow. The business was commenced in August 1924 by Evelyn Puttergill, who took delivery of XU 5585, a Strachan & Brown-bodied Dennis called Shanghai. Puttergill, who then lived at 146 Mayall Road, Herne Hill, duly obtained a licence to operate his bus on weekdays on the 34/37B/73A and 173E. On Sundays he normally ran on the 69A. The vehicle was in the attractive livery much favoured by independents, red with white window frames & brown rocker panels with the fleet name in gold lettering.

94

Puttergill traded as the Shanghai Motor Omnibus Company until 1926 when, on February 3rd, there came the incorporation of a limited company, E. Puttergill Ltd. of 76 Atlantic Road, Brixton, Puttergill's home address by this time. The authorised share capital of £1,000 was held entirely by Puttergill and members of his family and Evelyn Puttergill was designated Managing Director. Subsequent changes of home address were accompanied by changes of registered office for E. Puttergill Ltd. By October 1926 it was 19 Jelf Road, Brixton and by March 1928, 68 Mervan Road, also in Brixton.

In 1928 two additions were made to the fleet, both Dennis E-type single deckers. UC 9525 of March 1928 vintage carried a Phoenix-built 30-seater bus body painted red & white which introduced a new fleet name to the London scene; Golden Arrow. YX 7689, which was six months its junior, had a green & black canvas-hooded coach body supplied by Strachan & Brown. This was acquired principally to work a contract service from the London area to Kingswood, Surrey on behalf of Heinemann Ltd., and was joined on this work in May 1929 by another new Strachan & Brown-bodied E-type coach, UU 1950. UC 9525 was obtained merely to provide a spare vehicle for the bus licence already held. By January 1929 XU 5585, the original Dennis double decker, had received the Golden Arrow fleet name and when a new Dodson-bodied Dennis, GN 5896, was licensed on March 1st 1931 to replace XU 5585, it was similarly named. Contrary to what might have been expected, this new arrival was not a Lance such as other Dennis operators had placed into service, but a now outmoded HV-type, the third and last of this model to enter service in London.

During the early part of 1928 the Puttergill vehicles were rehoused at the Stockwell Service Station at 189 Clapham Road, S.W.9. They probably stayed there for only two years at the most for by February 1931 W. Christmas was managing the Puttergill buses from his garage at 363 Clapham Road along with the Cardinal and Summerskill fleets. In January 1933 a pair of new coaches arrived for the Heinemann contract from which they displaced the Dennis E's. The newcomers were JJ 1836/7, a pair of cream & black Duple-bodied Dennis Lancet 32-seaters. Though operated by W. Christmas, these two were not generally kept at his premises but were boarded out at P. H. R. Harris's garage at 55 Paradise Road, Stockwell, for which a rental of 35/- a week was paid. It appears that Harris, who had formerly operated the PHRH and Liberty buses, by then had financial control of the Puttergill business of which his wife Kathleen was secretary.

The only other development of significance to record prior to the acquisition of the business by London Transport was the commencement of a second weekday schedule in March 1931. UC 9525 began to run on route 202, which was then still unrestricted, but only on weekdays; on Sundays it operated as hitherto on the more profitable 69A.

The assets and licences of E. Puttergill Ltd., including the Kingswood express service, passed to London Transport on November 24th 1933 for which the arbitration tribunal awarded £13,500 to E. Puttergill Ltd. on December 5th 1935.

MERCURY/OXFORD/AGS

An operator who shared garage accommodation with Puttergill for much of his bus career was Alfred George Summerskill who, in August 1924 when he bought his first bus, lived at 33 West Cromwell Road, S.W.5. Summerskill was a Geordie, and had only recently arrived in London from Newcastle-on-Tyne having quit the family motor business started by his father some years earlier and incorporated on September 20th 1915 as George Summerskill Ltd. The business was left in the hands of Summerskill's former co-directors, Thomas Lee and John C. Graham Jnr., under which it survived for a further seven years.

Summerskill's new bus was XU 5449, a dark red Dodson-bodied Dennis licensed on the seventh of the month with the fleet name Mercury. A second, identical bus (XW 3474) was purchased in November 1924 and was called Oxford. Mercury is thought to have been garaged initially somewhere in Warwick Road, S.W.5., but by the time Oxford was delivered Summerskill was operating from Samuelson's garage in Page Street, Westminster. A further change of address came about in the summer of 1925 when the vehicles were moved to 297A Brixton Road. Summerskill meanwhile had changed his home address twice, and when A. G. Summerskill Ltd. was formed on September 9th 1925 to take over the business he was living at 8 Raleigh Gardens, Brixton Hill, the address which was used as the company's registered office. 2,002 £1 shares were issued out of a possible 2,500 of which Alfred Summerskill held all but eleven which were in the name of his wife, Diana Patricia Summerskill. The limited company took over operations on September 30th for £250. Just prior to this the two buses had forsaken their original fleetnames in favour of the letters AGS intertwined to form a monogram.

On May 21st 1927 the registered office of A. G. Summerskill was changed to 171 Brixton Hill when the Summerskills moved house yet again. Before this, in February 1927, the original Dennis had been replaced by a new, identical vehicle YE 6281, and in June 1928 the second Dennis departed on the arrival of YW 4483, another new but by now antiquated-looking vehicle of the same type. XU 5449 was sold and became a lorry; it was one of the first standard London-type Dennis double deckers to go. XW 3474 appears to have been retained to enable operation to commence at an unknown date (but by October 1928) on unrestricted route 266. This operation involved a lengthy "when working" journey from London Bridge via route 10 to reach the nearest terminus of the 266 at Leytonstone.

Until 1929 Summerskill took an active part in the operation of his buses, but this ceased when he obtained the Richmond Bridge Garage at 421 Richmond Road, East Twickenham. He ran a garage and coal merchant's business from there with a man called Montagu Levy as manager, later replaced by Morris Mostyn Brown. The Twickenham address became the registered office of A. G. Summerskill Ltd. in October 1929, and the company took out a yearly tenancy on an office in the Richmond Bridge Garage for £75 per annum. It was probably at about this time that AGS buses were placed under Mr. Christmas's control and operated for the remainder of their career from 363 Clapham Road.

96

New Titans were purchased in February 1930 (GC 5781) and February 1932 (GW 1285), both carrying Birch-built 56-seat open staircase bodies. The latter, after a successful bus career during which it was rebodied during the war whilst in the ownership of Cumberland Motor Services Ltd., became a showman's vehicle and was still active in its native London in the late nineteen-sixties. The arrival of the first Titan was followed by the sale of XW 3474 which, like its former partner, became a lorry. In 1931 a spare bus became available for the first time when the working on route 266 was abandoned as uneconomic. Summerskill had unsuccessfully tried in January 1929 to exchange this schedule for one on a Peckham-Nunhead circular route (the one proposed by F. H. Bruce), but this application was turned down. When GW 1285 was delivered the newer of the two remaining Dennisses, YW 4483, became the spare vehicle but YE 6281 remained on the company's strength though delicensed and still on solid tyres.

London Transport acquired the AGS business on November 24th 1933. In addition to the four buses a 20 hp Rover saloon PL 1406 passed to the new owners. At the end the AGS operations were on the 58E/173E on weekdays augmented by the 59C on Saturdays only, a pattern of operation which had remained largely unchanged for about six years. The final Sunday workings were on 184C, though in earlier years the 17 had been much favoured. £20,000 was awarded to the Summerskills by the Arbitration Tribunal, after which they left London altogether to take up farming in Berkshire and later, for many years, at Felpham near Bognor Regis.

The Brixton Motor Works, 287/291 Brixton Road

Close to no. 297A Brixton Road was the Brixton Motor Works Ltd. at 287/291. This garage—now demolished in favour of flats—housed the Phoenix bus of G. W. Glascock whose career was mostly spent at Toler's but whose early days (from January 1924 to about January 1925) were at Brixton. Concurrently with this the depot was used as a coach garage by C. H. Whale who ran various excursions from the Brixton area.

Shaw & Berry's Garage, Porden Road, Brixton
Prince of Wales Garage, 20 Church Road, Brixton
Cedric Garage, 181 Brixton Hill
Ferndale Garage, Ferndale Road, Brixton

Three of the small motor car garages to the south of Lambeth Town Hall, Brixton, provided accommodation for private bus owners. Local government offices now cover the site of Shaw & Berry's former garage on the north side of Porden Road at its junction with Buckden Road whence Holiday, Bangs & Dengate once operated. The Prince of Wales Garage run by the Bull Brothers at 20 Church Road—now renamed St. Matthew's Road—was where Wilson's Optimist bus was kept in its last few months of operation in 1926/7 and it also housed for a while, as we shall see later, Charles Buchan's bus The Lea Rig. A housing estate now covers this site and also the spot where the Cedric Garage once stood at 181 Brixton Hill on the corner of Calders Row. This was the base for F. J. Nunn's Venture bus. Another small motor garage in Brixton, but this time a little to the north of Lambeth Town Hall, was the Ferndale Garage in Ferndale Road where Mrs. F. V. Brailey housed her Fleur de Lys buses in 1925/6.

WILSON/OPTIMIST

No. 81 Waller Road, New Cross was the business address from which Wilson, Waterman & Wilson ran their Wilson bus in its early days. The vehicle in question was XU 9110, a Hickman-bodied Daimler delivered in September 1924 in an unimpressive all-red livery. The licensee and senior partner was George Edward Wilson of 20 Amersham Road, New Cross. Early returns made by Wilson show the bus to have been kept at 81 Waller Road but this was highly unlikely as this address is a terraced house with no accommodation for a bus at the rear. By September 1926 it was garaged at the Prince of Wales Garage in Church Road and could possibly have been there much earlier. An advertisement for the Prince of Wales Garage appeared on the back of the tickets during the bus's latter days.

Initially the Wilson Daimler worked over many services before settling down on the 15A (Mondays to Fridays) and 36 (Saturdays). The only known Sunday workings were on 295. In due course XU 9110 was renamed Optimist, an event which probably occurred on its annual overhaul in August or September 1926. Its independent career came to an end on July 29th 1927 when it passed to Public for £2,750.

VENTURE

Frederick John Nunn of 81 Approach Road, Brixton owned two buses which he ran under the fleet name Venture. Both were red & white Strachan & Brown-bodied Daimlers. Nunn purchased XR 4058 as a "new" vehicle from J. M. Roberts in February 1924. It was licensed on the 29th of that month, it being leap year, and was examined by the police on March 7th. XR 8933 was bought by Nunn in October 1924 when it was only six months old. Its original owners were Statham & Roberts who had run it as the J.S. & S.R. before merging with Julius & Lockwood who had replaced it with a new Dennis.

Nunn submitted a whole list of routes on which he intended to run prior to receipt of his first Daimler. These were 12, 25, 33, 34, 36, 37, 45, 59, 77 and 88 and were followed shortly afterwards by the 17 and 128. The latter, if operated, would probably only have been a Sunday and Bank Holiday service. After the regulation of schedules under the London Traffic Act Nunn's Monday-Friday workings embraced 45A and 59A, and the Saturday schedules 58B and 59A. Nunn had only one weekday schedule, the second vehicle being a spare. Throughout his career the Venture buses were housed at the Cedric Garage.

On February 25th 1928, almost exactly four years to the day after the first Venture bus was licensed, Nunn sold his two vehicles to Public. It is not thought that Nunn was in any way connected with Venture Transport (Hendon) Ltd., the well-known company started by Clare Culverhouse and Robert Marsden in February 1927 despite the fleet name common to both.

142/146 Brixton Hill
Waterworks Road, Brixton Hill

Also on Brixton Hill, but nearer to Lambeth Town Hall than the Cedric Garage, were nos. 142 and 146 which housed Cambrian Landray who sublet to four other operators, Cambrian (with whom they were connected at one time), Percy Frost-Smith, Ingarfield & Bright (Tally Ho!) and Mrs. F. V. Brailey.

CAMBRIAN LANDRAY
THE LEA RIG

Cambrian Landray Ltd. was the name given to a new company incorporated on August 11th 1922 to acquire two associated Brixton-based transport businesses. One was a coaching firm known as F. C. Landray & Co. the owners of which were Frederick Charles Landray, James George Guyatt and Guyatt's son with the same christian names. The Guyatts were also haulage contractors and this was the second business acquired by Cambrian Landray. Two premises were involved in the deal. No. 146 Brixton Hill was a small garage owned by Landray which was capable of holding three charabancs with an office above. Close by, but separated from no. 146 by Waterworks Road, was 142 Brixton Hill, an extensive site owned by the Guyatts whose lorries shared it with some of F. C. Landray & Co.'s charabancs. The authorised share capital of Cambrian Landray Ltd. was £15,000 in £1 shares of which £10,750 was issued initially. Just under half the issued capital was held by Landray and the Guyatts; the remainder (£5,500) was held by Athole Murray Kemp-Gee and James Coventon Moth, on behalf of the Cambrian Coaching & Goods Ltd., hence the "Cambrian" part of the Cambrian Landray fleet name. For their part, Landray and the Guyatts held shares in Cambrian equivalent to those held by the Cambrian directors in Cambrian Landray. An operating agreement was drawn up between Cambrian and Cambrian Landray whereby the former would be run by Kemp-Gee and the latter by F. C. Landray, with a pooling arrangement for their coaching receipts. The registered office of Cambrian Landray Ltd. was initially 620-621 Ulster Chambers, 168 Regent Street, but in December 1922 it was changed to 52 High Street, Tottenham Court Road, Cambrian's headquarters. Cambrian Landray Ltd. began to operate from the retrospective date of June 1st 1922.

Details of the operations of Cambrian Landray Ltd. in its first two years are sparse, though the firm appears to have traded profitably. The main line of business was charabanc operation to south and east coast resorts but additional income was obtained from haulage work, particularly of timber from the docks in 1922/3. Lorry hire accounted for a small part of the company's income and further revenue was obtained by renting garage space to other operators including the bus operators whose names we have already noted. Cleaning, servicing and refuelling was carried out by Cambrian Landray on their behalf in a fine brick building erected at the rear of no. 142. This garage, which still stands largely unaltered in 1975, was capable of housing open-top double deckers and was entered from Waterworks Road. Initially Cambrian Landray Ltd. leased both 142 and 146 Brixton Road but on January 1st 1924 it purchased the freehold of the former from Guyatt senior.

The harmony between Kemp-Gee and Landray was short-lived, and so was the pooling agreement. After a board room disagreement Kemp-Gee resigned as a director of Cambrian Landray Ltd. in October 1923. Landray was allotted 150 additional shares in lieu of salary due to him as Managing Director, and Guyatt junior was allotted the same number of shares in lieu of money advanced to the company. By this means Landray and the Guyatts achieved a 50% shareholding in the business, which henceforth operated completely independently of Cambrian. Early in 1924 a claim was made against Cambrian for £1,772 9s. 2d., said to be outstanding on coach hires, the supply of petrol, sale of rolling stock and garage rent. Certain units of the Cambrian bus fleet had been garaged at Cambrian Landray's from the start of operations in August 1923 and stayed until Cambrian obtained its own depot at Tulse Hill early in 1924. On February 14th 1924 the registered office of Cambrian Landray Ltd. was transferred to 146 Brixton Hill.

In view of the subsequent downfall of Cambrian, the directors of Cambrian Landray were proved right in severing their connection with Kemp-Gee's empire. The Cambrian Landray coach business flourished, and from July 1924 buses were introduced into the fleet. Harmonious relations were established with other coach-owning bus operators such as F. J. Nunn (Venture), Ingarfield & Bright, and Holliday, Bangs & Dengate, and inter-company hiring of coaches regularly took place. In January 1926 the LGOC became, in effect, half-owner of Cambrian Landray when it took control of Cambrian (who still held half the Cambrian Landray shares), but it did not interfere in the operation of the company's affairs.

Cambrian Landray was unique in being the only small independent to operate Tilling Stevens double deckers on its bus services. In May 1924 a contract was made with the Hickman Bodybuilding Co. Ltd. to provide bodies for five reconditioned Tilling Stevens TS 3A chassis which had formerly been used as charabancs. The first vehicle was completed in time to be inspected by the police on July 22nd, and the bus fleet was completed by March 1925. The vehicles concerned were IT 292/293/301/302 and XM 2992. Note the Irish registration numbers which were to be found on many charabancs at the time, and particularly on Tilling Stevens. The registration numbers were issued 'en block' by a dealer and the vehicles concerned never, in fact, operated in Ireland. The Hickman bodies on the Cambrian Landray buses were 48-seaters and were painted red & white with a blue band upon which the fleetname was carried. The overhaul of the first chassis to be rebodied by Hickman (IT 292) was carried out by J. M. Roberts, who probably overhauled the other four also.

Cambrian Landray was normally associated with routes 59 and 159 which it worked daily with four buses, the fifth being a spare. They ventured further afield on December 4th 1925 when one bus (usually IT 292) commenced to run route 532A from Oxford Circus to Warlingham. Even this was closely connected with route 59 which it paralleled as far as the Swan & Sugar Loaf at South Croydon. There were three return journeys each day, leaving Oxford Circus at 11.00 a.m., 2.15 p.m. and 5.50 p.m. Cambrian Landray's fares slightly undercut those of East

Surrey between Croydon and Upper Warlingham, but receipts were not too good and the service was withdrawn on January 25th 1925 without the company feeling the benefit of summer traffic which was always heavy over the country section. From May 1925 certain journeys bore the route number 459 which ran from Oxford Circus to the Red Lion at Coulsdon and was virtually a short working of the 59. Also from about May 1925 the 286C was added to the Sunday itinerary.

In November 1925 control was obtained of the bus formerly run by Charles Alexander Buchan of 32 Dawes Road, Fulham and operated weekdays on route 14 and Sundays on 230. Like Conacher of the Waverley, Buchan turned to the writings of an author from his Scottish homeland when seeking a fleetname. From the pen of Robert Burns had come the love song "The Lea Rig" (which, in English, means a fallow field) and this was the name which Buchan borrowed to grace the sides of XW 4774. The vehicle in question was a red & white Hickman-bodied Daimler which is thought to have been fitted with a Tylor engine, and it was registered for service on December 4th 1924. It had originally been garaged in Craig's Garage at 224 Fulham Palace Road but by October 1925 it had been rehoused at the Prince of Wales Garage, Church Road, Brixton. As a means of transferring ownership the Brixton Motor Omnibus Co. Ltd. was registered on November 4th 1925 with a nominal capital of £500 in £1 shares. Buchan retained an interest in the company by holding five shares; he was also a director and secretary. The remainder of the shares became the property of Landray and the younger Guyatt, who were also directors. After its acquisition The Lea Rig was run to all intents and purposes as part of the Cambrian Landray fleet, whose colours it probably received.

During 1926 the LGOC, who—it will be recalled—were now financially interested in Cambrian Landray, approached the directors with a view to purchasing the whole of the business. Suitable terms were arranged, and the LGOC assumed operational control on January 1st 1927, though they did not obtain financial control until March 2nd. Control of the Brixton Motor Omnibus Co. Ltd. passed to General at the same time. In addition to the five Tilling Stevens buses and the Daimler, a fleet of seven Cambrian Landray coaches passed to General. It is probable that they never ran for their new owner and all were disposed of fairly quickly. Four were Tilling Stevens (XB 9888, IT 413/4/8) and in addition there was a De Dion (IT 303), a Leyland (LX 8984) and a small Unic 14-seater (XH 2265). Prior to their acquisition, the LGOC arranged with Thomas Tilling Ltd. for the latter to take over the Tilling Stevens chassis in exchange for an equivalent number of Straker Squires from the Tilling-controlled Timpson fleet. The five Cambrian Landray double deckers quickly became Timpson buses and were joined by XB 9888, which was rebodied by Tillings with a second-hand Dodson double deck body from a Frost-Smith petrol electric. They were replaced as Cambrian Landray buses on January 21st 1927 by five K's (119, 124, 833, 851, 904) in General livery. On the same date operation was transferred to the LGOC garage at Old Kent Road (P). The Brixton Daimler departed at the end of March in favour of K160 which was operated from Putney Bridge (F) garage.

101

The Cambrian Landray schedules were operated only up to October 20th 1927 following which the vehicles were transferred back to LGOC ownership. The schedules were then held in abeyance until January 1st 1928 when the Brixton Motor Omnibus Co. Ltd. and the non-operational Cambrian Landray Ltd. were absorbed by the LGOC. The ex-Cambrian Landray garage in Waterworks Road was subsequently used by General and later by London Transport as a central garage for Green Line and private hire coaches. This garage still survives to the present day, as do F. C. Landray's old premises nearby at 146 Brixton Hill.

FS PETROL ELECTRIC

Percy Frost-Smith, M.I.M.E., M.Inst.T., M.I.A.E., A.M.I.E.E. had become quite a legend within his own lifetime due to his long and varied career in the transport industry. In his youth he first showed his talents as a pupil of Alfred Dickinson, a Birmingham consultant and civil engineer, from whom he received a course of instruction both in the works and in the drawing office. His career in transport began in 1895 when he went to Spain in connection with the conversion to electricity of the tramway systems in Madrid and Barcelona. On his return to England in 1898 he joined the surveying staff of the British Electric Traction Co. Ltd. who appointed him works manager to the Motor Traction Co. Ltd. in the following year. From Walnut Tree Walk, Kennington, he ran two chain-driven Canstatt Daimlers with iron tyres in a premature attempt to establish a Kennington to Oxford Circus motor bus service. This ceased after about fifteen months whereupon Frost-Smith took up an appointment with Milnes Daimler Ltd. under H. G. Burford, for whom he organised a Liverpool to Manchester motor parcels service and early motor bus services at Hastings and Eastbourne.

1903 saw Percy Frost-Smith as works manager with J. G. Petter & Sons on the production side of the industry, but early in 1905 he was called back to London by H. G. Burford to consider an offer from Thomas Tilling Ltd. to become chief engineer and manager of their motor department. He took up his duties with Tilling on February 1st and under his management the motor department underwent rapid expansion. He was in charge when the pooling and sharing agreement with the LGOC came into force on May 6th 1909, and he was also partly responsible for the design of the highly successful fleet of petrol electrics operated by Tilling. When Tilling Stevens Motors Ltd. was formed early in 1912 he became its chief engineer, though still connected part time with the parent company. Appointment as joint managing director followed in April 1915, a post from which he resigned in August 1920 after designing the post-war fleet of Tilling Stevens buses. He then became a consulting engineer at 64 Victoria Street, S.W.1. On his headed notepaper he described himself as a "specialist in commercial motor vehicles, petrol electric transmission, trackless trolly omnibuses and passenger transport." In his Victoria Street office Frost-Smith made plans to build and operate his own fleet of petrol electric buses in London.

In preparing the designs for his new chassis Frost-Smith worked in conjunction with Phillip V. Powell, a colleague of twelve years' standing.

On the drawing board there emerged a vehicle which Frost-Smith was confident would compete successfully against his former employers. He registered the FS Petrol Electric Equipment Company to assemble the vehicles in a rented railway arch at Highbury and started off by ordering sufficient units for an initial production run of six vehicles. These six were to be for his own use though he was prepared, indeed willing, to accept orders for further vehicles from other users. The Frost-Smith design was a fairly conventional petrol-electric vehicle though certain features were incorporated including a combination control gear for which patent letters were pending. This comprised a box bolted to the dash board slightly left of the driving column from which, by the simple movement of a lever, the driver could operate forward, neutral, electric brake and reverse directly without the need for intermediate rods. The FS chassis was really only an assembly job as all parts were bought in from outside suppliers. Who many of these were, has not been recorded, though it is known that the engine was a standard Dennis 45 hp built by White & Poppe with a Scintilla magneto and Solex carburetter; the propeller shaft, rear axle (except casing), universal joints and steering column were built at Huddersfield by David Brown & Sons Ltd. and Kirkstall supplied the steel forging for the back axle.

The first FS chassis was mobile and had completed tests successfully at the Public Carriage Department by the third week in September 1922, and then went to Dodson's factory for bodying. By October 16th two buses had been completed and Frost-Smith anticipated putting them into service on November 1st. They were fitted out as 48-seaters but on test it was found that they contravened the maximum laden weight limit of 8 tons. This was rectified by the removal of four seats, but the delay that this involved meant that they were not licensed until October 30th as XM 2056/7. Police approval was given on November 2nd which was after the date on which Frost-Smith had hoped to start operating. The third bus, XM 3064, had to be downseated similarly before it was licensed on November 3rd. When operation finally started on November 12th 1922 Frost-Smith could have had no inkling that his scheme was doomed to bring him to the verge of financial collapse. His three buses looked a brave sight in their blue & white livery with the fleet name PETROL FS ELECTRIC emblazoned proudly on their sides.

The fleet was quickly increased to six. XM 4568, which had been built as a 44-seater, was found to be 2 cwt. lighter than its predecessors and was increased to a 46-seater prior to being licensed on December 4th. XM 5302 dated from December 19th and was a 47-seater as was XM 5761, the sixth and last FS petrol electric whose log book was issued on December 29th. The last three were reduced to 44-seaters in June 1923, possibly as a result of weight increase due to chassis strengthening.

Frost-Smith was dogged with bad fortune from the start. His buses were relentlessly shadowed by Tilling vehicles which even travelled with them as far as their garage which, in the first instance, was White's in Porson Street, Lewisham. Before he began operation Frost-Smith had spent some time studying possible routes and evolved a pattern of operation which soon proved unsatisfactory in practice. He had come to the conclusion that he would do best to break away from the traditional

103

pattern of LGOC routes and to run two services of his own between Lee Green and Liverpool Street via Victoria. He inaugurated the two services in November 1922, both un-numbered. They were identical between Lee Green and Victoria, which was by way of Lewisham, New Cross, Peckham, Camberwell and Vauxhall. From Victoria one route was via Victoria Street, Charing Cross, Ludgate Circus and Bank and the other via Hyde Park Corner, Marble Arch, Oxford Street, Holborn and Bank. A third variant, introduced in December 1922, was via Hyde Park Corner, Piccadilly, Shaftesbury Avenue, Holborn and Bank. The most lucrative part of these operations soon proved to be within central London, and after a few weeks the FS fleet was concentrated between Victoria and Liverpool Street following the line of the LGOC's route 11. It will be recalled that Frost-Smith's office was in Victoria Street, this having been specifically selected—he claimed—as being ideally suited for studying bus operation along route 11. It did not go unnoticed, however, that much of his "studying" was done in the bar of the nearby "Prince Albert" whence he would sometimes emerge to "borrow" money from the conductors' cash bag on one of his buses as it passed.

The Victoria—Liverpool Street operation lasted only a matter of weeks before Frost-Smith had another change of mind and commenced the service for which he is probably best remembered. Starting in mid-January 1923, he linked Ealing Broadway in London's western suburbs with Farnborough (Kent), far in the south. The through operation may have proved too lengthy, as before long buses were working the service in two sections, Ealing—Charing Cross and Oxford Circus—Farnborough. Like its predecessors, this venture was also short-lived, and it was followed by a spell of operation in true "pirate" style over a whole variety of services. For example, on April 17th, a day when all six buses were roadworthy, they could be found on General's routes 9, 12, 33, 36 and 47. Subsequently Frost-Smith reverted to a single service, this time the 88, on which his buses remained for the remainder of their career. With the shift away from Lewisham-based services Percy Frost-Smith found it necessary to rehouse his buses which, by June 1923, were operating from railway arch 194 in Hercules Road, Lambeth. A second move was made in about July 1924 to Waterworks Road where the FS fleet lived out the remainder of its career.

Chasing by combine operators was by no means the only problem encountered by Percy Frost-Smith. To make matters worse his buses did not prove as reliable as he had anticipated and breakdowns were far more common than they should have been. They suffered from pronounced overheating despite strict orders to drivers to avoid racing. Further trouble came from the back axle assembly which was not heavy enough to stand the torque of the electric motor. On several occasions stranded passengers from a broken-down FS petrol electric were rescued by a passing Chocolate Express whose owners were probably glad that they had resisted Frost-Smith's exhortations to buy one of his bus petrol electrics and wisely remained faithful to their infinitely superior Leylands.

A shortage of capital may have been the reason for the formation on March 19th 1923 of the FS Petrol Electric Omnibus Co. Ltd. which had a

104

nominal capital of £15,000 in £1 shares. Percy Frost-Smith's office at 64 Victoria Street, S.W.1. became the registered office of the new company which, by an agreement of March 27th, took over the buses for £10,051 3s. 9d. of which £6,000 was in shares and the rest in cash. 12,002 shares were issued initially; half to Frost-Smith and the balance to John Macfarlan Mitchell, a Kelvinside, Glasgow, sales representative. In September 1923 Mitchell was allotted 765 more shares and became the major shareholder, though Percy Frost-Smith remained as Chairman.

Although the FS chassis was offered for sale to the public no orders were ever received. In fact no further FS petrol electric buses were built after the original six, probably because of the firm's deteriorating financial position. The books began to look very red in 1924, so much so that at an Extraordinary General Meeting on November 22nd it was resolved to wind up the company because its liabilities made it impossible to carry on. Sidney Herbert Clinch of 119 Moorgate, E.C.2., was appointed liquidator and on December 3rd his address became the company's registered office. Bus operating ceased on December 1st after which the vehicles were put up for sale. In March 1925 they were bought by Alexander Timpson who put two of them into his bus fleet and converted three others into charabancs. The sixth remained, as far as we know, unused.

Percy Frost-Smith lost everything with the collapse of the company. The transport world was shocked to hear that, on Christmas eve 1924, less than a month after his buses were withdrawn, he had died of cancer after a brief illness of only one day. His widow and children were left completely unprovided for and in the following month a fund was started by W. J. Sharp of Edward Sharp & Sons Ltd., the Maidstone sweet manufacturers, to assist them.

The disposal of the assets of the FS Petrol Electric Omnibus Co. Ltd. was handled by Goddard & Smith and took place in March 1925. The six buses fetched between £150 and £175 each and a dismantled Dennis engine sold for £51. Sundry items brought the total to a pitiful £1,200 or thereabouts. The FS Petrol Electric Omnibus Co. Ltd. was wound up on December 5th 1925.

TALLY HO!/I & B
William Fielder Ingarfield of 37 Aytoun Road, Brixton, was in partnership with Lester Harold Bright in the Tally Ho! bus, which was garaged at Waterworks Road when new in February 1925, though it had moved to Toler's at Camberwell by September 3rd of the same year. They were also coach operators and sometimes hired vehicles to Cambrian Landray. The Tally Ho! was XX 1514, a Hickman-bodied Daimler which was first registered on February 17th 1925. It wore a red & white livery, and carried the fleet name in gold block letters surmounting an illustration of a hunting horn. In February 1926, when the vehicle was overhauled and repainted at Roberts' works in Shepherds Bush, the Tally Ho! design was replaced by the star symbol of the West London Association. After the Association ceased to function it is believed to have carried the fleet letters I & B standing for Ingarfield & Bright, the name under which the partners traded.

Ingarfield & Bright operated principally on route 526, often with Ingarfield conducting, and they were the last independent to survive on this route except for Birch. In April 1928 they received an offer from the latter to purchase the bus, which they accepted. It was operated by Birch out of Cathcart Street from April 5th 1928 although no immediate transfer of licences took place and Ingarfield remained the licensee on behalf of Birch. A limited company, Ingarfield & Bright Ltd., was formed on July 7th 1928 to take over the operation and on October 18th its fleet was doubled when a new vehicle was licensed as a spare for the Daimler with a view to its ultimate displacement. The vehicle in question was XV 1153, a Leyland Lion single decker in full Birch livery apart from the legal owner's panel which carried the name Ingarfield & Bright Ltd. A schedule was obtained for XV 1153 on unrestricted route 214, upon which it ran when not required as a substitute for the Daimler on the 526D. The Daimler continued to run in its red & white livery until March 1929 when it was withdrawn for overhaul. After the overhaul was completed Birch advertised it for sale quoting the date of manufacture as 1919, this presumably being a reference to the year in which the chassis was constructed for the War Department.

On February 1st 1929 Birch absorbed the I & B workings. Ingarfield & Bright Ltd. was retained as the operating company for Birch's private hire activities, being renamed Birch Brothers (I.B.) Ltd. in November 1949 and Birch Brothers (Transport) Ltd. in November 1954.

6-10 Tulse Hill, Brixton
Wise's Garage, 43 Effra Parade, Brixton

Two further garages in Brixton remain to be mentioned. At 6-10 Tulse Hill, Cambrian Coaching & Goods Transport Ltd. had its south London garage to which were allocated twenty-six buses from about April 1924 to July 1925. This substantial garage building was erected by Cambrian who provided a yard at the side for additional open-air accommodation together with a separate workshop at the rear. The premises were afterwards used for over forty years by Northern Motor Utilities Ltd. and, only slightly modernised, are still giving good service to a firm of egg distributors. At 43 Effra Parade there used to be a garage owned by J. J. Wise & Son, a firm of haulage contractors. In the last four years of independent bus operation the Wises rented garage space to three operators, Adelaide, H & B and Pembroke. Descriptions of the Adelaide and Pembroke buses are given on pages 147 and 86 respectively. H & B now follows.

IMPERIAL/H & B

H & B started off in August 1924 as Imperial, and at that time it was run not only by H & B but by D also. These initials stood for William Charles Holliday, Percy Rawlings Bangs and William Henry Dengate. Holliday was the licence holder and the company's 'office' was his home at 9 Branksome Road, Brixton. The three men operated in a small way for about three years with a single Hickman-bodied Daimler, XU 5524, which had been licensed on August 11th 1924. As far as is known they usually ran—at least on weekdays—on the 59 or parts thereof though in their earliest days the partners obtained plates for the 11, 27 and 37. In about December 1925 they dabbled for a short while in the 532A (Oxford Circus-Warlingham) but this would have been a Sunday operation. Railway arch 192 in Hercules Road was the Daimler's first garage, but from the latter part of 1927 there followed a spell in Porden Road, Brixton. The HB & D bus was painted in an all-over red livery and carried the fleet name Imperial in large, gold script letters which originally sloped upwards from the "I" towards the final "l" though on its first repainting the name was placed on an even keel. The partners also ran at least one charabanc at this time, but no particulars of it have so far been traced.

November 1927 saw the delivery of a new bus, Birch-bodied Dennis YU 4689, which relegated the Daimler to spare. It perpetuated the all-red livery and carried the fleet name H & B written as a monogram. D was omitted because Dengate had departed for Sussex. The Dengate family's buses which operated from the garage at Beckley to destinations such as Rye and Hastings were a feature of the East Sussex scene for very many years, and right up to 1974 the Dengate name was still in evidence though the Rye-based firm running the buses had no family connection with the Dengates.

Things really began to happen for Holliday & Bangs in 1928 when they ventured into the field of long distance coaching after an attempt to expand their bus interests with a new Thornton Heath Pond—Waddon service had proved abortive. They started up "The London & Kings Lynn Limited Stop Pullman Coach Service" and from Church Road, Brixton a coach left daily via London (Victoria), Chelmsford, Braintree, Halstead, Sudbury, Bury St. Edmunds and Thetford. Two new Reo Pullmans worked the service between them at first, augmented after a short while by a Thornycroft 20-seater. The coach fleet further expanded in 1930 with the arrival of some small Dennis 18-seaters. This additional rolling stock enabled an extra journey per day to be introduced in each direction, the morning journey from London operating north of Bury St. Edmunds via Thetford and Northwold and the afternoon journey via Brandon and Downham Market, the reverse applying on journeys from Kings Lynn. During the winter months of 1930 only one journey per day was operated, this being via Thetford. The Kings Lynn via Brandon service was later abandoned in favour of a new operation which paralleled the old as far as Bury St. Edmunds and then operated via Ixworth, Hopton and Swaffham to terminate at Fakenham, the pattern of service then being one journey daily in each direction to Kings Lynn via Thetford and one to Fakenham, augmented by extras at busy periods. The title of the service was simplified to "Limited Stop Pullman Coach Service".

With their entry into the realms of long distance coaching, the partners found it necessary to obtain an office from which to organise seat bookins, etc. They established a Control Office, as they called it, first of all at 14A Acre Lane, Brixton, and from September 29th 1930 at nearby 3 Tulse Hill. Prior to this the expansion of the fleet had dictated the move in January or February 1929 to Wise's garage.

A surprising addition to the fleet came in May 1930. The Dennis HS chassis of GJ 5506 was fairly normal for a London vehicle, though never a particularly popular model in the metropolis. The surprise was the Birch-built body which carried an open-top. Apart from the vehicles purchased by Pickup this was the only independent open-topper to enter service in London in the nineteen-thirties. In anticipation of its arrival the original Imperial Daimler was withdrawn on March 25th and sold. GJ 5506 was the last double decker to be purchased, and on December 5th 1933 it passed to London Transport together with YU 4689, which was now the spare bus and was still on solid tyres. The compensation was subsequently fixed at £8,800. The final operations were: weekdays 59A/B/F; Sundays 59A/B/C.

The partners did not immediately dispose of the coach business. As Holliday & Bangs Ltd. (registered office 9 Southampton Street, W.C.1.) they continued to operate the Kings Lynn and Fakenham services until 1934 when they were sold to Eastern Counties. In December 1935 Percy Bangs applied for employment with London Transport but he was refused on the grounds that, at 43, he was too old.

★　　★　　★　　★

In Stockwell, which adjoins Brixton to the west, were once two very important independent bus garages (55 Paradise Road and 363 Clapham Road) and one of less importance (189 Clapham Road).

55 Paradise Road, Stockwell

PHRH
LIBERTY
Philip Henry Roper Harris had been a taxicab owner since 1908 and could be expected, with his wide knowledge of London, to know where the best passenger traffic was to be found. Harris was the owner of seventeen Unic taxis when he decided to diversify his interests and run buses as well. His start in buswork came on July 3rd 1924 when the first of three Dennises which he had on order was licensed. This was XU 767, and it was followed in September by XU 7430 and XU 9057. They all carried red & white bodies supplied by Dodson with the fleet name PHRH in the form of a huge letter P within the extended loop of which were the other three initials.

At first Harris's buses ran from the garage where his taxis were kept at 1/3 Brixton Road, Kennington, but in the first half of 1925 he obtained his own freehold premises at 55 Paradise Road, Stockwell. These comprised a cottage in which Harris and his wife lived, a garage and a petrol pump. A laundry business had once been conducted from there, but in about 1917 a motor builder and engineer by the name of Richard Allan moved in. It later became known as the Studley Garage, a title which Harris retained when he bought 55 Paradise Road. The Studley Garage was no stranger to independent buses for the Service bus of Allery & Bernard had operated out of it from the time it was new in mid-1923 until it moved, at an unknown date, to the Red Rose garage in Vauxhall Bridge Road. The history of the Service bus is outlined in chapter 4. Prior to Harris's purchase of it, the Studley Garage had existed mainly on the servicing and repairing of private cars, and he continued this line of business as well as running his buses and taxis from there.

The PHRH buses were often to be found on routes 11, 34, 36, 59 and 74 and licences were secured under the London Traffic Act to run three buses on the 11E, 34 and 49A on weekdays. Sunday workings have not been recorded except that they included the 284 from April 1925. When Harris wished to expand his operations in 1925/6 he did so by placing a pair of new single deckers in service on unrestricted routes. The vehicles concerned, both Dennises, were small pneumatic-tyred vehicles seating 26 in the case of YL 2999 of August 1925 and 25 in YP 7106, which was new in July 1926. YL 2999 entered service in September 1925 on 547 but this proved unremunerative and the bus was transferred to join the Clarendons on route 297 upon which it was augmented by YP 7106. The last new double decker to join the fleet, Dennis YE 5277, came in February 1927 and was a spare vehicle. Like all Harris's buses it had a Dodson body.

Meanwhile Harris had acquired the Liberty bus, operated by Reginald Scott Quickett whose address has been variously quoted as 46 Upper Gloucester Place, Dorset Square and 60 Alexandra Road, Gipsy Hill. This bus had started off life in a rather unusual way and owed its existence to the whims of F. A. Macquiston, K.C., the Member of Parliament for Argyll. This gentleman had very definite views on the way buses should be run in London and attributed the traffic congestion, which was then—as now—a serious problem in the capital, as being in a large degree due to the buses run by the combine being confined to their defined routes from which they did not stray even when traffic conditions got bad. He unashamedly advocated that buses should be run like taxis, wherever the trade justified it, and likened them to taxis even further in that whereas, in his view, owner-driven taxis were the hardest and most efficiently worked, so this should also be the case with buses. Another theory of his was that the combine was making very large profits on its bus services, and he wanted to test this out. Macquiston ordered a bus chassis from Leyland and a body from Dodson, which he arranged should be painted blue & primrose and named Liberty. Then he looked around for someone suitable to run it for him.

The man he found was Quickett. He was a young ex-flying officer and was a first-class motorist and mechanic. He regarded the project with enthusiasm. Macquiston arranged for Quickett to buy the bus from him for the price he paid for it—by instalments—and advanced him some working capital as well as paying the third party insurance. Leyland were three months late delivering the bus, but it was ready to be licensed on March 13th 1923 as XN 1344. Quickett arranged for it to be garaged in a railway arch in Hercules Road, though by December 1923 he had moved north of the Thames to Harmood Street, Chalk Farm.

As anticipated, the Liberty bus worked over a great variety of routes in its early days. When opposition from the LGOC's chasers got too intense Quickett would switch to another service and operate on it until the Combine's officials located him again and put on another batch of chasers. He obtained approval at various times to run on sections of numerous routes. For three days from June 4th to 6th 1924 he worked on the 70 in connection with Epsom races. Under the London Traffic Act Quickett had to settle down to a regular pattern of operation and he selected the 284A as being a profitable one to concentrate on. Perhaps he found the restriction of being tied to a schedule too much for him, or maybe he was unable to make the bus pay under the new system. Whatever his reasons, he decided in 1925 to sell to P. H. R. Harris. In order to do so he created the Liberty Bus Co. Ltd. on July 23rd 1925 with a capital of £1,000 of which Harris and his wife became the sole directors. The vehicle's home was then changed to Harris's address at Paradise Road but it retained its old blue & primrose Liberty livery. From Harris's point of view this bus was an odd man out, being a Leyland, so in February 1926 Harris swopped it with City for XR 9753, a Dennis which was non-standard in the City fleet.

Harris was in due course approached by A. T. Bennett to sell out to Public, which he agreed to do. His vehicles passed to Public on September 29th 1927, together with the Paradise Road premises, for a total of £24,000. 55 Paradise Road became a Public garage for a while and Harris took an appointment with the company as Assistant General Manager.

Harris's stay with Public was short-lived. He acquired back the property in Paradise Road in June 1928 and began to run a number of long-distance coach services from there. On July 21st 1928 he formed Coachways Ltd. which, in its year of maximum operation, 1929, ran daily services with four Dennis E's from London (Aldwych) to Harrogate via Bradford & Leeds, and Torquay via Salisbury and Yeovil. The Yorkshire service, which was operated in conjunction with the Hale Garage Coach Co. Ltd.—a successor to the Meteor buses—was cut back to Leeds by 1930 and the highly competitive Torquay operation was abandoned. Harris also ran a London-Worthing service under the title of Fairway Super Coaches. In 1927 he purchased control of the Varsity Omnibus Co. Ltd. from S. F. G. Collier and renamed it Fairway Coaches Ltd. on October 3rd 1928. This company assumed control of the Worthing service. From about 1931 until it was taken over by the LPTB Harris had a financial interest in E. Puttergill Ltd., the operator of the Golden Arrow buses. Harris's coaching interests extended still further in 1932 when he became a director of Upminster Services Ltd., which was formed on June 15th after a battle, both on the road and in the law courts, over the Aldgate-Upminster service. The formation of the new company marked an uneasy truce between Harris and the forceful Edward Hillman, who was appointed a co-director with Harris, and shortly afterwards the latter sold his interest in the business to Hillman. Despite his coaching activities Harris still found time to keep his taxi fleet going, and in 1932/3 he had twenty on the road. In April 1933 the London-Leeds service was sold to the Yorkshire "pool" of operators. This was followed by the sale in December 1933 of the Fairway company to Southdown, who liquidated it on February 21st 1934. The old premises in Paradise Road continued to be used for housing taxis but are now lost under a housing scheme built by the LCC in the nineteen-fifties.

The disposal of Fairway followed Harris's untimely death on August 26th 1933 at the age of 47. His estate, which amounted to £5,982, passed to his wife Kathleen, who had helped him in his bus activities, "for so long as she remains my widow. If she remarries or allows any other man to usurp my place and affection, the whole of my estate has to pass to and be divided equally between my three children . . . My reason for this is that if my wife wishes to remarry, which she is entitled to do, her husband should work for her as I myself have done." Philip Henry Roper Harris was a hard taskmaster to the last!

363/5 Clapham Road

363/5 Clapham Road, S.W.9, was the headquarters of the Commercial Motor Garage & Repair Co. Ltd. for over two decades. Only after the 1939-45 war did it change hands when it became a London depot for Transport Equipment (Thornycroft) Ltd. It is now part of the Mayflower filling station, the entrance to the old garage being on the left, as you face it, of a one-time private house behind which is the extensive garage building itself. As its name implied, the Commercial Motor Garage & Repair Co. Ltd. specialised in dealing with commercial vehicles, both goods and passenger. It was under the control of William Christmas, a man well respected in the industry and with many years of motor vehicle experience to his credit. Christmas had formerly worked for Dennis Brothers and naturally specialised in Dennis products. He overhauled many of the Dennis buses running in London, and even operators as far afield as Romford District Motor Services brought their Dennises to him. His works were first used as a bus garage for a few months in 1927 to house the Pullman bus, but in the closing years of the independent era Christmas expanded his bus activities considerably and assumed control of eight buses on behalf of three companies based on verbal agreements with them. They were the Cardinal Omnibus Co. Ltd. (3 buses), A. G. Summerskill Ltd. (3) and E. Puttergill Ltd. (2). He provided most of the services required by these proprietors, the last concerning themselves only with banking and accounts, and the provision of tickets and waybills. All work on the buses was carried out by Christmas's staff, and he also supervised the crews and their work. This side of his business ceased as Tuesday, January 16th 1934 drew to a close. Next day the buses, which Christmas had worked on behalf of London Transport since November 1933, were to be found running from the Board's own garages following the overnight reorganisation which had merged all the previously acquired independent businesses into the Board's main network of operations.

The Stockwell Service Station, 189 Clapham Road

The Stockwell Service Station at 189 Clapham Road has already been recorded in the history of the British Lion Omnibus Co. Ltd. Puttergill's buses were kept there for a short while from about March 1928 until they moved to no. 363. A Volkswagen dealer now uses the premises.

14 Stockwell Park Road, Stockwell
(also 6A Neville Street, Kennington)

In Stockwell Park Road, which used to link Stockwell with Brixton but has now largely disappeared, lived Mrs. Blanch Pinch at number 14. She was one of the proprietors of the Peraeque buses.

PERAEQUE

Peraeque Transport Co. Ltd. was the name of a company incorporated on March 3rd 1927 with a capital of £500 to purchase for £450 the three-bus business run by Simpson, Cox & Pinch of 1 Guildford Road, Stockwell. The partners were Arthur Simpson, Mrs. Blanch Pinch and Thomas F. Cox. Arthur Simpson was licensee until the limited company came into being with Blanch Pinch as Managing Director and Secretary. Mrs. Pinch virtually ran the company and was amply qualified to do so. She was a middle-aged, well-educated, forceful and astute business-woman who might well have been a suffragette in an earlier age or a women's liberation leader were she here today. She was well known amongst the bus fraternity and attended all their social functions even though she was a cripple and had to move around with the aid of a walking stick.

The first Peraeque bus arrived on the scene in May 1924, and was a dark red & white Daimler, XT 5611, with Strachan & Brown bodywork. The Peraeque fleetname was in white letters on a black panel with scrolled ends. A second bus joined it early in 1925 and was similar except that the body was by Hickman. MF 8001 was new in May 1924 and had been unsuccessfully operated by Harry Ball under the title Kathleen. Like many others of their breed, these two Daimlers proved unreliable in their operation, and a written battle commenced between Mrs. Pinch and J. M. Roberts which ended up in the law courts. As no satisfaction could be obtained from Roberts the partners ordered a pair of new Leylands to replace the Daimlers, and these were delivered in February 1926 and licensed on the 12th as YM 8086/7. They carried Dodson bodies, as indeed did all subsequent Peraeque buses and upon their arrival the two Daimlers were returned to Roberts. About a year later a third Leyland was purchased. YR 5805 had been delivered new to A. H. Young for operation by the Empress Omnibus Co. Ltd. of Wood Green in November 1926, just before Empress sold out to the LGOC, but it was not included in the takeover and was sold by Young to Peraeque having seen little if any service up to then. The fleet strength rose to five with the purchase of Peraeque's only Dennis, YT 8381, on September 1st 1927, and their only single-decker, Leyland PLSC-type Lion UC 4756 in February 1928.

The original garage for Peraeque was Toler's in Lothian Road from which they moved to the A.B. Garage at 6A Neville Street, Upper Kennington Lane, owned by Mr. C. Kempton. A yearly tenancy was taken from December 26th 1925 at £15 3s. 4d. a month. At first part of the garage was sublet to Enterprise but later, with the Peraeque fleet expansion, the place was filled to overflowing and additional accommodation had to be provided for two buses at the side of Mrs. Pinch's house at 14 Stockwell Park Road where a petrol pump was installed. A formal agreement was subsequently drawn up whereby the Company leased the land upon which the buses stood (which measured approximately 75ft. by 20ft.) and the pump for £104 per annum terminating on June 23rd 1941. A private telephone was installed by the GPO to connect 14 Stockwell Park Road with the Neville Street premises.

Modern double-deckers began to join the fleet in August 1929. Between then and September 1931 no fewer than six Leyland TD1's were purchased (UV 7395, UW 8539, GK 8779/80/9834, GT 1083). Only four replaced existing Leyland and Dennis double-deckers; two were additions to the fleet which thus reached its maximum of seven.

The authors have not been able to reconcile the number of buses owned with the number of schedules operated because of lack of sufficient detailed information on the latter. It is known that the first two Peraeque buses worked principally on routes 15, 34 and 73; the third was purchased for route 525. Subsequent fleet expansion was obtained by placing the additional vehicles on such unrestricted routes as 26E, 50, 203 (the single-decker) and 292. At the end the routes worked on weekdays were 50 (with "when working" journeys from Vauxhall to Streatham), 15A/B/E & 525 ("when working" Elephant & Castle to Limehouse), 293/A/B ("when working" Stockwell to Barking) and 34/B/73A/D/ 173D/E ("when working" Kennington to Liverpool Street). Sunday operation at this time was entirely on 69A/B.

London Transport took over on December 5th 1933 upon which date the seven buses passed into their ownership together with YX 6759, a disused Ballot car of 1928 vintage. £47,500 was awarded as compensation in 1935. Mrs. Pinch's husband, who had latterly been Traffic Manager-cum-driver, and Arthur Simpson were both found employment by the Board.

95 Windmill Road, Croydon
REGAL
MAGNET/FELIX/FLEUR DE LYS

An outpost of independent bus operation was 95 Windmill Road, Croydon. This was the headquarters of a bus, coach and lorry business owned by James Thomson. A substantially-built garage at the rear of no. 95 housed Thomson's vehicles and the coaches of the well-known local firm Bourne & Balmer with which he was associated. Access to it was from Queens Road. Thomson was a man of some financial substance and unlike most small operators he was able to buy all his vehicles outright and was thus always free of hire purchase commitments. He bought the first of six Dennis buses in December 1923 and chose for it the fleet name Regal which was applied in "General" style. RK 678 looked particularly handsome in a livery of yellow with white window frames, brown lining-out and black mouldings. The second Regal bus, RK 1004, was chocolate & white when new in February 1924 and subsequent buses were in the red & white livery into which the first two were duly repainted. RK 1509/10 arrived in April 1924, RK 7521 in August 1926 and RK 8899 in March 1927. The first four were bodied by Wilton, the fifth by Dodson, and the last by Birch.

The 59 group of routes naturally proved a magnet for Thomson's buses, Croydon being ideally suited for placing buses on this long trunk route, but he was not slow to try out others in the early days. The local 12 and 75 were obvious ones to try, but Thomson also applied for many others some of which, like the 8 and 29, were far removed from Croydon. During the 1924 exhibition the Regal buses reached Wembley by way of route 49 and on Sundays they operated as far south as Reigate. Applications to work over the Southmet tram routes from West Croydon to Crystal Palace and Sutton were rejected on the grounds that there were obstructions, but the 408A (West Croydon to Beddington)—an East Surrey service—soon proved a happy hunting ground for Regal. After the London Traffic Act came into force the weekday routine was 58F, 59A, 258 and 408A on Mondays to Fridays supplemented by the 75E on Saturdays. Sunday operation appears to have been mainly on variations of the 59 group including the 532. On September 22nd 1925 a limited company was formed to take over the Regal buses under the title of Thomson Motor Services Ltd. Nominal capital was £500 and the registered office was 95 Windmill Road. James Thomson was the sole director and held all but one of the five hundred shares.

Little is known about Thomson's coaching and haulage activities. In January 1926 he owned at least three "Bourne & Balmer" charabancs and also had a new Saurer on order. Though Thomson ran a profitable business, the maintenance of his vehicles in good condition was not his strong point. As early as the end of 1924 the Regal buses were reputed to be in a bad way, and when RK 1004 was sent to Birch's for overhaul in December 1926 its body was found to be in such a bad condition that they recommended its replacement by a new one.

The year 1925 saw the acquisition by Thomson of the two buses owned by Mrs. Fernande Virginie Brailey of 11 St. Saviours Road, Brixton. Mrs. Brailey had started business in April 1924 with the purchase of a new Thornycroft which she christened Magnet and housed in Hole's garage at 81A Page Street. Magnet was painted purple & cream and was registered as XR 9847 on April 14th, appearing at Scotland Yard three days later. In correspondence of the time a Mrs. Larthe is mentioned as being connected with the business. Who she was is still not known but it is possible that she was related to Edward Larthe who was a junior partner in the Pirate bus. Both vehicles were Thornycrofts and were kept at the Fleet Garage, and to carry a possible connection one stage further, Henri Leon—the principal owner of the Pirate—and Mrs. Brailey were both of French origin. It is a wild guess, but perhaps Mrs. Brailey was Mrs. Larthe "renamed". Mrs. Larthe's name had disappeared from the scene by August 1st 1924 when Mrs. Brailey's second bus was licensed. It was XU 4809 and was a Hickman-bodied Dennis in red & yellow livery carrying the fleet name Felix. Felix was kept at the Fleet Garage from new. Magnet was also housed there by then, its stay at Page Street having been of very short duration. Early in 1925 Mrs. Brailey made a contract with Cambrian Landray for her two buses to be housed at their Brixton Hill premises. This arrangement worked happily until March 5th when the Magnet Thornycroft was involved in a fire at the garage. It was established in court that the fire had been caused by a Cambrian Landray

114

employee smoking too close to the petrol tank of the bus as he refuelled it. After this episode the Brailey buses moved home once again, this time to the Ferndale Garage, a railway arch premises in Ferndale Road, Brixton.

It was probably when XR 9847 was repainted red & white after the fire damage was repaired that it received the fleet name Fleur de Lys. The Thornycroft was definitely carrying this name by May 1925, when it was to be found mostly on the 27 and 59 groups of routes. XU 4809, the Felix Dennis, was also renamed Fleur de Lys at an unknown date. During the latter part of 1925 Mrs. Brailey negotiated for her buses to be taken over by James Thomson and in order to buy the Brailey buses Thomson formed a limited company under the title of Brailey Ltd. of which he and Mrs. Brailey were designated joint Managing Directors. The company was incorporated on January 4th 1926 with registered office at 95 Windmill Road and took over the operation of the Fleur de Lys buses from March 1st. These then ran from Thomson's Croydon garage on to their scheduled weekday workings which by this time were on the 17B, 34 and 170B. Initially 1,802 £1 shares were issued out of an authorised 2,000, and of these Thomson held 1,301 and Mrs. Brailey the remainder. At some time in 1927 Thomson obtained complete control of the business.

The Fleur de Lys Thornycroft was the odd man out in the otherwise all-Dennis fleet owned by Thomson and he decided to dispose of it. In April 1925 he had bought a spare Dennis second-hand from Mr. & Mrs. Hoare who had traded as the Royal Toots. In 1926 he transferred its legal ownership to Brailey Ltd. although it continued to carry the Regal fleet name, and it displaced the Thornycroft which subsequently joined the many other ex-London vehicles of this make in the service of Thames Valley.

Thomson was the first to grasp the opportunity of selling to Public whose offer of £24,250 for the two businesses he readily accepted. A. T. Bennett took over the Regal buses on June 23rd 1927 on behalf of Public whose incorporation had not yet been finalised, and by arrangement with Thomson continued to use the Windmill Road garage as a base for Public's Croydon operations until these were transferred to the LGOC in May 1928. The Bourne & Balmer coach business was reorganised on June 14th 1928 as Bourne & Balmer (Croydon) Ltd. Thomson played no active part in it thereafter but was a substantial debenture holder and leased the Windmill Road and other premises to them. The Bourne family retained control until November 27th 1953 when it was acquired by Timpson's, then a B.E.T. subsidiary. The old Windmill Road garage is still largely unaltered from its condition in Regal days, though lying empty at the time of writing.

34 Ethelburga Street, Battersea

South-west London was peculiarly sparse as far as bus operators were concerned, but it included one of the most famous independent garages of all. In Battersea, at 34 Ethelburga Street, was the home of the pioneer independent bus operator, the Chocolate Express Omnibus Co. Ltd.

EXPRESS

If it were possible to nominate the best-remembered independent of all, the honour would probably fall to the Chocolate Express Omnibus Co. Ltd. This pioneer of post-war independent bus operation embodied all that was best in private enterprise and deservedly won a reputation second to none for service, cleanliness and reliability. Even in the roughest London weather its buses appeared spotless, and there was probably no other city operator anywhere in the country whose buses were swept out at the end of each journey.

Three ex-servicemen ran the business. The dominant personality among them was Arthur George Partridge, a Gloucestershire man who in pre-war days had been a driver with the London Road Car Co. Ltd. His skill and ability, together with his intense interest in buswork, soon led him to become a leader amongst London bus owners. He was for some years Chairman of the Association of London Omnibus Proprietors and represented them on the London & Home Counties Traffic Advisory Committee and other bodies. As an eloquent after-dinner speaker he was outstanding, and his business acumen was acknowledged and admired even by his competitors. In 1933 the shrewd Frank Pick even offered him a managerial post with London Transport, a gesture he extended to few other independent proprietors. Partridge did not take the job. He told a meeting of the Omnibus Society in February 1933 that, before the first Express bus was put on the road, nearly a year was spent investigating the possibilities and best methods of operation, by a man who had spent fifteen years in public transport in London. He strongly held the view that if more independent owners had done this there would have been fewer failures and the business would have been held in higher esteem.

Partridge was accompanied in the new venture right from the start by Albert Sydney Griffin who had been his wartime comrade in Egypt. Within a few days of going into business they were joined by David Francis Jermyn. As the business developed Jermyn became the Company's Traffic Superintendent and Griffin its Garage Superintendent besides acting in alternate months as drivers or conductors or assistants to Partridge. Partridge, as Managing Director, looked after the administration of the Company as a whole.

Plans for running buses were first made by Partridge in the early post-war period. London was experiencing acute transport difficulties and the bus services provided by the Combine on central London routes were grossly inadequate in many areas, especially at peak travel periods. He realised that in running buses he would encounter stiff opposition from the LGOC and its associates, but his conviction that there was ample room for both led to the commissioning of his first bus. An order was placed through Dodson for a new Leyland chassis, to be bought on hire purchase. Construction was completed in July 1922 and on the 25th it was presented to the police who did not pass it immediately as they required certain minor modifications to be made. One of the police officials was overheard to remark, however, that it was the finest bus that had yet been inspected by them. On August 2nd the vehicle was finally approved by the police and was licensed as XL 7513. Resplendent in chocolate & primrose with gold lining and mouldings picked out in black, it entered service on Saturday August 5th and in doing so sparked off an era in London's transport history that was to be one of the most interesting and colourful ever. The fleetname selected was Express with the initial E written in the greek style like a small 'c' with a horizontal central bar. The Express was soon making headlines in the national press and was plagued with chasers stationed fore and aft by the LGOC.

As the days went by and turned into weeks the LGOC's chasing persisted unabated and the partners began to get despondent. One day, in desperation, they turned abruptly into the cobbled forecourt of the Houses of Parliament. They were evicted but not before they had complained bitterly to interested Members about the persecution to which they were subjected. The incident came to the ears of the Home Secretary who called for a report. This was duly made but availed the owners of the Express little. Eventually it was public opinion, aroused by the Press, which forced the General to abandon its tactics. Headlines like "FAIR PLAY FOR THE EX-SERVICEMEN'S BUS" could not be ignored even by an organisation as vast and powerful as the LGOC.

For the first few weeks of its existence the business ran as a partnership and the first Express bus was licensed in the name of the Express Omnibus Company. It was transferred to the ownership of the Chocolate Express Omnibus Co. Ltd. after this was incorporated on September 22nd 1922. The word "chocolate", which made the company's title so characterful, only came as a kind of afterthought. The Registrar of Companies refused to permit the registration of the name first submitted because the title Express Bus Co. Ltd. had been registered earlier in 1922 by another concern. The partners, who became the limited company's directors, then added the word "chocolate" which was of course derived from the basic colour of their new bus. The fleetname on this and all subsequent vehicles remained plain Express though the buses were as often as not referred to by those who knew and travelled on them as the Chocolate Expresses.

As first registered, the new company was a public one and had an authorised capital of £15,000 in £1 shares. Its registered office was at 181 Queen Victoria Street, E.C.4. A prospectus was issued offering 11,250 shares at par. According to the prospectus the plan was to purchase, as a start, six more buses with Leyland chassis on exceptionally favourable terms and with quick delivery when required. Each "will be equipped with the celebrated Dodson body" and will be the last word in comfort and efficiency. The prospectus gives some interesting statistics of the first seven weeks operation from August 5th to September 22nd inclusive, when the gross traffic receipts were £568 14s. 10d. giving an average gross income of £81 a week. If this rate of takings continued the annual revenue per bus for one year would be £4,212 against expenses (including a substantial sum for depreciation) of £2,526, giving a surplus of £1,686.

The scheme to "go public" was not a success. Initially the response had been good but a newspaper article describing the scheme as speculative effectively sounded its death knell. At an Extraordinary General Meeting on January 15th 1923 a motion was approved to turn the company into a private one. The three directors then purchased the few shares for which members of the public had subscribed so that, by December 1925, they were in possession of all the issued shares (totalling 6,853). On November 27th 1926 the registered office was changed to 34 Ethelburga Street, S.W.11. and on December 21st 1926 it became 64 Victoria Street, S.W.1., the address at which the late Percy Frost-Smith had formerly had his office.

The company's fleet never grew to the size originally hoped for, through lack of capital in the first instance, and later because of the restrictions imposed by the London Traffic Act. A total of five Leyland LB's was owned. XN 6774, XT 4951, XU 7498 and UC 8658 joined the fleet in May 1923, May 1924, September 1924 and March 1928 respectively. Like all Express buses they bore Dodson bodies. The chassis of UC 8658 was of particular interest in that it was assembled by the company itself from parts supplied by Leyland after production of the LB model by the manufacturers had ceased.

The Express will always be remembered in connection with the famous route 11 upon which its buses mostly plied, initially without route numbers. But from the early days there were two early morning journeys on route 19 leaving Clapham Junction at about 6.40 a.m. and 8.20 a.m. for the Angel, Islington, whence they ran light to the Liverpool Street terminus of the 11. Apart from a few journeys on the 11 Sunday operation was almost entirely on the 33D from July 1925 onwards. Even before 1925 the company experimented very little with routes other than these. They made application for route 49 in about March 1923 but, if they worked it at all, it could not have been for long. By 1924 they had developed an interest in the 70. Much of the Sunday mileage was on it prior to July 1925, though Epsom was probably the furthest point south to which Chocolate Express worked. They endeavoured at one stage to extend from Epsom to Long Grove Asylum but the police held the proposed route to be far too dangerous and rejected it. The 70 was essentially a fair-weather service which proved unprofitable in the long run to several other operators; Chocolate Express may have suffered likewise. In later years the Company operated a special service jointly with the LGOC during the Wimbledon Tennis Championships, this being one of the few recorded instances of co-operation between an independent and the Combine.

The property at 32/34 Ethelburga Street was where the Express buses were always kept. At first a weekly rental was paid to the South Western Transport Co. Ltd., a firm of automobile and general engineers run by Charles H. Winteringham. On September 28th 1927 Partridge purchased a leasehold interest in the property which he named the Ethelburga Garage. The main income was from the garaging of the Express buses, to which the garaging and repair of private cars was always subsidiary. In March 1929 Partridge secured the freehold, which he offered to sell to the Company. His co-directors disapproved of the idea but agreed that the company should garage there indefinitely at £8 5s. 0d. a week for six buses plus £28 per annum for office accommodation. In addition it would purchase all its petrol and oil requirements at market prices which were then 1s. 2½d. a gallon for petrol and 3/- a gallon for oil. A formal agreement to this effect was drawn up in November 1931 but was not ratified until November 29th 1933, after London Transport had made it clear that it would not acquire the garage. On January 8th 1934, Partridge granted a lease to the Company for 21 years on a portion of the garage 52ft. 6ins. × 48ft. 3ins. In not purchasing the freehold from Partridge in 1929 the company made the biggest and possibly the only mistake of its highly successful career. We shall revert shortly to its fruitless endeavours to establish in law that London Transport should acquire the garage along with the bus business, and thereby pay the appropriate compensation for it.

On July 30th 1929 the Company's first Leyland Titan (UV 9097) was licensed. On its lower saloon bulkhead, beneath the clock, were emblazoned proudly in gold lettering the words "CHOCOLATE EXPRESS OMNIBUS CO. LTD. Est. 1922." Its success was instantaneous. A second Titan arrived in November 1929 (UW 6157) and a third (UW 6987) was licensed on December 30th after having been shown on the Dodson stand at the 1929 Commercial Motor Exhibition at Olympia. GC 6087 followed in February 1930 and GO 1636 in March 1931. Five Titans replaced four Leyland LB's, XU 7498 remaining as a spare vehicle, giving two spares for four service buses. By present day standards the retention of a 50% float of spares would be hopelessly extravagant. It was more so in the case of the Express whose maintenance standards were so high that breakdowns were very rarely encountered. The Titans worked wonders for the company's income which rose from £13,600 in 1928—the last full year of LB operation—to £17,620 in 1930. All five new Titans were bought out of revenue. Three of the displaced LBs found renewed employment with provincial operators; XL 7513 (which in October 1929 received the chassis of UC 8658) and XN 6774 went to the Enterprise Omnibus Co. of Clacton and later to Eastern National, whilst UC 8658 (with XL 7513's chassis) joined the Skinner fleet in Hastings. XT 4951 was converted to a lorry for the company's use in March 1930 but was sold less than a year later. An attractive feature of the second, third and fourth Titans was the application of the Company's name in full along the length of the bus above the lower deck windows in addition to the usual Express fleetname on the lower panels. On the newest bus, GO 1636, the name was affixed in gold letters along the glass window louvres.

In August 1932 Chocolate Express achieved the distinction of becoming the first motor bus operator in London to achieve ten years of independent operation. Its twelfth birthday arrived five days before compulsory acquisition by London Transport on August 10th 1934. This was a sad day indeed for the bus industry and for the travelling public alike; one of the most efficient and enterprising concerns the bus world has known was eliminated overnight by the stroke of a pen. Partridge, Jermyn and Griffin retired from buswork as wealthy men judged against the standards of the day. Thanks to the buses Jermyn and Griffin had both been able to move from their small houses in Crab Tree Lane, Fulham, to more expensive residences at Barnes and Gunnersbury, whilst Partridge bought himself a pleasant house in Chatto Road, Clapham. Each of the three had a son who found employment with the firm and became directors in November 1929; Dudley Partridge and Ronald Griffin were clerks and Charles Jermyn was a conductor.

119

The Chocolate Express staff were better treated than any others, not excluding those of the General. This was reflected in the long service which many of them could boast at the time London Transport took over, and compared well with the constant changes of staff which typified some of the other independent concerns. Two of the men taken over by London Transport—G. Wilson, a driver, and A. Richards, a washer—had been with Chocolate Express since August 6th 1922, the day after the first bus first ran. Alone amongst London bus operators the company ran a staff pension fund, created to enable employees to receive £1 10s. 0d. a week on reaching the age of 65. There was also a sick club giving £1 a week benefit for the first six weeks of sickness and 10/- a week for the following six weeks. As no pension and sick fund schemes were operated by London Transport, they were wound-up and the monies distributed amongst the Chocolate Express staff before the day of takeover.

The "appointed day" upon which the Chocolate Expresses were to disappear from the roads of London was Friday August 10th 1934. At 55 Broadway at 3.30 p.m. on the day before, Partridge signed the legal documents handing over the company he and his colleagues had worked so hard to build-up. Mr. S. L. Poole, who remembers the company well, wrote the following description of its last few hours.

"First thing in the morning on the final day GO 1636 and UV 9097 made the last of the "19" runs, saying goodbye to the regulars of years, then on to the 11 until the evening when the last two buses left Bush House for the last time. UV 9097, the first of the Titans, made a last run from Liverpool Street as if following them all off the stage, to the garage for a farewell party. There the staff removed all route boards, numbers, fareboards, everything that had anything to do with the Express—the Board did not want them.

Farewells are always sad things. Each went his way leaving the buses alone in the garage, the silence broken only by the creaking and cracking sounds of contracting metals as the engines cooled off. Just before 8 o'clock next morning the six buses lined up outside the garage for the last time, the white glass of the front stencil holder seeming to stare ahead like a sightless eye. Mr. Partridge passed down the line, shaking hands with all the 34 men who had made up the staff, including the garage staff and others in the open topper, which was to lead the way to Chiswick.

As the clocks struck 8 engines were started, amid a cheer from quite a crowd of people who had come to see this last act played through. They drove away, one by one, until only a faint haze of blue smoke remained, dwindling away as the memory of the Express was to do."

In a sense the battle which had once raged between the Express and the monopoly flared up again, but this time the scene of action was transferred from the streets of London to the Law Courts. The Arbitration Tribunal had offered £31,000 in compensation for the business which, though in itself fair, allowed nothing for the Ethelburga Garage, which London Transport maintained it need not acquire as the formal document committing the company to garage there had not been

120

executed until November 29th 1933, seven months after the passing of the London Passenger Transport Act. The Chocolate Express company put its case to the Arbitration Tribunal on February 19th 1934 but the Tribunal held that no property acquired after the date of passing of the Act (April 13th 1933) was to be compulsorily transferred to the Board, and that the company was merely a weekly tenant of the garage so therefore the Board need not acquire it. The Company appealed against this decision, and became the first independent to appeal against an award of the Arbitration Tribunal. Meanwhile, in an effort to settle out of court, London Transport offered to accept the obligation of the lease up to Michaelmas 1935, but this was refused by the company. The appeal was heard by Lord Justices Scrutton, Greer and Maugham and concluded on June 20th 1934. Judgement was given on Monday, July 2nd when the appeal was dismissed with costs to be paid by Chocolate Express.

On April 14th 1936 at 32 Ethelburga Street a special resolution to wind-up the company was passed, there being no creditors, and R. T. Cuff of 10 New Court, Carey Street, W.C.2. was appointed liquidator. The winding-up must have been carried out in a very dilatory manner, for it was not until February 16th 1954 that the Chocolate Express Omnibus Co. Ltd. ceased to exist. Like many other former independent bus garages in south London, the Ethelburga garage has long since disappeared. A new building for the housing of lorries and taxis, with accommodation above, had been erected in 1936 in place of the old garage, but this met a sudden end in the closing stages of the war when a Nazi rocket reduced it to rubble. Now the site is almost impossible to locate for the area has been completely redeveloped with a small town of shops and flats.

★　　★　　★　　★

Before Partridge bought the Ethelburga garage its previous owners, the South Western Transport Co. Ltd., accepted three other bus operators (LCOC, Alma and Superbus) as tenants besides Express but all had gone out of business before Partridge took over. During Partridge's ownership the only buses he housed other than his own were the two Leylands which comprised the Triumph fleet.

LCOC

The rise and fall of the Newlands District venture of F. H. Bruce has been outlined in some detail in chapter 2. Bruce's previous venture, though endowed from the start with similar dreams of grandeur, was no more successful. Both attempts by Bruce to establish bus operation on a grand scale finished up in the same way, with the vehicles being seized without notice because of unpaid hire purchase instalments.

January 8th 1923 marked the start of Bruce's first excursion into the world of independent bus ownership when he formed the London Circular Omnibus Co. Ltd. His co-partners at this stage of the venture were a pair of London business brokers, Frederick William Major and Thomas Delaney, and their office address at 88 Fleet Street, E.C.4. was used as the registered headquarters of the new company. The authorised share capital was set at £2,000 divided into 1,500 ordinary £1 shares and 2,000 deferred at 5/-, and would have been completely inadequate had Bruce's plans fully materialised. Bruce himself owned 251 ordinary and 1,000 deferred shares with a total value of £500, and the business brokers each held 500 deferred shares worth £300 altogether. Their main task was presumably to find subscribers for the remaining ordinary shares in order to provide enough capital to get the business started. They were unsuccessful in disposing of all the ordinary shares and 434 remained unissued. Five subscribers took 815 shares the greatest portion of which—200—went to Ernest William Colbrook who became company secretary and was later appointed a director.

It is not known why the company's unusual title was chosen. Rumours say that Bruce intended each bus to make a complete circle of London in its day's work. An equally likely explanation is that it was chosen because the initial letters were as close to those of the LGOC as Bruce could possibly get. His first step in making the company operational was to order a Leyland on hire purchase from Dodson, having made arrangements with Charles Winteringham for it to be garaged at 34 Ethelburga Street. The bus was delivered in April 1923; licensed as XN 5034 on the 15th and presented at Scotland Yard two days later. Bruce had already applied to the police for plates for no fewer than twenty-five Leylands which he proposed to run on the following services:-

C1	Putney High Street to Liverpool Street
C2	Clapham Junction to Liverpool Street
C9	Barnes to Liverpool Street
C11	Shepherds Bush to Liverpool Street
C19	Balham High Road to Highbury Barn
C25	Victoria to Seven Kings
C33	Richmond to Liverpool Street
C37	Richmond to Peckham

With the exception of the C1 and C2 these were all existing LGOC services to whose route number Bruce had added his own 'C' prefix. Clearly XN 5034 was intended as only the start to much bigger things.

XN 5034 was in a maroon livery with cream window frames. Initially it bore the letters LCOC entwined in a circle but later this was replaced by a yellow diamond edged in black bearing an initial letter in each corner. The staff were provided with uniforms bearing the intials letters on the collars.

Things did not go as planned. There were boardroom changes which resulted firstly in Colbrook becoming a director on May 17th, followed by the departure from the board of Bruce himself and later of Major and Delaney. The company's financial situation was far from happy and the directors took the precaution of cancelling a contract for a further five new Leyland buses which had been ordered in March 1923. On November 12th 1923 the registered office was transferred to 34 Ethelburga Street and at the end of the same year the sole directors were Colbrook and a fellow shareholder, Cecil Martin.

In May 1924 the financial crisis came to a head. The South Western Transport Co. Ltd. gave the company notice to quit by the 31st because

122

they had not been paying for the rent and petrol supplies. New accommodation was not obtained because, before the notice expired, Dodson's representatives arrived at the garage one evening to remove the bus to Willesden as the hire purchase repayments were seriously in arrears. They quickly found a new purchaser for XN 5034 which appeared in mid-June as the Omega. Dissolution of the London Circular Omnibus Co. Ltd. was given by formal notice in the London Gazette on July 16th 1926.

SUPERBUS

A bus with a particularly uneventful history was XU 4371, the Superbus. Its only real feature of interest was that its owners were mostly in various branches of the clothing trade which was not an industry from which aspiring bus proprietors normally emerged in the 'twenties. Of the eight shareholders in Superbus Ltd. Isadore Stanley Benson, David Edgard, Jack Charkin, Harry Edgard and Phillip Kosenberg were tailors or milliners; only Sophie Fishman, Joseph Benson and Deborah Edgard were otherwise engaged. Superbus Ltd. was incorporated on July 10th 1924 with a registered capital of £1,500. Isadore Benson and David Edgard were its directors and Isadore Benson's business address at 72/74 Paul Street, Finsbury, was used as the Company's registered office. Day-to-day affairs were conducted from David Edgard's premises at 239 Kings Road, Chelsea.

Superbus's one and only bus was licensed on July 29th 1924 and was bought outright for £1,270 15s. 0d. It was a Strachan & Brown-bodied Dennis, in a red & off-white livery with brown rocker panels which were later repainted red. Its fleetname was written in "General" style. Tickets appear to have been normally purchased from the Westminster Omnibus Co. Ltd. It worked solely on 11, 14 and 73 (latterly only 14 group) and its independent career came to an end on August 4th 1926 when General purchased the entire share capital of Superbus Ltd. The vehicle was immediately transferred to General's Putney Bridge (F) garage and in early January 1927 it was replaced by K759 which was one of the last K's to enter service in independent colours. The Dennis joined the Redburn fleet after being overhauled at Chiswick, and K759 continued to work the Superbus schedules until they were merged into the LGOC on January 1st 1928.

TRIUMPH

The Triumph bus came into being thanks to the enterprise of four LGOC drivers from Hammersmith (R) garage; Messrs. Tegg, Reynolds, Stephens and Pauling. Alfred Tegg was the leader of the quartet, and conducted the Triumph Omnibus Company from his home at 5 Branksea Street, Fulham. On May 12th 1923 their new bus was licensed. XN 8524 was a Dodson-bodied Leyland resplendent in a livery described as violet with white window frames and white-edged tyres to match. By about the end of 1924 it had become red & white. In its earlier years the Triumph bus was one of many garaged at the Shepherds Bush premises of General Auto Services Ltd. and it was also in Craig's Garage at 224 Fulham Palace Road at one undefined stage in its career. At an unknown date (definitely by July 1929 at the latest) it moved to Ethelburga Street. Throughout its entire career the Triumph Motor Omnibus Company ran mostly on route 14 and variants thereof, and from 1925 it concentrated entirely on that route. Weekdays were spent on 14A and Sundays principally on 14B/D/F.

In 1929 the partners considered that the time had come to buy a new, up-to-date bus. They selected the newest and most up-to-date of all, the Leyland Titan. This model, which turned out to be excellent in so many respects, was completely untried in London when Triumph ordered theirs. UV 5764 was licensed on July 30th and shared with its stablemate, Chocolate Express UV 9097, which was licensed on the same day, the honour of being the first bus of its type to be purchased for use in London. The Dodson bodywork on UV 5764 was to a design that was destined to become a classic amongst independent London buses. The arrival of UV 5764 meant that XN 8524 was relegated to spare.

In 1930 the original four-man partnership broke up. It had lasted since May 16th 1923 on which date a formal partnership agreement had been drawn up giving each of the four an equal share in the business. W. Stephens wished to leave and was paid out on September 27th 1930. Shortly before this T. Reynolds had died, and on October 27th 1930 his executors received the financial equivalent of his share in the business. Stephens and Reynolds were not replaced, and thereafter Alfred Tegg and Stephen Pauling were to remain the sole proprietors.

The old Leyland, XN 8524, became unserviceable in 1931. It would appear that it suffered a chassis defect of some sort, for the partners looked around for a replacement chassis. City came to their aid in July 1931 when they let Triumph have the chassis of their YL 417. This was fitted with the overhauled body from XN 8524 whose chassis passed to City in November but was never used by them. Triumph paid City £75 for the LB chassis but got £25 of this back for XN 8524.

Triumph operated until November 1933 when, on the 24th, the business was taken over by the LPTB. In addition to the buses a 1929 Austin 16 hp saloon car, XV 8746, passed to the Board. An arbitration award of £8,000 was made to the former owners of the Triumph buses in February 1936.

Mansell Mews, Wimbledon

SHAMROCK

To the south-west of Battersea, at Mansell Mews, Wimbledon, was the garage for a short period of an ill-fated operator, the Shamrock Traction Co. Ltd.

"Miss Helen Jane O'Farrell Kelly is the first woman in London to own a fleet of omnibuses" wrote the Daily Chronicle in November 1924. "Though she is only 26, she has an ambitious scheme of getting together a really big "pirate" fleet. She told a Daily Chronicle representative last night that she has three buses running and three more on order."

Miss Kelly owned only a quarter share in the Shamrock Traction Co. Ltd. and was not the sole proprietor as the newspaper report would tend

124

to suggest. Nor was she the first woman bus proprietor, having been beaten for this honour by Fernande Brailey's Magnet bus. She was, however, the youngest of London's small band of lady bus proprietors and she was also the person most actively engaged in running the Shamrock business. She was herself an experienced driver of commercial vehicles, an art which she had learned during the war. With a name so attractively Irish it was only fitting that the buses should be called Shamrock and painted in an appropriate shade of green (officially Mall Green) with cream window reliefs. Her co-directors in the business were her widowed mother, Mrs. Helen Dolores O'Farrell Kelly and her two cousins, Francis Edward Croucher, a retired Indian Army captain, and his brother, Hubert Roland Croucher. The family interests had previously been in house property, but when it looked as though bus ownership would prove more lucrative some of the money was used as a deposit on the purchase of three buses.

The Shamrock Traction Co. Ltd. was incorporated on June 28th 1924 at 27 Church Street, Chelsea, and had a nominal capital of £4,000 in £1 shares of which only 304 were ever issued, resulting in the company being undercapitalised for its size. Three Dodson-bodied Thornycrofts had already been placed on order and arrangements were concluded for these to be housed in Toler's Garage at Lothian Road, Camberwell. The Thornycrofts, XU 2191-3, were delivered early in July and licensed on the 12th. They are believed to have run at first on route 36, but application was made from time to time for a variety of others including 15, 18, 19, 22, 25, 33, 37, 38, 40 and 49. With the introduction of regulated schedules the pattern of operation was stabilised into Mondays-Fridays on 14A. 14A was also operated on Saturday mornings, but from about midday the buses moved to route 70, taking the Shamrock buses deep into the Surrey countryside. Latterly on Sundays the buses could be found on 74 though an interesting earlier operation had been 205A.

Throughout its career the Shamrock company was plagued with difficulty in finding a suitable garage. By January 1925 the buses had left Toler's and moved to S. H. Motors Ltd. who ran the A1 garage in Estcourt Road, Fulham. This was on the site where an old LGOC horse bus depot had been from March 1885 to October 1910. July 1925 saw the Shamrocks in 1-5 Fitzalan Street, Kennington Road, and three months later they were in Craig's Garage at 224 Fulham Palace Road. This unsatisfactory situation clearly could not continue and the company came to the conclusion that the only answer was to obtain its own premises. On November 23rd 1925 a mortgage was taken out on a leasehold garage in Mansell Mews, Wimbledon, previously occupied by Alexander Soul, a jobmaster.

Accommodation was not the company's only problem. As early as April 1925 it became clear that the profits for which it hoped were not being made. One of the buses, XU 2191, was impounded for debt and passed to Cambrian in the latter part of the month reducing the active fleet to two units although three schedules were retained, one unworked. Extra capital had to be raised and this was done through the issue of debentures. But the situation continued to worsen. Bad management and pilfering by staff combined to make collapse inevitable. Early in 1926 the remaining two Thornycrofts were seized, and a new owner found for them in the shape of H. C. Motor Works Ltd. of Hull. A Receiver & Manager was appointed by the shareholders for the now-busless company. He was Henry Charles Merrett of Merrett, Son & Street, who we shall meet later in connection with the Batten group of companies and who had behind-the-scenes connections with the LGOC. Prior to his appointment as Receiver & Manager, Merrett had provisionally arranged for the sale of the business to the LGOC, who immediately put in hand the preparation of three K-types to work the Shamrock schedules. On February 22nd K650, 947 & 1038 were licensed in the name of Miss H. J. O'Farrell Kelly and delivered to Chelverton Road (AF) garage ready for operation from there the next day. They were in full Shamrock livery and re-introduced green & cream to the fleet, the Thornycrofts XU 2192/3 having been repainted red & white in December 1924, at which time the script style fleetname had been replaced by one in block capitals underlined in 'General' style.

On March 19th 1926 the registered office was transferred from 38 Perham Road, W.14 (its location since September 1925) to 55 Broadway and on April 22nd 1926 General formally took over ownership, having operated on behalf of the Receiver & Manager since February 2nd. Apart from the transfer of the three buses to Putney Bridge (F) garage on June 29th 1927 there is nothing further to record. The licences for the three Shamrock buses passed to the LGOC on January 1st 1928, though the Shamrock company was not wound up until November 10th 1930, over two years later than all the other acquired companies. Merrett had meanwhile ceased to act as Receiver & Manager on May 31st 1928.

Like so many of the independent bus owners, Miss Kelly had dreamed of owning a large fleet of buses, all earning big profits. Her dream never came true, and she and her co-partners finished up poorer people than they had begun.

35 Merton Road, Wandsworth
WALKER
TURNER

A little-known service, 207, once linked the Railway Hotel at Barnes with the golf club house in Richmond Park operating outwards from Barnes by way of Upper Richmond Road, Priory Lane, and the park itself and returning from the park via Clarence Lane and Roehampton Lane. The distance from end to end was less than 1½ miles and there was little housing en route to stimulate trade. Even so two buses served this short route at weekends providing a 10 minute headway for people wishing to visit Richmond Park. On Mondays to Fridays one bus was used and was capable of maintaining a quarter-hourly frequency. The through fare of 3d. was distinctly high by the standards of those days.

The earliest operator on the route appears to have been a Mr. John Henry Walker who had a small, green & white, dual entrance Bean, the seating capacity of which could hardly have exceeded ten. Beyond the fact that he issued tickets carrying the name "Walker" nothing more is known about him.

The route was defunct in September 1928 when Henry Arthur Turner came on the scene. He was a motor engineer who lived in comfortable circumstances in Down Lodge, a detached house (now demolished) in its own grounds at 35 Merton Road, Wandsworth. Inside the grounds he had a garage capable of holding three vehicles but it was not a public garage in the usual sense though he presumably carried out repair work for other people there. He had acquired in 1928 a Bean Model 5 chassis of 1926 origin which was minus a body and which had recently been overhauled by its makers. It had been registered when new as YN 4594 but it is not known what it was used for in 1926/7, nor is it known what type of body it carried. It may well have been a lorry but on the other hand it is just possible—but this is pure supposition—that it was the Bean previously used by J. H. Walker. Turner arranged for Birch to build a new 12-seater body on to the chassis of YN 4594; one that would comply with Metropolitan Police regulations so that it could be used on the 207. Birch's terms were a deposit of £20 followed by twenty-three monthly payments of £8 and a final payment of £5, making £209 in all. They collected the chassis from Turner early in October and began construction straight away. In addition to the body Birch also fitted a front bumper to increase the overall length by two inches, which was necessary under the regulations then existing in order that an offside seat for seven persons could be fitted.

YN 4594's new body was still under construction when, towards the end of October, Turner asked Birch to supply in addition a complete new vehicle based on the Bean 30-cwt chassis. The total cost for this was agreed at £513 (body £190, chassis £323), Turner to make a deposit of £100 on delivery plus the balance at 8% in twenty-nine monthly instalments of £15 plus a final payment of £13 4s. 0d. Construction began almost immediately. On December 11th YN 4594 was passed by Scotland Yard followed at the end of the month by the second vehicle, which was registered by Birch on January 14th as UL 1771. Both were delivered to Turner in January 1929 and they entered service in either the latter part of that month or in February.

The bodies on both were almost identical in appearance, having rear entrances to comply with police requirements. Both had longitudinal seating in green leather; YN 4594 seated twelve and UL 1771 held fourteen as it was based on a slightly longer chassis. Their external livery was dark green relieved by a grey roof.

Very little time elapsed before Turner started getting into arrears with his hire purchase repayments. The service simply did not pay and by December 1930 Turner was in a precarious financial position. He had virtually lost everything, and as a last desperate resort he advertised the business in the Evening News as a going concern, hoping that by selling he would raise sufficient money to cover his debts. No takers came forth immediately and, before Turner had a chance to advertise again, Birch sent their works manager, Mr. Hardman, to seize the vehicles. He was by this time £252 16s. 0d. in arrears with his repayments, and his indebtedness to Birch increased by a further £53 11s. 8d. in March 1931 after the two vehicles had been returned to Bean's for overhaul, Turner having allowed them to get into an indifferent condition.

127

Birch advertised the two Beans for sale, the older one for £90 and the other for £210, but they were unsuccessful in finding buyers at the prices asked so court action was resorted to against Turner to retrieve the outstanding debt. The case was heard in April 1932 when Birch were awarded damages against Turner. After the hearing UL 1771 was submitted for auction by Aldridges Ltd. and in June 1932 it passed to F. E. Nutt, a haulage contractor of Ashbourne Way, Golders Green, who intended starting a service from Golders Green along Colin Deep Lane to Colindale. The Metropolitan Police approved the route, but with the spectre of the LPTB looming on the horizon Nutt thought better of the venture and resold the vehicle to W. F. Church of 102 Station Road, New Southgate for use as a nursing home bus. It is still in existence having been purchased in the middle 1960's for preservation from a bungalow owner at Wendover, Bucks, who had used it for over twenty years as a garden shed. It still displays the original destination blind reading "To & from RICHMOND PARK Golf Club". The fate of YN 4594 is not known, but in view of its age (six years was an advanced age for a Bean in 1932) it was probably broken up.

After Turner's buses were seized in December 1930 route 207 again lay dormant until August 30th 1931 when the LGOC began to run on much the same basis as Turner had done previously with little or no change to the frequency. Two Dennis Darts were allocated to Mortlake (M) garage for the service. It was abandoned early in September 1939, a few days after the outbreak of war, and no bus service has ever operated into Richmond Park since.

CHAPTER FOUR

INNER LONDON

137 Elephant Road, Elephant & Castle
SOUTH LONDON COACHES

"One Set Purpose—Your Satisfaction." This was the motto used by the South London Coaches for a number of years. In the years immediately following the end of the Great War three charabanc operators worked in conjunction to form what was then called South London Coaching Services. These three were R. Baxter, Pavey Brothers and E. Burmingham & Co. Ltd. They combined to run the usual range of seasonal tours and race excursions, and in the summer months operated daily services from Soho Square to Brighton, Hastings and Margate. By 1924 Baxter and the Paveys had ceased to run and the South London Coaches were operated solely by E. Burmingham & Co. Ltd. whose head office and garage was a railway arch at 137 Elephant Road, little more than a stone's throw away from the Elephant & Castle.

E. Burmingham & Co.Ltd. was incorporated on February 6th 1922 to take over an existing coach business carried on by Edward Charles Burmingham and Ernest Edward Burmingham who, as near as we can tell, began coach operation in April 1919. In their earlier days the Burminghams favoured Commer coaches but also ran a Wolseley converted from a private car chassis. The later 'twenties saw Maudslays predominantly in the fleet. Most of the coaches were painted light blue, and this was the colour applied to the Company's only London bus, XU 7405, a Strachan & Brown-bodied Dennis purchased new in September 1924. The vehicle looked most attractive with window frames in off-white and with lining-out, both on the panels and on the main mouldings, in black. The fleet name SOUTH LONDON COACHES was applied in "GENERAL" style. XU 7405 did not become red & white until its third overhaul, in October 1927.

Under the arrangements of the coach fleet manager, J. H. Lowe, XU 7405 ran in true independent fashion, operating several services within a day. Even when schedules had to be submitted late in 1924 under the London Traffic Act, a complicated one was compiled by which on Mondays to Fridays the bus operated on no fewer than five routes each day, i.e. 17B, 34, 59B, 159D, 170B. On Saturdays 34, 59B and 159D were operated. The vehicle was also, at times, seen on 12C and 112B, but this may have been on Sundays when operations were not restricted.

During 1927 Harry Heast, a Cheshunt bus and garage proprietor, obtained a controlling interest in the business and almost at the end of the year, on December 12th, XU 7405 was sold to Public for £3,000 of which £1,529 went immediately in satisfying debentures, the interest payment of which was already a year in arrears. By 1930 South London Coaches had ceased to trade under the auspices of E. Burmingham & Co. Ltd. and were shown as "Proprietor: H. Heast." By this time, also, the coaches had left their railway arch home at 137 Elephant Road for better accommodation at 1 Avonmouth Street, just off nearby Newington

Causeway, which also served as a coach station. Daily services were now operated to Brighton, Hastings and Margate, supplemented by a weekend service to Norwich and Great Yarmouth plus a wide range of day and half day excursions. On Monday, September 26th 1927 the company joined the ranks of those operating medium distance express services with a daily service from Charing Cross and Victoria to Farnham via Camberley and Aldershot. Starting with one journey a day each way (9.30 a.m. ex Farnham and 6.0 p.m. from Charing Cross) the service built up to a maximum of four journeys a day each way (three on Sunday) by 1929, including a late night journey to Farnham leaving Charing Cross at 12 midnight.

Unfortunately for Harry Heast his coaching enterprise did not pay off. The British Motor Trust seized some of his best coaches for non-payment of hire purchase instalments, and on September 16th 1933 he was declared bankrupt.

5/11 Vauxhall Bridge Road, Pimlico

RED ROSE
TRINITY/J.H.
SERVICE

Red Rose Motor Services Ltd. was one of the more ambitious of the smaller independent undertakings and was owned by men already successful in other fields. The company was registered on January 4th 1924 with a share capital of £6,000 which was increased two months later to £10,000 and further increased in July 1926 to £15,500. The owners were all Welshmen living in London. Rees Thomas Davies, Edward Owen, Ivor Griffith Pugh and John Pugh were all by profession dairymen and David John James was a grain merchant. Originally Rees Davies was managing director, David James, chairman, and John Pugh secretary, but in practice John Pugh was the one who devoted most time to running the business and he subsequently became managing director. While the business was in the planning stage it had been the intention to call it the Red Dragon Motor Services Ltd.; perhaps the Red Dragon of Welsh heraldry had inspired the title as a patriotic gesture. However the less fiery but only slightly less colourful title of Red Rose was thought more appropriate and this was the name applied to the sides of the buses. A sixth director joined the business in March 1924 just as the buses were being delivered. He was Thomas William Cross, a Kingston upon Thames brewer's grain contractor. He remained with the business until the end although Davies and Owen sold out their interests to the others in July 1927.

The company started out by taking a lease on extensive garage premises at 5/11 Vauxhall Bridge Road which they later called the Rosemex Service Station. This duly became the company's registered office replacing, in about July 1924, the original address of 3 Thames House, Queen Street Place, E.C. The occupants immediately prior to the arrival of Red Rose were United Transport (London) Ltd., the well known haulage contractors and general engineers. Nearly fifty years earlier, in October 1873, the premises had been opened as the depot for

130

the London Tramways Company's isolated route along Vauxhall Bridge Road and the ramp by which the horses reached the upper storey stables could still be clearly seen. Indeed, though a full century has now elapsed since the tramway opened, much of the original structure still remains including the ramp. Even the old trackwork at the entrance was still visible until as late as about 1950. The premises ceased to function as a tram depot when the L.C.C.'s electrified service commenced from Victoria through to Camberwell and beyond in August 1906. Under Red Rose's ownership petrol was retailed under the title of Rosemex and on October 21st 1925 a separate company, Rosemex Oil Fields Ltd., was created to take over the assets other than the buses. These included general engineering and haulage departments and all the normal functions of a filling station.

To revert to Red Rose, its first commercial venture was to place a contract with Dennis for the supply of eight chassis, the bodies for which were ordered from Strachan & Brown. They were all delivered in March 1924, and were registered in pairs between the 8th and the 28th as XR 4899/4900, 6675/6, 7152/3, 7518/9. The first one was presented at Scotland Yard for examination on the 11th and entered service soon after. Before operations began plates were obtained for routes 6, 15, 22, 33, 38, 42, 76, 77, 88 and 96 and in July 1924 additional services were added: 11, 12, 16, 17, 28, 37, 39, 46, 52 and 73. Each bus must have carried a huge stock of route boards! The company pioneered two 'Sunday only' routes of its own between Strand (Aldwych) and Hampton Court, one via Great Smith Street, Vauxhall, Clapham Junction, Putney, East Sheen, Richmond, Teddington and Bushey Park, the other via Victoria, Vauxhall, Clapham Junction, Putney, Roehampton and Kingston. Under the London Traffic Act Red Rose held eight weekday schedules which embraced routes 6, 11, 14, 15, 36, 59, 77 and 88. The company continued to favour Hampton Court as the objective for its Sunday workings which reached there by three separate routes, 205, 217 and 295. Though the Act effectively prevented the acquisition of extra suitable schedules a further bus was purchased in December 1925 to provide a spare which, somewhat incredibly, the company did not seem to have considered necessary earlier. YM 3395 was, like its predecessors, a Dennis but it was distinguishable from them by its Dodson body.

During its career Red Rose took over two small concerns running one bus apiece. The first was the Allber Omnibus Co. Ltd. which had been registered on February 11th 1926 to take over the bus business of Arthur Edward Allery and René Bernard (a Frenchman) and almost immediately afterwards came under Red Rose control. Their bus, which ran under the fleetname Service, pre-dated Red Rose's own fleet by almost a year. It had been bought in May 1923, was registered XO 479 on the 30th and passed the police examination on June 1st. Initially it carried a very pleasant livery officially described as orange & chrome, which was actually dark orange with fawn window frames. Sadly it was later repainted dark red all over. Its fleetname was in gold block capitals with the "V" much larger than the other letters. The partners both lived in Ravensbury Road, Earlsfield but their business address was 30 Thornsett Road, Earlsfield where they had their own garage business, the Allber

Garage. Allery was the senior partner and the bus licences were held in his name. The bus appears never to have been kept at the Allber garage, instead it was garaged by other bus proprietors who probably attended to its day to day running on behalf of its owners. At first it was housed at 55 Paradise Road, Stockwell, moving at a later date to the Red Rose garage. It was after it had been there for some while that Allery and Bernard agreed to sell it to Red Rose for which purpose the Allber Omnibus Co. Ltd. was formed with a nominal capital of £1,200 in £1 shares. The Red Rose directors replaced Allery and Bernard on March 24th 1926 and four days later the registered office moved from 30 Thornsett Road to 5/11 Vauxhall Bridge Road.

The Service bus is thought to have been the first independent to reach Epsom (on route 70). This was one of the initial routes sought by Allery and Bernard before operation commenced, along with the 11, 19, 28 and 31. The partners sought permission to work the 70 to its extreme southern destination at Dorking but were refused approval beyond Epsom because of the poor turning lock on their early-type Leyland. Police schedules deposited late in 1924 restricted weekday operation to 49A/77B Mondays to Fridays and 28A/77B Saturdays.

The second acquired bus was the J.H. owned by John Hough. The youngest of the trio of firms, this originated as the Trinity bus registered on October 2nd 1924. It was a Wilton-bodied Dennis, XU 9497, and its title was inspired by John Hough's home address which at that time was 1 Trinity Rise, Tulse Hill. The bus was always painted red & white and operated firstly from Toler's garage in Camberwell before moving to Vauxhall Bridge Road. Its principal operations were on the 49 although initially it by no means confined its activities to this. Later on John Hough moved to 57 Shrubbery Road, Streatham and at an unknown date the Trinity title gave way to the initials J.H. The pattern of takeover was much the same as that for the Service bus. Firstly a limited company was incorporated on April 12th 1926 with a share capital of £1,200 and registered office at 5/11 Vauxhall Bridge Road. The Red Rose directors purchased the shares, in this case on May 17th 1926.

The buses belonging to the acquired companies operated in full Red Rose livery and could be distinguished from buses belonging to the parent fleet only by the legal owner's name on the rocker panel. The Service Leyland may never have been repainted by its new owners. It introduced a non-standard chassis to the fleet and a new Dennis was immediately ordered to replace it. YP 8995 was licensed on September 1st 1926 whereupon the Leyland chassis was converted by the company into a lorry for Rosemex Oil Fields Ltd. The new bus carried a Dodson body which may well have been the same one formerly carried by the Leyland. Two further buses joined the combined fleets in May and July 1927 respectively as spares. The first, YH 3745, was registered in the name of John Hough Ltd. whilst the other, YT 2578, was officially owned by the Allber Omnibus Co. Ltd. Both were on new Dennis chassis but the bodies were second-hand ones built by Straker Squire and taken from chassis of the same make which had been withdrawn from service by other operators, though it is not known which two vehicles these bodies came from.

The Red Rose buses came to the end of the road on March 3rd 1928 when Public took them over. The three companies were duly wound up; Allber and John Hough on June 18th 1928 and Red Rose itself on December 8th 1930. Rosemex Oil Fields continued in business at the Vauxhall Bridge Road premises and was renamed Rosemex Service Station Ltd. in January 1958. The last of the original Red Rose men left in the business was John Pugh the former bus manager. He died in May 1962. Financial difficulties later beset the company and the appointment of a liquidator was ordered in May 1972. The garage is now thriving again under new management under the title of Vauxhall Bridge Road Service Station.

81A Page Street, Westminster

No great distance away from 5/11 Vauxhall Bridge Road was, at one time, a garage known as 81A Page Street, Westminster. An early 'thirties development of flats now covers the site where, early in the century, Christopher Dodson Ltd. once had a coachbuilding works and, later, S. H. Hole ran a thriving coach and garage business.

SAMUELSON

It has been popularly quoted that the second independent operator was Primrose. This was not so. On September 7th 1922 Sidney Harold Hole, trading as the Samuelson New Transport Company, began a service with double-deckers between Northfields and Ealing (Argyle Road) via Argyle Road itself, which was then unserved by buses, and thereafter via LGOC route 97 for the rest of the way. This was only one month after Chocolate Express began to operate on route 11 and two months before Adams bought his Primrose Straker Squire. Hole was no newcomer to the realms of public transport, having formerly served with the LGOC where he rose to the rank of Superintendent at Forest Gate garage.

S. H. Hole had shortly before this purchased certain of the assets of the Samuelson Transport Co. Ltd., a public company, which had been under a Receiver and Manager since April 1922. Formed on April 14th 1921 by George Berthold Samuelson, a film producer, Sydney Charles William Blythe, a works manager, and a cinema agent with the unusual name of Harry Harry Lorie, the Samuelson Transport Co. Ltd. had made staggering progress within a very short time. In August 1921 it became a public company, by which time it had expanded the original six-coach fleet of May 7th (the first day of trading) to ninety-nine, to which could be added 23 vans used for transporting coach passengers' luggage from door to coach free of charge in the same manner as Cambrian. Of the ninety-nine coaches in stock forty-three were fully paid for, as were all the vans. The assets of Silver Star Services Ltd., a fifteen-coach Brighton business, had been purchased and a London to Brighton express coach service was run jointly with them in addition to many other scheduled coastal runs. Further capital was needed to implement a planned fleet of parcels lorries which were intended to leave London each night for business centres within a 200 mile radius of the capital, hence the reason for going "public." The remarkably successful first few months of operation attracted hundreds of small investors to put their money into the business, which continued to prosper for a while. In March 1922 the British Ex-Officers Travel Association Ltd., a firm of coach operators and booking agents, was acquired. Then the bubble burst and, after two successive Receiver and Managers had been appointed by dissatisfied debenture holders, it was finally decided in September 1922 that the company could not by reason of its liabilities continue in business. Though the business had had great potential the directors, who were not experienced transport men, had probably committed the proverbial error of trying to run before they could walk.

Though the Samuelson company was in difficulties which forced its winding-up the organisation which it had created continued trading though in a drastically pruned condition. S. H. Hole, who lived at Taplow, Berkshire, purchased some of the assets including the lease of the garage at 81A Page Street, Westminster and the right to use the Samuelson title. He traded as the Samuelson New Transport Company and in June 1923 endeavoured to form a public limited company to take over and develop the business. It was to have a capital of £15,000 in 50,000 preference shares of 4/- each and 100,000 ordinaries at 1/-. Shareholders in the old Samuelson company were offered one fully paid ordinary share as a free bonus with every two preference shares subscribed in the new company. The scheme did not immediately catch on and it was not until August 18th 1928 that the Samuelson New Transport Co. Ltd. finally came into being.

The operation of the bus service in West London had been decided under the old regime though it was S. H. Hole who put it into operation. Three former charabanc chassis, two Daimler Y-types (XB 9972/9986) and one Dennis (XB 9984) were fitted with double-deck 34-seater bodies formerly used by Thomas Tilling Ltd. on TTA1 chassis and now repainted in an all-over brown livery. Being garaged at Page Street, they had a long distance to travel to the nearest point on their Ealing to Northfields service. They ran in service between Victoria and Acton Vale when 'running out' and also carried passengers on the return journeys at night. Normally the service seems to have been worked by two buses but sometimes all three were in evidence. Before long the service along Argyle Road was discontinued and the Samuelson buses then ran exactly as route 97.

The competition provided by General on 97 proved too much for Samuelsons, and the buses appear to have been withdrawn on December 15th 1923 after which the three vehicles reverted to coaches. The bus service had never, in any case, been more than a minor part of Hole's activities which were centred mainly around his coaching operations. The Samuelson name was until recently seen on "National" sightseeing coaches though the Samuelson New Transport Co. Ltd. has not been associated with S. H. Hole for many years, having been sold to London Coastal Coaches Ltd., representing Tilling & B.A.T. interests, in July 1937. It is now a constituent member of the National Bus Company. A sister organisation, Samuelson Saloon Coaches Ltd., ran a daily London-Birmingham-Liverpool express service which came under the control of the Red & White organisation on September 14th 1931.

Though Sidney Hole ceased local bus operation under the Samuelson title as early as December 1923 this did not mean that he had lost all interest in this type of work. Starting in June 1923 he had begun to operate buses from his Westminster premises on behalf of other owners and himself became a bus proprietor again for a short while in 1925/6 as part-owner of the A1 bus. He would have developed his bus interests further had a November 1925 attempt to gain approval to run on the suburban route 518 (Hounslow, The Bell to Southall Town Hall) been successful.

Hole's A1 bus passed to LGOC ownership in March 1926 and he was successful in putting other acquisitions in the way of the LGOC from amongst the buses garaged at Page Street. It may have been because of this that in March 1926 Frank Pick gave an undertaking to find work for Hole's depot resulting in acquired fleets being placed under his control. The A1 and Marathon buses ran in this manner up to August 17th 1926 when they were replaced at Page Street by the whole of the thirteen-vehicle EP fleet which was standardised on Straker Squires. Formal agreements were drawn up between Hole and the LGOC under which the former was to provide every function expected of a proprietor operating on his own account including the maintenance, overhaul, operation and staffing of the vehicles; everything, in fact, except the letting of advertisement spaces which was handled by the LGOC. Daily records of cash takings and service mileage were forwarded to the LGOC, plus monthly statements as to maintenance and overhaul costs and tyre mileages. All operating and maintenance charges were deducted from the traffic takings, against which Hole was also allowed £7 15s. 0d. per bus per week for management and other expenses. Uniforms were purchased by Hole and invoiced at cost to the LGOC, who themselves supplied all tickets, waybills and tyres to Hole. They also insured the buses whilst Hole insured the staff against workmen's compensation, employers' liability and similar claims. Hole's connections with the LGOC ceased on March 16th 1927 when the EP's were moved from Page Street into one of General's own garages at the termination of their contract with the Samuelson company.

Details of the independent companies based at 81A Page Street, most of which were operated by S. H. Hole on behalf of their owners, now follow.

MARATHON

The first man to garage his buses at Samuelson's was Hugh Sutherland Valentine Paterson of the Buckingham Palace Mansion Garage at 11 Eccleston Street East, Victoria. The premises next door to his, at no. 10, were owned by L. M. Turnham, the charabanc proprietor who also ran the Victoria Road Car bus which is described in chapter 7. Turnham may well have evoked Paterson's interest in passenger transport, and almost certainly took a hand in running Paterson's two buses as his name sometimes appeared on documents relating to them. Paterson bought a pair of new Leylands from Dodson in June and July 1923 (XO 1942/4835). They were in a livery of very dark green with cream window frames and carried the name Marathon in large letters extending almost the length of the bus. After an uneventful career, mainly on the 17C, 184C, 185A and 286, Paterson's buses were sold on June 18th 1926 to the LGOC who purchased the share capital of the Marathon Omnibus Co. Ltd. of 41 Finsbury Square, E.C.2., which had been formed on April 17th 1926 to enable the change of ownership to take place.

Under the LGOC's auspices the Marathon buses continued to run from the Page Street garage until August 17th 1926 when they were transferred to Shepherd's Bush (S). In March 1927 they were replaced by a pair of K's, K104 & 167, and the Leylands, after overhaul, joined the Vivid (XO 1942) and Atlas (XO 4835) fleets which were then Batten-controlled companies and were standardising on Leylands. Marathon ceased to operate on January 1st 1928 when the assets were absorbed by the LGOC.

FLORENCE

Walter Hardwick Holden Green of 49 Brook Green Road, Hammersmith, W.6. was the proprietor of Hammersmith Coaches which he ran from a garage at 113 Dalling Road, Hammersmith. Late in 1923 he ordered his first bus from Strachan & Brown on a Dennis chassis. It materialised in January 1924 and was licensed on the 26th as XR 888, having been passed at Scotland Yard the day before. XR 888 was red & cream and carried the fleet name Florence. It was joined in June 1924 by XT 6628, an identical vehicle. The two Florence buses were run on Green's behalf by S. H. Hole and were always garaged at Page Street. Their first routes varied widely and included 25, 33, 36 and 37, but the London Traffic Act restricted their weekday movements to 12C/112B and 49A/B. The Florences could generally be found on the 112A on Sundays.

Green used the rear of his Florence bus tickets to advertise his Hammersmith Coaches. On July 11th 1925 the coaching side of Green's business was reorganised as Hammersmith Coaches Ltd. with registered office at 49 Brook Green Road. The fleet at this time comprised four vehicles, two 28-seaters and two 14-seaters. The buses were not included in the reorganisation, and in 1926 Green decided to dispose of them to the LGOC. On July 24th 1926 he formed the Florence Omnibus Co. Ltd. of Lennox House, Norfolk Street, W.C.2. with a share capital of £2,000. Control passed to the LGOC on September 3rd and the head office was thereafter changed to 55 Broadway. The two buses operated from Hammersmith (R) garage from September 8th and they departed in January 1927 for overhaul en route to Redburns and were replaced by K5/320 in General colours. These lasted on the Florence workings until January 1st 1928.

* * * *

Enterprise, Orange and Westminster, also The Jockey, all ran from Page Street from the early part of 1924 but their stay was short-lived except for Westminster who remained until 1926, and their histories are dealt with elsewhere.

DISTRICT

District was the name given by William Hampton to the two buses he purchased in mid-1924. Both were red & cream Dennises and were licensed in May (XT 5917) and July (XU 1748) respectively. Hampton lived at 16 Gower Mews, W.C.1. and was for a while partnered by a man called Stedman, though Hampton was always the licensee. The 9, 15, 29 and 33 comprised some of the earlier District operations, but later the two buses were scheduled to operate on weekdays as 15A and 173E and on sections of the 15 and 295 on Sundays. Like most of the other Page Street operators, Hampton arranged the sale of his business to the LGOC, and on May 17th 1927 formed the District Omnibus Co. Ltd. with registered office at 55 Broadway. Control passed to General on Thursday June 2nd and the two buses were transferred into the garage at Willesden (AC). This allocation was inappropriate and after only a week the vehicles moved once again, this time to Holloway (J). On January 1st 1928 the two District Dennises were absorbed into the LGOC.

ROYAL TOOTS

A. G. Summerskill, whose activities we have already dealt with in Chapter 3, was in Page Street for a few months from about November 1924 onwards. The next arrival after him was XW 5626, a Dodson-bodied Dennis which was christened Royal Toots and licensed on December 17th 1924. The un-bus-like title indicated a light-hearted approach to buswork which was further enhanced by the yellow & cream livery and the little painting of a puppy seated on a cushion between the ROYAL and the TOOTS. Mary Rose Helen Hoare and her husband Theodore of 8 Hyde Park Gate, Kensington, owned Royal Toots which Hole ran for them, apparently without success, for by April 7th 1925 XW 5626 had gone south to Croydon to join the Regal fleet of J. Thomson.

T & W

Next came T & W, the Dennis of Cyril Charles Alfred Thornelow of 95 North Side, Clapham Common, and F. Wilson. The T & W bus was XX 1756 which was bodied by Dodson and licensed on February 19th 1925. Its first schedule combined routes 514 and 523 in a similar fashion to the Dominion and Beattie buses but by almost mid-1925 its exclusive terrain had become the 514 on the busy Uxbridge Road. Calamity struck in the shape of the "Uxbridge Road Order" effective from March 29th 1926 under which all licences for route 514 were revoked leaving the operators holding them with nowhere to run. No replacement licence on an alternative restricted route was immediately forthcoming and the proprietors last ran their buses on March 28th. Fortunately for them the LGOC expressed a willingness to buy their business, their aim in doing so being to prevent them springing-up as competition elsewhere, which they could quite conceivably do when alternative licences were granted by the police.

On April 13th 1926 the T & W Omnibus Co. Ltd. was formed at Lennox House, Norfolk Street, to take over the now unused but still licensed XX 1756 which was lying in 81A Page Street. The shares were acquired by the LGOC on May 17th. The new owners had already decided not to request an alternative service from the police; they were content having bought the bus to, as it were, kill it off. Its plates were removed on May 18th and it never again ran as T & W. After some months had elapsed the T & W Dennis was overhauled for service with Redburns, and on January 1st 1928 the business was officially absorbed into the parent company without having operated at all during its twenty months as an LGOC subsidiary.

DOMINION

A similar case to T & W was that of the Dominion Omnibus Co. Ltd. This had been registered—again like the T & W Omnibus Co. Ltd.—on April 13th 1926; it was acquired by the LGOC on May 17th 1926 and remained dormant. Dominion had begun under the auspices of taxi-owner William Henry Cook of 27 Huntsworth Mews, W.1. in April 1925 with two all-red Dodson-bodied Dennises, XX 8837/9591, bearing the name Dominion in General-style gold lettering. The two Dominion buses were removed from service on the Uxbridge Road route 514 the same time as the T & W, and after lying unlicensed for a while were transferred to Redburn in November 1926. W. H. Cook was connected with S. H. Hole in the purchase of the A1 bus in September 1925, and the association between the two men continued after the sale of the London buses, Cook being a co-director in the Samuelson business until control passed to Red & White.

W. H. Cook was particularly successful as a taxi proprietor and the firm that bears his name, W. H. Cook & Sons Ltd. flourishes today at Huntsworth Mews and also at the former Goldhawk Garage in Brackenbury Road, Shepherds Bush, which was once the home of several of his contemporary bus proprietors. W. H. Cook himself, now in his early nineties, lives in retirement in Sussex. To the transport man a poignant reminder of Mr. Cook's Dominion buses and of the independent bus era in general exists in the shape of XX 9591, the newer of his two Dennises, which has been restored by publisher Prince Marshall. Though at present in General livery, perhaps it may some day be repainted back into its original Dominion red.

A1

An office at 29 Mincing Lane, near the Tower of London, was the headquarters of S. W. Collins & Co., a firm of rice brokers. Early in 1923 its proprietors, S. W. Collins himself and his partner W. G. Amis, decided to diversify their interests and turned from food to transport when they placed in service the A1 bus. This vehicle was kept at the Fleet Garage, 96 Hackford Road, Brixton for the first stage in its career and did not arrive at Page Street until 1924 when it was bought by Guy Harry Warwick Wright who lived at Frinton-on-Sea, Essex. XO 8668, which was licensed on August 3rd 1923 and was examined at Scotland Yard the same day, was the very first of the many Dennises that were to run so successfully on London streets. It was chocolaty-maroon & cream and carried a blue diamond on the side panel upon which was written the fleetname. To quote "Commercial Motor", the fleetname was "brief and to the point, but somewhat reminiscent of a well-known sauce".

138

In September 1925 ownership of the A1 bus changed again. By this time the London Traffic Act was well and truly in force and a straightforward sale of the bus was no longer acceptable to the police; first the A1 Omnibus Co. Ltd. had to be formed on September 9th. It was a company with £1,000 capital and its registered office was at 81A Page Street. The original directors were G. H. W. Wright and George Thomas Mash, the latter being Hole's transport manager. Hole himself had a small shareholding in the new company but its principal owner was W. H. Cook of the Dominion on whose behalf Hole had arranged the sale. The A1 bus came under the control of the limited company on October 1st and shortly afterwards Wright severed his connection with it for a cash payment of £925.

On Tuesday March 30th 1926 the A1 bus changed ownership yet again. Its fourth proprietor in less than three years was the LGOC who purchased the entire share capital of the A1 Omnibus Co. Ltd. from Cook and Hole. At about the same time they concluded the agreement with Hole whereby the A1 and certain other acquired buses would continue to be garaged, serviced and operated by Hole from 81A Page Street. At this time the main weekday service operated by A1 was the 73E with odd journeys on 173D, 173E and 12C. Sunday operation was on the 5C. Before the regulation of schedules the bus had been seen on many other services including 2, 3, 11, 12, 27, 29, 34, 77, 112 and 127, and for a short while after the Act came into force the 514 had been on the itinerary. General continued to run the A1 bus from Page Street until the night of Tuesday August 17th 1926 when it was transferred to Nunhead (AH) upon the arrival at Page Street of the fleet of E.P. Straker Squires. In February 1927 XO 8668 went for overhaul and on to Redburns, its place being taken by K 993 which maintained the service until January 1st 1928.

114 Draycott Avenue, Chelsea

FAVOURITE
The removal, warehouse and cartage business known as W. J. Pike Ltd. was a family concern incorporated on January 25th 1910. In its origins it went much further back than this and had only become a limited company upon reorganisation after the death of its founder, William James Pike himself. From small beginnings as a furniture remover in 1840 Pike built up a thriving concern owning about eighty horses. The sole director of the company from 1910 until it was again reorganised in 1927 was John Heavans, the other members of the family who held the entire share capital jointly with Heavans being William H. Pike, Albert Frank Heavans Pike and their sister, Mrs. Helen E. Mogford. They ran their business from 114 Draycott Avenue, Chelsea, on which they had purchased the freehold in 1911 after the expiry of a twenty-one year lease which William Pike had previously held. The business was completely separate from, but had family connections with, Pike Ltd. who are still in the removals and warehousing business to this day in the Fulham Road.

After world war I the removals fleet was mechanised with petrol lorries and coaching is believed to have become one of the company's activities early in the 'twenties. A natural sequel to this was the purchase of a trio of buses between May 1924 and April 1925; XT 2643, XT 9480 and XX 8348. These were three identical Dennises for which Wilton constructed the bodies. They were painted in Panhard red with cream window surrounds, and they carried the fleet name Favourite. XX 8348 was unfortunate in meeting a tram head-on at Willesden Green whilst on the 526 on August 16th 1925 when it was only four months old. The damage to the bus was extensive, but was repaired in due course.

The original operations varied, but the first two buses are known to have included routes 11, 30 and 73 in their wanderings and they also carried route boards for 14, 17, 19, 33 and 73. Weekday schedules obtained when the London Traffic Act came into force were for the 14A and 49A. The third vehicle was licensed after this date and worked on the 526D, the West London Association service.

By the spring of 1926 the directors had come to the conclusion that they would do best to dispose of the buses and concentrate on their other activities. Negotiations for sale were commenced with General and reached an advanced stage before they abruptly fell through. So close were they to completion that, on April 22nd, the company wrote to the West London Association to the effect that they had sold their buses and would be withdrawing from the 526. It seems that bus operation ceased completely for a few weeks, but by June 9th the Favourites were back on the road on their original timings. The eventual sale of the buses, on much more favourable terms than had been previously negotiated with General, came about on August 17th 1927, when Public took them over on payment of £9,000.

Following the sale of its buses, the business was reorganised in December 1927 as W. J. Pike (1927) Ltd. In 1952 the Pike family retired after having been connected with the business for more than a century, the new owners being the proprietors of Mountain Transport Services Ltd. A further change of management took place in November 1955 when the business came into the hands of Road Services (Caledonian) Ltd. At an Extraordinary General Meeting held in Glasgow on February 3rd 1960 the decision was made to wind the company up. It is doubtful whether, by this time, there was anybody still connected with the business who could recall the far off days of the 'twenties when it ran buses on London streets.

287/289 Camden High Street, Camden Town
1-12 Harmood Street, Chalk Farm
(also Bridge Wharf Garage, Kentish Town Road)

Walter James Dangerfield was a big, blunt man. He was a forceful character and a power to be reckoned with in the bus-world of the mid-twenties. From farming at Mill Hill he progressed to owning taxis at Camden Town though horticulture remained in his blood and he could always be relied upon to produce a goodly supply of potatoes and other vegetables for sale to his staff. The carting of pig offal by motor lorry from Smithfield market was another of his sidelines. He was a leading light in the Mohawk Motor Cab Co. Ltd. which was formed on July 20th 1922 to take over the Mohawk Garage at 1-12 Harmood Street, Chalk

Farm, almost opposite the LGOC's Chalk Farm (CF) garage. In December 1923 the freehold property nearby known as the Bolton Garage at 287/289 High Street, Camden Town, was rented by the Mohawk company from the Regents Canal & Dock Co. and was purchased from them on March 17th 1925; this was renamed the Carlton Garage by its new owners. The Mohawk and Carlton garages traded in unison stabling taxis and carrying out overhauls and repairs to all manner of vehicles.

The pirate bus was much in the news in early 1923 and inevitably Dangerfield's attentions turned towards it. While he was making arrangements to finance a fleet of Leylands of his own the owners of two other pioneer buses, X-service and Carlton Association, came forward with a request to house their vehicles in the Mohawk Garage in February and March respectively. Thereafter Dangerfield's buses and those of other proprietors co-existed side by side in varying degrees of harmony at 1-12 Harmood Street (and later also at 287/289 High Street) for the next few years. Apart from the two mentioned above, the others known to have garaged with Dangerfield are, in order of arrival, Universal, Majestic, Drake & McCowen, Nulli Secundus, The Fountain, Alberta, The Adelaide Service, Dauntless and Pickwick.

Before passing on to the story of Dangerfield's buses, it is well to pause here to look at the background to his two garages as both had been connected with passenger transport in earlier years. The Harmood Street property was originally built for Christopher Dodson and was probably used by him as his main coachbuilding works right up to May 1921 when the extensive new premises in Cobbold Road, Willesden were ready for occupation. We know for sure that it had become the Mohawk Garage by mid 1922. The garage at 289 High Street, Camden Town alongside the canal had been a jobmaster's premises for many years. It also housed a booking office from which, in August 2nd 1872, Samuel Crews began to run a horse bus service on behalf of the Metropolitan District Railway to Gower Street Station using hired vehicles. This lasted for only about a year, when the railway took over operations itself, but Crews later ran on his own account, together with services on behalf of the Railway from Piccadilly Circus to Baker Street and Portland Road Stations. These ceased in 1895. The premises were afterwards Associated Omnibus Company stables and the last tenant before Mohawk took over was a motor engineer by the name of Henry Samuel.

Both the Dangerfield garages have survived the ravages of time and late in 1975 presented much the same appearance to the world as they had done five decades earlier except that the narrow approach to the Camden High Street garage from the main road has now been considerably widened.

CARLTON
OVERGROUND
NULLI SECUNDUS
NORTHERN

A company entitled Dangerfield Ltd. was incorporated on February 9th 1923 with a share capital of £2,000 comprising 1,970 7% preference

141

shares of £1 and 1,000 ordinaries of 1/- each. Dangerfield was Managing Director for life and his co-directors were Robert Henry Mills, a Mill Hill architect and surveyor who also had a financial interest in the Mohawk company, plus two glass merchants, Maurice Bateman and Gerrit Willem Coenraad Van Der Hock, a Dutchman. The nominal share capital was increased to a total of £13,000 in November 1923 though this was not entirely taken up. The value of investments in the Company by the respective shareholders was: Mills and his wife Hannah £3,170, Bateman and Van Der Hock £3,115 each, and Dangerfield £105. The registered office at 27 Cross Street, Hatton Garden was also that of the Carlton Window Cleaning Company from whom it is thought the fleet name Carlton, which was used on the buses, was derived.

The first Carlton was XN 3091 and it was licensed on March 27th. Like the seven buses that subsequently joined the fleet in 1923 it was a Dodson-bodied Leyland. The main body colour was officially crimson lake but was usually described as brown and was relieved by off-white window frames. Various operations were applied for, those directly comparable with LGOC operations being 28 & 31 followed by 24, 27, 29 and 59. Dangerfield Ltd. probably became best known in its early days for its Muswell Hill (Queens Avenue) to Victoria service to which it gave the route number 4, recalling a short-lived pre-war LGOC route of 1912 between the same places which was also numbered 4. The Carlton buses endeavoured to maintain a fairly regular service on the 4 in what was the first real attempt by a London independent to obtain operational stability on a service of its own.

May 1924 was the most significant month in Dangerfield's bus career as it saw the entry into service of the first of the famous Overground buses. XT 3927 was licensed to Dangerfield as an individual and was the forerunner of a fleet of no fewer than twenty units purchased up to January 1925, all of which were Dodson-bodied Dennises. The source of inspiration for the OVERGROUND fleet name was obvious, and such was its success that the Carlton fleet was later renamed likewise and given the same red livery. The Dangerfield Ltd. fleet also expanded in 1924 with the Autumn arrival of a new Leyland and three new Dennises. The two fleets were worked under Dangerfield's command as one unit. In 1925 he allocated fleet numbers, his own Dennises becoming 1-20 and the Dangerfield Ltd. fleet 21-32. No. 33 came second-hand from Lionel Punnett's X-service in July 1925 and was the only Overground Straker Squire.

With the shadow of the London Traffic Act looming large he joined with Birch Bros. Ltd. in a joint application for four services:-

Potters Bar	—	Hampton Court
Hadley Highstone	—	Elephant & Castle
Muswell Hill	—	Victoria
Potters Bar	—	Victoria

These were approved on October 6th 1924. The scheme for co-ordinated operation with Birch came to nothing and at the start of 1925 the fleet was to be found still on route 4 which, under the Bassom renumbering, had become 285. Very early in 1925 this was abandoned in favour of daily operation on the well-known 284A, which was to become a popular route with independents, plus weekday morning peak journeys on 279B. These particular morning journeys were very profitable and also attracted vehicles from the Burlington, Western and Majestic stables.

From 1925 expansion was more or less out of the question as all the best routes became restricted and the few new vehicles that were bought thereafter came as spares or replacements. In late 1925 two new Leylands were licensed to W. J. Dangerfield and took fleet numbers 34/35, and a similar vehicle of 1926 became 33 in place of the Straker Squire of that number. The last to arrive, no. 37 of February 1927, was a new Dennis for Dangerfield Ltd.

Two acquired businesses came into the Dangerfield camp in mid 1926, bringing one bus apiece into the combined fleets and consolidating Dangerfield's position on the 284A, upon which they both worked. The Nulli Secundus bus was a Dodson-bodied Leyland XP 4908, similar to Dangerfield's own; the Northern was a product of Straker Squire, XP 2039.

Nulli Secundus was the name chosen in October 1923 by William James Royle Martin and Edward Albert Routledge for their crimson lake Leyland which was licensed on November 2nd to the Nulli Secundus Omnibus Company of 1-12 Harmood Street. Its early career was spent mainly on route 29 along with a multitude of other independent buses. Edward Routledge seems to have left the business after about a year and nothing more is heard of him. Not so, alas, for poor Royle Martin who hit the headlines in June 1924 when he was sent to prison for a month by the Bow Street magistrate for being drunk in charge of his bus. Pleas by his father that he had been a public schoolboy, then an Army Captain who had won the M.C. in 1917, and had later served in the Indian Army which he had left with the highest honours, were of no avail. A police witness had seen the driver of the bus, in Chandos Street, about to start the engine. He swayed to and fro, and then fell on the bonnet. At that moment Martin, who was the conductor, came down the stairs of the bus and staggered towards the driver, very obviously drunk. Two women passengers were sitting inside at the time, no doubt wishing they had chosen a bus with a somewhat more conventional crew.

The business survived Martin's Chandos Street escapade and branched out with a second bus on February 1st 1926. The newcomer was YM 6965, a small Dennis 25-seater which was bought to run with the Orange buses on the 550. It had a sister vehicle, YM 6966, which was owned by the Farwell Omnibus Co. Ltd. and was also on the 550 and indeed, apart from supplying the money for the new bus Martin appears to have had little to do with the bus. It was run for him by Farwell and garaged with Farwell's buses at Coventons garage in Junction Road, Holloway. Like its sister, YM 6965 passed to Orange on March 25th 1926 although it continued to run for its new owners in Nulli Secundus colours until April 1927.

Shortly after the disposal of his short-lived second bus, Martin arranged the sale of his double decker to Dangerfield for £1,550. He formed the Nulli Secundus Omnibus Co. Ltd. on June 2nd 1926 with head office at 54 Coleman Street and Dangerfield, Mills and Bateman as directors. An agreement for sale was drawn up on June 8th 1926 to be effective from September 1st on which date the Nulli Secundus bus became a subsidiary of Dangerfield Ltd.

The Northern bus had been launched on to the streets of London in September 1923 by Walter Faulkner of 139 Stroud Green Road, N.4. Apart from holding the licences Faulkner played no active part in running the bus but employed, as manager-cum-driver, the former proprietor of a small fleet of BSA sidecar taxis, Clement Preece. These had traded under the title of Sidecar Hire Co. Ltd., and as a sideline to these Preece had done haulage work with an ex-army Pagefield until it met an untimely end on the Bath Road near Chippenham when it went up in flames. The Northern bus was housed at 256 Archway Road for which an advertisement was carried on the ticket backs. This was where Preece's sidecar taxi business had been based and it was owned by S.E.M. Harte's Bulwark Manufacturing Company which later ran an unsuccessful London-Dunstable express coach service. Harte suffered heavily in the 1929 collapse of the Cambrian coaching combine with which he had become financially involved. Like the Nulli Secundus, the Northern bus was frequently to be found on the 29 in its younger days though many other services, notably the 27, also received its spasmodic attentions before scheduled operation commenced on the 284A. An accident in Kentish Town Road, when the bus nearly overturned in trying to avoid a motor cyclist whose machine had cartwheeled in front of it, brought to an end Preece's career as a London bus driver. He had been at the wheel and suffered badly from shock afterwards. Soon after this Faulkner agreed to sell the business to Dangerfield and to facilitate transfer of ownership the Northern Omnibus Co. Ltd. of 139 Stroud Green Road was incorporated on April 29th 1926 with a share capital of £800. Under an agreement of May 5th this took over the Northern bus from an unspecified date for £798 by share allotment. On June 18th the registered office was transferred to 54 Coleman Street and on the same date Dangerfield (as an individual as distinct from Dangerfield Ltd.) became the principal shareholder. The Northern Straker Squire henceforth worked from the Dangerfield garages but there is no evidence to indicate that it was ever repainted in Overground livery. Faulkner continued in his main career of photographic dealer and his former manager, Clem Preece, after a spell of traffic management for Dangerfield and a year or two working on Cadillacs in the U.S.A., joined his friend S. E. M. Harte in Kingston & Modern Travel Ltd. which was associated with Cambrian. Sensing financial trouble ahead, he left to join Royal Blue in the management of which he spent a long and distinguished career, retiring from the position of Commercial Traffic Manager for the Western National group of companies in 1965.

On May 10th 1926 Overground Ltd. was incorporated at 54 Coleman Street to take over the 23 buses licensed to W. J. Dangerfield. The company records relating to Overground Ltd. have long since been destroyed and it is not known when the limited company officially took control. It was probably not until November or December 1926 when

Dangerfield was appointed Managing Director. The shares were allotted in December, mainly to Dangerfield.

An interesting event occurred on May 27th 1927 as a prelude to what followed soon after. Most of the shares in Overground Ltd. were transferred from Dangerfield to Christopher Dodson. The deduction which can be made from this is that Dodson was the source of Dangerfield's capital from which the Overground fleet was created. We would hazard the guess that Dangerfield now wished to sell his bus interests and, in order to put the books straight, Dodson's shares were transferred into his own name as distinct from being held by Dangerfield as a nominee as hitherto. In the following month, on June 8th 1927, the company was sold to the LGOC, the effective date of takeover being June 1st. 55 Broadway became the head office.

On the same date that it took over Overground Ltd., the LGOC also acquired the Dangerfield, Nulli Secundus and Northern companies. In the case of the latter W. J. Dangerfield remained the main shareholder until December 10th when the position was regularised by the transfer of his share allotment to Dangerfield Ltd. A condition of sale to General was that Dangerfield should remain as Manager and licensee of the companies formerly controlled by him. It is not known if this was an agreement for life or for a specified period because unfortunately no copy of it seems to have survived. Dangerfield continued in sole charge as hitherto, the only principal alteration being that on January 1st 1928 the assets of the Dangerfield, Nulli Secundus and Northern companies were sold to Overground Ltd. Prior to this, in July 1927, the Northern Straker Squire had been replaced by ex-Empress Dennis MH 9159. The three companies were put into voluntary liquidation and were wound up on August 27th 1928.

The story of Overground—General's unique subsidiary—from January 1928 onwards will be continued in a later volume.

X SERVICE

A pleasant-looking khaki & red Straker Squire XM 9591 took the road on February 20th 1923. It was a Dodson-bodied 46-seater with the fleet name X-service incorporating a large X placed between a smaller SER and VICE proclaiming that its owners had formerly been commissioned in His Majesty's Service. The operating company, which traded as X-service Omnibuses, was owned by Lionel St. Elmo Schuyler Punnett, Captain Charles G. Kemp-Small and Coltman S. Clarke. Having mentioned these three impressive names, two of them thereupon fade out of our history, Clarke almost immediately and Kemp-Small after about a year, leaving Punnett in sole command of the business. Their Straker Squire, XM 9591, ran from one or other of the Dangerfield garages. To start with a group of six services was applied for, each with its own X-service route number, viz:

1. North Finchley (Tally Ho) to Liverpool Street Via Golders Green, Baker Street & Bank.
2. North Finchley (Tally Ho) to Liverpool Street via Golders Green, Swiss Cottage, Camden Town & Bank.

3. Swiss Cottage to Victoria via Baker Street & Piccadilly.
4. Victoria to Liverpool Street via Bond Street & Oxford Street.
5. Hammersmith to Victoria Embankment via Kensington, Marble Arch & Regent Street.
6. Shepherd's Bush to Liverpool Street via Notting Hill Gate, Oxford Street & Bank.

Before long the X-service was pirating on established LGOC services, and on one day alone in April 1923 was seen on the 2, 13, 31 and 84, and by January 1924 it had joined the many others plying mostly on the 29. An interesting feature of Punnett's activities was regular Wednesday and Sunday trips out to Napsbury Hospital. A second bus similar to the first was licensed as XR 8763 on April 5th 1924.

Punnett did not remain in the bus business for very long. In February 1925 he arranged to sell out to E. E. Farwell, the proprietor of the Reliable and Dauntless buses. The deal initially fell through and was not finally implemented until July. This delay arose because neither party fully understood the legal barriers prohibiting the transfer of schedules from one proprietor to another. The case is more fully outlined in chapter seven wherein is described how Farwell, though having paid Punnett cash for his schedules, never derived any benefit from them. One X-Service Straker, XR 8763, passed to Farwell, the other saw further service in the ownership of Dangerfield.

CARLTON ASSOCIATION

The second independent owner to join Dangerfield in Harmood Street was Arthur Edward Ewen of 143 West End Lane, West Hampstead. Ewen's first bus was, like Punnett's, one of the rare breed of Straker Squires to carry a Dodson body and was registered as XN 912 on March 10th, 1923. It carried the fleet name Carlton Association which presumably meant to indicate that it was running in association with Dangerfield's Carlton buses. The bus is reported to have wandered widely, but the 29 group of routes was always high on its list of priorities and it eventually settled down to a regular working—on weekdays at least—on the 529C.

Ewen did not stay at Harmood Street for much more than two years. He moved to 54 Iverson Road, Brondesbury probably because it was nearer his home, and was already running from there when he took delivery of a new bus in November 1925. This was number YM 1060 and replaced the Straker Squire which later saw service in Hull. For some unaccountable reason YM 1060 was sold to another Iverson Road operator, Overington, after only a year and replaced by a further new Dennis, YR 4523. This bus was the last purchased by Ewen prior to the sale of his business to Public on July 8th 1927 for £2,750. Public took over operation of the bus on June 1st before completion of the sale, and took Ewen on to their payroll.

DRAKE & McCOWEN/DRAKE/W. R. DRAKE

The first of a pair of very smart Leylands which ran out of Harmood Street was licensed on August 31st 1923 as XP 435. It was followed on

May 20th 1924 by XT 4608. They were handsome in a striking colour scheme of creamy-yellow & black. The latter colour has been reported by some observers as navy blue and it is of course possible that this was substituted for black at one stage. The fleet name DRAKE & McCOWEN was carried in large gold letters with the cream panel as the background and occupied almost the length of the lower saloon. Robert McCowen left the business in about 1926 whereafter the fleet name was shortened to Drake, still in block capitals. The application of a mundane red & white livery in 1928 brought with it a further fleet name revision to W. R. Drake in script-style lettering. William Richard Drake of 245 Great (now Royal) College Street N.1. had been the senior partner from the start and combined bus ownership with his second-hand furniture business.

One of the principal routes worked by Drake & McCowen right from the start was the 27, their variant of it being renumbered 206 with the introduction of the Bassom numbering system in December 1924. Under the London Traffic Act one bus was scheduled on the 206, the other on the 284A. One of the buses, XT 4608, achieved notoriety when it was overturned by protestors during the General Strike. Even so it reappeared in service next day with its windows boarded over with planks of wood. Drake survived the mass acquisition by General and Public during the 1926/7 period and when the Dangerfield garages were no longer available the two buses were rehoused at the Bridge Wharf Garage in Kentish Town Road, adjacent to the Regents Canal and now a depot for A.B.C. bread vans. Finally Drake disposed of the business to Birch Brothers Ltd., the last day of operation under the old regime being October 26th 1928. Birch continued to run the Drake buses as a subsidiary until they, together with the two Ingarfield & Brights, were absorbed completely on February 1st 1929.

THE FOUNTAIN

Arthur Ingram Bland of 33A Gladstone Park Gardens, Dollis Hill, was the proprietor of The Fountain, a rather drab-looking Dennis which was painted all-over red with the fleetname in a large whitish rectangle on each side. It was registered XR 3546 on February 29th 1924 and presented to the police for inspection on the same day. Dangerfield housed it until about January 1926 when it was moved to Coventon's garage at 112A Junction Road, Holloway. After schedules were introduced, it could be found on weekdays on the 27A. It passed to Public for £2,850 on August 11th 1927.

THE ADELAIDE SERVICE/ADELAIDE

The only one of the many operators who garaged at Dangerfield's to remain independent to the end was the Adelaide. Frederick William Hayes was the owner of this business which led an uneventful career from November 1924 until November 1st 1933 when the LPTB took it over.

Hayes lived at 355 Bensham Lane, Thornton Heath, but the first bus was garaged at Camden Town, presumably for convenience of operation since it ran principally on the 27 group. It was XW 2210, a red & cream

Dodson-bodied Dennis with brown rocker panels, and it bore the name The Adelaide Service in large block capitals along the length of the main side panels. Later in its life it became red & cream only and was fitted with pneumatics; it was then called just plain Adelaide. At an unknown date, but almost certainly by June 1927 when General took control of Dangerfield's interests, the Adelaide bus ceased working from 289 High Street. By January 1930, when a new Leyland Titan was delivered, Wise's Garage at 43 Effra Parade, Brixton, was the operational base.

GC 3354 was the new Titan, which carried an open-staircase body by Dodson from whom, like its predecessor, it was bought on hire purchase. The livery employed was largely red with cream bands. The Dennis was not disposed of with the arrival of the Titan but remained as a spare vehicle. The routes operated varied a little over the years, although the 27 was always the centre of activities. In August 1927 weekday operations were scheduled on the 127 and the 206. At the time of acquisition by London Transport the weekday services operated were 3A, 127A/B, 227E/F, with Sundays on 3A and 127B. The Adelaide showed a very low profit in relation to the capital employed when compared to most of the other independent buses which survived through to 1933. Even so, the modest profit was probably sufficient to satisfy Frederick Hayes, who was an elderly man and not in the best of health, and his two sons, who worked on the bus. Unfortunately the profit factor reflected in the compensation payment received from the LPTB which, at £5,250, was considerably less than many others received for similar-sized businesses.

PICKWICK
The last of Dangerfield's bus-owning tenants to be recorded is Ivan Maxton who began to run his Pickwick Dennis XX 195 on route 27 in February 1925. Maxton's schedule later passed to the Paterson Omnibus Co. Ltd. of Ilford as we shall see in chapter 8.

7/9 Rochester Mews, Camden Road
CLARENDON
Lying inside the 'V' formed by the junction of the Camden Road with Royal College Street is Rochester Mews. This narrow thoroughfare had long been connected with the motor industry, and even before the first world war Harold Miles Merry had been in business there as a garage proprietor. The building concerning us is no. 7/9, where today stands the very modern Clarendon Garage with its main frontage to the Camden Road. In 1923 its predecessor was also called the Clarendon garage and was under the control of Harold Joseph Barnett who, in 1925, was prosperous enough to take over nos. 4/6 Rochester Mews also. A near neighbour at no. 21 was the British Automobile Traction Co. Ltd. who ran the fleet of green "British" Daimlers on route 24. At the height of the private bus boom Barnett decided to buy a fleet of buses. With his own garage and repair facilities he was better off than many of his contemporaries, and what better route could he choose than the busy 29 which almost passed by his door.

A modest start was made in September 1923 with XP 440. a Leyland, which took its fleet name Clarendon from Barnett's garage business.

148

It soon became well known for the clock which it bore in its lower saloon. The second and third Clarendon buses were licensed in March and August 1924 respectively and were registered XR 4807 and XU 6691. The first was a Leyland like its predecessor; the other a Dennis. August 1st 1925 saw the completion of the fleet in the guise of two little pneumatic-tyred Dennis single-deckers YL 965/6. This pair pioneered the short but useful new route 297 between Tufnell Park and Kings Cross on which they were later joined by PHRH. An 'A' suffix was added to the weekday 297 when Clarendon extended southwards on Sundays to Charing Cross in December 1925. Like all Clarendon buses the two newcomers bore Dodson-built bodies. The livery of the fleet has been variously described as maroon or chocolate & white.

After receiving a tempting offer from A. T. Bennett, Barnett sold his five Clarendon buses to Public on August 11th 1927 and received £14,000 for them. Coaching then attracted Barnett's attentions though the Clarendon garage remained his main source of business and he was also a hire car and taxi proprietor. In 1928 he worked one coach on the London-Bedford service in conjunction, latterly, with Birch who acquired Barnett's times in January 1929. He also took an active interest in the New Empress Saloons from July 1928 until October of the same year when City took over control.

79/91 Pentonville Road
(also 105 Marsham Street, Westminster)
& St. George's Yard, Blundell Street, Islington)

CLAREMONT

Situated at 79/91 Pentonville Road, next to Claremont Square, is a recently-opened wine and spirits cash and carry in the building known for many years as Cattermole's Garage. In October 1924 it opened to the public under the title of Claremont Garage and two months later it became the home of a fleet of five new buses which were named after it. There are three central characters in the complicated Claremont story; William Moriarty, Francis Joseph Wood and John Pike.

Moriarty, who as his name suggests was of Irish descent, was the owner of the Claremont Garage. He was very experienced in the motor trade and ran a haulage and general contracting business known as the Midland Garage at 30 York Road, Kings Cross out of which he operated a large fleet of 120 taxis. As early as April 1923 William Moriarty had been interested in the possibility of running buses and, together with Walter Woolf Levy with whom he was in partnership in the Midland Garage, applied to the police for ten plates. These initial plans for running buses were subsequently dropped and a year and a half was to elapse before the name of William Moriarty appeared as legal owner on the side of a London bus.

Moriarty had an acquaintance in the form of Frank Wood, a wealthy Lancastrian from Burnley who was a successful motor factor and held the sole concession for the sale of Straker Squires in his part of the world. The two men discussed the idea of each putting a bus on London streets

149

and, having decided it was a good idea, suggested to John Pike that he may care to do likewise and also to take charge of the running of the buses.

John Pike, who lived at 37 Wincott Street, Kennington, had been a friend of Moriarty's since boyhood. Before the war he had been employed by W & G du Cros at Acton as a driving instructor and during the war served in the mechanical transport section of the Army Service Corps. In Palestine he was injured and came close to losing a leg; that he did not do so was thanks to a very lengthy spell in hospital after the war ended. In 1924 he was fully recovered and seeking a permanent future for himself. He had decided to go in for taxi ownership but changed his plans when the opportunity for running buses was put before him.

An order was placed for three buses—one each—with Dodsons who were to supply the bodies on Dennis chassis and would arrange the hire purchase terms. Before they were delivered Moriarty and Wood decided to buy one more apiece. Quick delivery was imperative as, with the London Traffic Act now a reality, they were anxious to get the buses on the road before the end of December. Dennis could supply two more chassis at short notice but Dodson's order books were full so Strachan & Brown were given the contract for the bodies. On November 28th 1924 two buses were licensed, XW 3890 (with Dodson body) to Pike and XW 3891 (Strachan & Brown) to Moriarty. Wood's first bus arrived from Strachan & Brown in time to be licensed on the 9th December as XW 5110. Dodson's order was completed when XW 5716/7 were licensed on the 18th to Wood and Moriarty respectively. All vehicles bore the red & white Claremont livery with the appropriate owner's name on the rocker panel. The receipts for each bus were kept separate and each week a statement of takings was supplied by Pike with a complete summary of results once a month. Operations were principally centred around the 73 group of routes which passed the door of the Claremont Garage, although Wood had certain Monday to Friday workings on the 15A whilst Pike's and Moriarty's buses had route 29 as their main sphere of Saturday operation.

The Claremont Garage was (and still is) an extensive building and merits a brief description. At its opening in 1924 it contained showrooms, coachbuilding works, repair shops, petrol sales and offices. A 24-hour garage and breakdown service was provided; Unic cars and vans were hired out and the company would supply any make of new car its customers required. In charge of the whole enterprise as General Manager was C. G. Carpenter who, like his employer, had studied the latest ideas in motor car sales and service in the U.S.A. The garage had cost a great deal of money to build and this cost was heightened by a last-minute decision to include an upper storey at the expense of the ceiling height in the ground floor garage and necessitating heavier foundations.

Moriarty's extensive financial resources were stretched by the cost of the Claremont Garage and in February 1926 he found it necessary to dispose of his two buses. Frank Wood was a willing buyer and on February 23rd the Claremont Omnibus Co. Ltd. was formed with a share capital of £2,000 and registered office at the Claremont Garage to take over Moriarty's operations, control of the limited company passing to Wood. Wood now controlled four buses and his stake in the London bus business was further increased in January 1927 by the purchase of the Reliable buses owned by the Farwell Omnibus Co. Ltd. which ran two Dennises (XW 2566/4334) on the 284A. A third bus was also owned as a spare. This was Straker Squire XR 8763 which, under Wood's auspices, found its way north to his home town of Burnley. Under Wood's ownership the Farwell buses were moved from their original garage at Coventons to the Claremont Garage and were run for him by Pike.

It had, in fact, been through the efforts of John Pike that Wood acquired the Farwell business. In the latter part of 1926 three of the five small operators remaining on route 284A were considering selling out to General. The activities of Dangerfield's Overground buses which predominated on the route had made their position very vulnerable. Pike arranged to meet the proprietors in the Woodman at Highgate on November 10th and persuaded them to give him first option, the option to expire on November 18th. E. E. Farwell was prepared to sell for £3,850. John Potter, the owner of the Cardinal bus, settled on a sum of £1,750 and A. T. Peggram, representing the Majestic Omnibus Co. Ltd., agreed on £1,850 as a suitable price. Having obtained signed options Pike was then faced with obtaining the required amount of cash within eight days. As we have seen, Wood financed the purchase of Farwell's buses. Pike purchased the Cardinal bus himself, but the option on the Majestic lapsed. The Farwell and Cardinal businesses passed to Wood and Pike respectively in January 1927.

Wood's purchase of Farwell's assets was a simple matter involving an exchange of shares in a limited company. In the case of the Cardinal bus a limited company had to be formed and the Cardinal Omnibus Co. Ltd. came into existence on November 26th 1926 with its registered office at 7 Fallow Court Avenue, North Finchley, and a share capital of £200. The first directors were John Potter and his mother, but they were duly replaced by Pike and the registered office transferred to Claremont Garage. The pre-Claremont Garage days of the Farwell and Cardinal buses are described in Chapter 7.

Wood's expansion of his bus activities was not yet complete. On April 1st 1927 he began running a frequent service between Burnley and Clitheroe under the title Claremont Omnibus Service. A fleet of no fewer than eight new Vulcan twenty-seaters was purchased and a network of services was developed radiating from Clitheroe and serving Preston, Grindleton, Chaigley and Pendleton. An hourly Clitheroe to Manchester service was inaugurated and two Burnley-Manchester services were operated, one via Todmorden and Rochdale, the other via Accrington and Bury. Under the title of Claremont Luxury Coaches of Bank Parade, Burnley, Wood intended to commence a London-Birmingham-Manchester service and applied in March 1927 to the local authorities concerned for permission to do so. He had a very ambitious scheme to run a coach every hour throughout the length of the route, but must have thought better of it after making his applications and never commenced operation.

151

Back in London, there was a rift in the harmony between Wood and Pike and the former installed his nephew as manager of his six London buses. The results on them thereafter took a downward plunge and on September 30th 1927 Wood sold the six vehicles to Public for a total of £18,000. On May 4th 1928 the Claremont Omnibus Co. Ltd. was renamed Claremont Omnibus Services Ltd. and its head office was transferred to Spring Gardens Mill, Craven Street, Burnley. The assets of the Lancashire-based bus and coach services were transferred to it. To bring Wood's story to a conclusion, his fleet grew to thirty-seven vehicles. These were 1-12/14-16 Vulcans TD 7980-85/8857-65, 17 Leyland PLSC CW 6365, 18-20 Studebakers CW 7624/81/2, 21-32 McCurds CW 7821-32, 33-38 Leyland Tigers CW 7833-8. After merciless competition from Ribble, Wood sold out in 1930 to the Rishton & Antley Motor Co. Ltd., which became a Ribble subsidiary and was itself absorbed by Ribble in October 1930.

Pike, now left with only two buses to manage, decided early in 1929 to make an excursion for himself into the fast developing field of long-distance express coach operation. March of that year saw the arrival of a pair of tan, green & black Dodson-bodied Dennis F's, UL 7590/7692, which traded as the Claremont Coaching Service on a once-daily London-Liverpool route via Oxford, Stratford-upon-Avon, Birmingham and Chester. The London terminus was the Claremont Garage which, in the late 'twenties, was used by a number of long distance operators as a coach station. The vehicles were very luxuriously appointed and carried only twenty seats though their potential capacity was greater. They were fitted with thermo-rad central heating and every passenger had a pull-down table in front of him and a rug to wrap around his legs. Four more coaches were ordered but, before delivery, Pike sold the service to his Liverpool Agents, the Vestey-owned Merseyside Touring Company Ltd. after a short spell of less than three months as an express operator. Just prior to this he had made a study on behalf of the Liverpool company of local bus operation with recommendations on how to improve and develop their local services which began on March 13th 1929 on a four-mile Bootle-Liverpool service with five TSM Expresses. Following receipt of Pike's recommendations the Merseyside Touring Co. Ltd. expanded its bus services rapidly so that, by June 1930, a network of ten were in operation radiating mainly from Bootle. Pike's two coaches did not pass to the Merseyside company when they took over his Liverpool-London service; instead they were sold to Westminster Coaching Services Ltd. who garaged alongside his vehicles at the Claremont Garage.

The Cardinal and Claremont buses continued to run much as before until late 1929 when a major change was planned. John Pike wanted to replace the two existing buses with new ones, at the same time keeping one as a spare. The difficulty was that, under the regulations as they then stood, the one spare bus would not be allowed to deputise for both the other two as they were technically in separate fleets. The problem was overcome on December 17th 1929 by reorganising the Cardinal Omnibus Co. Ltd., whose nominal capital was increased to £2,000. The Claremont bus was then transferred to the ownership of the Cardinal Company, whereafter both buses ran for Cardinal but carrying the Claremont fleet name. This arrangement also had the advantage that only one set of accounts need be kept instead of two. The share capital, of which £1,000 was issued, was held by John Pike and his mother.

Also in 1929 Pike was forced to look around for new accommodation because he planned to buy covered top buses and the headroom in the Claremont Garage was too low to accept them. William Christmas, who had latterly been overhauling the buses, offered garage space at 363 Clapham Road which was accepted in August 1929. This was much less favourably placed in relation to route 73, on which both buses were now scheduled, and involved long "when-working" journeys. Henceforth crews changing over at mid-day reported at, and paid in to an office for which a room was set aside in the house where Pike now lived in Canonbury Square. In January 1932 the limited company's address was amended to 363 Clapham Road.

Pike's first covered top bus was a Leyland Titan—UW 6734—which, though delivered in time to be licensed on November 29th 1929, does not appear to have entered service until the end of January 1930. The older (ex-Cardinal) Dennis then became the spare bus until the following December when it was ousted from the fleet by a second new vehicle, GK 8667. This one was a Dennis Lance and it bore a Dodson body similar to that on the Titan and was one of only two open staircase Lances in London. The original Claremont Dennis then became the spare and the other was sold in December 1930.

With his departure from the Claremont Garage John Pike finally severed his business connections with his former colleague, Bill Moriarty. The latter, alas, never recovered from his huge financial outlay on the Claremont Garage and finally went bankrupt. He struggled for many years as a taxi owner-driver. After working long hours throughout the war he had finally fought his way back to owning a fleet of about twenty-five vehicles when his life ended prematurely with a heart attack.

John Pike's buses were removed from him on the appointed day, November 1st 1933 and compensation was later awarded of £18,000. At the end the company's weekday operations were on 73A, 73E, 173D and 173E with Sunday operation on the 229. Together with the three buses, London Transport inherited GC 8623, a 1930 Humber car which the Company had purchased second-hand in 1932. Later, John Pike and his drivers and conductors held a farewell dinner at Gennaro's Restaurant, and they went on from there by four-wheelers and hansom cabs to the Garrick Theatre's Old Time Varieties. The evening concluded over farewell drinks and a chat over old times at the Cafe Monico. John Pike, now 79, lives in retirement in Hertfordshire after a successful career as Managing Director of Metal Sprayers Ltd., from which he retired in 1961. One of his most prized possessions is a cocktail cabinet, the largest that could be found, which—stuffed with glasses and bottles of all kinds—was presented to him by his former staff in memory of their days as independent busmen.

★   ★   ★   ★

A few other independent bus concerns also garaged at the Claremont Garage from time to time though its inability to accommodate covered-top double deckers mitigated against its use by bus companies from 1929 onwards. Its main use, at least as far as p.s.v.'s were concerned in the late 'twenties and early 'thirties, was as a garage and coach station for many of the long distance express services which sprang-up in this golden era of coaching. The histories of the Tower, R.A. and Westminster buses follow. One further operator, Pullman, stayed at Claremont Garage only for a few months in 1926/7 as part of its frequent wanderings from one base to another. These are described in detail in chapter 5.

TOWER

The Tower Carriers Ltd. of 13 Earl Street, Westminster dated from October 6th 1920 and was at first, as its title implied, principally a haulage business. It was the successor to the Tower Bridge Transport Company and the Gorchart Service Company, both of which were run by a man called William Reginald Jackson. By the middle of 1922 effective control of the business had passed to Robert Godfrey Monro who lived at Claygate, Surrey and was by profession a civil engineer, and Lt. Col. John Duncan Munro, an engineer and director of Beddington Brickworks Ltd. Besides its haulage activities the company carried out vehicle repairs and acted as dealers in lorries. They overhauled for sale quite a large number of second-hand Thornycroft 4-tonners at a satisfactory profit. Unfortunately the company did not prosper as well as had been anticipated due to unwise investment of its capital in unprofitable sidelines notable of which was a firm called Radio Slot Machines Ltd.

In March 1924 the company's address became 105 Marsham Street, but this was merely a renumbering of the original premises. All but one of the outside shareholders had sold out to the Monros just before this. At about the same time a decision was made to enter the field of bus operation and three vehicles were ordered from Thornycrofts, the choice of chassis being no surprise considering the company's successful operation of many lorries of this make. The buses were delivered in May (XT 3717) and July (XU 2148/3280) and were painted in a very pleasant tangerine & cream livery with the fleet name Tower on each side. At the time the company had insufficient money to pay for the vehicles so they were bought by the Monros and leased from them, eventually becoming the property of The Tower Carriers Ltd. on December 31st 1925.

In their early career the Tower buses roved widely. Even from 1925 onwards each of the three buses worked on a different route on weekdays, one being on the 73, one on the 76 and third on the 88. Sunday details are not known except that in March 1926 route number 288 was allocated to Tower's variation of the 88 which ran from Mitcham to Kew Gardens. At first they ran from the company's Marsham Street garage which was well situated operationally for two of the three buses, but by March 1926—and possibly much earlier—they had moved to the Claremont garage. One unfortunate feature was that the tangerine livery lasted only until the first annual overhaul when it was replaced by an uninspiring red & white.

154

December 1st 1926 saw the purchase of The Tower Carriers Ltd. by General. The new owner required only the buses, and the remaining assets were sold back for a previously agreed sum to the Munros who had formed a new company entitled Tower Transport Ltd. to take them over. General immediately moved the buses to its own garage at Battersea (B) whence they ran for the first time on December 1st, and lost little time in withdrawing the Thornycrofts. The last one ceased to run on March 8th 1927 and the Tower fleet then consisted of K's in General livery. The vehicle on the 88 was of note in that it was the only combine-owned bus on the route carrying the General name, the remainder were all Metropolitans. On Wednesday June 29th 1927 the Tower buses were dispersed to garages more suitably located for their operation. The 73A/173D bus went to Hammersmith (R), the 88 to Merton (AL) and the 76 to Tottenham (AR).

January 1st 1928 saw the absorption of the Company into the LGOC.

R.A.

R.A. were the intials which appeared on the side of a Daimler XW 2849. This bus, in dark red livery except for dark brown rocker panels and greyish-white window frames, could be found on Mondays to Fridays on the 6A and at weekends on the 42A. Its owner was Clifford George Ray Boreham and its base was the Claremont Garage. "Ray" Boreham was an army captain during the war, and this gives an indication of the reason for his choice of fleetname. Immediately prior to becoming a bus owner in November 1924 he had been the licensee of the "Duke of Clarence" at 140 Rotherfield Street, Islington.

A limited company entitled R.A. Motor Services Ltd. was incorporated on November 13th 1925 with a registered office at 76 Shepperton Road, Islington where Boreham then lived, and a capital of £1,500. Boreham was joined by Bertram C. Crang and Geoffrey Boreham who owned an old-established firm of auctioneers, valuers and estate agents in the East India Dock Road. Ray Boreham had fallen behind with his monthly hire purchase repayments of £66 13s. 4d. to J. M. Roberts since the previous August and the capital provided by his new co-directors helped to tide him over an awkward situation. He was designated Managing Director with the option of being appointed conductor of one of the Company's buses at £5 per week!

As things were not going too well the obvious course of action was to find a buyer for the bus. General came along with an offer which was accepted and the bus changed hands on Friday March 19th 1926. There was no immediate sign of any change of ownership, and the R.A. Daimler continued to run from the Claremont Garage as before for the next five weeks, the receipts being taken by an inspector to Dalston (D) garage each day. Meanwhile a K was being prepared for work in the same livery as the Daimler. The latter ran for the last time on April 26th and on the following day K458 ran the service but from the General's Hackney (H) garage. It continued to run the R.A. working until it was absorbed into the Tramways (Metropolitan) Omnibus Co. Ltd. on January 1st 1928. The withdrawal of the old R.A. Daimler did not mean its end as a bus, as happened to so many others of its type. After its sale on August

155

21st it passed to E. W. Young and soldiered on as a unit of the Aylesbury Omnibus Company for some years afterwards.

WESTMINSTER
BELGRAVIA

Three partners began the Westminster Omnibus Company in April 1924 with the purchase of XR 9000, a Strachan & Brown-bodied Dennis. The trio who owned the bus, and worked full-time in the business during its subsequent highly successful career were James Holland Rich, Francis Harold Rose and William John Coleman. The latter's home address at 16 Clonmell Road, Tottenham was used as the company's office in the first place though later an office was rented at 19 Pentonville Road where crews reported for duty and paid in. Initially 81A Page Street was used as the garage but this was not altogether satisfactory and in about June 1926 Rich was introduced to the Claremont Garage by John Pike, a former colleague of his at W. & G. du Cros in pre-war days. It remained there until late 1929 when the need for greater headroom brought about a move to St. George's Yard at 18 Blundell Street, Islington, formerly the home of a cartage firm J. & W. Jay Ltd. On September 26th 1932 came the third and final move to Flight's Garage at 47/9 Parkhurst Road, Holloway, where Westminster rented a complete depot building for which they paid 15/- a week per vehicle for up to twenty vehicles. Any over this number were not charged for. Rooms in the house at the front of the site, officially numbered 45 Parkhurst Road, were also rented. The company could have been securely settled in these ideal premises for many years had not the all-embracing London Passenger Transport Board come on the scene.

XR 9000 was bought through F. H. Rose, which would suggest that he was a motor dealer, and was licensed on April 8th 1924 and entered service two days later. In a search for profitable operation it ran at various times in almost every area of London. A second bus, XU 8451, was licensed on September 18th and had begun running by October 6th on the same wide variety of routes as its predecessor, to which it was identical. Meanwhile a limited company had been incorporated on July 17th 1924 with its registered office at 8 Sherwood Street, Piccadilly. After the London Traffic Act received Royal Assent it was necessary for the company to deposit schedules for its two buses. This meant that the directors had to make up their minds which of their former various operations would be the most profitable. They settled for routes 73 and 76 for which schedules were submitted in December. From December 7th the two buses began to run morning peak journeys on route 76 up to about 10.0 a.m. at Stoke Newington. Then the 73A was served up to about noon after which the buses ran shorts on route 173E until the evening peak. From about 4.30 p.m. at Kings Cross they ran light to route 76 which was worked until the peak was over, reverting thereafter to the 173E and also partly to 173D until the close of service just after midnight. From February 2nd 1925 one bus worked a late night journey on 12C (Oxford Circus to Dulwich) but this was probably not a great success as it was discontinued after April 11th. Sundays were spent entirely on route 73A.

Despite the introduction of Restricted Streets Orders, the company wished to expand. They ordered four Dennises from Dodsons, which were delivered in pairs in February and April 1925 (XX 1161/2; XX 8326/7). The problem was—where could they be operated? Retrospective legislation had eliminated the best Central London routes. Finally it was decided to try route 70 which was still at this time unrestricted and on April 6th XX 1161/2 were put to work on it. XX 8326/7 joined them eight days later. On Sundays, when the Restricted Streets Orders did not apply, all six buses could be found on 73A. The 70, which became restricted on June 3rd under the second Order, proved to be a loser and James Rich, who was now Managing Director, appealed to the London & Home Counties Traffic Advisory Committee for their support in enabling him to transfer the four buses from route 70 to more profitable operations. He had, he said, been hoping all along for a dispensation to run on a profitable service, and it would simply be ruin unless he could do so. His appeal was based on the grounds that he was in possession of the four buses in question before the date finally specified as the deadline for the first Restricted Streets Order; February 17th 1925. The truth of this is doubtful; nevertheless after further appeals to the Minister of Transport Rich got his way, and on October 8th 1925 the four buses in question were transferred to the 73/76 where they ran the same pattern of services as the two already working on these services. In obtaining this dispensation Westminster were much more fortunate than many other independent operators whose powers of persuasion were, perhaps, not so forceful.

The original partners could not finance the whole of the expansion themselves, and in March 1925 they took on an additional director, James Desmond Gabb. Gabb, a retired army captain then living in South Devon, became the Company's assistant treasurer (later redesignated cashier). We have already recorded that Rich was Managing Director; Rose (an Australian) was secretary and Coleman treasurer.

Not content with six buses on the 73/76, the firm wished to develop further. Again there was the problem of where to run additional vehicles profitably. Two extra vehicles were bought, and for some while they ran regularly only on Sundays on the 73A, acting as spare buses on other days. YO 60 of July 1926 was an identical Dennis to the previous four, but YF 6944 of April 1927 was a very different thing altogether. Following the trend set by a few other operators, the new bus was a pneumatic-tyred single-decker which seated 30 in its Dodson body and was based on the successful Dennis E-type chassis. Regular weekday operation of these two did not start until November 21st 1927 and the then unrestricted route found for them was 26D which involved a lengthy "dead" journey between the Claremont Garage and Ilford. On January 9th 1928 the single decker was transferred to the 203 which was also unrestricted at this time.

Westminster purchased only one existing business during its successful career. This was Frederick Robert Hort and Alfred Henry Law's bus which ran daily on the 73A and was aptly named Belgravia after their trading address, 47 Sussex Street, which was situated in the heart of the Pimlico area sometimes known as Belgravia. Hort & Law started

157

business in October 1924 with XU 8984, a scarlet & white Leyland which they garaged firstly at 147 Hercules Road, Lambeth and later at Toler's in Lothian Road, Camberwell. Early in 1927 Westminster negotiated to buy the Belgravia and, as part of the process for changing ownership, Hort & Law registered the Belgravia Omnibus Co. Ltd. on February 21st 1927 with a share capital of £2,000 and its headquarters at 47 Sussex Street. Westminster took control on about March 21st and transferred the registered office to its own address at 222 Strand. 1,996 of the Belgravia shares were held in the name of the Westminster Omnibus Co. Ltd. and the remaining four were held one apiece by Rose, Rich, Coleman and Gabb. On November 23rd 1927 the Belgravia bus was absorbed into the parent company though Belgravia remained in existence as a non-trading subsidiary. In October 1928 the ex-Belgravia Leyland was swopped with MH 3812, a Dennis of the Prince Omnibus Co. Ltd. to permit standardisation on Dennises.

Further profitable expansion of the London bus business, except on Sundays, was clearly now out of the question, so the company had to look further afield for its future new operations. At the time the air was buzzing with rumours that great profits were to be made in long distance coach operation, and the Westminster company set covetous eyes on the London to Cambridge road. Two coaches were ordered, and in the Autumn of 1927 the service began, probably just before a similar one operated by Varsity Express Ltd. who became one of Westminster's main competitors on services to East Anglia. The Cambridge route ran under the title of Westminster Coaching Services and on February 13th 1928 a separate company entitled Westminster Coaching Services Ltd. was formed as a prelude to further developments in coaching. The new company took over two coaches, a Gilford and a Dennis. These were Gilford UC 5468, which was Westminster's first coach and carried a remarkable-looking biscuit & black coloured body with a clerestory roof, and YU 9391, a Dennis. The clerestory-topped body on the Gilford had been built by Redhead's Garage of Lewisham High Street; the builder of the other is not known. February 28th 1928 saw the extension beyond Cambridge to Bury St. Edmunds and in July a prong was added from Cambridge to Huntingdon via St. Ives. In April 1929 this was diverted away from Huntingdon to Wisbech via St. Ives and March. The Bury St. Edmunds Service reached Lowestoft by way of Diss, Bungay and Beccles on March 3rd 1929 and very quickly thereafter was extended to Great Yarmouth. London to Ely began on May 7th 1929 and for the 1929 season only, two journeys on the Great Yarmouth service by-passed Cambridge and ran via Ipswich and Southwold. London-Cambridge-Thetford-Norwich began in October 1929 and was the last major new service to be introduced. A summer extension beyond Norwich to Sheringham was unsuccessful and was not repeated after 1930. This vast expansion of services was brought about by using new normal-control Gilfords. These were soon supplemented by Dennis F's and most were later replaced by a new fleet of forward-control Gilford 1680T's. A high standard of vehicle maintenance was never one of Westminster's strong points, and Mr. Arthur Hadingham, who recalls the coach fleet well, recently recounted seeing YX 5782, a Dennis coach, passing through

Bungay on a rainy day in June 1932 with the passengers sitting inside it with their umbrellas up, so much rain was coming through the roof!

When the time came for the modernisation of the London bus fleet the company had to depart from its previous practice of standardising on Dennises. The Lance had not yet been introduced and the H-family, which was then Dennis's answer to the Leyland Titan, was no match for it in performance or design. Westminster accordingly ordered seven Titans on hire purchase from Dodson. UW 2308-11 and GC 3170-2 were licensed between October 1929 and January 1930. A further similar vehicle, GN 184, arrived in January 1931 and in May 1932 another was received in the form of GX 2602. These nine new vehicles replaced seven of the earlier, open-top Dennises. Because of this the company was able to put an extra bus on to the 73A on Sundays from May 4th 1930 bringing its operations to their maximum of nine buses on weekdays (7 on 73/76, 1 on 26D and 1 on 203) and ten on Sundays.

The only remaining open topper, YO 60, was replaced in February 1933 by the most famous of all London independent double deckers, JJ 9215. Dodson was responsible for the body on this handsome and enormous-looking S.M.C. Sikh six-wheeler. With a seating capacity of 64 it was the largest bus running in London at the time. Its large body weighed only 2 tons 6 cwt. and the unladen weight of the whole vehicle was only 7 tons 5 cwt. 3 qrs. This low level of weight was achieved by reducing the thickness of the wood employed in the main body framework and by substituting metal reinforcement to achieve sufficient strength. A windscreen was not fitted on this otherwise very modern vehicle because, in the opinion of Mr. Rich, the managing director, windscreens did not make for the utmost safety and the draughts they created affected the health of the drivers. He deemed a metal cowl and storm apron sufficient protection. This was Westminster's second attempt to operate a Sunbeam six-wheeler. In 1931 a vehicle of the same type but with an older style of Dodson body had been painted in Westminster colours. It had been built to fulfill an order by the Harnett family for their subsidiary Sphere Omnibus Co. Ltd. but did not enter service with them. On March 17th Westminster, jointly with the Sunbeam Motor Company, submitted it for police tests to ascertain its suitability for routes 73A and 76, and it passed. The reason Westminster did not take it into stock is not known. With the registration UK 7456 it later served as a demonstrator with Mansfield District, Midland General and the Corporations of Derby, Birmingham and Northampton. It was scrapped in 1940. JJ 9215 preceded it to the scrapyard by about a year. It's career with London Transport had been short lived and its last recorded work thereafter was as a private bus for the Wigan & District Subsistence Production Society of Standish in 1937/38. Whilst in London it had proved a smooth runner, but it was spoilt by a tendency to boil quickly.

With the formation of London Transport looming close, the directors of Westminster had to consider very seriously the future of their undertaking. Under the terms of the Act they would be able to claim compensation for severance if they retained the coaching business. On the other hand the coaches were infinitely less remunerative than the buses, which had been averaging an annual profit in the region of £8,000 in their later years, and the coach services may not have justified retention on their own. The owners decided that, rather than wait to collect severance money, they would endeavour to find a buyer for the coach business. They thought that Thomas Tilling Ltd. would probably be interested. Tillings wished to obtain a monopoly on the London-Cambridge route and were already negotiating for the purchase of Varsity Express, with which concern Westminster Coaching Services Ltd. now had an operating agreement. Tillings were, indeed, very interested, and negotiations which began in June 1933 were completed within the following month. The twenty-three Westminster Dennises and Gilfords passed to Tilling control in July 1933, and on October 1st they were taken over by Tilling's East Anglian subsidiary, the Eastern Counties Omnibus Co. Ltd.

Denuded of its associated coach business, the Westminster Omnibus Co. Ltd. continued in being until July 11th 1934 when its fleet of eleven once well-maintained but now rather scruffy red & cream buses passed to the LPTB. Along with them went the services of sixty-eight staff and three miscellaneous vehicles. XB 9722, a Dennis breakdown van fitted with crane and run on trade plates, was once a charabanc for Albert Ewer. YL 5024, a 13.9 hp Morris van, and YF 3426, a Sunbeam saloon car, completed the trio. London Transport paid compensation of £77,000 and at the final reckoning £68,297 7s. 6d. remained to be distributed to shareholders. The Westminster Omnibus Co. Ltd. was formally wound-up on November 30th 1936.

12 Phoenix Place, Mount Pleasant

Situated in the Mount Pleasant area of Clerkenwell was the Phoenix Place garage of Cambrian Coaching & Goods Transport Ltd. It was one of several garages owned or rented by this wide-ranging company who occupied the premises from about 1921 to 1925. The garage, which faces the Post Office Corporation's huge sorting complex and is now bounded on each side by areas of semi-dereliction, was later used by various firms of motor engineers and is now leased to a large firm of building contractors. Cambrian's history is revealed in chapter 9.

21-23 Old Nichol Street, Shoreditch

F & K

F & K was the fleetname used by John Robert Fallowfield and Joseph Redvers Knight, charabanc proprietors who entered the field of bus operation rather late in the day and stayed in it for only a short time. From their premises at 21-23 Old Nichol Street, Shoreditch—an old, low brick-built structure which is now in the hands of a furniture dealer and still virtually unaltered externally—they ran a pair of Maudslay ML3 buses on route 263 (42A Sundays) from December 1926 until May 1927. YR 8860/1 were 30-seaters with dark red & yellow bodies by Hall Lewis, a builder who also supplied charabanc bodies on Maudslay chassis to Fallowfield & Knight. An approach from A. T. Bennett to sell the two buses to the proposed London Public Omnibus Co. Ltd. led to an attractive offer of £5,000 which was sufficient inducement for the partners to end their bus-operating career only six brief months after it had started. Bennett began to operate the buses from May 29th 1927 (before Public itself was incorporated) although the sale was not completed until July 28th. Fallowfield & Knight were among the few independent proprietors to take up an offer of shares in Public.

Coastal coach services and hire work were continued, and on February 6th 1928 a limited company was formed entitled Fallowfield & Knight Ltd. to take over the business. In 1945 a merger with W. & J. Britten's Superb Coaches resulted in the formation of Fallowfield & Britten Ltd. This came under the control of George Ewer & Co. Ltd. in 1952 and traded for over a decade afterwards as a subsidiary of Grey Green.

Whiston Street, Haggerston

ALBERT EWER

In the early nineteen-twenties Albert Edward Ewer broke away from the family business to branch out on his own as a haulage and coaching contractor. The family firm he left had its origins back in 1885 when his father, George Ewer, began trading as a proprietor and hirer of horses and carts in Shoreditch. This developed by the turn of the century into general haulage work from which the growth of the great Grey Green coach empire came as a natural development. George Ewer died before the first world war but left the business in the hands of a daughter and four sons, of whom Albert was one. Albert Ewer's solo venture in the 'twenties was a success and he established a fleet of lorries ranging from one to twenty tons. He also became the operator of nine London buses, but his coaches, called "The Royal Blues" were then the major part of the business and many different makes of vehicle passed through the fleet including Thornycrofts, A.E.C.'s, Lancias, Leylands, Beans and Maudslays; the latter apparently being a particular favourite of his. The business was run from headquarters at 152 Curtain Road, Shoreditch, though the haulage department had its own offices at Tower House, 40 Trinity Square, E.C.3. The principal garage was in Whiston Street (nowadays known as Whiston Road) in Haggerston. Memories of the old Ewer days lingered there in the shape of his old garage, a large and substantial building which, though used as a motor works, was long verging on decay and was finally demolished in 1974.

Bus operation commenced in October 1924 with the purchase of XW 478, a Dodson-bodied Leyland. It was followed by five more vehicles of the same type (XW 1634/2993/5572, XX 488, YL 5450), the last of which was licensed on October 1st 1925. Almost three years elapsed before any further additions were made to the bus fleet. YX 7083/4 arrived in August 1928 and were a pair of identical Dodson-bodied Leyland Lions of the PLSC3 type with pneumatic tyres and seats for thirty. The ninth and final bus was IA 6573, a Maudslay ML-type 32-seat single-decker of unknown origin. All the buses bore a red & white livery in contrast to the blue of the coaches and carried the fleet name Albert Ewer on a cream panel on the main body sides.

Ewer's buses outlasted the takeovers of 1926-8, but in 1929 it was decided to dispose of this side of the business to the LGOC for the tempting sum of £24,000, which could be more profitably re-invested in the company's booming coastal coaching activities. The nine buses passed to the LGOC who also took over the services of the 38 people employed thereon (1 inspector, 18 drivers, 18 conductors and a lady clerk). At the time of the takeover the company's scheduled operations required six double-deckers and two single-deckers, there being one spare single-decker. The routes scheduled were as follows:—

	MON.-FRI.	SAT.
26D/E	1 s/d	1 s/d
38A/B/C/D/E	4 d/d	3 d/d
231A	1 s/d	1 s/d
266	1 d/d	1 d/d
525	1 d/d	2 d/d

On Sundays all vehicles were working on routes 69/A/B/C at the time of takeover although earlier in the same summer some Sunday journeys had been worked on the 238 which was Ewer's own variation on the 38 theme.

The purchase was completed at 3.00 p.m. on Monday September 30th 1929 and the vehicles began to operate under LGOC control on the following day. Up to October 8th the operations remained unaltered, even to the extent of still running from Ewer's Whiston Street garage. The operations on all except the 38 and 69 (Sundays) were then abandoned, the four vehicles required for the 38 being operated from the LGOC's Holloway (J) garage from October 9th, the date upon which Ewer's licences were officially transferred.

Albert Ewer remained in the coach business and expanded his activities in March 1931 by taking over the coach side of Joseph Eva's activities, the two coach fleets being combined under the title of Eva's Motor Coaches Ltd. The combined fleet, which totalled over forty units, came under fierce competition from Grey Green and other operators, and in May 1934 Albert Ewer sold out to Grey Green. Thereafter he stayed active in road haulage for another quarter of a century.

CHAPTER FIVE

WEST LONDON

335 Portobello Road, Notting Hill
Golden Cross Garage, 244 Portobello Road, Notting Hill
Pamber Street Garage, Ladbroke Grove

RED LINE

In and around the Portobello Road, now famed for its antique and curio shops, were garages used to house the substantial road transport fleet operated by E. Brickwood Ltd., a company registered on May 17th 1911 with a capital of £1,000 of which £802 was issued. Originally a firm of cartage contractors, it later turned mainly to the ownership of buses and coaches. Edward R. T. Brickwood was the Managing Director and Secretary of the company which bore his name. The family owned property at 335 Portobello Road, on the corner of Golborne Mews, at the rear of which, in Golborne Mews itself, were small garage premises in which Brickwood's vehicles were housed. With the expansion of the business these became inadequate, and Brickwood rented space in two garages controlled by the large local business firm of Walter Hildreth Ltd. The main one was the Golden Cross Garage at 244 Portobello Road. The small and seemingly insignificant garage entrance at this address belied the fact that, behind it, lay a large and very substantial garage whose main entrance was from Basing Street. This was the only garage used by Brickwood which was capable of housing covered top double deckers. Hildreth's second garage was the Pamber Street Garage, just off Ladbroke Grove, in an area now blighted by the presence of an overhead motorway-style road. The Pamber Street Garage had formerly housed the well-known coachbuilding firm of Carrosserie Latymer (1915) Ltd., and earlier still it had been stables for the London Road Car Company. The freehold belonged to Birch Brothers Ltd. All three garage premises mentioned here still exist. The Pamber Street Garage and the Golden Cross Garage still trade under their old names, though the latter has been substantially rebuilt since independent bus days. The original Brickwood premises in Golborne Mews are now used for residential purposes.

Brickwoods' were already established as coach operators when they entered the bus world by ordering two Thornycrofts, the first of which XP 7023, was licensed on December 1st 1923 and presented for police inspection three days later. Its sister vehicle, XT 6131, was licensed on May 30th 1924. Both were bodied by Strachan & Brown and were distinctive in being the only London-type Thornycrofts to have bodies other than Dodson. They bore the legend Redline written as one word, though very soon the fleetname was split into two words—Red Line—in which form it remained until the end. After their initial wanderings the two Thornycrofts settled down to work on the 247A and later the 218E which was the former renumbered. The bus fleet never expanded beyond two scheduled units and was always outnumbered in numerical terms by the coach fleet which consisted of a variety of vehicles of Daimler, Dennis, Tilling Stevens and Gilford manufacture.

163

In 1928 the firm decided that the time had come to replace the two Thornycrofts. The first to go, XP 7023, was replaced by a new Dodson-bodied Dennis E-type 30-seater, UC 3013. This vehicle did not last long with Red Line; it was licensed on February 1st 1928 and sold in March 1929. Probably its seating capacity had proved inadequate for the busy Harrow Road. It, and the remaining Thornycroft which was the last of its type in London service, departed upon the arrival of a pair of ungainly Dennis H-type Dodson-bodied 56-seaters which entered service in March and May 1929 respectively as UL 7670 and UU 4830. The Dennis H family was by this time outdated in design and in deciding to purchase a thoroughly modern new bus late in 1929 Red Line trod new ground with a Daimler CF6, a model for which Brickwood's acted as dealers at the time. GC 1684 was registered on January 7th 1930 and provided a spare vehicle for the bus fleet. Its Birch-built 56-seat body carried an experimental closed windscreen and bore the title RED LINE OMNIBUS CO. above the lower saloon windows. Sad to relate it was not a success. The light construction of the chassis rendered it unsuited to the hammering it was expected to take as a London bus. Red Line persevered with it for no more than two years after which they removed the body and placed it on to a new AEC chassis. The CF6 was then sold and subsequently ran for a Bristol owner as a lorry. Meanwhile, in April 1931, a second Daimler had been purchased, but this was of the altogether more heavy variety designated CH6. Registered GO 5538, the new Daimler was of great significance in introducing to London the preselective gearbox and fluid flywheel, a design which was later to become synonymous with London buses. It proudly carried the wording DAIMLER FLUID TRANSMISSION on the rain shields over the lower deck centre windows. Unhappily GO 5538 did not run as satisfactorily as Brickwood had hoped and this may have been the reason why a second CH6, which he was strongly rumoured to have ordered, was never delivered. It was underpowered and suffered from much overheating which led to lubrication trouble with the sleeves, whilst to make matters worse the bands of the preselector gearbox tended to stick. Red Line's CH6 was bodied by Birch who had purchased from Red Line one of the 1929 Dennises, UL 7670. Birch did not use it themselves although they may have intended to as they gave it an overhaul. After doing so they received an enquiry from the Earlswood Bus Co. Ltd. of Central Garage, Westgate-on-Sea, Kent, for a double decker and offered UL 7670. After fully enclosing the cab and repainting in Earlswood's Oxford blue & cream livery, the bus passed to its new owners on March 23rd 1931.

Brief mention has already been made of the AEC Regent bought in 1932. GW 2294 was one of the longer wheelbase variety as also bought by Pickup, and it eventually became the well-known STL 558 in London Transport days. It was unique amongst London independent AEC's in having, like the CH6, a Daimler preselective gearbox and fluid transmission. The chassis was delivered in January 1932 and the body from the CF6 was placed upon it. On the 11th the complete vehicle was driven to Birch's works at Kentish Town where considerable work was carried out to modernise it. A completely new open cab was fitted, the board indicators were replaced by blinds, and a revised seating pattern installed reducing the capacity from 56 to 51. This was done to bring the

Photo No. 6
A blue-liveried Frost Smith petrol electric. The side route board indicates that it is paralleling the eastern end of the famous LGOC route 11.

Photo No. 7
One of Samuelson's trio of double-deckers. The Dennis bonnet looks disproportionately long against the short ex-Tilling body which seats only 34.

Photo No. 8
Charles Turner Clarke's grey Unity bus ran for little over a year before being sold to Royal Blue. The Straker Squire body could be easily identified by having five side windows all of equal length.

Photo No. 9

Brand new, and awaiting its police inspection at New Scotland Yard, is the first of Redburn's large fleet of semi-forward-control Straker Squires. The route number aperture carries the inscription "REDBURN'S SERVICE 1", illustrating Redburn's original intention of introducing their own route numbering scheme.

Photo No. 10

The largest member of the Admiral consortium was A. T. Bennett & Co. Ltd. They led the Fair Fares campaign and their first Straker Squire, ME 7240, is shown here carrying the slogan "MAINTAIN FAIR FARE COMPETITION" on the top rail.

Photo No. 11 (*top left*)

The Leyland LB was one of the most successful of independently-owned buses. The characteristic Leyland radiator is clearly seen in this view, taken inside Strachan & Brown's Acton factory, of the long-lived Carswool bus which became almost a legend in its lifetime for its antiquity.

Photo No. 12 (*top right*)

A smart creamy-yellow and black livery adorned the two Dodson-bodied Leylands purchased by Drake & McCowen. The newer of the pair, XT 4608, was photographed after McCowen had left the partnership.

Photo No. 13 (*centre right*)

Dodson bodywork is also seen on this green Rapid Leyland, one of eight operated by Passenger Transport Ltd. The treatment of the last lower saloon window varied from time to time on Dodson bodies, hence the difference between this bus and the Drake one.

Photo No. 14 (*below*)

G. F. Ambridge purchased both Leyland and Dennis for his two bus Veleta fleet. Some of his staff pose here beside the Leyland just before setting out for work on a sunny morning. The business later passed to City.

Photo No. 15
George Frederick Buck, his bus and staff, photographed in a quiet Peckham side street. The bus was originally called Genial, and was later again renamed St. George. Its body is by Wilton. A photo of this vehicle in later life appears in fig. 103.

Photo No. 16
Percy Chiswell and his "fleet" of Dennises on parade in Loughton. PU 7282, on the left, was destined to be the shortest-lived of all London Dennises. It carries a Dodson body, its stable mate having been bodied by Strachan & Brown.

Photo No. 17

A typical one-bus outfit was the Cardinal whose youthful owner, J. M. Potter, poses sternly by his vehicle. Above the route number on this Dodson-bodied Dennis are the words "NORTH LONDON ASSOCN.", recalling the short-lived and loosely knit operators' association on route 284.

Photo No. 18

Birch-bodied Dennises were a rarity. YU 4689, seen standing in the sunshine by the pond at Thornton Heath, is in the H & B fleet of Holliday & Bangs. The plain red livery, devoid even of any lining-out, does not enhance its appearance.

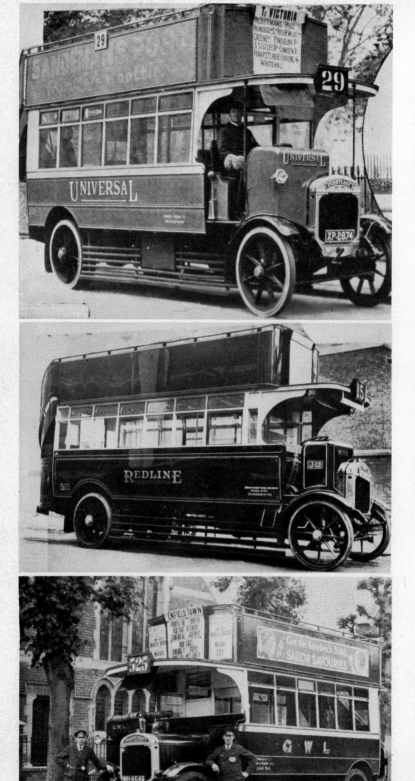

Photo No. 19
Despite its seatin
capacity of 50, th
Thornycroft J-typ
never achieved gre
popularity with th
independents. Jame
Llewellyn Craig'
Universal bus wa
photographed on th
29, a favourite hun
ing ground for man
operators.

Photo No. 20
The two Redlin
Thornycrofts o
E.R.T. Brickwoo
were the only one
to carry Strachan
Brown bodies; a
the other Londo
Thornycrofts wer
bodied by Dodso
This photograph
taken before ent
into service, show
clearly the diffe
ences between th
two body style
when compared wi
the Universal vehic
above.

Photo No. 21
The 525 was
popular service wi
independents. Th
best known vehic
on it was probab
the GWL Thorn
croft which boile
its way betwee
Cubitt Town an
Enfield in the se
vice of the Lewin
ton family fro
March 1925 until
was taken over b
Public in July 192

Photo No. 22
The Matchless Daimler had an unsettled early history, its original owner, Fred Mason, lasting little over a month before quitting the bus business. Its Hickman body can be recognised by the small central window, but it lacks the distinguishing deep driver's canopy featured on many Hickman bodies.

Photo No. 23
Strachan & Brown-bodied Daimlers had an extra-wide window over the rear wheel arch. This is one of a pair of such vehicles operated under the fleet name Independent by Marcus Aurelius Giovanni Salvatore Forno.

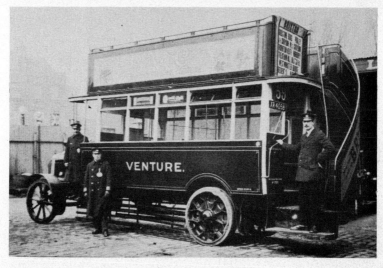

Photo No. 24
The cobblestone yard of its Brixton garage is the setting for this view of Strachan & Brown-bodied XR 4058, one of a pair of Daimlers comprising F. J. Nunn's Venture fleet.

Photo No. 25 (*top*)

The 2½-ton Dennis was the first pneumatic-tyred model to enter London service in any quantity. Admiral had the largest fleet of these of which no. 19, a Dodson-bodied 26-seater, is seen here on the short-lived route 280.

Photo No. 26 (*bottom*)

James Weaver used AEC B-types with home made bodies on his Southall & District service in the western suburbs. Formerly B2681, this 20-seater was bought from the naval authorities at Devonport Docks and was converted by Weaver from its former use as an ambulance.

Photos No. 27 & 28

A contrast in body styles on Dennis 2½-tonners. The Strachan & Brown body (fig. 27) on RO 1596 of Biss Brothers is notably more modern than Dodson's version purchased by Havelock (fig. 28). Both are photographed operating on services pioneered and worked by numbers of independents, Biss on the 551 and Havelock on the 263.

Photo No. 29 (*bottom*)

Two Waltham vehicles and their crews. The little Fiat and the Dennis both originated with Charles Dunford's Barnet Motor Services from whom the Fiat was purchased direct by Waltham, the Dennis joining it later after a spell in the Admiral fleet.

Photos No. 30 (*above*) and 31 (*below*)
For operators requiring something in the 30-seat range in the middle 'twenties, the Dennis E and Leyland PLSC represented the most popular choices. Typical examples of each are the Prince E-type (fig. 30 *above*), and Nil Desperandum's PLSC (fig. 31 *below*). The Prince vehicle carries a Dodson body incorporating quarter lights which were omitted from later vehicles; the Nil Desperandum was bodied by Birch. Both were photographed on typical independent-inspired services, one at the Angel, Edmonton, and the other at Surrey Docks.

Photo No. 32 (*above*)
Dennis E's were not a success when employed, like this Dodson-bodied Red Line example, on services running into central London. Photographed at Sudbury prior to departure for Kings Cross, UC 3013 lasted just over a year in Red Line service.

Photo No. 33 (*below*)
High Street, Barkingside, in pioneering days, with a Birch Dennis E scurrying through an area soon to be changed beyond all recognition by the building developers.

Photo No. 34
(*above*)
Several of the inde
pendents supple
mented their incom
by running coache
This Tilling Steven
TS3A petrol electri
was operated b
Birch and bore
typical char-a-ban
body of the earl
nineteen-twenties

Photo No. 35
(*left*)
E. Gray & Son
Ltd., one of whos
fleet of Leylan
buses is shown
fig. 58, were amon
the earliest users
Gilford coaches. Th
Redhead - bodie
saloon coach o
1927, bought fo
Gray's Londo
Oxford service
depicts the grea
advance made
coach bodywork
the seven year
since the Birc
vehicle (*above*) wa
built.

vehicle within the existing weight regulations and was necessary because of the heavier chassis now employed. The biggest job carried out on the body was the extension of the rear to provide for the enclosure of the open staircase. The original staircase remained in position and the enclosing walls were built round it.

London Transport took over the bus business of E. Brickwood Ltd. on December 5th 1933 inheriting the mixed fleet of Dennis H, Daimler CH6 and AEC Regent, of which there was one each, plus a 1933 Lanchester car AGP63. The Arbitration Tribunal duly approved an award of £19,000 for the business, which included severance payment. One of Edward Brickwood's co-directors of the time, Percy Sleeman, later became a top name in the London coaching world through his connection with Valliant Direct Coaches Ltd. Red Line continued as a coach operator and on February 10th 1937 the business was taken over by a new company entitled Red Line Continental Motorways Ltd. which was owned by John and Margaret Brennan. It operated from Brickwood's old address of 335 Portobello Road, which was then owned by F. & R. Hildreth Garages Ltd. The business passed to B.E.T. control on August 31st 1953 and was liquidated in 1968, the goodwill being sold to East Kent on September 19th of that year.

K.B.B./EAGLE

Red Line was not alone in the Golden Cross garage; it was shared with the Eagle buses owned by Benjamin Butler. This business had started in June 1924 under the title K.B.B. and was then owned by King & Butler Bros. of 28 Blagrove Road, North Kensington. Their bus was XT 9231, a Dodson-bodied Dennis. Benjamin Butler was the licensee and within a year he was running the business alone. Under his auspices the vehicle was renamed Eagle and moved from its original garage, General Auto Services at Shepherds Bush, to Hildreth's. XT 9231 was at this time painted in a chocolate livery with creamish-white window frames and bore the fleet name Eagle in gold lettering on a biscuit-coloured panel. The business was reorganised on June 13th 1927 as a limited company with a capital of £200 under the title of Eagle Omnibus Co. Ltd., and its registered office at 28 Blagrove Road was a room rented from Mrs. Charlotte Butler for 10/- a week. The charge for garaging at Hildreth's was £1 5s. 0d. a week per vehicle. The Eagle became associated with route 15, upon which it worked exclusively from 1925 onwards. Prior to that application had been made for numerous services including 6, 7, 15, 17, 27, 49, 52 and 73.

A second vehicle was purchased in 1929 to provide a spare in case of emergencies. UU 1907 was a new 30-seater Dennis E bodied by Dodson and registered on May 16th. This soon proved to be too small for its intended purpose of being Eagle's front-line vehicle, and before long the company found itself ordering a new double-decker upon whose arrival the original Dennis could be disposed of and the single-decker relegated to spare. GC 7388 was licensed on February 27th 1930 and the unusual choice of chassis—Daimler CF6—was clearly influenced by Red Line's purchase of a similar vehicle, and it bore an identical Birch body to that on the Red Line unit. Like Red Line, Eagle experienced considerable trouble with their CF6 which is reported to have required no fewer than six new engines in its first eighteen months. Unlike Red Line, Eagle kept their CF6 to the end, but from July 1932 onwards it worked only occasionally as a spare, Eagle having taken delivery of a new Leyland Titan MV 6306 with a Dodson body. This last addition to the fleet replaced the Dennis E which had been sold to G. H. Allitt & Sons Ltd. a short while earlier.

On November 10th 1933 Eagle's business was taken over by London Transport. The Arbitration Tribunal approved an award of £8,000 on November 29th 1935.

13/14 Ledbury Mews West, Notting Hill

ROBT. THACKRAY
THACKRAY'S

Robert Thackray was a highly successful businessman. From his farm at Calcot, near Reading, he controlled the Ledbury Garage at 13/14 Ledbury Mews West, part of which had been an LGOC horse bus depot from 1866 to 1910. Thackray added a substantial brick-built garage which, in addition to its main entrance via the archway into Ledbury Mews West, had access at the rear to Lambton Place which led on to the main Westbourne Grove. The premises, barely altered externally despite the passage of time, are now occupied by a motor company. Thackray also had properties nearby at 16 Colville Road and 13A Colville Mews from which he ran a fleet of hire cars and taxis, also a general garage business with a twenty-four hour service. Thackray had been in business in the Westbourne Grove area since at least 1908 as a jobmaster and had widened the scope of his activities as time went by. In December 1924 he added bus operation to his list of business interests.

This began with the delivery of a quartet of new Dodson-bodied Dennises (XW 5667-70) carrying a red & white livery with the fleet name Robt. Thackray in gold script. It was later replaced by the West London Association insignia for operation on route 526. Fleet additions were made in the form of further Dennises in February 1925 (XW 68/XX 906) and January 1926 (YM 4719) bringing the total to seven, of which six were scheduled to run on routes 15A and 526D, leaving one as a spare. A second spare bus was purchased as late as May 1927 (YF 5623), only five months before the firm ceased running buses. Thackray had intended in late 1926 to expand his bus activities if possible, and applied for police permission on November 4th to operate an ingenious new service almost entirely over unrestricted roads between Pimlico (The Gun) and Hampstead Heath (Freemasons Arms) via Sloane Square, Kings Road, Gunter Grove, Finborough Road, Warwick Road, Holland Road, Holland Park Avenue, Clarendon Road, Lancaster Road, Ladbroke Grove, Chamberlayne Road, Brondesbury Road, High Road Kilburn, Swiss Cottage, College Crescent, Buckland Crescent, Belsize Park, Haverstock Hill and South End Green. Two routes were proposed between Pimlico and Sloane Square. Thackray approached Birch Bros. Ltd. with the proposal that they should operate the service with him, which they agreed to do in the event of it being approved. Police approval was not however forthcoming, the main reason for their refusal being that the service would cause inconvenience to other traffic by crossing many busy thoroughfares. It was probably this recalcitrant attitude on the part of the police towards independent operators that led Thackray to sell his buses to Public.

As far as we know Thackray normally ran his buses from his premises at Ledbury Mews, where they were joined for a while in 1925-7 by the fleet of the Premier Omnibus Co. Ltd. The buses appear to have traded for a while under a partnership called Thackray & Syms but from Janurary 6th 1926 the business was run as a limited company under the title of Robert Thackray Ltd. The registered office was 6 Colville Mews and the company had a share capital of £3,000 which was entirely held by Thackray. Thackray's manager for his bus activities was H. J. Buchan who later became the Paddington depot manager for Public.

The company also ran another Dennis bus XX 3882 which, though for all operational purposes was regarded as part of the Robert Thackray fleet and was numbered 5 in the Thackray series, was separately owned by Robert Thackray's brother, James Deighton Thackray. Purchased in March 1925, it ran on the 526D and for most of its career carried the West London Association's diamond-shaped badge on its sides though for a few early months it bore the fleet name Thackrays. It is reported to have been seen operating on route 142 when new.

The buses of Robert Thackray Ltd. were sold to Public on October 6th 1927 for £20,300 and J. D. Thackray's bus passed to them five days later on October 11th for £3,000. It is interesting to recall that Public paid no less than £1,876 for Thackray's stock of spare parts, which must have been by far the most extensive held by any London bus operator for a fleet of only seven vehicles. The buses continued to operate from Ledbury Mews under their new owners under a leasing agreement which lasted until May 23rd 1928 when the Public operations were stabilised in garages in West Green and Enfield.

The firm of Robert Thackray Ltd. still continued in existence though based in Reading from 1961, but it has never again operated buses. The sale of the buses in 1927 did not mean, however, that the passenger transport industry had seen the last of Robert Thackray. His London taxis continued to operate and in 1929 he commenced a London (Oxford Circus) to Reading coach service using red & cream Gilford "super saloon" coaches. This soon became the famous Thackrays Way service which was run hourly by Ledbury Transport Ltd., a company registered on July 25th 1929 and controlled by Robert and James Deighton Thackray. Their headquarters was a modern garage where the Oxford and London roads meet, and incorporated a booking office, waiting rooms, a restaurant for two hundred people and a park for a hundred coaches. The original London service, which operated via Maidenhead, became very popular and was soon operating half-hourly. A second London service, via Ascot, operated with one journey an hour, and a successful half-hourly Reading-Newbury service was also operated. Local bus services were acquired including Cordery's one from Reading to Riseley, and Thackrays Way also ran between Maidenhead and Henley via two routes. A variety of vehicles including Chevrolet,

Delahaye, Dennis and Thornycroft were replaced in due course by normal-control Gilfords upon which the company standardised. The London to Reading via Ascot service was discontinued in September 1931 by order of the Traffic Commissioner, and on December 19th 1935 the Thackrays sold Ledbury Transport Ltd. to Thames Valley, who kept it as a separate entity until the licences were applied for by the parent company in December 1949.

Meanwhile, in London, Robert Thackray Ltd. continued to run its taxi business until quite recent times. The Ledbury Mews garage was let to other operators for a while as an additional source of income. In 1930/1 it was used by the Skylark Motor Coach Co. Ltd. and from March 1st 1932 was leased for a short while by London General Country Services Ltd. for Green Line private hire coaches. From 1933 onwards it served as the base for the Thackray taxi fleet.

Property investment later became one of Robert Thackray's interests and a business which he formed in 1937 under the title of Robert Thackray's Estate Ltd. still continues in business to this day and controls properties both locally in Reading and in London. Robert Thackray lived on his farm at Calcot until his death on June 26th 1950.

The Cremorne Garage, Ashburnham Road, Chelsea
2A Parsons Green Lane
National Furniture Depository, 546 Kings Road, Chelsea

RED ROVER

The Royal Borough of Chelsea was sparesely populated by independents, probably because of a lack of suitable accommodation. The Cremorne Garage (latterly a V.I.P. filling station but now closed) in Ashburnham Road near its junction with Cremorne Road was for a short while the home of the Red Rover bus until it moved to 2A Parsons Green Lane, the previous occupier of which was the British Vacuum Cleaner Company. We have not established the precise location of 2A but assume that it was one of a row of mews buildings in Bridges Place which is alongside no. 2 Parsons Green Lane. By 1928 additional parking space had been obtained in the yard of the National Furniture Depositories Ltd. at 546 Kings Road, a building which has long since disappeared.

Red Rover had a most unusual and interesting career, and of all the many London independent bus companies, is the only one to have continuously run bus services up to the present day although Aylesbury, forty miles from London, is now the centre of its activities. Until recent times Red Rover was owned by the Cain family whose career in bus and coach operation can be divided into three distinct overlapping sections.

From July 1924 until compulsory acquisition by the LPTB on February 14th 1934 a 'pirate' bus was operated in London. Next came an express coach service between London and Aylesbury which started in 1928 as the Red Rover Saloon Coach Service and lasted until November 29th 1932, when it was sold to London General Country Services Ltd., an LGOC subsidiary. In the late 'twenties a bus service was commenced between Aylesbury and Buckingham to which was added a North Marston service with shorts to Weedon with the acquisition of P. J.

168

Simmonds' business in 1933. The disposal of the London coach service and the enforced sale of the London bus provided capital for the further extension of operations radiating from Aylesbury, where the red & creamy-yellow Red Rover buses are today still very much in evidence.

It is the London bus business in which we are here concerned. It began when Edward Maurice Cain, a taxi owner-driver of 11 Farlow Road, Putney, bought a new Strachan & Brown-bodied Dennis XU 3346 which he put to work on routes 14 and 49. Although entitled Red Rover, it roved around far less than many of its contemporaries, and even in its early days its operations remained fairly static. In buying a combination of Dennis/Strachan Cain established a tradition that was to last for many years. It was perhaps fitting that the last new double-decker purchased while Red Rover was still controlled by the Cain family, OPP 857 of 1950, carried the same combination of Dennis chassis and Strachan body. The products of the Guildford factory, including EV's, Arrows, Aces, Lances and Lancets, served the Cain family well during three decades.

The London operation never extended beyond one vehicle, probably because further licences on profitable services became almost impossible to obtain. On July 28th 1927 a limited company was incorporated with the unusual title of Red Rover Omnibus Ltd. and a nominal capital of £200. Its directors were Edward Cain, his wife Elsie and his brother Reginald Arthur.

The original bus, XU 3346, was replaced on August 1st 1930 by a covered-top Dennis HV, GH 5342. This vehicle stayed only two years at the end of which its duties were taken over by GY 1961, the last new Dennis Lance to enter service in London. It had the last type of all-enclosed Birch body with straight sloping front and roof route number box. Unfortunately only three bodies of this type were built, the other two being for Birch themselves on Titans GX 131/2. The Red Rover Lance, in addition to being the last new Lance in London, was also the last double decker of the era with a new Birch body. Shortly after it was built Dennis agreed at Red Rover's request to fit the Lance with self-changing gear mechanism; it is not known whether this modification was ever carried out. At the close of operations this bus was running solely on route 14, the operation on the 49 having been discontinued at some time between 1927 and 1931.

After February 1934, when the London-based bus passed to the LPTB, the company entitled Red Rover Omnibus Ltd. remained dormant for three years, the Aylesbury operations being carried on under the title of Red Rover Saloon Coaches, which had also been used for the London-Aylesbury express coach service. On July 1st 1937, Red Rover Omnibus Ltd. was reactivated to take over the Aylesbury bus services. It operates today with a fleet consisting mainly of modern AEC double and single-deckers and for much of the post war period has also included second-hand double deckers of the RT family which once, like Red Rover itself, ran in central London. Since December 29th 1955, when the Cains retired from the business after thirty-one years, it has been under the control of Keith Garages Ltd., who run it as a subsidiary to this day.

Farm Lane Motor Works, Fulham
Cobbold's Garage, 88 High Street, Fulham
456 Fulham Road, Fulham

OMEGA

At no. 101 Farm Lane, Fulham, in the Farm Lane Motor Works, was the home of the Omega bus firm from 1924 onwards. These premises, which housed several small business concerns, had once been connected with motor buses in the early pioneering days. Before that they had housed the ten horse buses of William Berg who sold out in January 1901 to the City & Suburban Motor Omnibus Co. Ltd. Motorisation began in September 1905 with two De Dions working Brixton-Oxford Circus and ended in March 1906. From November 1905 the Arrow buses of the London & District Motor Bus Co. Ltd. and later the London & Provincial Motorbus Traction Co. Ltd. were at Farm Lane. On April 1st 1907 these came under the control of Vanguard who vacated the premises after operations on January 5th 1908. In those days the street number was 13. Albert Mills of 10 Lorrie Road, Fulham was the last generation of bus owner at Farm Lane. He arrived there in June 1924 when he bought a second-hand Leyland from Dodson and called it Omega. Registered XN 5034, it had previously been used by the unsuccessful London Circular Omnibus Co. Ltd. It ran daily on route 14 and was sold in July 1931 to Arlington's in part payment for GP 3379, the new Dodson-bodied Leyland Titan which took its place; a smart machine with white-walled tyres.

Later in his career as a bus proprietor Mills moved to Cobbolds Petrol & Service Station at 88 High Street, Fulham which is still a service station but now owned by Tanner's. It was almost certainly in Craigs Garage at 224 Fulham Palace Road at one stage. July 1931 saw the Omega garaged at Twickenham in (it is thought) A. G. Summerskill's Richmond Bridge Garage in Richmond Road facing Cresswell Road. In about May 1932 Mills made his final move to the Goldhawk Garage, Brackenbury Road, Shepherds Bush where he stayed until November 10th 1933 when his bus passed to the LPTB from whom he received £7,600 in compensation.

Another operator reputed to have run from Farm Lane is Celtic who started off at 456 Fulham Road in January 1924 and may have moved to Farm Lane later. If it did, it was probably from no.101 which it operated, these being the only likely premises in Farm Lane in which a bus could be housed.

CELTIC

Strachan & Brown bodied a Daimler, XR 1195, in January 1924 which they delivered to Lewis & Green of 9 Averill Street, Fulham. It was painted red & grey, later red & white, and carried the fleetname Celtic. It was garaged at 456 Fulham Road, probably in the buildings at the back of no. 456 in Garden Row which were once LGOC stables and which, in the period under review, housed a number of small commercial concerns. As we have seen, it was probably later garaged in Farm Lane, Fulham.

By a gradual process the ownership of the Celtic bus completely changed during the twenty-nine months of its independent existence.

170

First of all Mr. Green, whose initials we do not know, left in June 1924, leaving Thomas W. Lewis to be joined by a new partner, Ernest William Beaumont. Then in September 1925 Lewis departed and was replaced by Henry Stewart. The last change of ownership came about on June 11th 1926 when Beaumont and Stewart sold out to the LGOC. Just prior to this, on May 28th 1926, a limited company was incorporated under the title of Celtic Omnibus Co. Ltd. with its registered office at Lennox House, Norfolk Street, W.C.2. and a share capital of £1,000. XR 1195 ran direct into the LGOC's Hammersmith (R) garage when it came off service on Friday June 11th, the Celtic company having become LGOC property during the day. The Daimler did not then run again for two weeks or so as it was urgently in need of overhaul.

Celtic operated initially on many of the routes in the Hammersmith area including all or sections of the 9, 11, 27, 33 and 73. Their latter day operations were 11A, 11C, 173D and 173E weekdays and 73/73A Sundays. It is noteworthy that the Celtic bus was allowed 60 minutes from Hammersmith Broadway to Kings Cross compared with the 45 to 50 minutes considered adequate by the LGOC. It is recorded by the Omnibus Society that the Celtic carried the running letters CE1 when first operated by the LGOC, but it latterly ran as R1. A K-type, K1069, replaced the Daimler in April 1927 and on January 1st 1928 the business was merged into the LGOC.

Craig's Garage, 224 Fulham Palace Road
(Also A1 Garage, Estcourt Road, Fulham)

At 224 Fulham Palace Road, almost facing Lillie Road, could be found Craig's Garage until it came under the hammer of the demolition men in 1971 to make way for a new filling station, also called Craig's. The proprietor in 1923 was James Llewellyn Craig of 19 Windsor House, Victoria Street, S.W.1, who was himself a bus owner, having purchased his first Universal bus, a Straker Squire, in May 1923. His Universal 'fleet' later grew to two as we shall see later. Other independent buses which were his tenants at 224 Fulham Palace Road from time to time were The Lea Rig, Lonsdale, Monarch, New Times, Omega, Shamrock, Swift, Triumph and White Star. Shamrock also spent a while at the A1 Garage in Estcourt Road, no great distance from Craig's Garage. This former LGOC stables is today approached from Haldane Road, the rear of the building having become the front due to the redevelopment of Estcourt Road in 1971/2.

NEW TIMES

Henry Owen Parmenter junior and William John Loveland were the instigators of the New Times Omnibus Company Limited. Parmenter was one of many taxi owners to enter the kindred business of running buses, and Loveland was proprietor of a catering business at 7 Great Chapel Street, W1. This address was used as the New Times headquarters for the first two years of the firm's existence. There is evidence that a little more planning than usual went into the New Times business, as practically five months elapsed between the formation of the company on December 6th 1922 and the delivery of the first bus. Proof that big things were expected to happen is that in May 1923 Parmenter applied to the police for no fewer than twenty plates to be affixed to Leyland omnibuses. As we shall see, the fleet never progressed in size beyond a tenth of the expected total.

Apart from Parmenter, who ran the business, and Loveland, there were two other directors at the time operation commenced. One was Parmenter's father, who was also Henry Owen Parmenter, and a cooper by trade, and the other was Robert John William Hawkins, a taxi driver whom we have already met in Chapter two. There had been others interested in the business at the outset, but they had backed out within a month or so.

XN 6976 was the first bus. It was a Dodson-bodied Leyland in an attractive livery of fawnish grey with red lines and was licensed on May 2nd 1923. Accommodation was secured for it at the Melhuish Garage, Blackstock Road, Finsbury Park, and by the last week of May it had commenced operation on route 29. Misfortune struck on August bank holiday Monday when, at about 8.30 in the evening, it was in collision with a private car at the top of Alderman's Hill, Palmers Green. The damage to the bus was extensive and it meant that, after only two months of operation, the firm had to go temporarily out of business until the vehicle could be made fit to run again. It seems that, after the incident, the New Times bus forsook the 29 in favour of a variety of routes which, generally speaking, had a West London bias. The 11, 15, 27 and 73 were all operated at various times and, even when the London Traffic Act came into force, several routes were scheduled during the day's work. By 1927 the sole remaining New Times bus ran on no fewer than five routes each weekday, viz. 3A, 11E, 12C, 59B and 112B.

A second bus was delivered in April 1924. XT 196 was a Leyland similar to its older brother but carrying a livery described by the operator as "Orriford Lake" offset with white windows and gold lining. The owners must have been satisfied with this new colour scheme as they had XN 6976 repainted similarly at its first overhaul in June 1924. Far from heralding a successful development of the New Times company, the arrival of XT 196 foreshadowed a board room split which resulted in the departure of Loveland and Hawkins. They both left in about October 1924 and Loveland took the older of the two buses with him as payment in kind for his share of the business. Both he and Hawkins began running buses on their own account, and though Loveland's career as a solo bus proprietor was comparatively short Hawkins built up a very prosperous and thriving business.

Loveland's departure meant that a new registered office had to be found. First of all Parmenter junior's home address at 30 Dancer Road, Fulham, was used, but in December 1924 the company's headquarters became 224 Fulham Palace Road. It has not been possible to establish with any degree of accuracy when the New Times bus was first based at Craig's Garage, but it is probable that it moved into there after the accident in August 1923. A final change of registered office came about in March 1927, the new address being Parmenter senior's home at 60 Colwith Road, Hammersmith. This coincided with the departure of the bus from Craig's Garage to the Victoria Works at Percy Road, Shepherds Bush.

In March 1928 the New Times bus was sold to Public, being one of its last acquisitions, and the New Times Omnibus Co. Ltd. was consequently wound up on February 28th 1929. It's career had not been a notable success despite the high hopes of the early days, and the reason was probably because, like so many others, the business was under-capitalised. The authorised share capital was only £100 and at the maximum the total shares issued had only totalled 165, but as these were 2/- shares it meant that capital of the company amounted to a mere £16 10s. 0d.

MONARCH

On February 27th 1925 a Daimler, XX 2024, was licensed with the fleet name of Monarch by Victor Perry of 32 Dawes Road, Fulham. Perry had come to England from Australia, and so brief was his bus career that he would probably hardly have been remembered by the bus owning fraternity had he not given a demonstration of throwing the boomerang at the Public Carriage Office which was talked about for long afterwards. Whilst there he deposited schedules to run on the 540, a service which was of doubtful value and which he failed to keep to anyway. He had hoped for better schedules on more lucrative routes, but was refused them. Perry was not alone in sinking his entire savings in the Monarch bus; he had two partners, whose identity has not been recorded, and they invested all their savings likewise. The investment quickly proved an utter disaster. The three rapidly found themselves in such dire financial straits that, after pawning everything, they had to consult the Guardians of the workhouse with a view to gaining admittance. On March 24th, after less than a month of bus ownership, Perry cancelled his road fund licence, and the next day ownership of the Daimler passed to Mrs. A. L. Drake who continued to run it as the Monarch. We take up the story of the Monarch bus again, together with that of Mrs. Drake's other bus, the White Star, in chapter seven.

General Auto Services Garage, Shepherds Bush Green

In contrast to the sparseness of independent garages in Chelsea and the complete lack of any in Hammersmith, there were three very important garages in Shepherds Bush the first and busiest of which was the filling station owned by General Auto Services Ltd. The garage has long since disappeared, but the site immediately east of the Central Line station is where it used to be. In the early days of the independents the garage became a veritable Mecca for bus owners of whom twelve based their vehicles there at one time or another during the period 1922-27.

NEW ERA

When Dodson accepted an order for a new Leyland double-decker it marked the beginning of a new era in the lives of four taxi cab owners who had decided to give up their own line of business to become drivers and conductors on their own buses. The prospects for the future looked very lucrative when they got together in the late part of 1922 to form the appropriately-named New Era Omnibus Co. Ltd. The leader of the group seems to have been Victor Arthur Hughes, and it was his taxi

173

address at 9-10 Kendrick Mews, Sussex Place, South Kensington, that was used as the company's registered office. His co-directors were Arthur Hildersham Hughes, Albert Edward Brookes and Stanley Ivor Handford. Though the company was formed with a share capital of £400 on November 24th 1922, its new bus was not delivered until March of the following year. XN 3322 was painted in a coat of light blue and was garaged at the Shepherds Bush Filling Station. It had commenced running by April 17th and worked mainly between routes 9, 11, 33 and 73 in the early days. Victor Hughes left the business in July 1923 to run his own buses under the name Commonwealth and this meant that the registered office of the company had to be changed. In fact it altered twice before the garage also became the registered headquarters in November 1925. Latterly A. H. Hughes was the company's secretary and licensee.

A second bus, XW 2158, came on the scene in November 1924. Though similar to the first it was painted red & white, a livery adopted by the first vehicle in April 1924. The original routes were abandoned, probably during 1924, in favour of the 17, and licences were duly obtained for two buses on the 17/286A.

Public took over operation of the buses on June 12th 1927 and a formal sale of the assets was completed on July 11th for £6,000. Two of the New Era directors took jobs with Public, Stanley Handford becoming an inspector and A. H. Hughes a depot manager. Albert Brookes had meanwhile returned to his old trade of taxicab driver. The New Era Omnibus Co. Ltd. was formerly dissolved on October 27th 1931.

SKYLARK
UNIVERSAL

The first Skylark, a Straker Squire XN 555 in a colour best described as crimson lake & yellow, was presented at Scotland Yard on March 2nd 1923 by Arthur Herbert Ansell; it was duly passed fit for service and licensed on March 5th. The trading address was firstly 48 Eynham Road, North Kensington, but it later became 20 St. Quintin's Avenue, North Kensington, Ansell's home address. Ansell later intended to take on a partner named E. A. Chapman to finance a second bus, but the partnership did not materialise and Ansell was joined instead by Charles Dobbs, a taxi proprietor who was connected at the time with the General Auto Services garage from which the Skylark bus operated. In its early days it was mostly to be found on route 11 though many other services were also applied for.

A whole year passed before the second Skylark put in an appearance. The Straker had probably given the usual crop of troubles resulting in the choice of Dennis for the second chassis. XR 4558 was licensed on March 5th 1924 and a sister vehicle, XU 319, joined it on the following July 1st. Both were red & yellow with Strachan & Brown bodies, and when it was overhauled in March 1925 the Straker was repainted in the same shade of red as these two. XN 555 ended its short life as a London bus just before the introduction of a third new Dennis in February 1926. This last vehicle was YM 8144 and had the Straker Squire body transferred from XN 555. An identical vehicle, YO 6917, joined the fleet as a spare bus in June 1926, but it is not known where the Straker body on this one came from.

Between the arrival of the first and second Straker-bodied Dennises the firm was reorganised as the Skylark Omnibus Co. Ltd., the date of registration being April 15th. Ansell and Dobbs were the directors and the registered office was at General Auto Services Garage. The registered capital of the company was £1,000, and out of the 750 £1 shares issued Ansell held 450 and Dobbs the remainder. The operational date of takeover by the limited company was May 12th 1926.

Before this happened the Skylark co-directors had become responsible for the operation of another omnibus company, the Universal owned by James Llewellyn Craig, the proprietor of Craig's Garage. He had commenced business as the Universal Omnibus Company on May 11th 1923 with a pale blue Straker Squire, XN 8444. This had run out of 1-12 Harmood Street, Chalk Farm initially but by January 1925 had moved to Craig's own premises at 224 Fulham Palace Road. After an initial period of fluctuation Universal settled down on the 29 from November 1923 onwards, and two schedules were taken out on this with the implementation of the London Traffic Act. By this time there were two vehicles in the fleet, XP 2874, a Thornycroft, having been licensed on October 2nd 1923. Ansell and Dobbs took over operational control of the two Universals on December 7th 1925, the date on which the Universal Omnibus Co. Ltd. was incorporated with head office at 224 Fulham Palace Road. Craig, Ansell and Dobbs were the directors but Craig remained a major shareholder along with Edward Fairweather junior, a shorthand writer who had been connected with the business previously. An outstanding hire purchase commitment of £250 on the Thornycroft was paid off and the buses moved to General Auto Service Garage to join the Skylark trio.

The next event came in October 1926 when the tenancy agreement with the General Auto Service Garage came to an end and both fleets were moved to the Victoria Works, Percy Road, Shepherds Bush. This had been used for the past few years by various firms of motor car body builders, and was later also the home in its last year of the New Times bus. Today a catering firm entitled V. Benoist Ltd. occupies the extensive premises. In April 1927 the registered offices of the Skylark and Universal companies were transferred to the Victoria Works. Just before the move of premises a new bus was received for the Universal fleet. It was YP 9836, a Strachan & Brown-bodied Dennis which, like its predecessors, was in the light blue livery. By this time bright liveries of this sort had become the exception rather than the rule amongst the independents. The Dennis ousted the Thornycroft, which was transferred to Skylark and repainted red & white. Perhaps it had proved too slow to maintain the somewhat hectic pace of route 29. In any event its stay with Skylark was short-lived and by April 1927 it had reached the fleet of the Enterprise Bus Co. of Newport, Isle of Wight.

Only one more new bus arrived before the demise of the Skylark and Universal fleets. This was bought as a replacement of the Universal

Straker Squire, which was relegated to spare, and was a pneumatic-tyred Dennis E single-decker, YH 3707. It officially belonged to the Universal company but was painted chocolate with a red bonnet and cream window frames and bore the Skylark fleet name. It was licensed in May 1927, less than three weeks before operation of the two fleets was taken over by Public, and its purchase was probably influenced by the apparent success of similar pneumatic-tyred single-deckers bought by Admiral for the 29.

Twice in its career Skylark endeavoured to start new services over territory largely devoid of buses. In November 1925 and again in June 1926 plans were put forward for a route from Bow Church to New Cross (Clifton Hill) via Rotherhithe Tunnel and Surrey Docks. April and June 1927 saw applications for a local service in Acton from Turnham Green via the Bollo Lane area to Northfields. Both were rejected by the police, even though the latter had the backing of the Acton Borough Council. The repeated failure to obtain new schedules and the seemingly bleak future for independents were probably the reasons for the sale of the Skylark and Universal buses to Public on July 8th 1927, operations having been in their hands since June 7th. £9,000 was paid for the three Skylark buses scheduled on the 11E, 17 and 286A and £6,000 for the pair of Universals on the 29A plus a further £1,414 for the spare bus. Both companies were wound up on February 20th 1929.

With the departure of Dobbs the independents lost a leading character. He had been a very vocal element in support of independent bus owners and was secretary of the Uxbridge Road Protection Committee. He was not lost to the transport industry though. In 1926 he had opened the Acton Town Garage in Gunnersbury Lane as a taxi depot and petrol station and from there he began his famous service of green Gilford coaches with which he pioneered cross-London express services under the banner of the Skylark Motor Coach Co. Ltd. whose history will be outlined in a later volume. He was also active in local affairs as an Acton Borough Councillor until he retired to live in the New Forest early in the 1939-45 war.

UNITY

The Unity bus was XN 3980, a Straker Squire in a striking all-grey livery with the fleetname in gold capitals blocked in red. Charles Turner Clark of 225 Uxbridge Road, Shepherds Bush was the proprietor and he arranged for his bus to be housed by General Auto Services. XN 3980 was licensed on April 5th 1923 and approved at Scotland Yard the next day. It had begun operation by the 17th and usually worked on the 9, 17 and 33 though 11, 18, 27 and 49 were also applied for. At an unknown date its garage was changed to the Acme garage at Southall. In Mid-1924 the licences were reapplied for by A. Boorer, Butson & Clark, but this partnership did not begin trading and by July 1924 the bus had been sold to Royal Blue.

ECLIPSE

Two new operators commenced work from General Auto Services Garage in May 1923. One was Triumph, who later moved via Craig's Garage to 34 Ethelburga Street, Battersea, and the other was Eclipse, who obtained two schedules on routes 17 and 286A. Robert Neal of 255 Acton Lane, Chiswick, was the owner of the Eclipse Omnibus Company and started in business with XN 8049, a Dodson-bodied Leyland in a livery called officially carmine & cream. A second Leyland, XW 1620, was licensed in October 1924 and differed from its predecessor in carrying a Strachan & Brown body. By this time Neal had moved to 37 The Approach, East Acton, whence he conducted the business, although the buses continued to be garaged at Shepherds Bush. Also at this time he worked in partnership with a man called Henry Stanley Percy Male about whom nothing is known except that the partnership was apparently short-lived. A third bus was bought in 1925 as a spare. It was a Daimler, PU 4769, formerly run by Fairlop and no doubt bought cheaply from Roberts. A fourth vehicle new in February 1927 was a pneumatic-tyred Dennis E-type single-decker YE 7373 with Dodson 30-seat body. It appears to have replaced the Daimler as the spare bus though the latter remained on the books, possibly unlicensed.

Neal sold out to Public on July 8th 1927 and received £6,000 for the two scheduled buses plus £1,272 14s. 0d. for the almost new Dennis and £274 7s. 8d. for the Daimler. The embryo Public organisation took over responsibility for operations as early as June 18th; three weeks before the contract was formally signed. With the money received from Public, Neal later began running coaches from the Goldhawk Garage, Brackenbury Road, under the title Eclipse Motor Coaches, and at the peak of his operations owned eleven Maudslays and a Ford. An Ealing to Yarmouth express service began in March 1929 and was sold to a consortium consisting of Valliant, Grey Green and United Service Transport in 1936, but Neal continued to operate a summer Ealing-Clacton run until 1948 when he sold it to Valliant.

COMMONWEALTH

When Victor Hughes left New Era he soon started in business on his own from the same yard, taking delivery of XO 6328, a Dodson-bodied Leyland. This was in a red & white livery on which the white extended below the window frames to the top of the rocker panel; the fleetname extended in large block capitals almost the length of the bus. XO 6328 was licensed on July 16th 1923 and was submitted to the police for their inspection the next day.

Hughes tried out routes 11 and 14 in his early days as the Commonwealth but he soon discovered the profitability of route 17. A second bus was bought in April 1924 (MF 6321) and a third in October of the same year (MH 1264). By the time these two arrived Hughes and his wife Clara had moved from their old home-cum-business headquarters at 61 Bolingbroke Road, Shepherds Bush, to 17 Churchfield Avenue, East Acton, a house which they appropriately called "Leylands". A limited company was formed under the title of Commonwealth Omnibuses Ltd. on August 22nd 1925 with "Leylands" as the registered office and a share capital of £3,500 divided into 1,000 preference and 2,500 ordinaries of £1 each. The company's business office was 33A Broadway, Acton where its Secretary, Miss M. E. Tibble, was situated.

In April 1926 Commonwealth made an unusual attempt to establish a service between St. Albans and Hertford. St. Albans City Council gave approval for the section within their boundaries provided times were co-ordinated with other operators but nothing more seems to have transpired. The company's main pattern of service was established as routes 17 and 286A. As late as March 1927 Commonwealth placed an additional scheduled bus into service on a new, short service numbered 298 between Acton (Churchfield Road) and the Willesden Junction Hotel at Harlesden. The rolling stock for this route was an almost new Leyland, YR 172, which had been built for Rapid only six months earlier. Another route unique to Commonwealth, apart from the 298, was the 300 which ran on football days between Harlesden and Queens Park Rangers' ground at Shepherds Bush.

By January 1927 Hughes had left his former colleagues of New Era days completely behind by taking his buses away from the General Auto Services garage and placing them in the Goldhawk Garage, Brackenbury Road. The days of Commonwealth drew to a close after the Hughes' received an offer of £15,500 for their business from Public. The latter took over on November 8th 1927, just four months after they had acquired New Era.

GLEANER

George Mais Finlay was the proprietor of the Gleaner omnibus which appeared towards the end of January 1924 and entered service in the following month. Finlay was by profession a motor engineer, and lived at 14 Fairlawn Park, Acton Lane. His red & white Dennis, MF 4499, was bodied by Strachan & Brown and garaged at General Auto Services. The profitable local services such as 11, 17 and 27 were the ones upon which the Gleaner bus normally operated in its earlier days.

Finlay wished to expand his business, and found Edward Hoiland, a Dane who had become British by naturalisation, willing to provide extra capital. Before embarking on the operation of a second bus the two men formed on September 3rd 1924 the Gleaner Omnibus Co. Ltd. with headquarters at 18 Coleman Street, E.C.2, which was the office address of Finlay's accountants. The share capital was £500. A second Strachan & Brown-bodied Dennis had meanwhile been ordered, and was licensed on October 1st. Both buses henceforth operated almost exclusively on routes 17 and 286A.

On April 29th 1927 there was registered at Companies House a new undertaking entitled Rural England Motor Coaches Ltd. Using General Auto Services garage as its base, the company inaugurated a daily London (Shepherds Bush)-Oxford-Gloucester express service under the slogan "The Brown Coaches". Rural England was controlled by Finlay, who was Managing Director, and Hoiland. It progressed well and very soon the two disposed of their Gleaner bus interests to Public to concentrate on the coaches. Public took the buses over on August 12th 1927 and paid £6,000 plus £45 for a Buick car which had, for book-keeping purposes, been part of the business. The Gleaner company was finally wound up on July 17th 1931, much later than had been originally anticipated, because of difficulties with the income tax authorities.

Their buses sold, Finlay and Hoiland were free to give their sole attentions to Rural England. They came to an arrangement with J. H. Watts, the forward-looking Gloucester bus pioneer, to run in conjunction with his Red & White coaches, the two concerns connecting and exchanging passengers at Gloucester. In April 1929 Rural England unwisely extended their own coach services from Gloucester through Red & White "territory" on two routes, one to Cardiff and the other to Merthyr. The joint-working with Watts naturally ceased and, about a year later, the Rural England Motor Coaches Ltd. itself went out of business. Its fleet at the end had consisted of five units; two Tilling Stevens, two Gilfords and a Studebaker.

OUR BUS

Charles Milner Bamford of 2 Bracewell Road, North Kensington, was the senior partner in Bamford & Curtis, a two-bus business which traded as "Auto Services" and ran latterly on the 17B, 170B and 286A. He owned the buses jointly with Arthur James Curtis, and garaged them at General Auto Services. XR 4395 was the first bus to be delivered and was a red & white Strachan & Brown-bodied Dennis carrying the fleet name "Our Bus". It was licensed on March 4th 1924 and was taken by Bamford for police inspection at Scotland Yard a week later. The second bus, XW 2996, was identical to the first, and entered service in November 1924. Public took over the two buses on July 8th 1927 for £6,000.

★　　★　　★　　★

In June 1924 King & Butler Brothers commenced to run their K.B.B. Dennis from General Auto Services Garage, but by August 1925 the vehicle had moved on to Hildreth's Garage at 244 Portobello Road which was closer to Benjamin Butler's home. The story of this bus, which later became the Eagle, has been recounted earlier in this chapter.

WHITE STAR/THE MATCHLESS

Fred Mason of 40 Granville Gardens, Shepherds Bush Green, enters our story on July 4th 1924 which was the date on which he appeared at Scotland Yard with XR 2651, a Hickman-bodied Daimler named the White Star. White Star was something of a misnomer, for the star on each side of the bus was in fact painted silver; the words WHITE and STAR were on either side of it in block capitals. XR 2651 was second-hand, its previous owner having been Sydney Moreton who ran it as one of his ill-fated "London" buses whose acquaintance we shall make in the course of the next few pages. It was joined in Mason's ownership after only a few days by the arrival of XU 2866, another identical Daimler but this time a new one. This vehicle was called The Matchless.

Despite the fleet names on the vehicles, Mason traded as the Star Omnibus Company and this name was carried on the back of his tickets which quoted his address as 229 Hammersmith Road, W.6. This was the coach booking agency from which Sydney Moreton had formerly worked and it is possible that the two gentlemen were in some way connected. Mason is known to have operated on route 73 but he probably also strayed on to other services. He applied to the police to run from Liverpool Street to South Harrow but the application was refused on the grounds of weight restriction in Sheepcote Road, Harrow.

Mason's bus career was even more impermanent than Moreton's. XU 2866, The Matchless, lasted little over a month in his ownership before it passed to T. H. Scaife who continued to run it under the same name. He ceased operation altogether at an unknown date—but probably in the latter part of 1924—with the sale of XR 2651 to Mrs. Annie Louise Drake.

PULLMAN
Pullman was a good choice for a fleet name, conjuring-up as it does a picture of smooth service combined with luxury. By today's standards the Dennis four-tonner of half a century ago was in appearance far from Pullman-like, but its seats were no less comfortable and its springing no less smooth than the current DM family of buses which Londoners now have to tolerate. Such is progress! The Pullman bus of 1925 was XX 874, a red & white Strachan & Brown-bodied Dennis which was licensed in February by William Francis McMahon of 132 Narbonne Avenue, Clapham. McMahon was the senior of three partners in a haulage business trading under the title of Road Services Company. Tom Lidstone and Arthur Widlake were his co-partners.

Because it entered service rather late in the day, the Pullman Dennis had a rather chequered early career. It started work on the 14 and was garaged conveniently for this route at Flight's Garage in Parkhurst Road, Holloway. The restrictions imposed by the police under the Road Traffic Act meant that the bus had to be withdrawn from the 14 and McMahon was offered the 527 as an alternative, which he accepted. His schedule for the 527C was approved on April 8th. At the end of April the bus was transferred to the Empire Garage at Boreham Road, Wood Green, where the terms were probably more favourable than those prevailing at Flights. The partners soon found out that the 527 could not pay its way and received approval in May to transfer to the 526D. Then came another change of garage when, after only six weeks at Wood Green, the Pullman moved to its third home in five months; General Auto Services. In July 1925 the Minister revoked the previous decision, debarring Pullman from the 14 and it returned to this service. From then onwards it worked on various sections of the 14 every day plus journeys on the 522D on Saturdays and 15A Sundays to add variety.

The acquisition of a more promising schedule did not herald a period of stability for the Pullman bus, for which further changes of garage lay ahead. By August 1926 it was to be found in the Claremont Garage in Pentonville Road and in May 1927 its zig-zag course of garages was extended still further when W. Christmas of the Commercial Motor Garage & Repair Co. Ltd. agreed to house it on his premises at 363/5 Clapham Road. This was the nearest that the Pullman ever got to the Clapham headquarters of the parent Road Services Company. It was destined to stay there for only a few months, for on November 24th 1927 it came under the control of General. This was the date on which McMahon, Lidstone and Widlake handed over the McMahon Omnibus Co. Ltd. which had been formed on October 28th 1927, with head office at 55 Broadway, as a preliminary to the transfer of ownership. As an LGOC subsidiary, the McMahon company ran from Putney Bridge (F) garage until it was absorbed on January 1st 1928.

The Pullman story nearly did not finish at this juncture, for in May 1928 McMahon, Lidstone & Widlake were seeking quotations for bodywork for a Dennis E-type 30-seater. It is not known what they planned to use the Dennis on and, as far as is known, no vehicle was purchased in the end.

BEATTIE/B & B

Cornelius Beattie attained a certain notoriety and—thanks to the national press—a large measure of public sympathy through refusing to bow down to the dictates of the Minister of Transport and the Metropolitan Police. These formidable opponents had instigated the drastic reduction of buses on the Uxbridge Road under the Order which took effect on March 29th 1926 and Beattie, like T & W and Dominion, was one of the small operators whose schedule was taken from him. The others acquiesced and ceased business; Beattie did not. He continued to run knowing full well that legal proceedings would be bound to follow.

To start the Beattie story at the beginning, he had been a latecomer to the bus industry and did not take possession of his only bus until March 1925. The vehicle in question was XX 3458, a red & white Wilton-bodied Dennis with the fleet name Beattie. He applied for a schedule on route 17 but, with the Restricted Streets regulations in mind, the police soon requested him to move from this on to the 523 which was a much less viable proposition. An Amendment Order later enabled him to return to the Uxbridge Road with a schedule combining 17D, 286A and 523. Everything went well from then onwards until the bombshell exploded in the form of the Uxbridge Road Order. Beattie had no intention of complying with the Order and carried on running as before. Predictably a summons was delivered in due course instructing him to appear at Ealing Police Court in September 1926 on a charge of failing to comply with the Minister's Order. Beattie counted himself fortunate when the case against him was dismissed and costs awarded against the police. This was a widely acclaimed decision, for Beattie had become a popular figure. Was he not a wartime hero who had been awarded the DCM for bravery? And was he not typical of so many men who had fought for their country in the war and had afterwards invested their savings in a small business to provide themselves with employment which was hard enough to obtain, even for heroes? The police, however, did not allow themselves to be influenced by sentiment. They appealed to the High Court where the previous decision was reversed and Beattie convicted. Beattie was not content to let the matter lie there. His case, which was in the nature of a test one, went to the highest echelon of British justice, but the luckless Beattie's appeal was rejected in the House of Lords.

181

Strangely enough, after the conclusion of the legal processes, the Minister of Transport had a change of heart and passed an Amendment Order allowing Beattie to resume his old schedule on the 17D, 286A and 523. Perhaps the pressure of public opinion had influenced him after all. Beattie's career as a bus proprietor was shortlived thereafter for, on July 19th 1927, he accepted an offer from Public to purchase his bus for the sum of £2,850. After his stormy and at times uncertain career as a busman, Beattie could hardly be blamed for grasping a good opportunity to leave the business for a reasonable price when it presented itself.

In its latter months the Beattie bus is thought to have carried the fleet name B & B, the second 'B' perhaps being another member of the Beattie family. Though Cornelius Beattie garaged his bus at General Auto Services he had relatives in the transport business with a garage at Bollo Bridge Road, Acton. Beattie's home address of 66 Gayford Road, Shepherds Bush (which replaced his earlier address of 44 Stronsa Road, Shepherds Bush), was used as the registered office of Beattie Coaches Ltd., a concern registered on June 4th 1928 to take over the family's transport activities. At the time of incorporation the company owned two Leyland and one Maudslay six-ton lorries which ran a regular bi-weekly service to Leeds and Manchester, and also had one Gilford and three Federal coaches on excursion and hire work. Though Cornelius Beattie was not himself shown as a shareholder of Beattie Coaches Ltd. he is believed to have been closely connected with it.

Goldhawk Garage, Brackenbury Road, Shepherds Bush

Westwards from Shepherds Bush Green was the Goldhawk Garage Ltd., the main entrance to which was at 2 Brackenbury Road though there was a side entrance from the main Goldhawk Road itself at no. 199. The Goldhawk Garage was a very large site in which there were a number of garage buildings. It has remained largely unchanged to the present day and is now occupied by W. H. Cook & Sons Ltd., the large firm of taxi and garage proprietors whose founder was once owner of the Dominion and A1 buses. A lesser number of independents occupied the Goldhawk Garage than were to be found at General Auto Services, but in housing six independent fleets it was a garage of no mean importance. One of the two operators who stayed at the Goldhawk Garage right through to LPTB days—Chariot—quoted the address as 165 Goldhawk Road. This was the filling station at the junction of the Goldhawk Road and Brackenbury Road and adjacent to the main Brackenbury Road Garage premises which were under the same ownership. The owners, at least during the latter part of the independent bus era, were Tankard & Smith Ltd.

LEGION

Legion was the name carried by MF 6914, a Thornycroft dating from April 1924. It was operated under the title of Legion Omnibus Company by George Pauncefoot of 81 Wellesley Road, Chiswick in partnership with Mrs. Violet McReadie. The Legion bus operated on a mixed bag of routes under the London Traffic Act prior to which it had been widely travelled but with the emphasis on route 18. Latterly its operations were:

182

Mondays-Fridays 12C, 112B, 73A, 173C; Saturdays 11A/E, 12C, 112B; Sundays 33B/D. It was garaged at Brackenbury Road until October 4th 1926 when it was transferred into the General garage at Hammersmith (R) as a result of their purchase of the business on that day. A limited company entitled Legion Omnibus Co. Ltd. had meanwhile been formed on September 16th 1926, with a registered office at Lennox House, Norfolk Street, W.C.2. to which the assets had been transferred.

Later in October 1926 Thames Valley made an offer of £350 for the Legion Thornycroft, which was accepted, and preparation work on a replacement vehicle began straight away. K 903 appeared on November 6th in the chocolate Legion livery and the Thornycroft was sold on the 10th. The K continued to run the Legion service until the business was taken over by the LGOC on January 1st 1928.

THE MATCHLESS/CLEVELAND

In August 1924 Thomas Henry Scaife of 11 Melrose Gardens, Shepherds Bush, started business with a second-hand Daimler, Hickman-bodied XU 2866. It was as good as new when Scaife bought it, having been with its previous owner for little more than a month. Fred Mason of the Star Omnibus Company had been the previous owner and had been responsible for the fleet name The Matchless which XU 2866 carried. Scaife retained this name until at least 1927 though he traded as the Cleveland Omnibus Company. The company became limited on April 24th 1926 with a share capital of £1,200 of which £1,002 was issued. Its registered office was 9A Rosedale Terrace, Dalling Road, Hammersmith; Scaife's address at the time. He was Managing Director, his co-owners from April 1926 being A. J. Ormiston and F. W. Bearman who both combined bus conducting with a small amount of administrative work. Scaife later quit the business, his shareholding being taken by Bearman's wife and son. Mrs. Bearman became actively engaged in the business, albeit on a part-time basis, following the death of her husband in April 1933.

Initially XU 2866 worked on 27, 33 and 73, and with the passing of the London Traffic Act its weekday workings were stabilised on various sections of routes 11 and 73. Sundays were usually spent on 33B/D. Only one weekday schedule was ever held, though a second Daimler bus was taken into stock in about December 1928. This was XT 5611 which had originally been used by Peraeque and later Independent and was bought as a spare. It carried the fleetname Cleveland, which was also applied to XU 2866 subsequently. XT 5611 was disposed of in 1930 upon the arrival of a new Dodson-bodied Leyland Titan GC 6664 which was licensed on February 27th of that year. The other Daimler was sold to the Chiswick Motor Company in May 1932 reducing the Cleveland fleet back to one for the remaining months of its career.

Cleveland had a haulage department in addition to its bus activities and advertised lorries for hire. These are believed to have been kept at New Cross where, according to Cleveland's notepaper, they had a branch office. The buses were garaged for several years at the Goldhawk Garage but at an unknown date (possibly in 1930) they were rehoused at 1

Oxford Road, Chiswick, which also became the company's registered office. The Chiswick premises were owned by the Chiswick Motor Company who, it will be recalled, bought the original Cleveland Daimler when its bus career was finished. The buildings are now used for light industry.

London Transport took over on December 5th 1933, inheriting an Armstrong Siddeley car MK 6178 in addition to the Titan. The Cleveland Omnibus Co. Ltd. in due course received £9,000 compensation for the loss of its business.

CHARIOT

Chariot Omnibus Services was the property of Ernest Gray Davison, A.M.I.M.E., A.M.I.A.E., a motor engineer of 21 The Vale, Acton. His was a one-bus business from October 1924 until June 1930 when a new AEC Regent arrived, increasing the fleet to two and relegating the original to spare. The Dennis with which Davison commenced bus work was MH 1595. It carried a Strachan & Brown body painted red with maroon rocker panels & white window frames and the fleet name 'Chariot' applied in 'General' style. The Regent was GJ 8501, a Birch-bodied open-staircase 56-seater in a red & white livery with black lining. It cost £1,939 when new (£1,219 for the chassis and £720 for the body) and in June 1932 a further £78 was expended on enclosing the staircase, a job carried out by Birch on the vehicle's second overhaul. Its colour scheme was altered at the same time and featured a much higher proportion of red, reliefs being confined to narrow cream bands below the windows on each deck.

Chariot was garaged firstly in the Goldhawk Garage, but by December 1926 it had moved to an unknown base in Wales Farm Road, North Acton. By mid-1930 it was back in the Goldhawk Garage which was now owned by Tankard & Smith Ltd., and it stayed there to the end. Davison favoured the 15 for his weekday operations and from April 1925 he seems to have concentrated on the 537 on Sundays. In 1927 the pattern of operation was:- Mondays to Fridays 15A; Saturdays 15A, 122E, 537; Sundays 537.

It may be recalled from chapter 2 that, for just over a year from March 1925, Davison was concerned in the management of the Henslowe buses and also, from February 1926, of the Swift bus. His own business was converted into a limited company on September 23rd 1926 with a capital of £1,000. The head office of Chariot Omnibus Services Ltd. was Room 23C, 82 Victoria Street, S.W.1. It was later 1A Rectory Road, Acton and later still 165 Goldhawk Road. The business survived until November 1st 1933 when the two buses passed to the LPTB together with a pair of miscellaneous vehicles; GK 2125 was a 1930 Morris Major car and BM 9201 was a 1921 Albion van used for breakdowns, etc. The latter vehicle was still on solid tyres and was disused at the time of takeover. MH 1595 was also on solids, being one of the few Dennis 4-tonners to pass into LPTB ownership still in this condition. The Arbitration Tribunal subsequently approved £10,000 compensation.

LONSDALE

Charles Ernest Hall of 76 Coningham Road, Shepherds Bush, laid the foundations of the Lonsdale Omnibus Company on November 24th 1924 when he signed an agreement with J. M. Roberts to buy Daimler XT 946 on hire purchase. This Strachan & Brown-bodied Daimler had recently been retrieved by Roberts from Sydney Moreton, for whom it had run as the "New London". Hall took delivery of the bus from Roberts almost immediately afterwards and had placed it into service before the year was out. A second reconditioned Daimler, this time a 'new' one, was provided by Roberts in January 1925, once again on hire purchase. XW 9413, also Strachan & Brown-bodied, was licensed on January 28th and brought the fleet to its maximum of two.

For the first few months the Lonsdale buses ran out of Craig's Garage but by April 1925 they had found a more permanent home at the Goldhawk Garage. They are also quoted as once having been kept in Leysfield Road, Shepherds Bush. The services operated varied at first, but the London Traffic Act quickly stabilised the position. On weekdays one bus operated on route 11A while the other was banished from its former operations on route 73 to the 526D. It remained on the latter only for just over two months and early in July 1925 it was allowed to return to its former service, its normal operation being 73A but with additional short workings on 73D and 173E. By early 1926 Sunday operation had become centred on route 27A and on football days a special service 271 from Shepherds Bush to the Fulham football ground was authorised. In mid-1925 Hall also owned a 28-seater charabanc for private hire work. He does not appear to have been actively engaged in the running of his vehicles; instead he employed a manager who, in later days at least, was a Mr. Butcher.

Lonsdale was another of the less-successful undertakings. By June 1925 hire purchase repayments had fallen behind on XW 9413, and the same thing had happened to XT 946 by October of that year. In an endeavour to re-organise things a limited company was formed under the title of Lonsdale Omnibus Co. Ltd. on December 16th 1925. Hall's accountant, George Hockley, became company secretary, and his address at 3 Bulwer Street, Shepherds Bush, was used as the registered office. In January 1926 Hall tried to transfer one of the buses back on to the 526D, probably because it was relatively competition-free compared with the 73, but the W.L.A. proprietors would have none of it. Arrangements were then put in hand to sell the ailing undertaking to the LGOC who announced their readiness to buy the assets as from March 23rd 1926. The acquisition date was later postponed and formal signing over of the assets did not take place until April 9th to take effect from the next day.

On Saturday April 10th 1926 the Lonsdale buses ran under LGOC control for the first time, and were that evening transferred into Hammersmith (R) garage. It is recorded by the Omnibus Society that they ran with running code letters LO for some while thereafter. The two Daimlers lasted a surprisingly long time under LGOC control, and it was not until March 1927 that they were replaced by K139/416 in General livery. Lonsdale ceased operation on January 1st 1928 when the assets were absorbed into the LGOC.

Only four other operators have been traced to the Goldhawk Garage. One was Commonwealth who spent the last ten months of their career there from January 1927 onwards. Cornwall and Bayswater were there from October 1925 to August 1927. The Omega bus of Albert Mills was there in the closing years of its career, 1932/3.

Roberts' Works, Cathnor Road, Shepherds Bush

On the west side of Cathnor Road, just across the main Goldhawk Road from Brackenbury Road, was the now-vanished works of J. M. Roberts. He had been in business there since about 1920 as successor to an earlier firm of motor engineers, Fonteyn & Caestecker. Besides supplying all the London-type Daimlers Roberts also garaged the buses operated by Sydney Moreton under the fleet names London and New London. As far as is known Roberts had left Cathnor Road by about 1930 and the premises appear to have then remained vacant for a number of years. Flats now occupy the site.

LONDON
NEW LONDON

Sydney Moreton was a persuasive gentleman who set out with the objective of getting wealthy at the expense of investors in bus companies which he would operate. Unhappily for the investors, the buses for which most of them had contributed did not materialise. Moreton took delivery of a token fleet of three buses though it soon became clear from complaints to Hammersmith police and others that he had received cash sufficient to purchase several more. Moreton was eventually arrested on a fraud charge, but before this happened his activities had reached the ears of the national press and a popular magazine of the day, John Bull, described how one un-named victim had been duped into parting with £77.

It would appear that Moreton had engaged an Estate & Business Transfer Agency called Fred Power to secure investors for him. This agency which was run by a Captain A. Duncan Ross, advertised in the daily press: "Motor-bus Driver required; Invest £150, secured, returnable: good wages, share of profits.—Power, 124 Uxbridge Road, Shepherd's Bush." The "victim" in question, an ex-soldier in the Mechanical Transport Corps, had like many others been finding difficulty in getting suitable employment and, having saved £150 from his army pay and gratuity, decided to answer the advertisement. The Fred Power firm seemed to him to be a reliable and well-managed organisation. According to its headed notepaper it had been established twenty years and was an agent for the highly-respected Sun Life and Fire Guardian and Commercial Union Insurance Companies. So when the ex-soldier received a letter from Fred Power stating that the position offered was that of a bus conductor who was to invest £150 to be secured by 10% debentures he agreed to be introduced to the principal of the bus company. This turned out to be Sydney Moreton who described himself as proprietor of the New London Omnibus Company of 229 Hammersmith Road, W.6. Moreton persuaded the ex-soldier to invest £150 and confirmed that he would be appointed to the position of bus conductor at £5 a week for a seven-day week with alternate Sundays off and an additional 2½ per cent of the profits of one bus. The ex-soldier paid £75 to Fred Power on account of an agreed investment in the first mortgage debentures to be issued by the New London Omnibus Company plus two guineas for the preparation of an agreement. Subsequently the ex-soldier found that there was no new bus on which to work so he asked Moreton for his money back. Moreton, as persuasively as ever, got him to unwisely sign an agreement accepting the repayment in instalments. The repayments were not made and he found it increasingly difficult to obtain further interviews with Moreton. He therefore appealed to Fred Power who informed him that Moreton had not been seen for two months and his whereabouts were unknown.

Moreton disappeared in about early-March 1925 at which time he had three buses in service. Two of these ran under the title London and the other was the New London. In much the same way that mystery shrouds much of Moreton's financial dealings, so details of his early bus activities are equally sparse. The first bus to carry the London fleet name appeared at Scotland Yard on October 12th 1923, and was a Straker Squire. Its owner's name was given as S. J. Fuller and its address was General Auto Services at whose Shepherd's Bush garage it was evidently intended that it should be kept. It is possible—but this is pure conjecture—that Fuller was the first to invest money in a bus for Moreton to operate. For some unknown reason the Straker Squire did not operate for Fuller (or Moreton), and it was presumably returned to its makers and re-sold to someone else. The identity of this vehicle has not been established. Nearly two months later, on December 4th, Fuller appeared again, this time with a Daimler which, after receiving the registration XP 7425, became the first bus to enter service under the title London. Fuller's address was now given as 180 The Grove, Hammersmith, which happens also to have been Moreton's address at this time. On February 15th 1924 a second London Daimler was licensed as XR 2651, this time in the name of Einar Tobiassen of 46 Royal Terrace, Kensington. The trio of buses was completed on April 17th 1924, when XT 946 was licensed, this time in the name of Sydney Moreton himself. This vehicle, like the other two, was in a red livery with white window frames, brown lower panels and silver bonnet. Its fleet name was New London.

All three buses ran out of J. M. Roberts' yard in Cathnor Road, Shepherd's Bush. Tickets were issued bearing "The London" or "The New London" down the centre front as appropriate. On the back all have the inscription "to hire apply S. Moreton, 229 Hammersmith Road, W.6" (a coach booking agency) except the 1d, 2d, 3d, and 4d New Londons on which the proprietor's name was misprinted as "Morton". As far as we know the buses ran mainly on the principal services radiating from the Hammersmith area such as 11, 27, 33 and 73, though approval was also obtained for routes 15, 19, 28, 31, 36, 49, 59 and 69.

The final date of operation is not known though it is thought to have been in about June 1924. It would appear reasonably certain that Roberts reclaimed the vehicles through non-payment of the hire purchase instalments. XP 7425 was bought by Houchin, Houchin & Howard and became the Vivid, XR 2651 passed to Fred Mason as the White Star and XT 946 became the property of Charles Hall who renamed it Lonsdale.

J. M. ROBERTS MOTOR SERVICE

As we have already noted, Josiah Morris Roberts of the Cathnor Motor Works was the unwilling recipient of a number of Daimlers from former customers who had found them unsatisfactory and had returned them, sometimes accompanied by the threat of legal action. Others he had impounded when hire purchase instalments fell into arrears. He had five such vehicles on the premises in May 1926 when the General Strike broke out and, ever willing to earn a quick penny, decided to take advantage of the temporary relaxation by the police of the route licensing system and become an operator himself. He chose a route between Victoria and Liverpool Street and began to run on May 6th. The first bus was in a red & white livery but soon MF 8001, an ex Peraeque vehicle, appeared on the service in green & white and carrying the fleet name J. M. Roberts' Motor Service. Other Daimlers known to have operated for Roberts were MF 9873 ex Lancastrian and XT 5611 ex Peraeque. A further Daimler, MF 7640 ex Convey & Clayton was also in Roberts' possession in May 1926 and could well have been used by him as it was licensed in his name up to September 30th and the same applies to ex Cosmopolitan MF 8159 which Roberts taxed up to December 31st. Operation would have ceased on or about May 12th as the strike drew towards its end. For MF 7640 and 8159 the scrapyard was their destiny but MF 8001 was later resold and eventually became the Chadwell whilst XT 5611 saw further service as the Independent.

Roberts subsequently became part owner of the Gretna business, of which more in chapter 8, and he also applied for a service of his own between Thornton Heath and South Bromley via Crystal Palace in November 1927, which was refused. His business interests led him to Staffordshire where he purchased W. K. Wynne (Hanley) Ltd. in January 1926 and renamed it J. M. Roberts (Hanley) Ltd. in July of the same year. The company ran buses on Tunstall-Longton and Stoke-Stafford services. The entire share capital was purchased in 1927 by the Potteries Electric Traction Co. Ltd. who continued to trade under the Roberts name until July 1928. Four vehicles passed to Potteries, one of which was XR 2651, the one-time London and White Star Daimler which now carried a single-deck body.

Victoria Works, Percy Road, Shepherd's Bush

The Victoria Works at Percy Road, Shepherd's Bush have already been noted as the home for a short period of the Skylark, Universal and New Times buses. The Leysfield Road factory complex nearby was well-known as the home of the substantial Premier fleet.

Leysfield Road, Shepherd's Bush

PREMIER
REGENT

Three men who fancied their fortunes in bus work were William Allen and the two Schiffers, Augustus John and Frederick Charles, father and son. William Allen ordered their first bus in October 1922 from Leyland but he became disillusioned by the slow delivery on the bus of his choice and cancelled the order, replacing it in January 1923 with one for two Straker Squires. These were ordered in the name of William Allen & Co. of 319A Edgware Road, W.2. and were constructed with Dodson bodies and not with bodies built by the chassis maker as was usual with this class of bus. The first was completed in its purple-red (officially mauve) & white livery with the fleet name Premier prominently displayed, and was examined at Scotland Yard on February 13th 1923. XM 9888 was licensed on February 27th and was quickly followed by XM 9995.

Three Premier buses entered service on March 3rd, working initially between Cricklewood and Liverpool Street, two points which were not directly linked by any existing LGOC service. Two of the three buses have been described. The third, XN 513, was outwardly identical and was run by Allen and the Schiffers' in conjunction with the other two, but it was owned as a separate venture by the younger Schiffer and Walter Harsant. It was erroneously registered in the name of William Allen Ltd. Further buses were quickly ordered by William Allen & Co. to expand the Premier fleet though no further Straker Squires were bought. Leylands had now become available and XN 1596/5018 were licensed in March and April 1923 respectively. They had Dodson bodies as, indeed, did all new buses bought up to 1927.

At some time during the summer of 1923 contacts were made with three gentlemen of means who professed themselves willing to invest substantial sums of money in the Premier business to enable considerable expansion to take place. These were Captain Percy Musker, Captain Sir Christopher Magnay, Bt., M.C., and Sir George H. Ussher Lacon, Bt., D.S.O. Together with William Allen and the Messrs. Schiffer, they incorporated the Premier Omnibus Company Limited, on October 12th 1923 with registered office at The Metro Garage, 29 Burne Street, Edgware Road. The authorised share capital of the Company was £10,000 in £1 shares of which £4,000 was subscribed initially, the remainder being taken up by February 1924. Under an agreement of October 12th the four existing Premier buses (XN 513 was not included) were taken over from September 17th for £4,500 comprised of £505 in cash and £3,995 in shares. Shortly afterwards an agreement was signed whereby the founders of Premier each became joint Managing Directors for life. This agreement specifically precluded Schiffer junior from expanding his bus interests outside the Premier company beyond the one vehicle jointly owned with Harsant. Captain Musker was appointed Chairman of the new Premier Omnibus Co. Ltd.

Five further vehicles arrived in 1923 to swell the Premier fleet to nine. XP 1957 was licensed on September 21st just before the incorporation of the limited company but was not included in the purchase agreement because this was backdated to September 17th. The next four vehicles were Dennises; forerunners of a fleet of twelve such vehicles bought by Premier. The choice of Dennis rather than Leyland was probably influenced partly by the quicker delivery but was probably mainly because, at £1,427, each complete Dennis was £186 cheaper than its Leyland counterpart. XP 2347/3760/4208 were new in October and MF 3319 in November 1923. The latter replaced for operational purposes

Straker Squire XN 513 which ceased to be treated as a member of the Premier fleet. Though it still remained in the joint ownership of Schiffer and Harsant its operation was taken over by Harsant who registered it in the name of the Regent Omnibus Company on December 29th 1923. It was repainted dark red with lemon window frames and given the fleet name Regent, and henceforth ran out of the Fleet Garage in Hackford Road, Brixton. Observers saw it on routes 5, 17, 18A, 27, 59, 73 and 77.

1924 saw five more Dennises enter the Premier fleet (MF 5862/6269/6399, MH 2138/2215). The last two were replacements for the Straker Squires which had been sold on November 3rd to Edward Paul. They fetched £650 each, which was less than half the £1,423 they had cost when new less than two years before. A week or two beforehand the partnership between Schiffer junior and Harsant had broken up and the Regent bus was also sold to Paul. Walter Harsant did not re-enter the bus business though he stayed in passenger transport as a charabanc proprietor at Doddington Place, Lewisham.

In the early days the Premier buses were mainly on the whole or part of routes 6, 9, 12, 33, 51, 73 and 142 and could be found at points as far apart as Stanmore, Dulwich, Wanstead and Turnham Green. From mid-1924 they were mainly on 11, 18, 60 and 73, and in common with many other independents Premier also ran to Wembley during the period the Empire Exhibition was open in 1924. When the company deposited its schedules under the London Traffic Act the routes selected were:

15A	6 buses in the evening
60	3 buses all day
202	5 buses Mondays-Fridays, 3 Saturdays—mainly middle day in each case
295	4 buses Mondays-Fridays, 3 Saturdays—mainly middle day in each case
522	9 buses in the a.m. peak and late evenings (Mon.Fri.), 3 all day and 6 a.m. peak (Saturdays)

This accounted for a total of twelve scheduled buses daily on weekdays. On Sundays Premier decided to operate on routes 33D (Strand-Hampton Court), 295, 73A and 202, although the operations on the two latter routes were abandoned after about the end of 1925. The 202 and 295 were routes pioneered by Premier and were unique in reaching Hampton Court by way of Bushey Park instead of going through Kingston upon Thames. Various minor alterations to the weekday services operated took place over the next few years. Starting from 2nd February 1925 the operations on route 15A were abandoned in favour of extra buses on route 295, whilst on the 4th April of the same year a part-day operation was begun on routes 33D and 73A, a short working of the 202. The total number of scheduled buses remained at twelve. Under the guidance of Premier's Traffic Manager, Mr. Albert Gray, the schedules were skilfully arranged to capture the best traffic possible throughout the day. Route 60, which was the only service upon which Premier operated all day on Mondays to Fridays, was always busy and provided many useful connections between the north western suburbs, the West End, and the City. Probably the most interesting Premier operation was that on route

522, which was exclusive to Premier except for some Saturday journeys by Orange. Nine buses would set out early in the morning on the 522 from Kilburn to Edgware. The first to leave Edgware southbound would be at about 7.10 a.m., after which the remaining eight buses would follow at two to three-minute intervals, five travelling to Aldwych and four to Aldgate. On arrival at Aldgate these four would immediately transfer to route 295 in time to pick up the second peak between Aldgate and central London. The five terminating at Aldwych would travel "light" through Lincolns Inn Fields and New Oxford Street to pick up their line of route on the 202 at Tottenham Court Road. These were then available to cater for the high traffic flows experienced to and from Hammersmith in the 10 o'clock hour. In this way the operation of route 522 was all over by 9 a.m., although as a matter of expediency some buses would work again on it in the late evening in order to return to the garage.

When the business was started William Allen rented space in an aircraft hangar at 39 Somerton Road, Cricklewood, which was the property of Handley Page. Premier buses operated from Somerton Road throughout the period of development in 1923/4 and the situation of this garage undoubtedly influenced the Company's choice of routes. In April 1925 a move was made to alternative rented premises in Thackray's Garage at Ledbury Mews, Westbourne Grove. Just under two years later a further—and final—move was made, to a garage at 2 Leysfield Road, Shepherds Bush. This property, which was also rented, included office space, and Leysfield Road became the Company's registered address. This substantial building was one of the largest of many on a factory estate and can still be recognised as the depot for the C & A van and lorry fleet. It is barely altered from bus days. The buses reached it via a narrow run-in between 36 Leysfield Road and 28 Greenside Road. On May 27th 1930 Premier purchased the freehold of the depot and its adjacent offices from J. M. Roberts & Son Ltd. (in liquidation) for £10,987. At the time it also rented accommodation in Goldhawk Road (probably at the Goldhawk Garage) and at Windsor.

Three more Dennises were bought in January 1926 (YM 5524), October 1926 (YR 2358) and February 1927 (YE 3930) and were the last Dennises and the last open-toppers to be bought new. These three were intended to provide spares as well as giving scope for increased Sunday operation. All Premier buses had one thing in common: this was their superb condition both mechanically and bodily in which they were only slightly inferior to the marvellously-maintained Chocolate Expresses. Breakdowns in service were very rare—a claim that some London "pirates" certainly could not make—and the paintwork was always immaculate. Mr. Allen was in charge of the mechanical side of things and saw to this. His co-Managing Directors concerned themselves with other aspects of the firm's business, Mr. A. J. Schiffer concentrating mainly on road supervision and his son on the office work. Although the number of staff employed was kept as low as possible a good standard was always insisted upon.

After the 1924 Act had restricted the development of the Company other outlets were sought upon which to invest the available cash resources. At a board meeting in February 1926 the directors decided to seek to purchase existing undertakings at a price not exceeding £1,500 per scheduled bus. This figure would indicate that the Premier board had little idea of the second-hand value of scheduled buses and it is not surprising that they only had one taker, and even then they had to raise their offer beyond the ceiling price to £1,820. May 10th 1927 saw the acquisition of the Victor Omnibus Co. Ltd. together with its one bus which plied daily on the 6D. The early days of the Victor bus are outlined in chapter 6. The change of ownership took place on June 23rd 1927 after which the Victor company was run as a subsidiary until January 17th 1928 when it was put into voluntary liquidation and the assets transferred to the parent company. During its time as a Premier subsidiary Victor was charged £60 per week for operation and upkeep. The Victor bus was XT 8841, a Dennis which was always readily recognisable, even after it had been repainted in full Premier livery, by its Strachan & Brown body.

After the schedule changes of April 1925 no more alterations were made, apart from the addition of the ex-Victor bus on the 6D, until the 1st May 1929 (although on the 7th December 1928 the 295 had been renumbered 233 and the 202 had become 573). On this date permission was received for the transfer of the solitary bus on the 6D to the 33D. No more existing companies were available for acquisition so instead Premier tried to open up new territory in the south-western outer suburbs. On the 30th January 1928 the Company approached the Minister of Transport for permission to operate a service of pneumatic-tyred single-deckers between Sunbury-on-Thames and Kingston, but permission was refused on the grounds that the route would traverse a lengthy section of tramway route. A year later Premier tried again, this time for a route between Kingston and Walton on Thames upon which it was proposed to operate eight single-deckers on a 15 min. headway. This was also unsuccessful, as was an attempt in October 1929 to obtain a 15 min. service of single-deckers between West Byfleet and East Molesey. In this latter case an appeal to the Minister followed the refusal, but this met with no success either. In yet another effort to expand, the firm branched out into taxi-operation for which six new Morrises were acquired in May 1929. These were only run for a little over a year and time does not appear to have recorded why they were abandoned as they are believed to have run at a profit.

The directors decided to pin their hopes for future growth on express coach operation. On April 18th 1928 at a board meeting the purchase of four saloon coaches was decided upon together with an increase in the share capital to £17,000 by the issue of 7,000 more £1 shares. The proposed route was from Hammersmith to Slough. However a new tax was placed on petrol in April 1928 and it caused the Company to think twice on the prospects of expansion into the coach field, and the idea was dropped temporarily.

September 1929 saw the delivery of Premier's first top-covered bus, UV 5096. This was a Leyland Titan carrying an open staircase Dodson body. Later in 1929 an order was placed for nine new coaches and a further double-decker. The company had finally committed itself to express coach operation and to finance it a further increase in the share capital was made to £30,000. The ten new vehicles arrived between December 1929 and February 1930. All were Leyland Titans with Duple bodies, GC 1205-13 being single-deck 26-seaters and GC 1214 a 52-seat double-decker. GC 1214 was the first double-decker built by Duple for London service and to all outward appearances could easily have been a Dodson product, its appearance was so similar. As soon as the order was completed six further Titan coaches were ordered followed by four more in March. Delivery took place between April and June of GC 6846/7, GC 7775/6/8, GJ 372/3, GJ 2350/97/8. The Premier coach fleet now stood at nineteen vehicles, outnumbering the double-deckers of which there were seventeen.

In ordering the new coaches the emphasis was placed upon comfort, with the result that only twenty-six seats were fitted in each instead of the usual thirty. These were all forward-facing and were arranged in pairs apart from the rear seat which held four; they were of the semi-armchair pattern with arm and foot rests. The joinery work was all of highly polished walnut, and an air of luxury was given by the curtained windows and the fibre mats on the floor. Externally the coaches resembled Duple's standard design of the period, and looked extremely smart in Premier's colours. They had two nearside doors, the front one of which was kept only for emergency use. Route indication was by means of single-line destination boxes at the front and in the curved rear waistrail, with roof boards on either side. Ample luggage accommodation was available in the side lockers and on the roof rack. The "Premier" name was carried on the front dash and on an oval box mounted above the destination indicator, whilst the inscription "Premier Line" was to be found on the sides and back. Although normally only used for double-deckers, the "Titan" chassis was chosen to give complete interchangeability between the double- and single-deckers in the fleet. Some of the coaches differed from others in bearing the "Titan" head on an oval enamelled plate on the top tank of the radiator instead of the "LEYLAND" plate.

A number of prospective coach routes were considered, and ones from London to Windsor and Aylesbury were definitely decided upon. Also contemplated were services radiating from London to Luton, Staines and Woking, and Byfleet and Woking. On the 6th January 1930 the first two of the new coaches were delivered, followed by a further three on the 27th. These were sufficient to open, on the 27th the Company's first express coach route from the Strand (Aldwych) to Windsor via Hammersmith, the Great West Road, the Colnbrook By-Pass, Slough and Eton. Lettered A, the new service operated at first on a 40 min. headway, which was reduced to 20 mins. on the 7th April and 15 mins. on the 12th June. On Sundays an eight minute service was operated. A minor change occurred on the 19th February when the route was diverted via Colnbrook Village although by October all coaches were again using the By-Pass.

Despite intense competition from Green Line, Highways and Thackray's Way the Windsor coach service did well and the directors viewed future coach expansion with optimism. It was decided to transfer the coaching assets to a new company which would finance future development. On October 1st 1930 Premier Line Ltd. came into being to take over the coach operations with effect from September 1st for £42,960 satisfied by the issue of fully paid ordinary shares. It was registered with an authorised capital of £60,000 of which £42,000 £1 shares were issued originally, increasing later to £57,406. All the shareholders were either owners of the Omnibus Company or their relatives, so Premier Line was in effect a complete subsidiary. Captain Percy Musker, William Allen and the two Schiffers were elected to the same positions that they held with the parent, and the head office shared the same address at 2 Leysfield Road. Express route A (London-Windsor) was transferred to the new Company and an immediate programme of expansion was embarked upon. The complex history of Premier Line Ltd. and its subsequent lack of financial success remain to be described in another volume. So, too, does the acquisition by the Premier directors of the Aylesbury Omnibus Co. Ltd. in October 1931.

Back in the metropolis, an influx of new rolling stock was scheduled to take place in the second half of 1930 with the delivery of a further twelve Duple-bodied Titans, making Premier the biggest Titan fleet in London. GJ 7536-8, GH 889/90, GH 2491, and GK 891-6 replaced the three Leyland LB's and all but four of the Dennises (XP 3760, YM 5524, YR 2358 and YE 3930). The fleet strength then stood at eighteen vehicles of which six were over and above the weekday schedules and allowed increased Sunday operation to take place, mainly on 33D and 233. No further buses were ever added to the fleet, which was reduced by three in November 1932 when all but one of the remaining Dennises were transferred to the Aylesbury Omnibus Company Ltd.

A few words about the Premier livery. The original purple-red was replaced at an unknown time by a darker shade of maroony-brown which was equally as handsome. One or two vehicles are reported to have operated for a short while, perhaps experimentally, in a highly-varnished shade of crimson and are said to have looked very beautiful.

The immaculate Premiers reached the end of the road on December 20th 1933 when the fourteen Titans and one Dennis became the property of the LPTB, together with two 1926 Buick cars (YO 7991 & YP 2867) and two Morris 10 cwt. vans (EV 4507 & XX 7176). Premier Line Ltd. was taken over on the same day, the Aylesbury company having been sold to Eastern National on May 11th 1933. Game to the last, however, the proprietors would not accept London Transport's valuation of the two undertakings and arranged to take both cases to the Arbitration Tribunal. The Omnibus Company's hearing began on the 6th March 1935 at the Incorporated Accountants' Hall on the Victoria Embankment and lasted for four days. The Hon. Sir R. Stafford Cripps, K.C., M.P., appeared on behalf of Premier and Mr. Walter T. Monckton, K.C., acted for the Board. The result of the hearing was an increase in the price to be paid by the LPTB for the undertaking to £199,500 although it was still far below the sum originally claimed. The Premier Line case did not go to arbitration after all, as both parties succeeded in reaching agreement on the very eve of the hearing. A memory of the Premier name is perpetuated in Premier Travel Ltd., the well-known Cambridgeshire company, much of whose original capital came from the Magnay family whose finances had helped the London Premier to prosper.

1 Oxford Road, Chiswick
Cambrian Buildings, Westfields Road, North Acton
Acton Town Garage, Gunnersbury Lane
Acme Garage, Pluckington Place, Southall

Independents based in outer West London were few and far between, in great contrast to the large number of operators who based themselves in the northern, eastern and south eastern suburbs. Cleveland's garage at 1 Oxford Road, Chiswick has been noted, and Cambrian's premises at Westfields Road, North Acton are described in chapter 8. Charles Dobbs, formerly of the Skylark, ran the Acton Town Garage in Gunnersbury Avenue where some of Mrs. Sayers' Royal Highlander buses were kept for a while. G. L. Hanson's Acme Garage in Pluckington Place, Southall, provided a base for Pioneer, Unity and, later, Public in the 'twenties. In May 1931 Mr. Hanson tried to start up a bus service himself on a route from Greenford (Hare & Hounds) to Hounslow (The Hussar). He claimed that a number of LPOC buses garaged with him operated over the restricted streets involved and as they were not now operated he wished to operate in lieu thereof. The application was refused. Hanson's garage can now be recognised as the Acme Works, an engineering shop in the old style with some interesting roof-mounted belt-driven machinery very reminiscent of the nineteen thirties.

★   ★   ★   ★

Chapter 5 closes with a brief mention of the Southall & District Traction Company. This was one of a number of bus enterprises of James Henry Absalom Weaver of Ledgers Road, Slough, who also ran services in Guildford, Woking, Windsor and Slough. The Southall & District operation called for three buses on a route between the Bell at Hounslow and the Broadway, Southall, which received the number 518 under the Bassom system. Because the vehicles were based with Weaver's Slough & District fleet at Slough, which geographically is far outside the limits of this volume, we have reserved the full description of his activities for a later volume. It suffices to record here that three AEC B-types (LH 8036/LN 4760/PP 491) with single-deck bodies ran the Southall & District service from about January 1923 onwards. Weaver built the bodies himself, with the help of a local carpenter, and the first one had a very pleasing, rounded back end. Unfortunately it did not please the powers that be, and no less a policeman than Bassom himself visited Weaver to tell him that the bus was eighteen inches over length. The round back gave way to a plain, flat one which did nothing to enhance the appearance of the bus but did not contravene the rules and regulations. In January 1925 Weaver applied for, and was granted, approval to operate additionally from Hounslow to Slough on route 81B but these may have been Sunday or garage journeys. Weaver decided to abandon all his bus interests after one of the vehicles, working in another area, was involved in a fatal accident. His various operations were sold piecemeal, the Southall one being the last to survive. It ceased when PP 491 ran into the depot for the last time on Friday April 23rd 1926.

CHAPTER SIX

NORTH WEST LONDON

Barnsdale Yard, Paddington
(also Pavilion Yard, North Pole Road, North Kensington)

Situated just north of the Harrow Road at its junction with Great Western Road, Paddington is Barnsdale Road. This mainly residential thoroughfare contained on its south side, a depot latterly used by the Greater London Council's housing department. Like much of Barnsdale Road itself, the yard has recently disappeared beneath new housing development. For a few years in the 'twenties the Barnsdale Yard was a hive of bus activity and the base for a number of independent operators. It was a well-placed yard from which to operate many of the trunk west London services. In 1924 the proprietors of the Bayswater, Cornwall, Dolphin, Overington, Royal, Victor and Varsity buses all made Barnsdale Yard their base, paying a weekly rental to Charles Randall, the owner of the yard. The Dolphin and Overington buses did not stay long before moving on to 54 Iverson Road, Kilburn, but the others remained until bought out by larger operators. They were joined for a few months in 1927 by the Glandfield bus which had been at 54 Iverson Road for the major part of its career. At the busiest period, the latter part of 1925, eighteen buses ran from Barnsdale Yard. Even after the buses departed in 1927/8 the yard served for a while as a base for passenger vehicles housing, among others, the Palanquin Coach Services vehicles which operated a London to Manchester express service.

ROYAL BLUE

Charles Randall, the owner of Barnsdale Yard, was also the proprietor of the Royal Blue buses which were once a familiar sight on route 247. At their maximum there were eight scheduled buses on this route on weekdays, and one further bus was held as a spare. Charles Randall, a rotund, red-faced man normally distinguished by his straw hat, was an established garage and taxicab proprietor before buying the buses and had a business address at 15 Chippenham Mews, Westbourne Park, as well as Barnsdale Yard. Earlier his taxis had been kept at Church Street, Paddington Green, a site long-since demolished to make way for a cinema.

Randall's first buses were Straker Squires, of which he bought three between June 1923 and March 1924 (XO 3124, XP 1193 and XR 4596). Like his taxis, Randall's buses were painted with a main body colour of royal blue and sported red wheels. The window frames on the buses were white and they carried the usual lining out in gold. Three Dodson-bodied Leylands followed the Strakers; they were XT 2864 of May 1924 and XU 5778/9 which were three months its junior. The only second-hand bus purchased by Charles Randall, Straker Squire XN 3980, came from C. T. Clarke in July 1924 after having run for just over a year as the Unity. Standardisation was clearly not Randall's strong point, for a third make of chassis appeared in the fleet in February 1925 in the form of Dodson-bodied Dennis XX 670. The ninth and last bus was licensed two months later as XX 9877. This was a very late Straker Squire, very possibly a vehicle built earlier against a cancelled order and being sold off cheaply, and it was one of the few examples of a London operator reverting back to a Straker Squire after buying vehicles of other makes.

By 1925 the taxicab trade had slumped and Randall's main sources of income were the buses and the garage business, both of which were doing well. A limited company was formed on August 31st 1925 with a nominal capital of £5,000 to take over the more profitable parts of the Randall business. Four thousand of the £1 shares were issued, the only shareholders being Charles Randall, who held 3,000 shares, and Thomas George Spain. The latter was a captain in the RASC and was not actively connected with the business. Originally it had been hoped to call the business The Royal Blue Omnibus Co. Ltd. but the Registrar of Companies would not sanction this. He objected to the use of the word "Royal", and the title with this word omitted would have been too similar to that of the Blue Bus Co. Ltd. of Neath to be allowed. So the limited company became Charles Randall Limited, although the buses continued to display the Royal Blue fleetname. The registered office was 15 Chippenham Mews, and when these premises were disposed of in March 1926 the registered address became Barnsdale Yard. Charles Randall appointed himself Managing Director of the business for a ten year period from November 30th 1925 at a salary of £600 a year.

Apart from the usual trial and error operations on all manner of routes in the early days the Royal Blue operations were particularly unvaried. They spent a short while on route 50 during the Wembley Exhibition of 1924, but otherwise concentrated all their weekday efforts on route 18 (later renumbered 247) on which eight schedules were held. On Sundays in 1925, and possibly later, workings were maintained on the 248 on which Royal Blue was the sole operator. The company even had its own private stand at Rugby Avenue, Sudbury. An inspector, George Perrin, was in charge of the buses on the road and was responsible for supervising the staff of about eighteen drivers and the same number of conductors.

The LGOC cast covetous eyes on the Royal Blue fleet, which was a fairly substantial one by London independent bus standards, and reasonably well run. An offer from 55 Broadway to purchase the business was accepted and on April 19th 1926 a meeting was held there to complete the formalities. Two days later the registered office was transferred to 55 Broadway though Royal Blue continued to run from Barnsdale Yard until April 27th, after which they moved into the LGOC garage at Middle Row (X). Before the year was over the whole fleet had been replaced by K's, suitably repainted in blue & white livery. The Leylands were transferred to Batten group companies and the Dennis was sold to Hull & District Motor Services Ltd. along with a similar bus (MH 9160) from the Cosgrove Omnibus Co. Ltd. The Strakers, which had been giving a good deal of bother in their later days due, mainly, to radiator and brake trouble, were sold for scrap. The nine K's which the LGOC drafted in remained until the business was absorbed into the LGOC on January 1st 1928. Subsequent to the sale of his bus interests Charles Randall continued in business for several more years as a taxi and garage proprietor.

197

THE ROYAL

Frederick Randall began to operate a bus from his brother's premises in July 1924 in partnership with Norman Joseph George Shepherd, their trading name being Randall & Shepherd. They chose a dark blue livery similar to that favoured by Charles Randall and the fleetname The Royal also bore some similarity. There were eventually two Royal buses, both Strachan & Brown-bodied Dennises. XU 1487 was licensed on July 8th 1924 and XX 8445 on April 4th 1925. The earlier vehicle worked on route 18 (later 247) and the other spent its time on the 526D as one of the West London Association vehicles and later adopted the Association's standard red & white livery. An interesting and probably short-lived Sunday operation for which approval was received in April 1925 was 528 Hammersmith (Brook Green) to Hatfield.

When the Royal Blue business was sold to the LGOC Randall & Shepherd decided to stay independent and continued to operate out of the Barnsdale Yard. On February 25th 1927 a limited company was formed with a nominal capital of £500 and registered office at Barnsdale Yard. Frederick Randall was its Managing Director. Later in the year an attractive offer was received from Public and the two buses were duly sold to them on August 17th for £6,000. Randall & Shepherd Ltd. was subsequently wound up on December 7th 1927.

CORNWALL
BAYSWATER

The Bayswater and Cornwall buses were linked throughout their whole careers through having as their manager a former taxi owner William Alliston. On March 11th 1924 he formed a limited company entitled the Cornwall Motor Omnibus Co. Ltd., with a nominal capital of £1,000 and ordered a Dennis double-decker on hire purchase from Strachan & Brown. Money for the new venture came in the first instance jointly from Alliston and his landlady, Rose Selina Dicks, who kept an apartment house at 22 Cornwall Road, East Acton, and whose husband, Sidney, worked on the bus and was later employed by Birch as one of the two inspectors supervising all operations on route 526D. The registered office of the new company was at the Cornwall Road address whence the Company's fleetname was derived. To those not in the know the fleetname Cornwall must have seemed somewhat unusual for a bus destined to run solely in London. However by the time the Cornwall bus was licensed on May 1st 1924 as XT 2093 Londoners were beginning to get used to buses with unusual fleetnames.

To start with space was found for the bus in the yard of the Pavilion Hotel on the corner of Wood Lane and North Pole Road, North Kensington, but this was only temporary and by July of the same year the Cornwall had found a more permanent home at the Barnsdale Yard.

The Company was only a few days old when its authorised capital was increased to £3,000. Two Chiswick gentlemen, Frederick Alfred Punter, a civil engineer, and George Knight had agreed to put money into the business. They joined Alliston and Mrs. Dicks on the board of directors, all four holding 650 shares each. Sufficient money was now in the kitty for expansion to take place.

198

Before further Cornwall buses took the road the Bayswater bus came on the scene. This was run by five people in partnership, trading as the Cornwall Omnibus Company (not Limited) but using the fleetname Bayswater, which was an appropriate title for a bus which operated mostly on one of the main Bayswater Road services, the 17. Two of the owners were Alliston and Mrs. Dicks, the others were railwaymen Thomas Henry Douglass and Charles William Letchford—an engine driver and fireman respectively—and bus conductor Charles Letchford. A contract for hire purchase of a bus was made by William Alliston with Strachan & Brown on July 11th 1924. The bus was XU 1368, a Dennis which had been registered four days previously. It is interesting to recall the terms of the hire which were an initial down payment of £400 followed by monthly instalments of £87 10s. 0d.

The original Cornwall bus must have shown promising results, for the fleet was augmented by no fewer than three extra buses in February 1925 (XX 979, 1478/9) followed by two more in April of the same year (XX 8832/3). All were identical Dennises to the first one and were painted in the same livery of red & white with brown rocker panels. They were numbered 3 to 7 respectively, no. 1 having been allotted to the original Cornwall bus and 2 to the Bayswater vehicle. Five out of the six scheduled buses worked on the 526D, Cornwall being the operator supplying the largest number of vehicles for the route. The sixth vehicle was scheduled to work routes 36 and 47.

The success story of the Cornwall buses was not repeated in the case of the Bayswater. Perhaps the 17 was less lucrative than the 36 and 526D. By the end of the first year the hire purchase repayments were in arrears to the tune of £175 and fresh capital was needed if the bus was to survive. The business was reorganised as the Bayswater Omnibus Co. Ltd. on July 15th 1925 with registered office at 22 Cornwall Road—its shares were fully subscribed for cash, Alliston and Mrs. Dicks taking 300 £1 shares each, the remainder being equally divided between Douglass and the two Letchfords to the extent of £200 each. William Alliston was appointed Managing Director of this as well as the Cornwall business.

The six Cornwall and one Bayswater buses ran from the Barnsdale Yard until the last week of October 1925 when they moved to the Goldhawk Garage, Brackenbury Road, Shepherds Bush. The only event of note subsequent to this was the purchase in September 1926 of a further Strachan & Brown-bodied Dennis, YR 143, the arrival of which meant that the Cornwall Company had a spare vehicle for the first time.

On August 17th 1927 the Cornwall and Bayswater fleets were sold to Public for £19,000 and £3,000 respectively. The sale comprised the seven scheduled buses, the spare bus, and a van which had been used in connection with the business. The last day of operation under Alliston's control was August 4th; from the following day the buses were operated by Public in anticipation of the completion of the sale. The directors of the two companies, having reaped a handsome reward from their sale, put the businesses into liquidation. Both were removed from the Register on May 8th 1928.

VICTOR

Two new buses, both with a name beginning with V, entered the Barnsdale Yard in June 1924. They were the Victor and the Varsity. Albert William Latham's and Victor James Mountney's Victor Dennis, XT 8841, was licensed on the 20th of that month, ten days ahead of Sidney Frederick George Collier's Varsity, XT 9991, which was also a Dennis. Mountney accompanied the red & white Victor bus to Scotland Yard on the day it was licensed. He was the senior partner and licensee and conducted the affairs of the business from his home address at 9 Albion Mews West, Hyde Park. He later moved to 118 Sutherland Avenue, Maida Vale and the "office" moved with him.

The Victor soon became a familiar sight on the 6D and though it did not do too well financially it had sufficient potential to attract the interest of the much larger Premier Omnibus Co. Ltd. who made an offer for it which Mountney and Latham accepted. To enable the transfer of ownership to take place they formed the Victor Omnibus Co. Ltd. on May 23rd 1927. This had its registered office at Mountney's Sutherland Avenue address and an authorised share capital of £2,000. May 31st was designated as the official date on which the limited company would take over the bus, and on June 23rd Mountney and Latham resigned from the business. The registered office was transferred to Premier's headquarters at Leysfield Road, Shepherds Bush and William Allen and Frederick Charles Schiffer of the Premier became the company's directors. At about the same time the bus was transferred to operate from Leysfield Road. The Victor ran as a Premier subsidiary under its old name until January 17th 1928 after which it was absorbed into the parent fleet. The Victor Omnibus Co. Ltd. was duly wound up on June 12th 1928. Mountney was later, from 1928 to 1932, a joint shareholder with Gerald and Irene Nowell in the Great Western Express Co. Ltd. running a daily service from London to South Wales.

VARSITY

Sidney Frederick George Collier lived at 37 Marylands Road, Maida Vale. This was only a few minutes walk from Barnsdale Road, so it was not surprising that he arranged with Charles Randall to garage his new Varsity Dennis there when it was delivered in June 1924. In fact it is thought that Collier was in some way connected with Randall's Royal Blue buses before branching out on his own.

Collier's first bus was XT 9991, a blue & white Dodson-bodied Dennis which bore the fleetname inside a wavy gold stripe extending the length of the vehicle. The bus was licensed on June 30th, but then over a week elapsed before it was taken to Scotland Yard for police inspection. It entered service on a number of routes including the nearby 18 and 27 and was also to be seen on the 33 and 73. A second Dennis, identical to the first and registered XX 5762, was licensed on March 24th 1925 and went into service on the 526D. XT 9991, meanwhile, had settled down to regular operation on the 247. In April 1925 Collier received permission to run 530 (Sudbury, The Swan to Chalk Farm Station) and 531 (Acton High Street to Chalk Farm Station), but these were Sunday workings and were of short duration if, indeed, they worked at all. A third vehicle was purchased in May 1926 as a spare. The bus in question was MH 2480 and it came third-hand from Henslowe. It was also a Dennis but the body-work differed from that of the other two Varsity buses in being of Strachan & Brown manufacture.

On February 25th 1927 the business was incorporated as a limited company under the title of Varsity Omnibus Co. Ltd. Six months later, on August 19th, Collier sold his two scheduled buses to Public for £6,000 plus £900 for the spare. He had meanwhile become interested in express coach work though he was not long in this sphere of activity before he sold out to P. H. R. Harris who renamed the company Fairway Coaches Ltd. on October 3rd 1928. As already recorded under the PHRH heading, the Fairway service between London and Worthing passed to Southdown after Harris's death. Collier was also connected with New Empress Saloons Ltd. for a short period from July 1928 until it came under City control three months later.

Wales Farm Road, North Acton

L.P.O.C.

The Citizoyne Bus Co. Ltd. had a career which was distinguished only by the swiftness with which it collapsed. Within nine short months it had been incorporated, had changed owners, changed title, gone broke and been wound-up. Registered on March 10th 1925 it was the property in the first instance of Clarke Williams, a Harringay motor contractor whose solicitor's address, 33 Chancery Lane, W.C.2., was the company's head office. A Dennis was ordered from Strachan & Brown, but before it was delivered Citizoyne had come under the control of John Joseph Horan, who became self-styled traffic manager. Horan proceeded to sell shares in the company, and by early May had found fifteen others interested in becoming bus owners. All the company's 1,200 £1 preference shares were taken up, and 700 out of 6,000 ordinary shares at 1/- were also subscribed for. Citizoyne therefore commenced business with a working capital of £1,235. Of the sixteen owners one, Horan, was traffic manager as we have already noted. No fewer than five of the others were designated manager's assistants, and the remaining ten were drivers and conductors. This was a formidable staff for operating the lone bus, XY 3470, which was licensed on May 4th 1925.

Even before the bus was delivered Horan had plans for achieving great things. Early in April 1925 every local authority in Greater London received a circular from the Citizoyne Bus Co. Ltd. notifying them of a proposal to inaugurate services, not only by buses but by motor-cycle taxis, and asking for information as to available stands. Shortly afterwards the Town Council at Aberystwyth was probably surprised to receive an application from Citizoyne for licences for six buses to ply in and around the town in summer months. The Council referred the question to its bus service committee, and there the matter seems to have faded gently away. London was not big enough; the whole country was to be Citizoyne's oyster. Horan may have even dreamed of building up an enterprise comparable to the highly successful National which was at the time expanding its activities in several parts of the country at once. At a meeting of members on May 2nd a proposal was put forward to change the company's name to the London & Provincial Bus Co. Ltd., and the new title was duly registered with the authorities on May 26th. The bus carried the fleet name L.P.O.C. (standing presumably for London & Provincial Omnibus Company).

The Company's garage was shown on their original licence application as being in Wales Farm Road, North Acton, and the only likely place this could have been would appear to be Strachan & Brown's works. Sadly for the Company it was too late on the scene to obtain schedules on profitable routes because of the Restricted Streets Orders, and the only route for which they are known to have successfully applied was 81B. This operated from the Bell, Hounslow, right out in the western suburbs, to Windsor and was far removed from the garage in Wales Farm Road. An application to work 518 (Hounslow—Southall Town Hall) was turned down as unsuitable for double-deckers. Despite, or perhaps because of, the Company's extensive management staff, receipts failed to exceed costs and on August 19th a special meeting was held to review the serious financial situation which had arisen. It was decided that, in view of its liabilities, the Company could not possibly continue and the only course available was to go into liquidation.

In all probability the L.P.O.C. bus did not run after the date of this special meeting. The vehicle quickly passed to Cambrian and on December 17th 1925 the London & Provincial Bus Co. Ltd. was removed from the Register. Though the company had the most grandiose title of all London independents, its operational career of at the most three months was one of the shortest on record. To the unfortunate owners of the company, who mostly lost between £50 and £250 each with its collapse, the provinces remained a goal which their buses never reached.

As we have already noted in chapter 5, Chariot garaged somewhere in Wales Farm Road—possibly at Strachan & Brown's—in the late 'twenties.

Colin Road, Willesden
COSMOPOLITAN/RYAN

Twenty years in the bus industry should, by rights, have qualified Irishman Joseph Ryan for success when he began to run a bus on his own account. He was, indeed, successful eventually, but in the early days it was very much a case of touch and go. Ryan, who lived at 7 Sandringham Road, Cricklewood, had worked for General from the horse bus days of 1901 up to 1921, first of all as a driver and, from 1912, as a foreman. A reorganisation in 1921 made Ryan redundant and he left with an **ex gratia** payment, after which he kept a shop for a while. The lure of bus work was great, and in 1924 Joe Ryan made up his mind to re-enter the bus business, this time as owner-driver. He paid a deposit of £250 to J. M. Roberts for a Hickman-bodied Daimler, and this proved to be his biggest mistake.MF 8159, which was licensed on June 2nd 1924 and bore the fleet-name COSMOPOLITAN in large gold letters on the red, brown & white body, was not one of the best of the reconditioned Daimler chassis to leave the Cathnor Motor Works. It gave very considerable mechanical trouble, which meant that Ryan lost a good deal of potential revenue. In

July 1925 his patience came to an end and he returned the bus to Roberts in disgust. A lengthy legal battle then ensued between the two which did not finally end until about 1930.

Ryan was then without a bus until September 1925 when a new Dennis was delivered to him by Dodson, from whom it was acquired on hire purchase. This bus was as good as its predecessor had been bad, and at last Ryan began to reap a return on his capital. MK 403 was painted red & white and carried the name RYAN. The former title, Cosmopolitan, was never used again, which was just as well as it had probably become associated in the public image with a bus that was always breaking down. Except when it was off for overhaul the Ryan Dennis could usually be found on the 218E (Kings Cross to Sudbury) except on Sundays when it worked beyond Sudbury to Greenford Green as the 218D. Ryan had initially deposited schedules for other services besides these, including 18A, but ran nothing but 218D/E from 1926 onwards.

In 1929 an event happened which convinced Ryan that he ought to have a spare bus. The Dennis was setting down passengers when a General ran into the back of it causing extensive damage. It was off the road for 4½ weeks while repairs were carried out and Ryan never received compensation from the LGOC for his loss of earnings. Furthermore the Dennis, though now on pneumatics, was rapidly becoming outdated, so early in 1930 Ryan ordered a Leyland Titan. Though the bus was bodied by Dodson, Ryan ordered it on hire purchase through Arlington who appeared to be offering better terms than Dodson at the time. MY 4650 was licensed on May 15th 1930 and relegated the Dennis to spare bus except on Sundays when both vehicles operated. Both were always smartly kept with their appearance enhanced by whitened tyre walls.

On January 1st 1931 Ryan took a three year lease on the garage which he had been using in Colin Road, Willesden. He had half of a semi-detached building for his exclusive use, his area measuring 80 ft. deep by 17 ft. wide. Its owner, a Mr. Harris, ran his own garage business from the other part of the building. Ryan had his own underground 500 gallon petrol tank installed and a Bowser pump. As the time passed he gave less and less personal attention to the business. He did not drive for long after the delivery of the Dennis, and from February 1930 the general running of the business was in the hands of Ryan's mechanic, Frederick Randall, who would report to or ring Ryan's home each day to let him know how things were going. Ryan rented an office at his Sandringham Road address from his landlady, Mrs. Wiseman, for £1 a week. During the last few months of its existence the Ryan Omnibus Company abandoned the Sunday Greenford Green extension numbered 218D and ran on route 218E daily. The end came on November 1st 1933 when, at a week's notice, Ryan's business was taken over by the London Passenger Transport Board for a sum later fixed at £8,204. The two buses passed to the new concern but Ryan retained MH 5701, an Austin tourer which had been used in connection with the business, for a payment of £10. Unlike most other acquired fleets of November and December 1933, the Ryan undertaking did not stay at its old garage, and under its old management, right up to January 17th 1934. The petroleum licence at Colin Road

203

expired on Tuesday, December 19th, and as the lease on the premises was also due to expire shortly, the Ryan buses were moved out and operated from the ex-General Willesden (AC) garage from the 20th. Today Ryan's former garage in Colin Road can be easily recognised as part of the premises of the Ryder transport group.

2 Westbury Road, Willesden
83 Denzil Road, Willesden

PIONEER

The Pioneer Omnibus Company was a pioneer in more than title alone; it was the first to run a London-type Thornycroft 'J' 50-seater which, at the time of its introduction into service in July 1923, was the largest bus in terms of seating capacity to run for a London independent. Brothers F. G. and J. F. Stevens of 3 Yew Tree Road, Shepherd's Bush were the proprietors and though the former was the senior partner for the first few years, he left to take over a public house. Thereafter the business was run solely by James Frederick Stevens, though his brother retained a financial half share in it.

MF 1001 was the original Thornycroft. It was painted in a livery of crimson lake & white with the fleet name in gold block capitals. On June 29th 1923 it was examined by the police at New Scotland Yard, and on July 3rd was licensed ready for driver training. A second Pioneer bus was delivered to the Stevens' in January 1924 but this time they forsook the two extra seats of a Thornycroft for the speed obtained from a Dennis. MF 4173, the bus in question, was fitted with sprag gear. The two Pioneers worked on various roads at first, switching their allegiance from time to time. Initially variations on routes 6 and 16 were favoured including an Edgware-Liverpool Street operation for which the route number 51 was carried. Route 17 figured prominently later but by the time police schedules were required to be deposited in December 1924 the 18 was the main Pioneer route and two schedules were secured for 18 and the associated 247.

Pioneer somehow managed to obtain a third schedule on the 18 group of routes in 1927, though how they managed to do so in the face of the Restricted Streets Orders remains a mystery. To cover this extra mileage a second Dennis, ML 6105, was purchased in July 1927. A third vehicle of the same type, MP 5211, was obtained in June 1928 and replaced the Thornycroft. MP 5211 was well out of date by the time it was delivered—pneumatic tyres and covered tops lay just around the corner—and was the penultimate standard London Dennis to be built.

Pioneer had at least three garages in its ten year career. The Thornycroft stood overnight originally in a yard at 83 Denzil Road, Willesden, which in 1923 led up to factory premises used by firms of electrical and mechanical engineers and is today used by a Chinese business concern. By about May 1924 the fleet, which now consisted of two buses, could be found at the Acme Garage in Southall. This was convenient for route 17 on which Pioneer was now largely concentrating. At an unknown date there came a move back to North West London when J. F. Stevens bought the freehold of a house and garage at 2 Westbury Road, Willesden. The tall, narrow corrugated iron-clad garage, and the house, were demolished in 1972 as part of a massive slum clearance project, whilst Westbury Road itself was obliterated in 1974 beneath the rapid spread of factory-built flats.

Three new Leyland Titans replaced the open-top fleet in 1929 (MY 1140/1315) and 1931 (HX 2492). Like all previous Pioneer buses they carried bodies built by Dodson. They were the last additions to the Pioneer fleet and maintained the operations until London Transport took over on December 5th 1933. At the time of take-over services operated were 18A, 218D/E on weekdays and 18A/218D on Sundays. The Pioneer business had been exceptionally profitable, and this was reflected in London Transport's payment to the Stevens of the high compensation figure of £29,000.

Grittleton Avenue, North Wembley

KATHLEEN

Parked beside 38 Grittleton Avenue, North Wembley, any night could be found a red & white Daimler called Kathleen. The occupant of 38 Grittleton Avenue was Harry Ball, and the bus he owned from May 1924 until about the end of the year was MF 8001. Ball was the first of several owners in this vehicle's interesting career. We shall probably never know who MF 8001 was named after, perhaps it was Ball's wife or daughter. Kathleen began work on about June 6th and could often be located on the 18 group although the bus is recorded as having made excursions on to the 11 and 27. Because it failed to earn its keep the Kathleen's career was short lived, and in due course Harry Ball went bankrupt. MF 8001 returned to J. M. Roberts before passing to Peraeque with whom she had arrived by the early part of 1925.

60 Lower Road, Harrow
103 Queens Avenue, Watford

LOUMAX
ROYAL HIGHLANDER

A comparative latecomer was the little Loumax bus owned by the brothers Grundel, Louis Paul and Max, of 543 Holloway Road, N.19. The Grundels ran a motor engineering business from premises then known as Beaumont's Yard at 60 Lower Road, Harrow, which is little altered today. It was from there that they pioneered a short but useful service from South Harrow Station to the Eastcote Lane council estate via Northolt Road, Corbins Lane, Eastcote Lane and Kings Road, at a fare of 2d. They started the service on October 10th 1928 with a vehicle of unknown identity, and were stopped by the police two days later for illegal operation. In their eagerness to start the service they had omitted to obtain a licence for it! They duly made formal application, which was initially refused, along with a similar one by Mr. B. Stratton of 15 Steven Crescent, South Harrow. Fortunately the police relented on the second time of asking and signified their approval on September 30th 1929, nearly a year after the Grundels' initial spell of illegal operation. Meanwhile a new 18-seater Duple-bodied Guy, MY 1336, was bought in September 1929 in anticipation of the granting of the licence. This was rather a quaint little vehicle with a rear entrance to comply with Metropolitan Police requirements and with its windscreen glass extending only half-way along the dash, just sufficient to keep the driver dry. Operation of the service, which was numbered 206A, recommenced, legally this time, on October 8th.

The Grundels ran their Loumax bus for only a few months before control passed in March 1930 to Mrs. Violet Florence Alicia Sayers, a widowed lady living in Shaftesbury Avenue, Harrow. The Loumax Omnibus Co. Ltd. of 60 Lower Road, Harrow, was incorporated on March 7th with a share capital of £750 to acquire the Loumax business. Mrs. Sayers held 125 of the company's "A" shares, the balance of 375 "A" shares and all 250 "B" shares being subscribed by a Mr. A. J. Smith. Under Mrs. Sayers' auspices a pair of new Guy single-deckers was ordered. MY 3390 arrived in March 1930 and MY 4117 a month later. These differed considerably from their predecessor and, though only twenty-seaters, were modern-looking forward-control vehicles of type ONDF. Unusually for London vehicles the bodies were built in the Lowestoft works of United Automobile Services Ltd., the ancestors of the present day Eastern Coach Works.

Mrs. Sayers had great plans for expansion and anticipated building-up a series of services with small capacity vehicles on outer suburban routes where roads were "unrestricted" and where there was no existing bus service of any sort. Two areas particularly interested her. One was newly-developing territory between Ealing and Greenford over which she obtained authority to operate a new service which received the number 210, and one of the Loumax Guys opened up the service which commenced on Saturday, November 8th 1930 as 210B from the Hare & Hounds at Greenford via Greenford Avenue to Hanwell Station (Park Hotel) which was the extent of the weekday operation. On Sundays buses worked through to Ealing Broadway as 210. The licence for this service was held by Mrs. Sayers in her own name and not in that of the Loumax company. A May 1930 application by Loumax for a North Harrow-Northolt service showed the other direction in which Mrs. Sayers' aspirations for development lay. This was allocated route number 211 but operation was confined to Sundays only. In July 1930 the route was re-defined as Pinner (Red Lion)—Northolt. This Sunday operation appears to have been short-lived, for in March 1931 the route number 211 was allocated to the well-known service between Greenford (Hare & Hounds) and Ealing Broadway via Greenford Avenue, Drayton Bridge and Gordon Road which was a successor to the 210. Gordon Road required the use of buses with specially-built narrow bodies to avoid overhanging trees. The service commenced in May 1931 and initially terminated at West Ealing Station on weekdays and only used Gordon Road on Sundays until September 1931 when the full length of route was operated daily.

Mrs. Sayers was short of money and needed to find someone willing to back her financially. At the beginning of 1931 she heard from her petrol supplier that another customer of his, Ernest George Hewitt, was prepared to invest money in bus developments. Hewitt was a bus proprietor on his own account and ran the Premier and West Herts services from his garage at 103 Queens Avenue, Watford. She approached Hewitt and told him that she was in a position to obtain a number of licences in the Metropolitan Police area on approved routes and sought his financial assistance. She could obtain ten licences in all; four for Ealing-Greenford and six for another service in which she had become interested; Uxbridge-Pinner. Hewitt agreed to finance the hire purchase of 6 Guy buses for Uxbridge-Pinner, Mrs. Sayers to provide the balance which would be Beans with special narrow bodywork for the 211. A partnership agreement was drawn up on March 27th 1931 under the terms of which Mrs. Sayers was to receive a retaining fee of £50 in respect of each of the six Guys (total £300) plus £1 per week, together with a further £50 per vehicle in the event of a subsequent profitable sale. Hewitt would operate the six Guys and take the remainder of the profits or bear the losses.

Hewitt immediately ordered six Duple-bodied Guy Victory 20-seaters which were delivered during 1931 as UR 9195/6, 9899, 9900, 9997/8. Mrs. Sayers however was unable to purchase her four Beans as the suppliers would not accept her as a credit risk, so Hewitt obtained two for her on an oral promise to pay the hire purchase instalments. These materialised in late March 1931 as HX 3466/7. They were little 14-seaters which, by special dispensation from the Metropolitan Police, had front entrances to run as one man vehicles. Because of the width restriction the Birch bodies were built so as not to overhang the wheels and the interior seating, which was in blue moquette, was arranged longitudinally. A third identical Bean, MV 933, arrived in December 1931 and was this time paid for by Mrs. Sayers who possibly disposed of the original Loumax Guy at this time in part exchange. The six new Guys and three Beans were in a red & white livery and traded as the Royal Highlander Omnibus Service with Mrs. Sayers as licensee.

The daily Pinner (Red Lion) to Uxbridge (Eight Bells) service 181A commenced in April 1931 but Mrs. Sayers obtained only three of the promised six licences so Hewitt used the balance of the vehicles to the best of their advantage on his own Watford services or on private hire. Thus Royal Highlander buses sometimes operated into London on the express service which Hewitt had earlier acquired from West Herts. The six Royal Highlander Guys were kept in Hewitt's garage in Queens Avenue, Watford, and so were the Loumax vehicles for the 206 from the end of January 1932. The Beans were housed at Charles Dobbs' Acton Town Garage in Gunnersbury Lane.

The partnership between Mrs. Sayers and Hewitt turned out to be an uneasy one. Relationships were strained right from the start because Mrs. Sayers was unable to pay the instalments on the two Beans which meant that Hewitt had to do so. By February 1932 Hewitt had got so incensed about the situation that he seized the two Beans but consented to put them back on the road after a week on the promise of a new agreement. This agreement was formally signed on February 29th by which time Mrs. Sayers was indebted to Hewitt to the extent of £863 1s. 11d. A new company entitled the Royal Highlander Omnibus Co. Ltd. was to be formed with Mrs. Sayers holding the licences and plates while Hewitt ran the services. Her debt to him was to be wiped out from the date of incorporation and £150 was to pass to Mrs. Sayers. Her salary as a director of the company was to be £3 per week and a third of the assets less liabilities in respect of route 211 were to pass to her as shares. The 181A route was to be included as part of the assets of the company but operated and controlled entirely by Hewitt. He was to begin operating the 211 from March 1st on behalf of the company.

On the same day that the Royal Highlander agreement was signed Mr. Smith, Mrs. Sayers' co-director in the Loumax company and its major shareholder, came to an arrangement with Hewitt to sell him the assets of the Loumax business. A formal agreement was signed on March 19th whereby Hewitt would purchase all the shares for £400.

With the two agreements signed and settled Hewitt's position looked much brighter than hitherto. Not so, however. Mrs. Sayers made no attempt to form the limited company so Hewitt had to keep on paying the instalments on the two Beans. After Hewitt had paid £348 of the £400 for the Loumax business Smith refused to hand the vehicles over so the balance remained unpaid. Early in May 1932, unbeknown to Hewitt, Mrs. Sayers offered the whole of the Royal Highlander and Loumax businesses to the LGOC for £11,000 a figure which subsequent negotiations reduced to £8,750 and comprised £7,160 for Royal Highlander and £1,590 for Loumax. In the middle of the month she visited Hewitt along with her accountant to inform him of the negotiations and offered him £2,500 which, she said, was half the purchase price though she would not produce documents to prove it. Hewitt said he would not entertain selling and claimed that Mrs. Sayers had the right to sell only one bus, MV 933 on the 211. Two officials of the LGOC called to inspect the vehicles at Watford on May 28th and it was only then that Hewitt realised the full strength of what was happening. A subsequent improvement of her offer to £3,500 by Mrs. Sayers did not change Hewitt's mind, so she then decided to try to wrest control of the vehicles away from Hewitt completely.

On May 28th Mrs. Sayers, against whom bankruptcy proceedings were now pending, issued a writ against Hewitt claiming she was entitled to the assets and effects of the Royal Highlander Omnibus Services on routes 181 and 211 and asking for an injunction to restrain Hewitt from interfering with the services, or from publishing that he was interested in the business, as that was damaging to her interests. Hewitt, infuriated, countered with an injunction against Mrs. Sayers to restrain her from selling the Royal Highlander assets and from interfering with his control of the vehicles. On June 7th, acting on legal advice, Mrs. Sayers wrote to Hewitt saying she had decided that he should no longer run the six Guys and that she would have no further use for his services. At the same time she posted a notice to drivers and conductors stating that the buses would in future be kept at the Acton Town Garage and all moneys would be received by her there and not at Watford. Anyone disobeying this would be subject to instant dismissal with no excuses accepted. The next day, June 8th, Hewitt issued a writ against Mrs. Sayers. On that date she owed him a total of £3,244 in unpaid hire purchase instalments, etc.

Aware of the legal wranglings between Mrs. Sayers and Hewitt, the LGOC deferred purchase negotiations for a while but these were resumed in July 1932 after Hewitt had accepted the inevitable and given permission for them to continue. Agreement was reached on August 2nd for the LGOC to take over from September 1st but Ministry of Transport approval for the exchange of licences was not forthcoming until September 8th so it was not until September 15th 1932 that the purchase of the two Loumax and nine Royal Highlander buses by the LGOC was completed. A fourth new Bean, which was partially completed in the Birch workshops, was not included in the deal.

During the last three months, while the vehicles had been completely under Mrs. Sayers' control, the condition of the two fleets had shown a marked deterioration. MV 933 was completely out of use because Mr. Dobbs was unable to get a new Bean back axle. Both Loumax Guys had ceased to run by the middle of August because their certificates of fitness had expired; previously, MY 3390 had been running with only single wheels on its rear axle. Two of the Guy Victorys, UR 9997/8, had been taken off for annual overhaul but no work was done on them. Just prior to the General takeover only one bus was available out of the three required for the Ealing operations. Two of the Royal Highlander Guy Victorys were at work on the Loumax route 206A and no service at all was running on the 181A. It should be mentioned that from May 1932 an additional operation had taken place in Ealing numbered 225 and the scheduled operations at the time of takeover were:-

LOUMAX
206 Harrow Met. Stn. to Eastcote Lane Council Estate   Sundays
206A South Harrow Stn. to Eastcote Lane Council Estate weekdays

ROYAL HIGHLANDER
181A Uxbridge (Eight Bells) to Pinner (Red Lion)   daily
211 Greenford (Hare & Hounds) to Ealing (Haven Green)   daily
225 Greenford (Rutland Road) to Ealing (Haven Green)   weekdays

The Hewitt v Sayers and Loumax case came before the Chancery Division of the High Court and Mr. Justice Farwell on Friday March 24th 1933. Hewitt sought declarations by the court that his agreements of 27/3/31 and 29/2/32 were valid and that the second succeeded the first, plus a separate declaration that his agreement of 19/3/32 for the purchase of the Loumax assets was also valid. He also sought enquiries at the foot of these declarations as to how the proceeds of the sale of two businesses were to be dealt with, the purchase sum involved being finally settled at £8,761.

Mrs. Sayers claimed before the Court that none of the agreements were valid. The original one of 27/3/31 did not constitute an agreement, she claimed, but was merely a list of heads of agreement from which an agreement should have been made but was not. She denied that there had ever been any partnership and said that as far as she was concerned Hewitt worked for her as Manager. The services were registered in her name and she was sole proprietor. She had no knowledge of the six Guy buses being bought on hire purchase and did not authorise it. She admitted authorising the hire purchase of two Beans but did not know until afterwards that the hire purchase agreement was in Hewitt's name. As for the 29/2/32 agreement, Mrs. Sayers' case was that it was signed when she was in a nursing home in imminent danger of death from pneumonia and that she was in no fit state to make a business transaction, therefore the agreement should be set aside. The Loumax agreement, she stated, did not exist and, if it did, Mr. Smith had no authority to make it therefore it was invalid.

Many witnesses—about thirty in all—gave evidence on Friday and on the following Monday. On the Tuesday Mr. Justice Farwell pointed out to counsel that the complexity of the case was such that there was every chance of it continuing for several more days. In view of the costs that would be involved he advised them to try to reach an agreement. Later in the day, after several hours of negotiations, agreement was reached. Payment to the defendants (Mrs. Sayers and Loumax) was to be £2,000 each, the balance of £4,761 to go to Hewitt. Each party would pay its own costs and any interest accrued would be divided proportionately.

Ernest Hewitt's subsequent bus and coach career remains to be dealt with in another volume. The Premier-Albanian coach fleet remains a major factor in the Watford/St. Albans area whilst Hewitt himself lives in retirement in Watford. Mrs. Sayers moved to the West Country but her enterprise in opening up fresh territories brought her no reward; the last stop in her bus career was at the Bankruptcy Court.

331 Pinner Road, Harrow

A & W

The suburban sprawl once known as "Metroland" nowadays reaches so far in a north-westerly direction that it embraces once-individual villages such as Ruislip, Pinner and Hatch End. In the early 'twenties, when the speculative builders were only just beginning to cast their eyes on this area of green fields and leafy lanes, such bus services as were required could mostly be provided by vehicles little advanced over the old country carrier's bus. In 1922 a diminutive Crossley 12-seater was bought by A. V. Ashley with money he had borrowed in an effort to provide work for himself after having been unable to find employment since coming out of the forces. On September 10th the little red Crossley began to run between The Case is Altered public house in Wealdstone and South Harrow Station. Early results proved encouraging, so much so that Ashley made plans to run to the George at Pinner in direct competition with the Metropolitan Railway who had stations at Harrow-on-the-Hill, North Harrow, and at Pinner itself. With additional capital provided by a Mr. Westwood, and an enlarged fleet, the service from Wealdstone through to Pinner began operating on May 6th 1924, it being presumed that the operation to South Harrow had been abandoned by this time. So sparsely was the area served by buses in the first half of the decade that the only bus link between Harrow and Pinner prior to the arrival of A & W was National's N16 which had started in September 1922 and ran hourly between Harrow and Northwood with a two-hourly projection thence to Watford. The LGOC did not come on the scene with its 104A (Edgware-Harrow-Pinner) until September 1924 by which time the development potential of the area was becoming fully realised.

The partners traded as "The A & W Omnibus Service" from a garage at 331 Pinner Road, Harrow. Their rolling stock consisted in 1924 of four Crossleys (ME 4953/9478, MH 1852 & OE 5780), some with twelve and some with fourteen seats, and all probably rebodied ex-War Department machines. They had an office at 208 Pinner Road, not far from their garage. A & W were lucky in being situated in an area where passenger traffic was steadily growing, and on Wednesday, January 23rd 1925 a second service was inaugurated. This ran from St. Anne's Road in Harrow to Hatch End every hour between 11.00 a.m. and 8.00 p.m., with an extra journey at 9.00 p.m. on Saturdays. The two A & W services were subsequently numbered at 140A (Pinner to Wealdstone) and 351 (Hatch End to Harrow Met. Station). In July 1927 both ran hourly from approximately 10.40 a.m. (2.35 p.m. Sundays) until 8.0 p.m. in the evening using one bus each. From 8.0 p.m. the vehicle from the 351 joined the other to provide a half-hourly service on the 140A until the close of traffic at about 11.0 p.m. A 1929 attempt to link Hatch End with North Harrow Station was thwarted by overhanging trees in Headstone Lane, but was approved in January 1930 as 353 (North Harrow Station to Pinner, Red Lion). It is thought that for a while in the period 1925-6, A & W ran a Saturday service between Watford and Rickmansworth.

Between 1926 and 1929 the dainty little Crossleys, with their spindly wire-spoked wheels, departed from the fleet as four larger vehicles arrived. Three—MK 6400, MP 5344 and MY 8142—were new Guy single-deckers; the fourth was the company's only double-decker, MH 1326, a Daimler 'Y' which had previously been used by H.F.B. Ltd. of Palmers Green. This was bought by A & W in September 1926 and could be found on the 140A when the weather was dry. It was sold some time in 1929.

On August 11th 1927 the A & W Omnibus Co. Ltd. was incorporated with a share capital of £200 and its office at 208 Pinner Road, Harrow. At the same time the bus service was unsuccessfully offered for sale as A & W wished to concentrate on other more lucrative activities which they had built up; coaching and furniture removals. Birch was among the operators approached as being a potential buyer, but they declined because the business was too small and too far away. The limited company stayed dormant for the remainder of 1927 but under an agreement of March 22nd 1928 it took over from Albert Vincent Ashley (Westwood having departed previously) the contracts, licences, insurances, stock in trade, petrol pump and three buses for £1,500 13s. 11d. comprised of 98 full paid shares and the remainder in cash. The three directors and shareholders of the new company were A. V. Ashley, Francis John McEwen—described as a motor engineer of 208 Pinner Road and Louis James Ashley, a Fulham engineer. A. V. Ashley and McEwen worked full time in the business, of which Ashley was Managing Director. The directors still wished to dispose of the bus services and in 1930 they were successful in negotiating the sale of them to the LGOC for £7,000. On Monday morning, June 2nd, the purchase was completed and the three Guys used on the bus services were transferred that same day to their new owner's Harrow Weald (HD) garage whence they worked for only a fortnight before being replaced by standard vehicles.

L. J. Ashley's interest in the business passed to A. V. Ashley in December 1936. After the death of the founder of the company, A. V. Ashley, on June 22nd 1937 his majority shareholding passed to Miss Phyllis McEwen. The McEwen's both went away in the war, Francis as an army officer and Phyllis as an LACW in the W.A.A.F., and in May 1946 the business was sold to C. B. Richardson and C. A. Thompson who, in March 1949, increased the authorised share capital from £200 to £25,000. A Receiver & Manager was appointed as a result of a winding-up order made by Mr. Justice Wynn-Parry on January 29th 1951 and the A & W Omnibus Co. Ltd. was deleted from the Register on February 10th 1959. Freehold property which it had latterly held at North Orbital Road, Maple Cross, passed in March 1951 to Valliant Direct Coaches Ltd., who also took over its excursions and tours licences. The old A & W garage site in Pinner Road, Harrow, now houses the modern coach garage of Venture Transport (Hendon) Ltd.

Station Approach, Pinner

THE PINNER BUS

Mrs. Winifred M. Winter was the proprietress of Winter's Taxi Service of Station Approach, Pinner. She lived in Vine Cottage in Marsh Road from whose back door she could step straight into the yard adjacent to Station Approach where her taxis were kept and petrol pumps and makeshift workshops were situated. Her cottage still survives, heavily disguised at the front but unaltered at the rear where the words Vine Cottage etched over the doorway serve as a reminder of the days long ago when Mrs. Winter lived there.

In 1929 she began negotiations with the police for their approval of a new service from Pinner via Pinner Hill to terminate in the front garden of the Pinner Wood golf course, the drive of which was to be the turning loop. The service was designed to serve the Pinner Hill estate and was on private roads from the junction of Pinner Hill with Potter Street to the golf club terminus. After an initial rejection, the police gave their agreement in October 1929, stipulating the Pinner terminus as the Red Lion and not the station as Mrs. Winter had originally intended. An 18-seater Bean was ordered from Birch who supplied MY 3496 in March 1930. It bore the title "The Pinner Bus". Coincidentally Mrs. Winter's service and that run by Henry Turner from Barnes both terminated on private property at golf-club houses and were both worked by Birch-bodied Beans. The Pinner Bean is of particular interest because, only a month before the London-type Birch body was placed on the chassis in March 1930, it had been fitted with a new Willowbrook body to the order of Bean Cars Ltd. The reason why this body was removed so soon, and its subsequent fate, is not known.

Mrs. Winter appears not to have been a true independent operator in the same sense as the others described in this book. Though she initiated the service and was responsible for ordering the vehicle and operating it, she seems to have done so as an agent of the LGOC. The latter allocated to the Bean an official LGOC body number (11104) when new though it was not included in their stock list, and they supplied Mrs. Winter with a replacement in the form of Dennis Dart DA2 from May 19th to 29th when the Bean was off the road. Mrs. Winter ran the service (which was numbered 208) only from March 28th up to September 10th 1930 after which General took it over themselves, operating it from Harrow Weald (HD) garage. The Bean continued to run on the 208 only until January 1931 after which it was transferred to the Morden Station Garage Ltd., an Underground-group company. The 208 was worked by a standard Dennis Dart thereafter.

84 Church Road, Hendon

BURLINGTON

As we shall see later in connection with the Western Omnibus Co. Ltd., two of its principals, S. E. Wootton and J. H. T. Holt, left at an early stage to form the Burlington Omnibus Co. Ltd. Registered on August 14th 1924 with nominal capital of £3,000, of which only £1,225 was issued, Burlington was owned and controlled by eight men who were all permanent directors subject to holding a minimum of 150 shares each. They were also the drivers and conductors of its two buses. In addition to the aforementioned Wootton and Holt, the board of directors consisted of Edward Coleman, Sidney Squires, Frederick Adams, Edwin Holt, Ernest Victor Faulks and Charles Bernard Faulks. With the exception of C. B. Faulks all lived in the Hendon area, conveniently placed for the Hendon Car Service Depot Ltd. at 84 Church Road, Hendon, where the buses were garaged. An Odeon cinema stands on the site nowadays.

Prior to the formation of the company a pair of new chocolate & white Dennises were ordered from Dodson. They duly materialised as MH 550/1 and were licensed on August 29th 1924. In time they settled down to a regular pattern of operation on routes 13C, 60D, 273A and 279B. J. H. T. Holt was the managing force behind the company and in August 1926 its registered office was changed from 20 Elms Avenue, Hendon—E. V. Faulks' address—to Holt's home at "Burlington", Garrick Road, West Hendon.

Burlington led an uneventful existence. It wished to expand and applied in 1926 for various new weekday services which were largely over unrestricted roads and which, if granted, would have provided useful new links particularly in Hampstead. The area around Hampstead High Street was completely unserved by buses (and remained so until the nineteen-sixties) and each route proposed by Burlington envisaged serving this area. The new routes sought, in order of application (and refusal) were:-

Hendon (Stag), The Hyde, The Burroughs, Brent Street, Golders Green, Hampstead, Haverstock Hill, Camden Town Station.
Hampstead High Street, Haverstock Hill, Great Portland Street, Goodge Street, Strand (Aldwych).
Hendon (Stag), The Hyde, Vivian Avenue, Queens Road, Golders Green, Hampstead, Haverstock Hill, Camden Town Station.
Hendon (Stag), Cricklewood, Kilburn High Road, Maida Vale, St. Johns Wood, Camden Town, Haverstock Hill, Hampstead High Street.

With its expansion blocked, the company decided to sell to Public, who took over on October 14th 1927 for the sum of £5,600. E. V. Faulks had meanwhile resigned from the Company in the previous month. On November 8th 1927 a meeting was held at "Burlington" at which it was decided to put the company into voluntary liquidation and it was finally wound up on December 5th 1928.

Before the buses were sold J. H. T. Holt had bought a Morris coach ML 4158 which he operated on his own account from May 1927. It was joined by a GMC, MP 3704, in April 1928. In the summer of that same year he commenced a daily express service between London and Manchester via Birmingham, Wolverhampton and Newcastle-under-Lyme. One journey a day was operated in each direction and the coaches were housed at the Chandos Garage in High Street, Edgware. Two new Gilfords, MT 1143/1664, arrived subsequently. Holt's service, which should not be confused with Holt Brothers' Yelloway Coaches, which ran via Manchester en route from London to Blackpool, continued to operate throughout most of 1929 but had ceased by the end of 1930. Competition on the Manchester run—there were six other services besides Holt's—may have proved too much for him.

Victoria Yard, Boundary Road, St. John's Wood

Boundary Road, St. John's Wood, was where the BB Motor Works had their premises in what was then known as the Victoria Yard. Arthur Bell Hewitt and William George Ball ran the BB business and had built up quite an extensive trade in motor engineering and garaging. The Victoria Yard lay behind the houses on the south side of Boundary Road and was reached by a narrow approach road next to the Victoria public house. From 1923 to 1927 the works housed buses from a number of independent fleets to whom BB supplied the usual facilities such as petrol, oil, cleaning and a breakdown service; they also undertook the annual overhaul of many of their tenants' buses.

Victoria Yard had previously been connected with the bus industry, albeit in horse bus days. For half a century, from 1859 to 1909, it had been used by the LGOC as a large horsebus depot. When the BB Motor Works vacated it in 1928 the London & Parisien Motor Company moved in. They were succeeded by the Standard Motor Co. Ltd. who used it as a service station until the present occupiers, Goodlass Wall, the Valspar paint makers, took over.

The first buses to operate from Victoria Yard were the light green Rapids owned by Passenger Transport Ltd. However, as their sojourn at Victoria Yard was short lived they are dealt with elsewhere. The Western, Paragon and Orange buses all remained for longer periods.

WESTERN

Western was the title chosen by a group of twelve LGOC busmen from Hammersmith (R) garage when they decided to go into buswork on their own account. They were led by Percy William Coe, a driver. The others were drivers Edward French, William Henry Glanville, Arthur Hignell, John Holloway and Frederick Reuben James together with conductors

Ernest Frederick Bye, John Henry Thomas Holt, Joseph Edward Insra, James Wallace Loin, Lewis Henry Midwinter and Samuel Edmund Wootton. They appointed Hammersmith accountant Ralph Augustus Slipper of 33A The Broadway to be their business manager and adviser.

The Western Omnibus Company's first bus was a chocolate & white Dodson-bodied Straker Squire which was licensed on April 30th 1923 as XN 6661. Its first appearance at Scotland Yard on April 13th (prior to its being licensed) was unsuccessful and it was eventually approved by the police on May 3rd. When it entered service its early operations ranged far and wide judging by the large number of route approvals which were asked for.

Coe arranged with Hewitt to garage the Western buses at the BB Motor Works. The original Straker was soon joined by two more, XO 939 and XO 2107, which once again were fitted with Dodson bodywork. The first was licensed on June 1st 1923 and the other on June 9th, by which time the Western Omnibus Co. Ltd. had come into being. The limited company was incorporated on June 5th with a nominal capital of £2,000 and registered office at 33A The Broadway, Hammersmith. The assets were absorbed into the limited company on July 9th. All the original partners became shareholders and further capital was obtained from Arthur Bell Hewitt, R. A. Slipper and others. Hewitt was appointed Managing Director and in effect took charge of the day to day control of the undertaking though most of the clerical work was undertaken by Ralph Slipper who sent one of his clerks daily from Hammersmith to Boundary Road to deal with the tickets and waybills, etc. Everything appertaining to the vehicles, including repairs and licensing, was completely in the hands of Hewitt who kept all the registration books at Boundary Road. Hewitt's colleagues on the board of directors were Coe, Glanville and Hignell.

No further new buses were ordered in 1923 although the directors gave a good deal of thought to the matter. An alternative make to Straker Squire was sought for future vehicles, and in January 1924 reconditioned Daimlers were inspected at Roberts' works in Shepherds Bush. The choice finally fell on Dennises, of which four subsequently joined the fleet. The first three, XT 110/4731/8982, were delivered in April, May and June respectively and had Wilton-built bodies. YM 8237 followed in February 1926 and was bodied by Dodson.

Two of the original members of the company, J. H. T. Holt and S. E. Wootton, left during 1924 to start the Burlington buses. Others of the ex-LGOC staff left in March 1926, just before the Western business was sold out to the LGOC, probably because they were fearful of their future back with the combine. Of the originals Bye, Coe, French, Hignell and Midwinter remained to be taken back as drivers and conductors by the General. The last morning of operation by Western as an independent concern was Monday, March 8th 1926. The contract of sale was signed during the day and when the buses ran in at night the company was LGOC property. The Western staff at the end comprised ten drivers, thirteen conductors, two composite men, three fitters, three washers, three electricians and a clerk. At the time only six buses were available for work as one Dennis chassis was being overhauled at Boundary Road and its body was away at Dodson's.

The Western fleet continued to run from Boundary Road until April 27th 1926. The next day the buses were transferred into the General's Cricklewood (W) garage. At this time the six scheduled weekday operations were on routes 60F and 247D with morning peak journeys on 279B. Earlier there had also been morning peak runs on 521C which was in effect a northwards extension from North Finchley to Hadley Highstone of the 279B. In February 1927 these were renumbered 279E and shortly afterwards they were omitted from the schedule altogether. Sunday work was almost entirely on the 247. Back in September 1925, when still independent, Western had proposed operating on the 526D on Sundays but the plan was abandoned after the West London Association, representing the established operators on the route, made clear its opposition.

In October 1926 the Dodson bodies were removed from two of the Straker Squires (XO 939/2107) to provide an overhaul float for the LGOC's acquired Dennises, and their places were taken by overhauled ex-Cambrian bodies as a result of which, for the first time, Western found itself with Strakers fitted with the chassis manufacturer's standard body.

Between December 1926 and April 1927 the original Western buses were replaced by K-types, the Straker Squires being disposed of and the Dennises transferred to the Redburn fleet. The Company's assets were absorbed into the LGOC on January 1st 1928.

PARAGON

The next bus operator to follow Western into the Victoria Yard was Edward Flower who became, in June 1923, the owner of a dark green Straker Squire registered MF 419 and called the Paragon. Flower lived at 21 Burton Road, Brondesbury, and was the proprietor of a garage and taxi business based at 3, 21 and 23 Bristol Mews, Warwick Avenue. His first bus was to be found on routes 8, 16, 18, 33, 37 and 51 at least, before settling down on the 247. By March 1924 its green livery had been replaced by red. A second bus, XW 8201, was purchased in January 1925 and was a red, Dodson-bodied Dennis for which a schedule was obtained on the 526D where its method of operation sometimes caused consternation amongst other memebers of the West London Association who at one time seriously considered asking Flower to transfer his bus to another route. It was joined in the Paragon fleet in June 1926 by an identical bus, YO 8528, which ousted the Straker Squire whose bus career came to an end after a short life of only three years.

A limited company was incorporated under the title E. Flower & Son Ltd. on November 2nd 1926 with a capital of £1,000 and registered office at 3 Bristol Mews. The shareholders were Edward Flower, his wife Emma, and his son who was also called Edward and was actively engaged in the running of the buses. On August 26th 1927 an offer from Public to purchase the bus side of the business for £6,000 was accepted, and the two Dennises passed to their new owner on that date.

216

THE ORANGE SERVICE

In May 1927 the LGOC took over one of the more dynamic of the independent bus concerns. This was The Orange Service of twelve buses run by George Barton Haywood and Gerald Nowell. The co-founders of the Orange business were both young ex-public schoolboys who met while working in the City of London for Lever Brothers. Haywood, who was 28, had been top in maths at Sutton Valence School. He worked for Lloyds Bank and later joined the army from which he was invalided out with the rank of captain. Nowell, 25, had been educated at St. Paul's School, Hammersmith. He was a lorry driver in the RASC, and was later in the RNVR. After a spell in the Foreign Office he joined Lever Brothers' advertising department, in which he worked for a while in Africa. They first ventured into business together in August 1923 by obtaining a licence to deal in cigarettes and tobacco. A fairly substantial trade was built-up in the sale of hand made cigarettes and the partners' customers included, amongst many others, members of Nowell's family in Brighton, one of whom owned the Gem Cafe in Preston Street. It is a far cry from selling tobacco to running buses, but Haywood and Nowell were convinced that the two trades could be carried on successfully side by side, and went on to prove they were right. They ventured into the bus business with the purchase of a new Leyland, XP 4355, which was licensed on November 1st 1923 having been passed by the police the previous day. It entered service on a single shift on November 1st, and soon The Orange Service bus became a regular feature of the London scene, often with Haywood at the wheel and with both partners taking turns at collecting in the fares.

Arthur Bell Hewitt agreed that the Orange bus could be housed at the BB Motor Works and it ran from there on to a variety of routes, most of which were favourites with the independents such as 2, 3, 8, 17, 27 and 76. At the beginning of 1924 the garage was changed to Samuelsons in Page Street as S. H. Hole was charging £2 15s. 0d. a week for garaging and cleaning compared with the £3 0s. 0d. required by Hewitt. When Hewitt reduced his terms at the beginning of October 1924 Haywood & Nowell moved back to Boundary Road. Soon there was enough money in the kitty to buy a second bus and in February 1924 XR 4129, another Leyland, was delivered ready to be licensed on the first of the next month. During 1924 the scope of routes operated was widened to include 11, 15, 16 and 18. The partners continued to work on the buses themselves until they could afford to employ other men. They finally gave up to concentrate on general management when their third vehicle was purchased in September 1924.

XU 8727 was a Dennis, and so was XW 473 which followed it less than a month later. The choice of chassis was probably influenced by the fact that Dennis were then asking £150 less per vehicle than Leyland. June 1925 saw the delivery of bus no. 5, YK 3657 which marked a return to Leyland. All five chassis in the fleet bore identical bodies by Dodson, from whom the buses had been bought on hire purchase. Weekday operations had now become stabilised on the 15, 27 and 76.

In addition to the buses and the tobacco business, Haywood & Nowell had their fingers in other pies at this stage. They advertised cars for hire, were agents for the Royal Insurance Co. Ltd. and others, supplied motor accessories and tyres, and were agents for the "Empire" automatic petrol economiser, a gadget made by the New Motor Speciality Co. Ltd. Their trading address was 119 Alexandra Road, St. John's Wood, Haywood's home.

The business was incorporated as a limited company under the title of Haywood & Nowell Ltd. on July 31st 1925, with a nominal capital of £4,000 and registered office at the Victoria Yard, Boundary Road. Haywood and Nowell were the first directors and they allotted themselves 1,750 £1 shares each. The limited company took over operation of the buses on August 31st, and on October 25th a man named Thomas Ernest Huntley was appointed to run the business and given the title Managing Director, although his shareholding was purely nominal.

In January 1926 buses 6 and 7 were ordered from Dodson's, and in the following month nos. 8 and 9 were also contracted for. All were on hire purchase, the terms being a deposit of £100 per bus on or before delivery followed by twenty-three equal monthly instalments. Unlike their forerunners the new buses were pneumatic-tyred single-deckers with chassis by Dennis. They were intended for new route 550. Fresh capital was required for this dramatic expansion of the business from five to nine buses and this was provided by Arthur Bell Hewitt, who took a major shareholding in the business and also became a director. Debentures were also issued, the holders being Haywood and Christopher Dodson.

The single-deckers ordered in January and February 1926 were quickly delivered. YM 5154/5 came during the same month in which they had been ordered and YM 9971/2 arrived at the beginning of March. They were normal control 25-seaters which proved to be reasonably reliable buses although faulty metal in the con-rods caused early troubles and the fan drive soon had to be converted from flat to whittle belting. These buses introduced a new colour scheme to the fleet. Instead of the attractive orange & white livery used hitherto they bore an even more striking combination of orange & black. Their owners must have been pleased with the result as they duly repainted their double-deckers orange & black also. In October 1926 a proposal to convert the Dennis double-deckers to pneumatic tyres was considered but rejected.

Two other operators arranged to run alongside the Orange fleet on route 550, each providing one vehicle apiece. YM 6965/6 were single-deckers identical to the Orange vehicles and were owned by A. J. R. Martin (Nulli Secundus) and the Farwell Omnibus Co. Ltd. (Dauntless) respectively. Both were licensed on February 1st 1926, but on March 25th they passed to Orange for the low sum of £170 each. Possibly their owners had not been impressed with route 550, which was slow to pick up at first. Both buses retained their red & white livery and original fleetnames until December 1926 (YM 6966) and April 1927 (YM 6965) when they were repainted in the standard orange & black colours.

The passenger takings on route 550 improved gradually, and from October 1926 season tickets were issued on it. But the route presented

218

other problems. The road surface was bad in places, especially in Leigh Road, causing damage to the buses. This was worsened because of speeding by the drivers due, probably, to a rather tight schedule. On the double-decker services, notably the 27/127 group, the Sunday operations were worrying due to low receipts and at one stage in the Autumn of 1926 fare reductions of up to 50% were considered. Luckily things improved and the reductions did not need to be implemented.

October 1926 saw the appointment of E. V. Faulks, formerly of the Burlington, as General Manager. In the same month the Company ordered from Dodson its last new bus, a pneumatic-tyred Dennis E-type. This 30-seater entered service towards the end of November and was the largest single-decker operated by Orange. One more new vehicle remained to be purchased; YE 1229. This was a Morris 8-cwt. van which was bought in December 1926 for £162. It had a Dodson-built body which looked very smart in a dark blue livery with the words "The Orange Service" on the sides. It replaced an old Belsize van, which had latterly been costing a lot in repairs. Apart from the arrival of the new van, December 1926 was a bleak month for the company as police stops were placed on no fewer than six out of the twelve strong fleet, and nos. 2, 4, 7, 8, 9 and 11 had to be taken out of service for repair. The 550 must have been badly hit with the non-availability of four out of the seven single-deckers.

1927 was the last year of independent operation by Haywood & Nowell Ltd. By then workings had settled down to eleven scheduled weekday operations, leaving one bus as a spare. On weekdays the double-deckers worked 15C/D, 27A, 76 and 522A (Saturdays only) and the single deckers worked principally on the 550 but also ran journeys on 6A (Saturdays), 15C and 60E. Sunday operations were usually on 127.

At a meeting at 55 Broadway on May 16th 1927 the entire share capital of the company was purchased by the LGOC, and John Christopher Mitchell became secretary in place of Gerald Nowell. Haywood and Nowell were temporarily appointed joint managers to continue operations from the Victoria Yard for the time being on the LGOC's behalf. They continued to train, clothe and supervise their men and, apart from using LGOC tickets from about the end of May, there was little apparent evidence to show that the business had changed hands. This arrangement continued until July 4th when the LGOC took over the operations itself, dividing the buses between their Chalk Farm (CF) and Cricklewood (W) garages. All the single-deckers went to Chalk Farm and the double-deckers to Cricklewood. The LGOC soon decided to replace the single-deckers and the Leyland LB's with standard K type 46-seaters. During September and October ten K's in standard General livery were drafted in to operate the Orange services. When Haywood & Nowell Ltd. was finally absorbed into the LGOC on January 1st 1928 only the two Dennises survived out of the original fleet.

Following the LGOC takeover of the Orange operation Barton Haywood left the bus industry but the name of Gerald Nowell was soon to the forefront once again. He became Managing Director of the Great Western Express Co. Ltd. (incorporated on July 30th 1928) and

219

inaugurated an all-night express service from London to Newport, Monmouthshire, using three Dodson-bodied Tilling Stevens. The first journey of the "Welsh Midnight Express" was launched with a bottle of champagne by actress sisters Renee and Billie Houston. The service was later extended to Cardiff. By a deed of sale dated December 8th 1932 the Great Western business was sold to Red & White from midnight on June 30th 1932. Nowell became manager of the group's combined London undertakings, and was in the early post war years Director and General Manager of South Midland Motor Services Ltd. until he became General Manager of the ill-fated Hants & Sussex Motor Services Ltd. and its various associated companies in 1949.

39 Somerton Road, Cricklewood

The former Premier garage at Somerton Road, Cricklewood, has been noted in Chapter 5. Premier's office and garage from February 1923 to April 1925 were inside the Handley Page factory which nowadays forms the extensive Cricklewood Factory Estate.

54 Iverson Road, Kilburn

At 54 Iverson Road, Kilburn, is a small yard with high railway arches at the rear now used by a variety of motor firms. Early in 1924 a lease on these premises was taken by Passenger Transport Ltd. who ran the Rapid buses. From then onwards it became the base, not only for Rapid, but also for the Overington, Dolphin, Glandfield and Carlton Association buses. The last mentioned operator had already been described in chapter 4; the others now follow.

RAPID

The foundations for the Rapid buses were laid in 1922 when, on November 29th, a company was registered with the title Rapid Bus & Transport Co. Ltd. at Jessel Chambers, 88-90 Chancery Lane, W.C.2. Its principal objectives were stated to be to carry on a business as owners and proprietors of buses, cabs, cars, carriages, vans and charabancs. The owners were Eric Whitehead Harris, a motor engineer by trade, and Charles Geoffrey Dodd. Both worked full time in the business, which was centred mainly around the operation of charabancs. It was, alas, a financial failure and had ceased to trade by August 1925. By this time it had no assets and no funds and its creditors were paid by Harris and Dodd out of their own pockets.

The Rapid Bus & Transport Co. Ltd. never ran buses, although it was the intention to do so. Towards the end of 1922, or early in 1923 a new Leyland double-decker was ordered from Dodsons, and was duly delivered in an attractive light green & creamy-yellow livery and bearing the fleet-name Rapid. This Leyland, still unlicensed at this stage, was presented at Scotland Yard on March 13th 1923 for plating. Before entering service, however, it was taken over by a new company who first licensed it as XN 2910 on March 27th in the name of Passenger Transport Ltd.

The old Rapid Bus & Transport Co. Ltd. had been under-capitalised, and in order to make their entry into the competitive field of London bus operation possible Harris and Dodd needed fresh partners with money to put into the business. They found their salvation in the forms of John Zuberbuhler (of Swiss origin) and John Hankins, both directors of the prosperous Middlesex Autocar Co. Ltd. The new company entitled Passenger Transport Ltd. was registered on March 12th 1923—the day before the first Rapid bus went to Scotland Yard—with a nominal capital of initially £100 but later increased to £1,000. The registered office was at the Middlesex Autocar Company's headquarters, 19 Woodstock Street, W.1. A further motor car dealer who became financially interested in the business was Eustace Watkins, who took shares on behalf of himself and Eustace Watkins Ltd. and later became a director. A sixth director was Captain Roger John Tweedy, a director of Burton & Tweedy Ltd., yet another firm of motor car agents. There was no lack of potential capital here. Eric Harris was appointed Managing Director and retained this position throughout the Company's career.

Harris and Dodd were the only directors actively concerned with the day-to-day running of the buses, and they saw the fleet expand from the original bus of March 1923 to eight by September 1926. On April 11th 1923 it was announced that the first Rapid bus would shortly be working on route 13 (Hendon "Bell" to London Bridge). Its exact first date of operation is not known but six days later, on April 17th, it was observed on parts of routes 2, 13, 9 and 33 according to where the heavy traffic was. Other routes which later attracted the attentions of Harris and Dodd included the 11, 12 and 25 before the company finally settled down on route 14. At its maximum in 1926/7 Passenger Transport Ltd. held eight weekday licences on this route.

There was a lull of five months between the delivery of XN 2910 and the arrival of further new buses. These materialised as XP 37 and XP 390 (licensed August 1923), XP 6211 (November 1923), XP 7074/5 (December 1923), XW 2215 (November 1924) and YR 172 (September 1926). Fleet numbers ran from 2 to 8 respectively and the buses normally operated on route 14 in chronological order of their fleet numbers. All were Dodson-bodied Leylands and all except the last one perpetuated the light green livery. However by November 1925 (and possibly earlier) a start had been made in repainting the fleet red & white and YR 172 was delivered in this livery.

Only one bus remains to be described. This is XN 5203, a further Leyland/Dodson, which was bought third hand in February 1927 from the ailing Henslowe Bus Company Ltd. They had acquired it from R. S. Connacher who had bought it new in April 1923 as the Waverley. For a very short while the Rapid fleet totalled nine, but it was very soon reduced back to eight when YR 172 was sold on March 1st to Commonwealth. The reasons for the disposal of this newest member of the fleet, or for the acquisition of a much-travelled bus three years its senior are not known. XN 5203 adopted the fleet number 8 vacated by YR 172. In addition to the buses a number of coaches were operated during this period, but details of most of them have not yet come to light.

The three earliest Rapid buses were first garaged at the Victoria Yard, Boundary Road. The firm did not settle there permanently for by March 21st 1924 it had obtained the lease on 54 Iverson Road. The Company also ran a garage at Kingston, the site of which the authors have been unable to locate. These latter premises were probably used more for the Company's coaching activities than for the buses although Kingston was a fairly useful base from which to supply buses to the southern end of route 14.

In June 1927 an offer to purchase the business on behalf of the proposed London Public Omnibus Co. Ltd. was accepted and the buses came under A. T. Bennett's control from the 25th of that month although ownership was not transferred until July 29th by which time the Public had officially come into being. Along with the buses there passed to Public the Iverson Road and Kingston garages and also a Sunbeam car and a Crossley light tender which had been used in connection with the business. Very considerable stocks of Leyland spare parts were also taken over. The money paid by Public was in the region of £26,000, part of which went to satisfy debentures of £9,000 which had been used to finance the development of the company and the purchase of premises. Passenger Transport Ltd. was formally wound up on December 16th 1927. Iverson Road was used by Public for just under a year, and later became the London base for the large fleet of coaches operated by Highways Limited.

OVERINGTON
DOLPHIN

The Overington and Dolphin buses both started their working lives in the Barnsdale Yard. The Overington was the first to enter service. Alfred Overington, a motor engineer of 57 Seymour Place, W.1., bought a new Strachan & Brown-bodied Dennis XU 3752 which he licensed and presented at Scotland Yard on July 25th 1924. Prospects seemed favourable and to raise money for the purchase of further buses, a limited company was formed on 21st October 1924 named Overington Ltd. with a nominal and fully issued share capital of £4,000. Alfred Overington and a fellow motor agent, Geoffrey Caithness, put up £1,500; the remainder was supplied by Eden Gawne, Bertram Watney and Philip Wentzell, Watney being the firm's largest shareholder with 1,500. The three last mentioned were directors but did not otherwise take an active part in the firm. They were distillers by profession. Overington was Managing Director and attended to the day-to-day running of the business.

The additional capital provided by Caithness and the trio of distillers enabled the company to operate two additional buses which Overington had previously ordered and which were delivered from the coachbuilders in October 1924, a matter of days before the limited company was formed. XW 287/758 were identical to XU 3752. With the London Traffic Act the Overington operations were stabilised from early 1925 onwards on the 247 whereas previously his buses had ranged far and wide including LGOC routes 6, 11, 14, 17, 18, 36 and 73.

In January 1925 the Overington buses moved out of Barnsdale Yard into 54 Iverson Road and the Dolphin bus moved with them. This was owned by the brothers A. A. & H. Dolphin who, at the time, traded from 32 Crawford Place, Edgware Road but later moved to 4 Garlinge Road, Brondesbury. The senior partner was Albert Augustus Dolphin and he, late in 1925, arranged to sell their one and only bus to Overington. It was an identical Dennis to the Overingtons and ran in company with them on the 247. Registered XW 633, it was built in October 1924. An official agreement of sale was prepared on January 26th 1926. This transferred the Dolphin bus to the newly-formed Dolphin Omnibus Co. Ltd. of which Overington, Caithness and Watney were the shareholders and Overington was Managing Director. The limited company had been registered on January 22nd and had a nominal capital of £2,000 of which £1,702 was paid-up. The Dolphin brothers continued to run the bus until March 2nd 1926 but the operation was deemed to be on behalf of the new company as from the previous January 1st.

On 22nd July 1926 Messrs. Caithness, Watney, Wentzell and Gawne parted company from Overington and sold their share in the bus businesses to him and his accountant, Sydney Jeffreys, with the exception of 250 shares in Overington Ltd. which were taken by Eric Whitehead Harris, one of the owners of the Rapid buses. At the same time the registered office of both Companies was transferred from 65 Great Portland St., W.1. to 57 Seymour Place, W.1., Harris becoming secretary of them.

A further bus was added to the Overington fleet in November 1926 in the form of a year-old Dennis. YM 1060 differed from the other buses in the combined fleets in having a Dodson rather than Strachan & Brown body. It came from the Carlton Association fleet of A. E. Ewen who had replaced it with a new vehicle of identical type. In due course Alfred Overington received an offer from Public to purchase the two businesses for a total of £18,000, and this was accepted. The transfer of the assets to Public was made on September 29th 1927 and the two companies were wound-up on June 15th of the following year.

The sale of the London bus businesses did not mean that the transport world had seen the last of Alfred Overington and Eric Harris. They realised the potential that lay in the development of express coach services and joined forces to form, on January 2nd 1928, the new firm of Overington, Harris & Ash Ltd. in which they were joined by C. C. Ash. The better known title of Highways Ltd. was adopted in November 1928. From an initial daily London-Yeovil-Plymouth service using six-wheeler Thurgood-bodied Lafflys, an extensive network of services was developed to destinations such as Ilfracombe, Newquay and Bournemouth. A frequent London-Windsor service was also operated at one stage. Despite its growth Highways Ltd. did not prosper financially, and its impecunious position led to the appointment of a Receiver who placed the business under the control of Southern & Western National in August 1933 in anticipation of its sale to Tilling.

223

GLANDFIELD

Glandfield was a one-bus business conducted from March 1925 onwards by Frank Murray Sherriff of 1A Ashburnham Road, Kensal Rise. Sherriff conducted the business in every sense of the word, for he was not only the proprietor but also the man on the back of the bus collecting in the fares. He purchased a red Dennis from Strachan & Brown, which was first licensed on March 26th. He arranged for it to be operated from 54 Iverson Road, and it ran uneventfully on the 526D as part of the West London Association. The business was operated as a limited company from April 5th 1927 when the Glandfield Omnibus Co. Ltd. was incorporated with Frank Sherriff and his wife Doris as the sole directors. They also held the entire authorised share capital of £500.

At an unknown date, but certainly by February 1927, the Glandfield bus had begun to operate from the Barnsdale Yard, and it was this address that became the registered office of the limited company. The bus was sold to Public on August 19th 1927 for £3,000 and Sherriff moved to 3 The Valley Green, Welwyn Garden City, Hertfordshire. The Glandfield Omnibus Co. Ltd. continued in business as a coach operator with a daily express service between Welwyn Garden City and London using a fleet of two which were kept firstly at Paragon Garage, Harrow Road and later at Jenner Parson's Garage in Welwyn Garden City. UC 1268 was a TSM of January 1928 and UC 5539, a Gilford, was a month newer. This was sold in June 1928 to make way for YW 7713, another TSM. Operation ceased in about March 1929.

CHAPTER SEVEN

NORTH LONDON

Leighton Road, Kentish Town
Royal Mail Yard, Cathcart Street, Kentish Town
(also Fortess Garage, Fortess Grove, Kentish Town)

The segment of London which we, for the purpose of this book, have called North London was more heavily populated by independent bus proprietors than any other. The main concentrations were in the Wood Green and Hertford Road areas where housing development had gone on apace. These areas of dense population were unserved by underground railways and were dependent heavily on trams which proved a natural target for the independents.

In the south-west corner of our "North" area, at Kentish Town, were two independent garages. City's erstwhile garage in Leighton Road is now a Shaw & Kilburn depot entitled Carmo House; its history is outlined in the City story in chapter 2. Though a large and substantial building, it was historically of much less significance than the complex of properties in Cathcart Street and in adjacent Holmes Road owned by the famous family firm of Birch Brothers Ltd.

ARCHWAY/BIRCH

On February 1st 1971 Grey Green Coaches Ltd. took over nine coaches from Birch. This in itself would seem an insignificant event if it were not for the fact that it brought to an end a connection between the Birch family and the passenger transport business which had lasted for almost two centuries. Of all the London independent bus operators of the nineteen-twenties and thirties Birch was the indisputable doyen for they alone could boast that their ancestors were running bus services in London before the LGOC was even thought of. Fortunately for us the various generations of Birch's maintained records of their business activities from which their history can be written in a fair degree of detail. Indeed the Birch story has been published in one form or another on a number of occasions in the last half century and for this reason much of the material recorded here is not "new". It is, however, placed on record once again for completeness and augmented by hitherto unpublished facts, to produce one of the most interesting stories of a single family's endeavour in the field of road transport.

In the last quarter of the eighteenth century the Birch's were a family of farmers at Stoke Damerel, Plymouth but William Birch, in addition to farming, was operating in about 1790 a stage coach service between Plymouth and Exeter. In about 1810 his son, also William, left the West Country to set up as a dairy farmer in Pimlico which was then still a patchwork of fields on the fringe of London. In 1815 he took a lease on premises in Horseferry Road which he subsequently bought and which later became the base for the family's transport interests. A third generation William Birch began to run cabs from these premises in 1832 at the early age of twenty and within a few years had expanded to a fleet about thirty strong. He died at a tragically early age two days after being

225

thrown from a gig on April 13th 1846 but his wife, an able businesswoman, carried on the family's cab interests after his death. In 1847 she joined with a trio of other cab proprietors, Messrs. Gamble, Hattersley and Langley, in the promotion of a new horse-bus service from Pimlico to Mansion House operated under the auspices of the Westminster Omnibus Association from which the four subscribers each received an equal share of the profits. In 1851 Mrs. Birch purchased four buses which she commenced to run on her own account. Two were placed on the Mansion House route on May 1st in the same chocolate livery as the Association buses; the other two were used to serve the Great Exhibition at Hyde Park. So enormous were the crowds visiting the Exhibition that the single-deck horse buses were quite unable to cope. As a result the famous knifeboard double-decker was evolved through the addition of a plank of wood to act as a seat along the centre of the roof.

The late William Birch's sons joined the business to help their mother run the new horse buses. John Manley Birch was 14 years old at the time and his brother William Samuel was 12. At the close of the Exhibition the two buses serving it were placed on the Mansion House route and, round about this time, Hattersley's interest in the Association came into the ownership of Mrs. Birch who now held a half share in it. The other half share passed to the LGOC in 1857 and a pooling and sharing agreement was instituted which lasted until 1909 when the Association was dissolved. In about 1865 a new bus service was commenced between Hanwell and London Bridge. Hanwell was chosen as the terminus as this was where Mrs. Birch now lived, and a new depot was built there for the buses. The 1850's and 60's were a period of great expansion in the cab as well as the bus business, and coachbuilding was added to the list of activities in this period. Mrs. Birch died in 1874 and her two sons were left to carry on in partnership. The sons discontinued the Hanwell service in 1876, unable any longer to counter the competition of the horse trams along the Uxbridge Road.

1878 was a big year of change for the Birch's. John and William dissolved their partnership and sold their times in the Westminster Omnibus Association. John purchased times in the Camden Town Omnibus Association plying between Chalk Farm Road (Adelaide Tavern), Camden Town, Russell Square and Charing Cross and acquired as his base freehold premises next door to the LGOC's depot in Cathcart Street, Kentish Town. William stayed on at Horseferry Road and joined the Atlas & Waterloo Omnibus Association whose lengthy route linked North Finchley, Childs Hill and Oxford Street. In 1885 he was joined by his son William Henry and renamed his business Birch & Son. In 1887 John Birch secured a contract for the night carriage of mails and parcels from London to Brighton and followed this with several other mail contracts. The Cathcart Street premises became known as Royal Mail Yard, and this title lasted right to the very end. In 1898 William Henry Birch branched out with a service of his own and for a short while there were three Birch concerns running horse buses in London.

In 1899 the brothers John and William joined forces again and on November 1st 1899 Birch Bros. Ltd. was incorporated with a share capital which eventually stood at £80,000, all fully issued and mostly held by members of the Birch family. In 1904 the company's first two motor buses were put into service. They were Milnes Daimlers and were forerunners of eleven buses of this make bought by Birch up to 1907. Three De Dions and two Crossley-Leylands were also purchased making the grand total of motor buses owned sixteen. In placing the original two Milnes Daimlers in service in 1904 Birch were amongst the pioneers of motor buses in London, but their pioneering spirit almost proved to be their downfall. Motor vehicles were in a very early stage of development and highly unreliable; furthermore mechanics and drivers experienced in handling them were in very short supply. Buses tended to spend as much time off the road as they did on it as, for instance, on February 19th 1907 when only six were running out of a fleet which then stood at fourteen. The Birch's were not alone amongst the smaller horse bus proprietors in experimenting with motor buses and they suffered the same fate as those who pioneered with them; heavy pecuniary loss. They had no alternative but to withdraw the motor buses. Of the eleven still remaining operational, nine last ran on November 2nd 1907 and the last two were withdrawn at the end of the day's operation on November 30th 1907. These were working on a Golders Green-Hendon (The Bell) service which ran under a railway contract, and were replaced on it by horse buses the next day. Birch also put up for sale the Finchley depot from which the motor buses had operated. Thereafter they maintained their horse bus services, although these were doomed by competition from electric trams as well as from motor buses as these became more reliable. The old omnibus associations crumbled, those on which Birch worked closing down in 1908. Birch's last horse buses ran on July 27th 1912 after which the Company concentrated its efforts on its taxicabs, mail contracts and coachbuilding. In that same year a contract was obtained for the maintenance of the bodies on the B.A.T. fleet operating in London and many new bus bodies were built in the Holmes Road bodyshops during the ensuing years for the B.A.T.'s provincial subsidiaries. The company's first motorised cab, Unic LA 5541, had been passed by the police on April 17th 1911 and this side of the business was steadily built up. Large numbers of lorry bodies were manufactured during the war on Locomobile, Pierce Arrow, Peerless and Saurer chassis for the Admiralty and War Department and a large contract was received from the LGOC for lorry bodies on Daimler chassis.

In March 1910 William Henry Birch joined his father and uncle and was appointed a director of the Company, having retired from his own horse bus business in the previous year. He became Managing Director in 1917 and was Chairman from 1936 to October 1949. Also in 1910 the Company enlarged its property interests in Cathcart Street with the purchase of the LGOC buildings which adjoined its own.

By 1919 Birch had gained much experience of motor vehicle operation through its fleet of taxis and felt capable of progressing back to larger vehicles. A fleet of seven ex-War Department chassis was purchased and fitted out with new maroon & black charabanc bodies in the Birch workshops for operation on "See Britain" tours, a venture which proved financially successful. The seven vehicles, six Tilling Stevens and a Leyland, bore the 'IT' registration letters so familiar on London area

227

charabancs at that time. In 1923 another new generation of the Birch family joined the business in the person of Raymond William Birch who was appointed director and engineer. He had been trained as an engineer and qualified from University College, London, in the early 'twenties and in 1922 he went to Leyland Motors' factory at Ham to gain practical experience prior to joining the family concern. By 1924 the Company felt the time was ripe to achieve its great ambition to re-enter the London bus business.

In September 1924 a contract was placed with Leyland for the supply of ten LB-type chassis. At the same time reconstruction commenced at the Cathcart Street premises to convert them into a modern motor bus garage, at a cost of about £2,300. Shortly afterwards the coachworks made a start on building the bodies for the ten chassis. Bearing in mind the sixty years of co-ordinated working with the LGOC during horse bus days, the Company approached the LGOC to enquire the possibility of working its ten buses in association with them either on an existing or on a new route. The LGOC, through its Managing Director, Frank Pick, rejected the proposal outright, leaving Birch with no alternative but to work in competition. Birch had meanwhile been approached by W. J. Dangerfield of the Overground with a view to working in co-ordination on four services for which both duly made identical applications. The services proposed were:

1. Potters Bar & Hampton Court
2. Hadley Highstone & Elephant & Castle
3. Muswell Hill & Victoria Station
4. Potters Bar & Victoria Station

Police approval was given on October 6th but Birch did not pursue the matter any further. In November they were approached by City who suggested they might join forces in a new Highgate-Brockley route via Oxford Circus and Victoria which was later to develop as the famous 536. The first chassis was received from Leyland on November 25th and the second soon afterwards. These first two Birch vehicles were completed in time to begin the Highgate-Brockley service on January 21st 1925 jointly with City and United.

Birch soon found themselves victims of the first retrospective Restricted Streets Order and, after making representation to the Minister which were initially unsuccessful, withdrew the two buses from the 536 and placed them on the 526 on April 11th along with three other new Leylands which had now been built. Thus began their connection with the famous West London Association service for which Birch prepared the schedules and provided the timekeepers. On June 18th the Minister informed Birch of his intention to make Amendment Regulations to the first Restricted Streets Order post-dating it from January 1st 1925 to February 17th. Birch were thus enabled to restore two vehicles to the 536 as they had been in service prior to February 17th; they returned to it on August 1st. The subsequent variations to routes 526 and 536 have been noted in chapters 1 and 2 respectively.

Birch took delivery of only six out of the ten Leylands ordered in the Autumn of 1924. This allowed for two to operate the 536, three the 526, and one spare. The London Traffic Act prevented further expansion on either of these services and as Birch had no plans at the time to diversify by opening new suburban operations on "unrestricted" roads, the balance of the order for ten was cancelled. The bus fleet was numbered in a series of its own, distinguishing it from the Birch taxis, which were classified C, and the coaches which were numbered from K1 upwards. B1/2 were in red & white livery when new and carried the fleetname Archway. B3/4/5 arrived in the same attractive colours as City and United (officially coffee, spanish brown & cream) as they were intended for the 536 and were plated-up for this service in March 1925 when brand new, though they subsequently started work on 526. B6 was red & white when built in line with other operators' vehicles on the 526. A seventh Leyland LB was received in 1927—the year in which Birch's last horses were sold—to enable the company's complement on the 536 to rise to three as a result of its extension in April to Elmers End over unrestricted roads. B7 arrived in brown livery and bore the fleetname "Birch", the old "Archway" name being discontinued. In 1928 the red & white vehicles on the 526 were repainted in City colours, which became the Birch standard, the West London Association having been abandoned with the demise of all the independents on it except for Birch.

In November 1926 Birch were approached by Robert Thackray with the offer to join him in applying for a new route from Pimlico to Hampstead Heath as outlined in chapter 5. At this time Birch were eager to extend their bus activities by pioneering completely new services and they agreed to join forces with Thackray in the new venture which unfortunately was rejected by the Commissioner of Police. This marked the start of a long struggle by Birch to establish new operations despite the thinly-veiled opposition of Authority to the independent operator; a struggle fraught with numerous set-backs from which Birch emerged only partially victorious. Between 1927 and 1929 efforts were made to get established in four distinct suburban areas. Each of these endeavours is of interest in showing the problems which the enterprising independent had to face when wishing to expand, and sometimes overcame.

Following upon the abortive joint attempt with Thackray, Birch proposed in March 1927 a Hampstead to Brook Green service via Bayswater in response to requests from the Paddington Borough Council, the Paddington & Bayswater Chamber of Commerce and local traders, notably Whiteleys Ltd., the large departmental store, for bus facilities between Maida Vale and Queens Road, Bayswater, following the withdrawal of LGOC route 74. The proposed route was later extended from Brook Green to Barnes at the suggestion of the Chamber of Commerce. It was duly turned down by the police because small sections were over restricted roads and in December 1927 Birch settled for a much modified service over roads which were not restricted linking Belsize Park with Kensal Rise. Because of overhanging trees and protrusions on lamp posts the service—which was numbered 203—was banned to double-deckers. The company wanted right from the start to extend the service from its badly placed terminal at Belsize Park to the natural traffic objective, the tram and bus terminus at South End Green, Hampstead Heath. From April 1928 onwards the Sunday service was extended to Hampstead Heath where it terminated at the Freemasons Arms in Downshire Hill and was renumbered 231. The extension was via Belsize Avenue, Haverstock Hill and Rosslyn Hill whence it looped through Pond Street, South End Green, South End Road and Downshire Hill back to Rosslyn Hill. South End Green was a restricted road which prevented a similar extension from taking place on weekdays. Undeterred, Birch sought dispensation for it in May 1928, offering to work it with no additional buses, thus giving a slightly wider headway over other parts of 231, some of which had now become restricted. The Minister's refusal came in June but in November he gave limited dispensation for a shorter extension to the Hampstead Town Hall in Haverstock Hill via Englands Lane and returning via Belsize Avenue. This was numbered 231A to bring the route number into line with the Sunday one. Birch still wished to extend daily to Hampstead Heath but meanwhile embarked on a scheme to extend westwards from Kensal Rise to serve the area beyond Chamberlayne Road. This was refused in December 1928 and so was a proposal to extend to the White Hart, Willesden in February 1930 though a Sunday service now ran to this point. In November 1930 the Sunday service to Hampstead was revised at the instigation of Hampstead Borough Council to run both ways via Pond Street and to terminate at South End Green thus avoiding the bad road surface in Downshire Hill. Towards the end of 1930 a scheme of co-ordination was agreed between Birch and the LGOC (of which more later) and following this the Minister agreed to the weekday extension of the route at both ends. Westwards it reached the Willesden Junction Hotel at Harlesden by way of Liddell Gardens, All Souls Avenue and Wrottesley Road and in the east it at last reached South End Green though operation was via Englands Lane and Haverstock Hill in both directions, Belsize Park Gardens and Avenue being omitted. Sunday operations were brought into line, and the revised service commenced on Wednesday, December 10th 1930. In June 1931 Birch applied for an extension to Park Royal which was refused for weekday operation though Birch were free to run it on Sundays which they did from August 8th. Success also evaded Birch in their efforts from mid-1931 onwards to persuade the police to allow the use of double-deckers on the 231 despite a protracted correspondence over two years. An offer to construct special double-deckers with the bodywork tapering inwards from the top of the lower saloon upwards was rejected in 1933 by the newly-formed Metropolitan Traffic Commissioners on the grounds that the service was scheduled to be acquired by London Transport, and for this reason Birch could not be allowed to improve its profitability as this would alter to their advantage the compensation to be paid in respect of it.

Though Birch pioneered the 203 they did not enjoy exclusive operation of it. In addition to their eight scheduled buses A. R. Brown worked two, Westminster one and Public four. In February 1928 Peraeque joined in with one bus and Public doubled its contribution to eight, whilst in March Albert Ewer placed one bus on the route, bringing the total scheduled by the six operators to 21. It was hopelessly overbussed with the inevitable result on receipts, and apart from Birch and Brown there was no attempt at regular operation. In May 1928, for example, Public's daily contribution only twice reached the scheduled eight and mostly varied from three to six buses each weekday. Westminster and Peraeque failed to appear at all and Ewer's bus showed up only once. The bad attendance record of the other independents is best illustrated by the fact that, in the five months February to June 1928, Westminster ran on only five days, Ewer also ran on five and Peraeque on three. In time Public withdrew and the others completely lost interest except for Brown whose business passed to Birch in due course.

In July 1927 Birch received a letter from the Great Western Land Co. Ltd. of Hanwell who had over 600 houses under construction in the rapidly expanding area between Ealing and Greenford. The development company was soliciting for a new bus service for its estate and found Birch ready to lend a willing ear to its needs. On September 24th Birch applied for five single deck licences for Greenford (Railway Hotel) to Ealing Broadway Station (Haven Green) via Greenford Avenue, Drayton Green Halt, Argyle Road, Cleveland Road and Castlebar Hill. Early in November a letter from New Scotland Yard informed Birch that the route could not be deemed suitable for bus operation because of excessive road camber and overhanging trees. Birch appealed to the Minister, instancing the fact that the police had recently given the LGOC approval for route 141 (Edgware to Borehamwood) upon which conditions were indisputably worse than on their proposed Ealing-Greenford route. Before replying, the Minister declared Haven Green, Castlebar Road and Cleveland Road as restricted thoroughfares as from November 8th, thus removing any possibility of Birch finding a suitable turning point in the vicinity of Ealing Broadway Station even if the rest of the route was approved. Despite this latest setback Birch still tried for approval, helped in their efforts by a petition to their M.P., the Rt. Hon. Major Isadore Salmon, by about 450 Elthorne Heights residents. This proved fruitless and Birch acknowledged defeat early in 1928. They had meanwhile purchased two new buses in anticipation of getting route approval and, rather than leaving them idle, placed them on unrestricted 26D/E in the eastern suburbs for which schedules were deposited on November 23rd 1927. One was later transferred to the 266 which proved badly unremunerative. Both routes involved unduly long garage journeys to Ilford and Leytonstone respectively. On the credit side they soon became "restricted" thus enhancing the value of the schedules which Birch were able to exchange for more suitable ones under the co-ordination scheme with the LGOC.

Birch had meanwhile been watching with interest the construction of the new Watford and Barnet by-pass road, and on the day that it opened, October 18th 1928, they made application to the Commissioner of Police for approval of a route between Hendon Central, Mill Hill and Edgware traversing newly-developed and partially-developed areas of housing. The route was eventually approved as 214 (Hendon Central to Canons Park) and began operation late in October 1928 with three buses. A fourth was added soon after and was licensed to Ingarfield & Bright Ltd., a Birch subsidiary. At first only three morning journeys operated through to Canons Park, the bulk of the service being Hendon to Edgware as 214A. On February 2nd 1929 the through service began to run all day and the next day the Minister declared portions of the route

231

(Queens Road and Hale Lane) restricted thus preventing any further vehicles being placed upon it. The route was an instant success and complaints were soon being received that it was inadequate over the Hendon-Mill Hill section. Birch applied to the Minister for dispensation to augment their operation by one bus but were refused an extra schedule. Much to their chagrin the LGOC was permitted to extend its route 121 over the Birch service from Hendon Central to Mill Hill, and they later rubbed salt in the wounds by terminating the 121 at Hendon again, replacing it with a 121E short working between there and Mill Hill using the latest T-type single-deckers which were employed to 'chase' the Birch's in best pirate tradition. Here was a reversal of the normal roles with General pirating on an independent's preserve. Birch sought retaliation by applying for a Mill Hill—Oxford Circus service in June 1929; needless to say this was refused. On September 30th 1929 the new Minister of Transport, Herbert Morrison, received a deputation from Birch in regard to the 214 and also its troubles on the 231, and he asked them to submit full details of their case together with copies of all correspondence, which they did on September 30th. Mr. Morrison, who was no sympathiser with the independents' cause, failed to give any reply for nearly seven months. When the reply came it was an outright refusal to grant Birch anything at all.

Whilst waiting to hear from the Minister, the Company had sought dispensation to revise the 214 to run from Hendon Central to Burnt Oak via the existing route as far as Edgware. This was not granted but a service was operated on Sundays—when dispensation was not required—as 215 from December 15th 1929. It was not a success and 214A (Hendon-Edgware) took its place after only three weeks' operation. On April 23rd 1930 the weekday service was cut back from Canons Park to Edgware (Premier Parade) in line with the Sunday service, the four scheduled buses thereby being concentrated on the major and most heavily trafficked section of route. An order came from the London & Home Counties Traffic Advisory Committee for Birch and the LGOC to get together and try to settle their differences amicably, and in November 1930 a scheme of co-ordination was agreed upon which the Minister subsequently approved to come into effect from December 31st 1930. One of the results of this was that, from that date, Birch withdrew their buses between Mill Hill and Edgware and were given exclusive rights to the Hendon-Mill Hill section which ran as 214C. This was suitable for double-deckers and was worked by them on all-day operations from then onwards though single-deckers helped out as peak hour reliefs until August 1932. Through bookings to the underground system via Hendon Central Station were available on the 214C.

A further attempt to branch out was made in April 1929 when Birch hoped to acquire a Romford (Mawney Road) to Rainham service. Licences had been granted by the Romford Urban and Rural District Councils in November 1928 to William Waterfall of 40 King Street, Camden Town. Waterfall was a Birch driver and the circumstances under which he acquired the licences are obscure. The theory could be advanced that he was acting by arrangement with his employer in obtaining the route, Birch not wishing to show their hand at the time. They intended to use Dennis 'E' B23 on the service, but the scheme came to nothing because Hornchurch UDC would not grant a licence for the section within their territory and the Romford UDC refused to transfer Waterfall's licence to Birch.

Three small operators came into the Birch orbit in 1928/9 starting with the one-bus concern of Ingarfield & Bright whose Daimler XX 1514 was the sole surviving independent on the 526 with the exception of the three Birch's. Operational control was assumed by Birch on April 5th 1928 but otherwise the bus ran as before with Ingarfield as licensee until July 7th when it came under the auspices of Ingarfield & Bright Ltd., a company incorporated with a share capital of £1,000 and registered office at 20 Cathcart Street. W. F. Ingarfield and L. H. Bright were shown as the first directors, but they were soon replaced on August 1st by W. H. & R. W. Birch. A new Leyland Lion, B20, was licensed in October 1928 in the name of Ingarfield & Bright Ltd. as a spare for the Daimler and a schedule was acquired for it on the 214 which it worked when not required on the 526. October 27th 1928 was the day W. R. Drake's two Leylands XP 435/XT 4608 were taken over, giving Birch valuable schedules on the 206 and 284A. Fleet number B18 was given to the Ingarfield & Bright Daimler whilst the Drake Leylands became B21/22. On February 1st 1929 the three schedules acquired in 1928 were transferred into Birch's name and the vehicles concerned absorbed into the parent fleet. This was followed on June 7th 1929 by the transfer to Birch of the two schedules on the 231 formerly operated by A. Brown's Maudslay single-deckers, UC 1816/7, to which Birch allocated fleet numbers B28/27 respectively. Birch had been providing supervision for Brown's buses since the previous August and had concluded an agreement with him for vehicle maintenance and repair in December 1928. Of the five acquired buses, the two Drake Leylands were similar to Birch's own fleet of LB's and remained until the time came for their normal replacement in 1930/1. The Daimler was advertised for sale in 1929 and the Maudslays, though only three years old, were traded in to Leyland's in part exchange for new vehicles in 1931 because they were non-standard.

The acquisition of Brown's two buses brought the Birch schedules up to their weekday maximum of twenty-three. Running letters and numbers were allocated to each schedule following the practice of the operators on the 526 and 536. In June 1929 the allocation was as follows: 526D A15 (ex Tally Ho)/19-21; 536B C1-3; 284A D1; 227 D2; 231A J1-8; 214/A M1-4; 26D/E Y1; 266 Z1. The 227 was a renumbering in April 1929 of the former Drake working numbered 206 to bring it more closely into line with the 127 which it paralleled all the way from Highgate to Hampton Court. On Sundays the ex-Brown operation on route 42 was retained and augmented to four vehicles (T1-4). Routes 27/127 and 73 were also operated on Sundays on acquired schedules as well as the regular Birch services.

It is now time to describe the co-ordination agreement worked out between Birch and the LGOC during 1930 which came into force on December 31st of that year. This agreement was unique in being the only one between the LGOC and an independent. As we have seen, it gave

233

Birch exclusive rights to the Mill Hill-Hendon route and, influenced by the fact that agreement had been reached, the Minister made Amendment Regulations enabling the 231 to be extended at each end though, even in its extended form, it always ran at a loss. Birch agreed to give up the acquired schedules on 26, 266, 227 and 284 to LGOC and Overground and also the Mill Hill-Edgware section of 214, and received two schedules on 526 formerly worked by General. One of the schedules Birch gave up, the 266, had been held in abeyance for some months as it proved too uneconomical to operate. Birch agreed not to expand its London bus operations beyond the total mileage scheduled at the date of the agreement (though this figure remained in dispute thereafter) and accepted through road-rail bookings on route 214C to the underground system. A further condition of the agreement was that Birch would not part with their London omnibus interests without first offering them to the LGOC. The agreement rested on an exchange of letters, there being no formal document drawn up. One unusual result of it was that on the Saturdays of the Royal Air Pageant at Hendon Aerodrome (June 27th 1931, June 25th 1932 and June 24th 1933) Birch contributed three or four vehicles to route 121 (Mill Hill-Peckham Rye) as their share of a co-ordinated supplementary schedule to cater for the large crowds visiting the pageant. From April 1931 onwards Birch and LGOC honoured each other's tickets on the 526 in the event of vehicle breakdowns.

For their last three years of London bus operation Birch's schedules encompassed 24 vehicles on weekdays which were distributed thus: 526 A1-6; 536C C1-3; 214C M1-5; 231B J1-10. Two of the 214 buses, M2/4, were peak-hour workings to reduce the headway from its basic 10 mins. to a 6 min. frequency. The final Sunday services were 27A, 42, 231, 526 & 536 supplemented in summer months by 127B. Sunday schedules were also deposited for 73A and 173D but had not been worked since 1931.

In 1932 John Manley Birch, Raymond's younger brother, joined the business after working for two years in the bus bodybuilding department of Brush at Loughborough. He later became the company's Deputy Chairman and Deputy Managing Director. In the same year the company's Chairman, W. S. Birch, retired from active participation at the age of 91.

We have followed the growth of the bus fleet up to the delivery of the last Leyland LB, B7, in 1927. The development of the 203 and 214 necessitated the use of single-deckers, so a fleet of 30-seaters was acquired in 1927 (B8-13) and 1928 (B14-17). B9-11/13 were red & white when new and B12 was maroon & cream (the Birch coach colours) but all were changed to the standard brown after about a year. These vehicles marked a change of allegiance to Dennis and were pneumatic-tyred E-types which served Birch well. A pair of Leyland Lion single-deckers was also purchased in 1928 as B19/20, but their transmission brakes proved highly troublesome where frequent stopping was required, and it was probably for this reason that they were converted to coaches in 1932. The 1929 deliveries brought the fleet of Dennis E's to twelve with the arrival of B23/4 and saw the entry into service of Birch's only two double-deckers from the Guildford stable, B25/6. These 54-seaters were the Company's first covered-top double-deckers and their success led to the re-equipping of the fleet with twelve new double-deckers in 1931/2. B25 passed the police noise test at Kingston Vale on March 19th 1929 and entered service on the 536 ten days later. Dennis H's were approved for the 526 in February 1930 and in latter years B25/26 ran mainly on this route. In 1929/30 the majority, if not all, of the Leyland LB's were converted to pneumatics.

The covered-top double-deckers raised a problem. Though the coachbuilding and paint shops were high enough to accommodate such vehicles, the main garage entrance from Cathcart Street was not. With a large scale conversion to such vehicles in mind for the not too distant future, the company was faced with the necessity to rebuild the entrance at considerable cost. While the work was carried out, accommodation for six or more vehicles had to be found elsewhere, and from April 1929 to March 1930 space was rented at 22s. 6d. per week per vehicle at the Fortess Garage in Fortess Grove, Kentish Town. These premises, on the north side of Fortess Grove, are now occupied by a firm of commercial vehicle dealers. In 1929 they were the service depot for W. D. Foster & Co. of 24/26 Hampstead Road, N.W.1., a firm of magneto repairers.

Birch reverted to Leyland when ordering its fleet of twelve new double-deckers. B29-31 arrived in 1930 and B32-8 in the following year. These carried open staircase bodies of standard Birch design and were 56-seaters. B39/40 of 1932 vintage were, like their predecessors, of the TD1 variety which had now generally been superseded by the updated TD2. The TD1 was specified in order to achieve standardisation within the fleet. They carried all-enclosed bodies with flat fronts in the latest idiom and had straight staircases resembling those on the General's LT and ST types. All the Birch Titans carried route number stencils at roof level. Only two of the old Leyland LB's, B1/7, survived this influx of Titans and lasted until London Transport days. Birch's last act of significance before the London bus fleet was compulsorily handed over to London Transport was the equipping of Titan B39 with a diesel engine at a cost of £269. City's far more extensive experiments excepted, Birch was the only independent to experiment with this form of motive power. B39 went into the Leyland depot at 47 New Kent Road on June 7th 1933 for its new engine and ran successfully thereafter until Birch operations came to an end. The company also experimented with heavy oil vapourisers on ten of its Gilford coaches with a fair measure of success.

The appointed day for the transfer of Birch's buses to the LPTB was February 21st 1934, the twenty-eight buses running under Birch ownership for the last time on the 20th. This was a double blow because it removed the major source of the Company's revenue. In terms of profit in relation to the capital invested, the motor bus department ranked roughly level with property investment as the most satisfactory side of the company's activities. The taxi and coach departments showed a very poor return on capital, and the coachworks, though trading satisfactorily, were clearly going to show an early decline as many of Birch's fellow independents, who were among its principal customers, were swallowed up. Birch took its claim for compensation to the Arbitration Tribunal which, in July 1935, awarded £191,241.

Birch decided to develop its coach operations as the future main source of income. A large range of coastal services and excursions was operated by the "Cream and Crimson Coaches." Starting back in November 1928 these had been supplemented by the famous London-Bedford Express service which was extended to Rushden in 1929 and Kettering in 1930. The single coach operated on the route by H. J. Barnett was replaced by a Birch vehicle in January 1929 and Beaumont Safeway's London-Bedford service was absorbed in September 1932. A policy of expansion in rural Hertfordshire, Bedfordshire and Northamptonshire resulted in the purchase of no fewer than ten small bus and coach businesses in 1938 and two further operators were acquired in 1944 and 1949. A modern garage was built in Rushden in 1937 and another at Henlow Camp in 1938, the latter serving largely as a base for the rural bus service network. During the second world war the London route, the famous 203, was cut back at its northern end to Rushden. The war also saw the reintroduction of double-deckers to the Birch fleet.

Hostilities over, the Labour government came to power and put the fear of nationalisation into the industry. Birch decided to separate the coaching activities from the buses so that, if the stage carriage services were compulsorily acquired by the State, they would not lose the coaches too. In January 1948 Ingarfield & Bright Ltd. was resuscitated to take over the coach business though the vehicles concerned retained the standard livery which was then cream & green. The company was renamed Birch Brothers (I.B.) Ltd. in January 1950 and was renamed again in January 1955 to Birch Brothers (Transport) Ltd.

The opening of the M1 motorway in 1959 saw the introduction of the 203M which provided a fast, non-stop service from London as far as Bedford. This was perhaps the last highlight in Birch's development, for the 1960's saw a gradual decline. On December 26th 1963 the last Birch taxi cab was withdrawn ending 131 years of continuous taxi operation with a fleet that, in 1937, had grown as high as 70 vehicles. Monico Motorways, a Kentish Town coach firm, was taken over in July 1966 but this temporary expansion was more than outweighed by the cessation of all remaining local country services on October 14th 1968 because, like so many rural operations, these had become unprofitable. Sadder still was the sale of the London-Rushden operations to United Counties on 14th September 1969 as this marked the complete end of Birch stage carriage operations. Less than twenty coaches then remained and these were used on various contract hires, largely transporting overseas visitors on sightseeing tours. These remaining operations were taken over by Grey Green on February 1st 1971 together with nine of Birch's vehicles. The Birch fleetname was retained by the new owners on a few vehicles which for the next four years could still be seen in and around London as shadowy reminders of a once-enterprising family business. After the coaches were disposed of Birch retained a small oil distribution business but this now also has ceased and the extensive Cathcart Street premises are split up into units used by a variety of business concerns.

Flight's Garage, 47/49 Parkhurst Road, Holloway

VICTORIA ROAD CAR

Flight's garage and petrol station at 47/49 Parkhurst Road, just down the hill from Holloway women's prison and close to the famous Nags Head, has long had connections with the bus and coach industry as a garage and coach station. These extensive buildings are perhaps best known for their connection over many years with Orange Luxury Coaches Ltd., and even today the housing of independently-owned coaches is one of the functions they perform. The first independent at Flight's was the Ambassador in December 1923. They were followed by a motor engineer, Leonard Mark Turnham who, on January 18th 1924, licensed a new Straker Squire XR 555.

Turnham was the senior partner in a garage and car hire business which traded as Turnham & Co. from premises at 10 Eccleston Street East, Victoria, on which he had taken a lease in about 1915. The premises had earlier been used by his father, nicknamed "Pop" Turnham, for housing the horses and broughams which he hired out to the gentry of the day. Len Turnham had earlier been a successful racing motorist and test driver. He had been a friend of the famous Percy Lambert, the first man to achieve 100 m.p.h. at Brooklands and, in the view of Charles E. Lee who knew Turnham well, Lambert's tragic death was probably the reason for Turnham's decision to retire from the race track. Mr. Lee recalls Turnham as a man with "a marked tendency towards individualism." Turnham's partner in Turnham & Co. was George Thomas Barrett. Their motor business was incorporated as a limited company entitled Turnham & Co. Ltd. on August 17th 1920 by which time coaching had become a prominent feature of the Company's activities.

Turnham bought his first charabanc, an AEC 28-seater, early in 1919. The Easter weekend found him touting along the railway queues at Victoria Station offering day return tickets to Brighton for £1; single fare 10s. 6d. He assured the would-be railway passengers that he could have them in Brighton quicker than they could reach their turn at the booking office window at Victoria Station. This was fact, not just a boast. After the war railway services were hopelessly inadequate and the purchase of a ticket at any of the main line termini could involve queueing up for many hours. Thus began the first daily London to Brighton coach service of the post war era. Soon afterwards Southdown began their daily service from the Brighton end and before long the two undertakings were co-operating with interavailability of tickets and reciprocal maintenance facilities in the event of breakdowns.

Before we come to Turnham's one and only London bus, let us trace his coaching career further. In 1920 Mr. Shirley H. James of Pickfords Ltd. had suggested the formation of a coaching pool to be known as London & Coastal Motor Services which was principally to co-ordinate services on the Brighton and Eastbourne roads. At first Pickfords administered the pool, but in the Autumn of 1921 Turnham & Co. Ltd. took it over. Its scope was widened considerably on April 30th 1925 when it developed into the famous London Coastal Coaches Ltd. with

237

Turnham as General Manager. Unfortunately Turnham's own company got into financial difficulties and the decision was taken on October 26th 1926 to place it into voluntary liquidation. Turnham & Co. Ltd. was wound up on February 28th 1928. Turnham's career now lay firmly with London Coastal Coaches who, under his control, opened the famous Victoria Coach Station in 1932 to replace a temporary station established in Lupus Street in April 1928. He was still General Manager at London Coastal Coaches at the time of his death on July 3rd 1944, after a painful illness, at the comparatively early age of 54.

It can be readily seen from the foregoing outline of Turnham's busy life that his London bus was but a minor item in his career. It was garaged at Flight's, the premises at Eccleston Street East being too low to accommodate a double-decker, even one of the open top variety. Turnham and "Tommy" Barrett both frequently worked on the bus, taking it in turns to drive and conduct. Flight's garage was conveniently sited for the 29 on which the bus mostly ran in its early days, though it graduated via such routes as 14 and 73 to the 27A and 38A on which it mostly ran on weekdays after the introduction of the London Traffic Act. Early in the Bassom era it worked also on a unique and potentially useful route 218 from Kings Cross to Victoria via Tottenham Court Road, Oxford Street, Marble Arch and Hyde Park Corner which turned out to be short-lived. Sundays were mainly spent on the 27/127 group of routes.

XR 555 was in a handsome royal blue livery and its fleetname revived a title from former days, the Victoria Road Car. It was owned by Turnham and Barrett as individuals and not by Turnham & Co. Ltd., and it bore the fleet number 551! It seems as though the Victoria Road Car title may have been a second thought, for the first tickets carried the inscription "London Road Car Omnibus Co." which, had it been applied to the bus, would have revived memories of an even more famous title from the past. Indeed Turnham originally contemplated also using the "Union Jack" fleet name which was the famous feature of the old London Road Car organisation. Towards the close of 1926 the decision was taken to dispose of the bus to the LGOC, a decision no doubt brought about by Turnham's financial troubles. The Victoria Road Car Co. Ltd. was incorporated on December 6th 1926 with 55 Broadway as its registered office, and its shares passed into LGOC hands three days later. The LGOC allocated XR 555 to the Page Street garage as from Sunday January 4th 1927 and it stayed until March 1927 by which time a replacement was available in the shape of K 227 which operated out of Holloway (J) garage. This bus was taken back into General stock on January 1st 1928 when the Victoria Road Car Co. Ltd. ceased to operate.

The next arrival at Flight's Garage was G. A. Adams of the Primrose, who ran from Parkhurst Road as a sort of half-way measure after leaving Wells' Garage in Cambridge Road and before arriving at Gray's in Tottenham High Road. He had started running from Flight's by May 1924 but had moved on by January 1925.

SCARBOROUGH/VICTORIA

Next, in July 1924, came Christopher Colebatch with his new Dennis XU 409. Scarborough was the name chosen to adorn the red & white

238

Strachan & Brown body. The choice of this very pleasant Yorkshire seaside town as a fleetname was not so odd as it might at first seem, for Colebatch lived at 22 Scarborough Road, Stroud Green. He selected a rather less pretentious fleet number than the 551 chosen by Turnham for his Victoria Road Car bus; Colebatch settled for 30! By October 1924 the fleetname had been changed to Victoria after a serious accident which attracted unwelcome publicity. Victoria was, in any case, a far more apt title for a bus which spent most of its time on the 29. Colebatch sold out to Public on August 5th 1927 for £2,700.

H. M. MERRY (lion insignia)

Harold Miles Merry was an older man than many of the independent proprietors. As early as 1912 he was in the garage business in Rochester Mews, where he had the Clarendon Garage which, in the 'twenties, was occupied by H. J. Barnett of Clarendon bus fame. Merry, who lived at 14 Hilldrop Road, Holloway, was in business as H. M. Merry Motor Transport Services at 99 Camden Mews, Camden Road and 3/4 Brandon Road, Kings Cross at the time he bought his first bus in March 1925. His main activities were those of hire car, taxi and garage proprietor and motor engineer and the buses appear to have been merely a sideline. As far as can be ascertained, Merry never kept the buses at his own premises, and chose Flight's garage as a convenient place to base them. His initial entry into buses was in partnership with someone called Butler, but the Merry & Butler combination was soon discontinued and before long Merry was running the buses alone.

XX 7200 was Merry's first bus. A royal red & white Leyland, its Strachan & Brown body carried no fleetname but had a small gold lion rampant emblem where the fleetname would have been. The most suitable service still available as late as March 1925 was the 525 and XX 7200 started work on this. Later in the year two additional buses were ordered, again from Strachan & Brown but this time on Dennis chassis. They were small, pneumatic-tyred 26-seaters for which Merry obtained approval in September 1925 to run on the 546 (Islington, Chapel Street-Camden Town) and in October 1925 on a variant of this numbered 548 (Islington, Chapel Street-Tufnell Park). YL 5595 was licensed on October 1st and YL 6476 six days later. The 548 lasted only a little longer than the 546 and by January 1926 both single-deckers were working permanently on the 551.

A limited company came into being on October 22nd 1926 to take over all Merry's business activities. H. M. Merry Motor Transport Services Ltd. had a share capital of £1,000 and was located at 3/4 Brandon Road, York Road, Kings Cross. Less than a year later, on August 5th 1927, the three buses were sold to Public for £8,000. The company continued trading only for about a year after this and was dissolved by notice in the London Gazette dated November 6th 1931.

★   ★   ★   ★

From February to April 1925 the Pullman Dennis was garaged at Flights, and July 1925 saw the arrival at Holloway of Crabb & Clarke's Sphere

239

Daimler. It was bought by the proprietors of Ambassador in October 1926 and in April 1927 they departed for other premises in Holloway. After the sale of the Victoria bus to Public in August 1927 no further independents stayed at Flights until September 1932 when Westminster rented accommodation for their sizeable combined fleet of buses and coaches.

Victoria Garage, Victoria Road, Holloway

ALMA

The Victoria Garage in Victoria Road (now Chillingworth Road), Holloway, has long since disappeared beneath a council housing estate. Back in 1924 it was a thriving business owned by Harry Laing whose principal tenant was the Truby Motor Haulage Co. Ltd. In addition to the Truby lorries there was ample garage space to house the independent buses running under the titles of Alma and Alberta.

The Alma was the first bus in the Victoria Garage. The principal figure behind the Alma buses and their licensee during their three year career was Raphael Edward de Casagrande. He was partnered in the venture by two other young men, Frederick George Davies and Leslie Frederick Flaxman. The latter was related to Walter Flaxman French, a motor transport pioneer and head of the United Services Transport Co. Ltd. for whom de Casagrande had recently been a driver. In pre-war days he had been a motor mechanic in a Kensington garage and later a chauffeur; during the war he was an army lorry driver. So, mechanically at least, he was well qualified to cope with the trials and tribulations of bus work. Between them the three partners bought a new Thornycroft which was registered XR 999 on January 31st 1924 and given the fleetname Alma.

The Alma bus ran first of all on routes 11, 19 and 49, which all ran conveniently close to 34 Ethelburga Street, Battersea. This was its first garage and the most convenient de Casagrande could find at the time in relation to his home at 102 Ebury Street, Victoria. In about May 1924 the Alma began to appear regularly on the 29 for which a schedule was obtained at the end of the year under the new London Traffic Act. In about March 1925 de Casagrande moved house to 122A Marlborough Road, Bowes Park. The landlord of his new flat, a Mr. I. Wolfe, had a son for whom he wanted to find a business. So, with a deposit of £500 provided by his father towards the cost of a new bus, Wolfe junior became a partner in the Alma. When he moved to North London de Casagrande arranged for the bus to be moved too, and the home he found for it was the Victoria Garage.

With the £500 provided by Wolfe a deposit was placed with Dodson on a new Leyland which was delivered promptly in time to be licensed as XX 8697 on April 6th 1925. This second Alma bus was in the same red & white livery as its predecessor and it found employment on the 526D. The Leyland proved to be a wise investment and before long it was decided to buy another one in place of the Thornycroft. In the latter part of July 1926 YP 5156 entered service carrying the fleet number 1 formerly borne by the Thornycroft which, like many other London buses of the same make, found its way into the Thames Valley fleet.

In 1927 de Casagrande received an offer from A. T. Bennett to buy the two Alma buses on behalf of Public. Though for his own part de Casagrande was not keen to sell and neither was Flaxman, Wolfe wished to, and from June 27th Bennett took over the operation of the buses. The actual purchase was completed on August 3rd 1927 for £5,850.

The partnership dissolved, the four young men went their separate ways. Indeed Davies may have left before the end. De Casagrande, who had run the business and worked full-time in it, had to make a new career for himself. For the first time in his working life he forsook motors and bought a confectionery shop in Seven Sisters Road, Holloway. Later he owned for many years a newsagents and confectioners business in Upper Edmonton. His death came sadly in 1966 as a result of being beaten up by shopbreakers.

How did the fleetname Alma originate? It is Latin for "beloved." Raphael de Casagrande had just got married when the first bus was bought. His widow thinks there may have been some connection and we would like to think so too, but we shall never know for sure.

ALBERTA

Albert Henry Hackman started the Alberta business in June 1924 when he put into service a new Leyland, XT 5386, on hire purchase from Dodson. The bus, in red & white livery, was licensed on May 30th and was submitted by Hackman to the police on June 6th. Further new Alberta buses followed which, though not the property of Hackman, were run by him on behalf of their owners, in much the same way as John Pike ran the Claremont buses for other people. XT 8752 followed the original Alberta Leyland by less than three weeks and was identical to it. The finance for this had been provided by a Westcliff-on-Sea factory manager, Gustavas Ernest Weber, who was licensee of the bus but probably took no active part in its operation otherwise. G. E. Weber also financed the third Alberta, XU 6822, which arrived in August 1924 along with XU 6823 which was the property of Gustavas's brother Louis Charles Weber. This pair were Dodson-bodied Dennises.

April 1925 heralded the arrival of three further new buses, bringing the combined Alberta fleet to its maximum of seven. XX 7606/8731 & 9344 were purchased under the auspices of the Alberta Omnibus Co. Ltd. which had been formed on February 6th 1925 with a share capital of £8,000 and with its registered office at Hackman's home address, 44 Petherton Road, Highbury. The company also took over the four existing Alberta buses. Its directors were Hackman and the two Webers plus a further Weber brother, William Valentine Weber, who was a director of the Punch & Ticket Co. Ltd. whose punches the company naturally used. Additional capital was obtained from George Foster, a Deptford butcher, George Carle, a retired butcher living in Wanstead, and Francis Alfred Pale, a stockbroker's manager, but these three did not hold directorships.

At first the Alberta buses were housed at 289 High Street, Camden Town—one of the Dangerfield garages—but at an unknown date they moved to the Victoria Garage. Their earlier operations were mainly on the 29 with 27/127 and 73 also coming into favour later. Stabilisation under the London Traffic Act saw them on 27A/C, 127, 206/C on weekdays. The last three to be delivered were placed into service on the 525 having been bought too late to go on to a central London service. Latterly Sundays were spent on 71/A, 127/A/B and 525. Besides the buses two private cars were charged up to the business, a Singer and a Studebaker.

The Alberta business does not appear to have been a particularly profitable one and it may well be that the owners were glad to sell out to General. The exchange of shares took place at 3.00 p.m. on the afternoon of Friday, November 5th 1926, and as the buses finished work that same evening they were sent to their new owner's Holloway (J) garage. Due to its high Dennis content the Alberta fleet suffered little change under LGOC control though all the Dennises changed bodies on overhaul in December 1926 and January 1927 (see appendix 5). Only two K's were brought in. K308, in General livery, replaced the older of the two Leylands in February 1927, the Leyland being despatched to the Batten-controlled Invicta fleet after overhaul. The remaining Alberta Leyland was withdrawn in July 1927, its replacement being K334. On June 29th 1927 three of the Dennises were transferred to Tottenham (AR) garage which was better placed than Holloway for the 525. Alberta was absorbed into General on January 1st 1928.

172 Marlborough Road, Holloway
AMBASSADOR
EMPRESS/SPHERE

Marlborough Road is an important thoroughfare linking the main Holloway and Hornsey Roads. At no. 172 stands the Marlborough Service Station, a curious looking structure with castellated roof line and with a steep run-down from road level to permit double-deckers to get inside its twin doors. A large house adjacent to the garage and an open yard next to the house form the extent of the property which, from April 1927 until the end of independent bus days, was occupied by the Ambassador buses owned by George Harnett and his elder sister Caroline. Prior to this an old-established wheelwright's business had been located on the site. In August 1928 the Harnetts were fortunate in purchasing the freehold and they then developed the Marlborough Service Station-cum bus garage, the total cost including purchase price being just under £3,000. It was the personal property of the Harnetts to whom their two omnibus companies (Ambassador and Sphere) paid a weekly rental. In 1933 a fourteen-year lease was executed by the Harnetts to the bus companies which required the latter to garage their buses there at 25/- a week for each bus plus the purchase of all petrol and oil.

The Harnetts' bus interests started with one vehicle in December 1923 in the shape of XP 7183, a red & white Dodson-bodied Dennis. Its fleetname Ambassador was chosen for no other reason except that it sounded "classy". George Harnett actually ran the bus, his sister Caroline's interest being merely financial as she was fully occupied businesswise helping her mother in their confectionery shop in Hornsey Road. Before the war George Harnett had served an apprenticeship with Napiers at Acton after which he had a variety of jobs including a couple

242

of choppy trips on a Grimsby trawler which convinced him he was not cut out for a seafaring life. After the war came a two-year contract to work for the Government in India. This finished and a new future had to be found. Harnett was toying with the idea of taxi driving when, one night, through the window of the Finsbury Park Tavern, he noticed an independent bus go by. Next day he ordered his first bus from Dodson.

The 29 was an obvious choice of route for the bus to work on and it duly entered service after passing its police test on December 18th. For just over a year Ambassador was a one bus fleet until the arrival of a second Dennis, XX 6678, in March 1925. This was prevented by the Restricted Streets Orders from joining its elder sister on the 29 so a schedule was obtained for it on the 525. The Harnetts garaged initially at Flight's in Parkhurst Road but in August 1925, because of a disagreement, they moved to the Empire Garage at Wood Green. They stayed there for only a month before moving on to a garage somewhere in Holloway before moving back to Flight's where they remained until a final home was found at Marlborough Road in 1927.

One of the Harnetts' neighbours in Parkhurst Road was the Sphere bus, a chocolate & cream Daimler, MF 9241, which had bodywork of Hickman manufacture. Arthur Edward Crabb and George William Clarke had been the owners of this bus since it was purchased from J. M. Roberts in July 1924. At first it was called Empress and ran alongside the buses of the Empress Omnibus Co. Ltd. of Wood Green with whose buses it was housed, first at the Whymark Garage and later at the Empire Garage, Wood Green. Renaming to Sphere took place at about the time that it moved to Parkhurst Road in July 1925. The partners did not get on too well and eventually approached Harnett to buy the business from them. He agreed, and on October 9th 1926 the Sphere Omnibus Co. Ltd. was formed with registered office initially at the home of one of the partners, 23 Sperling Road, Tottenham, and a share capital of £200. Shortly afterwards the Harnetts took control and immediately replaced the Daimler, which George Harnett considered useless, with a new Dennis (YR 3672) in October 1926. The Daimler passed via Roberts to a Cork operator, Capt. A. Morgan, and was reregistered TI 1802. He also owned another ex-London Daimler, the much-travelled MF 8001. The new Dennis was in the same red & white livery as its Ambassador contemporaries and is believed to have carried the Ambassador fleetname from new, the wording Sphere appearing only on the legal ownership panel. Clarke stayed on with Harnett as a conductor; Crabb was later one of the first drivers on New Empress Saloons.

Ambassador became a limited company with £1,000 capital on October 20th 1927 under the title Ambassador Bus Co. Ltd. The sole directors were George and Caroline Harnett and they used their home address, 44 Hornsey Road, as the registered office. Following this, the next major event was the obtaining of an extra bus in November 1928, giving the company a spare for the first time. XV 3453 was a Dennis H-type and was the first vehicle owned by Harnetts to have covered top and pneumatics. Indeed it was only the second independent top covered bus, the first being City's Guy G1. When new it bore the Sphere name on the rocker panel though this must have been an error as the bus appears to have always been on the books of the Ambassador company. Its Dodson body seated 54 and was rather ungainly, but this was a criticism that could be levelled at all the London covered-top Dennis H's and was caused by the high chassis line which gave them an overall height of 14 ft. 8 ins. compared with the 14 ft. 3 ins. of the Leyland Titan and Dennis Lance.

An interesting event occurred in 1930. It was widely recorded in the trade press at the time that a six-wheeled 66-seater S.M.C. with Dodson bodywork had been ordered for Sphere. Along with other London operators, the Harnetts had been approached by Sunbeam, who were very anxious to break into the London bus market with their "Sikh" six-wheeler. They placed an order for one, which was duly built and painted in full Ambassador livery. It had an enclosed staircase body. Prior to delivery it was given a preliminary police test over routes 212 and 294, but the police refused to grant approval, stating that the vehicle must be tested again when it was licensed. The Harnetts may have been unwilling to risk its eventual rejection by the police and cancelled their order for the vehicle which was then repainted in the livery of the Westminster Omnibus Co. Ltd. who were also potential Sunbeam customers.

After the Sunbeam episode the Harnetts remained faithful to Dennis. They ordered a pair of Lances for delivery in November 1930. The first to arrive was destined to work for the Ambassador company on the 29 and was due for delivery on the 17th, the other was for the Sphere working on the 294 and was scheduled to arrive on the 24th. They were licensed as GK 7167/6 respectively on December 2nd and replaced only one of the older Dennises, leaving another to make a second spare in a combined fleet of five. The newcomers had enclosed stairs but retained the traditional open driver's cabin. They were not, however, an identical pair. GK 7166 had a body built by Dodson whose products had already given such good service. For GK 7167 Harnett went to Birch for the reason that he thought the Birch-built body had more style. Both were 56-seaters. The last and finest vehicle in the fleet was GX 143 and was delivered to the Ambassador Bus Co. Ltd. in March 1932 as a belated replacement for Dennis XP 7183. Again a Dennis Lance, its body was of Dodson's last and most handsome style and it would have been a fine vehicle indeed had the overall effect not been marred by the omission of a windscreen.

London Transport took over the Ambassador and Sphere businesses on August 29th 1934. The combined fleets at takeover totalled the five Dennises, of which only three were scheduled on weekdays, plus a 1928 Arrol-Aster 16.6 hp car UR 1669 which had been bought second-hand in June 1931 and was on the books of the Ambassador company. The final route workings were: Ambassador—29 daily, 525 weekdays; Sphere—294 weekdays, 212 Sundays.

The Harnetts received the handsome sums of £20,500 for the Ambassador business and £8,000 for Sphere. These payments were purely in compensation for vehicles and services as no property changed hands. George Harnett later bought an Essex farm at Wickham Bishops

Photos Nos. 36, 37 and 38

Several of the types of double-decker favoured by the independents failed to fulfil their promise in one way or another; indeed, only the Leyland and Dennis could be regarded as truly successful. The Straker Squire A-type (fig. 36) faded out fairly early, the last one being Supreme's, seen here with a Dennis of The Reliance behind it. Some firms courted disaster by running rebuilt Daimlers supplied by J. M. Roberts. Julius & Lockwood (fig. 37) realised their deficiencies early on and quickly bought themselves a Dennis as their front line bus. The brand new Dennis is seen, as yet unlicensed, and behind it stand the Strachan & Brown-bodied Daimler which it is shortly to replace with, in the background, a Hickman-bodied vehicle of the same make. The Thornycroft J-type was reliable but slow. However on this occasion (fig. 38) Henri Leon's H.L. bus was not going slow enough to avoid running into the back of a char-a-banc, throwing its canvas hood into a state of disarray.

Nothing marked the individuality of the independents more than their choice of fleet names, some of which were very bizarre indeed. Here are a few of the unusual titles which must have left the travelling public mystified as to their significance.

Photo No. 39 (*right*) Photographed, not in the Far East, but at Kings Cross, is Evelyn Puttergill's Shanghai, a Strachan & Brown-bodied Dennis. The authors have not to this day established the significance of this fleet name or the reason why it was chosen.

Photo No. 40 The derivation of the name Uneedus is clear enough for all to follow, and is in much the same mould as Hav-a-ride and Our Bus. This Uneedus vehicle, identical to the Shanghai above, is pictured outside the National Gallery in Trafalgar Square.

Photo No. 41 New Times dawn with a brilliant rising sun. But new times for whom? The owners of the business benefited little from their enterprise. This, the second and last new vehicle purchased by New Times, is a Dodson-bodied Leyland.

Photo No. 42
Royalty was bound to figure somewhere in the annals of independent fleet names, though there is nothing regal in the appearance of Randall & Shepherd's blue Dennis. This bodybuilder's photo shows The Royal prior to its introduction into the rigours of London service.

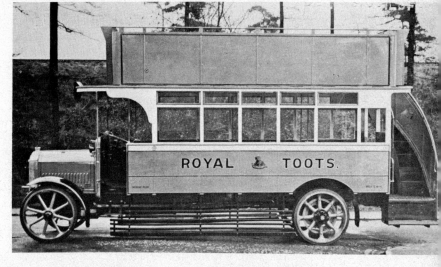

Photo No. 43
Still irreverently on the subject of royalty is the Royal Toots. The Hoare's yellow Dodson-bodied Dennis led a brief three month career as the Royal Toots before passing to James Thomson whose fleet name Regal continued the same theme.

Photo No. 44
Several operators chose superlatives of one sort or another for their fleet name, but the title selected by the Webber brothers probably beat them all. In those days the Empire was an institution for Britons to be proud of, not to decry. The Empire's Best bus is a Dodson-bodied Leyland.

Photo No. 45 (*left*)
The star insignia of the West London Association.

Photo No. 46
All too seldom the independents pulled together in their common battle against the "Combine". A rare example of independent co-ordination at its best was route 526, the West London Association service. Above (fig. 46), at the Swan & Pyramids terminus in North Finchley, three WLA vehicles lay over before returning southwards to Wandsworth Bridge. From left to right they are Cornwall's no. 5, a Strachan & Brown-bodied Dennis; Birch's B3, a Leyland with body built by the operator; Robert Thackray's XW 5668, a Dodson-bodied Dennis.

Photo No. 47
The side view of Randall & Shepherd's Dennis No. 2 shows the standard red and white livery of the West London Association. The same bus is seen in its original livery in fig. 42.

Photo No. 48

The success of route 551 proved that independents did not necessarily need to form an association to make a service prosper. This view at the Griffin, Whetstone, where the 551 had its western terminus, shows Prince's Dodson-bodied Leyland PLSC on its stand outside the pub. Arriving at the terminus is a once-independent Dennis 2½-tonner now in the service of Public, the firm which many mistakenly saw as forming a bastion of independent operation for years ahead.

Photo No. 49

Cambrian was very publicity minded in its earlier, more successful days, and used this motor cycle and sidecar combination to stress to the travelling public the reasons why they should use the Cambrian buses. The sidecar is built in the shape of a miniature char-a-banc, complete with fleet number A1, and the outfit is seen in less than pristine condition at Epsom Downs on a wet Derby day.

Photo No. 50
There was a fair crop of failures amongst independent operators, but two were put out of business through no fault of their own but because of legislation aimed at protecting trams. One of them was Dominion, the newer of whose two Dodson-bodied Dennises, XX 9591, is seen in the Uxbridge Road bound for Hayes on the ill-fated 514. XX 9591 survives today as a runner thanks to a preservation scheme.

Photo No. 51
Undoubtedly the biggest financial disaster was the collapse of Cambrian. Here Strachan & Brown-bodied Dennis D7 is seen after the rescue bid by General. It still carried Cambrian green livery but the garage running stencils and the legal wording "JOHN CHRISTOPHER MITCHELL—SECRETARY" are both reminders of who the real owners now are.

Photo No. 52
The final insult—an LGOC K-type wearing independent colours stands at Kings Cross on the once strongly-independent 247. K 691 was one of nine such vehicles drafted into the Royal Blue fleet, and is seen operating out of the LGOC's Middle Row garage.

Photo No. 53
other K type, this ne operating in en livery on be-lf of Cambrian. K S seen picking up Hammersmith oadway with a neral S-type be-hind it.

Photo No. 54
Tilling initially retained Timpson's silver livery and distinctive style of fleet name even though Tilling Stevens petrol electrics were drafted in to replace the original fleet. One of the first replacement vehicles was IT 302, a one-time Cambrian Landray bus with Hickman body.

THE GREAT **COMBINE WANGLE**—IT'S UP TO **YOU**
—— FOR **LIBERTY'S** SAKE ——
SIGN THE PETITION.

Photo No. 55
Anti-Combine leaflet distributed in about 1924 by the Association of London Omnibus Proprietors.

Photo No. 56
Some leading independents saw investment in new trams as a threat to their livelihood. Overground Dennis No. 19 in the precincts of the Houses of Parliament with anti-tram propaganda prominently displayed on its windows.

near Witham and, ten years afterwards, began yet another career as a hotel and property owner in Clacton. His sons now run the hotel business while George Harnett himself lives in retirement there. Caroline and her mother also lived latterly in Clacton until their deaths, the latter only a few months short of 103 years old.

112A Junction Road, Highgate
CENTRAL

The Central Omnibus Co. Ltd. was a business that might have turned into something big, but didn't. There was no lack of capital here, for it was controlled by Commercial Car Hirers Ltd., the substantial company allied to Commercial Cars Ltd., the builders of Commer vehicles. A ready-made operating base existed at 112A Junction Road, Highgate, the headquarters of Coventons Ltd., a heavy freight and haulage firm also associated with Commercial Car Hirers Ltd.

John Beaumont Parrington, the Fleet Superintendent of Coventons Ltd. and a director, was in charge of operations. His fellow directors on the Central Omnibus Co. Ltd., which was incorporated on March 9th 1923, were Edward Percy Williams and James Jackson Ure. These were also Coventons directors, and they were joined on the board in October 1923 by James Coventon Moth, the well-known managing director of Commercial Car Hirers Ltd. Central's registered office, which it shared with the other companies in the group, was Albion House, 59A New Oxford Street.

In a businesslike manner, a report on the best possible routes upon which to operate was commissioned from an 'expert' before the buses were delivered. This expert was Percy Frost-Smith, and in the light of his own subsequent failure, it might be thought that he was perhaps not the best person to pick for the job. It seems that he recommended route 27, with the 11 and 25 as next best alternatives, as the board of directors duly decided to run on the former but to carry boards on the buses for the other two.

Three buses, XN 7386/7891/8771, were delivered in May 1923 and bore the fleet letters A, B and C. They were Straker Squires, and wore a rather attractive light brown livery (officially described by Central as khaki) & white. The first two passed the police Noise Committee on May 8th and the third was presented soon after. Bus D was a similar vehicle (XP 849) delivered in the following September.

Frost-Smith's recommendation to run on route 27 could not have been too ill-conceived, as the buses appear to have done quite well for themselves. In October 1923 the directors decided to keep them on this route and to extend beyond the LGOC's terminus at Highgate Station northwards to Barnet. Later an interesting working was introduced at Kew whereby four journeys in each peak on Mondays to Fridays were projected off the usual line of route over a private road to serve the Ministry of Labour offices at Leybourne Park. Central was the only company to operate thus.

Like so many other independents, Central exchanged their individualistic livery for a mundane red & white when the vehicles went

245

for their first overhaul. C changed colour in February 1924 followed by B in March, A in May and D in August. The work was carried out by Birch whose quote was £37 per bus to "Repaint light red relieved by a suitable colour as selected. Revarnish & clean insides. Line-out and write." In October 1924 the Company's registered office was transferred to the garage at 112A Junction Road.

Early in December 1925 a new bus was ordered, probably as a replacement for one of the Straker Squires as the London Traffic Act would have prohibited any additional operation on route 27. It was a Dodson-bodied Leyland, but it was not destined to run for Central. Shortly after it was ordered the directors decided to dispose of their bus interests to General. Though the Central ran at a profit, it is likely that its directors had become disillusioned with bus operation by the failure of the other bus concern in which they were also financially interested, the ailing Cambrian Coaching & Goods Transport Ltd. The disposal of Central enabled them to concentrate on their road haulage and allied activities.

At the Engineers' Club in Coventry Street on January 29th 1926 Coventon Moth met representatives of the LGOC and fixed up the sale. On February 1st the Central Omnibus Co. Ltd. ceased to be controlled by Coventons Ltd. and became instead a subsidiary of the LGOC. Three of the Straker Squires were removed into Holloway (J) garage whence they maintained the Central operations for only twenty days. The fourth Straker was away at the manufacturer's works being repaired after a bad smash and probably did not return in time to rejoin the Central fleet before it was replaced by K's in the interests of standardisation. The Straker Squires went to Cambrian, which may indirectly account for the fact that the four Central K's were delivered in a green livery. These could well have been repainted for Cambrian before it was decided that, temporarily at least, acquired Straker Squires would be concentrated on the Cambrian fleet. As for Central's new Leyland, this never operated for Central nor, indeed, did it run in service in London at all. Though delivered in Central livery and licensed by them on January 29th 1926 as YM 6649, it remained in store (and unlicensed after February 12th) until it was sold on March 1st to Lee & Beaulah of Elloughton for operation in the East Riding of Yorkshire. Central was one of the very first LGOC acquisitions and at this stage the General would not have known that, in the months to come, it would acquire many other similar Leylands which it would prefer to retain rather than the Straker Squires.

At the time of takeover the Central's rather complex operations on the 27 were as follows:-

27A Highgate to Twickenham   Daily
27C Highgate to Hammersmith Bdy.   Daily
27D Highgate to Kew Gardens   Weekdays
27E Hammersmith Bdy. to Twickenham Mon. to Thurs. and Sat.
127 Highgate to Hampton Court   Sundays

Immediately after the LGOC took control the heavily used Leybourne Park journeys on the 27D were discontinued on the instructions of the police, the last journey being during the morning peak of August 9th.

246

Under LGOC control the operation of the Central buses was uneventful. The same vehicles, K11/42/70/980, remained until the firm was wound up although they were repainted in standard LGOC livery in due course, retaining the Central name only on the rocker panels. Complete acquisition by General took place on January 1st 1928.

It might have been expected that, with all its facilities, Coventon's garage at 112A Junction Road might have provided a home for several of the local independents, but this was not so. Apart from the Central buses, the only known independents to be based there were E. E. Farwell and A. I. Bland. The latter owned a Dennis called the Fountain which we have already met in 1-12 Harmood Street. It was garaged at Coventons from about January 1926 until the Public took it over on August 11th 1927.

RELIABLE/DAUNTLESS

The Farwell Omnibus Co. Ltd. had originated in November 1924 when Ernest Edward Farwell of 46 Bickerton Road, Holloway, bought a Dodson-bodied Dennis, XW 2566, which he ran mainly on the 284. He kept it originally at Dangerfield's garage in Harmood Street, Chalk Farm, but soon moved to Coventon's. Oddly enough Farwell did not use his own surname as a fleetname although it would have been most appropriate. Instead he christened his bus Dauntless. A sister vehicle, XW 4334, was licensed on November 29th, also for the 284, and received the name Reliable.

Farwell had visions of expanding his bus business, and in February 1925 he agreed to purchase the two bus businesses owned by L. S. St. E. Punnett trading under the name of X-Service. Ignorant of the law, Farwell paid cash for Punnett's pair of Straker Squires and the schedules upon which they operated, only to find out that the latter were not transferable. Punnett had little choice then but to remain in business while Farwell made a second attempt to carry the acquisition through. He had obviously found out that the only way of gaining access to someone else's schedules was through an exchange of shares in a limited company, so on July 1st 1925 he formed such a company entitled the Farwell Omnibus Company Ltd., the directors being Ernest Farwell and his wife Marie. Initially Punnett was allotted £175 worth of shares and £50 in cash for his business, which he undertook to transfer, so far as he legally could, to the Farwell Omnibus Company Ltd. Unfortunately for Farwell he had once again got it wrong. Punnett's was the business which should have been turned into a limited company, in which Farwell could then have taken over the shareholding. Instead, after the new purchase agreement had gone through, the X-Service schedules were surrendered by Punnett only for Farwell to find that they could not be transferred to his company and that they had, instead, become null and void.

Though Farwell gained no extra schedules out of his abortive purchase of the X-Service, he found himself with additional rolling stock which he had no use for. Fortunately for him he had eventually only purchased the newer of Punnett's two Strakers, XR 8763, the other having been taken over by Walter Dangerfield who, it is suspected, impounded it to clear outstanding debts for services rendered such as garaging and servicing.

247

Farwell had arranged with Dodsons for the delivery of a new double-decker to operate the second Punnett schedule, an order which he promptly cancelled when he realised that the deal had gone wrong. It is thought that Farwell ran the Straker Squire illegally on the 27 for a while, and it later became a spare for the 284. Punnett's shares in the business passed to Ernest Farwell in December 1925, Punnett having abandoned all interest in London bus operation in favour of a resumed career in the Royal Air Force. After its acquisition by Farwell the Straker carried the fleet name Dauntless until June 1926 in which month the Dauntless name was discontinued, the whole fleet thereafter being called Reliable. This was just after Farwell had emerged from an unsuccessful new enterprise on route 550, a service over unrestricted roads pioneered by Orange. A new single-decker Dennis 25-seater, YM 6966, had been delivered for the route which Farwell ran only during February and March 1926. This Reliable single-decker was a sister to YM 6965 which Farwell operated on the 550 on behalf of Nulli Secundus. When the venture failed to come up to expectations both vehicles were sold to Orange, for whom they continued to run for a time in their original liveries. In May 1926 Farwell applied for and was granted a new route 554 linking Hendon Central Station with Colney Hatch Lane, Wilton Road (Muswell Hill) but no evidence exists that this ever operated.

Farwell negotiated the sale of the company to John Pike of the Claremont in November 1926 though it was Pike's business accomplice, F. J. Wood, who actually paid for and took it over in January 1927. The vehicles then moved out of Coventon's into the Claremont Garage in Pentonville Road. The subsequent brief history of the Reliable buses is told under the Claremont heading in chapter 4.

Today anyone walking down the old entranceway between the shops in Junction Road to look for Coventon's garage would be disappointed. The whole extensive site now lies under a complex of new flats.

256 Archway Road, Highgate

256 Archway Road was a rather drab-looking shop which formed the headquarters of the Bulwark Manufacturing Co. Ltd. The company had been formed in 1917 to make aircraft castings and was subsequently converted into a firm of motor engineers and suppliers, haulage contractors and coach booking agents. It acquired several adjacent properties including shops on either side at nos. 254/258, and later a garage was constructed at nos. 260/8. In the middle 'twenties Bulwark took in as a tenant Walter Faulkner's Northern bus which garaged there until May 1926 when control of it passed to Dangerfield as outlined in chapter 4. The bus occupied a part of premises (in effect no. 258 Archway Road) which was a converted shop where, once inside, the top of the bus just missed the rafters of the roof. The old Bulwark premises are all still in existence to this day basically unchanged by the passage of time, the actual building in which the Northern was kept now being a coin-op laundry.

CARDINAL

Two independent operators were based in Whetstone at the 1197-1207 High Road garage of Billy Thompson. This was later known as Trounson & Knights and is now incorporated in the premises of the Standard Tyre Company. The two operators were Cardinal and Majestic. Cardinal came first in the form of MF 9904, a red & white Dennis first licensed on July 30th 1924. Its owner was 25-years old John MacDonald Potter of 7 Fallow Court Avenue, North Finchley who, after several years as a cinema projectionist, punctuated by war service, was looking around for a new career. After talking to Lionel Punnett of the X-Service he decided on bus work and borrowed £250 from his mother Annie for a deposit. Hire purchase terms were arranged with Christopher Dodson who built the bodywork and also suggested the fleetname Cardinal.

Potter had next to no mechanical knowledge so he enlisted the services of James F. Ridley of 6 Regents Parade, North Finchley to work on the bus as a mechanic and as a conductor. Ridley had previously been with the Express Dairy as a fitter. Potter promised Ridley that, when the monthly instalments of £44 12s. 0d. on the bus were paid up, he would take him on as a partner. Meanwhile, as a token of security, he nominated Ridley as the licensee and it was the latter's name that appeared on the side of the bus.

At the start the Cardinal bus plied mainly between Highgate and the West End or Richmond, sometimes travelling as far afield as Hampton Court according to traffic. No route number was carried until the London Traffic Act brought stabilisation and the Cardinal settled down on the 284A.

A major catastrophe hit Potter in 1926 when, because of cash discrepancies, he dismissed Ridley. Ridley retaliated by surrendering the licences which meant that the bus could not operate. It was off the road for several weeks before the police would re-issue the licences in Potter's name. Meanwhile the dismissed man had introduced court proceedings seeking a declaration that he was part owner of the business which should be wound up and the proceeds divided. In the absence of any written confirmation as to the existence of a partnership the case failed.

As we have seen in chapter 4, Potter decided to dispose of the bus in November 1926. He was reluctant to sell to General or to anyone who, like Walter Dangerfield, he suspected of having connections with them. The vehicle passed to John Pike in January 1927 and lost its Cardinal fleetname though the title of Cardinal lingered on until the end of the independent era through the limited company to which Pike transferred all his bus assets.

After his bus career John Potter had a variety of jobs including a period as a Southdown coach driver from 1934 up to the war. He now lives in retirement at Finchley after having been employed the last twenty years of his working life at the local swimming baths.

MAJESTIC

Arthur Thomas Peggram, a quiet, reticent man, was at the wheel of a chocolate-coloured Leyland, XO 7581, when it appeared at Scotland Yard for plating on July 27th 1923 under the title of the Albion Omnibus Company. The business address of the company was Peggram's home at that time, 3 Herbert Terrace, Long Lane, Finchley. It is not known why Albion was chosen as the fleetname and it never ran as such. Rumour has it that Albion Motors Ltd. objected to the use of its registered trade name, causing the bus to be renamed Majestic before it entered service.

Peggram held only a minor cash stake in the bus, as did an individual by the name of T. W. Carter. The majority of the capital was supplied by Mrs. Hyacinth Adeane Rose Morrison, a Finchley widow. Peggram, a motor engineer, was responsible for its operation and described himself as Manager. It ran initially from the Dangerfield garage at 1-12 Harmood Street where it was joined in May 1924 by a second Leyland, XT 3142. The Majestics were mostly to be found in their early days on various sections of the main Finchley Road routes 2 and 13 with Sunday outings to St. Albans. It is not known why, but when schedules became necessary under the London Traffic Act only one was obtained although there were two buses. This was on the 284A and also included a morning peak journey on 279B. Sundays were normally devoted to the 27. By this time the buses were housed at Whetstone and Peggram had moved the business address to a new house at 27 Mayfield Avenue, Finchley.

Towards the end of 1925 George Ellis Askew a Loughton businessman and coach operator, appeared on the scene and arranged with Mrs. Morrison to buy the Majestic buses. He planned to leave one at Whetstone under Peggram's control for the 284A and intended to make better use of the other by running it on a then-unrestricted East London route from his own premises at Forest Road, Loughton. So that he could take over the 284A schedule Askew arranged for Mrs. Morrison to form the Majestic Omnibus Co. Ltd. of which he became the major shareholder. 1,002 £1 shares were allotted out of the authorised 2,000 of which Askew had 995, Peggram 6 and Mrs. Morrison 1. The company was incorporated on November 10th 1925 and had its head office at 27 Mayfield Avenue.

The limited company took over only the newer of the two buses, XT 3142. The other, XO 7581, was transferred into the ownership of George Askew who began running it on the 100A, still with the fleetname Majestic. In August 1926 it was relicensed with Peggram's name and address but we do not know what it was used on and can only surmise that he operated on an unrestricted route in north London which he thought would be more profitable than the 100A. Peggram continued to work closely with Askew. He remained in charge of the bus on the 284A and also acted as an agent for Askew's fleet of four or more Lancia coaches. On March 1st 1926 XO 7581 passed back from Peggram to Askew for the 100A and in November 1926 came an abortive attempt to sell the assets of the Majestic Omnibus Co. Ltd., including XT 3142, to John Pike. A restriction Order was placed on the 100A on July 30th 1927 and five days later both Majestic buses passed to Public who paid £4,000 for them. Though the date of takeover was officially August 3rd the buses had been under Public control for just over a fortnight before this.

The Loughton-based bus was run by them from July 11th onwards and the Whetstone-garaged vehicle from July 13th.

With the departure of the Majestic buses George Askew continued with his coaching and other activities as outlined in chapter 8. Peggram also dabbled in coach operation in a small way though his main connection with the coaching world was the "Majestic" booking office on the corner of Mayfield Avenue and High Road, North Finchley, of which he was the proprietor. The only coach he is known to have owned was YV 3577, a brown Gilford which he bought new in March 1928 and retained until June 1933. For part of the time it was registered in the name of a partnership, Peggram & Marshall.

East Barnet Road

BARNET MOTOR SERVICES

Northwards along the Great North Road from Finchley lies the town of Barnet. In the 'twenties Barnet, like Harrow, was still separated from the built-up area of suburban London by a short stretch of countryside, though speculative builders were soon to rectify this. The town was well-served from many directions by buses of the National and General as well as various independents, in addition to the electric trams of the M.E.T. But these were mostly main-road operations emanating from other towns or suburbs of importance and there was no purely local operator in Barnet until Charles William Dunford, proprietor of the Parkbridge Nurseries in Park Road, New Barnet began running from Hadley Highstone to the Prince of Wales in East Barnet, via Station Road. According to contemporary police records operation started on March 8th 1923. Apart from his horticultural interests Dunford was already an established charabanc operator with a marked preference for Fiats. He traded, appropriately enough, as Barnet Motor Services.

Dunford's first recorded Fiat was a charabanc, NK 1885, and this was followed in January and June 1923 by NK 5070/5752. NK 8696 of 1924 vintage may have replaced NK 1885. They were all small capacity vehicles of twelve to fourteen seats and may each have been used on the bus service from time to time. Some, or maybe all, were in a yellow-brown livery with maroon linings. Very early on Dunford successfully applied to extend his service northwards from Hadley Highstone to the village of Potters Bar. It is not known if his buses ever reached Potters Bar; if they did the extension did not last long enough to have merited mention in the local papers or elsewhere.

Under the London Traffic Act Dunford's pioneer route was in due course numbered 352. A second service commenced on Monday June 2nd 1924 and was first allocated route number 519E, though this was later amended to 354. Starting, as in the case of the 352, from the Two Brewers at Hadley Highstone it ran via Barnet, Whetstone, Oakleigh Road, New Southgate Station and Bounds Green Road to terminate at Lymington Avenue, Wood Green. The service ran only on weekdays with ten journeys in each direction giving a headway of approximately every 1½ hours. One bus was sufficient to maintain the published timetable on this service; another was needed for the 352. These little yellow/brown

251

Barnet buses looked incongruously small alongside the multitude of double-deckers, both independent and combine, serving Wood Green at the time and were dwarfed by the M.E.T. trams. From November 2nd 1924 the service was curtailed to run from the Bull & Butcher at Whetstone to Wood Green as 354A with fifteen journeys each way and Sunday operation began with journeys running right through from Hadley Highstone to Wood Green.

The fleet was modernised in October 1924 with the purchase of its largest-ever vehicle, a new Dennis NK 8877. The Dodson body of this seated twenty and, though still only a small bus by normal standards, it looked large beside the diminutive Fiats. Presumably, after its entry into service, the Dennis maintained the Wood Green run most of the time.

In January 1925 Dunford submitted revised schedules for his two services. The 352, still bearing the same number, was to be extended northwards to Hadley Wood Station. The extension commenced on Monday March 2nd from which date the service consisted of fifteen journeys in each direction on weekdays and eight on Sundays. Probably on the same date the Wood Green service was diverted at Whetstone to terminate at Totteridge War Memorial under the route number 353. July 1925 saw Dunford applying for a new service between Palmers Green and Muswell Hill via Whetstone and Colney Hatch Lane, but the police refused to grant a licence for it.

Dunford ceased running his services at the end of 1925. The Dennis passed to A. T. Bennett & Co. Ltd., the proprietors of the Admiral buses, under whose auspices the 353 appears to have operated for almost another year. The 352 was abandoned, and between January and March 1926 NK 5070/5752, and probably also NK 8696, were sold to the newly-formed Waltham Motor Services Ltd. The Dennis was later sold by Admiral to Waltham where it met up once again with the Fiats which had been its stable mates in Barnet days.

The East Barnet Road garage where Dunford kept his buses faded into memory many decades ago. A Northmet electricity office and showroom marked the site for many years and by 1972 this, too, had been demolished to pave the way for a Budgen supermarket.

114A Blackstock Road, Finsbury Park

John Melhuish & Coy. Ltd., of 114A Blackstock Road, Finsbury Park, were the proprietors of a very spacious garage and filling station where they carried out the usual range of vehicle repairs and overhauls. They were taxicab and commercial vehicle suppliers and provided garage accommodation for these types of vehicle. They do not appear to have been particularly keen to establish themselves with bus operators though New Times was one of their clients from May to about August 1923. Next door was Pickfords' furniture department, and nowadays Pickfords are in the former Melhuish garage also.

Whymark Garage, Whymark Avenue, Wood Green
Empire Garage, Boreham Road, Wood Green
Syree's Garage, 7/9 Commerce Road, Wood Green
(also Central Garage, Hedge Lane, Palmers Green
and Lloyd's Garage, Station Road, Wood Green)

Wood Green was inevitably a popular centre for independents because of the attractiveness of route 29 and its various offshoots, all of which passed through the centre of the borough. Within a comparatively short distance of each other were three garages whose stories are linked, not by ownership, but by the movements of bus proprietors from one to another.

The earliest of the three to house buses was the petrol station in Whymark Avenue, little more than a stone's throw from the Wellington public house, a well-known bus terminal point before the advent in 1932 of Turnpike Lane tube station. The two Newstead buses were the first at the Whymark Garage in December 1923 and they were joined by four other operators including three trading under a common name of Empress. These three were the Empress Omnibus Co. Ltd., F. F. Downes and Crabb & Clarke. The fifth independent at Whymark Avenue was Mason Brothers who owned the Uneedus bus. The number of buses at the Whymark Garage was at its peak of seven vehicles amongst the five operators in July and August 1924. In the latter month the Empress Omnibus Co. Ltd. moved into its own purpose-built garage in Boreham Road, taking the whole Whymark Garage clientele with them except for F. F. Downes who, in September 1924, transferred to the third of the major Wood Green garages, Syree Brothers' in Commerce Road.

The Empire Garage at the back of the houses at the northern end of Boreham Road, near the Wood Green/Tottenham boundary, was a comparative rarity in having been built by a small independent bus operator to house its own buses and those of others. The Empress Omnibus Co. Ltd. who built it was a go-ahead concern which met with less success than its efforts deserved. They had the garage built after experiencing at first hand the plight of bus owners in finding suitable accommodation and workshop space. Buses first ran from it on August 28th 1924 and by the middle of 1925 no fewer than eleven concerns were based there. In addition to the four we have already noted at Whymark Avenue there was (in order of arrival) Field Marshal, Lancastrian, Perkins, The Leader, Empire's Best, Stanmore and Alexandra. Some such as Uneedus and Empire's Best moved out to other garages where better terms were offered whilst others failed to make the grade and went out of business. Two later arrivals were Ambassador and the much-travelled Pullman but neither stayed long. In December 1926 the Empress Omnibus Co. Ltd., about to sell out to the LGOC, gave notice to their last remaining bus tenants, Field Marshal and Perkins, to leave by the 21st of the month. They went to Syree's garage where they joined up once again with several other ex-Empire Garage tenants.

Syree Brothers' garage was at 7/9 Commerce Road. The Syrees were for many years motor body builders and they also ran a general motor and garage business. On the crest of the coaching boom of the nineteen-twenties, they established a booking agency for a wide range of express services. The first bus to arrive was H. C. Durell's D. M. Thornycroft in July 1924. F. F. Downes followed two months later after vacating the Whymark Garage, and afterwards came Hav-a-ride, Direct, Empire's Best, Empire (Newstead), Field Marshal and Perkins, the last four all being ex-Empire Garage. All except Perkins sold out to larger operators in 1926-8; Perkins departed in 1931 when their own garage was built in Enfield.

Nowadays there is no garage at 7/9 Commerce Road. Extensive "redevelopment" has seen to that. Syree's old garage was demolished in April 1970 after having lain empty for some while. Fortunately the Whymark Garage still exists virtually unaltered as a used car showroom, and the accommodation for the buses of fifty years ago can be seen at the rear. The Empire Garage, too, still stands. After passing into LGOC hands it was used mainly for storage until becoming, for a short time, a body overhaul shop for their subsidiary, Public. The freehold was sold on November 11th 1930 and for many years afterwards it was the home of the D. O. Transport & Garages Ltd. A firm of building contractors now occupies it and recalls its past ancestry by naming it their Empress Works.

EMPRESS

The first the north London public knew of the Empress was when the Middlesex County Council received a letter from a "Putney bus firm" offering to run a service between Finsbury Park and New Southgate via Wood Green and Bounds Green Road. In 1923 Bounds Green Road was served solely by tram route 21 which had been the subject of much public criticism because of its irregularity. The writer of the letter was Albert James Agg, a motor engineer whose firm entitled Ward & Co. was based at 51 Upper Richmond Road, Putney. It may seem strange that a west London firm should have offered to run a local service in north London, but the explanation for this was that the Empress Omnibus Co. Ltd. which was about to be formed had A. J. Agg as its future Secretary and director. The other two directors were local men, and the more active of the two was Arthur Herbert Young, formerly a conductor at the LGOC's Palmers Green (AD) garage, who lived in Hornsey and was probably the instigator of the Bounds Green Road idea. Charles George Leaphard was the third director and his home address, 50 Solon Road, Wood Green, became the company's registered office in place of Agg's in August 1923. Like Young, Charles Leaphard was a former LGOC man at Palmers Green garage, from which he was dismissed after ten years' service when his employers found out about the Empress venture. He worked as a driver on the Empress, doubling up as company secretary from May 1923.

The Empress Omnibus Co. Ltd. had been registered on February 17th 1923 with a nominal capital of £6,000. It was probably purely coincidental that, at the same time, another Empress company was being contemplated in east London by the Stanton family. The Cambridge Heath concern was the first to receive a bus, its Straker Squire entering service twelve days before XN 4477. This chocolate & cream Leyland was registered on April 10th 1923 and started work on Monday April 23rd. The Empress Omnibus Co. Ltd. was in business and intended to expand.

Its initial application for three routes embraced Winchmore Hill to Finsbury Park, Putney High Street to Southgate, and Hadley Woods to Victoria, but when operation began it was on the Finsbury Park-New Southgate link which had been offered to the Middlesex County Council earlier. It soon turned out to be a poorer proposition than anticipated and lasted only about a week. By the beginning of May the Empress had been diverted at Wood Green to run via Palmers Green to Winchmore Hill, again a tram route. Then came a succession of applications for various workings via combinations of existing tram and LGOC bus routes such as Winchmore Hill to Crystal Palace, Wood Green to Edmonton via Bruce Grove, St. Albans to Camden Town and Winchmore Hill to Hammersmith via Moorgate, Elephant and Hyde Park Corner. The directors were trying to feel their way on to the most profitable operations and for a while the Empress bus appears to have run in "pirate" fashion wherever the money appeared to be. After a few weeks of this it settled down mainly on the 29 along with many other independent buses. Empress became deeply involved in the fare war then raging on route 29 and in August 1923 was offering the most ridiculous of all bargain fares; 2d each way between Palmers Green and Charing Cross between 10.30 a.m. and 4.00 p.m. Mondays to Fridays.

First of all garage accommodation was found for the bus at the Central Garage, Hedge Lane, Palmers Green, but before long a yearly tenancy was taken on L. A. Lloyd & Co.'s garage at Station Road, Wood Green, which lay on the north side between the railway embankment and Bradley Road. Early in 1924 the garage owners asked Empress to change the tenancy to a weekly basis, which they agreed to do for a consideration of £25. Lloyds then lost no time in giving Empress notice to quit, which they received on February 21st. It was upon receipt of this that the directors of the bus company decided that the best thing they could do would be to build their own depot in view of the uncertainties of renting accommodation. Meanwhile they found a third temporary base at the Whymark Garage and it was during their stay there that a short-lived scheme was inaugurated whereby two other operators (Crabb & Clarke and F. F. Downes) also adopted the Empress title and livery. On February 13th 1924 the Company's registered office changed from Solon Road to 212 Wood Green High Road when Charles Leaphard moved house.

March 1924 was a big month for the Company. To start with a new bus was ordered from Dodson's, this time on a Dennis chassis. Then a builder by the name of Wakeling was contracted to erect a garage on a plot of land to be purchased in Granville Road, Wood Green. The Granville Road project was not approved by the Wood Green Council so instead plot no. 886 in nearby Boreham Road was purchased from the British Land Company. Council approval for this revised project was received in June and construction began the following month amid an outburst of protest from Boreham Road residents against the building of a bus garage in a residential area. Actually the garage could hardly be seen from Boreham Road itself, it was behind the houses on the eastern side of the road and was reached by an approach road little wider than a bus. Construction of the depot was completed in about September 1924, progress having been marred only by Wakeling going bankrupt and the delay in finding another builder, a Mr. Rowley, to finish things off.

The company was one of the very few small independent concerns progressive enough to build its own depot. The name Empire Garage was chosen for the building, and was specially appropriate as 1924 was the first year of the great Empire Exhibition at Wembley. It was renamed Empress Garage on December 18th 1925 by which time the topicality of the Empire Exhibition was swiftly on the wane. The Empire Garage became the company's registered office on August 23rd, before the builders had moved out. Besides becoming the operation base for the Empress buses (of which there were now two) the garage also served as a public filling station and car repairs were carried out there. Arthur Young was in charge of the garage and sometimes worked right through the night as a 24-hour service was maintained for a while. Like Charles Randall of the Royal Blue, Young could normally be distinguished in the summer months by his straw hat, and his liking for a glass or two of beer was legendary. The main function of the garage quickly became the housing, fuelling and general maintenance of other operators' buses. The first to move in were the Mason Brothers whose tenancy began on August 27th 1924 with the arrival of their first Uneedus bus. For a while the Empire Garage became highly popular with bus owners and by the middle of February 1925 no fewer than eleven concerns were running out of it. In addition to buses, many car, van, lorry and charabanc owners garaged at Boreham Road for varying lengths of time.

The Empress Omnibus Co. Ltd. must be credited with an unusual and possibly unique enterprise. In the summer of 1924 it operated a regular once-weekly service from Wood Green to Margate using one of its double-deckers. Each Sunday at 7.45 p.m. the bus would leave Wood Green High Road, and at 5.00 p.m. it would begin its return trip from Margate, where passengers had spent about four hours by the sea. Seats had to be booked in advance, either at agencies or with the company's conductors. The upper deck was reserved for return fare holders only at 9/- a time. Children at half price, single ticket holders, and those with 8/- returns travelled downstairs.

The new Dennis ordered in March 1924 was delivered at the beginning of July and licensed on the 4th as MH 9159. It was put to work soon afterwards on the 29. A third bus was now planned and it was agreed that it would be bought by Agg who would arrange for its hire purchase to the Company. With a surprising disregard for standardisation the choice of chassis fell to Thornycroft who duly supplied one of their sedate J-types in time to enter service before Christmas 1924. It was registered MH 2516.

Like so many otherwise well-conceived schemes, the Empress suffered because capital was insufficient to match the business aspirations of its owners. In time this proved to be the Company's downfall. Meanwhile, on November 6th 1924 when the finances were hard pressed, the Company's nominal capital was increased by £250 to permit the allotment of shares to Mrs. Eleanor Strongman, a teacher living at Southgate, who joined the board of directors. From the start of 1925 the restrictions of the London Traffic Act made themselves felt through regulated schedules which prevented the buses from chasing traffic as hitherto. It might have been thought that the stability which this brought would have benefited Empress as it had done for many other independent undertakings, but this was not so. Empress's weakness lay in the fact that it was entirely committed to route 29 and its various offshoots, on which the receipts remained disastrously low as a result of the earlier fare-slashing campaign. Prior to 1925, though the 29 had been the spine of the Empress workings, buses had branched out at the northern end to serve North Finchley, the Southgate area, Winchmore Hill or Edmonton. Forced to settle down, the Company selected the 294 (Lower Edmonton) operation for weekdays and the 29 (Hadley Woods) on Sundays. A diversion to Bruce Grove as the 270 in 1925 was short-lived. On May 25th 1925 Charles Leaphard left the board of directors shortly after it had been found necessary to mortgage the Empire Garage to secure adequate working capital.

The start of 1926 saw little improvement in the general financial position, and in February the purchase of another bus was deferred. Later in the year a Mr. Woodward came forward with extra capital which he was willing to put into the business, whereupon he was accepted as an additional director. On the strength of his financial contribution a further bus was ordered from Dodson's, this time a Leyland. This was in September, but in the October it became clear that the position could not be redeemed by the addition of extra capital and Woodward was told not to pay any money in. Young took over responsibility for the new Leyland which was registered YR 5805 in his name on November 12th but was in Empress livery. Meanwhile he had approached General with an offer to sell out to them. The LGOC first of all proposed a figure which was disappointing, but in early December an improved offer was made which the Empress directors decided to accept. At a board meeting on December 10th the transfer of all shares but one to Agg was decided upon, the single share going to C. A. King, a chartered accountant empowered to come to terms with the company's creditors. Agg became secretary and had the task of arranging the transfer of the business to General. On December 23rd 1926 control of the company passed to its new owners and at the end of service on that same night three of the Empress buses were transferred into Chalk Farm (CF) garage together with seven drivers and nine conductors from the Empress staff. YR 5805, the new Leyland, was not included in the sale and remained Young's property until it was purchased by Peraeque a month or so later.

Very soon after the change of ownership the Empress Thornycroft was disposed of, being replaced on January 18th 1927 by K1003. This vehicle was noteworthy in that it was the first K-type to operate on an ex-independent service in full General livery save for the legal lettering on the rocker panels. Prior to this the independent fleetname had been carried on the main panels of the K-types at the insistence of the police, and the change of policy introduced by K1003 followed a relaxation of this rule. The Dennis left the Empress fleet on July 1st and the Leyland followed just under a fortnight later. Thereafter the operations were continued with three K's in General colours until the Company was wound up on January 1st 1928.

After the Empress business was sold to General, Agg passed out of the passenger transport scene but Young, and Leaphard—who, it will be recalled, had left the Empress board a year earlier—tried hard to get back into the industry. Both submitted a number of applications for new services which the police systematically rejected on one pretext or another. In January 1927 they applied jointly for a back-street route between Stamford Hill and Finsbury Park. December 1927 saw an application by Young for an Edmonton to Romford service and in July 1928 Leaphard sought to run Friern Barnet to Highams Park. He was still trying in January 1929 when a proposal for a service from the New Cambridge Road (Lordship Lane) to Tottenham was turned down and his last application in April 1929 (Stockwell, Hammerton's Brewery to Norwood) was no more successful. Clearly they would get nowhere in suburban London but, back in April 1927, they explored the possibilities of a Wood Green-Romford-Southend service which would operate on an express basis within the Metropolitan Police area. Licences were obtained for six vehicles but before operation could begin on May 27th 1927 Leaphard and Young had parted company and it was the latter who started the new venture as sole proprietor. First of all a service of eight journeys a day ran between the Jolly Butchers at Wood Green and Borough's garage at Southend under the title of the "Empress Bus" but before long the more famous title of New Empress Saloons emerged. Young met with severe competition on the Southend Road but his hand was strengthened by the formation on July 3rd 1928 of New Empress Saloons Ltd. in which he was joined by two former independent bus proprietors, H. J. Barnett and S. F. G. Collier. In October 1928 control passed to the City Motor Omnibus Co. Ltd. (as we have seen in chapter 2). Young remained a director for a while and then stayed on a little longer as a driver, his pioneering days at an end.

After severing his connection with A. H. Young, Leaphard began an unhappy spell as a bus and garage owner in Essex (as we shall see in the Perkins history later in this chapter) and in 1932/3 he was employed as a driver by Sunset Pullman of Brentwood and by Romford District Motor Services. His fortunes reached their lowest ebb when London Transport took over Romford District and he was immediately discharged as redundant. At 46 years of age and with a family to support, the dole was a grim prospect in 1934.

NEWSTEAD ESTABLISHED 1860/EMPIRE
We shall shortly be meeting the famous Admiral buses, which were once held out as being a shining example of independent bus operation at its best. One of the participants in the Admiral fleet in its earlier days, before A. T. Bennett obtained exclusive use of the name, was Lyle Mill Newstead of 76 Falkland Road, Hornsey. With two Dodson-bodied Straker Squires, ME 9689 and MF 180, Newstead had joined Admiral in May 1923. In December of the same year he parted company with Bennett and moved to Whymark Avenue whence he began running the

258

two vehicles on his own, still mainly on route 29 though he also applied for plates for routes 14, 19, 21 and 73. Suitably repainted in an all-over dark red, easily distinguishable from the former navy blue & white, the two vehicles were operated by Newstead until September 1924. The most memorable thing about them was their fleetname which, in a bold white panel announced Newstead: established 1860. The "established 1860" is thought to have been a reference to a useful horse bus service formerly operated up to about 1911 by Mill Newstead, Lyle's father, between the People's Palace and Oxford Circus via Commercial Street & Theobalds Road. In time Newstead decided to dispose of his two Straker Squires, and ordered a new vehicle from Leyland for October 1924 delivery. He found Cambrian willing to buy the Straker Squires, and on September 22nd they paid Newstead £1,300 for the pair. Newstead was then without a bus until the delivery in October of MH 1705. This new Leyland carried a chocolate & white body built by Strachan & Brown, and with it Newstead began the third stage in his bus operating career.

MH 1705 was called Empire, and was the second Empire bus to run in London, having been preceded two months earlier by F. J. C. Kirk's Dennis. There was no connection between them, and indeed the two probably hardly ever met as Newstead's bus was mainly on 294 and later the 529 whilst Kirk's stayed in East London on the 511. The choice of title was probably quite coincidental and was no doubt inspired in Newstead's case by the fact that his bus was based in the Empire Garage at Boreham Road, his move to which coincided with the purchase of the new Leyland. It stayed at Boreham Road until May 1926 when Newstead moved to Syree's Commerce Road garage.

On November 21st 1927 Newstead sold his bus to Public for £3,000, leaving Kirk in sole possession of the title Empire.

EMPRESS/F.F.D./HORSESHOE

Frederick Francis Downes of 46 Russell Avenue, Wood Green, was no newcomer to transport when he ordered his two Daimler buses from Roberts in the March of 1924. He had spent twenty years as a conductor on the MET trams and was now aged 48. He spent his life savings of £500 as the deposit on the two buses, agreeing to repay the balance of the total cost of £2,900 by monthly instalments of £133 6s. 8d.

The title chosen by Downes for the first of the two buses was Empress and, as we have seen in the preceding pages, it ran originally from the Whymark garage in conjunction with the Empress Omnibus Co. Ltd. MF 7349 was licensed on May 7th 1924. By the time Downes' second Daimler, MH 1261, was delivered in October 1924 he had broken off contact with the Empress business of Young, Leaphard and Agg and moved to Syree's garage in Commerce Road. The second Daimler was easily distinguishable from its brother as it bore a red & white livery with Downes' initials as the fleetname; F.F.D.

At an unknown date, but probably fairly early in 1925, Downes moved to garage number three. He had arranged with a man called Harry Holmes to park his buses next to the blacksmith's shop at 3 Culross Road, West Green, where Holmes traded as Henry Holmes & Son. His old-world smithy had survived like a relic from the past in a drab corner of suburbia, and much of his work still consisted of shoeing horses. So it was small wonder that, in May 1925 when Downes had MF 7349 repainted red & white, he renamed it Horseshoe. MH 1261 followed suit soon after. It is interesting to record that, as demand on the blacksmith's business began to tail off, Harry Holmes turned in 1928 to coach operation starting with a second-hand Lancia for which he also used the fleetname Horseshoe. Horseshoe Coaches Ltd. are still active in West Green to the present day though their old Culross Road base exists no longer.

Downes' buses usually ran on route 29 and its various short workings though he applied for approval to run on others from time to time. He was unlucky because both buses proved to be highly unreliable and constantly in need of repair. Many days were spent off service and because of this his takings averaged only about £42 a week which was barely sufficient to meet the hire purchase payments and left almost nothing for the many other operating expenses. Because money was short, repairs were often skimped leading to further breakdowns and further loss of revenue. To try to extricate himself from this spiral Downes ordered a new Leyland to replace one of the Daimlers, but too late. By March 1926 he could no longer carry on and arranged to sell the business to the LGOC. For this purpose the Horseshoe Traction Co. Ltd. was incorporated on March 20th with a nominal capital of £2,000 and registered office at 41 Finsbury Square, E.C.2. The shares passed to the LGOC on Thursday April 1st 1926 and the office was transferred to 55 Broadway.

On July 28th 1926 a Receiving Order was made against Downes, the petitioner being J. M. Roberts who contended that Downes owed him £1,132 13s. 2d. for repair work carried out on the two buses. Downes duly appeared at the offices of the Official Receiver on Friday August 13th (an unfortunate choice of date!) when it was revealed that the LGOC had paid him £2,450 for his business of which £300 was used to clear outstanding hire purchase payments on the buses. He told the Receiver that the remaining £2,150 had gone on general hiring expenses and to pay off sundry creditors—he could not remember who—and that gross liabilities were now £1,137 5s. 1d. as against assets of £16 14s. 11d. Judgement was obtained against him for £1,000 for repairs, etc. and an execution levied on household furniture. This, however, was claimed by his wife whereupon the execution was withdrawn and bankruptcy proceedings instituted. There then followed a series of appearances in the Bankruptcy Court where it transpired that Downes had falsely claimed to have spent the whole of the £2,450 received from the LGOC in clearing debts and on general living expenses whereas, up to September 1926, he still held it all in cash. From September 26th onwards he had lost £800 of it through investing unwisely on slow horses! These losses, which he had been afraid to tell his wife about, were sometimes as high as £80 a week. Poor Downes' Horseshoe had certainly not been a lucky one.

After the LGOC took over Horseshoe they continued to run from Culross Road until Wednesday April 21st when the vehicles were transferred into Tottenham (AR) garage. The new Leyland, which had been ordered by Downes, was delivered at about this time and was licensed on April 29th as YN 3800, the registration number being the last in a large block reserved by the LGOC. It replaced MF 7349.

The two Horseshoe buses remained at Tottenham until absorbed into the LGOC on January 1st 1928 although by this time K's had replaced the other vehicles. The Leyland had been withdrawn in August 1926 prior to going to Grangewood, and the remaining Daimler had been withdrawn at the end of the following March.

Downes' misfortunes as a bus owner did not deter him from applying in August 1928 for a licence to operate from Hatfield to Cockfosters via Potters Bar. His bad luck stayed with him, however, and permission was refused.

FIELD MARSHAL

The independent bus owners were, by and large, an imaginative lot when it came to selecting fleetnames, and it was perhaps inevitable that sooner or later one of them would go one rank better than General and call his bus Field Marshal. The one-upmanship extended in this case to the use of fleet number 72 for the one and only bus ever owned by the Keech's and Boorers.

MH 866 was a red & white Strachan & Brown-bodied Dennis which was licensed on September 16th 1924. It was bought by Arthur Keech and Alfred Boorer who were cousins and had both spent many years working on the Great Northern Railway. Keech was an engine driver on the east coast main line but Boorer preferred to drive local trains from the nearby Hornsey depot. The two bought the bus, which was on hire purchase, for their sons to work on. Victor Alfred Boorer was already a busman and drove for General at Palmers Green (AD) garage. Wilfrid Arthur Keech was a hairdresser and tired of his profession. He was named as licensee of the bus as well as being its conductor, and his home address of 19 Southcote Road, Tufnell Park, was also the company's address. The Field Marshal was housed in the Empire Garage and normally worked on the 29 though, before the London Traffic Act came into force, it occasionally strayed on to the 73, sometimes reaching as far westwards as Hampton Court on Sundays and Bank holidays. At one time the purchase of a charabanc was considered but the idea came to nothing.

On January 16th 1925 Boorer senior was tragically killed on the railway when he was run down by a locomotive in fog and his interest in the business passed to his widow, Edith Alice Boorer. In 1926 the Keech's decided to quit and offered to sell their share in the bus to Percy Constant, another LGOC employee at Palmers Green garage. The Field Marshall Omnibus Co. Ltd. was incorporated on July 9th 1926 with a share capital of £750 and an agreement was made on July 18th for completion on the 30th whereby the Keech's and Boorers would sell the bus to the new company for the allotment of 748 fully paid up shares. Percy Constant owned half the shares whilst Mrs. Boorer and her son, Victor, held the remaining half between them. Constant's address at 78 Westbury Avenue, Wood Green, served as the Company's registered office. The use of two l's in Marshall in the title of the limited company should be noted; it is of no great significance except to indicate that

261

someone was having trouble with their spelling! The bus carried the name correctly spelt.

With the sale of the Empress Garage (as it was now called) to the LGOC Field Marshal had to find another home. Their last day at Boreham Road was December 20th 1926 after which they moved to Syree's Garage. In July 1927 Percy Constant enquired about the purchase of a new Karrier WL6/2 68-seater with a covered top but this came to nothing and on February 17th 1928 the Field Marshal bus was sold to Public for £2,800. The company was dissolved on May 17th 1929.

Victor Boorer became a driver with Public but was turned down for employment by the LGOC, supposedly on medical grounds, when the latter absorbed Public. He then drove for Birch and subsequently for London Transport until his retirement. Percy Constant was more ambitious and began the first regular London to Bedford service under the title of Constant's Super de Luxe Coaches in March 1928 with five journeys a day in each direction (six on Saturdays). Constant stayed at Syree's garage for this venture which was short-lived, the service being withdrawn in December of the same year. An interesting feature of it had been a facility for day trips from Bedford to France via Constant's coach to London; truly a mammoth day out! A fresh start under the title Arcadia's Super-de-Luxe Coaches was made in May 1929 between London, Bedford and Wellingborough on a twice-daily basis, but this lasted only a few weeks. For this venture Constant based his activities at the Whymark Garage.

LANCASTRIAN

Somewhere along Perth Road, Wood Green, probably at its junction with Crossways where a Salvation Army hall now stands, is reputed to have been a site used by Thomas Morris of 23 Leith Road, Wood Green, as a base for his bus and charabanc business. His first bus, MF 9873, a chocolate & white Daimler with the fleetname Lancastrian, was licensed on July 28th 1924. In October 1924 he arranged for the bus (but not his charabancs) to be housed at the Empire Garage, where he stayed until March 1925. Like Geninazzi of the Alexandra and Perkins & Edwards of The Leader, he left owing money which in his case was not fully repaid until December 1926.

Morris's bus operations were mainly centred around routes 29 and 294 though in his early days he submitted applications to work on 4, 27, 71 and 73 etc. This was in the pre-London Traffic Act days and there is no indication that Morris actually worked on all or any of these services. Under the London Traffic Act Morris never held more than one weekday schedule which was on 29/294. During the early part of the second year of the Wembley Exhibition Lancastrian offered a direct service from the Wellington, Wood Green to Wembley on Tuesdays to Fridays inclusive for 1/- single. There were six journeys a day each way and as seats had to be pre-booked at the Premier refreshment bar opposite The Wellington, it may have been that the service was worked by a charabanc. In July 1925 Morris applied to run from Edmonton (Sparklets Works) to Whetstone (Griffin) via the new North Circular Road over what later became the famous 551. His pioneer application for this service was

262

turned down because of the bad state of Bowes Road, Palmers Green, but this decision was reversed by the police in the next December after roadworks had taken place. Morris could never have actually ran on the 551 as he did not own a single-decker suitable for it.

In July 1925, at its first overhaul, the original livery of the Daimler was replaced by red & white and in January 1926 a replacement bus, MK 2119, was acquired in the shape of a new Dodson-bodied Dennis. A limited company was registered on June 3rd 1927 to acquire the bus side of the business. It had a capital of £500 and its registered office was at 23 Leith Road. The secretary of the company was Walter James Lovegrove, one of Morris's conductors. The bus and its schedule were taken over by Public on August 5th 1927 together with one spare Dennis engine, the whole ensemble costing the Public £2,800. It is not known when Morris ceased his coach operations, but it was almost certainly prior to February 1929 by which time he had left the area. The Lancastrian Omnibus Co. Ltd. was wound up on December 9th 1930 after lying dormant for three years.

PERKINS
The most perfect example of a family bus business ever to run in London between the wars was Perkins. It was founded in November 1924 by Frederick Henry Perkins whose one bus was worked by his four sons, Clifford, Leslie, Victor and Alexander, as and when they became old enough to do so.

F. H. Perkins, who lived at 52 Mannock Road, Wood Green, was a complete stranger to bus work before the purchase of his new Dennis, MH 2118, from Strachan & Brown in November 1924. Covent Garden market was where he had worked previously and his departure from there came as a result of being cold-shouldered by his fellow workers through refusing to join a trade union. His bus, which was aptly called Perkins, entered service on December 1st 1924 on route 529 on which it remained exclusively except on Christmas days when it ran to St. Albans on the 71. Perkins arranged for the bus to be garaged at Boreham Road, and it stayed there until the Empress company went out of business in December 1926 whereupon alternative accommodation was found at Syree's in Commerce Road. A limited company entitled the Perkins Omnibus Co. Ltd. was formed on September 29th 1927 to take over the business as from October 8th. Its registered office was the Perkins' family home which was now 115 Hoppers Road, Winchmore Hill. Frederick Perkins' wife, Kate, was the company secretary.

The Perkins bus worked profitably and the temptation to sell out to General or Public was resisted. Indeed Perkins was the only one amongst the many Wood Green area independents to survive into the nineteen-thirties. The new decade was entered upon with a new bus, MY 2177, a Leyland Titan which had been delivered from Dodsons in December 1929. Its arrival meant the sale of the old Dennis which, only a year previously, had been converted to pneumatics. It went to C. G. Leaphard, formerly of the Empress Omnibus Co. Ltd., who was now proprietor of the Thundersley Park Garage on Bread & Cheese Hill in Thundersley, Essex. Painted brown, it ran for Leaphard on a works service from Pitsea to the Ekco Works near the Southend boundary, Southend-on-Sea council having refused Leaphard permission to run within the borough. Leaphard's garage business lost money and he found himself unable to keep up his payments to Perkins for the Dennis. Finally, in October 1930, Perkins bought the Thundersley business, including the freehold land, garage and bungalow, from Leaphard for £1,433 and old MH 2118 once again became a Perkins vehicle. The Perkins Omnibus Co. Ltd. subsequently found the Thundersley business as unprofitable as Leaphard had done. A 1931 application to run an hourly bus service on weekdays between Vange (Gales Corner), Pitsea and Southend, could have brought profitability to the Thundersley business had it been approved, but it was not.

Early in 1931 Perkins senior bought a plot of allotments in Lancaster Road, Enfield for £600. He built a substantial brick bus garage with its entrance into Kynaston Road at one end of the site and at the other a pair of cottages called Oakleigh and Fernleigh and later numbered 70/72 Lancaster Road. These were occupied by two of Perkins' sons who had only to walk the length of their back gardens to get to work. The total cost of the land and buildings was a mere £2,650 and in October 1933 a conveyance on the whole property was made to the Company for this same sum.

Unhappily Frederick Perkins died on July 31st 1931, being one of the few independent bus proprietors to die "in harness". After its founder's death the Perkins business was carried on by the rest of the family until August 29th 1934 when the Leyland Titan was compulsorily handed over to the LPTB from whom the Perkins family later received £7,200 in compensation. Two of the Perkins boys took employment with London Transport. Another, Victor, stayed on at the Lancaster Road garage which was converted to a filling station and repair shop for private cars. In 1937 the houses and garage at Lancaster Road were transferred out of the books of the Perkins Omnibus Co. Ltd. preparatory to it being wound up, and the Thundersley business was sold. Possibly due to the intervention of the war the omnibus company was not finally dissolved until August 16th 1946.

Today little remains of the Perkins business but memories. The Lancaster Road properties were sold for demolition in about 1966 for £24,000. A Barclay's bank and a Budgen supermarket now occupy the site. The garage at Thundersley, which had been partly rebuilt and renamed, was demolished in 1972/3. Perhaps the best surviving memento is in the possession of Mr. Leslie Perkins, who nowadays runs a car hire business in Enfield. He has the menu card of a farewell dinner which was held at the George Hotel, Enfield, on Saturday February 10th 1934. The many regular passengers on the Perkins bus had clubbed together to hold the function as a tribute to the owners of the Perkins Omnibus Company Ltd. and to show their appreciation for the reliable service the Perkins bus had provided over the past years. This little family firm had built up a liaison with its regular riders of which it could justifiably be proud and which it would be impossible for today's big combine to emulate. It is perhaps sad that the march of progress can apparently only be made at the expense of the personal touch.

THE LEADER

The Leader bus was owned by Arthur Reginald Perkins and F. G. Edwards and its career was short-lived. Little is known about the business except that the only bus owned was a red Strachan & Brown-bodied Dennis, MH 2480. It was licensed on December 15th 1924 and worked from the end of that month until the first week in March 1925. Route 294 seems to have been the only one upon which it operated, and it issued Empress Omnibus Co. Ltd. tickets. Throughout its very brief career The Leader was kept in the Empire Garage. MH 2480 passed to Henslowe.

EMPIRE'S BEST

The brothers Webber, Ernie and Edwin, of 57 Seymour Road, Hornsey, made their first business acquaintanceship with the Empress Omnibus Co. Ltd. at the end of December 1924 when they arranged for their new Leyland to be housed at Boreham Road. MH 2484, a red & white Dodson-bodied vehicle, was licensed on the first day of 1925 and entered service on the 294 soon afterwards. The title of Empire's Best, which the vehicle carried in bold block capitals, was perhaps not as curious as it may at first seem as the Empire was much to the forefront of people's minds at the time thanks to the Wembley Exhibition. Besides, there were already eight operators at the Empire Garage when the Webber brothers arrived there and they no doubt thought theirs was the best of the lot. Be that as it may, this unusual title was later to become a household name through much of north London and parts of Essex thanks to the Webbers' highly successful London-Clacton coach run. Even today in these final crumbling years of the Empire, the blue & white coaches remained until 1975 to remind us of past glories, though they ran as a subsidiary of Banfield's Coaches after the Webbers went into retirement in July 1960. The Banfield empire itself duly crumbled, and the Clacton service is now run by coaches in Bee Line colours.

The Empires' Best bus ran solely on the 294 on weekdays throughout its career, with short workings introduced from April 11th 1925. Approval was obtained to operate also on route 14 but appears not to have been taken up, and in February 1925 route 206A was sought, which was also approved but apparently not operated. The bus ran a more varied itinerary on Sundays. It ran first on the 294. In June 1925 it was transferred to the 21, in October 1925 back to the 294, in April 1926 to the 69, in December of the same year to the 29 and finally, in April 1927, back to the 69.

In March 1926, after a year and three months at Boreham Road, the Webbers found a new home for their bus in Syree's Garage at 7/9 Commerce Road. In the following year arrangements were practically completed with Public for the sale of the bus but negotiations were discontinued and the eventual purchaser was the City Motor Omnibus Co. Ltd. Webber brothers ran it for the last time on March 1st 1928 and City took over the operations the next day. A few months later the Webbers entered the next stage of their career when they inaugurated their famous London-Clacton daily express coach service.

Though the Webbers never expanded their bus business beyond one vehicle, their coach service enjoyed much greater success. The coaches ran from a garage at 44 Commerce Road which had previously been called James' Garage and had been used by a firm of motor engineers. The first of a fleet of Leyland Tigers was delivered in July 1928, and by May 1930 the Empire's Best fleet of coaches numbered nine units (4 Leyland, 2 Gilford, 1 Chevrolet, 1 Daimler and 1 Star). A Clacton-Birmingham service was commenced in 1930 but was later discontinued by order of the Traffic Commissioner under the Road Traffic Act 1930.

ALEXANDRA

A comparative latecomer to the London bus scene was the Alexandra Omnibus Co. Ltd. The man behind the business was Felix Geninazzi, a Southgate property dealer who incorporated the £600 Company on January 10th 1925. Geninazzi's office at 25 Hampstead Road, N.W.1. was used as the registered office of the Alexandra company. A new red & white Strachan & Brown-bodied Leyland was ordered, which materialised as XW 9375 and was first licensed on January 30th 1925. It was based at the Empire Garage and was operated for Geninazzi by the Empress company using Empress tickets. Unfortunately, being a latecomer, no satisfactory schedules could be obtained for the Alexandra bus because of the London Traffic Act. It ran for a while, illegally, on the 294 but ceased operation entirely in May 1925 after a working life of only three months. The bus was sold in July 1925 to Lee & Beaulah of Elloughton, passing in December 1926 to East Yorkshire Motor Services Ltd. The Alexandra Omnibus Co. Ltd. was finally dissolved on May 31st 1929.

STANMORE

Empire Garage was a veritable home for lost causes, and housed three in all. The short-lived Alexandra, and the even shorter-lived The Leader, were joined on February 2nd 1925 by the Stanmore bus. MH 3380, the vehicle in question was a red Dodson-bodied Dennis which was licensed on January 29th 1925 by Arthur (or Alfred) S. Stanmore. Early in February this gentleman received written permission to operate a schedule on route 29A and he put his bus into service accordingly. On February 11th he was asked by the police to make some adjustments to his schedule, which he agreed to do, returning it to the public carriage office with the required alterations inserted ready to receive official sanction. He must have been shocked beyond belief to be then informed that his schedule as amended was refused altogether and that his bus must be withdrawn from service. Stanmore ceased running on February 17th, the embittered victim of one of the most underhand manoeuvres ever recorded being taken by the police against an independent operator. He left the Empire Garage owing £11 8s. 10d. for rent and petrol, his career as a bus owner having lasted little more than a fortnight. Stanmore's was, indeed, the shortest-lived of all the independent bus operations, a record not to be envied. In all probability MH 3380 was returned to Dodson's. Towards the end of the month it reappeared in much the same locality, this time in the ownership of Convey & Clayton of Edmonton, who had been without a bus for a month after returning their Daimler—an unsatisfactory vehicle—to J. M. Roberts.

D.M./D.M. LTD.

Harold C. Durell started in business at Commerce Road in July 1924 when he purchased XU 2699 and began to trade as the Durell Bus Company. The bus was a new red & white Thornycroft and it bore the letters D.M. which stood for Durell Motors. As far as can be ascertained the D.M. bus ran mainly on route 29 and its various short-workings although Durell sought approval to run also on 18, 21, 25 and 73 in his early days.

A limited company entitled Durell Motors Ltd. was incorporated on October 22nd 1926 with registered office at Durell's home address, 46 Burma Road, Stoke Newington. The secretary of the new company was a man named Henry Collier who henceforth managed the business. Indeed he may even have purchased it from Durell hence the formation of the limited company, but in the absence of any records relative to Durell Motors Ltd. this theory cannot be confirmed. Collier lost little time in negotiating for a new bus to replace the Thornycroft and decided on a Dennis with Birch body. This was constructed in January 1927 and licensed on February 15th as YE 6365. Like its predecessor it was red & white lined out in black, but the fleetname was revised to read D.M. Ltd. in gold script letters inside an oval. The Thornycroft which it displaced has never been traced and it was one of the few London buses of its type not to end up with Thames Valley. The new Dennis had only a short career with Durell Motors Ltd. for on November 11th 1927 it was sold to Public for £3,250. In October 1930 Durell Motors Ltd., whose address was now given as 82 Victoria Street, S.W.1., unsuccessfully applied to run a St. Albans to Hitchin bus service which the St. Albans and Harpenden authorities refused to sanction on the grounds that adequate facilities were already in existence. Apart from this, nothing is known of the later history—if any—of Durell Motors Ltd.

HAV-A-RIDE/H.F.B.

As quaint a fleetname as any was Hav-a-ride. The man behind the name was Harold Ernest Briskham of 12 Palmerston Crescent, Palmers Green, and the bus carrying the name was MH 1326, a Daimler Y of October 1924 origin. In his early days as a bus proprietor Briskham kept surprisingly clear of the 29 route, one of the favourites amongst independents which in theory possessed the great advantage of passing within a few yards of the Commerce Road garage. He is recorded as having been seen on the 9, 11, 15, 16, 38 & 42 and, with the introduction of schedules at the end of 1924, settled down on the 284A which involved a fairly long "running-out" journey to Camden Town. In June 1925 the Hav-a-ride title was exchanged for the less imaginative one of H.F.B. The H and F represented the christian names of Harold Briskham and his son Frederick; the B standing, of course, for Briskham. On June 21st 1926 a limited company was incorporated under the title of H.F.B. Ltd. with a share capital of £500 and its registered office at 12 Palmerston Crescent. The company took over the bus and also a car hire business which the Briskhams ran at the time.

267

H.F.B.'s Daimler was the only vehicle of its type on the busy 284A and it was so short of pulling power that it could always be relied upon to run late, if at all. Naturally the Briskhams' receipts suffered and in time they fell behind with their repayments to Roberts. In the summer of 1926 the Daimler passed back to Roberts' possession, but whether he seized it or the Briskhams returned it of their own accord is not known. In September 1926 a new H.F.B. bus took to the road, MK 7335. It was a Leyland which was in all ways as good as its companions on the 284A. It would seem that it did not redeem the Briskhams' failing fortunes, for by the latter part of 1927 almost the entire share capital of H.F.B. Ltd. had passed to Christopher Dodson from whom the Leyland was on hire purchase.

On October 7th 1927 the bus was sold to Public for £3,000. The younger Briskham continued as a bus conductor, firstly with Public and subsequently with the LGOC. His father retained the car hire business for, perhaps, two years from stables which then fronted the Cock Tavern public house near his home. He had gone out of business by the autumn of 1930 and thereafter worked for very many years in a newsagents and travel agency business in Palmers Green. H.F.B. Ltd. was dissolved on February 2nd 1932.

DIRECT

The Batson brothers were comparative latecomers to the competitive world of London buses. Cyril Rhodes Batson of 19 Stanford Road, New Barnet was licensee and driver; his brother Reginald of Trinity Road, Wood Green, was the conductor. They paid the Syree brothers 17/- a week for garaging and servicing the bus and bought petrol and oil from them. Their new Strachan & Brown-bodied Dennis, MH 5193, was registered on April 1st 1925 and it entered service on the 525, a purely suburban route but one of the few in the area still available on which a profit could possibly be made. The Batsons called their bus the Direct, although it was no more direct than any of the others on the somewhat circuitous 525. Cyril Batson applied for approval to run on two other services besides the 525. He was granted permission to operate Muswell Hill-Tottenham Hale (533) but as far as is known never did so. An application to link Wood Green with Golders Green (it is not known by what route) was turned down.

The Direct had been running for less than a year when the Batsons offered to sell it to the LGOC. A purchase price was agreed and the Direct Omnibus Co. Ltd. was formed with a capital of £1,000 on March 29th 1926 to enable the transfer of ownership to take place. The registered office was initially 41 Finsbury Square, E.C.2., but this was changed to 55 Broadway when the LGOC obtained control on April 13th. The Direct bus was last run under the Batsons' auspices on Monday April 12th; it recommenced operation on the 14th under the LGOC's control, from their Tottenham (AR) garage. Eight days before takeover, Reginald Batson was assaulted by a couple of drunks while the bus was standing at the Enfield Town terminus. He raised laughter in court by saying, "They were just a little **abbreviated**, but not properly drunk."

Operation under the LGOC was uneventful except for the replacement, in December 1926, of the Dennis by K756. The Dennis, after overhaul, was transferred to Redburns. On January 1st 1928 the Direct Omnibus Co. Ltd. was taken over by the Tramways (MET) Omnibus Co. Ltd.

112 Mayes Road, Wood Green

RELIANCE

Charles Churchman was in business with his son Henry as a removal contractor before his first bus was bought. The chocolate Leyland ME 8109 which arrived in March 1923 was named Reliance, and on March 29th it began working on routes 29 and 42. Rumour had it that Churchman was also at the time considering operating on the 22. By early April the Reliance had settled down on the 29 and its various short workings, and from about February 1925 it was working on the 529. In his early days Churchman applied to run from Barnet to Richmond and he later applied to work on the St. Albans service 71. Both would probably have been Sunday or Bank holiday operations. Churchman kept his bus at 112 Mayes Road, Wood Green, where he also housed his removal lorries. Nowadays a Department of Health & Social Security building is on the site.

In 1924 Churchman appears to have actively considered buying a Thornycroft and even applied for approval to operate such a vehicle. There must have been a change of plan, for in November 1924, when his second bus was licensed, it appeared as a Dennis, MH 1862. His fleet thereafter remained at two, both of which were scheduled under the London Traffic Act to spend weekdays on 529. On August 18th 1927 Churchman sold his bus interests to Public for £6,000 and concentrated thereafter on his removals business until 1930.

Regent Garage, Regents Avenue, Palmers Green

UNEEDUS

The Mason brothers of 95 Conway Road, Southgate, dreamed up the fleet title Uneedus. It was proudly carried by MF 8953, a red & white Dennis which carved out a successful career for itself on route 29. Bertram William Samuel Mason and his brother, Frederick Kenneth, came from a family who had been active in the processed food trade for many years. The fame of Mason's Potted Meats had spread far beyond their native Finsbury Park, and the war years had been particularly lucrative ones with the factory fulfilling large orders for the fighting troops. When the young Mason brothers expressed a wish to branch out into a completely different line of business their father assisted by putting up the finance for the purchase of the first bus in June 1924.

After two months at the Whymark Garage the Masons moved to the new Empire Garage which they made their headquarters in August 1924. Their stay there lasted only until February 1925 when they moved to the Regent Garage at Palmers Green, owned by McNab Mackintosh. The main Regent Garage (nowadays known as the Texaco Garage) is on the North Circular Road which was newly built when the Uneedus started to run. The Uneedus fleet, which grew to five vehicles, was housed in a sturdy brick building, which was then part of the Regent Garage premises, facing the end of a private road known as Regents Avenue. This building was a literal stone's thrown from the LGOC's Palmers Green (AD) garage, and still exists largely unaltered although the fields that reached almost to its walls have long since vanished. It is nowadays owned by a local laundry, having until recently served as a chassis steam cleaning works for commercial vehicles.

A second new Dennis, MH 1353, joined MF 8953 on the 29 in October 1924. At about this time the Masons sought to run through to Enfield Town via the MET tram route, but permission was refused for operation north of the existing terminus at Winchmore Hill (Green Dragon) on the grounds of dangerously overhanging trees. No increase in fleet size took place until January 1926 when a pair of new vehicles was licensed. These marked a distinct break from London bus tradition in being a pair of pneumatic-tyred Guy single deckers of the BB type which was proving popular in the provinces. These 24-seaters, MK 2245/6, were ordered for route 551, a cross-country route which was beginning to attract the attentions of independents at the time. When a further vehicle was required for the 551 in December 1926 the choice fell on a 30-seater Dennis E-type, ML 1169. The Uneedus fleet had then developed to its maximum of five units, all of which had Strachan & Brown bodies.

In mid-1927 the brothers decided to sell to the LGOC and accordingly formed the Mason Omnibus Co. Ltd. on June 13th with a capital of £2,000 and registered office at 55 Broadway. General took over on July 6th 1927 and the five Uneedus buses and twenty staff (many of whom were quickly dismissed) were moved into the General garage across the road. Before the month was out the two Guys had been replaced by K's, the only instance of single-deckers of this type being transferred to an acquired operator. The Guys were overhauled and re-allocated to National who already ran buses of this type on their country services operated on behalf of General. The three Uneedus Dennises remained until the company was absorbed into the LGOC on January 1st 1928.

Their buses disposed of, the Mason family carried on with the potted meat business until 1945 when their shareholding in the firm bearing their name was disposed of. Mason's Potted Meats Ltd. ceased trading in 1950.

Willow Walk, West Green

ADMIRAL

The independent fleet usually hailed as being the supreme example of what could be achieved by private enterprise was the Admiral. This fleet of immaculate navy blue buses has not infrequently been described as having been the brainchild of Alfred Temple Bennett, a notion actively fostered in later years by Bennett himself. In fact it was Bernard Golden Daniel Cosgrove of 77 Princes Avenue, Palmers Green who thought up the name Admiral and placed the first Admiral buses on the road.

Cosgrove had formerly been associated with the Ware firm of Harvey & Burrows and had several years' experience of running buses in rural

Hertfordshire. He decided to branch out on his own account in London and, after looking around for some while, came to the conclusion that route 29 could do with more buses. The choice of fleetname was logical. The army had been well represented on the streets of London for many years, thought Cosgrove, so why not the navy also? He firstly placed an order for two Straker Squires which were ready to appear at Scotland Yard on December 8th 1922. His reason for selecting Straker Squires was two-fold; he already had experience in running vehicles of this make, and their factory was conveniently near the garage from which he arranged to work, A. T. Bennett & Co. Ltd. at Willow Walk, West Green. In a contemporary interview with "Commercial Motor" Cosgrove reported that he had two further similar buses on order and intended to expand ultimately to a fleet of ten. This, he thought, would be the top limit if he were to retain individual control and keep within his own working capital. He stated that he had put £15,000 into the business.

The first two buses entered service on the 29 on December 14th with ex-LGOC men at the front and back. Initial results were encouraging and average takings per bus were in the region of £10 for each ten hour shift. ME 6185/6 were the two original vehicles and they were smartly turned out with chromed wheel hub caps and radiators glistening as part of the image Cosgrove wished to build up.

The success of Cosgrove's venture in its early stages did not go unnoticed by A. T. Bennett, a shrewd and prosperous businessman who headed his family firm of A. T. Bennett & Co. Ltd. This had been formed on February 15th 1922 with a capital of £6,000 to take over as a going concern the engineering, motor body building and other activities carried out at Willow Walk as from January 1st 1922 for £6,000 in shares. The "other activities" included a prosperous coal merchants business and a fleet of taxis which ran under the title of "B & S" Cab Company (B & S standing for Bennett & Son). A. T. Bennett's brothers John and William were directors and minority shareholders in A. T. Bennett & Co. Ltd.and so were his two unmarried sisters, Georgina and Sophia.

A. T. Bennett's business career had been an interesting one. He had served his apprenticeship with Richard Moreland & Son Ltd. where he was mainly concerned with heavy pump-engine work. He stayed with them for eleven years and then, in 1902, left to start in general engineering on his own account at Willow Walk. The early years were principally spent in the manufacture of automatic fog signals for Trinity House but in 1909 he diversified by starting in the taxi business. The war years saw the works wholly devoted to the production of parts for aircraft engines. After the war a general engineering service was developed with well equipped workshops, the emphasis being on motor engineering. The company had the contract for maintaining Harrods' fleet of Albion and Lacre vans and used ex-Harrods chassis when mechanising its coal delivery fleet, which was yet another branch of the Bennetts' activities. Petrol sales and lock-up garages were further useful sidelines. Early in 1923 work was put in hand to convert much of the extensive Willow Walk premises into a bus garage.

271

The Bennett family were keen churchgoers and A.T. and his brothers had been connected with St. James' Presbyterian Church at Wood Green since their Sunday school days. A. T. Bennett married his wife at St. James' in 1906 and they celebrated their diamond wedding there on May 1st sixty years later. He was an active freemason and keenly interested in public life. He served on the Wood Green Juvenile Court Bench in the years leading up to World War II and was appointed a Justice of the Peace for the County of Middlesex on 26th July 1940. He became Deputy Chairman of the Edmonton Petty Sessional Division in 1950 and finally gave up active work as a magistrate in January 1954, two days before his 75th birthday. In his bus owning days A. T. Bennett was looked upon with mixed feelings by some of his fellow proprietors who took a jaundiced view of his church activities and of the fact that he was a degree or two more abstemious than they.

Bennett started off his bus career by ordering a pair of Straker Squires identical in all respects, including the navy blue Admiral livery, to Cosgrove's two. ME 7240/7364 were approved at Scotland Yard on February 20th 1923 and licensed the following day. Both proprietors placed further buses in service in the next few weeks starting at the end of February with ME 7351 (Cosgrove) and followed in March by ME 7886 (Bennett) and in April by ME 8598 (Cosgrove) and ME 8829 (Bennett).

ME 8598 was the last Cosgrove-owned Admiral to enter service. His plans for a fleet of ten remained unfulfilled, four buses being the maximum he ever owned at one time. Cosgrove's failure to expand his fleet of Admirals as planned was to an extent offset by the addition in May 1923 of a third proprietor to the consortium of Admiral operators in the shape of Lyle Mill Newstead of 76 Falkland Road, Hornsey. His Straker Squire ME 9689 was licensed on May 17th, the same day as Bennett's fifth bus, ME 9690. A second Newstead bus, MF 180, joined the fleet on May 31st. Newstead's two buses had Dodson bodywork as did ME 9690, the only Bennett-owned Straker not to carry the chassis manufacturer's own body. One, at least, of the two Newstead buses originally carried the legend "Bennett & Newstead" on the rocker panel, but no proof has ever been found that there was any financial link between the two. Admiral operations at this time were completely on the 29 except for some Sunday journeys to St. Albans on the 84 which appear to have ceased after 1923. A southward extension of the 29 from Victoria to the Gun at Pimlico was inaugurated in June 1923.

Bennett put MF 691 into service in June 1923 and this was followed in July by MF 1020. This vehicle was the property of the fourth and last proprietor to join the Admiral line, G. J. Heast. His arrival brought the grand total of Admirals up to thirteen for a few brief days. By the middle of July Cosgrove had withdrawn from the fleet he founded and taken delivery of a pair of new brown Straker Squires licensed to the Edmonton Omnibus Company. His four Admiral buses were sold, two to Harvey & Burrows and two to C. W. Pallant, possibly via Straker Squires. December 1923 saw the departure of Newstead who moved his two buses to the Whymark Garage and repainted them red. The Admiral rolling stock then remained at seven (6 Bennett and 1 Heast) until the spring of 1924 when expansion began to take place once again.

The Bennett fleet was augmented by three further Straker Squires—its last—in March (MF 5397), April (MF 6432) and May (MF 7881) 1924. These were followed in July by MF 9171 which was owned by Heast and was the last Straker of all to enter service in Admiral colours. Bennett was already planning to switch his allegiance to Dennises and MH 473 arrived in August 1924 to break the Straker Squire monopoly of the Admiral fleet. A further five Dennises (MH 3883/5256/5449/5450/5555) were purchased by Bennett in the early part of 1925. Meanwhile Heast had decided to cease bus ownership and put his two Straker Squires up for sale. They passed to the EP fleet in January 1925 and thereafter left Bennett in undisputed possession of the Admiral title.

Bennett's vigour in expanding his share of buses on the 29 group must have been a worry to the LGOC. Bennett pioneered an all-year round daily service on the 29 northwards to Hadley Woods which the LGOC had served only at times to suit the needs of day trippers. But the main battle really raged on the more heavily populated section of route from Palmers Green southwards. On Saturday, June 23rd 1923, Admiral fired its first volley in the famous "Fair Fares" campaign by introducing extended 1d. fares on the 29. General retaliated three days later by introducing reductions so substantial that they brought the fare scale almost down to pre-war levels. A cut of 33 1/3% gave three stages for 1d. instead of two, reducing the through fare from Victoria to Hadley Woods from 1/- to 8d. These reductions were applied only to routes 24 and 29 which were the worst hit by Admiral competition, and the fact that they thus became anomalous with parallel routes did not appear to worry the General unduly. July saw Admiral introducing an intermediate 1½d. fare covering four stages. An example of the effect of this was that the important journey from the Finsbury Park tube terminus to Wood Green became 1½d. on Admiral compared with 2d. on General.

The fares war was becoming almost suicidal, coinciding, as it did, with the flooding of the 29 with numerous extra General buses not to mention the many small independents seeking a livelihood on it. These small people were caught up in the battle but many had neither the capital nor the staying power to see it through and were forced elsewhere. Some tried to drum up trade by reducing fares still further, and we have already seen as an example of this the 2d. midday fare charged by Empress between Palmers Green and Charing Cross in August 1923. Even Bennett, realising that discretion was the better part of valour, moved some of his fleet off the 29 and on to the Muswell Hill-Victoria run in October 1923 though he did not stay long on it. However the 29 remained the main Admiral route and in September 1924 Bennett was able to report to the South Tottenham Branch of the National Citizens' Union that, even at their reduced level, the fares were still at a paying rate despite the fact that his crews were paid higher than the recognized standard. He produced documentary evidence that Admiral buses ran to a timetable as a counter to strong criticism of the operating methods of the independents.

At an unknown date in 1924 Admiral started a daily service between North Finchley and Tottenham Hale which was numbered 274 by Bassom. It may have been withdrawn in February 1925, the month which saw the start by Admiral of route 529. This variant of the 29 to serve Winchmore Hill had been worked by independents on and off for almost two years, but before long a regular 12 min. service was operated augmented by other private buses such as Reliance and Meteor. The 529 soon became an independent route to be reckoned with, and an increased service of MET trams over the same ground came as no surprise. On April 14th Bennett announced a new "Fair Fares" scheme and also declared his intention of operating northwards from the Winchmore Hill terminus to Enfield.

On May 13th 1925 the police gave approval for route 280 which began to run soon afterwards. It linked Finsbury Park (where it terminated via Isledon Road) with Enfield (The Holly Bush). A month later it was extended northwards to the pond at Forty Hill. In September 1925 it was revised to meet traffic demands to run from Stroud Green to Forty Hill as the 538 upon which the Admirals worked alongside Redburns on a co-ordinated timetable. A great deal of fresh capital was injected into the bus business to finance the purchase of no fewer than twelve new vehicles in May and June 1925. These were little 25 and 26-seaters based on Dennis 2½ ton chassis and bodied by Dodson (MH 6323-5/6468-70/7956-8/8182-4). The great significance of these vehicles lay in the fact that they were pneumatic-tyred. Bennett claimed the honour of being the first bus proprietor in the Metropolitan Police area to run buses with pneumatic tyres, though this claim was not strictly accurate as Barnet Motor Services had forestalled him with their small Fiats. Bennett's achievement was, however, significant in that he pushed pneumatic tyres well into the Metropolitan Police area whereas the Barnet vehicles had run only on the fringe. They were highly successful and undeniably paved the way for the introduction a few years afterwards of pneumatic tyres on a large scale.

In July 1925 Admiral announced a new service between the "Hope & Anchor" in Angel Road, Edmonton via the New Arterial Road, Village Road, Winchmore Hill and Enfield, but the scheme appears to have been abortive. An earlier operation with double-deckers that was very much alive was 58 which linked Finsbury Park with the Wembley Exhibition during the 1924 season. A service was also operated from Wood Green to Wembley at certain times, mainly in the evenings and on Saturdays, under the route number 58A. The Northern bus also participated in the 58A and so, probably, did other independents from time to time. In June 1925 a proposed extension of the 529 from Victoria to Cheyne Walk was turned down by the police.

In December 1925 a seventh Dennis double-decker was purchased (MK 1572) to cover one of the schedules vacated by Heast. This was followed soon afterwards by MK 2236/3072. MK 6959 was received in August 1926, and in February 1927 ML 2140 arrived to become no. 4. This was the last new double-decker to enter the Admiral fleet and it brought their total stock of 4-ton Dennises up to eleven. Further 1926 deliveries comprised a quartet of Dennis 2½ ton 25-seaters (MK 3401/3700/3701/7066).

Admiral's only second-hand vehicle, NK 8877, a little 20-seater Dennis formerly operated by Barnet Motor Services, was taken into stock on the

274

last day of 1925. Its sphere of operation had been route 353 which Admiral appear to have worked as successors to Barnet Motor Services for the next twelve months. Any such operation was, in fact, illegal as the schedule was non-transferable under the stringent regulations then imposed by the police. It is not known whether Admiral came into dispute with the police over this; however operation of the 353 ceased at the end of 1926 and in the latter part of January 1927 the little Dennis was sold to Waltham Motor Services Ltd.

The last new vehicle delivery of 1926 was ML 539. This was an E-type Dennis 30-seater on pneumatic tyres and its entry into service in October 1926 was significant in that it marked the use of four-wheel brakes on a London bus for the first time. Previously the police had steadfastly refused to sanction the use of brakes on the front wheels of buses in the metropolis. It is thought that their objection was based on the danger of all four wheels locking in a skid. Bennett had approached the police at the beginning of the year with the suggestion that they should test a vehicle but at first the police refused to move in the matter. When they finally tested ML 539 it was on a smooth concrete surface made slippery with a coating of soft soap upon which the bus was raced at 25 m.p.h., turned sharply this way and that, and braked suddenly. It sailed through the tests with flying colours, so much so that the police were powerless to withhold sanction any longer. Servo-assisted four-wheel brakes had come to stay.

Bennett planned a fleet of Dennis E's. ML 539 was the first of an initial order for seven, the remaining six of which were confirmed with the builders as soon as the police tests proved successful. Bennett had come to the conclusion that pneumatic-tyred single-deckers would pay better than solid-tyred double-deckers. They were faster and more comfortable and would not waste so much time at stops. In his opinion small speedy buses would greatly reduce London traffic congestion and this theory impressed a number of other independent operators who also ordered Dennis E's for central London operation. Unfortunately the theory proved to be unsound as far as the economics of bus operation were concerned as several operators found to their financial detriment. With only thirty seats per bus the lucrative peak hour trade was diminished and the small extra speed made possible by pneumatic-tyred buses was insufficient to get in extra journeys to help offset the loss in peak hour revenue. In one respect Bennett was a visionary. He foresaw single-deckers with separate entrances and exits, but over forty years were to pass before such specimens became common in London in the shape of the infamous MBS and allied types.

ML 539 entered service on the 529 on Tuesday, November 2nd. It was joined subsequently by ML 1582-4/1812/1813/1924 which were built in January 1927. Some were used to inaugurate a new service which began in mid-January numbered 201 linking Finsbury Park with the Tottenham LCC estate. The respective termini were the "Stapleton" in Stroud Green Road and the junction of White Hart Lane and the New Arterial Road (now known as the Great Cambridge Road). Admiral sought a 6 min. headway but the police were only willing to sanction a quarter-hourly service. After a month the route was extended to a new eastern terminus at the Sparklets Works in Angel Road, Edmonton.

275

Let us take a look at Willow Walk in February 1927 when the Bennett business was at its zenith. The company's bus fleet alone stood at thirty-eight units (11 Dennis & 4 Straker Squire double-deckers; 23 Dennis single-deckers) and the taxi fleet was also substantial with twenty-six vehicles on the books. The private-hire car fleet numbered five and there were two charabancs and five lorries, the latter being used principally in connection with the coal merchants' business. The works which maintained these seventy-six vehicles and also did much outside work, covered over an acre and employed three hundred men in three shifts on a day and night basis. The company was agent for Dennis Bros. and carried some £1,500 worth of stocks of spares in the stores. The coach-building and repair shops were well equipped and there was a separate paint shop. The company was practically self-sufficient as regards the overhaul and maintenance of its own vehicles and could completely strip a bus to its chassis, overhaul it and get it back on the road within ten days whereas most independents, who had their overhauls carried out by commercial concerns, could reckon on having a bus off the road for at least a fortnight.

A. T. Bennett inevitably came to be regarded as a leader amongst independent busmen. He accepted the responsibility of unofficial leadership and lost little opportunity to publicise their cause. Like most of his fellow proprietors he felt stifled by the London Traffic Act which he described at a public meeting in the Hazelwood Lane school in Palmers Green on Wednesday March 10th 1926 as having been "passed by the Labour Government almost under the bludgeon of Lord Ashfield". At this same meeting he disclosed that he had received an exceptionally tempting offer to sell but was determined not to do so and would not let his patrons down. Shortly after this, on April 8th, it was announced in the London evening papers that Bennett had been asked to stand as a candidate for Parliament in the West Ham constituency so that he could fight the battle of the independent bus owners at a higher level. He declined, saying that the bus fight could be carried on in a better way than by an incursion into Imperial politics. The firm's dinner at The George, Enfield, on Saturday December 17th saw Bennett in an outwardly confident mood for the future, but as subsequent events proved, he was already planning to sacrifice his independence as a bus owner. He predicted in his after dinner speech that the end of the trams was nearer three months than three years. He commented that small companies were being bought out but "we came into the business successfully and we are stopping in it, and we are going to stop in it on our own" (Applause).

In the spring of the new year a communication from Bennett dropped through the letter box of every independent bus owner, and Bennett's scheme for the future thereby became common knowledge. A new company was to be formed to amalgamate the activities of the independents who would sell their businesses to the new company for cash or shares. The new company would be completely independent of the LGOC and large enough to fight it on its home ground. Bennett was negotiating with the Metropolitan Police and the Minister of Transport for the relaxation of existing restrictions so that licences could be transferred to the new undertaking; these negotiations eventually proved successful. The entire capital would, said Bennett, be put up privately and there was no question of a public issue for at least six months after the formation of the new company. The aim would be to co-ordinate what was formerly individual effort into a regular service on several routes using a new fleet of six-wheeled pneumatic tyred double-deckers. The London Public Omnibus Co. Ltd. was incorporated on July 8th 1927 with a share capital of £600,000 and with A. T. Bennett as Managing Director, but even before this some sixty bus owners had expressed their willingness to sell and contracts with several were already drawn up awaiting signature. The Public was offering a tempting £3,000 or thereabouts for each scheduled bus and for many of the independents, apprehensive of the future, this was an offer too good to be resisted.

Bennett's own company formed the nucleus of the new Public concern although in his case completion of the purchase was not finalised until August 17th 1927. A. T. Bennett & Co. Ltd. received £130,000 which included the freehold property at Willow Walk, West Green. This thereupon became the main Public garage and workshops, and all the other activities formerly carried on there ceased. Thirty-seven Admiral buses passed into the Public fleet of which 32 were scheduled on Mondays to Fridays and 33 on Saturdays on the 201, 529 and 538. The firm of A. T. Bennett & Co. Ltd. was formally wound up on May 9th 1928.

On August 2nd 1927 Admiral obtained approval to operate new route 602 from Muswell Hill Broadway to the Sparklets Works at Edmonton, and so did the LGOC. By this time Admiral was to all intents and purposes controlled by Public and had been completely absorbed before operation of the 602 began. Admiral also left Public another legacy; a fleet of eight new vehicles was on order at the time of takeover. Seven were Dennis E's; the eighth was a six-wheeled, covered-top, pneumatic-tyred double-decker of an advanced design which Bennett had ordered from Guy Motors Ltd. as the precursor to a fleet of such vehicles. Bennett had made London bus history by getting the first permit from the police for pneumatic-tyred, six-wheeled double-deckers to operate in the capital in respect of a limited number of Guys. The permit was obtained on June 15th 1927 but the first vehicle did not enter service until September 9th under the auspices of Public. It received much publicity but its thunder had been stolen by the LGOC's LS1 which had started work in London just beforehand.

From the very time that Bennett's scheme was announced there had been mumblings in some quarters that all was not as above-board as Bennett would have it seem, and some held suspicions that the LGOC was somewhere in the background. The enormity of the capital needed to finance the scheme was suspicious in itself. A City group, headed by the financier Clarence Charles Hatry—whose imprisonment after a sensational trial following the collapse of an artificial silks concern at Alexandria, Dumbartonshire, gained him notoriety in later years—was responsible for raising the finance. The capital for the undertaking was indeed guaranteed by the LGOC though no public announcement of the

277

LGOC's control was made until March 1928 by which time they had bought out the small number of minority shareholders. Public's Chairman was the Marquis of Winchester and it is suspected that it was he who induced A. T. Bennett to launch the "Public" scheme. The two were later connected in other business affairs such as the Metropole Gramophone Co. Ltd. which had controlling fingers in other pies and at one time was negotiating for participation in the talking picture industry. Public was run as an autonomous body from its headquarters at 5 Gordon Square though major policy decisions naturally came from 55 Broadway. It was in a similar position to the Overground empire run by W. J. Dangerfield and the highly interesting story of both will be told in a later volume.

Bennett's post-1928 business career was mainly with the Marshalsea group of engineering companies of Taunton and Ilminster with which he had been connected since 1912. He was Chairman of the group until his retirement in September 1968 when he was appointed Group President. He died on May 22nd 1969 at the age of 90. His wife, who had shared sixty-two years with him, had died in the previous December.

CRITERION

Apart from the Admirals, there was only one other independent bus at Willow Walk; this was the red & white Criterion owned by Horace Arthur Wells of 20 Pyrland Road, Highbury. It came to Willow Walk at an unknown date, having formerly been kept at Tankard & Smith's garage in South Tottenham. Bennett supplied petrol and oil and also serviced the Criterion for Wells who worked on it as a conductor. The vehicle was a Strachan & Brown-bodied Dennis first registered on December 22nd 1924 as MH 2594. Under Wells' ownership it ran entirely on route 29 and its various short workings. Usually the full route from Victoria to Hadley Woods (29) was operated only on Mondays to Fridays. On Saturdays the bus ran from Victoria only as far north as the Cherry Tree, Southgate, as 29B, whilst on Sundays the bus was further curtailed to run Charing Cross to Palmers Green (29C).

The Criterion's career was uneventful. In due course Wells decided to sell out to the LGOC, forming the Criterion Omnibus Co. Ltd. on April 23rd 1926. The nominal capital of the limited company was £1,000 and its registered office was Lennox House, Norfolk Street, W.C.2. The shares were acquired by the LGOC on May 19th and the registered office was thereafter transferred to 55 Broadway. The bus was allocated to Tottenham (AR) garage but did not actually operate from there until June 5th. It had been in mechanical trouble prior to the LGOC takeover, and it took almost a fortnight to get it running satisfactorily. In December 1926 MH 2594 was replaced by K809, and after overhaul was sent to join the Redburn fleet. K809 remained the Criterion bus until the LGOC absorbed the business completely on January 1st 1928.

Culross Road, West Green

The Culross Road depot where F. F. Downes kept his Horseshoe buses has already been noted. It lay in the 'V' formed by Culross Road and Woodlands Park Road, close to their junction with the main West Green

Road. In preparation for extensive housing development, the garage was demolished in 1972, and in the following year Culross Road itself was swept away as part of the same scheme.

Beaconsfield Road (?), Tottenham

IMPERIAL

Arthur Wellington Priest and his brother, Ralph William, were the proprietors of the Imperial Motor Services, a haulage firm founded in April 1919. The next step was the ownership of charabancs (in 1924/5 there were two 28-seat Thornycrofts and two 14-seaters, a Chevrolet and a Studebaker), and from charabancs the follow up was to buy a bus. In October 1924 the red & white Imperial bus, Strachan & Brown-bodied Dennis MH 1693, took the road.

The Priest brothers' operating base has not as yet been traced. According to the LGOC it was in Clyde Road, Tottenham, but as far as the authors can tell, suitable premises did not exist in Clyde Road back in the nineteen-twenties from which commercial or large passenger vehicles could have been operated. A possible clue to their garage lies in an advertisement on the back of the Imperial bus tickets for the Beaconsfield Garage at 32A Beaconsfield Road, a thoroughfare which leads into Clyde Road. These premises, which nowadays house lock-ups, were certainly spacious enough to accommodate Imperial's vehicles, but the approach road through an archway linking two houses would today preclude the passage of an open-top double-decker because of insufficient headroom. The possibility exists that the headroom has been reduced over the years through the building up of the road surface, but it is of course just as likely that Imperial garaged somewhere entirely different. The business was run from a rented office at 298 West Green Road, close to the old Imperial cinema which inspired the company's name.

The first services applied for by Priest Bros. were 11 and 29 and they were subsequently scheduled to operate 29C and 39A on weekdays, Sunday operation normally being on the 29 when the full northward extension of the route to Hadley Woods was covered. The brothers paid 5/- a week to a Mr. F. Perring for the privilege of standing on his private plot of land at the junction of Silver Street and Fore Street, Edmonton, when working on the 39A.

When the brothers decided to sell their London bus to the LGOC in 1926 a limited company was formed under the title of Priest Brothers Ltd. Share capital was £1,000 and the registered office was Lennox House, Norfolk Street, Strand. The company was incorporated on June 15th and was taken over by the LGOC during Wednesday, June 23rd. The next day would have been the first day of operation under the auspices of General and it was planned that the bus would for the time being continue to operate from Imperial's Tottenham premises. However it was unfit for service and had to be sent to Chiswick for repairs, and when it returned it was allocated to Tottenham (AR) garage. On January 28th 1927 the Dennis was replaced as the Priest Brothers Ltd. bus by K1041 and, after an overhaul, was transferrred to Redburn's. The business was absorbed into the LGOC on January 1st 1928.

R. W. Priest remained in business as Imperial Motor Services and in 1927 advertised charabancs for hire including new 1927 All-Weather saloons with 32 & 35 seats. "Most luxurious coach in London, fitted with card table, bucket seats, electric lights, etc." He was now trading from Viney's address at 32 Summerhill Road, Tottenham. In November 1927 he started an express service between London and Luton, still under the title of Imperial Motor Services. There then followed a complex career of coach operation starting in February 1928 with an extension northwards to Bedford after which, in September 1928, an entirely new Bedford service was commenced via Hitchin, and the original cut back to Luton. Both routes were sold in March 1929 and, two months later, a London-Slough-Reading service began, followed in June 1930 by London-Sevenoaks. Both were operated as Safeways and were withdrawn in August 1930 after which Ralph Priest subsequently became Manager of the coaching business of W. D. Beaumont of Enfield. In May 1933 he joined Strawhatter of Luton and passed, on their demise, to London Transport with whom he was a Green Line Controller in post-war years.

Meanwhile Ralph's brother, Arthur, re-entered the coaching world in July 1929 as Regent Motor Services on a London-Hertford service which was later sold to J. S. Ray of Harringay. November 1929 saw the start of a London-Dunstable service called, like his brothers' Reading one, Safeways. He later joined forces with W. D. Beaumont and between them they operated as Beaumont-Safeway on London-Bedford and London-Dunstable-Leighton Buzzard. The Bedford service subsequently passed to Birch and the Leighton Buzzard one was sold to London Transport in April 1934. Arthur Priest found himself, like his brother, working for London Transport, but he was dissatisfied with his lot. He felt that a mechanic's job at Luton garage for £3 10s. 6d. a week was poor recognition for several years experience of passenger vehicle ownership and operation, not to mention youthful years spent with A.E.C., Daimler and Commer.

Hebbs' Garage, 2 Defoe Road, Stoke Newington

In Stoke Newington there was a garage which once served as a home for a small number of buses. Hebbs Motors Ltd. were located at 93 Church Street. This was the office address of the garage business and is today a sewing machine depot. The garage building was at the rear and had the address 2 Defoe Road. Next door to it was the site of the house where once lived Daniel Defoe, the author. Hebbs' garage has long since faded into oblivion and the garage site is now part of a large council depot yard. Hebbs' two best bus customers were Smith & Oates, whose bus "The Hawk" lived out its life span at Defoe Road from December 1924 to September 1927, and F. A. Rasey, who kept his F.A.R. bus there from November 1924 until he moved to Tankard & Smith's in South Tottenham in 1927. A customer of shorter duration was Moses Edelman whose M & E bus was based at Hebbs' for about three months from November 1924 to February 1925.

THE HAWK

George Peter Smith of 147 Dynevor Road, Stoke Newington was the licensee and senior partner in Smith & Oates. He and Harry Oates bought XW 6538, a Hickman-bodied Daimler, late in 1924 and licensed it on December 30th. Its livery was red & white and it carried the fleetname The Hawk in gold script-style lettering. Initially on local routes such as 69 and 73, it was soon transferred to the 511. Smith & Oates were both working partners and could frequently be found along with the many other owner-drivers and conductors on the popular 511. As we have already seen, they garaged exclusively in Hebbs' at Stoke Newington.

In April 1927 the partners diversified their activities with the purchase of a coach, YF 6379, which was a Roberts-rebuilt Daimler 26-seater. Five months later, on September 7th 1927, they sold their bus to Public for £2,550 to concentrate on coachwork. A new TSM, YV 2158, was purchased in March 1928 and a second TSM, UL 4084, replaced the Daimler in January 1929. Smith & Oates continued to run their coaches until about September 1937 and are thought not to have expanded beyond a fleet of two. From about 1932 onwards they were at Jerome's Garage in Hackney.

1/3 Tottenham High Road, Stamford Hill

GRAY

The Gray family was at one time very prosperous and had fingers in two pies; they ran a bus, coach and haulage business at 81 Harrowgate Road, Hackney on the corner of Cassland Road, and also had a hat-shape manufacturing business at 149 Hackney Road. In the summer of 1924 they moved their transport activities to a splendid new garage-cum-coach station at 1/3 Tottenham High Road, Stamford Hill, which, though in 1975 a depot for Corona, the soft drinks people, still looks every inch a bus garage. The principal of the business was Edward Gray of 160 Hackney Road. His large family included five sons, Bertie, James, Frederick, William and Charles who were all connected with the businesses in one way or another. Charles Gray managed the transport undertaking and William was manager of the garage. James was also connected with the transport side of things while the others were employed in the hat-shape business. Gray's most important employee was James Leach, an ex-LGOC man who, though designated foreman, was also inspector and cashier. He had an office at the back of the Stamford Hill garage and he lived with his wife in a flat over the top of it.

The earliest recorded passenger vehicle owned by the Grays is XA 8819, a Y-type AEC charabanc bought in 1920. Little is known about their coaching activities or the vehicles owned during the period 1920-25 though one charabanc of interest which is recorded as having belonged to them in 1925-26 was MH 5495, a Garford which was sold to E. B. Horne for conversion into one of the first Gilfords. The decision to run a fleet of buses was made in 1923 and eight Dodson-bodied Leylands were licensed in two batches of four. XP 9079/9776, XR 481/658 were new in January 1924 and MF 9645/9846, MH 304/402 arrived in July and August. The change from LCC to Middlesex registration letters for the

281

second batch was necessitated by the move to Stamford Hill. One further identical vehicle was bought in May 1925 (MH 7206) to provide a spare for the other eight. Five of the scheduled weekday workings were on routes 6, 8 and 38 and the other three were on the 69. Gray had, additionally, applied for journeys on 520 at the start of scheduling under the London Traffic Act but, like those run by G. A. Wright of the British Lion, they were soon abandoned. At about the same time Gray also applied to operate northwards to Hertford, and this received the route number 275 under the Bassom numbering scheme. There is no trace of Hertford Council giving approval for such an operation, but Gray is known to have worked into Hertford—possibly illegally—on at least one Saturday.

In addition to the bus fleet there were at least seven coaches in stock at one time. Gray was one of the earliest buyers of Gilfords and standardised on this make for coaches bought from January 1926 onwards. The company was a pioneer of medium distance coach operation relying on police plates to take fares on the coach without the necessity to pre-book, and two London to Oxford services introduced by them on March 12th 1928—one via Amersham, Beaconsfield and Henley and the other direct via Uxbridge, Beaconsfield and Stokenchurch—led to great developments by other operators. The coaches ran under the title of "Red & Black Coaching Service." The longer-way-round service to Oxford was soon abandoned, but the direct one was developed to six journeys a day (fewer at weekends) of which two were extended via Burford and Cheltenham to Gloucester by October 1928. The London terminus for these operations was Bush House, Aldwych, which also became the starting point for new once-daily services to Paignton via Salisbury, Exeter and Torquay and to Margate.

As far back as June 12th 1924 the two distinct sides of Gray's business activities had been reorganised as limited companies. E. Gray & Sons (Hackney) Ltd. was the title given to the hat-shape business, whilst the transport and garage activities came under the wing of Edward Gray (Transport) Ltd. This title was changed to E. Gray & Sons (Transport) Ltd. in October 1924, though tickets issued by the company's buses bore the incorrect title of Grays Ltd. Each of the male members of the family held shares in both companies.

Grays' survived the wholesale demise of independents in 1926/7 but the fleet suffered a general rundown in condition and no new buses were ordered. The probability is that the company had overstretched itself with its coaching activities and had insufficient capital available for renewal of the bus fleet. When freshly painted the Gray buses looked resplendent in their red livery with greyish-white window frames, gold lining and black mouldings, but by 1929 their condition was shabby. Bad publicity was received when a bus overturned at the junction of Shirland Road and Sutherland Avenue, Maida Vale, on April 10th 1929 in an accident which was similar in many ways to an earlier Tottenham Hotspur one (see page 291). It was 8.40 a.m. and the bus was laden with people going to work. It overturned when the driver tried to avoid an accident and about forty people were injured, some seriously. Very fortunately no-one died.

By the beginning of 1930 negotiations were in hand for the sale of the buses to the LGOC. These negotiations were handled by A. T. Bennett and Edward Matthews, formerly proprietor of the Meteor buses and now part-owner of the Hale Garage at Tottenham Hale. A price was agreed and the takeover arranged for February 21st 1930. The intention was to run the ex-Gray buses on Gray's licences until March 12th on which date the licences would be transferred to General who would immediately substitute six of its standard buses and operate from its own garage at Dalston (D). The three licences on route 69 were to be allowed to lapse. Meanwhile the Gray buses had to vacate the Stamford Hill premises as soon as the takeover was completed, and it was arranged that they would operate temporarily from the Hale Garage at a rental of 15/- a vehicle per week. However the condition of the Gray buses had deteriorated to such an extent that K-types ex-Dalston had to be substituted on March 6th, six days earlier than had been intended. So run down had the condition of the Gray fleet become that on the previous morning (the 5th) none of the nine vehicles was in service. One was off the road for annual overhaul and was still in Gray's garage, six had mechanical defects and two had been the subject of police stops. Of the six with mechanical trouble, three had left the depot in the morning but were soon brought back because of defective piston, differential and clutch respectively.

Forty-five former Gray staff passed into LGOC employment. In addition to Mr. Leach there were eighteen drivers, eighteen conductors, three night fitters, two day fitters and three washers. The nine Leyland buses were taken to Chiswick Works to await disposal.

The hat-shape business had ceased in about 1927, possibly to provide capital for the expansion of the family's coaching activities, and the Gray coaches had been disposed of prior to the end of 1929, but it has not proved possible to trace the date upon which coach operation ceased. The firm of E. Gray & Sons (Transport) Ltd. was wound up on November 15th 1932 after unsuccessful attempts by the Registrar of Companies to trace its owners. E. Gray & Sons (Hackney) Ltd. had been similarly dissolved seven days earlier.

PRIMROSE

Gray's garage at Stamford Hill exceeded in size the firm's own needs, so space was rented out to other operators, one of whom was George Albert Adams of 22 Elmore Street, Islington. His Primrose bus was one of the earliest independent vehicles, XM 3527—a Straker Squire—having been licensed on November 14th 1922. This attractive-looking bus in its yellow & white livery commenced working a service from Edmonton to Victoria via route 76 to the Bank and then via route 11. This was unnumbered initially but Adams later gave it the number 8 though it bore no relation to the famous LGOC route 8. In February 1923 the Primrose was also on the 29 but competition on this route may have proved too fierce for, by April 1923, it had moved away and was recorded working in many different parts of London. Indeed Adams was a most prolific applicant for police plates for a wide variety of services, some entirely covering existing LGOC routes such as 6, 9, 11 & 33, and others embodying

283

combinations of them. Among the more interesting in the latter category were Old Ford-Clapham Common, Hackney Wick-Victoria and Wormley-Victoria. During the 1924 exhibition Adams worked to Wembley on routes 6 (from Hackney Wick) and 8 (from Old Ford). The eye-catching yellow livery lasted only until March 1923 when the main panels were repainted bright red, the only primrose then remaining being around the windows plus a yellow strip on which the fleetname was painted. A second red Primrose was purchased in May 1924, XT 4176, a Strachan & Brown-bodied Dennis. From 1925 onwards both worked solely on route 69/A on weekdays. As for Sundays, Primrose applied for its own version of the Victoria-High Beach run in April 1925 and this received the number 288, but by 1926 it had been abandoned in favour of the 69 as on weekdays.

Adams operated out of three garages in fairly quick succession. First of all he was in C. A. Wells' garage in Cambridge Road, Hackney. By May 1924 he was operating from Flight's garage in Parkhurst Road and by the beginning of January 1925 he had moved to Gray's garage.

In March 1926 Adams offered to sell his buses to General. A limited company was duly formed on the 15th of the month with registered office at 41 Finsbury Square, E.C.2, and on April 1st 1926 the Primrose Omnibus Co. Ltd. was taken over by the LGOC. Though the negotiations for sale had been carried out as discreetly as possible news of it leaked through to the staff at Gray's garage, who showed their displeasure with little acts of sabotage on the Dennis. Luckily the Straker Squire was away for overhaul at the time, otherwise it would probably have suffered the same fate. A worried Adams informed the LGOC of what was happening and they had no alternative but to house the bus in one of their own garages. When it came off service on March 25th it ran into Tottenham (AR) garage whence it operated for its last six days in Adams' ownership, establishing the unique record of being the only independently-owned bus ever to operate out of an LGOC garage.

Operation continued from Tottenham garage after takeover until January 1st 1928 when the Primrose business was absorbed into the Tramways (MET) Omnibus Co. Ltd. Meanwhile, on December 1st 1926 the Dennis had been sent away to Chiswick for overhaul prior to joining the Redburn fleet. Its replacement was K 805 in red livery with a primrose central panel. The Straker Squire was replaced in March 1927 by a second K-type, K74, but this one was in full General livery except for the legal owner inscription. Between them K74 and 805 maintained the Primrose workings until the end.

CRESCENT

A. A. Mathews of 60 Grosvenor Road, Edmonton, was the licensee of a blue & white Straker Squire with which he began in business in May 1924 as the Crescent Omnibus Company. He had as junior partners men by the name of Crompton and Nicholls about whom nothing else is recorded. MF 7694 was first licensed on May 19th and worked initially on route 73, and possibly also the 13 and 38, transferring in the following year to the 69A. Little is known about the Crescent bus except that it was garaged firstly at Straker Squires. Then, about a month later, it moved to

284

Ponders End where it was possibly in Walter's yard along with the B.C. and C.W.P. buses before moving to take up more permanent residence at Grays'. It was repainted red & white by an early date—certainly by October 1924—and was sold to Public on July 8th 1927 for £2,000.

POPPY

Also to be found at Gray's garage was MF 7628, a red & white Leyland bought in May 1924 by Wainwright & Winter. It was christened Poppy and was the only bus they ever owned. On May 20th T. H. Winter took it to Scotland Yard where it was passed for service by the police; it subsequently ran on the 69 on weekdays and Sunday operation was probably also on this route. The firm's business address has variously been quoted as 83 High Road and 217 High Road, Tottenham. Probably one was Wainwright's home address and the other Winter's. After an uneventful career of just over three years, operation of the Poppy was taken over by Public on June 9th 1927, who ran it under Wainwright & Winter's licences until July 28th when the transfer of ownership was formally completed for £2,500.

★   ★   ★   ★

Grays' had another tenant, Alfred Sneiman, who kept his Gordon buses there for about two years from the Autumn of 1924. Sneiman had his own garage built in Lea Bridge Road and when this was ready for occupation he vacated Grays' premises.

Tankard & Smith Ltd., 226-232 High Road, South Tottenham
The Hale Garage, Tottenham Hale

METEOR

Until quite recent times Tankard & Smith Ltd. was a well-known name in London motor circles as a large firm of motor car distributors, dealers and repairers with several branches in the suburbs. Their premises at Peckham and Shepherds Bush have already been noted as the home of several south and west London operators. Nos. 226-232 High Road, South Tottenham (demolished in March 1973) was another of their branches which housed independent buses during the boom years of the 'twenties. Foremost among them was the Meteor fleet which began in December 1923 and was the brainchild of Edward Matthews, formerly of the Royal Flying Corps, who lived at 17 Bedford Road, West Green.

Meteor bus number 1 was a Leyland in a rather drab colour scheme of all-over red with the Meteor fleetname in gold script on a black panel, a livery which all subsequent Meteor buses also wore. It was licensed as MF 3646 on December 19th 1923, and appeared at Scotland Yard on the 21st, entering service for the first time later in the same day. A Dennis, MF 8611, arrived in June 1924 followed by a further Leyland, MH 1435, in the following October. April 1925 saw the fleet expand to its maximum of five vehicles when MH 5536/7, a pair of Dennises, entered service. Initially Matthews had tried out several routes including, of course, the 11, 15, 25, 29, 33, 69, 73 and 76. He finally settled down on the 529, for which he held five Monday to Friday licences, plus the 69A on Saturdays.

285

On September 4th 1925 a limited company was incorporated to take over the Meteor buses, with its registered office at Rood House, Cross Lane, E.C.3, Matthews' solicitor's address. 3,702 shares were issued out of a possible 5,000. Edward Matthews held the majority of 3,241, the others being owned by his brothers Harold Frank Matthews, a schoolmaster, and Percy Barnard Matthews, a fish salesman.

It eventually became clear to the Matthews that they would have to obtain their own garage if the business was to run satisfactorily. Harold Matthews was fortunate in obtaining a large piece of freehold ground at Tottenham Hale, on the junction of The Hale and Ferry Lane, which contained only a shed formerly used by the church to give under-privileged children a day out. A garage was erected for the buses, and petrol sales were also made to the public from which a highly profitable business developed. The buses moved from Tankard & Smith's to the Hale Garage in February 1927.

Even with a garage of their own, the Meteor buses failed to make the profits that the Matthews had hoped for and Edward Matthews began to foresee a much brighter future in long-distance coach operation. Meanwhile A. T. Bennett, acting on behalf of the proposed Public organisation, offered the attractive sum of £13,750 for the buses plus £700 for stock in trade. This was early in June 1927 and on the 16th of that month operational control of the buses passed to Bennett. The actual purchase was not, however, completed until August 18th so the five ex-Meteor vehicles continued to run with "Meteor Omnibus Co. Ltd." as their legal owner inscription until then. Edward Matthews went to work for Public as an engineer and he was one of the few independent bus proprietors to take shares in Public. He accepted 3,500 preference and 3,500 ordinary £1 LPOC shares as part of the purchase price.

On July 21st 1928 the Hale Garage Coach Ltd. was formed with a nominal capital of £6,000 to take over the Hale Garage business of Henry Matthews and to operate a London-Leeds-Bradford coach service under the title of Hale Coachways jointly with Coachways Ltd., a company formed on the same date by P. H. R. Harris. The idea of running coaches was Edward Matthews' but it was left to Henry to run them as Edward was at this time working for Public. Two Dennis E's were purchased, the first, MT 65, in August 1928; MT 1273 followed in December. Operations were short-lived. Obtaining the many licences then required to run the service proved a costly business and trade did not come up to expectations. In April 1933 the vehicles and licences were sold to the Yorkshire Pool of Great North Road operators (East Yorkshire, Yorkshire Woollen District, Yorkshire Traction and West Yorkshire). Henry Matthews continued to own and run the Hale Garage for the next thirty years and Edward became a successful consulting engineer. The Hale Garage Coach Co. Ltd. was recently wound up. The Hale Garage is today owned by Ray Powell Ltd., British Leyland dealers, who have retained the old bus garage buildings as a workshop.

WW

We now revert to Tankard & Smith's to meet the three Wards, Frederick Walter, Francis Walter and Arthur Francis, who, together with Robert

Punnett, owned the W & P Omnibus Co. Ltd. The business was started on December 1st 1924 by Frederick Walter Ward; the others did not join him until later. He bought a Dodson-bodied Dennis, MH 2239, which was in an attractive livery of scarlet & white with lightish-brown rocker panels and the fleetname WW. His home and business address was 71 Lordsmead Road, Tottenham. The bus was housed at Tankard & Smith's and began work on December 13th on the 29. Just over a month later its operation was changed to the 69 (where competition was a little less fierce) though it is known to have also operated on the 11 on occasions. It was repainted red & white, probably on its first overhaul. The limited company was formed on September 25th 1925, the directors being the three Wards and Punnett who between them held the entire issued share capital of £1,247. The fleetname on the bus continued to be WW.

At an unknown date the WW bus moved from Tankard & Smith's to Howard Barrett's garage in Claremont Street, Upper Edmonton. Amongst the operators already there were Daniel George Edward Cosgrove and his brother Terence St. Patrick Cosgrove who had previously run, together with their uncle Bernard Cosgrove, a fleet of four buses but who were now reduced to one. This was a Dennis, MF 9160, which was employed on the 69. The proprietors of W & P were offered this bus which they agreed to purchase, taking the Cosgrove brothers on as employees to continue to work it. The Cosgrove Omnibus Co. Ltd. was incorporated on September 20th 1925 with a nominal capital of £1,000 to take over MF 9160 at a purchase price of £800. The Wards and Punnett held all but two of the 802 issued £1 shares but Daniel Cosgrove remained the licensee of the bus. The first registered office was his home address of 40 The Crescent, Tottenham, but this was changed on December 30th to Punnett's address, 1 Wards Terrace, Broad Lane, Tottenham.

Towards the end of 1925 the Wards and Punnett expanded their bus operations more than three fold by purchasing the five-bus business of Tottenham Hotspur from the Viney family. The Tottenham Hotspur Omnibus Co. Ltd. had been incorporated on December 7th to enable the purchase to take place, and on 1st January 1926 the five Tottenham Hotspur buses were formally purchased for £100, though obviously a further unrecorded cash transaction took place to adequately repay the Vineys. The whole of the authorised share capital of £1,000 in £1 shares was issued and, apart from £120 held by the Vineys, the remainder were all held by the Wards and Punnett. Significantly a debenture issue of £3,000 at 5% was made on December 12th 1925 to Nimrod Armitage Barrett who owned a butcher's shop in Fore Street, Edmonton. He was a relative of Howard Barrett, the owner of the garage where the WW, Cosgrove and Tottenham Hotspur buses were kept. Once at his garage, the day-to-day operation of the buses came under his control and it was not long before he was arranging to take over financial control also. On April 29th 1926 Barrett's Garage became the registered office of all three and he was then designated Managing Director. Barrett, however, appears from the outset to have been acting on behalf of C. W. Batten, who may well have been the source of his capital. Batten was a former

287

independent proprietor who, having sold his own business to the LGOC, was now quietly purchasing control of others on their behalf. As this chapter progresses we shall pick up the threads of the various Batten-group companies in the Edmonton area. The ultimate destiny of all of them, including the WW bus, is described on page 297.

M & E/MORFAY/EMBASSY

Moses Edelman was the proprietor of a pair of Dennis's which he licensed in November 1924 (XW 2324) and February 1925 (XX 1007). They were bought on hire purchase from Christopher Dodson and were called respectively M & E and Morfay. When XW 2324 was new it stayed for a short while at Hebbs' Garage in Defoe Road, Stoke Newington, but by the time XX 1007 was delivered three months later "home" for Edelman's buses had become Tankard & Smith's. Edelman later left for a new base at Barrett's Garage in Upper Edmonton. Various routes were operated from time to time including 73, 76 and 525, but by 1927 weekday operations were confined to 73A, 138 and 173D. In June 1926 Edelman moved to his fourth and last garage, Jerome's in Downs Road, Hackney.

Edelman, who lived at 64 Fountayne Road, Stoke Newington, decided in due course to form a limited company with an authorised capital of £1,000. On February 4th 1927 Embassy Motors Ltd. was incorporated at 92 Stoke Newington Road—Edelman's solicitor's office— and Edelman's wife, Fanny, became holder of 800 out of the 803 £1 shares which were issued. Embassy had become the fleetname for both buses shortly before this. Embassy Motors Ltd. functioned for only eight months, for on October 24th 1927 Public purchased the business. After paying off outstanding hire purchase commitments to Dodson the Edelmans were left with £6,253 2s. 10d. Their Embassy Motors Ltd. was finally dissolved on January 23rd 1931 after having lain dormant since the sale of the buses.

SB

The brothers Sear entered buswork in 1924 though they were by no means newcomers to the motor industry, having owned for some while a small motor car repair business which they conducted from a corner site at 149 West Green Road where it joins Elmar Road. Encouraged by the apparent success of local independent bus owners, Henry and Edward James Sear decided to expand their activities to include bus operation and ordered a Dennis from Dodson. This was delivered in October 1924 and was registered in the same month, as MH 1257. This, and the Sears' subsequent buses, were almost certainly housed throughout their career at Tankard & Smith's; probably the Sears did not have the space or equipment to run them from their own premises. The brothers chose the traditional combination of red & white for their colour scheme and the bus carried no fleetname as such but bore the initials SB entwined in a circle. MH 1257 was usually to be found on the 29 and its short workings, for which weekday licences were duly obtained, though it was also observed on the 69 and 212 on occasions, probably on Sundays.

MH 1257 remained the sole SB bus until May 1926. The brothers wished to expand their bus interests and, there being no suitable unrestricted double-deck routes then available in the area, they decided to buy two single-deck Dennises for the 551 which was at that time developing in a very promising way. MK 4483/4 were a pair of Strachan & Brown-bodied 24-seaters which soon became regular performers on the Edmonton-Whetstone road. When a larger bus was required to augment the service in March 1927 a 30-seater E-type, ML 2421, was supplied by Strachan & Brown. With the delivery of the latter vehicle the Sear Brothers' fleet reached its maximum of four which, while sufficient to cover the three weekday licences on the 551 and the one on the 29, left no spare bus to cover casualties.

A limited company entitled Sear Brothers Ltd. was incorporated on December 17th 1927 with a nominal capital of £3,000 and with its registered office at 149 West Green Road. To get advice on how to form a limited company the Sears had approached Arthur Gannon, the proprietor of the Prince buses, who was brother-in-law of one of them. Edward and Henry Sear were the sole shareholders and they held half the capital each. Just after this they applied to the police, jointly with Prince, to extend the 551 eastwards to Walthamstow via the recently completed Lea Valley Viaduct, but approval was refused in February 1928 due to alleged obstructions on the roads over which they proposed to operate in Walthamstow. In May 1928 (the exact date has not been established for certain but it may have been the 19th) the buses were sold to Public securing for Sear Brothers Ltd. the doubtful honour of being the last independent operator to be purchased by that concern. After disposing of the business the brothers resolved, on June 1st 1928, to wind the company up, and it was finally dissolved on May 30th 1929.

FAR

The only independent to remain at Tankard & Smith's until the London Transport era was Frederick Arthur Rasey of 40 Grayling Road, Stoke Newington. First of all Rasey's bus ran from Hebbs' Garage in Stoke Newington but later moved—in about July 1927—to Tankard & Smith's where Rasey paid a weekly rental of 8/-. Rasey always operated on sections of routes 38 and 73 on weekdays and latterly ran solely on the 73 on Sundays though he had tried the 69 in his earlier days. The actual operations in the last days of the business in 1933 were:-weekdays up to 3.30 p.m. 73A/173D, after 3.30 p.m. 38A/E; Sundays 73A/173D.

Only two buses were ever owned, and both carried Rasey's initials as their fleetname written as FRA, the 'R' being larger than the other two letters. The first was XU 8988, a red & white Hickman-bodied Daimler registered on September 29th 1924. By 1929 this was in need of replacement and Rasey made arrangements through a local distributor, H. Humbert Ltd., for the supply of a new Dennis HS covered top bus with Birch 54-seat bodywork. Meanwhile, on Wednesday July 3rd, Birch lent Rasey one of their own covered top vehicles for police trials on this type of vehicle over the whole of Rasey's routes. Police approval was given in August and MY 1689 was licensed on October 25th. In Rasey's case the trend towards plainer liveries was reversed, as MY 1689 was in

289

an attractive scheme of chocolate with creamy-yellow window frames & a pink waist rail.

Rasey, who lived latterly at 10 Mafeking Road, Tottenham, ran his bus until November 24th 1933, which was the day appointed for its transfer to the LPTB. Rasey was in due course awarded £4,000 compensation for his business.

Other operators who are known to have been based at Tankard & Smith's were Edwards & Convey, proprietors of the Daisy bus, H. A. Wells of the Criterion, Cosgrove and Earl. All are described elsewhere in this chapter.

30 Markfield Road, Tottenham
32 Summerhill Road, Tottenham

TOTTENHAM HOTSPUR

The name of Viney was connected with transport in the Tottenham area for well over half a century and was once as synonymous locally with transport as Tottenham is with Hotspur. The founder of the business was H. B. Viney but in the early years of this century affairs were in the capable hands of his son, Henry Francis Viney, a shrewd businessman who ran the family haulage and furniture removal business in Tottenham. He had irons in another fire too, being proprietor of a Hertfordshire farm at Standon Green End which was run for him by a bailiff. The farm was useful in providing feeding stuff for the Viney cart horses. In about 1910 Viney left the haulage business and bought a country pub, the Bull & Horseshoes at Potter Street, but his departure from the transport scene proved to be only temporary and two years later he bought his old business back. The Great War saw the firm of H. B. Viney & Son really prospering. In addition to the traditional horse transport three steam lorries were owned but many others, sometimes up to thirty, were hired at times to cope with government contracts. Viney's vehicles were for many years housed in the railway arches at 30 Markfield Road, Tottenham. These were augmented during the war when Viney acquired a large house at 32 Summerhill Road, Tottenham, which he made his home and also used as an office. Next to the house there was a covered yard where vehicles could be housed under a corrugated iron roof, and at the rear stood a two-storey workshop.

1919 was the year of Viney's entry into the passenger business with the purchase of some five or six Tylor-engined AEC chassis, mostly surplus War Department vehicles, upon which charabanc bodies were mounted. The livery was a brownish red with crimson band along the top of the body lined in gold, and the fleetname chosen was Tottenham Hotspur. A charabanc called Greyhound was also operated for a while, having been purchased second-hand from a Mr. Nosworthy, the licensee of "The Greyhound" in Lea Bridge Road. Coaching proved very prosperous and had expanded sufficiently to justify the opening of a booking office at 264 High Road, Tottenham, in May 1923. By this time the charabanc fleet consisted of five AEC 28-seaters, a brand new Lancia 18-seater and a Crossley 14-seater. A 2-ton Straker Squire with the fleetname Tottenham Belle is reported as having been owned prior to this but probably did not last with Vineys for very long. Apart from the charabancs, motor landaulettes were kept for hiring out and the haulage department consisted by now of petrol, steam and horse vehicles of many sizes.

The coaching department was managed by one of Viney's three sons, Bertie Charles Viney. He also appears to have owned two Lancia coaches on his own account, a Tetraiota called "Flying Fox" and an older pre-war or wartime Z-type named "Little Ronnie" after his son who was born in 1922. Another brother, Reggie, is also thought to have owned a coach at one time. He alas came to an untimely end when he fell from a ladder and broke his neck. When, in 1923, H. F. Viney senior sold his farm to finance his entry into the bus business, Bertie was appointed to take charge of the buses also. The bus fleet, which totalled five at its maximum, perpetuated the name Tottenham Hotspur which was applied in a variety of styles, perhaps according to the whim of the signwriter. The vehicles were basically red in colour, with window frames which varied from time to time between grey & brick yellow. The fleet was supplied by Straker Squire over a period of nine months starting with MF 4166 and MF 4463 in January 1924. MF 7044 arrived in April followed by MH 295 in August and MH 1095, the last, in September. The buses were housed with the haulage fleet at Markfield Road and, after a spell on routes 29, 73 and 69, finally settled down to run exclusively on the latter. The licences were held in Bertie Viney's name.

An unwelcome notoriety was achieved on Wednesday, June 17th 1925, when MF 7044 overturned suddenly in Kingsland Road during the morning rush hour. This bus was laden with City-bound passengers and travelling along at a steady speed when a lorry came suddenly out of Englefield Road into its path. The bus driver, H. Forrest, swerved to avoid the lorry and almost immediately the bus toppled over to an accompaniment of breaking glass and cries of alarm. People from the top deck were thrown out amongst the busy Kingsland Road traffic as the bus fell. Most of the passengers were injured and nine were detained in the Metropolitan Hospital. One died. The scene was soon one of morbid excitement and a large crowd quickly gathered to see the spectacle. The whole road was blocked. Hackney Borough workmen who were tar spraying nearby at once set about extracting the inside passengers, and boards were grabbed from some concrete mixing work to lay the injured on.

This section of the Tottenham Hotspur story finishes on a sad note. In July 1925 H. F. Viney was taken ill with dropsy and from then onwards his involvement in the business declined progressively. In the closing months of 1925 he negotiated the sale of the buses as from January 1st 1926 to the Ward brothers and Punnett who already owned two buses, the WW and the Cosgrove, as we have seen earlier in this chapter. In December he moved to Hoddesdon and in February 1926 the Summerhill Road premises were put up for sale by auction. He died on March 18th 1926 at the age of 53. The haulage business was wound up but Bertie Charles Viney carried on in coaching. He did not possess the same business flair as his father and never progressed beyond a modest sized fleet. In June 1948 the business was reconstituted as Viney's Motor

Coaches Ltd. Bertie Viney himself left in 1952 and his fellow directors, who were all members of the Viney family, disposed of the business to George Ewer & Co. Ltd. on October 26th 1964.

We revert now to the history of the Tottenham Hotspur buses. In order to make the change of ownership possible the Tottenham Hotspur Omnibus Co. Ltd. was formed on December 7th 1925 with its registered office at 1 Wards Terrace, Broad Lane, Tottenham, with a nominal capital of £1,000. Initially Bertie Charles Viney was appointed secretary and Henry Francis Viney was Chairman, but within a few days H. F. Viney had relinquished his position and Frederick Walter Ward, Arthur Francis Ward, Francis Walter Ward and Robert Punnett had joined the board. On December 16th a debenture issue of £3,000 was made to Nimrod Armitage Barrett who, it will be recalled, had supplied capital similarly to the W & P company. The buses were transferred upon purchase to Barrett's garage in Claremont Road, Edmonton, and operated from there henceforth as part of the "Batten" group. We pick up the threads again on page 297.

SILVER STAR

One further brief excursion by Bertie Charles Viney into the bus business remains to be recorded. When his coach "Little Ronnie" became too costly to repair Viney ordered a new vehicle from Strachan & Brown to replace it. On October 27th 1926, ML 611 was licensed. It was a Dennis 24-seater of the standard London bus type; it carried a red & white livery and bore the title Silver Star. Its arrival enabled Viney to re-enter the bus world and he promptly placed it on route 551 though on Sundays and on "when working" journeys it could be found on the busy Hertford Road route 69A where it looked tiny alongside fleets of double-deckers. Viney had obtained possession of the Summerhill Road Yard formerly owned by his father and the bus was garaged there. This second enterprise as a bus operator was short-lived and on May 20th 1927 the Silver Star was taken over by the LGOC for £1,500. A limited company was incorporated on May 6th with a nominal capital of £1,000, and registered office at 55 Broadway. The bus was allocated by the LGOC to the ex-Redburn garage at Ponders End (RS) for operation, the Silver Star Omnibus Co. Ltd. being finally absorbed into the LGOC on January 1st 1928.

Straker Squire Works, 67 Angel Road, Edmonton
Grove Court Garage, 57A Fore Street, Edmonton
Barrett's Garage, Claremont Street, Edmonton

Adjoining Tottenham to the north is the former borough of Edmonton in the part of which, known as Upper Edmonton, were three major bases of independent operation. They were not all used simultaneously. The earliest one was in Angel Road in the works that once formed part of Ely's cartridge factory and which, after considerable reconstruction by the government during the war, had been leased by Straker Squire Ltd. The company's production of bodies and chassis, of which the famous A-type predominated, did not take up all their available covered accommodation, so one very large building, which resembled an aircraft hangar, was used as a public garage and housed, amongst other things, the buses of six independent operators. These were Cosgrove, CWP, Crescent, Fairlop, Prince and Supreme. A seventh, Biss Brothers, was also there for a short while following a fire in their premises at Waltham Cross. Not all the vehicles garaged at 67 Angel Road were Straker Squires; the Fairlop bus was a Daimler and the Prince a Leyland.

With the demise of Straker Squire Ltd. those tenants who still remained had to find new homes and two almost adjacent garages in Upper Edmonton came into prominence. One was the Grove Court Garage run by Ernest Knifton Ltd. at 57A Fore Street, on the main north-south bus and tram route through Edmonton. E. F. Knifton was a road haulage, sewer and general contractor who had occupied the premises since at least the early 'twenties. He provided garaging facilities for bus operators right up to the end of independent operation, and a petrol station still occupies the site today, though in a much modernised form. Facing the Grove Court Garage is Claremont Street where, a few yards from Fore Street on the Western corner of Clive Avenue, were the premises of Howard C. Barrett, a motor-car dealer and general garage proprietor since before the days of the independent buses. A department store car park now occupies the site. Several small operators ran from Claremont Street, and in the early part of 1926 Barrett himself became a bus owner by obtaining control of the Tottenham Hotspur, Cosgrove and WW buses from the Wards and Punnett. As we have already seen in connection with the WW bus, he appears to have done so as an agent for Charles William Batten who was himself acquiring bus companies as a "secret" agent of the LGOC. In June 1926 Batten formally took control of the three companies and the LGOC purchased the garage from Barrett though the transfer of ownership of the premises to them was not immediately apparent as it was made through the Cosgrove Omnibus Co. Ltd. When the true identity of the new owners became known to the other tenants at Claremont Street most made arrangements to move across the road to the Grove Court Garage. Two of Knifton's tenants at Grove Court, Loveland and White Star, moved across the road too, but in the opposite direction, when they became LGOC-owned under Batten's control.

Before describing the various operators in Edmonton, it is appropriate at this stage to outline the organisational set-up concerning the group of companies usually referred to officially at the time either as the "Batten Group" or the "Merrett Group". Batten, as we have already seen, was formerly a bus owner himself and was responsible for building-up the successful Atlas fleets based in East Ham. Howard Charles Merrett was a chartered accountant and senior partner in the firm of Merrett, Sons & Street. Batten's responsibility in the group was for operational matters, including the hiring and firing of staff whilst Merrett was mainly responsible for financial and general business affairs. At the maximum there were eleven companies in the group, five at Edmonton and six at East Ham. There appears to have been little or no interchange of vehicles between the group's two garages at East Ham and Edmonton, though major overhauls on the Edmonton based buses were carried out at East Ham. For accountancy purposes the Cosgrove Omnibus Co. Ltd. was used as the parent company for the other four at Claremont Street and all takings, purchases, etc., passed through its books, and it was to the Cosgrove company that the independent operators outside Batten's control paid their rents for such time as they remained at Claremont Street. A single administrative staff was established for the whole group under the supervision of a Mr. Sefton, who was designated Traffic Manager, and Mr. Williamson, the group's cashier. Both these gentlemen were located at Edmonton.

The earlier history of two of the companies, the Tottenham Hotspur Omnibus Co. Ltd. and the W & P Omnibus Co. Ltd. has already been traced up to 1926. We shall pick up the threads again after reviewing the Cosgrove, White Star and Loveland Companies which made up the Batten group of five at Edmonton.

B.C./COSGROVE
CWP

After Bernard Cosgrove parted company with A. T. Bennett and left the Admiral business which he had founded, he disposed of his first four Straker Squires to start afresh with new vehicles. Four new Straker Squires were delivered over a period of six months starting with MF 1297/8 in July 1923. The first of them was inspected by the police on July 20th and, like its partner, was in a chocolate livery with yellow upper parts. Both were licensed to Bernard Cosgrove who traded for a month or two under the title of Edmonton Omnibus Company, which the buses carried on the rocker panels. No fleetname was carried. They began work on the 69 group and were garaged at the Straker Squire works.

Bernard Cosgrove was assisted by his nephews, Daniel George Edward Cosgrove and Terence St. Patrick Cosgrove. When the third new Straker, MF 2143, arrived in August 1923 it was licensed to Daniel and is believed to have been jointly owned by him and his brother. It was in an identical livery to MF 1297/8. Also connected with the Cosgrove trio was Charles William Pallant, a commercial motor engineer and charabanc proprietor at 248 Romford Road, Forest Gate. He purchased from Bernard Cosgrove the newest two of his earlier Straker fleet, ME 7351 & ME 8598 (the other pair—ME 6185/6—went to Harvey & Burrows of Ware) which, it is thought, Cosgrove ran on his behalf. The reason for thinking this to be so is that all applications made by Bernard Cosgrove, Daniel Cosgrove and Pallant for permission to run on various services are identical and were made at the same time. The date on which Pallant bought his two buses from Cosgrove is not known for certain, but it was probably some time in July 1923. Pallant retained the blue Admiral livery but had his own initials painted on the sides in place of the former fleetname. One bus carried CWP in equal sized white capital letters; the other had the C and P in large red letters with a smaller brown W in-between.

The three Cosgrove and two Pallant buses stayed largely on the 69 during the winter of 1923/4 though they also appeared on 13, 35, 38, 73 and 76. Summer Sundays in 1924 saw the Cosgrove buses, at least, extending their already lengthy journey from Brixton Station northwards from the usual terminus at the Globe, Wormley to Hertford, Bernard

Cosgrove's old "home territory" of his former days with Harvey & Burrows.

A fourth new Straker Squire arrived for the Cosgroves in January 1924 in the shape of MF 4511 but despite this the fleet strength remained at three as MF 1298 had been sold in the previous month to Redburn's in whose fleet it was numbered 13. It is thought to have run for them for a while in its original brown livery but with the Redburn fleet name added. MF 4511 was painted red & white but it is not known if it carried any fleetname at first. It was put to work on the 29 and by June 1924 was bearing the fleet letters "B.C." Of the other two Cosgrove-owned Strakers one, at least, was still in brown livery without a fleetname in September 1924.

In about January 1924 the Cosgrove and Pallant buses moved out of the Straker Squire works to an open yard in the Hertford Road near its junction with Southbury Road, Ponders End. This is now (1975) a garage owned by Walters Motors Ltd. whose present Chairman then owned the plot. He then worked as a foreman and fitter for Redburn's at their Green Street premises. After a short stay at Ponders End the buses are believed to have moved back to Straker Squires.

During the last week of June 1924 a further new bus was presented to the police and was subsequently registered on July 4th as MF 9160. It was red & white and bore the "B.C." fleetname, being licensed to Bernard Cosgrove, and appears to have replaced MF 4511 which was sold off at a very early age to become a lorry. The position by January 1925 thus was that Bernard Cosgrove was operating two vehicles with the fleetname "B.C." (MF 1297/MF 9160) whilst his nephews owned one vehicle, MF 2143, which now carried the fleetname Cosgrove in block capitals.

Meanwhile, in about September 1924, Pallant parted company with the Cosgroves. In October he applied for plates to operate on his own account a Straker Squire from Victoria to Chadwell Heath under his business title of Forest Gate Motor Transport, but it is not known if he actually did so. The two double-deckers were returned to Straker Squires about then, and in November they emerged in the ownership of Cambrian, their third owner in two years. Pallant had obtained two new Straker Squires in the summer of 1924 (AN 6404/6520) but these were charabancs and probably ran from his premises at Forest Gate.

At an unknown date the Cosgroves removed their buses from Straker Squires going firstly, it is thought, to Tankard & Smith's at South Tottenham. Bernard Cosgrove probably stayed there to the end of his operating career but his nephews subsequently moved to Claremont Street. Bernard Cosgrove went through bad times domestically and financially. In August 1924 he was taken ill and had to spend some time in hospital at Orpington. Whilst there his wife Jessie learned of his misconduct with another woman and his marriage broke up in May 1925 after less than three years, to end in divorce six months later. At about this time his Dennis, MF 9160, passed into the ownership of Daniel and Terence who gave it the "Cosgrove" fleetname and disposed of their Straker Squire, leaving Bernard Cosgrove with but one bus, MF 1297. In due course he was forced to sell this to the Wilson family in January

1926, with whom it formed the nucleus of the Earl Motor Omnibus Co. Ltd. Bernard Cosgrove later committed suicide by drowning himself in a tributary of the River Lea near Tottenham Hale.

The Cosgrove brothers sold their Dennis to the Wards and Punnet in circumstances already described, having formed the Cosgrove Omnibus Co. Ltd. on September 25th 1925. They became employees of the new owners and Terence Cosgrove subsequently spent forty years in transport, retiring eventually as a senior road official with London Transport.

WHITE STAR/MONARCH

On September 7th 1926 Mrs. Annie Louise Drake's interesting career as a bus owner came to an end when her White Star bus joined the Batten Group. Mrs. Drake's bus career had commenced late in 1924 when she bought XR 2651, a third-hand Hickman-bodied Daimler whose last owner, Fred Mason, had run it as the White Star. Mrs. Drake kept XR 2651 in its White Star livery and arranged for it to be housed at Craig's garage in Fulham. It was there that she encountered Victor Perry who was anxious to dispose of his Daimler XX 2024 called Monarch after the very briefest of flirtations with the bus world. Mrs. Drake negotiated to buy Perry's bus, and it came into her ownership on March 25th 1925, retaining the title of Monarch.

The London Traffic Act and its retrospective road restrictions adversely affected Mrs. Drake, who was obliged to move on to unprofitable services. Both buses were observed on the 527 on its first day of operation and Monarch, at least, was later seen on the 523. White Star ran for a spell on 525 before the authorities relented and allowed one bus to revert to its former workings on the 11 and 73. The second vehicle had been placed in service too late to qualify for a schedule on a profitable route even after the retrospective restrictions were lifted so Mrs. Drake reduced her fleet to one by selling XR 2651. By November 1925 XX 2024 had been renamed from Monarch to White Star in its place.

November 1925 saw Mrs. Drake operating out of an unknown garage at Vauxhall and 1926 saw her in Edmonton at the Grove Court Garage. A limited company, the White Star Omnibus Company Ltd., was formed on September 17th 1926 with a capital of £1,000 in order to enable the LGOC to purchase the bus through C. W. Batten, the registered office being 188 Fore Street, Edmonton. On October 7th XX 2024 moved into Barrett's garage in Claremont Street.

LOVELAND (shield insignia)

Like H. M. Merry, William John Loveland did not use a fleetname but preferred an emblem which in his case consisted of a red shield on which were gold crossed swords with a crown above and an eagle below. Loveland's earlier career with New Times and his connection with R. J. W. Hawkins have already been outlined in Chapter 5. When he left New Times in about October 1924 he took Dodson-bodied Leyland XN 6976 with him. For a few months the New Times title was retained, but in the early part of 1925 it was replaced by the emblem, the significance of which is not known. Loveland issued tickets with the title Hawklove, believed to have been adopted because of a projected joint operation with Hawkins which never came into being. The route upon which XN 6976 had run during its New Times days was the 73 and it remained basically on this service under Loveland's control as it would have relied on the same weekday licences. It has also been reported as having been seen on the 4A and 69; these were probably "when-working" journeys. After leaving New Times, Loveland moved to 57A Fore Street and, on August 19th 1926, to Claremont Street. The latter move occurred a week after the Loveland bus had come under LGOC control, a limited company having been formed on July 30th 1926 under the title of Loveland Omnibus Co. Ltd. for this purpose. Loveland received £1,700 for his £1 shares from the LGOC, who placed the bus under Batten's control.

V.C.N.

The LGOC adopted a policy of standardising the Batten fleets on Leylands which were drafted in from other acquired companies. The first two to arrive were allocated to Claremont Street to replace two of the Tottenham Hotspur Straker Squires which were despatched, after overhaul, to join the E.P. fleet at Page Street, which was being standardised on vehicles of this make. The new Leyland arrivals were XU 5778/9 formerly run by Royal Blue and they displaced MH 295/1095. They, in turn, replaced YL 8115 and YM 6664 from the E.P. fleet and these two arrived, duly overhauled, in October 1926 to replace two more Tottenham Hotspur Strakers, MF 4463/7044, which were delicensed and thereafter stood disused in the Claremont Street garage. Meanwhile, in August, a third ex-Royal Blue Leyland had arrived in the shape of XT 2864 and it replaced the Cosgrove Dennis MF 9160 which was sold for operation in the East Riding of Yorkshire. The last remaining Tottenham Hotspur Straker Squire, MF 4166, soldiered on until December 1926 when it was withdrawn between the 15th and 29th with no immediate replacement. A chocolate & white livery was adopted as standard and applied to all vehicles when overhauled. An interesting feature at this time was the use of the fleetname V.C.N. which was carried by all the six Leylands at Claremont Street (4 Tottenham Hotspur, 1 Cosgrove and 1 Loveland). V.C.N. stood for "Vul-cold-Nize", a product for repairing motor tyres and other rubber outfits, the secret process for the manufacture of which had been registered under this name in 1925. Merrett purchased the manufacturing rights and in June 1925 formed a limited company entitled Vul-cold-Nize Ltd. to market the firm's V.C.N. repair kits. We can only assume that the application of the letters V.C.N. on the buses was part of a publicity exercise by Merrett to further the prospects of the Vul-cold-Nize company which, in the event, failed and had ceased business by 1928.

Control by Batten and Merrett was short-lived, for on December 31st 1926 their management was terminated and the whole group taken directly under LGOC control. Claremont Street garage continued to function but as a subsidiary of the LGOC's Tottenham (AR) garage, and was given the code letters UE, standing for "Upper Edmonton".

297

Henceforth there was no operational connection between the former Batten companies at Edmonton and those at East Ham. Under LGOC management the replacement of the remaining non-standard vehicles continued. Leyland AN 6120 arrived in January 1927 from Ubique as a belated replacement for the last Tottenham Hotspur Straker Squire, and the White Star Daimler departed early in April with the arrival of K103. Between July and October 1927 the Leylands were all replaced by K's, details of which will be found in the appendix. These all ran in full LGOC colours except for the legal owner's name. The only original bus remaining at Claremont Street after this was MH 2239, the WW Dennis.

The Claremont Street garage was closed to bus operation after the run-in on Tuesday February 8th 1927 and the vehicles were transferred into the parent garage at Tottenham. On June 29th the Loveland and White Star buses were transferred once again, this time to Hammersmith (R) garage, which was a little better situated than Tottenham for operating route 73. On January 1st 1928 the Cosgrove, Tottenham Hotspur and W & P companies were absorbed by the Tramways (MET) Omnibus Co. Ltd., and the White Star and Loveland concerns were taken over by General.

This concludes the review of the Batten group companies in Upper Edmonton. We now turn to the other operators in the southern part of the borough, starting with Smith & Potter.

SUNBEAM/SUPREME

W. J. Smith and E. H. Potter owned the Sunbeam bus, MF 5720, which was a Straker Squire and operated first of all from the manufacturer's works in Angel Road. It was first licensed on March 24th 1924 and began work soon afterwards. Its activities ranged far and wide and included routes 11, 18, 38, 73, 76 and 106, though later—probably from early 1925 onwards—Smith & Potter concentrated on the 511 on weekdays and the 69 Sundays. In 1925 the partners moved to Barrett's Claremont Street garage and in June 1926 they made yet another move to 57A Fore Street where they were destined to stay until London Transport days.

The fleetname Sunbeam was short-lived. It is thought that, as in the case of the Albion bus, the vehicle manufacturer of the same name objected to the use of his registered trade name on a motor vehicle not of his make. By April 21st the bus was running without any title, and it was not until about February 1925 that it appeared as the Supreme. A month later a second bus was delivered. The Straker had suffered from the usual crop of troubles associated with this make so Smith & Potter wisely chose a Dennis when expanding their fleet in March 1925 with MH 5040.

Smith and Potter were both working partners. Smith, who had previously been a driver at the LGOC's Tottenham (AR) garage, attended to the running of the buses on the road, and to their maintenance. The licences were held in his name although, according to the records of the Association of London Omnibus Proprietors, Potter was the senior partner. Potter was a grocer and had no previous bus experience. His work in the firm was mainly administrative, and he attended to the schedules, tickets, waybills, cash and so on. A limited company was incorporated with a capital of £2,000 on March 8th 1927 with Smith and Potter as the sole directors. The registered office of the Supreme Motor Omnibus Co. Ltd. was 31 Wakefield Street, Edmonton, which was Smith's home address at the time.

The first modern bus to be purchased was MY 2742 in January 1930. This was a Dodson-bodied Leyland Titan and it received fleet number 3. No bus was sold as a result of its purchase but MF 5720, the Straker Squire, became a spare, increasing the fleet strength to three. It had by this time acquired the distinction of being the last of the once-numerous Straker Squires to operate as a London bus. It was finally withdrawn in March 1931, two months after the delivery of a second new Titan, HX 2643. This was very similar to its predecessor except that it seated 56, as against 52 in the earlier vehicle. Both had open staircases. The Dennis was duly relegated to spare, having recently been fitted with pneumatic tyres.

Supreme survived the formation of the LPTB by only four months. On November 1st 1933 the Board took over the three buses and the Supreme Motor Omnibus Co. Ltd. came to an end. Compensation was later fixed at £16,000.

EARL

The Earl Motor Omnibus Co. Ltd. was registered on January 14th 1926 to take over the last remaining bus owned by the ill-fated Bernard Cosgrove. The vehicle in question was MF 1297, a Straker Squire scheduled to run on the 73. The new Company's registered office was 18 Pelham Road, South Tottenham, which was the address Cosgrove then shared with the Wilson family. Cosgrove was the company's first secretary and its Managing Director was Thomas Wilson, who had put up the money to keep MF 1297 operational. After Cosgrove's death Leonard Frank Wilson, who was probably Thomas's son, became secretary and a director. The nominal share capital of the Earl Motor Omnibus Co. Ltd. was set at the unusual figure of £806 in £1 shares. The Earl bus ran firstly from Tankard & Smith's but was very soon rehoused at Barrett's garage in Claremont Street where it met up once again with MF 9160, the Dennis which was once also owned by Bernard Cosgrove. It stayed there only until July 1926 when it transferred to 57A Fore Street where the company remained until the end. The end nearly came fairly quickly, for in October 1927 Wilson almost completed negotiations with A. T. Bennett for the sale of the business to Public for about £3,500. At the eleventh hour the deal fell through and Earl remained in business.

Wilson proved that he had the business flair which Cosgrove had lacked. His first major act was to order a more reliable vehicle than the Straker Squire and his choice fell on Leyland. ML 1800 was acquired on hire purchase from Dodson's and was licensed on January 25th 1927; it was one of the last examples of its type to enter service in London. The Straker Squire was kept on as the spare bus until February 1930 when a new red & white Leyland Titan arrived, again on hire purchase from Dodson. This was MY 2806, and it replaced the earlier Leyland on all-day service, the latter being relegated to become the spare. Earl never operated more than one scheduled bus on weekdays. The final pattern of service was 73A, 173D and 573 (formerly 202) on Mondays to Fridays, 69 and 229 on Saturdays, and 69 on Sundays. The Company's tickets carried the incorrect inscription Earl Motor Bus Co. Ltd.

The LPTB took over on November 24th 1933 and the proprietors subsequently received the very satisfactory sum of £8,000 for the loss of their small one-bus-plus-a-spare business.

DAISY/CC

D. F. Edwards and Bernard Convey presented themselves at Scotland Yard on May 16th 1924 with a Hickman-bodied Daimler resplendent in its livery of red with cream window frames & brown rocker panels. Its fleetname, written in script style, was Daisy. Daisy was licensed on May 27th and probably ran in its early days on the 29, 72, 73 and 76, which were the routes for which Edwards obtained plates. The garage chosen by Edwards & Convey was Tankard & Smith's at South Tottenham.

Within a matter of months Edwards had left the business and his financial stake in it was taken over by Charles Wesley Clayton. 39-year old Clayton had been a conductor on the Daisy bus right from the start of operation, a task he shared shift and shift about with Convey who was six years his junior. The new partnership traded as Convey & Clayton using Convey's home at 113 Antill Road, South Tottenham and, later, 88 Brentwood Road, Tottenham, as its trading address. At an unknown date the firm moved from Tankard & Smith's to Barrett's Garage and, in January 1927, it left Claremont Street to go to 57A Fore Street. Convey & Clayton was the last independent operator to run from the then LGOC-controlled Claremont Street garage.

The original Daisy Daimler was dispatched back to J. M. Roberts in January 1925, indicating that its performance had been less than satisfactory. Roberts used the vehicle himself until September 1926, possibly mainly as a works runabout or towing wagon, after which it was scrapped. Convey & Clayton were without a bus for about a month after the departure of the Daimler, and they were fortunate in obtaining, late in February, a Dodson-bodied Dennis MH 3380. Though it was second-hand, its condition must have been as good as new as it had seen only a fortnight's use with its previous owner, A. S. Stanmore. It bore the same livery as the Daimler but had the fleetname CC inside a gold circle. It worked week-days on route 39 and was unusual in this respect. The 39 was not a popular route with independents and in the period 1928-33 the CC bus was the only one to break the LGOC monopoly on it. On Sundays it worked the 212C.

By November 1930 a new Dennis Lance had been placed on order. This arrived early in December registered HX 2171, and carried a 54-seat Dodson body in a red & cream livery. It entered service on the 39 in time for Christmas, but the older Dennis was retained as a spare bus, bringing the fleet total to two. November 10th 1933 was the date duly appointed for the LPTB to take over the Convey & Clayton bus. The partners were subsequently awarded £7,800 compensation for their loss of business, a figure which compared well with the £5,500 which the LPTB had put forward as their final offer in October 1933.

WA

The career of the Wilton bus has already been recorded in chapter 2. It will be recalled that it was owned jointly by Harry Francis Jolly of 89 Curtain Road, Shoreditch—the senior partner—and William Albert Wells. The vehicle was a Wilton-bodied Dennis, XT 5708, which ran from Toler's Garage from June 1924 until May 1926 when the partnership broke up. Jolly left the bus business and Wells found himself another partner, H. Allen. XT 5708 was renamed WA and moved north to Barrett's Garage which was more conveniently situated than Toler's for Wells who moved house from Kennington to 19 Elmhurst Road, Enfield Wash. Wells had latterly been the licensee in the bus's Wilton days and remained so when it became WA. It continued to work on routes 69A, 73A, 173D on Mondays to Fridays and 69A Saturdays. It probably ran over all or part of the 69 on Sundays also. The WA did not stay long at Barrett's. On July 9th 1926 it moved out, possibly to 57A Fore Street.

Maintenance on the bus appears to have been lax. It was examined by Birch's in February 1927 when a quotation was required for its overhaul and they found it to be in a very bad condition coupled to which the seats did not comply with police regulations. The partners were probably glad to receive an offer of £2,750 for the business from A. T. Bennett, who absorbed the WA bus into his Public fleet on September 2nd 1927.

Wells' career in transport did not finish there. By 1929 he was part-owner with E. L. Vine, the former proprietor of the Crest bus, of Modern Super Coaches of Edmonton, becoming a director when a limited company was formed on January 28th, 1930.

PRO BONO PUBLICO
AJM

Pro Bono Publico—for the good of the public—was the title chosen by Albert John Maffey of 31 Carpenter Gardens, Winchmore Hill. His chocolate-coloured Dennis, MF 8186, was supplied by Dodsons and licensed on June 2nd 1924. Four days later it was submitted for police inspection, and entered service later in the same month, principally on route 29. It had been suggested that Maffey's bus was garaged with the Prince vehicles at South Street, Ponders End, but this requires confirmation. In March 1925 Maffey purchased a new Leyland, MH 5067, in replacement of the Dennis. This vehicle was in a red & dark grey livery and carried the fleetname AJM inside a circle. It ran on route 529C until October 26th 1927 when it was purchased by Public for £3,000. Maffey stayed on for a while with Public but later became better known as a dealer in commercial vehicles, including many ex-London buses.

The disposal by Maffey of his original Dennis did not mean the death of the Pro Bono Publico title. In April 1925 the vehicle came into the hands of an ex-LGOC man John Frederick Brown of 61 Albion Road, Dalston who, retaining the original livery, placed it in service on route 511 which was at that time still unrestricted. Brown made an agreement with The Bell Punch Co. Ltd. for the hire of a punch on April 24th, so it was probably shortly after that date when his bus commenced operation. Brown garaged at Claremont Street until October 21st 1926 after which he moved to Whittington, Cox & Co.'s garage at 736 Lea Bridge Road, Leyton. Meanwhile, on August 17th 1925, a limited company was incorporated under the title of Pro Bono Publico Ltd. The 1,500 £1 shares were all held by members of the Brown family. J. F. Brown became Managing Director, and was accompanied on the board of directors by John Samuel Brown and Frederick James Brown.

In June 1928 Pro Bono Publico Ltd. doubled its operations by placing a new Dodson-bodied Leyland PLSC-type Lion 32-seater, VW 5135, on route 263. The operation was presumably not a financial success as the vehicle had been disposed of by May 1930. A Maudslay coach was also operated for a while in the form of VX 5149. The company's main operation remained that of the double-decker, whose daily appearance on route 511B was augmented on Sundays by the operation of a second bus on route 69B from September 1930 onwards when an additional double-decker was purchased. This was a comparatively rare specimen among independent operators, an AEC Regent. VX 7553 was a Dodson-bodied 53-seater and had an enclosed driver's cabin and open staircase. When a second modern double-decker was purchased in April 1932 the choice of chassis fell on Leyland, and EV 5860 emerged from Dodson's factory as a handsome, all-enclosed TD2-type 53-seater. Between them the Regent and the Titan maintained the company's operations until November 10th 1933, the day appointed for London Transport to take over. In November 1935 the Arbitration Tribunal awarded Pro Bono Publico Ltd. the sum of £11,000 in compensation for the loss of its business.

Tramway Avenue, Edmonton

CREST

Matthews & Vine was the trading name of the partnership which, in July 1924, placed the Crest bus into service. A. A. Matthews, the owner of the Crescent bus, was the senior partner but the licences for MF 9629, their red & white Dodson-bodied Dennis, were held by Ernest Vine. He lived at 4 Tramway Avenue, Edmonton, a cul-de-sac best known for its connections with the MET trams and, later, London Transport's trolleybuses. There was and indeed still is, a small garage-cum petrol station at the western end of Tramway Avenue, less than a stone's throw from Vine's house, and this is where the bus is thought to have been parked overnight. It ran first on the 76 but very soon switched to the 69 and 73 and was latterly on the 69 only. In the late part of 1926 Matthews was replaced in the partnership by Vine's brother-in-law, William Pruden, who lived next door to him at 2 Tramway Avenue. Vine had other business interests besides the Crest bus but Pruden worked full-time on it as a conductor. On August 5th 1927 Pruden & Vine sold out for £2,500 to Public who had been running the Crest bus from the Biss garage at Theobalds Grove since July 1st.

The partners both continued in transport. Pruden became a conductor for Public, later transferring to the LGOC, and Vine became, in April 1929, a partner with W. A. Wells (formerly owner of the WA bus) in Modern Super Coaches. A limited company was registered to run the two-coach fleet on January 28th 1930. The "Modern" coaches ran for thirty years under the control of Vine, Wells having left before or during the war. The entire capital was held in the immediate post-war years by the Vine/Pruden family, E. L. Vine and William Pruden being the largest shareholders. In the bus shortage of 1947-9 Modern coaches were hired to London Transport for peak-hour journeys mainly on route 34 (the successor to the old independent route 551). On November 2nd 1959, just before his 67th birthday, Vine relinquished the reins and Modern Super Coaches Ltd. was sold to the Holmes family, the owners of Horseshoe Coaches Ltd.

Falcon Road, Ponders End

PRINCE

Arthur Gannon was a strict but shrewd employer who built up a successful fleet of buses and coaches under the name of Prince. He subsequently achieved the honour of being the last of the central area independents to succumb to the LPTB, thanks mainly to the delaying methods which he successfully employed over the valuation of his coach service licences which the LPTB were not anxious to take over.

Gannon commenced in business as the Prince Omnibus Company in June 1923. Earlier, like so many thousands of others, he had been demobilised from the army in 1919. He found employment with the LGOC as a driver, first at Hendon (AE) and then at Tottenham (AR) garage. With three fellow drivers he planned to buy a bus and go into competition with their employer, each of the four to put £500 into the business. A new Leyland was ordered but, before delivery, the three backed out of the scheme leaving Gannon to run the bus alone. With MF 399, a Dodson-bodied Leyland resplendent in chocolate & cream, he began his highly profitable career as a bus proprietor.

The Prince joined many other independents on such favourite routes as 9, 11, 38 and 73. In addition Gannon obtained approval to operate some interesting services such as Winchmore Hill to Crystal Palace and an Edmonton Town Hall to Tottenham "frying pan" service with a loop from Tottenham High Road via Bruce Grove, Lordship Lane, Wood Green High Road and West Green Road back to Tottenham. A proposed route from Chingford to Barking was refused by the police. Expansion was slow at first and a second identical bus did not materialise until March 1924. This was MF 5214. When schedules were required to be deposited at the end of the year two were obtained on 38E and 173D. The third Prince bus was delivered too late to join its stablemates on central London operations and was put to work on the 511 in February 1925. MH 3812 was Prince's only Dennis double-decker and it lasted in the fleet only until October 1928 when it was exchanged with Westminster for a Leyland of approximately the same age as itself, XU 8984. The Prince operation on the 511 was initially of short duration and before long the schedule had been exchanged for one on the 525, but at an unknown date—certainly by mid-1927—the vehicle had reverted to the former route.

303

Straker Squire's factory in Angel Road was Prince's first garage, but in 1924 Gannon was fortunate in obtaining a 21-year lease on a site at 143 South Street, Ponders End where there was a dwelling house and a large vacant plot of land. He had a useful if somewhat ungainly corrugated-iron clad garage built on the vacant plot fronting Falcon Road; this garage was extended twice as the Prince operations grew. Though the house at 143 South Street has since been demolished, the garage still exists, looking much as it did in Gannon's days, and provides a home for the London Borough of Enfield's fleet of Karrier school buses. The lease was taken out in Gannon's name, but after the formation of a limited company the rent and rates were paid by the company.

After the purchase of Dennis MH 3812 the double-deck fleet remained at three until the advent of new Leyland Titans in 1930. This did not mean that Prince's expansion programme had come to a halt, for he joined the ranks of local operators on the promising 551 which required single-deckers. A pair of new Dennis E's was obtained in November 1926 (ML 754) and February 1927 (ML 2078). At the time it was new ML 754 was, with its 30 seats, the largest vehicle so far operated on the 551. A Leyland Lion, MP 1844, was added to the single-deck fleet in January 1928 enabling one bus to be kept as a spare. Mention must be made of the Sunday and Bank holiday workings of Prince which were, throughout the Company's career, almost exclusively on the 69 and its allied route 229.

Coaching began in a small way in 1926 with the purchase of a Lancia, but the climate was right for the expansion of this side of the business and by 1931 the number of coaches owned exceeded the number of buses. The original Lancia was joined by three others and in 1929 replacements came in the shape of four new Bamber-bodied Maudslay MLs. A substantial range of regular coastal services was featured in the firm's coaching itinerary, the destinations including Bournemouth, Southampton, Hastings, Folkestone and Portsmouth from Enfield, Edmonton and Tottenham. There were excursions to Bognor Regis, Clacton and Southend and the usual race course trips to Kempton and Hurst Parks and Epsom. On Sundays a special service ran from the Broadway, Edmonton, to Harefield Sanatorium. Business was sufficiently brisk to justify Prince having its own booking office at the Broadway, Edmonton. Starting on January 1st 1930 an irregular semi-express service was commenced between London, Chigwell and Ongar using a single-decker with the destination painted in whitewash on the windscreen. The service operated for some while but was withdrawn at an unknown date after failing to secure a road service licence.

The growth of the business warranted the formation of a limited company on March 3rd 1927. This was entitled the Prince Omnibus Co. Ltd.; its nominal capital was £3,000 and registered office 143 South Street. The sole directors and shareholders were Arthur Gannon and his wife Hilda. The Company entered into considerable capital expenditure in 1930 when no fewer than five new vehicles were bought. Following upon the introduction of the four new coaches in the previous year, this showed the financial success which Gannon was enjoying. Two of the

304

new arrivals were Leyland Tiger coaches with Duple bodywork; the others were a trio of new Leyland Titans, which were the company's first top-covered double-deckers. These bore Dodson open-staircase bodies and were registered MY 2663/2917/4043. The year 1931 saw the purchase of another pair of Leyland Tiger/Duple coaches, which brought the coach fleet to its maximum of eight vehicles.

Just before Christmas 1931 a new single-decker bus was delivered from Duple's factory and entered service as the most modern vehicle on the 551. Somewhat unusually MV 1019 employed a double-deck Leyland Titan chassis of the TD1 variety. Upon its arrival the newer of the two Dennis E's, ML 2078, was delicensed and put into store. Prince's fourth Leyland Titan double-decker, an all-enclosed Dodson-bodied TD2, MV 1376, was put into service in January 1932 and was the last vehicle purchased by the Company. The writing was now on the wall as far as London independents were concerned and further expenditure on new vehicles was probably not considered worthwhile. In any case the fleet was almost entirely composed of modern-style vehicles, the oldest serviceable bus being ML 754, the Dennis E of 1926.

Wednesday December 5th 1934 marked the end of operation by the Prince Omnibus Co. Ltd. for it was the designated "Appointed Day" upon which London Transport was to take over. The event was a sad one and meant more than just the reluctant demise of yet another bus operator, for Prince was the last to go. Independent bus operation in central London had come to an end; an era was closed. The 4th was the last full day of operation under Gannon's command, and in the early hours of the 5th he and his wife were at the garage to welcome the last vehicle home. A contemporary newspaper report described the event. "London's last private omnibus made its last journey last night. It set out from Victoria and early this morning garaged at Ponders End—one of the chocolate coloured vehicles of the Prince Omnibus Company. Today it will emerge with a red coat of paint and the words "London Transport." Said Driver Pettit this morning:- "I got out at Ponders End with a lump in my throat." Said Conductor Hampton:- "We shall miss the thrills we have had. Our last passenger gave me his ticket as a memento."

The LPTB took over eight buses, including the unlicensed and partly dismantled Dennis E-type ML 2078; eight coaches of which only HX 4158 was licensed, it being the off-season; a 1925 Daimler car RW 1566 and a Ford van HX 7298. The goodwill of the coastal service licences was immediately re-sold, mainly to George Ewer & Co. Ltd., as London Transport had no powers to operate them. The Board did not acquire the South Street premises which, though leased by Gannon to the Company in November 1933 after the LPTB had objected to taking them over, were held by the Arbitration Tribunal to be not transferable under the Act, the Company's position being merely that of a tenant paying an annual rent to Gannon. Gannon received £49,250 for the business and the Prince Omnibus Co. Ltd. was finally dissolved on May 31st 1949.

His buses and coaches gone, Arthur Gannon started a new career by purchasing the heavy haulage firm of Risdon, Semper & Co. Ltd. whose main activity was a London-Liverpool service using a fleet of Armstrong

Saurers. It was partly moribund when he took control but by the time he sold it in 1941 he had built it up to an efficient and profitable fleet of about 45 units. Thereafter Arthur Gannon had a succession of business interests ending with a large garage and petrol station at Peacehaven, Sussex, from which he retired in 1961 at the age of seventy.

Walters' Yard, Hertford Road, Ponders End

Walters Motors Ltd. run a garage business in the Hertford Road, near Southbury Road at Ponders End. For a short while in the early part of 1924 the site, which was then an open yard owned by the Walters family, was used as overnight accommodation for the buses owned by the Cosgroves and C. W. Pallant. Crescent possibly also garaged there for a month or two in mid-1924.

68 Green Street, Ponders End

REDBURN'S MOTOR SERVICES LTD:

The Redburn family had been established in the haulage business at Ponders End for over fifty years before they bought their first motor buses. Thomas Redburn, the founder of the business, had arrived in the Enfield area from his native Abingdon, Berkshire, in 1870. He had passed away by the time of our survey but not before he had himself made a brief excursion into the field of buswork. Back in 1880/1 he had run a pair-horse bus—a double-decker—between the railway station at Ponders End and "The Bell", Enfield Highway charging what would then have been the very high fare of sixpence for the full journey. At the start of the period in which we are interested T. Redburn & Son was in the capable hands of his elder son Leonard Thomas Redburn whose activities included, in addition to general haulage work, the hire of charabancs, petrol distribution and the reconditioning and sale of surplus War Department lorries. When the first buses were ordered, Redburn shopped locally, obtaining four 44-seaters from Straker Squire.

The Redburn concern was financially bigger and stronger than most of the others who entered the London bus business. There was no intention to merely dabble in buswork; Len Redburn intended to run buses in a big way. In early 1923 there were very few bus services of any sort in the Ponders End area of Enfield, the obviously lucrative passenger traffic of the main Hertford Road being served exclusively by the trams of the Metropolitan Electric Tramways, an LGOC-associated company whose inadequate and uncomfortable tram service was the subject of much adverse comment. Redburn intended to compete with the trams and was confident that he would win trade away from them. He intended to run a service from Enfield via Ponders End, Edmonton and Tottenham to Finsbury Park, entirely along tram roads, and made application to the police accordingly. The LGOC got wind of this scheme and hurriedly introduced a new route numbered 58 between Tottenham and Victoria via Finsbury Park and Oxford Circus to scare Redburn's off. This started on May 2nd 1923 and covered what the LGOC considered to be the most remunerative part of the Redburn route. Redburn's counter-intelligence must have been at least as good as the LGOC's, for they hurriedly changed their plans and at the last moment began working on the direct route from Waltham Cross to Elephant & Castle. Thus the highly popular 69 route came into being, almost by accident. Redburn's must have been delighted to note that General's route 58 did not do well, and was withdrawn on December 4th 1923, though they would have been less pleased that General began to run on the 69 in competition with them between Edmonton (The Angel) and London Bridge from June 27th 1923.

Redburn's next big step after ordering the first buses was to form a limited company to run them. Redburn's Motor Services Ltd. was incorporated on May 3rd 1923, the very day on which the first Redburn bus was licensed. The registered office of the company was at Drivers Hall, 68 Green Street, Ponders End, where the Redburn family had a large garage and work shop. The company's nominal capital was £6,000 and there were several shareholders the principal ones being, in descending order of shares held, L. T. Redburn; Benjamin Cross, an Enfield builder; Alfred Goodwin, a Ponders End farmer and merchant; Len Redburn's brother Archie and his sister Constance. Len Redburn was later appointed Chairman and Managing Director for life.

On May 8th 1923 ME 9102 was passed by the police and Redburn's were ready to go into the bus business. More Straker Squires were ordered and deliveries continued steadily throughout the year at an average of just under two a month. By the end of August there were eight in service and at the end of December the total had grown to fourteen, one of which had been bought second-hand in that month from Bernard Cosgrove. This was the only second-hand bus ever purchased by Redburn's as an independent concern. More Strakers came during the first half of 1924, and the last of a long line of twenty-two such vehicles was placed into service in June. The chocolate & white livery which was used initially was replaced on new vehicles delivered from mid-December 1923 onwards by the more usual red & white. The style of fleetname varied too, and continued to do so as time went by.

Redburn remained faithful to the 69 and later extended it northwards to Wormley and, on certain Sundays in 1925 northwards still further to Hertford as route 275. Southwards it was extended to reach Camberwell. With twenty-two vehicles on the books they were able to maintain a quite attractive frequency, and other operators' vehicles augmented the Redburns and contributed towards the success of the 69. But Redburn had not finished expanding although by mid-1924 the troubles usually associated with Straker Squires had caused him to look elsewhere for new rolling stock. An order was duly placed for Dennis and Strachan & Brown to supply five vehicles which were delivered between August and December 1924 and were the last new buses received for the 69.

As well as the 69, which might be regarded as Redburn's trunk route, there were two local services in Ponders End which the company obtained approval to operate in about August 1923. The 515 (as it later became known) was a mainly factory service from Green Street, Enfield Highway to Brimsdown and the 516 was a short operation linking Ponders End via Nags Head Road with the railway station, a revival of part of the old horsebus service.

Owing to Restricted Streets Orders, development after December 1924 had to be on more lightly trafficked routes and when, in the Spring of 1925, a further order was placed for new buses, the choice was six 26-seater pneumatic-tyred single-deckers based on the Dennis 2½ ton chassis with Strachan & Brown bodies. These were licensed in June and July and enabled the company to contribute towards routes 280, later 538 (jointly with Admiral) and 551 (shared with Uneedus, Merry, Prince, BB and SB). Contemporary police records also show Redburn as operating a service from late June 1925 numbered 278 between Forty Hill and Edmonton (Blue Anchor), extended on July 28th 1925 to Sparklets Works. Little is known of the 278 which probably did not last for long.

With thirty-three buses the Redburn fleet was the fifth largest independent one in London. It appeared to be prospering and all looked well for the future. So it came as a surprise when the LGOC announced, on Monday October 18th 1926, that it had concluded negotiations for the purchase of Redburn's Motor Services Ltd. from that day and that these negotiations had been going on for some time. 161 staff passed to the LGOC including Chief Inspector Bradley, three inspectors, four timekeepers, four clerks, 73 drivers and 76 conductors. Over forty of them were soon afterwards discharged despite strenuous efforts by the local Member of Parliament to save their jobs. General arranged with Redburn to lease part of the Green Street premises and allocated to it their code letters RS. The Redburn family retained its lorries and associated activities.

The LGOC erected a temporary building on the Green Street site to accommodate its Redburn buses. Needless to say the fleet did not stay unchanged for long under LGOC control. A certain amount of body exchanging took place at first on the Straker Squires but only MF 4401/6405 ran in service with replacement (ex Cambrian) bodies. General had apparently had a change of plan and, instead of keeping the Strakers operational, decided to replace them as soon as possible and to use the Redburn fleet as a repository for some of the many Dennises which it had acquired. So, from November 1926 through to March 1927, Dennises from other concerns ousted the Straker Squires. These were all newly-overhauled vehicles which emerged from Chiswick Works with second-hand bodies, the LGOC having set-up a float of four spare bodies to speed up the overhaul procedure. Had they not done so the renovated chassis would have had to stand around waiting for their own bodies to be made ready, body overhauling being a much more lengthy process than chassis overhauling. Full details of all the body exchanges involving Strakers and Dennises are given in appendix 5. The first ten Dennises to arrive bore the Redburn's fleetname, but subsequent arrivals were in General livery except for the writing on the legal ownership panels. All the original Redburn Dennises stayed in the fleet until it was finally absorbed into the LGOC on January 1st 1928.

The last, somewhat tenuous, connection between the Redburn family and the bus business was broken on May 23rd 1928 when General ceased to run from Green Street. On that date the new garage at Ponders End (E) was opened by General for its subsidiary, the London Public Omnibus Co. Ltd., and this became the main "combine" garage for the area. The LGOC vehicles at Green Street were transferred into Tottenham (AR) garage on the same day.

579 Hertford Road, Enfield Highway

GWL

Lewington's Cycles Ltd. at 579 Hertford Road, Enfield Highway is a thriving retail business devoted nowadays mostly to the sale of sports goods and toys. Few, if any, of its present day customers would ever dream that nearly half a century ago the Lewingtons also ran a Thornycroft bus from the same premises. In those days the shop occupied a frontage of only 15ft. and there was ample room at the side and back for the bus to stand overnight.

The Lewington family business was started by George Lewington who had come to Middlesex from Basingstoke. He originally had a bakery business near Turkey Street but cycles and motor cycles had long been his hobby and inevitably the bakery was given up in favour of a cycle shop. The idea of buying a bus originated with the eldest of the three Lewington sons, Wilfred John Lewington, who was working for Redburn's as a mechanic. He saw that, despite their troubles with the Straker Squires, Redburn's were making money and envisaged an opening in the business for himself and the next eldest brother, Edgar Leslie, who was three years his junior. Lewington senior agreed the idea was a good one and on January 28th 1925 he formed the Comfort Omnibus Co. Ltd. with registered office at 147 Hertford Road, Enfield Wash. It had a share capital of £100 of which only £12 was ever issued as shares; George Lewington held ten and his two elder sons one each. A bus was ordered from Thornycroft, a somewhat unusual choice in which George Lewington is believed to have been influenced by an allegiance to his home town's products, plus a particularly good sales representative who promised quick delivery. It was built in March 1925 and licensed on the 24th as MH 4646. Despite the Company's official title the bus never bore the fleetname Comfort. Instead it carried the letters GWL in block capitals standing for George, Wilfred and Leslie.

The red & white GWL was a latecomer to buswork and its operations were thus limited to outer London. The Lewingtons chose the 525 upon which their bus soon became well-known as the only Thornycroft for miles around. On Sundays it penetrated the central area on the 69. Both Wilfred and Edgar Leslie Lewington worked regularly on the bus and both held composite licences. Their bus-owning career was short-lived and on June 16th 1927 the vehicle came under the control of Public from the Biss garage at Theobalds Grove preparatory to the sale of the business to them on July 8th for £2,300. The Comfort Omnibus Co. Ltd. was wound up on February 18th 1928.

The two Lewington brothers both went with their bus to Public but Wilfred stayed for only about a year. Leslie stayed to be taken over by the LGOC but left in about 1930. Afterwards they ran a fleet of six tipping lorries—Peerless, Packard, Dennis and Leyland—serving local gravel pits. Their partnership broke up after about five years but both continued in the sand and gravel business though after the war Wilfred

309

changed to engine overhauling. Both now live in retirement. The family cycle business is now run by their youngest brother who succeeded to it on the death of George Lewington in 1948.

Theobalds Garage, High Street, Waltham Cross
(also 37 High Bridge Street, Waltham Abbey)

BB

Waltham Cross was the northernmost extremity of the London electric tramway system. In the High Street, beyond the tramway terminus and by the railway station now known as Theobalds Grove, was the Theobalds Garage. In 1975 a firm of contractors occupied the site. Except for a brief spell when a small garage by Waltham Cross station was used, this yard was the headquarters for the buses run by the enterprising Biss family who owned The Old English Gentleman public house at Waltham Abbey and who had various other interests between them. They purchased the Theobalds Garage, which was freehold, on January 22nd 1924. The money for the family's venture into the field of bus operation was subscribed by James Stanley Biss, who had worked in a local powder mill and in the insurance business before this and who was a competent motor mechanic, Robert Warland Biss, the proprietor of a builder's business, and Percy Robert Biss who managed the family's pub. The first of these three, generally known as Stan and a keen greyhound trainer, ran the buses. He lived at the Queen's Head, Waltham Abbey, which was the company's first trading address.

Coaching had been a side-line with the Biss family for a year or two before bus operations began with a pair of chocolaty-maroon & cream Straker Squires PU 1124/5. They were licensed on November 30th 1923 ready to begin work early in the following month. The 69 was the only prosperous route in the area and the buses were naturally operated mainly on this. They could be distinguished by their gold BB in a white oval which on later buses was enhanced by the addition of four "ears". Besides the 69, Biss Bros. also applied to run Sundays on such trunk services as 29, 38 and 73 and their applications for Sunday services included in October 1924 one from Elephant & Castle to Hertford. This involved applying to the Hoddesdon, Ware and Hertford authorities for licences for eight buses and fourteen drivers and conductors. Biss were soon in trouble with these authorities for not adhering to the timetable which they had submitted. The trouble was that they were being harassed by National who allocated four "chasers" which lay in wait for the Biss buses at Ware on their journeys from Hertford and at Waltham Cross on the northbound run. In 1925 this service ran under the route number 275 and Redburn's also took part in it. It is believed to have been withdrawn late in that year because, so it is rumoured, of a disagreement with Ware Council.

The Biss family's association with the products of Straker Squire was short-lived, and the next six double-deckers were Strachan & Brown-bodied Dennises (PU 1998, 2667, 3225; NK 8082, 8605/6). These were all delivered in 1924 and were painted dark red & white into which

310

livery the two Strakers were repainted in about June 1924. With the delivery of NK 9295 in January 1925 Biss Brothers now contributed nine buses to the lengthy route 69.

In addition to his own buses, which prospered, Stan Biss provided maintenance facilities for other local independents such as Crest, Crescent and HH. When the Waltham buses started up in business in March 1926 they were garaged with the Biss fleet at Theobalds Grove. For a short period, the dates of which are unknown, the Biss vehicles were garaged temporarily in the Straker Squire works at Edmonton following a fire at the Biss Garage.

A limited company was formed under the title of Biss Brothers Ltd. on November 10th 1924 with registered office at Theobalds Garage. The 3,000 £1 preference and 10,000 10/- ordinary shares were all held by members of the Biss family. Under the auspices of the limited company a pair of small, pneumatic-tyred single-deckers was purchased in August 1925, further expansion with larger vehicles on the 69 no longer being allowed. RO 1471 and RO 1596 appeared as 26-seaters on route 551 and perpetuated the combination of Dennis and Strachan & Brown. A larger single-decker, RO 5230, was a Strachan & Brown-bodied Dennis E delivered in December 1926 and two more similar vehicles were ordered in April or May 1927. These would have been fleet numbers 13 & 14, but only the first of them was built. RO 7186 was placed on service in June 1927 by which time negotiations had been almost completed for the sale of the business to Public on whose behalf A. T. Bennett took over control of the Biss buses as from May 31st, the Public company itself not having been officially incorporated as yet. The Biss vehicles were in fact the first to come under the control of the embryo new company with the exception, of course, of the Admirals themselves. RO 7186 was too close to completion for its delivery to be stopped and it arrived in full BB livery; the order for its sister vehicle was cancelled. Both this vehicle and RO 5230 were unusual for London buses in having sliding roofs. Biss's received £39,600 for their bus fleet and a further £3,000 for the freehold of the Theobalds Garage, which became a Public depot. The official date of the transfer of ownership was August 3rd 1927 and the firm of Biss Brothers Ltd. was formally wound up on September 30th 1929.

Public took over twelve scheduled buses on the 69, 212C and 551. Along with these they acquired a large stock of spares and two vans, a Ford and a Morris. Initially the Biss's took shares in Public but these were later sold to the LGOC. The family took up poultry farming in the Waltham Cross area and continued in the building trade. They did not return to the psv industry until March 1950 when Monk's nine vehicle business at Bishops Stortford was purchased. Today the next generation of Biss Brothers, R.D. and S. G. Biss, run a thriving bus and coach business at Bishops Stortford and are also active in Harlow and Waltham Cross. On October 20th 1952 they attempted to enter their old territory of the 'twenties with a stage service to Waltham Abbey from the Black Swan at Roydon using a Bedford OB 29-seater. Unfortunately this enterprising service did not prosper and nowadays Biss's nearest stage services to London are at Bishops Stortford.

WALTHAM
WAYMAN/CW

Waltham Motor Services Ltd. was a company incorporated on January 28th 1926 on the inspiration of a motor mechanic and former Air Force man, Basil Ringrose. With a capital of £1,000 and with registered office at Ringrose's home, 24 Oakhurst Road, Freezywater, the company was formed to run local bus services radiating from Waltham Cross. Two routes were operated. The 306F (Waltham Cross to Epping Forest, Wake Arms) ran in opposition to National whose service running eastward from Waltham Cross was a successor to one formerly operated by Charles Wayman. The other service, 352, was operated solely by Waltham although National unsuccessfully sought permission for it in February 1927 but were refused because their 24-seaters were too heavy for the bridge over the New River in Church Lane. The full length of 352 was from the Green Man at Waltham Abbey to the now-demolished White Horse Inn in the small village of Flamstead End; shorts from Waltham Cross to Flamstead End were designated 352A.

Operations began with two, maybe three, buses. Small buff Fiats NK 5070/5752, formerly the property of C. W. Dunford's Barnet Motor Services, were definitely acquired and it is very probable—but not confirmed—that a third similar bus, NK 8696, also passed from Barnet to Waltham. Curiously one of the routes on which these unusual little buses ran in Barnet days was also 352, the number having been re-allocated by the Metropolitan Police to the Flamstead End service after it ceased to be used in the Barnet area. The Fiats were bought by Waltham on or before March 8th 1926 and one of them later became the subject of a County Court action by Dunford against Waltham for non-payment of £47 10s. 0d. being part of the purchase price. Waltham's counter claim that bad material and workmanship used by Dunford had kept the vehicle off the road for a total of forty-seven days was accepted and the final judgement resulted in Waltham paying only £26 10s. 0d. of the amount claimed.

Waltham Motor Services Ltd. had a variety of shareholders, few of whom held more than a £50 stake in the firm. The largest shareholders were James Kirby, a warehouseman, and his son, a stoker, who between them held £450 of the capital. Ringrose himself never held more than fifty of the £1 shares. Only £802 was taken up out of the authorised share capital of £1,000. The company's directors throughout its two year career were Basil Ringrose, George Albert Shelitoe, a retired police officer, and Herbert Thomas Finch, an accounts clerk.

It may be of interest at this stage to recall the earliest independent operation on the Waltham Cross-Epping Forest road under the auspices of Charles Wayman. Wayman had been a motor engineer at Waltham Abbey since pre-war days, working from his premises at 37 High Bridge Street upon which he took out a lease on November 27th 1913. In 1920 he began bus operation using a single-decker B-type formerly used by the LGOC. Still in General colours but with the word Wayman on the side in large block capitals, B 2697 began to run a shuttle service between Waltham Cross and Waltham Abbey. It is thought that several buses passed through Wayman's hands during the course of his career, though few details have so far come to light. The identity of a second B-type single-decker has yet to be discovered, but two double-deckers are known definitely to have been operated. A double deck B-type, B 1300, was in his possession in November 1920 and a Straker Squire, NH 1805, worked for him from March 1924 to July 1926.

By mid-1923 Wayman's service had been extended at each end to run between Enfield Town and Epping Forest (Volunteer). By June 13th 1923 Wayman had branched even further afield and obtained permission from Hertford Council to run three buses within the Borough, presumably on a service from the Waltham Cross area, and he kept these licences up until well into 1924 and possibly later. One single-decker had, by July 1924, been repainted red with cream windows and bore the letters CW inside a white circle. Very plain tickets were issued which bore only the value and serial number. In January 1924 National began its service N13 between Watford Junction and Waltham Cross, and in August 1924 they started route N30 (Waltham Cross to Waltham Abbey). These routes, which were renumbered 306A and 306B respectively in December 1924, covered much of Wayman's Enfield—Epping Forest operation. Wayman withdrew on July 1st 1926 and in September of the same year National took out a lease on his former garage in High Bridge Street as the base for its Waltham Cross area services.

We now revert to the story of Waltham who, as 1926 drew to a close, negotiated to buy two larger vehicles. Both were bought on hire purchase, but one was new and the other second-hand. The second-hand vehicle was 20-seater Dennis NK 8877 which had originated in 1925 with Barnet Motor Services and had spent a year with Admiral before passing to Waltham in January 1927. It kept its blue & white Admiral livery to which was applied the Waltham fleetname. Its arrival was preceded by the delivery in December 1926 of Waltham's first and only brand new vehicle, RO 5240. This was a London-type single-deck Dennis 24-seater with the usual type of Dodson body fitted to these vehicles. It was chocolate & white in colour, and it provided useful additional seating capacity on the 306B though it was probably not as speedy as NK 8877 which was regarded as a little flyer. The Dennises worked together on the 306B and the Fiats continued to maintain the 352.

Waltham is thought to have always garaged its buses at Biss's. In fact the firm was operated, at least latterly, as though it were a Biss subsidiary, the crews for the Waltham buses being included in the Biss duty rosters. When Biss sold out to Public in 1927 the proprietors of Waltham had little alternative but to do likewise. On the same day that Public officially took over Biss Bros. Ltd., August 3rd 1927, it also absorbed Waltham whose vehicles had been running under Bennett's control since June 9th. The Waltham fleet had diminished in its later days to only two vehicles—the Dennises—for which Public paid £3,000 plus a further £80 15s. 0d. for spare parts. The operation on the 352 had been abandoned some months earlier and the little Fiats disposed of. Waltham Motor Services Ltd. was wound up on September 22nd 1930. Meanwhile Basil Ringrose, the man who had been its inspiration, had joined the Rhodesian Air Force and later settled in East Africa, to return to Britain and a new career in shopkeeping after the death of his wife in tragic circumstances some years later.

313

York House Garage, Windmill Lane, Cheshunt

HH

Harry Heast and his wife Louise lived in the village of Cheshunt when it was still untouched by the large-scale housing development of latter years. Heast owned the York House Garage in Windmill Lane. In 1975 the garage building and Heast's old petrol pumps were there and in the hands of a firm of fuel oil distributors. In October 1924 Heast bought himself a bus; a red Dodson-bodied Leyland with the fleetname "HH" and registered NK 8710. It joined the numerous others serving route 69 and may also have worked the 29 on occasion as Heast applied to the police to run on this also. Although Heast was himself a garage proprietor he appears to have contracted with Biss Bros. to carry out all overhauls and major repairs on the bus, probably because this was a heavier type of work than his own garage facilities were capable of.

A limited company was incorporated on April 4th 1927 with a share capital of £1,000 under the title of H.H. Omnibus Co. Ltd. The registered office was at York House Garage and the directors were Mr. & Mrs. Heast. As we have seen in chapter 4, Harry Heast had by this time secured an interest in the South London Coaches business run by E. E. Burmingham and there are indications that Burmingham may have had a reciprocal interest in the H.H. business.

The H.H. Omnibus Co. Ltd. sold its bus to Public on December 12th 1927, the same date on which the latter also bought South London Coaches' only London bus. Public paid the handsome sum of £4,400 for the Heast bus business and spare parts, a payment well in excess of what they normally made for one-bus businesses. They also purchased Heast's property in Cheshunt for £1,600 though there is no evidence that they ever used it. Heast thereafter concentrated his attentions on South London Coaches. These, as we have seen, hit hard times a few years later, leaving him bankrupt.

CHAPTER EIGHT

EAST LONDON

Empress Garage, Canal Sidings, Cambridge Heath
Havelock Garage, 113 Albion Road, Dalston

EMPRESS

The main East London garage in terms of the number of operators using it was the Empress Garage at Canal Sidings, Cambridge Heath. In the middle nineteen-twenties it housed the buses of at least nine operators including Empress Motors Ltd. themselves and it has achieved the unique status of being the only garage owned by an independent operator of the 'twenties still housing the same company's vehicles to this day. Forty to fifty years ago the Empress Garage was a mixture of purpose-built garages and railway arches but the arches have long since ceased to be used by Empress. Empress Motors Ltd. survived the removal by the LPTB of its four London buses on February 1st 1934 by concentrating on its coaching activities. Its present modern fleet of Bedfords and Fords is still owned and controlled by the descendants of Edward Thomas Stanton, a one-time driver for Vanguard and LGOC, who started it all when he bought his first bus in March 1923.

XN 3270 came from the Straker Squire factory in a brown & white livery and began work on April 11th 1923 on route 42. At the time Stanton lived at 128 Albion Road, Dalston and used this as his business address. He did not acquire the garage at Canal Sidings until about December 1923 prior to which he garaged at Wells' Garage in Cambridge Road, Hackney. When XN 3270 was given its first overhaul in about March 1924 its colour was changed to red & white and a new vehicle, XT 2588, was delivered like this in May 1924. This was the second and last Straker Squire bought by Stanton who went to Dennis for his third bus, YP 9564, which was licensed on September 1st 1926. The solid tyre and open top era was completed on March 1st 1927 with the arrival of a second Dennis, YE 8274, which ousted the original Straker Squire and also took its body.

The most significant event in Stanton's career was the purchase in April 1928 of a trio of new Dennis coaches in a livery of maroon & black which would contrast strongly with today's all-over cream. The coach fleet quickly overtook the buses numerically and occupied the spaces at Canal Sidings formerly rented to other independent bus proprietors, most of whom had moved away or sold out by then. In February 1934 the coach fleet stood at seven units (four Dennises and three Morris Commercials). The London Traffic Act inhibited the growth of the bus fleet. When YP 9564 arrived in the Autumn of 1926 it had to go on the outer suburban 26D/E as it was not allowed to join its two stablemates on the 6A and 42A except on Sundays. The fifth new bus, YX 7335, came solely as a spare, and an endeavour to find it regular weekday work on the south London route 50 in 1931 proved unprofitable and caused it to revert to being a spare. The vehicle in question dated from August 1928 and was a Leyland Lion; Empress's only single-deck bus.

315

As the 'twenties drew to a close the time came to replace the remaining Straker Squire with something more modern. It was one of the last of its type to remain in London service and was succeeded in May 1929 by a heavy-looking Dennis H, UU 1056. The two Dennis open-toppers came to the end of the road in mid-1932 when GX 2692/3 arrived on the scene. This handsome pair were the latest TD2 type of Leyland Titan and maintained Empress's trunk workings until the end came less than two years later.

The present limited company was incorporated on January 13th 1926 with a share capital of £2,500. The Empress Garage at Canal Sidings was its registered office and the sole directors and shareholders at the time were E. T. Stanton and his wife Agnes. The company took over the freehold garage and also the two buses then owned, and in January 1928 it took out a twenty-one year lease from Louis Solomons of the garage and workshop at the rear of the Havelock public house at 113 Albion Road, Dalston. Solomons had previously been connected with Havelock Motors Ltd. who had sold out to Public in August 1927. Empress used the Havelock garage as its workshop until the building was destroyed by bombing during the war.

The Empress buses ran in for the last time on the night of January 31st 1934. London Transport took over all four the next day and also took MM 9288, a Morris van used in connection with the bus business. In April 1936 the Arbitration Tribunal awarded Empress Motors Ltd. £24,000 for its bus business plus a further £500 severance payment. E. T. Stanton ceased active interest in the business some years later but remained the major shareholder until his death on November 12th 1953.

HAVELOCK

Shortly after the end of the 1914-18 war Charles Daiber and Frederick Ernest Mallindine entered into the sphere of coaching when they bought XB 8451, an AEC B-type charabanc based on a chassis of pre-war origin. Full details of their coaching activities are not known but they are recorded as having at least two AEC 28 seaters (XH 9682/XK 7608) by 1922 in addition to XB 8451. They had an arrangement with Louis Solomons, the licensee of the Havelock public house at 113 Albion Road (nowadays called Albion Drive), Dalston, whereby they garaged their vehicles at the back of his premises where they also had a workshop and jobmasters business entitled the Havelock Motor Works. The pub still stands presenting much the same appearance to the world as it did half a century ago but the motor works at the rear can now only be seen in imagination beneath the grassed surround to a block of flats.

December 1923 saw the appearance on London streets of the first Havelock bus. XP 7888 was a crimson lake & white Dodson-bodied Dennis which was soon repainted red. Almost a year later, in November 1924, it was joined by XW 3304, an identical vehicle. Daiber & Mallindine obtained schedules for these at the end of 1924 on the 6A and 42A though a variety of other services (e.g. 6, 7, 8, 9, 11, 22, 30, 38, 69, 76) had been tried earlier. The buses were housed from the start at Canal Sidings though repairs were carried out at the Havelock Garage.

Expansion was in the air, and on January 6th 1925 Havelock Motors Ltd. of 113 Albion Road came into being. The 4,000 £1 shares were all taken up, the majority by Louis Solomons who was to provide the capital for expansion. The new company took over from Havelock Motors as from January 1st 1925 and inherited the lease on the workshop and stables at the rear of the public house which had originally been made between Solomons and Whitbread & Co. Ltd. and dated for 21 years from June 24th 1921. Eighteen months elapsed and then, in June 1926, three new buses took the road and were joined six months later by two more. YO 8392-4 and YR 8400/8601 were all Dennis 2½-tonners with 25-seat Dodson bodies and, with their arrival, the livery changed to chocolate & white. All five were put to work on the 263 and additionally on the 555 Sundays.

On August 4th 1927 the entire business including the charabancs, a van and a car, was sold to Public who paid £17,500. The fate of the charabancs is unknown but the buses had been operated on Public's behalf since June 30th. The leasehold premises passed to Public who subsequently transferred the lease back to Solomons who, in turn, sold it to Empress Motors Ltd. Afterwards Mallindine stayed in the motor trade as an engineer but Daiber forsook it to become Solomons' manager in the Havelock. Havelock Motors Ltd. was dissolved on June 29th 1943.

WELLINGTON

Except for Empress and Havelock, the other operators at Canal Sidings were all on route 511 though in most cases they had tried out a variety of other workings first. The full list of 511 operators at Canal Sidings is: Eastern, Empire, Lea Valley, Wellington, The Jockey, Nelson, The Reliance. The Jockey and Nelson later moved to Baltic Yard, Walthamstow and are dealt with under that heading. The Reliance is better known for having run from its own garage at Chingford later in its career and a full description is given further on in this chapter. Of the others the first to garage with Stanton was Frederick Ernest Reeves who owned the two Wellington buses.

Reeves was licensee of a public house at 36 Arcola Street, Dalston before the urge to become a busman caused him to order a new Leyland from Dodson. His pub was called the Duke of Wellington and in choosing his fleet name he retained a link between his old life and the new. He was helped by his wife and two sons and the latter worked on XR 2730 when it entered service in February 1924. Reeves moved home to 71 Shacklewell Lane which became his business address but he garaged throughout his career at Canal Sidings. In March 1925 his second bus, another Dodson-bodied Leyland, entered service as XX 5413. The original bus ran during its first ten months or so on the 8, 11, 38 and 42 but from 1925 onwards Reeves concentrated solely on the 511.

After less than three years as a bus proprietor Reeves decided to return to being a licensed victualler and arranged for the sale of his buses to General. The Wellington Omnibus Co. Ltd. was formed on November 6th 1926 with its office at Lennox House, Norfolk Street. On November 18th the sale of the shares to General was completed and on the evening of the 19th the two buses ran for the first time into their new owner's

317

Leyton (T) garage. In October 1927 they were replaced by K 471/499 and on January 1st 1928 the Wellington business was absorbed into the Tramways (MET) Omnibus Co. Ltd.

EASTERN

Samuel Attwell Boon spent an uneventful career as the proprietor of the two Eastern buses. He was helped in the business by his brother, a former taxi driver who did not—as far as we can tell—have any share in the ownership of the vehicles. Both were older than the usual run of independent busmen, fiftyish, and were au fait with all the tricks of the trade. S. A. Boon's trading address was firstly 21 Mayola Road, Clapton and later 263 Vicarage Road, Leyton. His short bus career saw him at three different garages starting with Emerson's in Bodney Road, Hackney. By June 1924 he was at Canal Sidings and January 1926 saw him in Jerome's Garage, Hackney. The two Eastern buses were XP 4850, a Leyland of November 1923, and XT 9535 a Dennis built in June 1924. Both carried red & white Dodson bodies. Though he ran firstly on central London routes such as 7, 8, 11, 29 and 42, Boon concentrated solely on the 511 from January 1925 onwards. On August 30th 1927 he sold to Public for £6,085.

EMPIRE

The Empire bus originated in August 1924 when Frederick John Charles Kirk of 109 Mildenhall Road, Clapton went into business with Edward Harman. Both were ex-LGOC men from Dalston (D) garage where Harman had achieved the honour of becoming the company's rowing champion. Their red & white Dennis, XU 5639, was to be seen in its early days on routes such as 8, 29, 33 and 38 though from early 1925 it worked daily on the 511A/B. Theirs was an unhappy partnership from the start. "Ginger" Kirk's temper was as fiery as his hair but Harman, a six-footer, was equally hot-headed when roused. Inevitably they parted company after a few months and Harman left to start up the Lea Valley bus. Kirk remained sole owner of the Empire business from then onwards. In September 1930 the Dennis was replaced by a new AEC Regent VX 7487, a 54-seater with enclosed cab and open stairs. Like its predecessor it was obtained on hire purchase from Dodson. Kirk always garaged at Canal Sidings and his stay there terminated on November 1st 1933 when his bus was taken over by the LPTB for a sum later awarded at £8,500. He subsequently retired to Jersey where, so rumour has it, he later became a thorn in the side of the German forces during their unhappy occupation of the island.

LEA VALLEY

Lea Valley was one of the few 511 operators whose career was spent exclusively on this route and who did not sample the delights of inner London operation previously. As we have already seen, Edward Harman parted company with F. J. C. Kirk after only a few months of running the Empire bus together. He joined forces with Alfred Burton in February 1925 to run as Lea Valley. Empress Motors' garage was the home of XX 1259, a Dodson-bodied Dennis, for its independent career which lasted only twenty months. On January 23rd 1926 the partners formed the Lea Valley Omnibus Co. Ltd. with a share capital of £1,000 to take over the bus. Harman and Burton were the sole directors and shareholders, and Harman's home address of 193 Graham Road, Hackney, was the company's registered office. He received the official designation of Managing Director. On the morning of Wednesday, November 3rd 1926, the shares in the company passed to the LGOC who allocated the Lea Valley Dennis to their Leyton (T) garage. Its body was exchanged with that on the Imperial Dennis MH 1693 in January 1927, and it was absorbed into the Tramways (MET) Omnibus Co. Ltd. on January 1st 1928. Harman returned to the employment of the LGOC with the demise of his bus and remained at Leyton garage with London Transport until his death.

260 Cambridge Road, Hackney
3/5 Bonwell Street, Bethnal Green

BROWN/A.B.

C. A. Wells' garage at 260 Cambridge Road, Hackney, housed three independents though in each case their stay was short lived. Adams' Primrose bus of November 1922 was one of the earliest of the independents and was joined at Wells' garage in March 1923 by Stanton's first Empress bus. This stayed for about nine months and moved out when Stanton acquired the garage at Canal Sidings. The next buses to arrive were those of Arthur Robert Brown of 64 Walton Buildings, Bethnal Green. Brown bought himself a pair of Hall Lewis-bodied Maudslay single-deckers which ran most days on the 203 (later 231A) but could be found on the 42A on Sundays. They were painted dark red & white and were first taxed on January 20th 1928. The fleet name consisted of a gold oval inside which was the name BROWN although UC 1816 carried at one stage the letters A.B.

During his short career Brown changed both his home and garage addresses. The former became 36 Huntingdon Buildings, Bethnal Green and the latter was changed after only a few months to 3/5 Bonwell Street, also in Bethnal Green. This was the headquarters of Plotts & Goldman's fleet of Gilford coaches trading under the name of Central London Motors.

Brown's buses ran on the 231A in conjunction with Birch who agreed to supervise them from August 1928 onwards because Brown was unable to do so himself. They concluded a further agreement in December 1928 to inspect the two buses on his behalf once a week to ascertain their mechanical fitness. By 1929 Brown had decided to dispose of his buses and, in view of his close connection with Birch, offered them the option to purchase which they were pleased to accept as it brought their monopoly of the 231A one stage nearer. Brown last operated on June 6th 1929 and Birch ran the two Maudslays from the following day.

Cambridge Road is now known as Cambridge Heath Road and the former Wells garage is today a B.R.S. depot. Brown's second garage, 3/5 Bonwell Street, served as an ice cream factory from the later 'thirties to the mid-fifties and is now a thing of the past as is Bonwell Street itself.

81A Harrowgate Road, Hackney

On the corner of Harrowgate Road where it joins Cassland Road, was once a yard which was used from the early 'twenties up to the time of the Blitz by a succession of small motor firms. It was probably land surplus to the needs of Daniel Lloyd who for many years was in business as a cowkeeper at no. 81. The Gray family of 160 Hackney Road used 81A as a base for their coach and bus business up to the summer of 1924 when they moved to their own purpose-built garage at the Stamford Hill end of Tottenham High Road (see Chapter 7).

Emerson's Garage, Bodney Road, Hackney
Jerome's Garage, Downs Road, Hackney

Part of Emerson's garage in Bodney Road, Hackney, was a one-time fire station and its appearance still gives a clue to its origins. The Emerson name is still proclaimed over the garage's other entrance from Pembury Place. Samuel Attwell Boon's Eastern bus spent its first few months there between November 1923 and about June 1924. Not far away, in railway arches at Downs Road, was Jerome's Garage run by Charles Gamgee where Boon spent the latter part of his career. Other occupants in the period 1927-8 were A. G. Cook's Reliance Omnibus Co. Ltd. and Moses Edelman's Embassy Motors Ltd.

736 Lea Bridge Road, Leyton
219 Lea Bridge Road, Leyton

There were two separate independent garages in the Lea Bridge Road, Leyton. The more easterly, no. 736, was the premises of Whittington, Cox & Company who housed Pro Bono Publico for several years until its absorption by London Transport. Gates of Woodford now use the premises as a Ford service depot. At no. 219 was the site where Alfred Sneiman built a garage for his Gordon fleet in 1926. The garage, which bore the Gordon name proudly engraved above the door until the latter part of the nineteen sixties, has now made way for a self-service petrol station exotically known as the Orient Autoway Centre. The Gordon garage was conveniently situated facing Kettlebaston Road where Sneiman lived at no. 83 throughout his bus career.

GORDON/GOC

When Alfred Sneiman left the LGOC and began bus operation in October 1924 it was from Gray's Garage at Stamford Hill that his Dennis first ran. XU 8376 was a Dodson-bodied vehicle carrying the fleet name Gordon. By April 1925 it had been joined by two more buses of the same type (XX 2572/7690), and before long all three were to be found on the 511A except on Sundays and Bank Holidays when 38B, 38E, 511 and 511B were favoured. On Sundays in 1925/6 he ran his own exclusive service 267 (Victoria to High Beach via Loughton). Sneiman was unpopular with his contemporaries because of his blithe disregard for the adherence to schedules. But his methods paid off handsomely to the extent of justifying the construction of his own substantially-built garage at 219 Lea Bridge Road, a site which he purchased in November 1926. A spare bus was bought in October 1926 in the form of TW 5863, a Dennis

E 30-seater which was the first pneumatic tyred vehicle in the fleet. It could be found on summer Sundays at the Bakers Arms touting excursions to High Beach at a shilling a head. It was followed in April 1927 by TW 8886, the first of six Lancias which Sneiman acquired for coaching work; a profitable sideline which later outstripped in numerical terms the scheduled bus fleet.

On March 3rd 1926 the Gordon Omnibus Co. Ltd. was incorporated with a capital of £3,000 to take over the business. Alfred Sneiman and his wife Elizabeth Ellen, were the sole directors and their home address in Kettlebaston Road served as the Company's registered office. For much of its career the company used an insignia on the sides of the buses instead of a fleet name. This comprised a wheel (within which was written the letters G.O.C.) surmounted by a pair of wings, the wheel being on a horizontal base inside which was the word 'London'. The winged wheel quickly appealed to the sense of humour of other independent busmen who nicknamed the Gordon's "Flying Ants".

In September 1929 and April 1930 two of the three scheduled workings on the 511A were taken over by modern covered-top double-deckers with the arrival of VX 2198 and VX 5169. These were Leylands, Gordon's first, and were of the then popular TD1 variety with open-staircase 52-seater bodies by Dodson. Modernisation was completed in November 1931 by the arrival of EV 3403. This bus had become famous even before entering service by being exhibited at the Olympia exhibition of commercial vehicles, and was unique in being the only Maudslay double-decker operating in London. A much-publicised feature of its all-enclosed Dodson body was the 'Plein Azur' sunshine roof on the upper deck; an innovation in London which must have been highly appreciated on fine Sundays when the 511 ran as far as High Beach in the heart of Epping Forest. Only the oldest of the three Dennises was withdrawn from service upon the arrival of the covered top contingent and this stayed with Gordon as a lorry. The other two (now on pneumatics) and the E-type single-decker stayed as spares and enabled a considerable augmentation to take place on Sundays.

Sneiman was one of the many bus operators who succumbed to the lure of short-distance coach operation and he began to operate a service between East Ham and Grays via Aveley, the latter being an area then claiming to be badly served by public transport. The date of introduction of the service is not known but it was probably late in 1932 or early 1933. It was maintained by units of the Gordon coach fleet which then consisted of six Lancias and a Maudslay, and was run without a licence. In mid-1933 the company endeavoured to regularise matters by applying for a road service licence to run a 30 min. service from East Ham to Grays, extended every 90 mins. to Tilbury. The application was refused by the Traffic Commissioners, and Gordon withdrew its coaches at the close of operation on Saturday, September 30th 1933.

The day appointed for the takeover by London Transport of the Gordon buses was December 15th 1933. Six buses changed hands (2 standard Dennis, 1 Dennis E, 2 Leyland Titan and 1 Maudslay ML7) and the Board also acquired the ex-bus Dennis lorry and a 1927 Moon open touring car HV 7599. Both were unlicensed at the time of takeover. The company was awarded £30,825 by the Arbitration Tribunal making Sneiman a wealthy man in monetary terms though his private life, culminating in divorce, was much less happy. He continued to run the Gordon coaches until about the outbreak of war. Just after the war the garage was taken over by Essex County Coaches Ltd. and after their departure in 1949 it became—like the ex-Gray garage at Tottenham—a depot for Corona, the soft drinks people.

Baltic Yard, Hoe Street, Walthamstow

The Baltic Yard at 213A Hoe Street, Walthamstow, presents much the same picture today as it did almost fifty years ago when, with the Good family as owners, it housed some of the east London independents. In the nineteen-twenties the owners traded as Good Brothers though the actual proprietors were Good senior— a man all out for business and the owner of several houses thereabouts—and his sons Leslie and Harold. Coaches and a plastics firm occupy much of the Baltic Yard nowadays. Its curious title is still proclaimed on a wooden board over the narrow entrance, but the origins of it seem to have faded into obscurity.

GRAFTON

The Grafton Omnibus Company of 279 Cambridge Road, Bethnal Green, came into existence in January 1925. The idea of purchasing a bus originated with Isadore Wolfsbergen (later known as George Welby), who had been an LGOC conductor for some years, latterly at Dalston (D) garage. His brother-in-law, Mark Cravitz, who was also an LGOC man and worked at Seven Kings (AP), agreed to join in and further support came from Isadore Wolfsbergen's brother David, together with Joel Edward Hart, Isaac Cohen and Harris Goldberg. Each of the six partners subscribed £100 towards the price of a bus, a hire purchase agreement being drawn up with Dodson for the remainder. Only the two ex-LGOC men and Goldberg worked in the business though Isaac Cohen, a civil servant by profession, acted as their accountant. Mark Cravitz, who lived at 279 Cambridge Road, Bethnal Green, was the licensee and he was also for a while secretary and spokesman for all the 511 operators, a thankless task which constant bickering and lack of co-operation forced him to give up.

The six partners were all members of the Grafton Athletic Club, hence the title given to XW 8641, a red & white Dennis. Weekday operation was always on the 511, but overbussing of this route on Sundays caused Cravitz to work the 25 group one winter and an excursion was later made on to the 69, but both suffered the same trouble as the 511. In the summer of 1925 the bus worked between Camberwell Green and Chingford on Sundays as route 513. To start with XW 8641 was kept at Lloyds Garage in Grove Road, Bow, but after a few months Good senior offered Cravitz the opportunity to rent a house in Pembroke Road, Leyton provided the Grafton bus was garaged in the Baltic Yard, an offer which Cravitz, who was living in cramped conditions in Bethnal Green, readily accepted.

In 1926 the partners decided that, to seek security for those who wished to remain in bus work, it would be best to sell out to the LGOC.

322

A limited company, the Grafton Omnibus Co. Ltd., of Lennox House, Norfolk Street, Strand, was incorporated on September 1st 1926 with a share capital of £1,000 preparatory to the transfer of ownership on September 27th. As it happened Mark Cravitz was the only partner who chose to remain on the buses and he continued to drive the Grafton bus from the LGOC garage at Leyton (T). Isadore Wolfsbergen accepted the offer of a job as a shop manager from his brother who had two businesses, and Harris Goldberg returned to the rag trade with which he had been formerly connected.

The new owners ran the Grafton schedules from Leyton (T) garage and in February 1927 replaced the Dennis—which went to Redburns—with K945. On January 1st 1928 Grafton was absorbed into the Tramways (MET) Omnibus Co. Ltd. Its former leading light, Mark Cravitz, remained as a driver and conductor with General and its successor, London Transport, at Leyton garage until his retirement in January 1964.

THE JOCKEY

The Jockey was as curious a fleet name as any. It was thought up by Albert John Robinson of 77 Sewardstone Road, Cambridge Heath and was applied to the side of his red & white Leyland, XT 4857, in gold script on a white panel. This made its debut at Scotland Yard on May 16th 1924 and was licensed ready for service on the 21st. Robinson's early operations are known to have included routes 11, 29 and 73. He also notified his intentions to run on 6, 15, 27, 33, 38 and 42 and may well have done so. He garaged first at 81A Page Street which was a suitable location for these central area services, but in January 1925 he moved to the Empress Garage at Cambridge Heath when he joined the various other independents on the 511. The date of his subsequent transfer to the Baltic Yard is not known.

Like the majority of other 511 operators Robinson decided to sell out to the LGOC and formed the Jockey Omnibus Co. Ltd. on September 17th 1926 as a preliminary to this. General purchased the £1,000 shares on October 12th and transferred the registered office from Lennox House, Norfolk Street to 55 Broadway. XT 4857 moved to the LGOC garage at Leyton (T) and in September 1927 was replaced by K485 which maintained the Jockey schedules, in General livery, until January 1st 1928 when the business was absorbed into the Tramways (MET) Omnibus Co. Ltd.

NELSON

The only Baltic Yard operator to last through to the nineteen-thirties was Nelson. Like The Jockey, Nelson was a 511 operator and was formerly at the Empress Garage, Cambridge Heath, but had reached Walthamstow by July 1925. Again in a similar manner to The Jockey, it had worked for a while on central area routes (8, 11, 33, 38 and 42 were applied for) before settling down on the 511. The first Nelson bus was XU 8538 of September 1924 origin, and it was joined by XX 5499 in March 1925. Both were identical Strachan & Brown-bodied Dennises with the popular livery of red with darker lower panels and cream window frames. The proprietors were Walter Thomas Marshall of 63 Nelson Road, South Chingford and Herbert Henry Clench who lived next door at 61. Marshall was the senior partner and held the licences; he also regularly drove the bus despite having a gammy leg which was shorter than the other. Clench was also a working partner.

Clench gained repute among his bus-owning colleagues as being a difficult man to get along with and in due course his partnership with the less dogmatic Marshall broke up. Clench left to form his own business in December 1926 and Marshall was meanwhile joined by Fred Churchward with whom he worked in harmony until the end. They formed a limited company, the Nelson Omnibus Co. Ltd., on January 14th 1927. Its capital of £3,500 was held in equal shares of £1,750 by the two proprietors, and the registered office was Baltic Yard.

A third bus was acquired in March 1928 as a spare, and it marked a swing in preference from Dennis to Leyland. YV 2305 was a Leyland PLSC Lion 32-seater which, like similar vehicles acquired by other operators, soon proved too small for busy journeys. A pair of new Leyland Titans arrived from Dodsons in January and February 1930. Registered GC 1804/7493 they replaced the two original Dennises and rendered the fleet all-Leyland. The last arrival, a handsome and modern TD2-type Titan, again bodied by Dodson, was GX 1914 which replaced the Leyland Lion in May 1932. This found a home in Somerset with E. J. Dunn of Bridgwater and later passed to Western National. Nelson survived the formation of London Transport only until November 1st 1933 when its assets passed to the new monopoly for £24,500.

H.H.C.

When H. H. Clench parted company with W. T. Marshall he tried to establish himself as a bus operator on his own account. He remained at the Baltic Yard and ordered three Dennis 2½-ton single-deckers from Dodson. YE 850-2 were small chocolate & white vehicles with the fleetname H.H.C., and they were taxed on the first day of 1927.

At this late stage it was inevitable that Clench would have difficulty in finding suitable routes on which his three buses could be profitably placed, and there is evidence that this proved to be a greater problem than he had anticipated. Before the buses had even been delivered the police had disallowed a proposed route between Clapton Pond and North Woolwich on the grounds that it used and crossed restricted streets. Clench settled for the 551 weekdays and 42 on Sundays. It was during his career on the 551, on March 4th to be precise, that he was apprehended for impersonating a police officer. It was a Friday and he had been standing at the Angel, Edmonton, to pay his crews as they came past. The men on one of his buses complained about the behaviour of staff on two vehicles that arrived at the same time as themselves, a Redburn and a Uneedus. Clench, pretending to be an official from the public carriage office, insisted on inspecting their timecards. The opposition crews became suspicious and hastened away to call the genuine police. Later in the same month, disenchanted with the 551, Clench tried the Rotherhithe Tunnel route 182 instead. This ceased on

Photo No. 57

The General Strike brought the Independents into their own with the virtual disappearance from the streets of the Generals and their associates. Albert Ewer's Leyland XW 5572, overloaded with passengers and with a bicycle escort, is seen working the Liverpool Street-Victoria section of route 11.

Photo No. 58

Windows on this Leyland from the Gray fleet are boarded up as protection against missiles thrown by angry strikers and their sympathisers. On the offside the boards project forward beyond the saloon windows to provide a minimum of protection for the driver.

Photo No. 59
The Dennis H family was an unworthy successor to the famous 4-tonner, and it lost Dennis almost all their lucrative London market. An early and particularly antiquated-looking H-type, thanks to its open-top Dodson-body, was this specimen purchased for The Reliance fleet of A. G. Cook.

Photo No. 60
Closed-top bodywork of rather more modern styling was fitted by Birch to this Dennis HS supplied to F. A. Rasey in the autumn of 1929. The chocolate and yellow livery was enhanced by the lower saloon waistband in pink, and by the white-walled tyres.

Photo No. 61 (*above*)
Martin were the foremost users of the Dennis H with a fleet of five, four with Hickman bodies and one—depicted above—bodied by Birch. Martin's red livery was one of the least attractive amongst the independents who survived through to 1933.

Photo No. 62 (*left*)
The curved-top radiator of the Dennis HV, though not particularly handsome, was markedly more modern than that of its predecessors. One of the few HVs in London service was Birch-bodied VX 7702 of BBP. This was one of the first independent concerns to invest in an enclosed cab for the driver and in roller destination blinds.

Photo No. 63 (*top*)
A variety of manufacturers sol
single-deck vehicles to th
independents in small numbe
late in the 'twenties. UC 181
(top, fig. 63), one of Brown'
two Hall Lewis-bodied Maud
lay ML3's, is seen just afte
takeover by Birch whose fle
number B28 is carried on th
bonnet side.

Photo No. 64 (*centre*)
MY 8142 was one of a pair
Guy FBB 32-seaters operate
by A & W and was the last ne
bus bought for that fleet. Dupl
provided the body.

Photo No. 65 (*below*)
G. H. Allitt & Sons Ltd. ran tw
Karrier JKL buses in addition
a quintet of coaches of th
same make. GU 2533,
Dodson-bodied specimen,
seen at Surrey Docks headin
for New Cross on the 202 whic
was pioneered by Allitt.

Photo No. 66 (*top*) Two suburban firms had particularly troubled careers. Newlands District (top, fig. 66) began its chequered operations with this small brown-liveried Bean which carries a 20-seat body by Holbrook. It is seen providing an ostensibly free service to the residents of Peckham.

Photos . No. 67 & 68

Centre and bottom (figs. 67 & 68) are seen two specimens from the Royal Highlander fleet. MV 933 was one of a trio of Beans with specially narrow Birch bodies for use in the Ealing area. UR 997 was one of six Guy OND 20-seaters with Duple bodies. It is seen running in Watford on hire to the Premier Omnibus Company whose owner financed its purchase. Beneath the fleet name on both is painted the tartan plaid which characterised all the Royal Highlander vehicles.

Photo No. 69
The operators running locally in Romford had a character of their own, and this was mainly because they did not have to buy vehicles to Metropolitan Police specification. The mixed Imperial fleet included this AJS Pilot with locally-built Metcalfe bodywork, seen here at the Upminster terminus.

Photo No. 70
The penultimate vehicle to don the green Imperial livery was this Gilford 1680T which was bought second hand in April 1933 when it was likely that the end lay only a matter of months away. The curtains at the windows are reminders of better days.

Photo No. 71
The Capitol enterprise ended in flames. This gear-driven Tilling Stevens, once a member of the Wendrome fleet before coming to Capitol, had its body destroyed by fire. It later saw service, rebodied, in Scotland.

Photo No. 72
Romford District vehicles carried a small star on their dash, perhaps denoting that they ran out of the Star Garage. The fleet contained three Dennis Darts of which this Metcalfe-bodied specimen was the First.

Photo No. 73
The Leyland Titan was the saviour of the independents, for there was really no other bus to match it in London. Most had Dodson bodies, the earliest style of which is demonstrated by Triumph's Titan, one of the first two to enter service in the capital. It is seen at Hampton Court.

Photo No. 74
Before long Dodson eliminated the lower deck quarter lights which had been incorporated in the first few Titan bodies. Seen terminating at Winchmore Hill is the Titan on which the Perkins family depended for their livelihood.

Photo No. 75
The Miller fleet eventually contained five Dodson-bodied Titans. VX 5859, the second to be purchased, is seen serving route 293, an east suburban route served almost exclusively by independents except for a few peak hour Generals.

Photo No. 76
Frederick Hayes favoured an enclosed cab for his Adelaide bus which had more red in its livery than most operators' Titans. It is seen at the Highgate terminus prior to setting out on the long run to Hampton Court. A newer, Birch Titan stands behind it.

Photo No. 77
Duple built thirteen bodies for Premier which were identical in almost all respects to Dodson's first style of Titan body. One is seen here outside the builder's Hendon factory awaiting delivery to the Company's Leysfield Road garage.

Photo No. 78
Also photographed at the coachbuilder's is a Birch-bodied Titan destined for service with A. G. Summerskill. As with Adelaide (fig. 76) this operator was in a minority at the time, at least as far as the independents were concerned, in specifying an enclosed driver's cab.

Photo No. 79
The Daimler CF6 was a failure in London conditions which were far too strenuous for it. Only two
served in the capital, one of which—Eagle's Birch-bodied GC 7388—is seen caught up in heavy traffic
in the Strand.

Photo No. 80
The only Daimler CH6 to run for a London independent was this Red Line vehicle. The Birch body built
for this has a style of its own and combines an open cab with an enclosed platform. The double front
windows with half-drops, the roof box, and the combination of board and blind indicators are all
features of contemporary LGOC practice.

Photo No. 81
The Dennis Lance was favoured by only a few London operators. Conway & Clayton's vehicle was the only Independent bus latterly on route 39 and was photographed at Its terminus at the Angel, Edmonton, on the site where a large cinema now stands. The Dodson body is of the six bay variety built for Titans and Lances from August 1930 onwards.

Photo No. 82
The Cardinal Omnibus Co. Ltd. bought a Lance and a Titan and was able to compare the qualities of both. GK 8667 was the eighth and last Claremont bus to enter service in London.

Photo No. 83
Dodson supplied the body for F. J. C. Kirk's AEC Regent, the Empire, which spent a busy working life on the streets of east London on the 511.

Photo No. 84
...d Line's famous ...ng-wheelbase AEC ...gent GW 2294 ...rried the much-...built Birch body ...nsferred from a ...imler CF6. The ...en cab and ...closed stairs are ... reversal of the ...ndition in which ... body saw ser-...vice previously.

Photo No. 85
Charles H. Pickup's five Park Royal-bodied AEC Regents were famous in their own lifetime by virtue of their open tops and their speed. GW 1224 is seen at Clapham Common bound for Richmond.

Photo No. 86 (*above*)
The first generation and the la[st?]
Birch's garage at Kentish Town is t[he]
scene of this photo of the Company['s]
original Leyland LB which, even wh[en]
fitted with pneumatic tyres, loo[ks]
really ancient compared with B39, [the]
diesel-engined Titan.

Photo No. 87 (*left*)
The last independent Lance was b[uilt]
to the order of Red Rover. Birch's fi[nal]
style of double-deck body is fltt[ed]
which, with its flat front and roof b[ay,]
hints that its designer was influenc[ed]
by current LGOC design trends.

Photo No. 88 (*far left*)
Heading a line-up of Ambassador vehicles outside the garage in Marlborough Road, Holloway, is
Dennis Lance GX 143. It carries Dodson's last style of London body which, at the request of the
operator, perpetuates the old fashioned open cab. Behind are Dodson-bodied Lance GK 7166, Birch-
bodied Lance GK 7167, Dennis H XV 3453, and Dennis 4-tonner YR 3672.

Photo No. 89 (*above*)
Empress had two of the later TD2 type Titans with all-enclosed Dodson bodies. GX 2692 and its crew
pose for the photographer outside the late lamented Finsbury Park Empire. Empress Motors Ltd. run
coaches to this day from their Canal Sidings garage.

Photo No. 90 (*below*)
The last generation of single-deckers is exemplified by this Duple-bodied 31-seater, the newest single-
deck bus in the Prince fleet. Although outwardly resembling the Leyland Lion it was, in fact, based
upon the double-deck Titan chassis. The Prince fleet was destined to be the last independent one in
London.

Photo No. 91
Despite its satisfactory performance under busy conditions, Go—
Maudslay was the only double-decker of this make to run in Lond
was the first vehicle to carry the last type of Dodson body wi
exaggerated piano-style front.

Photo No. 92
The London bus that never was! The SMC Sikh built for Ambas
but never purchased by them carried enclosed staircase De
bodywork which was an elongated version of the standard bo
supplied on many Titans.

Photo No. 93
Westminster's famous 64-seater SMC was a most impressive vehi
appearance if not in performance. Its Dodson body had a style
own though its otherwise excellent appearance was marred I
open cab favoured by Westminster even as late as 1933.

April 20th in favour of the 100A/F and in May 1927 he applied for the 96D before concentrating the three vehicles on the 263 shortly before it was declared restricted. Sundays in the summer of 1927 saw him running unlicensed, and therefore illegally, to Epping. On August 5th 1927, after seven brief, unsettled months of operation, the three H.H.C. buses passed to Public. The new owners, who worked them on Clench's schedules from July 25th, paid him £5,600 for them.

Clench left London and went to live at 13 Cutcliffe Grove, Bedford. The payment he received from Public enabled him to set-up in business as the Dreadnought Omnibus Co. Ltd. starting with TM 2460, a 20-seat Berliet in March 1928. In May 1929 the Bedford council refused Dreadnought permission to ply for hire in Bedford any longer and Clench, at the age of 37, found the second stage of his bus-owning career at an end. His next recorded enterprise is in 1930 when he was part-owner of Lion Motor Services who, from an administrative base in South Chingford, ran a service from London (Bishopsgate) to Ongar. Ownership changed hands in January 1931 when the service was sold to Associated Coaches (Ongar) Ltd. after which the name of H. H. Clench at last disappears from the transport scene.

FAIRLOP

B. D. L. Burton was one of the proprietors who, like Alliston of the Cornwall and Marshall of the Nelson, took the name of the road in which he lived as the fleetname for his bus. A tall, softly spoken man, Burton lived at 10 Fairlop Road, Leytonstone, and worked in the early days in partnership with a Mr. Hollywood. He started his bus career in September 1924 and is believed to have run on a miscellany of routes including, predominantly, the 69 for a couple of months. When it became necessary to submit schedules under the London Traffic Act he selected route 39A for Mondays to Fridays and 69A for weekends and these became effective from December 6th 1924. Only a month later, on January 4th 1925, he switched his sphere of operation entirely and began to work the 511. His complete pattern of operations from then onwards was as follows. He ran daily on the section originally numbered 511 and later renumbered 511A between Stratford Broadway and Chingford Mount with a projection to the Royal Forest Hotel, Chingford, in the summer months of 1925-7 and a further Sunday extension to High Beach in the summers of 1926 and 1927. A short-lived Sunday operation on the 513 took place in November and December 1925.

Originally Burton secured accommodation for his bus at Straker Squire's works in Angel Road, Edmonton. He is thought to have departed from there in January 1925 when he moved to the 511. It is not known where he garaged from then onwards though Baltic Yard is the most likely place he moved to.

The first Fairlop bus was a Daimler, PU 4769, which Burton bought in September 1924 and retained for only nine months. He sent it back to Roberts in June 1925. PU 8660 arrived to replace it and was a new Dennis which must have been infinitely more successful as it maintained the Fairlop schedules to the end. Burton's last day in business was January 30th 1929. On the following day the bus was taken over by City as part of its expansion policy of buying-up other scheduled operators. His bus sold, Burton turned to a new life as proprietor of an off-licence.

The Reliance Garage, Folly Lane, Chingford
THE RELIANCE/RELIANCE

Arthur George Cook was the senior partner in A. G. Cook & Company of 10 West Side, London Fields. Cook and his wife, who was somewhat younger than he, had been better known for their tally business which they kept going after starting the buses. Indeed some of their drivers and conductors are reputed to have been among their best customers! Cook's co-partners in A. G. Cook & Company were Frederick May and Arthur John Hayworth. Between them they ordered a Straker Squire for delivery in March 1924 under the title of The Reliance. XR 7078 was joined in December 1924 by XW 6378/9, a pair of Dodson-bodied Dennises which were followed in March 1925 by XX 5800/1. The Dennis/Dodson combination was again favoured with the arrival of YM 2955 in December 1925, and in April 1927 complete standardisation was achieved when YF 6913 appeared on the scene to oust the Straker Squire.

Cook & Co. worked originally from the Empress Garage at Canal Sidings, but the growth of the fleet to six units by December 1925 meant that additional accommodation had to be found elsewhere. As a result some buses were kept at Jerome's Garage in Downs Road, Hackney. With further deliveries of new buses planned for the latter part of 1928 it was obviously essential to find somewhere to house the entire fleet under one roof, and in September 1928 the problem was overcome by the purchase of a plot of land at Chingford in Folly Lane at its junction with Walthamstow Avenue (now the North Circular Road). The land, which was in an area then largely undeveloped, cost only £175. The construction of the building cost another £2,577 and the purchase of furniture required a further £85. Thus for total outlay of only £2,837 the company had a freehold garage capable of taking the whole fleet.

Some time before this the business had been incorporated as a limited company with a share capital of £3,000. The Reliance Omnibus Co. Ltd. was formed on December 2nd 1925 with its head office at 10 West Side, London Fields. The original three partners were directors together with Cook's wife Frances Annie Cook and a Mr. Edward Richard Bates.

Before the new Folly Lane Garage came into use in about June 1929 the fleet had expanded from six vehicles to ten and now included three single-deckers. YX 7619/20 were Leyland Lions of September 1928 vintage and XV 3915 was another vehicle of the same type delivered two months later. December 1928 saw the arrival of a Dennis H, XV 6848, which had an open top although this feature was going out of favour at the time. With a seating capacity of 56 it was the largest capacity vehicle ever owned.

At the very start the routes worked by The Reliance varied and are thought to have included those most favoured amongst the Hackney area operators such as 6, 8, 11, 22, 35 and 42. Like most of the others at Canal Sidings, The Reliance concentrated on the 511 from early 1925 onwards and obtained five weekday schedules for its six buses. The fleet growth of 1928/9 saw the company working the 266 in company with Ewer, Summerskill and Miller but this lasted only from September 1928 until December when The Reliance began its own lengthy 366 route between the Green Man, Leytonstone and Brentwood. The four new vehicles of 1928 were used on this plus the older spare Dennis, and the service was later augmented further as the fleet strength rose to its maximum of fourteen, all of which had schedules. On Sundays the 366 vehicles worked on the 69. 1930 saw the company taking an interest in route 50 which involved a herculean journey from the Chingford garage to Streatham Common. As late as May 1934, after many of their colleagues had already succumbed to the LPTB, Reliance surprisingly tried to secure a new service numbered 510 between Chingford Mount and Waltham Cross on which they planned to run two buses. Permission was refused on the grounds that Reliance were themselves shortly to be taken over. The company's final pattern of operation was: Weekdays 511—5 buses, 366—6 buses, 50—3 buses; Sundays 511—5 buses, 69—9 buses.

Seven "modern"-type buses joined the fleet from October 1929 onwards starting with UW 4198, a Leyland Titan. Like all other buses ever purchased, except the original Straker Squire, they had Dodson bodies. Three replaced earlier Dennises (XW 6378/9, XX 5801) and the remainder swelled the scheduled fleet. The Titan was followed by a pair of Dennis Lances (VX 8363/4), the first in London, which had enclosed stairs and a peculiar combination of roller route blinds at the rear and boards at the front. The front destination was in the roof. They bore a close external resemblance to GK 7166 of the Sphere Omnibus Co. Ltd. which was also constructed by Dodson in November 1930. When the order for them was placed with Dodson, external staircases were specified. This was amended during construction with the result that the vehicles carried outside-type stairs within an enclosing wall which, from inside, looked clearly as though it was added as an afterthought. These were the last Dennises to join the fleet, and for the last four new vehicles the preference swung back to Leyland. TD2-type Titans were received in June 1932 (EV 6510/6692) and October 1932 (EV 8335) and had the last style of Dodson body though they retained the traditional open cab. A single-decker of the similar TS4-type Tiger variety (EV 8334) completed the quartet, also in October 1932. Vehicles later bore the fleet name Reliance in "General" style instead of the former title of The Reliance. At the end the fleet comprised ten double-deckers (3 Dennis 4-tonners now on pneumatics, 1 Dennis H, 2 Dennis Lances and 4 Leyland Titans) and 4 single-deckers (3 Leyland Lions and 1 Leyland Tiger). A pair of Austin cars (YH 8911, GT 2397) were also on the books.

Reliance was one of the last independent fleets to survive. The last day of operation was November 6th 1934. Next morning, in the rush hour soon after daylight had dawned, the unusual spectacle could be seen of the whole Reliance fleet running in a fourteen-vehicle convoy to Chiswick, having left their old Chingford home for the last time. They were mostly looking decidedly down at heel after several months of minimum maintenance, but the Leyland Tiger, which led the convoy, proudly carried a laurel wreath on its radiator.

327

The Folly Lane garage did not pass to London Transport when the bus fleet was absorbed, though Reliance endeavoured unsuccessfully to prove to the Arbitration Tribunal that it should do so. It had been in Mr. Cook's name and not the company's up to December 1933 and was thus not eligible for transfer under the Act. The Cooks received £25,500 for their bus business and later retired to Hampshire. Three decades have almost elapsed and their old buildings have all been demolished but the Reliance name lingers on as the title of a filling station which now stands on the Folly Lane site.

25 York Hill, Loughton

THE PC

The Chiswell family have been long established in business in Loughton and the antique and reproductions business of Chiswell Brothers still flourishes in Forest Road. The father of the Chiswell Brothers, Alfred Chiswell, was for many years a cabinet maker at 25 York Hill. A natural development from this was furniture removals, the two trades being complementary to each other, and contacts made in furniture removing led naturally on to an interest in antiques. The two Chiswell sons joined their father in the family business and one, Percy, expanded his interests still further in 1922 when he bought a little Ford model-T charabanc, NO 6211, which is still remembered by some of the older folk in Loughton. The next step was the purchase of a full sized bus in June 1924 followed by another in April 1925.

Percy Chiswell's two buses were painted red & white and carried the fleet name THE PC. Both were Dennises but they differed from each other in their bodywork, the earlier of the pair, PU 3549, having been built by Strachan & Brown whilst PU 7282 was a Dodson product. Chiswell's first route application was Elephant & Castle to Epping Town followed shortly afterwards by Victoria to Loughton and High Beach. Other early operations included routes 10, 11, 38 and 76 but from January 1925 onwards the buses plied regularly on the 511. The Chiswells had a garage for their furniture lorries at the rear of the York Hill shop, just in Queens Road, and the buses were also housed there though it is possible that they were also sometimes kept in a yard at Westbury Lane, Buckhurst Hill. There is still, today, a garage on the site though this is a later building than the one used by the Chiswell's in the 'twenties.

Towards the end of 1926 Percy Chiswell negotiated the sale of his buses to the LGOC and formed the P.C. Omnibus Co. Ltd. for this purpose on December 1st 1926. Share capital was £2,000 and the registered office was Lennox House, Norfolk Street. Under an agreement of December 2nd the two buses were sold to the limited company for £3,300 to be satisfied in full by the allotment of 1,998 £1 shares in the company. The buses were in a very run-down condition and when the police learned of the change from private to company ownership they refused to allow the buses to be relicensed in the company's name until they received an overhaul. Chiswell was reluctant to pay the cost of the overhauls and on December 23rd he dismissed the staff and ceased operation. This must have come as a severe blow to the men concerned only two days before Christmas and with little prospect of finding

328

re-employment easily. General acquired the share capital of the P.C. Omnibus Co. Ltd. on January 11th 1927 and collected the buses five days later, despatching them immediately to Chiswick for overhaul. PU 3549 was overhauled and fitted with a second-hand body ex Superbus, ready to resume the PC operation from Leyton (T) garage on January 25th. Its own body later went on to the one-time Florence Dennis which became a unit of the Redburn's fleet. PU 7282, though less than two years old, never ran again. Its chassis provided a source of spares for other Dennises and its body, like that of PU 3549, went into the Redburn's fleet, this time on the ex-Superbus chassis from which PU 3549's body had recently come. PU 7282 was not immediately replaced, its schedule lying dormant for nearly a year. A replacement finally arrived in the form of K60 on December 15th 1927, just over a fortnight before the PC workings were absorbed into the Tramways (MET) Omnibus Co. Ltd. on January 1st 1928. K60 was, needless to say, the last K to be transferred to a one-time independent undertaking.

The Chiswell brothers continued with their other interests although, in recent times, the furniture removals have been sold to Wilkinsons who now occupy the York Hill premises. Percy Chiswell, now in his eighties, still lives in retirement in his native Loughton.

Forest Road, Loughton

MAJESTIC (continued from chapter 7)

Just as well-known in and around Loughton as the Chiswells were the Askew family. In recent times they were the last surviving hay & straw merchants in the area and their business in High Road, Buckhurst Hill, did not finally close its doors until as late as 1971. The Askew with whom our story is concerned is George Ellis Askew who, in 1925, ran his business from his house at 86 Smarts Lane, Loughton under the old-established title of Askew & Son. Facing the house and extending through to Forest Road, which runs parallel to Smarts Lane, was an extensive property owned by Askew which included a large corrugated iron clad garage with a frontage in Forest Road. From here Askew & Son ran a jobmaster's business. For nearly half a century the Askews had run horse brakes from their home village which were well renowned throughout Essex until motor charabancs finally ousted them. For the benefit of East Enders in need of fresh country air Askews' brakes ran at weekends from the Rising Sun at Whipps Cross to the Kings Oak Hotel at High Beach, in the heart of Epping Forest, for 1/-. Parties would be picked up at Walthamstow or Leyton for excursions to Epping, Lambourne End or Abridge; a wonderful ride on a fine day, and even if it rained the canvas hood and side sheets could be unfurled to make it very cosy inside. The spotless brakes, with their glistening hub caps and huge, burnished-brass lamps, made surprisingly long journeys at times. Laden with food and beer they would set out for week-end excursions to Essex coastal resorts as far afield as Clacton. The Askews had to move with the times and inevitably their yard in Loughton began to echo to the backfiring of motor lorries and charabancs. The earliest charabanc so far recorded is NO 8233, a 14 seat Metcalfe-bodied Fiat of March 1923. In November 1925 George Askew became financially interested in the two

Majestic buses as we have seen in the last chapter, and for much of the time between then and July 1927 one of the Majestic double-deck Leylands, XO 7581, worked out of Askew's Loughton premises on the 100A (Elephant & Castle-Epping).

After the sale of the Majestic buses to Public Askew continued with his coaching activities using a fleet of Lancias. The Majestic Omnibus Co. Ltd. in which he was now sole shareholder lay dormant for a while and at one stage Askew intended to wind it up. He changed his mind and in January 1929 it blossomed forth under the new title of Superways Ltd. under which Askew placed all his coaching activities. For a brief spell Askew & Son, and later Superways Ltd., ran an express coach service from London, Bush House, to Plymouth via Andover, Salisbury, Yeovil, Exeter and Torquay. A noteworthy feature was the use of two special six-wheeled Gilfords delivered for the service in November 1928 and which between them maintained a daily service, one coach leaving each end at 8.30 a.m. and arriving at its destination in time for the evening meal. These splendid 33-seaters carried Duple full-fronted coachwork in which the seat next to the driver was reserved for a courier. The many trimmings included an automatic machine on the front bulkhead which dispensed chocolate, cigarettes and matches to travellers wishing to indulge their fancies. A second and less adventurous service had been introduced with ordinary four-wheeled Gilfords by September 1929. This ran four times a day (five on Thursdays and two on Sundays) from London, Woburn Place, to Cambridge, Gonville Place via Saffron Walden. As far as we know these ventures were not successful and when Superways Ltd. ceased trading in 1930 it marked the end of Askew's connection with the passenger transport industry. Superways Ltd. was wound up on November 15th 1932.

202 Barnardo Street, Stepney
CENTRAL

We now turn to East London proper as our survey of independent proprietors draws to its close by moving eastward from Stepney and Bow out as far as Romford. Railway arch 202 under the former London, Tilbury & Southend main line at Barnardo Street, Stepney was the base for a service which, strictly speaking, falls outside the scope of this book in that its outer terminus was Southend-on-Sea. However the dual facts that it worked on penny fare stages inside the Metropolitan Police area, and employed double-deckers of the standard London type render it worthy of a brief description.

The service was the brainchild of Philip Parsons who, in addition to being proprietor of Ye Old Town Dining Room at Leigh-on-Sea, was owner of the Royal Blue Car Company which ran charabancs, buses and hire cars from a garage at 1A Tylers Avenue, Southend. Together with two partners, Messrs. Hall and Keen, Parsons arranged to run a regular daily bus service between Southend and London under the title of London & Southend Central Motor Services. In December 1924 they licensed a Roberts Daimler XW 5644, which was in the same Royal Blue & white livery as Parsons' other vehicles except that it carried the fleetname Central in gold on a red panel. It was joined by a similar bus,

330

Southend-registered HJ 4671, in May 1925, and as far as is known these were the only two vehicles ever licensed to London & Southend Central. A limited company had been formed on February 14th 1925 under the title of London & Southend Central Motor Services Ltd. with W. E. Prime as secretary and A. J. H. Hubert as its manager.

Operation began early in 1925 and under the numbering system administered by the Metropolitan Police the service was designated 359 (Aldgate to Southend-on-Sea). Trouble was encountered right from the start because the Watch Committee of the County Borough of Southend-on-Sea refused to grant licences for operation within the town. The company, who had sought licences for four vehicles, appealed to the Minister of Transport and, pending his decision, operated the service illegally. Eventually the Minister upheld the company's appeal, and on August 11th 1925 the Watch Committee granted the licences subject to the provision that no passenger should be both picked-up and set down inside the borough boundary, within which there was to be a minimum fare of 7d. The service ran its full length only on Sundays; weekday operations were confined by the Restricted Streets Orders to a terminus in the eastern suburbs of London at the Spotted Dog, Barking and were numbered 359A, though one garage journey in each direction penetrated inwards as far as Stepney. The 1925 timetable, which is shown in abbreviated form below, indicates that one bus was housed overnight at each end of the journey. Both were kept fully occupied and the Sunday timetable was so arranged that vehicles spent alternate weeks housed in London and Southend.

WEEKDAYS

STEPNEY	8.10			
BARKING	9.00	12.00	3.30	6.20
SOUTHEND	11.35	2.35	6.00	8.45
SOUTHEND	9.00	12.20	3.20	6.30
BARKING	11.25	3.00	6.10	9.00
STEPNEY				9.45

SUNDAYS

ALDGATE	9.00	1.00	5.00
SOUTHEND	12.30	4.40	8.20
SOUTHEND	9.00	1.00	5.00
ALDGATE	12.20	4.20	8.20

The route took the Central Daimlers from Barking to Southend by way of Rainham, Purfleet, Grays, Stanford-le-Hope, Vange, Pitsea and Hadleigh. The through fare from Barking was 2s. 1d.; from Aldgate 2s. 6d. The fate of the service is not known. It probably faded quietly away some time in 1926, the two Daimlers being transferred to duties in the Royal Blue Car Co. fleet. This business subsequently passed to Westcliff-on-Sea Motor Services Ltd., who themselves built up a strong network of Southend to east London operations in the late nineteen-twenties in addition to their many other operations radiating from Southend. Having disposed of his Royal Blue Cars, Philip

Parsons—joined by his former colleague W. E. Prime—set up in business as Victoria Coaches, initially still at 1A Tylers Avenue but from 1935 at 246 Elm Road, Leigh-on-Sea.

Jacob's Garage, 343/A Mile End Road, Bow

DIAMOND/OLYMPIC

Colman Kurash lived in Bow at 38 Ridgdale Street, and when he ordered a bus he chose to run it from a local garage which had—and, indeed still has—a long and venerable transport background. Jacob's Garage at 343/A Mile End Road was a family concern going back many years. The Jacobs once ran a horse bus into London on a season ticket basis and had long owned cabs and hired out horses. It became motor orientated with the arrival of mechanical transport and thrives today under the twin banners of Alfred Jacob & Son (Jobmasters) Ltd. and Alfred Jacob & Sons (Car Sales) Ltd.

Kurash decided to trade under the title of the Diamond Omnibus Company, and the Diamond bus materialised early in March 1924 as XR 4559, a red & off-white Thornycroft on which the fleet name was carried inside a white diamond. After a matter of four weeks had elapsed, ownership of the bus passed to Joe Kurash. The relationship between the two is not known; perhaps they were father and son. Early route applications included 10A, 15, 25, 29, 33 & 101 but by 1926 the pattern of operation had become 15A/C/E Mondays-Fridays and 25/C/D Saturdays & Sundays.

At an unknown date the fleet name was changed to Olympic. This probably occurred when the bus received its first annual overhaul in about March 1925. A year after this the business passed to General who acquired the share capital of the Olympic Traction Co. Ltd. on April 10th 1926. The limited company had been formed in preparation for the takeover on March 18th 1926 and its registered office was 41 Finsbury Square, E.C.2. The Olympic staff of two drivers and two conductors—including Joe Kurash himself—passed into the service of the LGOC at Athol Street (C) garage. Not so the Olympic Thornycroft which went into Chiswick Works preparatory to its sale to Thames Valley. Its replacement, K89, was available on April 27th 1926 and worked the Olympic schedules until the company ceased to be a separate entity on January 1st 1928.

Old Tramway Yard, Grove Road, Bow

E. A. Lloyd & Sons' garage at Grove Road, Bow, was another place with an interesting transport background. A clue to its former glory lay in its postal address which, in the nineteen-twenties, was Old Tramway Yard. The trams referred to were, of course, the horse variety run by the old Northmet.

The depot site was an extensive one as can be witnessed by the size of the large modern warehouse which occupies only part of it at the present day. In the independent bus era it was used by a variety of industries concurrently. Lloyd's, who provided accommodation in their early days for Renown (October to December 1924) and Grafton (January 1925 to the middle of 1925), were a firm of haulage contractors. Also resident in the Old Tramway Yard at the same time were a farrier's business and a paint company.

366-368 Station Road, Forest Gate
UBIQUE

Sidney George Miller was a car dealer who made his entry into the bus business in October 1923 when he took delivery of AN 6120, a new Dodson-bodied Leyland. It was delivered in the name of the Ubique Omnibus Company, but before it was licensed it was taken over by a limited company formed by Miller to embrace his proposed bus activities and his existing second-hand car business. The Ubique Omnibus Co. Ltd. of 10 Little Ilford Lane, Manor Park was incorporated on October 22nd 1923 with a share capital of £2,000 in £1 shares all of which were distributed among Miller's large family, six of whom were still living at home unmarried. S. G. Miller was company secretary and William Frederick Miller, who is thought to have been his eldest son, was designated Managing Director.

The Ubique garage consisted of railway arches 366-8 in Station Road, Forest Gate which are today used by a granary company. From the start Miller usually favoured routes based upon his own area and his scheduled operation in 1926 was: Mondays to Fridays 25/D, 101B; Saturdays 101A/B; Sundays 101B. In February 1924 it was decided to buy a new Thornycroft if suitable terms could be obtained, and this materialised as AN 6452 registered on July 1st. The fleet still stood at two buses on April 9th 1926 when the share capital was acquired by General who promptly transferred the buses to Forest Gate (G) garage. The Thornycroft was quickly replaced by K412 and sold, and the Leyland departed to join the Tottenham Hotspur fleet in January 1927 to be replaced shortly afterwards by K572. The Ubique fleet remained as K412/572 until January 1st 1928.

Atlas Garage, 439 Barking Road, East Ham
Atlas Garage, Tilbury Road, East Ham
Invicta Garage, Wellington Road, East Ham
Atlas Garage, Hertford Road, Barking
East Ham Garage, Barking Road, East Ham

A whole cluster of independent garages could once be found in East Ham, all within a short distance of each other. Included amongst these were the Atlas garages at 439 Barking Road and in Tilbury Road and the Invicta garage in Wellington Road which became part of the "Batten" group of LGOC-owned companies whose Edmonton branch at Claremont Street we have already noted in chapter 7. Not all the East Ham operators became Batten-controlled, but those that did are dealt with first.

ATLAS

On May 8th 1923 Charles William Batten appeared at Scotland Yard with a chocolate coloured Leyland called the Atlas which was duly plated. Thus commenced the Atlas London Omnibus Service (to quote

Batten's original notepaper headings), not to mention an association between the name of Batten and public transport in East London which lasted right through to the nineteen-sixties.

Batten was a one-time official of the LGOC and an experienced motor engineer who had been running the Atlas motor garage at 439 Barking Road, East Ham. This was where the original Leyland XN 7748 was kept, and it was joined there two months later by an identical vehicle registered XO 5617. This second bus was jointly owned by Charles Batten and his son, David. After a lapse of nine months further new buses began to arrive, and between March 1924 and February 1925 no fewer than fourteen were delivered. Like the first two, they were all Dodson-bodied Leylands. Though outwardly all part of one fleet, the sixteen Atlas buses were, in fact, the property of a variety of people all of whom had been persuaded by Batten to invest money in buses which he would run on their behalf. Thus bus no. 3 was owned solely by C. W. Batten; 5, 8 and 12 were owned jointly by C. W. Batten and Oswald de Rosario; 4 was owned by William John Binfield; 13 was owned jointly by David Batten and Harold John Staines; and 6, 7, 9-11, 14-16 were the property of the Atlas Omnibus Co. Ltd. The registration numbers of these vehicles are given in the fleet lists.

The Atlas Omnibus Company Ltd. was formed on July 29th 1924 and had a nominal capital of £3,600. The principal shareholders were members of the wealthy Davis family of paint and varnish manufacturers who owned a factory at South Hackney. They were Henry John, Herbert Gladstone and Edwin Ernest Davis. As additional money was required to finance the purchase of further vehicles the company's authorised share capital was increased until, after three increases, it stood at £16,000. Except for £100 shares owned by Charles Batten the whole of the remainder were owned by the Davis's. Initially it had been intended to transfer Batten's original bus, XN 7748, to the new company on September 17th 1924 as his contribution to its assets, in which event it would have been the first bus owned by the Atlas Omnibus Co. Ltd. However the transfer was delayed until 1925 after it was found that the police, as was customary in the case of buses changing ownership, insisted on its being overhauled first. Next eight new buses were purchased, the last being delivered towards the end of February 1925. The other seven Atlas buses were, late in December 1924, transferred from their separate ownership by individuals to a new company in which all the people concerned were shareholders. Its title was the East Ham Omnibus Co. Ltd. and the date of registration was December 30th. The whole of the original nominal capital of £4,000 was issued together with a further £1,700 approved immediately after the company was formed. The largest shareholder was C. W. Batten with 2,418 £1 shares, and the others were likewise issued with shares in proportion to the number of buses or parts of buses previously owned. Thus de Rosario held 1,209 shares, David Batten and Binfield 806 each and Staines 403. It appears that the company did not initially fare as well as anticipated because more capital to the extent of £4,000 was needed at the end of 1925. This was issued in the form of 7% preference shares and was mainly held by a man called Edmund Harrington, although there were other small holders including the Davis brothers.

The Atlas and East Ham companies both originally had their registered office at 119 Moorgate, E.C.2. This was the address from which Staines worked as a chartered accountant. The address was changed to 111 Moorgate in October 1925.

As the combined Atlas fleets expanded there came a need for more accommodation than was available at 439 Barking Road, and C. W. Batten managed to acquire a freehold garage nearby, in Tilbury Road, from Ynyr and Florence Burges. This building had a frontage of 90 ft. on the north side of the Tilbury Road and extended about 125 ft. along the adjacent Wellington Road. The original conveyance of the property to Batten was made in July 1924, and on 27th August 1925 a limited company was formed to take it over and develop the garage business. Entitled C. W. Batten & Co. Ltd., it was owned by Batten (who held 3,000 shares) and the three Davis brothers (who held 1,000 each). The car repair and general garage business continued at 439 Barking Road.

The limited companies were run to all intents and purposes as one unit by Charles Batten who was Managing Director of all three. Fares were pooled from December 1924. The weekday operation was centred around the 15 route from 1925 onwards, the only deviation being to work journeys on the 101B and also on the 122F and 186F and 186A Saturdays. Sundays were more varied and included the 519A (which was exclusive to Atlas) in 1925 and the 122E in 1926. Prior to 1925 numerous routes had been included in the Atlas itinerary including such popular East End runs as the 10, 23, 25, 40 and 86.

In May 1925 Charles Batten approached the LGOC, ostensibly with a scheme for a working agreement for the two concerns on route 15. As far as is known no working agreement ever materialised, but instead Batten arranged a sell-out of the undertakings, the arrangement being that they would continue to appear to operate as independent entities under the continued management of Batten, although the shares would be held by LGOC nominees. The companies would continue, with their own separate administrative, scheduling and banking arrangements, and all hiring and firing of staff was to be carried out by Batten as before. The exchange of shares, giving the LGOC control, took place in April 1926. The shareholders and directors became Percy Scott Reid and Henry Charles Merrett, both chartered accountants of Merrett, Son & Street, and C. W. Batten who retained his shareholding and position of Managing Director but now as a nominee of the LGOC. Reid was appointed secretary to all three companies. Initially the registered office of each company was moved to Merrett, Son & Streets' address of 41 Finsbury Square, E.C.2., but in July 1926 it was changed again, this time to the Atlas Garage, Tilbury Road.

There was no visible sign that the Atlas buses had become part of the LGOC. Even the petrol station business continued as hitherto although it was outside the LGOC's usual line of business. Possibly many of the Atlas staff were unaware of the change at first. The reason for the continuance of the Atlas buses as hitherto, and Batten's continuing control, appears to be that Batten had been commissioned by the LGOC to acquire further independent operators who would be opposed to selling out to the combine but would not mind allowing Batten as an

335

individual to take over. Clearly some form of management contract was drawn up between Batten and the LGOC, but no details of it have yet come to light.

During 1926 nine independent companies joined the Batten Group, as it became known. Four were East End concerns (Britannia, Invicta, Grangewood and Vivid) and the other five were the companies described in chapter 7 which ran from the Upper Edmonton branch of the short-lived Batten empire.

BRITANNIA

This was the first east London operator to come under Batten control. The Britannia Traction Co. Ltd. was registered on March 26th 1926 with a capital of £5,000 and registered office at 41 Finsbury Square. This marked the transfer of ownership to the nominees of the LGOC from the original proprietors, William Henry Brown and Arthur James Painting. Brown, of 8 St. Andrew's Road, Ilford, was the licensee and their first bus, HM 3519, was licensed on August 24th 1923. The business made a slow start and continued with only one bus until February 1925 when there was a dramatic increase to five with the delivery of HM 4695/4698/4745/4746. The Britannia business was closely connected with Batten right from the start. It was garaged at 439 Barking Road and also at Hertford Road, Barking—another Atlas Garage—and later at Tilbury Road, and run by Batten for Brown and Painting who latterly lived at High Barnet and Shenfield respectively and were unable to be active in the business themselves. The vehicles were in a chocolate livery similar to the Atlases and, like them, were Dodson-bodied Leylands. Their operations were more widespread and comprised the 15A, 23, 86, 101B, 122F, 123F, and 124C on Mondays to Fridays with the addition of the 186 on Saturdays. On Sundays in 1925 the 524 was worked and also the 541A/B (in which the Atlas buses also participated) and in 1926 the 122F was worked on Sundays through to Rainham in conjunction with Atlas, plus the 15A, 23, 86 and 186. The acquisition of the business in March 1926 gave the LGOC control of five useful weekday schedules. As with the Atlas companies, Batten, Reid & Merrett were the directors and shareholders and, similarly, the registered office was transferred to the Atlas Garage, Tilbury Road on July 28th 1926.

BLUE BELL/INVICTA

The Invicta fleet was an even more useful acquisition as, in addition to its four buses, it brought an almost new garage into the group. The Invicta Traction Co. Ltd. was registered on April 6th, 1926, with £4,000 capital and head office also at 41 Finsbury Square. Thereafter its history was the same as that of Britannia. The concern originated with the appearance for plating of a peacock-blue Straker Squire on February 27th 1923. HM 2996 was appropriately called Bluebell and was owned by Arthur Albert Henniker of 152 Burges Road, East Ham. It ran in its blue livery only for a year. When it emerged from its first overhaul early in March 1924, the main colour had been changed to red and the Bluebell fleetname, no longer appropriate, had been relinquished in favour of Invicta written in Old English lettering. The fleet grew to three in

September 1924 with the delivery of Leylands HM 4481/2, and these were followed in March 1925 by another Leyland, HM 4820.

Henniker originally ran from 439 Barking Road, but he was a little more ambitious than most of his fellow proprietors and on October 19th 1925 he bought a plot of land at 56/60 Wellington Road, East Ham from a Louis Sydney de Ritter on which he had his own garage built. It was called the Invicta garage, and it was only just around the corner from Batten's Tilbury Road premises. With dimensions of approximately 104 ft. x 46 ft., the garage contained more than ample room to house the fleet of four. The surplus space in the Invicta garage made its acquisition by the Batten group a desirable proposition and on May 18th 1926 ownership of it was conveyed from Henniker to the Invicta Traction Co. Ltd. which was controlled by Batten. By 1926 the Invicta operations were on the 23, 112F and 123F although in earlier days other services had been tried including 9, 11 and 25. An interesting proposal in about July 1923 was for a circular service from East Ham Town Hall via High Street North, Manor Park Broadway, Romford Road, Ilford Broadway, Ilford Lane, Barking Broadway and Barking Road back to East Ham. It is not known if it ever operated. Under Batten control the 537E linked Barking with Dagenham on summer Sundays in 1926 along with the acquired Grangewood bus.

VIVID

The Vivid Omnibus Co. Ltd. was registered on April 10th 1926 at 41 Finsbury Square with a capital of £1,000. On this date the LGOC nominees secured control of a family business which had been run for the past year or so by William and Cyril Houchin and Mrs. Daisy May Howard from the Houchins' address at 46 Prestbury Road, Forest Gate. For £1,136 Houchin, Houchin, & Howard disposed of their interest in XP 7425, a Daimler called Vivid licensed to run daily on the 25. It was red with maroon rocker panels & white windows and was purchased in about December 1924. XP 7425 had been bought second-hand, having started life with "London" after whose collapse it languished in Roberts' works for a few months before becoming the Vivid. Vivid's garage was Batten's in Tilbury Road.

ESSENTIAL/GRANGEWOOD

The Grangewood bus added further variety to the Batten group in being a Thornycroft. XR 4694 was bought by Thomas William Lacey in January 1925 from Lewis Myers who had run it as the Essential. Under Lacey's control it later lost its blue livery in favour of red but retained the fleet name Essential. It could be found mainly on the 23 group of routes plus the 101B, though summer Sundays in 1925 saw it reaching Havering-atte-Bower on the 539. Lacey was the proprietor of a cab and motor business in Barking Road, East Ham, but he garaged the Thornycroft firstly at the Atlas Garage in Hertford Road, Barking and later nearer home in the East Ham Garage which was next door to the Atlas Garage at 439 Barking Road. After running the bus for a little over a year Lacey negotiated its sale to Batten who initiated an unusual procedure for taking it over. Back in 1924, on December 17th, C. W.

337

Batten and H. J. Staines had registered the Grangewood Omnibus Co. Ltd. with a share capital of £500. There must then have been a change of plan, for the company did not start trading. It remained dormant and on two occasions Staines began the winding up procedure. When Batten and his colleagues negotiated for the purchase of the Essential bus they presumably decided to make use of the Grangewood company in preference to going to the trouble and expense of registering a new one. But first it was necessary for the bus to be renamed Grangewood whilst still under Lacey's control. Under police regulations it was permissible to rename a scheduled bus provided the owner remained the same, but a change of ownership could only be made through an exchange of shares in a limited company if the right to the schedule was to be maintained. As soon as the bus was renamed Grangewood it was possible for the Laceys to transfer it to the ownership of the Grangewood Omnibus Co. Ltd., which was activated on March 19th 1926 with Lacey and his wife Amelia as shareholders. On April 19th Batten, Reid and Merrett replaced them and the change of ownership was complete. The history of the company, and its registered offices, followed the same pattern as the other east London companies in the group from then onwards. The Grangewood bus was moved into the Invicta Garage in Wellington Road upon coming under Batten's control.

Having disposed of his Thornycroft, Lacey continued running his taxis and hire cars and also started up his successful coach operations, which still perpetuate the Lacey name in east London. He was partnered during his period of entry into the sphere of coach operation by Oswald de Rosario, one of Batten's former colleagues in the Atlas consortium, and between them the two formed the limited company of Lacey's (East Ham) Ltd. on January 13th 1930.

★   ★   ★   ★

Batten remained in charge of the twelve companies only for a comparatively short time. The thirty-six vehicles in the combined fleets were standardised on Leylands in a brown & cream livery which so far as the East Ham companies were concerned, meant the disposal of the Grangewood Thornycroft, the Invicta Straker Squire and the Vivid Daimler which went in that order. Their replacements were YN 3800 (ex Horseshoe) on August 31st 1926, XT 5386 (ex Alberta) on March 3rd 1927, and XO 1942 (ex Marathon) on April 5th.

Batten relinquished control at the end of the day's operations on Thursday, December 30th 1926, and from the next day the Edmonton companies were divorced from the East Ham ones for administrative purposes and henceforth came under the control of Tottenham (AR) garage. The two East Ham garages continued to be used by the LGOC and received the garage codes EH (Tilbury Road) and E (Wellington Road). On January 1st 1927 the registered office of all the companies was transferred to 55 Broadway. In the same month Sefton, the Traffic Manager at Edmonton, was sacked because he had interests in other bus companies and soon afterwards Binfield and de Rosario departed likewise and for the same reason. Until then both had been working in the general office at East Ham.

One further Leyland remains to be recorded before the wholesale influx of K-types took place. XO 4835, another ex-Marathon vehicle, arrived at EH on April 11th 1927 as a spare bus for the Atlas Omnibus Co. Ltd. Between July and October the whole Leyland fleet at the two East Ham garages was replaced by K's whose details are given in the fleet lists. On January 1st 1928 the companies ceased to trade and operations were absorbed by the LGOC.

ARO

Batten must have incurred intense displeasure at 55 Broadway when he re-entered the bus business in June 1926 in a private capacity despite the fact that he was working on behalf of the LGOC as head of the Batten Group. Perhaps the abrupt end to his regime in December 1926 could be attributed to this. He was joined in his new venture by his 20-year old son Ronald Charles and also by H. J. Davis, E. E. Davis, O. de Rosario, H. J. Staines and W. J. Binfield—all formerly partners with him in the Atlas and East Ham companies—plus A. J. Painting ex Britannia. Early in 1926 these eight got together to plan the Aro Omnibus Co. Ltd. which came into existence on April 26th with a share capital of £10,000. Head office was H. J. Staines' premises at 111 Moorgate. Batten's garage at 439 Barking Road was to be the operational base as this had not passed to LGOC ownership as had the Tilbury Road premises.

Seven buses were ordered and they represented a complete change from former Batten policy in being Dennises and single-deckers at that, though the tradition of Dodson bodywork was maintained. The specification was for pneumatic-tyred 25-seaters suitable for working the 263 which was then still unrestricted. Schedules for this had been obtained in May 1926 by C. W. Batten in the name of the new company, whose first three chocolate & cream vehicles were licensed for service on June 1st. They were HM 6445-7 and they were joined on August 1st by HM 6749-51 followed lastly by HM 7040 on December 2nd. Seven schedules were held for the 263/A on weekdays. On Sundays the Company started off with its own route 553 from the Essex County cricket ground at Leyton to Hampton Court but after about only two weeks it was shortened and diverted to Clapham Common as the 555. A southwards extension of the 263 to Moorgate was refused in September 1926 because it crossed too many restricted streets. A month earlier the purely suburban route 533 had been approved but appears never to have operated.

In due course the 263 became a restricted route and Aro's seven schedules on it were regarded as valuable by Public who offered £17,500 for the undertaking. This was accepted and Public assumed operation from July 10th 1927 though the sale was not completed until August 3rd. The Aro Omnibus Co. Ltd. was wound up on August 16th 1928.

The name of Batten afterwards remained prominent in transport circles for many years thanks to the enterprise of Ronald Batten. The express coach service from Aldgate to Tilbury operated by Amalgamated Omnibus Services & Supplies Ltd. (formed March 8th 1929) under the fleet name of Battens Luxurious Coaches was well used up to the time the twelve coaches operating it were sold to London Transport in December

1933. This was only part of Batten's coaching activities which included many long-distance services developed from a three times daily London-Colchester run inaugurated on May 31st 1928.

Nowadays the old Batten group garage in Tilbury Road is still clearly recognisable. With one bay added on to the three original Atlas ones, it is currently used for light industrial purposes. The old Invicta garage in Wellington Road also lasted substantially intact until as late as 1974, having been known as the Prince Regent Laundry up to 1966, then becoming a sales and service centre for portable power tools up to the time of its final demise. The original Atlas garage at 439 Barking Road is now gone and renumbering of the premises in the Barking Road has made its site difficult to pinpoint. It was, in fact, on the corner of Latimer Avenue where a Mobil filling station now stands. The East Ham Garage—not owned by Batten—where Lacey's bus was housed for a few months, and which was next door to the Atlas Garage, now lies in memory beneath a modern discount warehouse.

Before moving on to the East Ham bus companies not connected with Batten the former Atlas Garage at Hertford Road, Barking, should be noted. This third garage in the Batten empire had, as we have already seen, housed the Britannia and Essential buses; it was also used by Martin and Gretna for part of their careers. It is now used by a firm of road transport contractors. Until as late as 1973 the name Atlas could still just about be discerned showing through several layers of paint on the side of the substantially built house (now converted into offices) which was part of the premises.

Monmouth Garage, High Street South, East Ham

The Monmouth Garage in High Street South, East Ham, on the corner of Monmouth Road, housed the Gretna fleet for part of its career. A recently-built filling station now stands on the site.

Wall End Garage, 446 Barking Road, East Ham

Piercy's garage at Wall End, 446 Barking Road (opposite Wall End Road) was the headquarters for several years of the Renown and Essex companies, and it also housed the Martin and Miller fleets for a shorter time. It was demolished as recently as 1972 in favour of a new Chevron filling station.

RENOWN

The Renown story is one of determined expansion despite the London Traffic Act and its related Restricted Streets Orders. Force of circumstances caused Renown to concentrate most of its efforts on outer suburban services and in doing so successfully it achieved what many others failed to do. It is true that the company was fortunate in serving an area of tremendous housing development which it was not slow to exploit. In the early 'twenties much of Barking and Dagenham was pure countryside, and weekend excursions to Rippleside and thereabouts brought a popular form of relief to many living in the oppressive slum areas of the East End. The London County Council's vast development plans transformed the area and between 1926 and 1933 the population in Ilford, Barking and Dagenham combined rose by 89%. In Dagenham alone the increase was 323%. Besides these happy circumstances, Renown was also lucky in having as its secretary and manager George William King who was a shrewd busman. As well as running the Renown buses he also helped and advised some of the other local bus proprietors. He was secretary of the Victory Omnibus Co. Ltd.; he assisted A. H. Martin in the formation of the Paterson Omnibus Co. Ltd., and he helped the Tatnall brothers to incorporate Tatnall Bros. Ltd. to run their Avondale coaches after their departure from the Gretna bus business. King's brother-in-law, William Llewellyn Reece, was the owner of the Renown buses. He was licensee of the Nottingham Hotel at 371 Prince Regent Lane, Custom House when the first vehicle was purchased. Dodson-bodied Leyland XU 9891 started work in October 1924 and was garaged briefly at Lloyd's Garage in Grove Road, Bow, prior to moving to the Atlas Garage at 439 Barking Road in December 1924. Its final move took it to Piercy's garage at Wall End, 446 Barking Road, East Ham by October 1926. A second, identical Leyland was registered on March 1st 1925 as HM 4754.

The first Renown bus entered service on October 12th 1924, five days after being licensed. It operated on route 15 which was then a favourite amongst independents and was duly scheduled for this route under the London Traffic Act. HM 4754 was less fortunate in that its anticipated delivery date was after the 15 had become restricted, so on April 12th Renown deposited a schedule for the 256 (weekdays) and 541A (Sundays). The 256 was not a success and before long Reece appealed to the Minister of Transport to transfer his bus to the 15. His representations must have been forcefully made for they were successful and this bus was given approval to transfer to the 15A from November 17th 1925.

No further expansion took place until 1927. Prior to this the Renown Traction Co. Ltd. had been incorporated on October 19th 1926 with a share capital of £3,000 and head office at 446 Barking Road, East Ham. The sole directors were W. L. Reece, who played no part in the business except to sign cheques and hold the licences, and his father William Reece who did no work for the company at all. Under an agreement of October 27th the two buses were sold to the Renown Traction Co. Ltd. for £2,500 satisfied by an issue of shares. W. L. Reece held 2,000 shares, W. Reece 300. Other minor shareholdings included fifty allotted to King.

The formation of the limited company heralded an expansion of the fleet from two to seven scheduled weekday buses by 1933. The entire expansion was financed by the issue of debentures co-inciding with the purchase of each new vehicle, Dodson being the debenture holder in almost every case. Firstly there came on to the scene two new double-deckers of the conventional type then becoming obsolete. HM 7440 was new in April 1927 and HM 8065 in September of the same year. The first was a Leyland LB; the other was the company's one and only Dennis. The Leyland was placed into service on the 292, which the Minister had already announced on February 4th would become restricted in Longbridge Road on April 14th. The Renown bus entered

341

service on the 13th, one day ahead of the Restriction Order becoming effective. The Dennis started work on September 30th on 26D, another route then enjoying a certain degree of popularity with the independents. This became restricted on January 27th 1928 which precluded Renown from any further expansion on it. It was becoming more and more difficult to find suitable routes for further buses, and when HM 8618 came in 1928 it was placed into service on the 266 on September 24th after being spare for five months. This new arrival was a Leyland Lion, the only single-decker ever operated by Renown. The 266 was a poor route, particularly in comparison with the lucrative 15 and 292, and its receipts in the first year averaged only 2.79d. per mile. Fortunately this figure had doubled by 1931 but was still not really satisfactory. Renown's contribution to the 266 was restricted to one bus due to a Restriction Order effective from October 31st 1928. So far in its course of expansion, the company had obtained three new schedules in two years, each shortly before the route concerned became restricted.

There now followed a lapse of just over two years before any further route growth took place. Meanwhile the fleet was almost entirely modernised with the arrival of six Leyland Titans between September 1929 and July 1931 (HV 93/453/702/898/1188/1540). This saw the withdrawal from service of the two oldest Leyland LB's and relegated the two remaining open toppers to spares. One Titan was also spare and another replaced the single-decker as the regular bus on the 266. Though the two earliest LB5's were withdrawn they stayed in the company's ownership. The original Renown Leyland was converted into a lorry after its bus career finished in September 1930. A purchaser was found for it, but it was away for only a short time before Renown seized it back for non-payment. Thereafter it remained unused in the garage alongside the second Leyland which was partially converted into a lorry in April 1931. A cab was fitted but the conversion then came to a halt and it, too, stood unattended thereafter.

Late in 1929, at the insistence of the Minister of Transport, conferences began to be held between the LGOC and the local independent bus proprietors in regard to providing adequate and co-ordinated facilities in the Dagenham area. Ultimately amendment regulations were made for Renown and the others (except for Martin) to go on to a new route 293 (Becontree Heath to Dagenham, Church Elm). In Renown's case it meant withdrawing from the 26D, 266 and 292 and placing all three buses on to the 293 (along with Miller, Peraeque and some peak hour Generals). This meant forgoing the handsome profit made on the 292 for the more modest one on the 293, but this deficiency was more than balanced out by the better use now being made of the ex-266 bus. Renown last worked the 26D, 266 and 292 on November 6th 1930 and began the 293 the next day.

Mention has not yet been made of Sunday workings which, after the abandonment of the 541A in November 1925, were mainly on the 15A though the 295 (later renumbered 233) was also operated. This continued only up to August 24th 1929 when operation was concentrated on the 15A. One bus was allocated to the 293 on Sundays after its introduction but was withdrawn in favour of the 15A in the summer of 1933.

Schedule no. 6 commenced on January 26th 1931 and to find it the company had to look south of the Thames to Rotherhithe and the 202. This was suitable only for single-deckers because of low bridges and so it was always worked by HM 8618, the Leyland Lion. It became restricted on April 29th and on May 16th the Lion caught fire in Rotherhithe Tunnel and burnt out, thus bringing Renown's contribution to the 202 to an abrupt and premature end after less than half a year. The body was a complete write off but the chassis was overhauled, presumably with the intention of putting it to further use. Somehow Renown's intentions with regard to the re-use of chassis always seemed doomed to failure, and the Lion was no exception. After overhaul it joined the two disused LB's collecting dust in the dark depth of Piercy's garage. The 202 schedule remained deposited but unworked until April 1933 when an Amendment Order was made by the Minister to allow Renown to work the 234, a short new route serving the factories along the estuary mud-flats in the Dagenham Dock area.

Much of the route, from the Chequers at Dagenham southwards, was over unrestricted roads. Renown was allowed two schedules on the 234 which were granted on the proviso that the unworked 202 schedule should be surrendered. Operation began on April 3rd, ten days before the London Passenger Transport Act received Royal Assent and effectively brought to an end any further development of independent bus operation in London. Renown had obtained its seventh and last new schedule in the nick of time. A new bus was bought to cover the additional schedule. HV 2822 was a TD2 Titan which cost £1,900, and when it was licensed on April 8th 1933 it brought to a close a whole era in London's transport. It was the last new bus delivered to a London independent and was also the last double-decker (possibly the last bus of any sort) to emerge from the Dodson factory at Willesden. This old established company, which had built London buses since 1842, had consistently refused to do work for the combine companies and with the bulk of its customers under threat of extinction, decided to close its doors for good. The body was of the old style so familiar on London Titans which had gone out of fashion when Dodson brought out its up-dated, piano-front body at the 1931 Commercial Motor Show. It was identical to the penultimate Titan, JJ 1269 of the St. George fleet, in having a nearside roller blind indicator which contrasted strangely with front destination boards, open cab and open staircase. It was almost certainly the last open staircase double-decker ever built in this country and it seems likely that both it and JJ 1269 were constructed from obsolete parts held in stock in the Dodson factory whose production was being run-down.

The Renown story now draws to a close with November 10th 1933 scheduled as the appointed day for the transfer of the business to London Transport. Ten buses, a Trojan runabout (TW 6952, bought in January 1929), and the Lion chassis passed to the Board.

At the end the scheduled Renown workings had been: weekdays—15A (2 buses), 234 (2 buses), 293 (3 buses); Sundays 15A (9 buses). The final weekly rental to E. W. Piercy (East Ham) Ltd. for the use of 446 Barking Road was 15s. 0d. per week for each bus plus £1 for the use of offices. G.

W. King, who had a contract of employment dated October 14th 1930 for fourteen years at a vast salary of £1,040 per year, passed to London Transport, initially as acting Depot Superintendent at Clay Hall (CL). In post war years he rose to become assistant Divisional Superintendent in charge of bus operations throughout north-west London. Renown took the matter of compensation to the Arbitration Tribunal with a lengthy and expensive case which occupied twenty-two days of the Court's time between November 1934 and the following February. On April 9th the Tribunal announced that compensation would be £29,772. The Renown Traction Co. Ltd. was finally dissolved on May 31st 1949.

ESSEX

Geoffrey William Nichol of the Essex showed none of the inclination to expand his activities like Reece of the Renown, who shared 446 Barking Road with him. But Nichol was first and foremost a haulage contractor and he probably regarded buses as a sideline. Nichol, who lived at 73 Holme Road, East Ham bought HM 4662 in February 1925. It was a red & white Dodson-bodied Leyland and it ran most of its career on variants of route 23. Its most ambitious working was probably the 545 in the summer of 1925. The bus later came under the control of the Essex Omnibus Co. Ltd. which was incorporated at 111 Moorgate, E.C.2. on March 26th 1926 with a share capital of £1,500. This was entirely held by Nichol and his wife Florence. On August 21st 1928 the registered office was transferred to 292 High Holborn, W.C.1.

In February 1929 the company started coach hiring with the purchase of a second-hand Maudslay, YF 1030, from the George Ewer fleet. A more important arrival was HV 190, a new Leyland Titan which took over the Essex bus schedule in December 1929 relegating HM 4662—now on pneumatics—to spare.

The two Leylands, and the now-unlicensed Maudslay coach, passed to London Transport on November 10th 1933 for a sum later agreed at £6,250. At the end the pattern of operation had been: Mondays to Fridays 151A, 223; Saturdays 23, 122F, 223; Sundays 122B, 223. On January 29th 1941 it was resolved to wind up the Essex Omnibus Co. Ltd. and a final dividend of £4 9s. 3d. per £1 share was paid out to the Nichols in January 1943.

49 High Road, Ilford

MILLER

On the London side of Ilford Broadway, at 49 High Road, was the service station owned by Frank Edgar Miller. A North Thames Gas Board car park now ingloriously marks the site. Miller was the owner of the red & white fleet of buses which bore his name. His bus history dates from February 1925 with the purchase of HM 4699, a Dodson-bodied Leyland. He lived at 5 Heynes Road, Chadwell Heath and, like Renown, originally garaged at 439 Barking Road, East Ham. He continued to garage at Batten's premises up to the latter part of 1926, by which time the bus normally rested overnight either in the Atlas garage in Tilbury

344

Road or just around the corner in the Invicta garage. Shortly before the LGOC took full operational control of the Batten empire, Miller transferred his bus to Piercy's garage. It was scheduled to spend weekdays on the 15A and 101B and is known to have run Sundays on the 295.

Nearly two years elapsed before Miller expanded his bus activities. In common with other principal east London firms, Martin and Renown, he was a late developer who was helped, as they were, by the rapid house building programme being carried on in the outer eastern suburbs. Before buying his second bus Miller inaugurated the Miller Traction Co. Ltd. on January 6th 1927 with its registered office at his home address. The whole share capital was held between Miller and his wife Florence Ellen Miller, who was appointed a director and was company secretary. Miller bought a new Leyland/Dodson HM 7254 in March 1927 which was placed into service on the 292. Thereafter he followed Renown's example by financing his expansion programme by the issue of debentures, and the first issue was made on July 27th 1927 to Christopher Dodson Ltd. to secure £1,350. This was in respect of HM 7855, a Dennis, the only one ever to join the Miller fleet. May 1928 saw the arrival of HM 8661, a Leyland Lion PLSC-type 32-seater which found employment on the 266.

In 1928 Miller bought the Ilford garage site and built a garage on it which was ready for occupation by the four buses in about March 1929. Part of it was let to the bus company at a weekly rental. It contained ample room to house seven buses, to which size the fleet eventually grew even though four was the maximum number of weekday schedules held. Four Dodson-bodied Leyland Titans came on the scene in February 1930 (VX 4269), May 1930 (VX 5859) and January 1931 (VX 8831/5). A TD2-type Titan, EV 7308, joined them in September 1932. It had the last style of Dodson body with piano front, and was all enclosed except for the driver's cabin. These five modern vehicles replaced HM 4699, the original Miller Leyland, and HM 8661, the single-decker whose low seating capacity probably dictated its sale to the Watford Co-operative Mutual Transport Co. Ltd. in February 1931. The number of spare buses on the books was reduced back to two in February 1933 when the lone Dennis, HM 7855, was sold to Martin as a replacement for a Dennis H wrecked in a collision with a tram at Ilford Broadway. In 1930 two Miller buses were transferred from the 292 to the 293 in circumstances already outlined in the Renown history. The Miller operation thus became for their last four years: Weekdays 15A/101B (1 bus), 266 (1 bus), 293 (2 buses); Sundays 15A/151B. In March 1932 the company applied jointly with Renown to operate an Upminster-Barking-Charing Cross coach service, but permission was not forthcoming and no vehicles were bought for it.

The six Miller buses passed to London Transport on August 29th 1934 and the Miller Traction Co. Ltd. was later compensated to the extent of £24,500.

16/17 Cecil Parade, High Road, Ilford
(also Plough Hotel, Mill Lane, Ilford)

MARTIN
M.T.T./GRETNA

The eleven-vehicle Martin fleet which was taken over by London Transport on June 13th 1934, ran in its latter days from a garage at Cecil Parade, Ilford High Road. Much of their operation was confined to east London and on weekdays the only vehicles to penetrate the central area proper were two buses on route 23. Though it contained no "modern" vehicles of the Titan/Lance/Regent era, the Martin fleet was a smartly kept one in a livery of red (officially described as carvermillion) relieved by ivory bands.

The legal owner of the Martin buses was the Paterson Omnibus Co. Ltd. into which had been absorbed over the years the licences of four separate groups of owners. The driving force was Albert Henry Martin of 58 Highland Gardens, Ilford, formerly an insurance agent. His entry into the bus world came in April 1925 with the purchase of HM 5039, a new Strachan & Brown-bodied Leyland first licensed on the 21st of that month. According to information supplied by Martin to the "Motor Transport Year Book" it began work the same day but this is doubtful. It ran firstly on 256 upon which it provided a 120 min. service but by 1926 it was on the 86, 123C and 186 which became restricted soon afterwards. Capital for the new venture was provided by Martin himself and by Sydney Robert Sargeant, who was also at the time working in insurance. It seems that Martin's first garage was probably the Atlas Garage at Hertford Road, Barking, though by August 1926 he had arrived at Piercy's Garage at 446 Barking Road, East Ham. By April 1928 he was back at Hertford Road where he stayed until transferring to Ilford in 1929.

The first takeover of another business came in November 1926 when, as we have already noted in chapter 2, Martin arranged to acquire A. J. Paterson's Daimler XX 1896 which traded as the Pat bus. It was necessary for Martin to form the Paterson Omnibus Co. Ltd. in order to secure the transfer of schedules, and he did so on November 11th 1926. Its nominal capital was £1,200 and the registered office was Piercy's garage at Wall End, 446 Barking Road, East Ham where Martin's Leyland was already kept and where it was joined by the Pat Daimler. The first directors of the Paterson Omnibus Co. Ltd. were Martin and Sargeant, and the nominal capital of £1,200 represented the amount paid by them to Paterson for the sale of his bus and transfer of its licences on the 23E, 86 and 186. The Martin Leyland, HM 5039, was duly transferred to the new company, which now owned two vehicles.

The business was successful and Martin wished to expand further. The 23 and 86 groups of routes were now restricted so he wisely decided to try his luck on the purely suburban 292. He was in fact the pioneer of this route for which the Paterson company bought two new Dennises, HM 7507/7999. The first dated from April 1927; the other was three months its junior. A third Martin bus began work in October 1927 on the 292 but, unlike its predecessors, HM 8092 did not belong to the Paterson

346

Omnibus Co. Ltd. It was owned by Martin in partnership with William George Aston, a Dorking businessman. For administrative convenience this bus was transferred to the Paterson company's ownership in March 1928 and in order to pay for it, but at the same time to avoid increasing the share capital of the company, Martin transferred certain of his shares to Aston. Not long after this Sargeant, who had retired to Portslade, Sussex, died and his shares passed to his executors. Two further Dennises new to the limited company were HM 8139 of October 1927 and HM 9043 of August 1928, a very late example of the old Dennis 4-ton type which, unusually for this type of chassis, carried a Hickman body.

The year 1928 saw the purchase by Martin and Aston of a substantial interest in the Gretna Omnibus Co. Ltd., a three bus concern. Like Paterson, Gretna was based at the Atlas Garage, Hertford Road, Barking to which the Martin buses had been transferred in about April 1928. Though Gretna held two good schedules and appeared to be a sound proposition Martin subsequently found that it was in a far from happy financial state.

The Gretna concern had been longer established in the bus business than either Martin or Paterson. It came into being in December 1923 and was originally called the M.T.T. Transport Company which was the name under which Edward Tatnall was in partnership with J. Mead. The partners owned two lorries for contract work on the construction of the Beckton gas works and the new Southend Arterial Road (A127). Business had at one time been so brisk that up to forty additional lorries had been sub-contracted, but as it slackened off considerably Tatnall began to see a brighter future in buswork. Tatnall contracted with J. M. Roberts to supply two Daimlers the first of which, XP 8185, was licensed on December 21st 1923 and presented at Scotland Yard for plating seven days later. The second vehicle arrived in February 1924 and was registered XR 1795. Mead left the partnership soon after this and the buses were subsequently renamed from M.T.T. to Gretna. This unusual title was chosen because it was the name of the Scottish border town where Edward's younger brother Sidney was living at the time. The business was conducted from the Tatnall family home at 7 Brampton Road, East Ham, and the buses were kept firstly at the Plough Hotel in Mill Lane, Ilford. A move was soon made to the Monmouth Garage in High Street South, East Ham, and later to the Atlas Garage at Barking. Gretna's two scheduled weekday workings were on 23, 122F, 123F and 124C. An interesting Sunday operation in 1925 was 544 from Stratford Broadway to Rainham, Essex.

Though he ran on services which others found profitable, Tatnall's financial position deteriorated steadily. This was due to the extreme unreliability of his two Daimlers coupled with the high cost of spare parts and the high casualty rate amongst these same items. In April 1925 he turned to his father, Thomas Tatnall, for financial help and in that month the latter became proprietor. In July 1925 his mother, Mrs. Susannah Tatnall, then widowed, assumed control. Even so the indebtedness to Roberts increased and in 1926 he asked for a half share in the business as a means of writing off the debts. The Tatnalls had no option but to accept and on May 19th 1926 the business was

347

reconstructed as the Gretna Omnibus Co. Ltd. with a share capital of £4,500. Under an agreement of June 14th the Gretna buses were sold to the new company as from June 1st for £3,000 by allotment of shares. Only £3,002 of the authorised shares were issued and were held equally by Mrs. Tatnall and Roberts who were also the sole directors. In about June 1926 Roberts drafted in a third Daimler which for the first time provided the Company with a spare vehicle and enabled some semblance of regular operation to be maintained. The vehicle in question was PU 5608 which Victory of Romford had sent back to Roberts on receiving a new Leyland. Though he was no longer the owner, Edward Tatnall remained as manager of the Gretna buses throughout this period.

Unknown to the Tatnalls, Roberts did a deal with A. H. Martin to sell him the Gretna business and in July and August 1928 he disposed of his shareholding to Martin and his colleagues who removed the vehicles from Edward Tatnall's control. In December 1928 Mrs. Tatnall acknowledged the inevitable and sold her portion of the business to Martin who now had one hundred per cent control. On September 11th 1928 the Gretna registered office had been removed from 7 Brampton Road to the Atlas Garage, Hertford Road, Barking, and on February 23rd 1929 it was transferred, along with that of its parent company, to the new premises at 16 & 17 Cecil Parade, High Road, Ilford.

As well as managing the Gretna buses Edward Tatnall also undertook coaching using a Daimler charabanc and continued to do so after the buses passed into Martin's control. Tatnall Bros. Ltd. was formed on June 24th 1931 to take over the coach business. Edward Tatnall's co-director in the new company was his brother Sidney whose full time occupation was conductor on the Martin buses, to which he had passed from the Gretnas. He later worked in the same capacity for London Transport. The fleet consisted of two Daimler coaches (HM 7707 & GU 2736) in 1931. HM 7707 had in fact, when new in April 1927, been licensed in the name of the Gretna Omnibus Co. Ltd. and it must have been sold to Edward Tatnall as an individual prior to the end of 1928. In June 1956 the Tatnalls retired and control of the company, which traded as Avondale Coaches, was taken over by W. T. Lacey & Sons Ltd., the successor to another London independent bus operator of former days.

In 1929 Martin made a start on replacing the non-Dennis vehicles under his control. These consisted of four Daimlers (3 ex-Gretna & 1 ex-Pat) and his own original Leyland. Four Dennis H's were ordered and carried the first covered-top bodies to be constructed by Hickman for London service. Indeed Martin was alone in ordering bodies from Hickman at this late stage. They had enclosed staircases, a feature new to London independents. VW 9014 was licensed on March 23rd and passed the police's Noise Committee on the 26th. Though in full Martin livery it was licensed to the Gretna Omnibus Co. Ltd. whose XP 8185 it replaced. Its life as a Gretna bus was short, for on April 1st the three buses and two schedules were absorbed into the parent company, and it never actually operated in service as a Gretna vehicle because police approval was not obtained for the operation of covered-top vehicles on the 23 group of routes until April 4th.

XP 8185, whose licence expired on the last day of Gretna operation, was scrapped by Martin and was not taken on the books by the Paterson Company. VX 97, VX 1361 and VX 3074 arrived in May, July and December 1929 respectively and they were followed by VX 5533 in April 1930. This was bodied by Birch, not Hickman, and it had an open staircase.

Mention must now be made of the Ilford garage from which the fleet operated in its last five years from February 1929 onwards. It consisted of a covered garage with a frontage of 110 ft. to the main road and a depth of 118 ft. capable of housing eight buses, space for the remainder being provided in an open yard adjacent to the garage. In addition a shop and living accommodation next door at 15 Cecil Parade was acquired in 1932. The freehold of the garage itself was owned by A. H. Martin Motors Ltd., a company registered by Aston, Martin and Sargeant on April 15th 1928, rent being charged to the Paterson Omnibus Co. Ltd. for housing its vehicles. The latter actually owned the freehold of the adjacent open plot of land and also of the shop. For all practical purposes the entire premises were treated as one unit, the differences in ownership being only apparent where book keeping entries were concerned.

Up to 1930 the backbone of the company's operations had been the three buses on the 23/86 groups of routes which were highly profitable. Starting in 1930 the receipts slumped to an alarming degree because of unregulated competition by parallel express coach services which were charging low minimum fares and operating as buses from Chadwell Heath eastwards. The Aldgate to Brentwood road became saturated with Hillman, Sunset Pullman and Green Line coaches, much to the discomfort of the established bus operators along it. At their maximum the combined coach services east of Stratford were averaging forty coaches per hour during peak times. Such were the inroads they made on the takings of the established bus services that receipts were halved between 1930 and 1933. The coach competition was regulated as to timetables, stops and fares in October 1933, but by this time the LPTB had been formed and the writing was on the wall for the Paterson concern. So when, in 1930, Martin saw what he regarded as the opportunity to obtain a further paying schedule, who could blame him for grasping it?

The history of this additional schedule dates back to February 1925 when Ivan Albert Maxton bought XX 195, a Dennis called Pickwick. Maxton ran it on the 27 group of routes from Dangerfield's Harmood Street premises (using Drake & McCowen tickets) until he was forced to withdraw it as a result of retrospective Restricted Streets Orders. The 525 was suggested to him as an alternative but he found this unprofitable and in about December 1929 sold the bus to Kingston-upon-Hull Corporation. He subsequently learned that the retrospective feature of the restriction order had been rescinded as a result of massive protests and that, had he remained in business, he could have returned to the 27. Somehow Maxton, who by 1930 lived in Laindon, Essex, came to the ears of Martin who agreed with Maxton—presumably for a small consideration—to resume operating Maxton's old 27 schedule on his behalf. Martin started running on the 27 on behalf of Maxton in June 1930 and on the 27th of the same month Maxton was notified that proceedings were being taken against him by the police under Section 7 of the 1924 London Traffic Act for doing so. During the lengthy legal procedures which followed Martin continued running the 27 until the case went against Maxton. The case against him was that, though he would have received permission to revert to route 27, he did not apply to do so and that, anyway, he was now entitled to no licence at all as he had allowed it to lapse for a lengthy period. An appeal was heard at the Ministry of Transport on May 24th 1932, the decision of which was that Maxton should be granted a schedule on a restricted route and that a schedule should be found for him. The schedule selected by the police was on the 525 to which Martin, no doubt with a little reluctance, transferred the bus on September 17th 1932. Shortly afterwards the schedule was changed from Maxton's name to that of the Paterson Omnibus Co. Ltd.

Court proceedings seem to have been almost a weakness with Martin. Apart from the protracted Maxton case in which he was intimately concerned, there was a dispute with Roberts over unpaid directors' fees from Roberts' days as a director of Gretna. He lost this one. Even the shop at 15 Cecil Parade came into the company's ownership as part settlement of another court action. For a long period Martin was at daggers drawn with the Hornchurch Urban District Council because he persisted in running through their area with vehicles not licensed to do so. The Council finally issued an ultimatum that legal action would be taken if Martin continued to run after March 24th 1930. Martin failed to comply and only avoided litigation in this case at the cost of agreeing to withdraw completely from route 186, to pay the Council's costs, and to pay into the poor box at court £9, this being the maximum penalty for each offence not mentioned to the justices.

Until the introduction into service of the "Maxton" bus on the 27 Martin's weekday schedules totalled eight of which three were on the 86/186 & 151, three on the 292 and two on the 23/123. Sunday operations were entirely on the 23. The 27 operation reduced the number of spare buses to one, and in 1932 Martin took the opportunity to increase it back to two when a two years old Dennis HV came on the market. GH 5342 was a Birch-bodied vehicle which Red Rover had purchased new in July 1930 and which they intended to replace with a Dennis Lance. Martin heard through Birch's, who were supplying the new Lance to Red Rover, that GH 5342 was to become redundant and he made an offer of £750 for it which Cain accepted. It joined the Martin fleet in time for the 1932 August bank holiday and held the unique position of being the only Martin vehicle with a windscreen. Not long after, the Martin fleet suffered a blow when VX 3074, the second newest of the Dennises, had to be written off after a serious collision at Ilford Broadway with an Ilford Corporation tramcar. A second-hand replacement was sought, and in February 1933 HM 7855 joined the fleet. This was an elderly Dennis four-tonner formerly used by Miller. With the spectre of the London Passenger Transport Board looming close it was probably thought not to be worthwhile buying anything better. Though quite a good vehicle, HM 7855 was not up to the condition of the rest of the Martin fleet which was always maintained to a very high standard. An extensive stock of Dennis spares was held at the Ilford garage including no fewer than four spare engines for a fleet of eleven vehicles!

The inroads into the receipts made by unregulated coach competition has already been mentioned. 1932 was a particularly bad year in which the profits slumped by 40% over those of 1931, which were themselves lower than in previous years. In November 1932 Martin approached the LGOC with an offer to sell the business. Preliminary discussions were held but the sale was not proceeded with, possibly because of the imminence of the London Passenger Transport Act. Martin was perhaps glad that he did not sell when, in 1933, receipts began to rise, and in 1934, after coach competition had been almost eliminated, the picture became very rosy. This upward trend was to reflect very favourably for Martin in the compensation calculations subsequent to acquisition by the LPTB. The "appointed day" was duly fixed as June 13th 1934 and on the midnight of the 12th the officials of the London Transport moved in and another enterprising bus undertaking ceased to exist.

London Transport acquired the eleven Martin Dennises together with a yellow 1921 Buick breakdown van with crane, XC 7609, which had been converted from a one-time ambulance. An unlicensed 1926 Chrysler saloon YN 69 and a 1927 Morris Oxford car TW 6666 also passed to London Transport. These had been charged to the business as directors' cars, mainly for taxation purposes. The weekday services acquired were on 23, 26, 86 and 292.

During its later days the Paterson Omnibus Co. Ltd. employed a staff of 71 men. There were 24 drivers and an equivalent number of conductors, together with no fewer than twenty "inside" staff. This latter figure would account for the high standard of maintenance always associated with the Martin buses, which put to shame the maintenance arrangements of some of the other London independents. Office staff was kept to a minimum with one clerk who also doubled as conductor when needed, and supervision on the road was mainly the concern of Frank Laurie, the only inspector. The Traffic Manager was Leonard Shute, who had joined in 1927 as clerk and assistant cashier and who became traffic manager in June 1933 when his predecessor, Charles Cordwell, who had been responsible for much of the development of the firm, died. Finally there was Albert Henry Martin himself, who was always active in the business, and was the only director to draw a salary which was £300 a year.

London Transport did not acquire the property in Ilford High Road although it took out a three month lease on the premises. These were later used for many years by the United Dairies as a milk depot and since 1971 have been used by a firm of building contractors. They are now known as 534 High Road. The Paterson Omnibus Co. Ltd. received a £46,000 compensation award in April 1936 and was wound up on March 10th 1939.

Chadwell Avenue, Chadwell Heath

In the nineteen-twenties Chadwell Avenue was only a short cul-de-sac off the main Romford Road at Chadwell Heath. On the western side was a dutch barn type of building erected in 1910 by Charles Gooch where formerly there had been an orchard. Gooch was a furniture remover, and his descendants are still in the same business in Chadwell Heath today, though the family's old premises were demolished in about 1966 to make way for flats. In August 1923, when R. R. Powell and his partners bought a Daimler entitled BBP, Gooch rented them space to house it at his premises, and in January 1925 it was joined by a Dennis with the fleetname Chadwell. In October 1930 Powell left Gooch's and moved his buses to Metcalfe's coachbuilding factory at Romford, whose freehold he owned.

Parsloes Avenue, Dagenham

PHILLIPS

Towards the end of November 1932 a new bus operator came on to the scene, much to the surprise of those who studied transport developments and thought that the days of fresh enterprise within the Metropolitan Police area were past. Horace Frederick Phillips of 4 Sandown Avenue, Dagenham, was the man behind the project. He lived in an area of considerable development which, even then, was overshadowed by the riverside works of the Ford Motor Co. Ltd., and he sought to provide a service from Heathway underground station (which had opened on September 12th 1932) to the Ford Works. He was not a complete newcomer to transport, having owned a coach since at least October 1931 which he used on general hire work and for which he held excursion licences from Dagenham to Clacton, Southend and Brighton. His application for a bus service was refused because of a street restriction in Heathway so he changed his plans and applied instead to link Dagenham Dock LMS Station with the Ford factory. Apart from a short portion in Chequers Lane the proposed route was over private roads the condition of which was sufficiently poor to deter the LGOC from considering a service. Police approval was received on November 23rd and the service began shortly afterwards.

Phillips had to buy a bus which complied with police requirements and obtained a second-hand Bean formerly run by W. A. Hart of Budleigh Salterton, Devon. DV 5364 was chocolate & cream and carried twenty passengers in its Tiverton Coachworks body. It was purchased through a dealer who took Phillips' Chevrolet coach RO 9162 in part exchange and scrapped it. DV 5364 was worked as a one man vehicle for which Phillips employed two driver/conductors on a shift basis. Contemporary records show it as being kept at The Garage, Parsloes Avenue, Dagenham. Though Parsloes Avenue is a long road there is no garage in its entire length today. The bus service ran only on weekdays, leaving the vehicle free for excursion work on Sundays.

The passenger traffic on route 232 was not great but Phillips struggled along. In September 1933 London Transport gave special consent for him to continue the service as they did not wish to take it over, but two months later he approached them with an offer to sell out. Phillips, who had meanwhile moved to 11 Suttons Lane, Hornchurch, was losing money steadily and on November 19th the bus ran for the last time. Its insurance had expired and there was no money in the kitty to renew it. On Wednesday, December 13th, London Transport paid Phillips a token £150 for the service and the bus but never ran either.

Holme Lodge Garage, London Road, Romford
VICTORY

Sydney Albert Simmonds of 4 Gordon Road, Chadwell Heath, was a one time ship's engineer whose interests turned to bus work in December 1924 when Roberts supplied him with PU 5608, a Hickman-bodied Daimler. Its fleet name was Victory which was an appropriate choice as any for a former man of the sea. The 25 was Simmonds' basic route of operation though he always maintained an interest in the 86. Early Sunday operations included 541 in 1925 and 552 in 1926, but he became less venturesome later in his career when Sundays were confined to 25E.

Less than eighteen months of Daimler operation almost bankrupted Simmonds, so often was it back at Shepherds Bush for repair. In despair he returned the Daimler to Roberts and threw himself at the mercy of Christopher Dodson who arranged for him to be supplied with a new Leyland instead. TW 3167 arrived from the Dodson factory in May 1926 and marked the start of a more profitable era for Simmonds. Meanwhile, the old Daimler passed from Roberts to Gretna, a concern which was to suffer particularly badly from its dealings with Roberts. A third Victory bus appeared in June 1928 and was a Leyland Lion, VW 5140, with 32-seat bodywork of Dodson origin. Initially it served as a spare bus but on May 14th 1929 it was observed to inaugurate a Stratford-Shenfield semi-express service. By April 1930 this had become Finsbury Circus-Upminster and was later stabilised as Stratford-Brentwood and lasted until about February 1932. The Leyland Lion had left the fleet by August 1930, the year in which Simmonds' greatest outlay on new vehicles took place. It began with the purchase of VX 4261, a new Dodson-bodied Leyland Titan, in February, and continued with the arrival of VX 6249/6250 in June. These were coaches and had Eaton bodies mounted on Crossley chassis, and they marked Victory's real start in coastal and private hire coaching. The Titan relegated the Leyland LB to a spare but it stayed to the end.

On July 28th 1927 the Victory Omnibus Co. Ltd. was formed at 4 Gordon Road, Chadwell Heath with a share capital of £500, all held by Simmonds and his wife Ellen Florence. In 1928 his brother, Herbert Augustine Simmonds, bought the Holme Lodge Garage at 134 London Road, Romford, into which Simmonds moved the Victory buses. Prior to this they had been garaged somewhere in Chadwell Heath. In December 1932 there was an amalgamation of interests when Sydney Simmonds became part owner of the Holme Lodge Garage and Herbert Simmonds became a shareholder and director in the bus company. The brothers granted a tenancy of the whole garage premises to the bus company at £20 a month and executed a fourteen year lease to it in November 1933. This state of affairs lasted until the two Leyland buses

353

(the older of which was still on solid tyres and unlicensed) plus a 1926 Austin car YM 4381 passed to the LPTB on November 7th 1934 for £8,250.

Shorn of its buses, the Victory Omnibus Co. Ltd. continued its coaching activities for the next two decades. Early in the war the Simmonds' left London and in December 1940 the company became a subsidiary of Gidea Park Coaches Ltd. one of whose directors was Albert Blane, a one-time Romford bus proprietor. The company was dissolved on May 10th 1968. The site of the Holme Lodge Garage now lies under part of Stewart & Ardern's modern Romford premises.

Metcalfe's Factory, Eastern Avenue, Romford

BBP

CHADWELL

Richard Rowland Powell of 21 Percy Road, Goodmayes was the licensee of PU 292 when it entered service in August 1923. He was the senior of a trio of partners of whom the other two were W. H. Bray and W. C. W. Bunning. PU 292 is worthy of special note because it was the prototype of the Roberts rebuilt Daimlers and its entry into service was three months ahead of the first of the main batch. Its Hickman body was unique in being of four window-bay construction instead of having the four-and-a-half window lay-out so familiar in the London double-decker of the time. Its livery was initially violet on the lower panels with greyish-white elsewhere except for the dash and bonnet which were silver, and it carried the fleetname BBP in intertwined letters. Its early route was mainly the 25 with journeys also on the 86 and the Sunday operation in the few summer weeks remaining in 1923 appears to have been Becontree (Three Travellers) to Chigwell Row; an almost entirely rural operation in those days. An interesting operation in summer 1925 was the 512.

In January 1925 Powell expanded his bus interests with the purchase of PU 6034, a Dodson-bodied Dennis. This was painted in a conventional red & white livery, as was PU 292 from September 1924 onwards. PU 6034 introduced the fleetname Chadwell and was jointly owned by Powell and a Mr. F. H. Whybrow who drove it. The name Chadwell was derived from Chadwell Avenue in Chadwell Heath where the buses were then housed alongside the furniture removal lorries of Charles Gooch. The fleetname Chadwell continued in use even though, in October 1930, Powell and his colleagues forsook Chadwell Avenue as their operating base and moved instead to the Metcalfe coachbuilding factory in Eastern Avenue, Romford (nowadays recognisable as the Acorn Works) of which Powell was the landlord. Each company paid Powell £65 per annum rent and also bought petrol and oil from him at ¼d. and 3d. respectively in excess of cost.

Powell worked the BBP and Chadwell companies as one unit, and on May 19th 1927 the BBP interests were reorganised as the BBP Omnibus Co. Ltd. of 111 Moorgate, E.C.2. (later 292 High Holborn, W.C.1.). The share capital of £1,000 was held entirely by Powell, Bray and Bunning. Two additional vehicles arrived in 1928, one new and the other second-hand. VW 5500 was the new one and it was a Leyland Lion

354

single-decker with Dodson 32-seat bodywork and the fleetname Chadwell. It was considerably more modern than MF 8001, a much travelled Daimler Y which was a most unusual vehicle for a London operator to buy second-hand as late as 1928. It later became even more unusual, almost infamous, in being the last of the notorious Roberts Daimlers to run in London, and even passed into the ownership of the LPTB who lost no time in arranging for its disposal. MF 8001 had begun life, it may be recalled, as Kathleen before going to Peraeque who duly passed it back to Roberts and shed no tears at its passing. Roberts ran it himself in the General Strike and then sent it across the Irish Sea to A. Morgan of Cork who presumably arranged for it to return once again to Roberts after he finished with it on June 30th 1927. BBP acquired it as a replacement for PU 292 which, for the latter part of its life at least, was powered by a Tylor engine as fitted to the AEC version of the Daimler Y-type chassis.

Powell & Whybrow now owned two Chadwell buses though only one weekday schedule was held. The BBP rolling stock was also increased to two in September 1930 when VX 7702 arrived. It was a Dennis HV with a Birch body similar to those built by the same coachbuilder on Leyland Titan chassis, and it was distinguished, like Martin's HV, by its brass radiator shell reminiscent of a fire engine.

On December 15th 1933 the BBP and Chadwell buses passed into LPTB ownership. At that time the schedules encompassed suburban routes 86A and 186A plus journeys to the West End on route 125 in the midday period on weekdays. BBP's MF 8001 and Chadwell's PU 6034 were both still on solid tyres and were unlicensed at the time of takeover. BBP also owned PU 8624, a Jowett car, which does not appear to have passed into the hands of the Board. Compensation for the BBP Omnibus Co. Ltd. was later fixed as £3,850, but the Board was required to pay only £1,250 for the Powell & Whybrow side of the business. Seemingly the Chadwell buses had not run at a profit in later years and the business thus did not rank for any payment in respect of goodwill in the final reckoning.

Star Garage, Eastern Avenue, Romford

ROMFORD DISTRICT MOTOR SERVICES

Romford was outside the Metropolitan Police's jurisdiction and was thus exempt from the London Traffic Act and its restricted streets provisions. Until the 1930 Road Traffic Act became effective in February 1931 licensing was still carried out by those local authorities who were empowered to do so under the Town Police Clauses Act of 1847. The authorities exercising these powers were the Romford Urban District Council, the Romford Rural District Council and the Hornchurch Urban District Council. At the start of our period Romford was a small country market town and it was not until the late 'twenties that it became increasingly connected to Greater London with the outward spread of bricks and mortar. Local bus services naturally sprang up to keep pace with the rapid building rate and for a number of years the green Imperials and the red Romford Districts played an important part in the transport system of Romford and its environs. The tiny vehicles which these operators started with reflect the rural nature of the Romford area

355

as late as 1927. Though the buses increased in size as time went by few progressed beyond the 26-seat stage because road improvements failed to keep pace with housing development and larger vehicles simply could not be worked satisfactorily on many of the services.

Though outside the Metropolitan area, the Romford local operators are included within this volume because their operations were absorbed into the Central Omnibuses department of London Transport in due course. Similarly the Aldgate to Romford night service of Fleet Transport Services Ltd. is excluded because it was taken over by the Country Bus & Coach department although entirely within the red bus area.

The earlier of the two major Romford operators was Romford District Motor Services. It originated with a single Ford model-T which came into the hands of Christopher Roberts of 26 Palm Road, Romford in January 1925. HJ 4156 received a new 14-seat bus body in December 1925, the same month in which Roberts was granted his first licences by the Romford Urban and Rural District Councils permitting him to run between Romford Station and Squirrels Health via South Street and Brentwood Road. This intermediate routeing was varied after three weeks to run via Victoria Road and Albert Road to Brentwood Road. On May 3rd he obtained permission to extend from Squirrels Health via Brentwood Road, Main Road and Straight Road to the Bear Inn at Noak Hill and in the same month he licensed his second bus, TW 3186. This was the first of four new Chevrolet 14-seaters with Romford-built Metcalfe bodies. Its arrival coincided with the start of a working partnership between Roberts and Richard Arthur Voss, a man more experienced in bus work than Roberts. Bus no. 3, TW 3969, was licensed in June 1926 when the service was extended from Romford Station through the town to Marlborough Road.

On August 31st 1926 a formal partnership deed was drawn up between Roberts, Voss and two others who provided £200 cash each but otherwise remained sleeping partners. One was Roberts' unmarried sister Alice who lived in Welshpool, Montgomeryshire, and the other was Ernest Hammer who owned the Pentowan Farm at Noak Hill. Christopher Roberts was put down as having a £600 (or fifty per cent) share in the partnership calculated partly as goodwill and partly as stock brought into the business. Voss was designated as holding a £200 (or one sixth) share for services rendered or about to be rendered. He put no cash into the partnership. Thus the Romford District Motor Services came into being.

More expansion was on the books for 1926. On August 30th Romford UDC gave approval for an extension northwards from Marlborough Road to Forest Road and, at the other end of the route, eastwards from Squirrels Heath to the district boundary at Ardleigh Green Road. The path was then clear for a further extension to Harold Wood whilst at Noak Hill the service was extended from the Bear Inn to the Pentowan farm. A projection early in the firm's career from Noak Hill to Ongar had been tried but was quickly found to be unjustified and a lesser extension on Wednesdays and Saturdays to Navestock was also unsuccessful. In about 1929 Romford District penetrated the Emerson Park Estate on what was to become the most profitable of its services.

356

Romford District's vehicles were always housed at the Star Garage, Eastern Avenue (now recognisable as Gosney's engineering works). On September 27th 1926 an agreement was signed with its owner, W.G. Rimmington, under which Romford District were allowed to build a garage to house five buses at the rear of the premises on a yearly tenancy of £65 per annum. Lighting was to be provided by Rimmington who in turn would be granted free garage space for his car. The rent later rose to 30/- weekly, probably with the increase in size of the fleet.

Further new buses were ordered. TW 5627 was licensed on the first day of October 1926 and TW 8532 in April 1927. These were the last of the four new Chevrolets. Further new buses were Dennises because the expansion of traffic meant that slightly larger and heavier vehicles were needed. However, before any more new buses were bought Romford District obtained two second-hand units from a dealer. VA 4584 entered the fleet in August 1927 and was a Strachan & Brown-bodied Dennis 20-seater, later downseated to 18. It was of Scottish origin to judge by its registration number, but its former history is unknown. Nor do we know the ancestry of PH 1973 which arrived in July 1928. This Chevrolet 14-seater was licensed to Romford District on July 17th in replacement of the original Ford which was sold for £40. In November 1928 PH 1973 received a new 14-seat body by Metcalfe.

On February 28th 1929 Voss terminated his interest in the business and was paid £350 for his share. Thereafter Christopher Roberts' interest was reckoned at £720 (or three-fifths) and his sister and Hammer at £240 (or one-fifth) each, which was the proportion in which they shared the profits. Voss left to set-up on his own as proprietor of the Capitol buses. His departure must have made things difficult for a while for he had been in sole charge of vehicle maintenance, timetables and the allocation of duties. Roberts, whose work had mainly been administrative such as accounts, buying and the preparation of ticket boxes, plus acting as relief driver, was forced to take over Voss's previous office activities and a foreman mechanic had to be hired. The sudden and unfortunate end to Voss's Capitol buses is described later in this chapter and he must have rued the day he left Romford District whose profits continued to spiral upwards in a most satisfactory manner.

Relative to the capital invested in the business, Romford District was one of the most profitable of all the independent bus concerns in and around London. Roberts was often criticised for paying low wages and for employing mere boys as conductors. Until the Road Traffic Act 1930 prohibited the employment of conductors under eighteen years of age Romford District took them at school leaving age of thirteen or fourteen. He answered these critisms by pointing out that he was providing employment where he need not do so. He had conductors working on 14, 18 and 20-seaters whereas the General (ex National) services with similar sized vehicles were one man operated.

In May 1930 Romford District reached its maximum operational fleet size of seven and settled to a route pattern which remained unaltered thereafter. They had always favoured a basic route from the Marlborough Road area of north Romford via Mawney Road to the centre of the town thence eastwards towards Gidea Park. The final pattern of three routes contained a long section common to all three between Marlborough Road and Gidea Park at which point the three forked. The services were:-

Forest Road to Emerson Park (Parkstone Avenue)
Marlborough Road to Harold Wood (King Harold)
Marlborough Road to Noak Hill (Pentowan Farm)

All three ran daily. The major service was the Emerson Park one which had a 20 min. headway (25 mins. on Sundays) and required three vehicles. The Harold Wood services ran hourly with one bus. Noak Hill was still almost entirely rural and was served by five journeys on Mondays to Fridays, seven on Saturdays, five on winter Sundays and seven on summer Sundays. A duplicate was allowed on three Sunday evening journeys as Noak Hill was a popular excursion spot for Romfordians on long, warm summer days. Rainham and Upminster were also once served by Romford District but were voluntarily abandoned at the instigation of the clerk to Hornchurch U.D.C., Mr. W. C. Allen. His council had become perturbed by cut-throat competition between Romford District, Imperial and National and in about 1929 called a meeting at which the parties agreed to allot routes and eliminate the competition to the benefit of everyone concerned, not least of all the travelling public.

The 1930's saw the purchase of six new Dennises, five of which were replacements for Chevrolets. GJ 2307 of May 1930 and VX 9897 of March 1931 were Duple-bodied GL's. There were two new arrivals in January 1932. EV 4010 was a 30 cwt. and received the 1928 body from PH 1973. EV 4011 was the first of three Dennis Darts with Metcalfe bodies. The other two were EV 5909 of May 1932 and ANO 794 of August 1933, Romford District's thirteenth and last bus. All the Chevrolets were withdrawn though TW 8532 remained on books in store at the garage, much cannibalised.

London Transport decided not to exercise its option to allow Romford District to continue in business as it wished to gain a monopoly on local transport in Romford, and served the firm with notice that it intended to take it over. The last day of operation by Romford District was Tuesday, July 10th 1934. London Transport took over the next day and soon found itself the centre of much adverse publicity. Of the fifteen operating staff taken over from Romford District all but four were immediately discharged to swell the number of unemployed in the area; a move which received a good deal of adverse publicity and caused much bitterness. One man to lose his job was C. G. Leaphard who had been one of the founders of the Empress Omnibus Co. Ltd. a decade earlier. New timetables were introduced which made the services inadequate and drew forth resolutions of protest from the Hornchurch Council and others. Noak Hill residents were up in arms because London Transport cut their service back to the Bear Inn, about a mile short of the former Pentowan terminus. No good traffic motive dictated the withdrawal, merely the fact that London Transport wished to operate "standard" ex-LGOC vehicles which the Traffic Commissioner would not permit to make the difficult turn by the cafe at the Pentowan. Eventually the new operator had to bow to public pressure on the Pentowan issue and the service was restored on November 28th 1934.

Not only was London Transport in trouble with the residents of Romford; it was also having difficulties with Mr. Roberts who insisted on dragging the issue of his compensation through the Appeals Board of the Arbitration Tribunal despite the LPTB's wish to avoid the expense which this involved. But for Roberts there was no alternative, because he valued his undertaking at £28,028 whereas London Transport thought it worth less than a third of that amount and would go no higher than £8,035. On July 22nd 1935 the Appeals Board set the compensation figure at £10,978 plus interest at five per cent which could be regarded as a moral victory for the Board as it was considerably nearer their valuation of the undertaking than it was to Roberts'.

115-9 Marlborough Road, Romford

IMPERIAL

Albert Edward Blane was as astute a busman as Christopher Roberts with whom he set up in competition with the granting of his first licences in April and May 1927. These permitted 27-year old Blane to run his green Imperial buses on the road from Romford to South Hornchurch by way of Hornchurch Road and Southend Road, a route over which Romford District was already running. In December 1927 Imperial was granted permission to link Romford with Rainham. This gave Romford District a chance to retaliate over Blane's invasion of their Hornchurch territory by putting buses on to the Rainham Road in competition with the Imperials. The 1929 meeting between the two competitors and National to create an orderly situation out of chaos resulted in Imperial concentrating on two basic services. These were from Marlborough Road to Rainham Cemetery and from Collier Row to Hall Lane, Upminster. In 1931 the Upminster service was extended to Cranham post office and the Collier Row terminus was projected from Hampden Hill to the White Hart bringing the Imperial operations to their maximum.

Like Christopher Roberts, Blane started with small vehicles manned by low paid staff and he made a very handsome return on his capital. The first Imperial Chevrolet was TW 9013, a 14-seater bodied by Thurgood. It was joined in July and August 1927 by VW 543/1212 which were similar though the bodybuilder is unknown. Expansion continued in 1928 with VW 3180, a Dennis GL and Imperial's first eighteen seater, and VW 7517, another 14-seater Chevrolet. 1929 saw only one arrival, YU 9022. This further Chevrolet had been built as a van in October 1927 and was given the Thurgood body from TW 9013 which became Imperial's van and maid of all work. A new tipping gear was fitted to it in October 1933.

Blane owned land at 115/7/9 Marlborough Road, Romford, on which he erected a depot with a frontage of 48 ft., depth of 290 ft. and width at rear of 64 ft. There were offices and stores, and late in 1932 he built a house at no. 119 to which he moved from his earlier home at 111. On June 24th 1933 the property was leased by Blane to A. E. Blane Ltd. for fourteen years on the most onerous terms which London Transport were obliged to honour when they insisted on acquiring the business in the following year.

Imperial began 1930 with five buses. Unlike Romford District, who reached its maximum in 1930 and whose fares and timetables remained completely unaltered thereafter, the Imperial fleet continued to grow right up to 1933. The purchase in February 1930 of VX 4253 was the first acknowledgement by Imperial that vehicles larger than twenty seaters were becoming essential to cope with the expanding trade. Metcalfe provided a 25 (later 26)—seat body on a rare forward-control A.J.S. Pilot chassis. Three Dennis 30-cwt. fourteen seaters followed which spent their latter days mostly on contract work and were the last tiny vehicles to be purchased. VX 6739/7354/7401 all arrived in 1930 and in the next year YU 9022, the Chevrolet with the body from the original Imperial bus, was rebodied though it was little used afterwards. March 1931 saw the addition of another 26-seater, VX 9932. This was a bonnetted version of the Morris Commercial Dictator and added further variety to an increasingly mixed fleet. EV 4760/6168 of 1932 were undoubtedly the pride of the fleet as well as being the largest vehicles ever-owned; they were Metcalfe-bodied Dennis Lancet 32-seaters. Last of all came a pair of second-hand Gilford 26-seaters which were bought on hire purchase from the British Motor Trust Ltd. in April (TR 8754) and June (TR 8755) 1933.

The timetable from 1931 onwards required three buses to cover the half-hourly daily frequency to Rainham and this route, in its later days, was usually worked by the two 32-seat Lancets and a 26-seater. The Upminster service also ran a daily half-hour headway and required two 26-seaters. This left a spare 26-seater and meant that latterly the small Dennises only made infrequent appearances on bus work. They found employment on a school contract to the Gidea Park College at Balgores Lane which had been worked since 1928, and from October 1931 onwards they also fulfilled a contract of a highly lucrative nature which called for two buses to run to the Ford works at Dagenham and back on weekdays.

The business was incorporated as a limited company entitled A. E. Blane Ltd. on December 31st 1931 with a nominal capital of £2,000. The registered office was 111 Marlborough Road, Romford. Blane and his wife, Mrs. F. B. Blane, were the sole directors. The day to day operations of the Company were under the control of A. M. Thrower who was Imperial's Traffic Manager and also their only Inspector.

London Transport planned to take over the Imperial operations on the same day as Romford District, but they reckoned without the stubbornness of Albert Blane who was reluctant to part with his buses and refused to agree over the amount to be paid as the initial deposit. He also proved a skilled negotiator as to the total valuation of the business, and London Transport's final payment of £16,375 was reluctantly made to avoid going to arbitration although well above their original valuation of the undertaking.

Imperial ran for the last time on Tuesday November 27th 1934. At the date of the takeover twelve buses were in stock though only nine were licensed. Two Chevrolets were disused on the premises, VW 1212 since March 1932 and YU 9022 since early in 1934. A 1930 Dennis, VX 7354, was the other unlicensed vehicle. The operational fleet consisted of three small Dennisses (VW 3180, which had received a new Metcalfe body in February 1934, VX 6739 & VX 7401), the A.J.S. (VX 4253), the Morris Commercial (VX 9932), two Dennis Lancets (EV 4760/6168) and two Gilfords (TR 8754/5). Both the unlicensed Chevrolets were partly cannibalised and Blane agreed to retain VW 1212 if London Transport took the other. The Chevrolet lorry, TW 9013, also passed to the Board, and so did a Morris Oxford saloon car, EV 6814.

The transport world had not seen the last of Albert Blane. He had already become associated with Gidea Park Coaches owned by Betts Blane Ltd. (later renamed Gidea Park Coaches Ltd.), and later became also a director of Victory Omnibus Co. Ltd., the former London independent, when it was taken over. He retired from Gidea Park Coaches Ltd. but found a new interest as major shareholder in Elm Park Coaches when it was incorporated as a limited company in January 1949. It took over the express services formerly operated by Gidea Park Coaches in 1956. Albert Blane took an active part in the life of Romford up to the time of his death on August 2nd 1963 and once had the honour of being Mayor. He had several business interests in the area and was a director of the Romford Football Club. His old Imperial bus premises in Marlborough Road still remain as a reminder of his enterprise and, slightly enlarged, are now used for light industry.

Emerson Park Sub-Post Office

STAR

Before passing to the last major Romford operator, Capitol, it is appropriate to include here a few brief notes about the earliest regular local service in Emerson Park. As early as 1910 George Heath of the Bull Inn, Hornchurch had distributed leaflets to announce a service of omnibuses or brakes on weekdays between Emerson Park, Great Nelmes and Squirrels Heath & Gidea Park Station in conjunction with the trains. This was mainly a morning and evening peak hour service but there were two mid-morning and afternoon journeys. The fare was 1d. By 1923 the service was being run by Gordon Duncan Glen of "St. Leonards", Butts Green Road, South Hornchurch. Glen was the sub-postmaster at Emerson Park, and he used a 14-seater of unknown make which he often drove himself. It is thought to have carried the fleetname Silver Grey. Glen's service, which was also mainly a peak hour operation at a 2d. fare, ran along Slewins Lane terminating at Burnt House Corner, Emerson Park. In December 1927 he sought the UDC's approval to extend via Heath Park Road and Victoria Road into Romford but because of terminal difficulties at Romford this was not approved. A revised application in March appears also to have been unsuccessful. By January 1931 the approved route was described as being from Gidea Park Station to Hornchurch (The Halt). In October 1927 Glen purchased VW 1798, a new Garner 32-seater (later reduced to 25 seats) called Star, which he kept until the operation was abandoned. Latterly, at least, the London & North Eastern Railway had subsidised the service, and when this subsidy was withdrawn so, too, was Glen's bus. This must have occurred early in 1933 for Glen disposed of the Garner in the April of that year.

Rear of 29 South Street, Romford
Romford Ice & Cold Storage Ltd., Church Lane,
Romford

CAPITOL

We now retrace our steps to pick up the threads in the story of Richard Arthur Voss, the partner who severed his connections with Romford District Motor services on February 28th 1929. He suspected quite rightly that there was great potential for a bus service northwards from Romford to the large village of Chipping Ongar and in March 1929 was licensed by Romford Rural District Council to operate two 14-seaters under the title of Capitol Omnibuses. A limited company was duly formed under the title Capitol Road Transport Ltd. An office was procured in the centre of Romford at 29 South Street and a pair of Chevrolets were placed on order with bodies built locally by Metcalfe. Garaging facilities were arranged at the rear of the London Co-operative Society and approached via a gap between the now defunct Victory Cinema at 19 South Street and a shop at no. 21. The two Chevrolets, VX 869/870, were licensed on June 13th 1929 and entered service shortly afterwards, the Romford terminus of the route being Rainham Road.

A second service was started on September 1st linking Romford with Abridge and paralleling the Ongar service as far as Passingford Bridge. Two further new vehicles (VX 2078/9) had been licensed a week previously. Again they had Metcalfe bodies and were in the same red & grey Capitol livery, but this is as far as the similarity with the Chevrolets went. In marked contrast to their predecessors, these were full-sized, forward-control vehicles based on the TSM Express chassis and their seating capacity of 32 was more than double that of the Chevrolets.

As a stimulant to traffic, books of tickets were sold at the company's office or by the conductors at the rate of fourteen for the price of twelve. This discount could hardly have been necessary as trade expanded naturally with the rapid growth of population in the Romford area as a whole. An extension of certain of the Abridge journeys to Epping in about March 1930 proved successful and a basic pattern emerged on weekdays of six journeys to Epping, seven to Chipping Ongar and 31 to Stapleford Abbots with a few journeys to intermediate points. On Sundays the respective journey totals were seven, six and eighteen. In most cases the Epping journeys started from Romford Station and not Rainham Road. During 1930 the passenger traffic completely outstripped the seating capacity of the Chevrolets and they were disposed of in about January 1931 when a pair of second-hand TSM's became available. These were KX 3852/4 and were new as recently as December 1929 having been formerly in the fleet of Wendrome Motor Services. They were 26-seaters and were built to much more of a luxury coach specification than VX 2078/9.

As with the other small Romford concerns the future for Capitol looked bright. But, early in the morning on Sunday July 12th 1931, tragedy struck. A youth was busy down a pit in the Capitol garage when, suddenly, the TSM on which he was working burst into flames. Another youth, who was washing a car down, tried to pull him clear and succeeded in getting the lad's fingers over the pit edge. But his energy was sapped by fumes and, as he escaped to save his own life, his mate died under the blazing bus. Someone called the fire brigade who arrived quickly but were unable to do anything. The garage was an inferno and burnt out completely. Two buses which were inside at the time, VX 2079 and KX 3852, were destroyed. At the subsequent inquest the youth who survived revealed that his colleague was smoking a cigarette outside the garage just before the fire, but he did not know if he was still smoking when he went down into the pit.

Though two buses survived, the Capitol service did not run again under the old management. On September 9th General began to operate the Capitol schedules using four S-type single-deckers (S384/866/873/884) which they garaged at the premises (which were demolished in 1974) of the Romford Ice & Cold Storage Ltd. in Church Lane, Romford. This prompted a petition from the residents of nearby Aveley and Dunton Roads to stop buses being garaged there in future. They presumably thought there was a likelihood of the General buses going up in a similar blaze! Though General purchased the two surviving Capitol TSM's along with the goodwill of the company they did not use them.

Legally General acted initially as managers of Capitol Road Transport Ltd. and the four S's ran with "on hire" labels. On November 13th the Traffic Commissioner gave his verbal approval for the transfer of the licences from Capitol to General and on Tuesday November 24th the Capitol licences were worked for the last time. The next day, November 25th, the services were absorbed by General who reorganised and ran them as G6A (Chipping Ongar) and G7 (Epping) using four buses from Hornchurch (RD) garage.

CHAPTER NINE

CAMBRIAN

We come lastly to Cambrian, the largest of the independents and worthy of a chapter of its own on this score alone. The main reason for omitting it from the main chapters is, however, that it had three major garages during its career as a bus operator, all of which come within different chapters in our volume.

The rise and fall of Cambrian is one of the most spectacular of all the independent stories. Cambrian was no small operator with inadequate backing; it was an extensive coach and haulage concern with resources sufficient to build up London's largest fleet of independent buses. In its short-lived heyday Cambrian's fleet of green & cream buses numbered fifty-two. Behind the whole enterprise was the flamboyant figure of Athole Murray Kemp-Gee whose name recurs time and time again in the coaching world of the nineteen-twenties. He masterminded a series of takeovers and mergers and his schemes continued unabated throughout the decade despite serious financial setbacks and lessening credibility.

Kemp-Gee, whose home was in Chesham, and who was a caterer by trade, burst forcefully on to the transport scene shortly after the close of World War One with his green Cambrian Coaches. His early exploits closely paralleled those of Samuelson, both having correctly diagnosed the great demand for coastal coaching after the restrictions of the wartime years. Both fleets expanded rapidly and included Ford vans for the collection and delivery of passengers' luggage. Very early in his career Kemp-Gee saw the potential of extended coach tours and by the 1922 season had an attractive range of seven tours of up to fourteen days duration. An eight-day tour of North Wales and the Wye Valley stopping at first class hotels for an all-inclusive charge of sixteen guineas sounds mouthwateringly cheap by today's standards. Cheap or not, a certain pioneering spirit was required to withstand the rigours of the solid-tyred and canvas-hooded charabancs of the day.

Unlike Samuelson, Kemp-Gee prospered, probably because he did not over-reach himself from the financial standpoint. But he wanted to expand, and a merger seemed the best way to bring in fresh capital. It also diversified his activities for Goods Transport Ltd., with whom he joined forces, was an established haulage concern as well as a coach operator. This undertaking had commenced on January 6th 1921 as the London & South Coast Transport Ltd. and was a subsidiary of Commercial Car Hirers Ltd. James Coventon Moth and George Ernest Marten, both of the parent company, were its first subscribers and its joint Managing Directors were Lt. Col. (retired) E. H. M. O'Farrell and E. F. Clements. The initial registered capital of £10,000 was soon increased to £15,000 and again to £17,500. By June 1921 eight lorries and twelve charabancs, all Commers, had been bought or placed on order.

It was now planned to expand yet further and, as part of the expansion, to separate the coaching and haulage activities into two companies. The existing London & South Coast Transport Ltd. was renamed Goods Transport Ltd. on July 12th 1921 to encompass the haulage business and it was planned to form a separate company, Motor Coaches Ltd., to take over the passenger vehicle assets from Goods Transport Ltd. Meanwhile debentures were issued to secure a further £15,600 to help towards the purchase from Commercial Car Hirers Ltd. of a fleet of 31 Commer lorries and two charabancs. The proposal to separate the coach business was not proceeded with because Kemp-Gee came on the scene with different plans.

Kemp-Gee and the Goods Transport directors agreed in November 1921 to negotiate the merger of their interests, and a month later the plan of campaign was decided upon. Goods Transport Ltd. would increase its share capital to £56,500 and would purchase Kemp-Gee's Cambrian Coaching Company, the title to be changed in due course to Cambrian Coaching & Goods Transport Ltd. Kemp-Gee was appointed joint Managing Director of the reconstituted company and was the majority shareholder (36,400). Commercial Car Hirers and its nominees held 15,675 of the remainder and Commer Cars Ltd. a further 2,000. Approximately forty-three lorries and seven charabancs—all Commers— were contributed to the joint fleet by Goods Transport Ltd. whilst the Cambrian Coaches rolling stock consisting of 45 charabancs (16 Commer, 13 Guy, 8 Vulcan, 5 Daimler & 3 AEC), 8 Ford one-ton vans, one Thornycroft lorry and one Lancia light van brought the joint fleet to well over one hundred units. The new title of Cambrian Coaching & Goods Transport Ltd. came into being on January 24th 1922.

Naturally a fleet of the size and diversity of Cambrian's required much organization. Its registered office was at Ulster Chambers, 168 Regent Street, W.1. but the main office was at Kemp-Gee's former headquarters at 52 High Street, Bloomsbury. This was also the chief booking office except for tours which were dealt with at 27 Denmark Street, W.C.2. The former Goods Transport Ltd. headquarters, which were at Commercial Car Hirers' premises at 112A Junction Road, Holloway, acted as north London office as well as a garage. Vehicles were also garaged at a number of other locations, notably 12 Phoenix Place, Mount Pleasant, which had been Cambrian's main depot. Cambrian vehicles had also been kept at the York Works in South Road, Southall, run by the Bicheno brothers, and at 52 Pakenham Street, Grays Inn Road. The lease on the latter was terminated very early in the enlarged company's career consequent upon the signing of a seven year lease from Christmas day 1921 of building no. 14 at the London Aerodrome, Hendon, from Graham-White Ltd. Henceforth this became Cambrian's main overhaul works and stores. A road haulage depot was later established in Market Road, Holloway, and lasted from 1923 to 1925. The company opened its own coach booking offices in Vauxhall Bridge Road and High Street, Lewisham, and established many agencies throughout Greater London.

The next major item on Kemp-Gee's agenda was the acquisition of a half interest in the assets of F. C. Landray and the formation of Cambrian Landray Ltd. The part-ownership of Landray's fleet of Brixton Belle coaches was obtained through a transfer of shares which resulted in Landray and James George Guyatt senior and junior acquiring 5,500 Cambrian shares between them. The co-operation between the two concerns, which Kemp-Gee had envisaged, never really came to much, in fact relationships between the two became increasingly unharmonious as we have seen in chapter 3. For a while the Cambrian Landray premises at Brixton provided another depot for the Cambrian fleet and was the first home for their London buses when they appeared in July 1923. The acquisition of Landray's interests necessitated a further expansion of Cambrian's nominal capital by £5,000 to £61,000, which took place on September 21st 1922. Also purchased in 1922 was the Vanguard fleet of Brighton Motor Conveyances Ltd., the first of several coastal coaching concerns in which Kemp-Gee was to have an interest. In December 1922 the registered office was moved to 52 High Street, Bloomsbury and a month later the Commercial Car Hirers representatives resigned from the board of directors though retaining their shareholdings. Kemp-Gee was now completely in charge and free to develop the business as he wished.

The way in which Kemp-Gee intended to expand his activities was made clear in his coaching timetable for 1923. Free to all passengers using the Cambrian coaches was a competition with six prizes totalling £100, plus a free coach ride. The prizes were to be awarded to those who suggested the three best routes on which Cambrian could place a new fleet of buses. Closing date was July 31st 1923 and the result would be announced in the Daily Express and Evening News. The competition literature is worth repeating in full, for it marked the start of a lengthy and unabating propaganda campaign by Kemp-Gee against the bus monopolists.

"Is it policy to permit a monopoly of the Bus routes of London? Does not clean competition ensure better service to the Public and keep down fares?

The "Cambrian" feel there is yet room for improvement and are consequently inaugurating a bus service in London. Not an oversized, unsightly, noisy, jerky, jolting starter vehicle, difficult to steer and a constant strain on the driver,

THE "CAMBRIAN" BUS

will be a bright modern, airy, easy starting, smooth running machine, built to carry a reasonable number of passengers without sacrificing space and comfort to the passengers in order to obtain an extra number of seats.

The lighting is such that you may read your paper with ease on any inside seat.

The question we now have to solve is—What is the best route?—Where are the most congested points so far as prospective passengers are concerned?—A route that is wanted morning, afternoon and evening?—a route that is not at present as well served as it might be?"

Entrants were advised to compile their lists after careful daily observations as to the points where passengers find most difficulty in obtaining accommodation. The route should be capable of convenient extension to an outlying district on a Sunday thus providing a pleasant trip into the country.

On May 1st 1923 Cambrian applied for fifteen plates for Straker Squires as the first stage of their bus campaign. Fourteen complete new vehicles were ordered from the Edmonton manufacturer, the balance to be made up by rebodying a 1920 charabanc chassis of the same A-type with a new Straker body. The first ten were ready for service by August 3rd 1923, the date on which Cambrian buses made their debut on the streets of London. Cambrian numbered its various types of vehicle in classes according to the chassis manufacturer and the first delivery of Straker Squire buses became S50-64. With the last four new Straker Squires and the rebodied one still outstanding for delivery Cambrian ordered thirteen Dodson-bodied Thornycrofts. T101 was licensed on October 23rd, four days before S61-4, and T102-113 followed between November 1923 and January 1924.

April to June 1924 saw the arrival of a further batch of new Straker Squires (S65-72) and in September and October a further seven of this make joined the fleet, bringing the stock of Straker Squires up to thirty. Of these latest arrivals S75-7 were new vehicles and S73/4/8/9 were second-hand. S73/4 were 1923 models previously run by L. M. Newstead and S78/9 were ex-CWP vehicles which had originated with Bernard Cosgrove, also in 1923. S74, at least, ran for a while for Cambrian in its original red livery with the Cambrian name painted on a green background covering the former fleetname.

Kemp-Gee now turned to Dennises, eight of which joined the fleet in November 1924 (D1-4) and July/August 1925 (D5-8). The last one was the former London & Provincial bus and was only three months old when purchased by Cambrian. It was also the last vehicle to enter the bus fleet under Kemp-Gee's control. One slightly earlier arrival remains to be recorded; T114, an ex-Shamrock Thornycroft which had passed to Cambrian in April 1925. August 1925 saw the bus fleet at its maximum of 52 units comprised of 30 Strakers, 14 Thornycrofts and 8 Dennises.

Two garages were used to house the Cambrian buses. At first the fleet was divided between the Cambrian garage at Phoenix Place and Cambrian Landray's premises at Brixton Hill. During 1924 a substantial depot was constructed at 6/12 Tulse Hill, Brixton, and it had been brought into use by the time S65 onwards entered service in April 1924. Its opening enabled Cambrian to cease garaging buses with Cambrian Landray. Petrol supplies to the garages were made daily by the company's own tank wagons which collected them from the Thames Haven refinery.

To Kemp-Gee's credit, it must be recorded that he intended from the outset to provide a frequent and reliable service on one major route with no question of pirating in the manner of many of his contemporaries. He selected the 17 as the route with the best potential. Despite strong advice from his inspectors that he should diversify his bus activities, Kemp-Gee adhered to the 17 and his only concession to the normal independent practice was that the buses garaged at Brixton operated on other services in the early morning and late evening when travelling to and from the garage. Even before the London Traffic Act came into force the Cambrian buses ran to a schedule and carried time cards. These indicated that the running time from Ealing to Liverpool Street was 70 mins. as against 74 allowed by the LGOC.

In July 1924, when the fleet stood at thirty-six units, the pattern of operation was as follows. Ten buses, all Thornycrofts, were garaged at Phoenix Place and worked exclusively on the 17. The morning run-out would be from the garage westwards to Shepherds Bush, Hanwell or Southall except for the last bus out which proceeded to Holborn Circus en route to Liverpool Street just ahead of the first bus back from Shepherds Bush. In the late evening all Phoenix Place buses ran in from Liverpool Street. Twenty-six vehicles were garaged at Tulse Hill including all the Straker Squires and a few Thornycrofts. These worked on routes 34, 59 and 88 before transferring to the 17 for the bulk of their day's work. Those on the 34 ran from Brixton to Thornton Heath, then to Liverpool Street, back to Brixton and then back again to Liverpool Street where they transferred to the 17. Buses destined for the 59 also worked southwards to Thornton Heath or to Streatham, from where they would make one direct run to Oxford Circus before becoming 17's. The 88's ran to Mitcham or Clapham Common before making a single journey to Oxford Circus. The evening run-in comprised a single journey per bus from Oxford Circus (as 59's or 88's) or Liverpool Street (as 34's). The evening service on the 17 was largely curtailed at Tottenham Court Road after 9.30 p.m., the only buses going through to Liverpool Street generally being garage buses making their last run before returning to Phoenix Place or Tulse Hill (via route 34). Sunday operations were liable to fluctuation and up to and including 1924 have not been fully recorded, although in that year Cambrian buses are known to have reached the Wembley Exhibition from Strand (Aldwych) and Brixton as routes 50 and 93 respectively.

On weekdays early turn crews finished work from 2.45 p.m. onwards and paid-in at the company's office at 52 High Street, Bloomsbury. The late turns reported for duty there but paid in at their respective garages at the end of the day. The changeover point was at the Old Queens Head in Soho Street. On Sundays crews worked a straight-through shift of about twelve hours enabling them to have one Sunday off a fortnight. Staff were paid a shade above union rates and received a bonus of ten per cent of takings over £4. In 1924 there were six inspectors including Chief Inspector Goodall, an ex-LGOC official, who was distinguished by having two gold bands around his cuff instead of one. Another ex-LGOC man, Mr. Butcher, was in charge of schedules. In overall control as Traffic Manager was L. W. Arnold. He resigned early in mid-1924 to join the abortive West End Bus Company and was replaced by R. B. Venables, but he later returned to his former post when his other plans fell through. The chief engineer was Leonard Bicheno who was also a director of the company from January 1923 onwards.

At the start the Cambrian staff were well turned-out in smart uniforms; discipline was strict and morale was high. The green Cambrian's soon became well-known on the 17, and it was quickly apparent that a regular clientele would let other buses go by in order to wait for a Cambrian. In mid-1924, after the service had been running for just under a year, Kemp-Gee gave a "breakfast" to all his staff. It was

368

given, he said, to enable him to become acquainted with his men, to explain his policy, and to ask in return that every effort should be made by every employee to encourage the company's progress on the 17. The more buses the company put on, the sooner tram competition would be eliminated.

Kemp-Gee was highly conscious of the value of good publicity and lost no opportunity to further the Company's name by gratuitous press reports or by advertising. The LGOC and its associates were always alluded to as the enemy and Kemp-Gee's advertising campaigns were always designed to malign the Monopoly. This extract from a February 1924 advertisement in "Time & Tide" is typical.

"The big battalions are arrayed against the pirate, but he is making a very gallant fight of it; so gallant that the big battalions of the enemy are demanding the aid of the licensing authority to enable them to encompass their victory. Torpedoing tactics, by themselves, have not availed; the upstarts, harried from pillar to post—followed and watched and their passengers snatched from them—yet manage to survive and keep the road . . . A year or two ago the monopolist bus driver would turn a blind eye, as a matter of course, to the would-be passenger who appealed for a halt from the pavement; and the tired and elderly, as well as the sturdy, were tacitly informed that they must wend their way to the nearest appointed stopping-place. We have changed that considerably since the advent of the pirate; to the glad astonishment of the would-be passenger, the blue, green or yellow bus condescended to stop when it was hailed."

Even the motor cycle & sidecar combination which went out to minor breakdowns with a few tools and a can of petrol carried slogans such as: "Have you had a better service on routes 17 and 59 since the Cambrian buses have been running?" and "Patronise the Cambrian and defeat the bus monopoly". The company obtained a little unwelcome publicity on October 3rd 1924 when someone mixed water with the petrol supply at Tulse Hill garage and the buses, laden with peak hour travellers, broke down one by one. As one newspaper report put it, "within an hour the dead hand had settled, and they were stilled."

Rumours about Kemp-Gee and his Cambrian buses were rife. At the height of his apparent success some said he was in a bad way financially; others said that this was a false rumour deliberately spread by Kemp-Gee himself to mislead the opposition. Cambrian were strongly tipped to be taking over Straker Squire when it became known in mid-1924 that the manufacturer was going into voluntary liquidation; a rumour which gained substance when it became known that two complete lorry loads of spares had been delivered from the Edmonton factory to the Cambrian works at Hendon. A new depot for fity buses was to be built at Southall, they said. The site was positively identified as being next to the Gem picture palace in The Green. Kemp-Gee's financial backing was from a firm of Welsh caterers called Jones and from his brother who controlled the Cambrian Oil Company—or so it was said. The truth of where his backing came from is still not fully known, though the Cambrian Catering Co. Ltd. is thought to have had something to do with it. As for the other rumours, Cambrian really was getting into a deteriorating financial state, it did not take over Straker Squire, and there was never any new depot at Southall. Yet another rumour, that twenty-five Dennises had been ordered, may have been correct but it never came to fruition.

It seems that Kemp-Gee underestimated the competition on the 17 or, alternatively, overestimated his own strength, for the buses did not prosper as they should have done. Competition was formidable especially from the LGOC and the London United Tramways with their vast joint resources. Kemp-Gee's fellow independents were also on the 17 in quantity. Take July 29th 1924, for example, when Our Bus, Pirate, New Era, Omega, Gleaner, Skylark, Cornwall, Tower, Eclipse, Magnet, Phoenix and K.B.B. were all to be found on it. Along with other independents, Cambrian indulged in a fares war on the 17 (and also on the 88) from December 2nd 1924 onwards, but this was largely self-defeating.

In July 1925 Kemp-Gee made what appears to have been a major blunder. He took a lease on a large building in Westfields Road, North Acton, which he named Cambrian Buildings. The idea was to centralise the bus fleet in a single depot, and the former premises at Phoenix Place and Tulse Hill were closed. These two had been ideally located for Cambrian operations; Phoenix Place was centrally situated and close to a busy section of the 17 and Tulse Hill was convenient for the lucrative journeys on the 34, 59 and 88. Westfields Road was far from convenient and the dead-workings to and from Brixton largely nullified the benefits formerly gained from the south London routes. The company had to go to the expense of running staff buses from North Acton to and from Brixton in the early morning and after the run-in at night. Furthermore the Westfields Road depot was badly equipped. There were no pits to enable proper maintenance to be carried out and there was no drainage, so that water from washing had to be swept by broom on to the approach road outside. This was of clay, so buses often sank up to their axles in it and lifeguards were frequently getting broken.

Gradually at first, and then at an accelerating rate, the mechanical fitness of the buses began to suffer. Breakdowns became more and more common, and as they did so regular customers began to desert in favour of more reliable transport. Even the crews, who had looked so smart in their new uniforms in 1923, began to look as dejected as the buses they worked upon because no further uniform issues were made. At the beginning of 1926 there were fifty-two buses in stock of which only twenty-seven (18 Strakers, 2 Thornycrofts and 7 Dennises) were serviceable. Of the remainder, thirteen were off for overhaul, but hardly any staff were left to carry out the work and the stock of spare parts had sunk to a critical level. The inspectorate staff had been reduced to three and there had been no attempt to adhere to the schedules for the past six months. There was nothing for it but to capitulate to the enemy. Cambrian wrote to General saying that they had found it necessary to make provision for further finance and asking whether the matter was of any interest to the LGOC. This phraseology did not fool the LGOC who were aware that the Cambrian company was going broke; their inspectors had been watching its run-down closely over the last few months. Based purely on its merits as a sound commercial venture, Cambrian was a very bad buy. But General was anxious to eliminate competition whatever the cost, and negotiations between the two parties were entered into accordingly.

On January 11th 1926 the LGOC acquired Kemp-Gee's personal shares in Cambrian Coaching & Goods Transport Ltd. in which they now held a massive controlling interest. Operation of the Cambrian buses came under LGOC supervision the very same day. D. Darvill—an LGOC man—was appointed as company secretary and Cambrian Buildings became the registered office until February 26th when it was transferred to 55 Broadway. Under an arrangement made by the LGOC with Kemp-Gee, he purchased from Cambrian all the vehicles which had been used by the haulage and coaching departments, a total of 102 vehicles, and he henceforth traded under the title of Cambrian Coaches from his old headquarters at 52 High Street, Bloomsbury. On February 1st the LGOC purchased the Cambrian shares held by Commercial Car Hirers Ltd. and at the same time took over the Central Omnibus Co. Ltd., a subsidiary of Coventons Ltd. who were themselves owned by Commercial Car Hirers Ltd. The financial affairs of Cambrian Coaching & Goods Transport Ltd. were found to be in a very complex state and on June 11th 1926, on the application of the LGOC and by order of Hon. Mr. Justice Astbury, Sir Gilbert Garney of 3 Fredericks Place, Old Jewry was appointed Receiver and Manager and Mr. Darvill was appointed Special Manager for the duration of the Receivership.

General soon set about reviewing the state of its new acquisition, which was one of the first of many and of great importance by virtue of its forty-seven weekday schedules. Sir Henry Maybury gave permission for thirty-four of the Cambrian fleet to be overhauled to work thirty schedules, the balance of schedules to be held in abeyance and considered as the Company's part of the reduction which was expected to be brought about on the Uxbridge Road under the London Traffic Act. It was originally intended to keep the fourteen Thornycrofts and eight Dennises in service, together with eight of the Straker Squires which were to be augmented by four ex-Central vehicles of the same make and in good condition. Twenty-two Cambrian Strakers could thus be put in store for ultimate disposal. This plan was revised when, in February 1926, it was discovered that Thames Valley would be prepared to take the entire batch of fourteen Thornycrofts, which meant that an equivalent number of Strakers had to be overhauled for further service. The four ex-Central vehicles (XN 7386/7891/8771, XP 849) were received on February 21st.

On December 1st 1924 route 17 had been re-defined under the Bassom numbering scheme and Cambrian's workings had been renumbered as follows:-

268 Liverpool Street to Uxbridge (Waggon & Horses)
286 Liverpool Street to Southall (Railway Hotel, Avenue Rd.)
291 Liverpool Street to Hounslow Heath

At the end of independent operation the deposited schedules showed the 286 and 291 to be the main Monday-Friday operations. The old-established operations still existed on sections of the 34, 59 and 88 though these had been expanded to run from aproximately 6.00 a.m. to 10.00 a.m. and again from 5.00 p.m. through to 1.00 a.m. at the expense of the Uxbridge Road. Since April 15th 1925 journeys had also been operated over route 38 during these same periods. The actual routes worked in each case being:-

34C Liverpool Street to Thornton Heath Pond
38A Victoria   to Walthamstow
59B Camden Town to South Croydon (Swan & Sugar Loaf)
88A Acton Green   to Mitcham

In addition, starting in May 1925, there were two daily journeys on 290A which left Strand (Aldwych) at 10.00 a.m. and 6.00 p.m. for Windsor. The basic allocation of buses was 29 to the 286 (some of which also worked 34C, 38A, 59B, 88A and 268) plus three spares, and 18 to the 291 (also 34C, 59B and 290A) plus two spares. Saturday workings were basically the same though the full service was provided on the Uxbridge Road until about 9.00 p.m. as against 5.00 p.m. on Mondays to Fridays, and the 290A Windsor operation worked throughout the day from 10.00 a.m. to 10.00 p.m. A new pattern of Sunday work had started up as late as December 6th 1925 with the introduction of Cambrian to the 549 (Southall to Stoke Newington) and buses were allocated thus:-

268   6 buses (also eve. jnys. on 286) + 1 spare
290A/291   19 buses + 2 spares
549   28 buses (also eve. jnys. on 286)

This schedule was obviously incorrect as it accounts for 56 buses (including spares) whereas the fleet total was only 52. A Sunday operation earlier in 1925 had taken Cambrian to Hampton Court from the Strand (Aldwych) under the banner of route 235A.

Under the LGOC's management the Cambrian weekday schedules were varied on a number of occasions though the number of buses scheduled never exceeded the new agreed limit of thirty. The first semblance of order came about on March 10th 1926 when revised schedules were deposited under which 20 buses were allocated to 286 (which also worked on 34C (8 journeys), 59F (3 journeys) and 88A (6 journeys)) and 10 buses to 291 (including 5 journeys on 290A). On March 31st 1926 route 185 was substituted for the 286 and was in effect a diversion of it at Southall to terminate at Western Road. At the same time the operations on 34C, 59F and 88A were discontinued. The 185 also operated shorts from Liverpool Street to Hanwell Broadway and Shepherds Bush as 185A and B respectively. On July 7th 1926 the 185 group was discontinued in favour of a resumed weekday service on 268 (Liverpool Street to Uxbridge) on a half-hourly headway and 286 which was now extended in Southall to the Swan Hotel, Norwood Road. On the same date Monday to Friday operation of the Windsor route 290A ceased. Only a fortnight later yet another batch of new schedules revived the 185 group on July 21st, and a further complete reorganisation a week later saw the return of the 59F journeys. This last schedule revision of July 28th 1926 introduced stability to the Cambrian workings at last, which henceforth were, on weekdays:-

185/A/B   18 buses including journeys on 268 and also on 184
Saturday evenings only.
291   10 buses including routes 286 and 59F Mondays to
Fridays and routes 286 and 290A Saturdays.

The main Sunday operation remained the 549 right through to the end of the Cambrian era.

A quick start was made on overhauling the vehicles, which appeared in full Cambrian livery but had the fleetname written in General-type lettering. Many of the vehicles never saw service again and General took the opportunity to remove the bodies from ten of the Straker Squires and these, after overhaul, were used as replacements for vehicles in the EP, Redburn and Western fleets. One Cambrian Straker, S58, received a body from an EP vehicle. For a few weeks the Company struggled on at Westfields Road but from the start of traffic on Wednesday, February 24th, the vehicles operated from the LGOC's Hanwell (HW) garage though they carried the garage code letters CA. On the same date the ex-Cambrian staff became LGOC employees, 79 being retained by the LGOC and 62 dismissed for various reasons. Under Cambrian's method of working each crew had stayed with its own bus, becoming spare when the bus was unavailable, but once in Hanwell garage this practice ceased.

As time passed by a variety of standard K-types were repainted green to replace Cambrian Straker Squires, and between January and March 1928 three Dennises were drafted in. By this time, however, the Cambrian livery was being dispensed with. Sir Gilbert Garney had been discharged from being Receiver & Manager on December 22nd 1927 and Mr. Darvill had likewise ceased to be special Manager and reverted to his former title of Secretary. The last minority shareholdings had been acquired by General in November 1927, making Cambrian a wholly-owned subsidiary and leaving them free to absorb it into the parent company. After all the other acquired companies were absorbed on January 1st 1928, Cambrian remained the sole ex-independent company still under General control (except, of course, Overground which was a special case). Repainting of the vehicles into General livery had commenced in December 1927 though the Cambrian name was retained on the legal-owner panel. Repainted buses were at first confined to the 291 to avoid confusion on other services where Cambrian fares differed from those of General.

On the night of April 30th 1928 the Cambrian business ceased to trade and next morning the operational fleet of 27 K's and 3 Dennises were all lettered General (except K610, 837, 844 which were away for overhaul). The final winding-up meeting of Cambrian Coaching & Goods Transport Ltd. was held on August 27th 1928.

In the meantime Athole Murray Kemp-Gee had not been inactive. He had concentrated mainly on his coaching activities which had blossomed if not flourished. On December 3rd 1927 he formed A.M. Kemp-Gee Ltd. with a nominal capital of £100. His Cambrian Coaches operated daily services from London to Kent coastal resorts and close headway local services were established from garages at Deal, Dover and Folkestone. By 1927 coastal towns from Whitstable, on the north Kent coast, round to Folkestone in the south, were served by Cambrian services, not to mention principal inland centres such as Canterbury and Maidstone. In 1928 a main central overhaul workshop was opened in Dover. The rate of expansion, which included the purchase of other operators, was very worrying to East Kent, the established major bus company in this south-eastern tip of Britain. But, as in London, Kemp-Gee over-reached himself and his empire collapsed. In May 1929 Kemp-Gee had announced that a new company was being formed under the title of London & Southern Counties Motor Services Ltd., with a capital of £350,000 to incorporate his own business and various other coastal operators from Torquay to Whitstable. The scheme was to be financed by the British Motor Trust Co. Ltd. who was a large creditor of certain of the proposed constituent concerns and particularly of A. M. Kemp-Gee Ltd. But, instead, the British Motor Trust Co. was responsible for forcing the liquidation in October 1929 of Kemp-Gee's empire. The liabilities of A. M. Kemp-Gee Ltd. had reached the astronomical figure of £82,000 of which BMT was a creditor for £57,000.

In November 1929 Cambrian Coaches was sold to East Kent and, though rumblings were subsequently heard from Kemp-Gee of further coaching schemes, these came to nothing and the coaching world lost one of its most colourful personalities.

APPENDIX I
SERVICES

a) Services inaugurated by independents

Prior to the coming into force of the London Traffic Act on January 1st 1925, independent operators almost always operated along all, or long sections of, existing LGOC services. In the early days route or service numbers were not normally displayed, but from the Spring of 1923 onwards, there was a growing tendency for independent buses to carry the LGOC service number pertaining to the journey they were making, or to the largest section of the journey if, at some point, they deviated or projected from the LGOC route. There were very few cases prior to 1925 where independents utilised service numbers or letters of their own, and such rare cases that did exist, such as with X Service, F. S. Petrol Electric, LCOC, City, Timpson and Overground, are described in the respective company histories.

The London Traffic Act stabilised weekday operations and meant that every service, even Sundays-only ones, had to be allocated by the police with a number. Under this system the numbers used by the LGOC and its associates were in the series 1 to 199, and services operated by independents followed on and were mostly in the two-hundred and five-hundred series. Sometimes a service was short-lived and its number was afterwards re-allocated, and in other instances numbers were allocated to services which, for some reason or another, the operator concerned subsequently decided not to introduce. In the list which follows all the independent services are listed together with the fleetnames of the operators known to have worked them. An asterisk (*) is used to denote routes which ran on Sundays and Bank Holidays only. Many had short workings with suffix letters, but the only ones shown here are those where the short working was the major operation, the complete route being worked only on occasions, for example only on Sundays. Several of the routes listed below never operated although they were approved by the police. These are included for the sake of completeness, and show the name of the operator who received approval for the service. Where no operator is shown, the service is one of those suggested by the police which no operator took up.

201	Swiss Cottage – Victoria (not operated)
201	Stroud Green – Edmonton (Sparklets Works)
	Admiral
202	Hampton Court – Stoke Newington
	Earl, Premier
	(renumbered 573 on 1/12/28)

202   New Cross (Achilles Street) – Rotherhithe
Allitt, Astoria & Nil Desperandum, Golden Arrow, Renown

203   Southall – Barking (not operated)
203   Kensal Rise Station – Belsize Park
Albert Ewer, Birch, Brown, Peraeque, Westminster

204   Old Ford – Sudbury (not operated)
204*   Tottenham (White Hart Lane) – Gordon Hill Station
204A   Edmonton (Silver Street) – Gordon Hill Station (applied for by Alberta; never operated)

205*   Hampton Court – Liverpool Street (Summer)
205A*   Richmond – Liverpool Street (Winter)
Red Rose, Shamrock

206*   Hampton Court – Hadley Highstone
206A   Teddington – North Finchley
206B   Twickenham Station – Hadley Highstone
Adelaide, Alberta, Archway/Birch, Drake & McCowen (renumbered 227 by 10/29)

206*   Harrow Council Estate – Harrow Weald (Red Lion)
206A   Harrow Council Estate – South Harrow Station
Loumax

207   Peckham – Dorking (not operated)
207   Barnes (Red Lion) – Richmond Park Golf Club
Turner

208   Liverpool Street – Coulsdon (not operated)
208   Pinner (Red Lion) – Pinner Hill (Golf Club)
The Pinner Bus

210   Winchmore Hill – Hammersmith Broadway (not operated)
210   Greenford (Hare & Hounds) – Ealing Broadway (via Uxbridge Road)
Royal Highlander

211   Victoria – Hampton Court (not operated)
211*   North Harrow – Northolt
re-registered July 1930 as
Pinner (Red Lion) – Northolt
Loumax

211   Greenford (Hare & Hounds) – Ealing Broadway (via Gordon Road)
Royal Highlander

212   Victoria – Wormley (not operated)
212B*   Victoria – Waltham Cross
Ambassador, CC, SB, Sphere

212C   Charing Cross – Waltham Cross
BB

213*   Plumstead Common – Westerham Hill
Timpson

214   Waterloo Station – West Ham (not operated)
214   Canons Park (Stanmore Circus) – Hendon Central
Birch, Birch (Ingarfield & Bright)

215* Victoria – Farnborough (may not have operated)
JL

217 Hampton Court – Strand (Aldwych)
Red Rose

218 Victoria – Kings Cross via Hyde Park Corner
Victoria Road Car

218E Sudbury (The Swan) – Kings Cross
Pioneer, Red Line, Ryan
(renumbered from 247A)

221 Hackney Wick – Victoria (not operated)

221 Peckham Rye – Peckham
Newlands District

223 Ealing (Argyle Road) – Hampton Court (not operated)

223 Marylebone Station – Dagenham (Church Elm)
Essex

225 Clapham Common – Harlesden (not operated)

225 Greenford (Rutland Road) – Ealing Broadway
Royal Highlander

227 South Croydon (Swan & Sugar Loaf) – Hadley Highstone (not operated)

227* Hampton Court – Hadley Highstone

227A Teddington – North Finchley

227B Twickenham Station – Hadley Highstone
Adelaide, Birch

229* Brixton Station – Wormley

229A Brixton Station – Lower Edmonton Station
Claremont (Suns.), Earl (Sats.), Prince (Suns.)

230 Harlesden – Tooting (not operated)

230* Wimbledon Common – South Hackney (Queens Hotel)
The Lea Rig

231 Clapham Common Station – Wormley (not operated)

231* Park Royal – Hampstead Heath (South End Green)

231A Harlesden (Willesden Junc. Hotel) – Hampstead Heath (S.E. Green)
Albert Ewer, Birch, Brown

232 Wimbledon Common – Dalston Junction (not operated)

232 Dagenham Dock Station – Ford Works
Phillips

233 Muswell Hill Broadway – Hammersmith Broadway (not operated)

233 Hampton Court – East Ham (White Horse)
Premier, Renown (Suns.)
(renumbered from 295 – 7/12/28)

234 Hadley Woods – Crystal Palace (not operated)

234 Dagenham Dock Station – Heathway Station
Renown

238 Highgate – Coulsdon (not operated)

238* Victoria – Epping Forest (Warren Wood House)
Albert Ewer

247 Sudbury (The Swan) – London Bridge (operated occasionally)

247A Sudbury (The Swan) – Kings Cross extended 1/4/25 as follows: —

247 Greenford Green – Kings Cross
247A Sudbury (The Swan) – Kings Cross
    Dolphin, Overington, Paragon, Pioneer, Red
    Line, The Royal, Royal Blue, Ryan, Varsity,
    Western
248 South Harrow – Kings Cross
    Royal Blue
256 North Woolwich – Cranbrook Park re-registered
    early 1926 as
256 Barking (Blakes Corner) – Lambourne End
    (operated occasionally)
256A Barking (Blakes Corner) – Chigwell Row
    Britannia, Essex, Martin, Pat, Renown
261* Hampton Court – Peckham (Lord Hill)
    C. H. Pickup
263 Muswell Hill (Alexandra Park – Edmonton Town
    Hall (not operated)
263 London Fields (Albion Rd.) – Leyton (Essex
    County Cricket Ground)
    re-registered by 1/4/29 as: —
263* Finsbury Park – Chingford (Royal Forest Hotel)
    (Summer)
263B* Finsbury Park – Chingford Mount (Winter)
    Aro, F & K, Havelock, H.H.C., Pro Bono
    Publico
266 Leytonstone (Green Man) – Chadwell Heath
    AGS, Albert Ewer, Birch, Miller, Reliance,
    Renown

267* Victoria – High Beach (Summer)
    Gordon
268 Uxbridge – Liverpool Street
    Cambrian
270 Pimlico – Bruce Grove Station
    Empress (Omnibus Co. Ltd.)
271 Shepherds Bush – Fulham Football Ground
    Lonsdale
273 Stanmore (Dennis Lane) – Liverpool Street
273A Edgware (The Boot) – Strand (Aldwych)
    Burlington
274 North Finchley – Tottenham Hale
    Admiral
275 Elephant & Castle – Hertford
    BB
278 Edmonton (Sparklets Works) – Forty Hill
    Redburn
279B North Finchley – Strand (Aldwych) (Weekday
    a.m. peaks) Burlington, Carlton, Majestic,
    Western, Overground
279E Hadley Highstone – Strand (Aldwych)
    Western
    (renumbered from 521C in 2/27)
280 Finsbury Park Station – Forty Hill
    Admiral, Redburn
284A Victoria – Hadley Highstone
    Cardinal, Carlton/Overground, Claremont,
    Dauntless, Drake & McCowen, Hav-a-ride

(later HFB), Liberty, Majestic, Northern, Nulli Secundus, Overground, PHRH (Suns.)

285 Victoria – Muswell Hill Broadway
Carlton/Overground

286 Southall – Liverpool Street
Beattie, Cambrian, Cambrian Landray, Commonwealth, Eclipse, Gleaner, Marathon, New Era, Our Bus

288* Victoria – Hackney Wick
Gray, Havelock, Primrose

288* Kew Gardens – Mitcham
Tower

289* Plumstead Common – Green Street Green

289A Plumstead Common – Bromley Common
Timpson

290A Windsor Castle – Strand (Aldwych) via Hounslow & Richmond
Cambrian

291 Hounslow Heath – Liverpool Street
Cambrian

292 Hounslow Heath – Liverpool Street via Northfields (not operated)

292 Poplar (Blackwall Tunnel) – Becontree Heath
Martin, Miller, Peraeque, Renown

293 Southall – Farnborough (not operated)

293 Dagenham (Church Elm) – Becontree Heath
Miller, Peraeque, Renown

294 Pimlico – Lower Edmonton Station
Alexandra Ambassador, City, Empire

(Newstead), Empires Best, Empress (Omnibus Co. Ltd.), The Leader, Sphere

295 Hampton Court – East Ham (renumbered 233 7/12/28)
District (Suns.), Miller (Suns.), Optimist (Suns), Premier, Red Rose (Suns.), Renown (Suns.)

297 Kings Cross – Tufnell Park
Clarendon
extended 12/25 as follows: —

297* Charing Cross – Tufnell Park
297A Kings Cross – Tufnell Park
Clarendon, PHRH

298 Acton (Churchfield Road) & Harlesden (Willesden Junction Hotel)
Commonwealth

300 Shepherds Bush (QPR Ground) – Harlesden (Willesden Junction Hotel)
Commonwealth

351 Harrow Met. Station – Hatch End Station
A & W

352 East Barnet War Memorial – Hadley Woods Station
Barnet Motor Services

352 Waltham Abbey – Flamstead End
Waltham

353 Wood Green (The Wellington) – Totteridge War Memorial
Barnet Motor Services

353 North Harrow Station – Pinner (Red Lion) A & W

354 Wood Green (The Wellington) – Hadley Highstone Barnet Motor Services

359* Aldgate (Mansell Street) – Southend-on-Sea
359A Barking – Southend-on-Sea Central

366 Leytonstone (Green Man) – Brentwood (Yorkshire Grey) Reliance

459 Coulsdon (Red Lion) – Oxford Circus (short working of LGOC 59) Cambrian Landray

510 Chingford Mount – Waltham Cross (never operated) Reliance

511 Stratford Broadway to Chingford Mount re-registered by 6/25 as:—

511* Stratford Broadway to High Beach (Summer)
511B Stratford Broadway to Chingford (Royal Forest Hotel) City, Eastern, Empire (Kirk), Fairlop, Gordon, Grafton, The Hawk, The Jockey, Lea Valley, Nelson, The PC., Prince, Pro Bono Publico, The Reliance, Supreme, Wellington

512* Stratford Broadway – Brentwood (Robin Hood) BBP

513* Camberwell Green – Chingford (Royal Forest Hotel) Fairlop, Grafton

514 Hayes Station – Shepherds Bush A1, Beattie, Dominion, T & W

515 Enfield Highway (Green Street) – Brimsdown Station Redburn

516 Ponders End (Durants Road) – Ponders End (The Alma) Redburn

517 Highgate (Archway Station) – Peckham Rye (Kings Arms) City, United

518 Hounslow (The Bell) – Southall (Town Hall) District (Weaver)

519 Wood Green – Hadley Highstone (probably issued in error – see route 354)

519 Elephant & Castle – Woodford Bridge (not operated)

520 West Kilburn (The Falcon) – Hackney Wick British Lion, Gray

521 Hadley Highstone – London Bridge (seldom operated)

521C Hadley Highstone – Strand (Aldwych) Western (521C renumbered 297E in 2/27)

522 Edgware (Station Road) – Aldgate
522A Cricklewood – Aldgate Orange (522A, Sats. only), Premier

523 Sudbury (The Swan) – Upper Tooting Beattie, Dominion, Monarch, T & W

524* Upton Park (Boleyn) – Chigwell Row
Britannia

525 Enfield Town – Cubitt Town
Alberta, Albert Ewer, Ambassador, Direct, Embassy/M & E/Morfay, G.W.L., H.M. Merry, Martin, Peraeque, Pickwick, Prince, White Star

526* Hadley Highstone – Wandsworth Bridge
526D North Finchley – Wandsworth Bridge
Alma, Archway/Birch, Clarence, Cornwall, Favourite, FW, Glandfield, Lonsdale, Paragon, Pullman, Robt. Thackray, The Royal, Royal Blue, Tally Ho!, Thackrays (J. D. Thackray), Varsity

527 East Acton (Ducane Road) – Hither Green Station
Buck, Clarence, ELMS, FW, Monarch/White Star, Pat, Pullman

528* Hammersmith (Brook Green) – Hatfield
The Royal

529 Victoria – Winchmore Hill
Admiral, AJM, Carlton Association, Empire (Newstead), Meteor, Perkins, Reliance extended from 27/11/29 viz: —

529 Pimlico – Winchmore Hill
Perkins

530* Sudbury (The Swan) – Chalk Farm Station
Varsity

531* Acton (High Street) – Chalk Farm Station
Varsity

532 Camden Town – Warlingham

532A Oxford Circus – Warlingham
Cambrian Landray, Imperial (Holliday, Bangs & Dengate, Suns.), Regal

533 Muswell Hill – Tottenham Hale (probably never operated)
Direct

533 London Fields (Albion Road) – Highams Park (probably never operated)
Aro

534* Westbourne Grove – St. Albans
Alberta, Robt. Thackray

535* Peckham (Hill Street) – Green Street Green
535A Peckham (Hill Street) – Bromley Common
British Lion (Suns.), Enterprise (Suns.), Henslowe, Standard (Suns.)

536* Highgate (Highgate Und. Stn.) – West Wickham
536C Highgate (Highgate Und. Stn.) – Elmers End
(The above is the final situation. For greater detail please refer to the City history in chapter 2).
Archway/Birch, City, United

537 Acton Vale – Rainham
Chariot (Sats. & Suns.), Essential/Grangewood (Suns.), Invicta (Suns.)

538 Stroud Green – Forty Hill
Admiral, Redburn

539* Finsbury Park – Havering-Atte-Bower
Essential

540	East Acton – Tooting (Mitre)
	Monarch
541*	North Woolwich – Lambourne End
541A	North Woolwich – Chigwell Row
	Atlas (Suns.), Britannia (Suns.), Renown,
	Victory
542*	East Acton – Keston
	Clarence
543	Uxbridge – Stoke Newington (probably never
	operated)
	Cambrian
544*	Stratford Broadway – Rainham
	Gretna
545*	North Woolwich – High Beach
	Essex
546	Camden Town – Islington (Chapel Street)
	H. M. Merry
547	Ladbroke Grove – Ebury Street
	PHRH
548	Tufnell Park – Islington (Chapel Street)
	H. M. Merry
549*	Southall – Stoke Newington
	Cambrian
550	Finsbury Park – Islington (Chapel Street)
	Nulli Secundus, Orange, Reliable
551	Whetstone – Edmonton (Sparklets Works)
	Astoria, BB, H. M. Merry, HHC, Prince,
	Redburn, SB, Silver Star, Uneedus
552*	Becontree (Chitty's Lane) – Chigwell Row
	Victory
553*	Hampton Court – Leyton (Essex County Cricket
	Ground)
	Aro
554	Hendon Station – Colney Hatch Lane (Wilton
	Road)
	(probably not operated)
	Dauntless
555*	Clapham Common – Leyton (Essex County Cricket
	Ground)
	Aro, Havelock
563*	Elephant & Castle – Honor Oak
	Newlands District
573	Hampton Court – Stoke Newington
	Earl, Premier
	(renumbered from 202 8/12/28)

b) *LGOC Services also operated by independents*

The LGOC and its associates had no copyright to the services which they developed and upon which they ran regular scheduled services. The independents were, therefore, quite at liberty to run in opposition on these services if they so wished, although their rights to do so became severely restricted after 1924 as far as weekday operations were concerned, due to the various

Restricted Streets Orders. Throughout the foregoing text LGOC service numbers are quoted where such services were operated by the various independents and the following list gives the extreme termini of each of these services. Letter suffixes are only included in relation to extensions or diversions from the basic service as operated prior to the London Traffic Act. It is not possible, in the space at our command, to quote the innumerable suffix letters introduced by Chief Constable Bassom from 1925 onwards

1.	Willesden (White Hart) – Sidcup (Wembley Summer 1924 Week only)
2.	N. Finchley (Swan & Pyramids) – Crystal Palace
3.	Camden Town – Crystal Palace
4.	Finsbury Park (Und. Stn.) – Greenwich Park
5.	Raynes Park (Junction Tavern) – Wanstead (George)
6.	Kensal Rise – Hackney Wick
7.	Acton Vale – Liverpool Street
7A.	Wormwood Scrubs – London Bridge Stn.
8.	Willesden (White Hart) – Old Ford
9.	Barnes – Liverpool St. (Week)
	Barnes – Barking or Becontree (Suns.)
10.	Elephant & Castle – Chipping Ongar
11.	Liverpool St. – Shepherds Bush
12.	South Croydon – Shepherds Bush
12B.	(later 112) Lower Sydenham – East Acton
13.	Hendon (Bell) – London Bridge Stn.
14.	Hornsey Rise – Putney
14A.	Hornsey Rise – Hampton Court (summer Suns.)
15.	Acton Vale – East Ham (White Horse)
15A.	Wembley – Strand (Aldwych) (Summer 1924)
16.	Cricklewood (Crown) – Victoria Stn.
17.	Hanwell Garage – London Bridge Stn. (Shoreditch Suns.)
17B.	Southall – London Bridge Stn.
18.	Willesden Garage – London Bridge Stn.
19.	Clapham Junction – Highbury Barn.
19A.	S. Croydon (Earl of Eldon) – Highbury Barn
21.	Wood Green – Sidcup (Black Horse)
21B	Wood Green – Farningham
22.	Putney Common – Homerton
23.	Wormwood Scrubs – Rippleside
23A.	(later 122) Wormwood Scrubs – Rainham
23B.	(later 123 weekdays & 124 Sundays) Wormwood Scrubs – Upminster
24.	Hampstead Heath – Pimlico
25.	Seven Kings – Victoria Stn.
25A.	(later 125) Becontree – Ebury Bridge
25B.	(later 26) Chigwell Row – Victoria Stn.
27.	(later 127) Highgate – Hampton Court
28.	Wandsworth Bridge – Hendon (Bell)
29.	Victoria – Hadley Woods
30.	Wimbledon Common – Hackney Wick
31.	Camden Town – Chelsea

383

32. Turnham Green – Wimbledon Common
33. Liverpool Street – Hampton Court
34. Liverpool Street – South Croydon
35. Kew Gardens – Highams Park
35A. Camberwell Green – Epping Forest (Wake Arms)
36. W. Kilburn (Falcon) – Hither Green Stn.
37. Rotherhithe – Hounslow Heath
38. Victoria Stn. – Chingford (R.F.H.)
38B. (later 138) Victoria Stn. – Loughton (Crown)
39. Southfields Stn. – Edmonton (Angel)
40. W. Norwood (Rosendale) – Epping Forest (Warren Wood House)
42. Clapham Common – Finsbury Park (Und. Stn.)
45. Clapham Common – Kings Cross
46. Kensal Rise – Victoria Stn.
47. Shoreditch – Green Street Green
49. Wembley – Lewisham
50. Streatham (Greyhound) – Lonesome
51. Cricklewood – Wimbledon Common (1923)
51. Cricklewood – Putney Bridge Stn. (1924)
52. Ladbroke Grove – Victoria Stn.
54. Oxford Circus – Riddlesdown (Summer 1924)
58. Walthamstow – Wembley
59. Camden Town – Reigate
59B. (later 159) Camden Town – Godstone
60. Colindale Stn. – Old Ford
68. Wembley – South Croydon
69. Camberwell Green – Wormley
70. Clapham Common – Dorking

71. Finsbury Park – St. Albans
72. Finsbury Park – Wormley
73. Hampton Court – Stoke Newington
73A. (later 173) Kingston – Stoke Newington
74. Camden Town – Roehampton
75. Croydon – Woolwich
76. Edmonton (Angel) – Victoria Stn.
77. Burgh Heath – Kings Cross
78. Shoreditch – Dulwich (Grove Hotel)
81. Hounslow Garage – Windsor
84. Golders Green – St. Albans
86. (ex 26) Stratford – Brentwood
186. (ex 26A) Stratford – Upminster
88. Acton Green – Belmont
93. Wembley – Wimbledon Stn.
96. Putney – High Beach
97. Ealing – Brentford
100. (ex 10A) Elephant & Castle – Epping Town
101. North Woolwich – Lambourne End
106. Finsbury Park – Blackwall Tunnel
128. Camberwell Green – Lower Kingswood
140. South Harrow – Watford Junction
142. Watford – Kilburn Park
146. Lewisham – Keston
170. Southall – Shoreditch
184. Southall – London Bridge Stn.
185. Southall – Liverpool Street
192. Harrow Weald – Wembley (1923)
408A West Croydon – Beddington (East Surrey)

The tickets of the London independent bus operators of 1922–34 were generally of a rather stereotyped pattern, at least as far as the fronts were concerned. For much of the period the majority of tickets in use were very similar to the numerical stage tickets used by the General for emergency purposes and on new routes before the geographical tickets for them were ready. Though many independent tickets had the operator's fleetname in the centre column with stage numbers running from 1 to 30 at the sides, quite a large number of operators always used pure "stock" tickets of this same layout but with the words OMNIBUS TICKET in the centre column. These could be bought on demand from most of the recognised ticket printers. Many were rescued from anonymity by the printed material on the backs. This would sometimes be the owner's address and telephone number, or an advertisement offering to hire the bus or buses. In some cases an appeal was made to passengers on patriotic or sympathetic grounds, while slogans advertising the particular service were sometimes used. Before 1925 ninety percent of the tickets used were of the Bell Punch Company's standard length, 2½ inches, and in almost the same ratio the colours used for the different ticket values were the same as those used by the General, particularly as regards the lower values from a penny to sixpence. However, there were individualists, as might be expected, and the first was the famous Chocolate Express.

Partridge and his partners were evidently determined right from the outset to be different. On their tickets the layout and value colours owed nothing to the LGOC. Their first set was printed by the Bell Punch Co. Ltd. and had the title EXPRESS OMNIBUS COMPANY in the centre column with stage numbers from 1 to 13 down on the left and 1 to 13 up on the right. Colours used at first were 1d. blue, 1½d. pink, 2d. green, 3d. grey, 4d. yellow, 5d. salmon, 6d. magenta (a somewhat lighter shade of the old LGOC 1/– colour). The 9d. was mauve and a later 1/– was blue, and other colours also differed. Over the years the colours varied occasionally, but not till the last years of Chocolate Express operation did the three lower values correspond with the LGOC colours of 1d. white, 2d. blue, and 3d. pink. Higher values remained different to the end. The fare value overprints on this first set and one or two later sets also differed in that instead of using a large skeleton figure, the value was expressed vertically down the ticket in a red overprint as 2d. FARE or whatever the value might be. After the first set, two sets followed of what were basically stock tickets with the words OMNIBUS TICKET in the centre, but with the same unusual type of fare overprint. Stage numbers were now 1 to 12. No other operator is known to have used this type of ticket, and if any did it is almost certain they would have been borrowed from Chocolate Express. A subsequent set was printed by Williamson of Ashton-under-Lyne, and another by the Punch & Ticket Company. After these tickets came two more sets, this time from the Bell Punch Company. These again had OMNIBUS TICKET in the centre but they carried more normal fare value overprints at first using large solid figures, but later came skeleton figures as used by the LGOC. Stage numbers now ran from 1 to 24 starting at the bottom left and finishing at bottom right as 24. These again were of a distinctive type not known to be used by any other operator. One or two values carried on the back an advertisement by Chocolate Express offering buses for hire. With one of these as a guide it is possible for the uninitiated to recognise the other tickets in the sets. After this titled tickets were used still with value colours above 3d. differing from the LGOC standard range.

Among other operators using rather distinctive tickets in the early days may be mentioned THE PRIMROSE, to use the title which appeared on them. Primrose used a numerical set by the Punch & Ticket Company of a type more common in the provinces. The penny value had stages from 1 to 17 gradually diminishing on each value till the 9d. which carried only stage number 1 on each side of the ticket. Later Williamson-printed tickets of this operator also differed from the more usual types used by others.

The Orange Service buses of Haywood and Nowell also had a distinctive type of ticket throughout their career. These, at the top of the ticket underneath the serial number, had an overprinted oblong orange block about 1 inch x ½ inch with the words THE ORANGE SERVICE in negative type. Although the centre column proclaimed the fact that it was an OMNIBUS TICKET the operator's name and address was also printed in tiny type. Many early Orange Service tickets carried adverts for one of the operator's other business interests, the manufacture and sale of hand made cigarettes.

New Era used tickets with rather unusual features. In the concern's earliest days Bell Punch tickets were used which appear to have carried the individual conductor's initials as the letters preceding the tickets' serials. Such combinations as AB, AH, SH, VH, continually occur on all lower values and can only be accounted for by studying the initials of several of the men concerned in running the buses involved. These were Victor Hughes (VH), Stanley Handford (SH), Albert Brookes (AB) and Arthur Hughes (AH). This system was discontinued on later sets, but another distinctive feature used on a second set of numerical stage tickets was the use of letters running through the alphabet from A to Z to denote the stage points, a method used by only one other independent, Commonwealth.

One particular type of stock ticket deserves special mention. This, as far as is known to the writer, was always produced by Bell Punch, and was to all intents and purposes a standard stock ticket, though sometimes of differing layouts. In the centre column the words OMNIBUS TICKET always appeared but at the bottom of that column was a tiny box in which the initials of the owner, or perhaps in some cases the manager, of the particular bus was printed. Known examples are WA (William Allen-Premier), RT (Robert Thackray), RN (Robert Neal – Eclipse), CWB (Charles William Batten – Atlas) and WHB (William Henry Brown – Britannia).

A further operator who was an individualist, both as regards his buses and his tickets, was C. H. Pickup. In his early days numerical

Williamson stage tickets were used on which the stage numbers ran from 1 to 26. The operator's initials and address were in the centre column on the fronts while the backs generally, but not always, carried Pickup's name and address. The colours up to 4d. were as LGOC, but above that the colours were entirely different. Unusually for a London independent, the ticket length was 2.3/8th inches. Generally speaking most other independent tickets were 2½ inches if produced by the Bell Punch Company or the Punch & Ticket Company, or 2.5/8th inches in the case of Williamson printings. Several different varieties of Pickup's Williamson printed tickets existed. In later days Pickup changed over to tickets printed by Bell Punch which, in the case of the numerical stage issues, were of 2¼ inch length. Pickup used "geographical" tickets on some of his operations. These tickets were individually printed for each service, and they carried full details of each farestage along the line of route. Geographical tickets had long been favoured by the LGOC but, as far as can be ascertained by the writer, they did not come into use by independents until 1925.

Pickup's geographical stage tickets varied in length according to their route. He used them on the three main services on which his buses worked, and a very distinctive feature was the means used to distinguish the sets from one another apart from the use of the service number. On route 37B, which carried stages from Richmond to Peckham, an overprinted green diagonal hatching was used covering the tickets' serial numbers. On route 70 (Clapham Common and Dorking) a solid green oblong overprint was used, while tickets on route 21D (Wood Green and Lewisham) were plain. The short Bell Punch numerical stage tickets were used on routes such as 36 and 73 where Pickup had odd journeys, and were also available for emergency use.

From 1925 onwards geographically named stage tickets were used by operators on service 17. The unusual feature of these was the printing of the first letter of the stage name in capitals sideways alongside the stage name. This method was used by all independents who used geographical tickets on the Uxbridge Road except Cambrian.

Certain special issues were made about which little information exists and which are difficult to clarify. Chiefly these are the returns, workman returns and exchanges used on route 511 from Chingford to Stratford Broadway. At least sixteen independent operators are known to have worked on this route from 1925 onwards and most of them probably issued return tickets which were available for return on the buses of any other owner. Some operators, among whom were Fairlop, Nelson and Pro Bono Publico, used at least for a time a series of return tickets headed NEW SERVICE OMNIBUSES. Others used returns and exchanges carrying the issuing operator's title. Some of this type of return listed on their backs the fleetnames of the buses on which the ticket would be accepted for the return journey. One well-known operator on the 511, Prince, did not appear among the 14 names listed, although some single tickets issued by Reliance stated on their backs "Cheap Return Tickets issued available on all buses on 511 route." As return tickets were torn in half and one half handed back with an exchange ticket, few 511 returns are known to exist.

The independents on 511 had another rare habit, the issue of half-penny value tickets, often titled. Only one other instance of this value of ticket being used by London independents is known. This was on route 297 where a halfpenny fare existed between Tufnell Park Station and Tufnell Park Hotel. Two operators were concerned, Clarendon and P.H.R.H.

Apart from the 511, return tickets from independent operators were rare. Only three other issues are known, namely those used on the City, Birch and United joint 536 service, a series used by Timpson's on 213/289 with a fare range from fivepence to ninepence, and some issued between Charing Cross and Forest Hill on route 12 by E.P. and Fleet jointly. On the 536, City return tickets are believed to have been used by all the three operators who worked it though Birch geographical exchange tickets are known.

In the earliest days of the London independents, three well-known printers catered for the whole of the ticket requirements. In all probability the Punch & Ticket Co. Ltd. and the Bell Punch Co. Ltd. did 85% of the work, the remainder being produced by Williamson of Ashton-under-Lyne. The Punch & Ticket Co. first possibly had a larger share of the work than the others, but the position changed after a year or two. Over the years the number of tickets printed by Bell Punch gradually increased towards the end of the independent era, and after 1930 the latter company produced probably as much as ninety percent of the tickets then in use. Very few of the operators who changed over to Bell Punch ever changed back. The position was complicated from 1925 onwards by the appearance on the scene of a London printer whose tickets were almost unknown outside the London area. This was John Knight of 62 New Road, Edmonton, who later traded as the Knight Ticket & Label Company of 857 High Road, Tottenham. Earlier tickets of Knight's bear addresses at 85 New Oxford Street, W.C. and 285 High Holborn, the latter being a ticket obviously printed by Williamson under sub-contract. Another bearing Knight's imprint is almost certainly a product of the Punch & Ticket Co. but with the wording "OMNIBUS SERVICE" instead of "OMNIBUS TICKET". Later tickets by Knight are quite distinctive and entirely unlike the productions of any other printer. Their chief feature is the very fine and tiny type used. On geographical tickets it needed someone with good eyesight to decipher the printed matter. This may have been due to the limitations of the Knight company's equipment, or in the interests of cheapness. Knight managed to compress on the face of a $2\frac{1}{2}$ inch ticket a quantity of printed matter which the others carried over to the back or for which they used a longer ticket.

Apart from Knight, the only other printer to produce tickets in any quantity for the London independents was for long a mystery to ticket collectors. Due to the researches of Mr. S. H. Hughes it appears they probably came from a firm at present known as Henry Booth (Hull) Ltd. or its predecessors. This firm makes a feature of supplying tickets to order to local printers and stationers who act more or less as sub-contractors. No ticket is known to exist which carries the Booth imprint and it is thought probable that the tickets were supplied to the operators by a firm no longer in existence. This was Harry Gilbert Ltd. of Newcastle-on-Tyne, who described themselves as mail-order printers and who are believed to have done a fair amount of trade in supplying Booth-printed tickets. These Booth tickets were used for some years (approximately 1927 to 1934) by Premier both on its London bus services and its allied Premier Line express coach services. City also used Booth geographicals for a time on the 536. City, Prince and Chocolate Express also at one time used at least certain values of numerical stage tickets printed by Booth.

Another very unusual ticket of which only one specimen has been seen by the writer is a numerical stage ticket for Timpson. This bears the imprint of Wilson of Woolwich and is obviously the production of a local printer.

The Premier Omnibus Co. Ltd. was unusual among independents in that, after using tickets printed by Bell Punch for the first four or five years, changed over to Booth tickets and never again, as far as is known, patronised Bell Punch as far as their London operations were concerned. Towards the end of its life Premier experimented with the "Trambus" machine, a primitive forerunner of the Setright Speed, believed to have been first used by the Public in its Guy six-wheeler introduced in 1927. Premier also used the inserted ticket type of Setright machine on its express services.

When dealing with the tickets of Premier, the position is complicated by the existence of the associated operations of Premier Line Ltd. and Aylesbury Omnibus Co. Ltd., and with tickets that have come to hand since 1934 it is not always possible to be sure from which sector of operations it originated. Something similar occurs with Red Rover. This operator's earlier London numerical stage tickets by Bell Punch carried the title RED ROVER but later tickets carried the words RED ROVER OMNIBUS CO. and are known to have been used both in London and on the operator's services in the Aylesbury district. It is sometimes possible to distinguish them by the advertisements on the backs of the tickets, but this is not an infallible guide.

Other than the return and exchange tickets already mentioned very few other categories of ticket are known to have been used by London independents. Timpson, in the early days of their bus service, used numerical stage penny and twopenny child tickets, while an OMNIBUS (CHEAP MIDDAY) TICKET of 2d value is believed to have been used by Premier. Cambrian also had penny cheap midday tickets distinguished by a skeleton red cross overprint, and probably twopenny values also existed.

The list which follows shows the titled or identifiable tickets issued by the independents. This is not claimed to be a complete list but it represents all those known to the writer. Nevertheless it is unlikely that many varieties have been missed. The route numbers listed are those in use in the period 1925–34, and in some cases these numbers do not appear on the tickets mentioned.

The FIRST column gives the title as displayed on the ticket. Asterisks indicate
that the ticket is basically a stock ticket, usually with 'OMNIBUS TICKET'
in place of the title, but which can be identified as shown in the end column.

The SECOND column indicates the printer—

BP	Bell Punch Co., London or Uxbridge
HB	Henry Booth, Hull
KN	John Knight, Holborn, Tottenham or Edmonton
PT	Punch & Ticket Co., London, N.1.
WA	Alfred Williamson, Ashton-under-Lyne.

The tickets printed by Henry Booth do not carry the usual printer's imprint
at the foot, but are distinctive by type of print used and the style of the
serial number.

The THIRD Column indicates the ticket layout:—

G—GEOGRAPHICAL		Stage names set out in geographical progression up or down each edge.
FB—FAREBOARD		Name of stage boarded set down one edge, with the name of the stage to which the ticket is available shown on the opposite edge.
N—NUMERICAL		Stage points indicated by numbers. The normal number of stages is 30 (15 on each edge); any variation in the number is shown in the fourth column.
L—LETTERED		Stage points indicated only by letters.
V—VALUE PUNCHED		Normally used for Exchange tickets, where the value of the return ticket tendered is indicated by the punch hole.

The FOURTH column contains notes of special interest or comment.

The Adelaide Service	WA	N	
Admiral Omnibus Company	BP	N	Stages 1–22
"A. J. M."	PT	N	
A. J. M. Omnibus Service	PT	N	
	KN	G	For Services 529 & 538
A. J. M. Omnibus Services	KN	G	For Service 529
"Alberta" Omnibus	PT	N	
***W. A.	BP	N	William Allen (See also Premier). Initials at foot of ticket
***Allery & Bernard	BP	N	Advertisement on back. Used fleet name 'Service'
Alma Omnibus	PT	N	
"The Ambassador"	PT	N	Stages 24–1
	PT	N	Stages 30–1
"Ambassador"	PT	FB	For Service 29
The "Ambassador" Omnibus Co.	KN	G	For Service 29
Ambassador Bus Co. Ltd.	BP	N	
Astoria			See Hawklove
A & W Omnibus Service	WA	N	
	BP	N	
Barnet Motor Service	BP	N	Stages 1–10
***C. W. B.	BP	N	C. W. Batten (Atlas). Initials at foot of ticket
C. R. Batson	PT	N	Used fleet name "Direct"
B. B. P. Bus	PT	N	
Beattie, Beattie & Beattie	PT	N	
A. T. Bennett & Co. Ltd.	PT	N	Stages 1–22
	BP	N	Stages 1–22
	BP	FB	Service 538 front, 529 back
	KN	G	Services 529 & 538

Birch Bros. Ltd.	***WA	N	Advertisement on back
	***BP	N	Advertisement on back
	WA	N	
	BP	N	
	WA	N	Special for Service 526
	WA	FB	Service 536) With various
	BP	FB	Service 526) alterations to
	BP	FB	Service 536) stage names and
	BP	FB	Service 214) terminals.
	BP	FB	Service 231
***Biss Bros.	BP	N	Identifiable by advert on back for Biss's pub, "Old English Gentleman"
Biss Bros.	PT	N	
Biss Bros. Ltd.	PT	G	Services 69 & 212
	KN	G	Services 69 & 212
Bluebell Omnibus	PT	N	Stages 24–1
E. Brickwood, Ltd.	PT	N	Used fleet name "Redline"
	BP	N	
***W. H. B.	BP	N	William Henry Brown (Britannia) Initials at foot of ticket
"British Lion" Omnibus	PT	N	
The Burlington Omnibus Co. Ltd.	BP	N	
Cambrian Coaching & Goods	BP	N	Stages 1–40
Transport Ltd.	BP	N	Stages 1–28
	BP	N	Stages 1–30
	BP	FB	Services 268 & 286
Cambrian Landray Coaching Ltd.	BP	FB	Service 59
Cardinal Omnibus Services	BP	N	
Carlton Association	PT	FB	Service 529
***Carswool Omnibus	BP	N	Title on back
"C.C." Omnibus	BP	N	
Central Omnibus Co. Ltd.	BP	N	
"Certainty"	PT	N	
Chariot Omnibus Service	PT	N	
Chariot Omnibus Services Ltd.	PT	N	
	BP	N	
***Express	WA	N	Stages 1–12 Identifiable by unique layout
	PT	N	Stages 1–12 Identifiable by unique layout
Express Omnibus Company	BP	N	Stages 1–13
Chocolate Express	KN	N	
***Chocolate Express Buses	BP	N	Stages 1–12 Title on back
Chocolate Express Omnibus	BP	N	Stages 1–24
Co. Ltd.	PT	N	Stages 1–24
	HB	N	Stages 1–24
City Motor Omnibus Co Ltd	***WA	N	Title on back (Omnibus Ticket on front)
	***HB	N	Title on back (Omnibus Ticket on front)
	***BP	N	Advertisement on back for City New Empress Saloons
	WA	FB	Service 536 Variations of terminal points
	HB	FB	Service 536
	BP	FB	Service 536
	WA	G	Service 536 Exchange ticket (Variations of terminal points)
	HB	G	Service 536 Exchange ticket
	BP	G	Service 536 Exchange ticket
Claremont Omnibus Services	PT	N	
	BP	N	

"Clarence" Buses	PT	N	
Clarendon Omnibus	PT	N	
	KN	N	
Clarendon	KN	N	
"Clarendon" Omnibus	KN	G	Service 29
	PT	FB	Service 29
Cleveland Bus Service	BP	N	
Cleveland Omnibus Co. Ltd.	PT	N	
Comfort Omnibus Co. Ltd.	PT	N	Used fleet name "GWL"
Commonwealth Omnibus Co.	BP	L	A–Z Untitled, but identifiable by lettered stages
	BP	L	A–Z With title on front
Commonwealth Omnibus Co.	BP	L	A–Z
	BP	G	Service 17
Commonwealth Omnibuses Ltd.	BP	G	Service 17
Cornwall Motor Omnibus Co. Ltd.	BP	N	
The Cosgrove Omnibus Co. Ltd.	BP	N	
"Crescent"	PT	N	
The Crescent	KN	N	
Daisy Bus	BP	N	
Dangerfield, Ltd.	PT	N	See also Overground
	WA	N	
Dangerfield's Overground Service	PT	N	
Dangerfield Overground Service	PT	FB	Service 284
	BP	FB	Service 284
Dispatch Bus	BP	N	
***District	PT	N	Advert for Hampton & Stedman on back
District Bus	BP	N	
District Buses	BP	N	
Drake & McCowen	PT	N	
W. R. Drake	PT	N	
The Durell Omnibus	PT	N	
Durell Omnibus	PT	N	
	KN	N	
The Durell Omnibus Service	KN	N	
H. C. Durell	BP	N	
Earl	KN	N	
Earl Motor Omnibus Co. Ltd.	BP	N	
***Earl Motor Bus Co. Ltd.	PT	N	Title on back
***Eastern	PT	N	1–24 Advert on back for S. A. Boon
"Eastern Omnibus"	PT	N	
Eastern Omnibus Association	PT	G	Stages for Service 511 Exchange ticket only, used by a group of operators named on the back of ticket
Edmonton Omnibus Company (Bernard Cosgrove)	BP	N	Stages 1–22
***Elms & Longman Motor Services	WA	N	Title on back
***Elms Longman Motor Services	WA	N	Title on back
***Empire	PT	N	Advert on back for F. Kirk
Empire	PT	FB	Service 511
Empire Bus Co.	PT	FB	Service 511
	PT	N	
"Empire" Omnibus	PT	N	
***Empress	PT	N	Stage 1–24 Advert on back for E. T. Stanton
Empress Omnibus	PT	N	

Empress Motors Ltd.	PT	N	
	BP	N	
The Empress Omnibus Co. Ltd.	PT	N	
Empress Omnibus Company Ltd.	BP	N	
The Enterprise Omnibus	PT	N	
	BP	N	
Enterprise Bus Co.	BP	N	
	PT	FB	Service 14 (from Putney)
	BP	FB	Service 14 (from Putney)
Enterprise Bus Company	BP	FB	Service 14 (from Hampton Court)
Essex Omnibus & Charabanc	BP	N	
Albert Ewer	PT	N	
Fairlop	PT	G	Service 511 (See also H. B.)
	PT	N	Exchange ticket only
E. E. Farwell	PT	N	Used fleet names "Reliable" & "Dauntless"
***Felix	BP	N	Identified by address on back. Also used by Magnet
"Field-Marshal"	PT	N	
	PT	G	Service 29
Fleet Omnibus Co. Ltd.	BP	N	
	PT	N	
"Fleet" Omnibuses	PT	FB	Return tickets only for Service 12
	PT	G	Exchange tickets only for Service 12
***Florence	BP	N	Identifiable by advertisement for Hammersmith Motor Coach Coach Service on back
Frith & Hope	PT	N	Used fleet name "Pembroke"
F. S. Petrol Electric	BP	N	Stages 1–26
***F. W.	BP	N	Address on back
***Gleaner Omnibus	BP	B	Advertisement on back
Gleaner Omnibus Co. Ltd.	BP	G	Service 17
Gordon Omnibus	PT	N	
Gordon Omnibus Co. Ltd.	PT	N	
	BP	N	
Grafton Omnibus Service	PT	V	Exchange ticket only – 2d/6d
	PT	G	Exchange ticket only – Service 511
Grays, Ltd.	PT	N	
	BP	N	
***Gretna	BP	N	Gretna Motor Coach advert on back
**P. H. R. Harris	BP	N	Advert on back – 2 different addresses
J. Hartley	PT	N	Title with and without address. Used fleet name "Regina"
The "Havelock"	PT	N	
	PT	FB	Service 263
The Hawk Omnibus	BP	N	
Hawklove	BP	N	Used by "Astoria" & "R. H."
H. B.	KN	N	See also "Fairlop" H. B. are the initials of the proprietors, Holliday & Burton
H. Heast	PT	N	Used fleet name "H. H."
Henslowe Bus Co. Ltd.	BP	N	
	PT	N	
H. F. Omnibus	BP	N	Used fleet name "Hav-a-Ride". The letters indicate the initials of the owners, H. & F. Briskham
H. F. B. Ltd. Service	BP	FB	Service 284
	KN	G	Service 284

***C. Holliday	PT	N	Advertisement on back
***Holliday & Bangs	BP	N	Identified by advert on back
Holliday, Bangs & Dengate	PT	N	
H. B. & D. Omnibus	PT	G	Service 59
H. & B Omnibus	PT	G	Service 59
Hooker & Irvine	PT	N	See also Overland
***J. Hough	BP	N	Name on back. Used fleet name "Trinity"
"J. H."	PT	N	
"Imperial"	PT	N	See also Priest Bros.
"Invicta"	PT	N	Stage 1–24
The Jockey Omnibus	BP	N	
J. S. & S. R.	WA	N	
***Julius & Lockwood	WA	N	Title on back
***Kathleen	BP	N	1–22 Advert on back for H. Ball
K. B. B. 'Bus	BP	N	
***C. Kurash	BP	N	Name on back. Used fleet name "Diamond"
Lacey's Motor Coaches	BP	N	Used fleet name "Essential"
Lancastrian Omnibus	BP	N	
Lea Valley Omnibus	PT	N	
The Legion 'Bus	BP	N	
Lewis Omnibus & Coaching Co.	WA	N	Used fleet names "Lewis" and "Essential"
"Liberty" Bus	BP	N	Stages 1–26
"The London"	PT	N	
London Circular Omnibus Co.	PT	N	Stages 1–24
Ltd.	BP	N	Stages 1–24
London & Provincial Bus Co. Ltd.	WA	N	
London Road Car Omnibus Co.	PT	N	Used fleet name "Victoria Road Car"
***Magnet	BP	N	Advertisement on back with address – also used by Felix
Majestic Omnibus	PT	N	Stages 1–24
Marathon Buses	PT	N	Stages 1–24
Martin Omnibus Co.	BP	N	
Martin Omnibus Service and Associated Cos.	BP	N	See also Paterson Omnibus Co. Ltd.
"The Matchless"	PT	N	
"M.-B."	PT	N	
"H. M. M."	PT	N	H. M. Merry
H. M. Merry Motor Transport Services Ltd.	PT	N	
***Meteor	BP	N	Advert on back for E. Matthews
Meteor Omnibus	PT	N	
	BP	N	
Meteor Omnibus Co. Ltd.	BP	N	
	KN	N	
	KN	N	Stages 1–22. Meteor Buses across top of front of ticket, also full title on left edge.
Miller Omnibus	BP	N	
Miller Traction Company Ltd.	BP	N	
	BP	FB	Service 15A)
	BP	FB	Service 293) Combined on 1½d
M. T. T. Buses	PT	N	
***R. N.	BP	N	R. Neal (Eclipse) Initials at foot of ticket
Nelson	PT	FB	Return ticket only – Service 511

394

Nelson Bus Co	PT	N	
Nelson Omnibus Co. Ltd.	PT	N	
	PT	FB	Service 511
New Era Omnibus Co. Ltd.	BP	N	
	BP	L	A–Z
	BP	G	Service 17
The New London	PT	N	
New Service Omnibuses	PT	FB	Return & Exchange tickets only
	PT	V	2d–6d Exchange tickets only,
	PT	V	5d–9d Issued by a consortium of operators on Service 511
L. M. Newstead	PT	N	
New Times Motor Omnibus Co. Ltd.	PT	N	
New Times Omnibus Co. Ltd.	BP	N	
Nil Desperandum	BP	N	
North East London Association	PT	N	Issued by operators on Service 263
Northern	BP	N	
"Nulli Secundus" Omnibus	PT	N	
"Omega" Omnibus	PT	N	
The Orange Service	BP	N	1–22 stages
	KN	N	1–22 stages
	PT	N	1–22 stages
	BP	G	Services 27A & 127
	BP	G	Service 76
	BP	G	Services 15, 522A & 6A
	BP	G	Service 550
"Our Bus"	PT	N	
	BP	N	
"Our Bus" Service	BP	G	Service 170
Overground Service	WA	N	See also under Dangerfield
Overland Omnibuses	PT	N	See also Hooker & Irvine
Passenger Transport Ltd	PT	N	Used fleet name "Rapid"
Pat Omnibus	BP	N	
Paterson Omnibus Co. Ltd.	BP	FB	Services 23 & 123d. See also Martin
	BP	FB	Services 186, 86a & 151c
	BP	FB	Service 292
Edward Paul, Ltd.	PT	N	Stages 1–24
	PT	FB	Return tickets only – Service 12
	PT	G	Exchange ticket only – Service 12
The "P.C." Omnibus	PT	N	
	BP	N	
"P. C."	PT	FB	Return ticket only – Service 511
Peraeque Bus	PT	N	
Peraeque	KN	N	
***Peraeque Motor Bus	BP	N	Title on back
Perkins' Omnibus	BP	N	
Phoenix Motor and Omnibus Company	BP	N	Stages 1–24
Phoenix Motor & Omnibus Co. Ltd.	BP	N	Stages 1–24
C. H. P.	WA	N	Stages 1–26 (Chas. H. Pickup)
	BP	N	Stages 1–26
	BP	FB	Service 21D
	BP	FB	Service 37B
	BP	FB	Service 70
W. J. Pike, Ltd.	PT	N	Used fleet name "Favourite"
The Pirate Bus	BP	N	
"Poppy" Omnibus	PT	FB	Service 69
Poppy Bus Service	PT	N	

***W.A.	BP	N	William Allen (Premier O.C.)— initials at foot of ticket.
The Premier Omnibus Co. Ltd.	BP	G	Services 60, 73, 233, 522 (Number not on ticket)
Premier Omnibus Co. Ltd.	HB	N	Stages 1–42
	HB	N	Stages 1–42 (Including Premier Line Ltd. in title) Also used "Tram-Bus" machine tickets – an early version of Setright Speed and also used Insert Setright tickets
Priest Bros.	PT	N	See also Imperial
"The Primrose"	PT	N	Stage numbers vary for each value
	WA	N	Stage numbers vary for each value
	WA	N	Stages 1–24 (One block for all values)
	PT	N	Stages 1–30 (One block for all values)
"The Prince"	PT	N	
	HB	N	
	PT	FB	Return ticket only – Service 511
***Prince Omnibus	BP	N	Title on back
Pro Bono Publico Omnibus Service	PT	N	
"Pro Bono Publico"	PT	FB	Service 511
	BP	FB	Service 511
"R. A." Motor Service	BP	N	
R. A. Motor Services Ltd.	PT	N	
Redburns Motor Services	BP	N	
Redburn's Motor Services Ltd.	BP	FB	Service 69A
Red Rose Motor Services Ltd.	PT	N	
Red Rover	BP	N	
Red Rover Omnibus Co.	BP	N	Also used on Aylesbury local services
The Regent Omnibus	BP	N	
Reliable Service	WA	N	See also E. E. Farwell
"Reliable Service"	PT	N	
Reliance Omnibuses	PT	N	Proprietor Chas. Churchman & Son
	KN	G	Service 529
"The Reliance"	PT	N	
Reliance	PT	FB	Return ticket only – Service 511
	PT	V	2d–6d Exchange ticket
	BP	V	2d–6d Exchange ticket
Reliance Omnibus Co. Ltd.	PT	N	
	BP	N	
	PT	FB	Service 511B
	BP	FB	Return tickets only – Service 511
***"Renown" Omnibuses	BP	N	Title on back
***Renown Omnibus Company	BP	N	Title on back
Renown Traction Coy. Ltd.	BP	N	
Renown Traction Company	BP	FB	Services 15A & 293 (for some values separate tickets for each service)
R. H.			See Hawklove
The "Rogue" Omnibus	BP	N	
Royal Omnibuses	BP	N	
****"Royal Blue" Omnibus Co.	BP	N	Title on back
***Royal Blue Omnibus Co.	PT	N	Title on back
	BP	N	Title on back
Royal Toots Omnibus	PT	N	
St. George Omnibus Co. Ltd.	BP	N	Title in both upper & lower case

***St. George Omnibus Co. Ltd.	BP	N	Title on back
Scarboro' Omnibus	PT	N	
	PT	G	Service 29
***Sear Bros.	BP	N	Title on back
Shamrock Traction Co. Ltd.	BP	N	
"Shanghai" Motor Omnibus	BP	N	
The "Silver" Omnibuses	PT	N	1–30 stages. See also Timpson's
	PT	N	1–34 stages
	††	N	Printed by Wilson, of Woolwich
Silver Star	PT	N	
Skylark Omnibus Co.	PT	N	
	BP	N	
Skylark Omnibus Company	BP	G	Service 17
Skylark Omnibus Co. Ltd.	BP	G	Service 11 (also with title mis-spelt Skylary)
	BP	G	Service 17
	BP	G	Service 29
South London Coaches	PT	N	
Sphere Omnibus Co.	KN	G	Service 29
Sphere Omnibus Co. Ltd.	PT	N	
	BP	N	
	PT	FB	Service 29
***Standard Bus Coy.	WA	N	Stages 1–24 Advert on back for A. R. Raper (mis-print for A. H. Raper)
	WA	N	Stages 1–30 2d has letters at foot for cheap mid-day fares
	BP	N	Title on back
"Star" Omnibus Co.	PT	N	Used fleet name "White Star"
***A. G. Summerskill	BP	N	Stages 1–20 Name on back
Sunbeam Omnibus	PT	N	Stages 1–24
The Sunbeam Omnibus Service	BP	N	
The Supreme Omnibus Service	BP	N	
	PT	FB	Service 511B
Supreme Bus Co. Ltd.	PT	N	
The Supreme Omnibus Co. Ltd.	BP	FB	Service 511B
***Swift Motor Omnibus Co.	BP	N	Stages 1–15 Title on back
***"Swift" 'Buses	WA	N	Stages 1–15 Title on back
Swift Omnibus Co. Ltd.	BP	N	Stages 1–6 Title across top of ticket
Tally-Ho	PT	N	
	BP	N	
***R. T.	BP	N	Initials at foot of ticket
R. Thackeray	PT	N	Name should be spelt Thackray
Timpson's	PT	FB	Services 213 & 289 (including returns)
	PT	G	Exchange ticket – Service 289
Timpson's Silver Buses	PT	FG	Exchange ticket – Service 289
Timpson's Omnibus Services	BP	FB	Return ticket – Service 289
	BP	G	Exchange ticket – Service 289
"Tottenham Hotspur"	PT	N	
Tottenham Hotspur Omnibus Co. Ltd.	BP	N	
***Tower Carriers, Ltd.	BP	N	Title on back
Triumph Motor Bus Coy.	BP	N	
H. A. Turner	WA	G	Only one ticket issued – 3d. Identified by stages (Service 207)
The Ubique Omnibus Co. Ltd.	PT	N	Stages 1–24
"Uneedus"	PT	N	
	PT	FB	Service 29
United Omnibus Co.	PT	N	

United Omnibus Co. Ltd.	PT	N	
	BP	N	
Universal Omnibus Ticket	BP	N	
Varsity Omnibus Co.	BP	N	
The Veleta Omnibus Service	BP	N	
The Veleta Omnibus Co.	BP	N	
***Venture	BP	N	Advert on back for F. J. Nunn
"Venture"	PT	N	
"Victor" Omnibus	BP	N	
Victoria Road Car Omnibus Co.	BP	N	
Victory Omnibus	BP	N	
Vivid Omnibus	BP	N	
Waverley Omnibus Company	BP	N	
Webber Bros.	BP	N	Used fleet name "Empire's Best"
The "Wellington"	PT	N	
Wellington	PT	FB	Return ticket only – Service 511
The Western Omnibus Co.	PT	N	Stages 1–24
The Western Omnibus Co. Ltd.	PT	N	Stages 1–24
Westminster Bus Co.	PT	N	
Westminster Omnibus Co. Ltd.	PT	N	
	BP	N	
"Wilson"	BP	N	
"Wilton"	PT	N	
The Wilton Service	KN	N	Title across top of ticket
The W. W. Services	WA	N	Stages 1–24 These tickets have printer's imprint of John Knight, Printer, 285 High Holborn W.C., but the tickets have obviously been printed by Williamson
X Service Bus	BP	N	Stages 1–26

APPENDIX 3

TOTAL NUMBER OF INDEPENDENT OPERATORS IN BUSINESS ON 31st DECEMBER OF EACH YEAR FROM 1922 TO 1932 AND ON 30th JUNE, 1933. FORMER INDEPENDENT OPERATORS RUNNING AS SUBSIDIARIES OF GENERAL AND TILLING IN 1926 AND 1927 ARE ALSO SHOWN

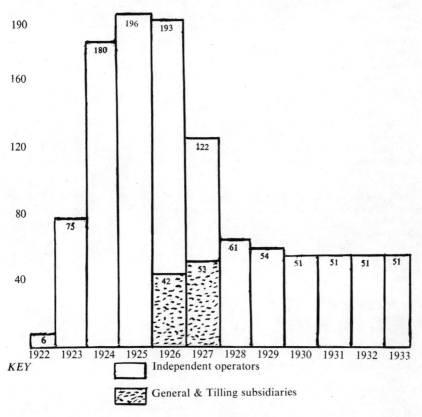

KEY   ☐ Independent operators

🔲 General & Tilling subsidiaries

APPENDIX 4

TOTAL NUMBER OF BUSES OF EACH TYPE IN SERVICE WITH INDEPENDENT OPERATORS IN THE METROPOLITAN POLICE AREA ON 31st DECEMBER OF EACH YEAR FROM 1922 TO 1932 AND ON 30th JUNE 1933.

This table excludes those Romford area operators whose services were entirely outside the Metropolitan area (i.e. Capitol, Imperial and Romford District). It also excludes Charles Waymann, about whose vehicles insufficient information is available, and Southall & District whose buses also operated on services outside the area and whose operations will be related in detail in a future volume.

Figures in brackets against the totals for 1926 and 1927 indicate the number of vehicles operated by former independent companies still trading under their own names but as subsidiaries of General or Tilling. These figures are additional to those outside the brackets.

399

DOUBLE DECK

	1922	23	24	25	26	27	28	29	30	31	32	33
Leyland LB	1	66	136	174	147(40)	108(13)	105	95	78	52	26	20
Straker A-type	3	83	128	119	17(70)	2(—)	2	1	1	—	—	—
Dennis (converted chara)	1	—	—	—	—	—	—	—	—	—	—	—
Daimler (converted chara)	2	—	—	—	—	—	—	—	—	—	—	—
Frost Smith	6	6	—	2	—	—	—	—	—	—	—	—
Dennis 4-ton	—	8	165	232	209(41)	92(73)	74	69	48	36	28	24
Thornycroft J	—	13	33	34	8(4)	4(—)	1	—	—	—	—	—
Daimler Y-type	—	4	30	33	19(6)	16(—)	10	8	2	2	1	1
Tilling Stevens TS3A	—	—	4	5	—(5)	—(20)	—	—	—	—	—	—
AEC K-type	—	—	—	—	—(42)	—(150)	—	—	—	—	—	—
Dennis H, HS and HV	—	—	—	—	—	—	2	12	16	16	16	15
City rebuild (4-wheel)	—	—	—	—	—	—	1	1	1	1	1	1
Guy FCX	—	—	—	—	—	—	2	2	2	2	11	11
Leyland Titan	—	—	—	—	—	—	—	22	72	106	127	129
Dennis Lance	—	—	—	—	—	—	—	—	6	6	8	8
Daimler CF6 and CH6	—	—	—	—	—	—	—	—	2	3	2	2
AEC Regent	—	—	—	—	—	—	—	—	4	4	10	10
City rebuild (6-wheel)	—	—	—	—	—	—	—	—	1	6	6	6
Maudslay ML7C	—	—	—	—	—	—	—	—	—	1	1	1
Leyland Titanic	—	—	—	—	—	—	—	—	—	—	—	3
SMC Sikh	—	—	—	—	—	—	—	—	—	—	—	1

SINGLE DECK

	1922	23	24	25	26	27	28	29	30	31	32	33
Crossley Tender	1	2	4	3	2(—)	—	—	—	—	—	—	—
Fiat	—	2	3	—	2*(—)	—	—	—	—	—	—	—
Dennis 2½ ton	—	—	1	26	48(6)	3(6)	—	—	—	—	—	—
Maudslay ML3	—	—	—	—	2(—)	—	2	2	2	—	—	—
Guy BB and FBB	—	—	—	—	3(—)	1(—)	2	3	—	—	—	—
Dennis E-type	—	—	—	—	6(—)	12(—)	16	20	20	19	19	19
AEC K-type	—	—	—	—	—	—(2)	—	—	—	—	—	—
Leyland Lion (PLSC type)	—	—	—	—	—	—	18	17	16	14	11	10
Bean	—	—	—	—	—	—	—	2	—	3	1	1
Karrier JKL	—	—	—	—	—	—	—	2	2	2	2	2
Guy OND & ONDF	—	—	—	—	—	—	—	1	3	8	—	—
Leyland Lion (LT type), Titan & Tiger	—	—	—	—	—	—	—	—	—	2	4	4

*possibly 3

BODY & STOCK NUMBERS ALLOCATED BY THE LGOC TO THE BUSES OF INDEPENDENT COMPANIES OPERATED AS SUBSIDIARIES IN 1926/27

The LGOC allocated body numbers to the vehicles of all companies acquired from April 20th 1926 onwards, commencing with the Clarence and Royal Blue fleets acquired on that date (body numbers 9173 to 9182), and followed by buses from companies already acquired. Stock (or bonnet) numbers were generally only allocated to Dennises and Leylands, although Tower's Thornycrofts received stock numbers as did the Uneedus Guys. The LGOC referred to Cambrian vehicles by numbers allocated by the former management and, indeed, used the Cambrian D-series as the basis upon which to number all subsequently-acquired Dennises. Vehicles in the group of LGOC-owned companies controlled by C. W. Batten were not allocated body numbers until December 31st 1926, the date on which Batten's control ceased. Certain of the vehicles concerned were Leylands transferred in from other LGOC subsidiaries. These vehicles (one Cosgrove and five Tottenham Hotspurs) lost their body numbers on receipt by Batten and were subsequently re-allocated new numbers. Vehicles with body numbers in the 8xxx series were charabancs. It was old-established LGOC practice to number charabancs, lorries and other miscellaneous vehicle bodies in a separate series from the buses. It should be emphasised that in many cases, both body and stock numbers were never actually carried on the vehicles themselves, the great majority of which were disposed of before their owning companies were absorbed into the LGOC and without ever receiving General livery.

The LGOC embarked upon a programme of overhauling the Dennises of its acquired companies. In order to speed up the overhaul process, a float of four spare bodies was created in November 1926. Three came from Straker Squires ME 8598 (Cambrian) and XO 939/2107 (Western) and the fourth was removed from the P.C.'s Dennis PU 7282 whose chassis was broken up for spares. For the next three months each Dennis chassis, on the completion of its overhaul, received a renovated body from another Dennis chassis, and in several instances this resulted in a chassis carrying a different make of body from that which had been originally fitted. When the float was discontinued in March 1927 four bodies became surplus. Three were scrapped (9355 ex T & W XX 1756, 9463 ex Florence XR 888, and 9497 ex Redburn's MH 846) and the fourth was sold to a dealer (9259 ex Western XT 110). A certain amount of body exchanging also took place on the Straker Squires. This was not done to create a float as in the case of the Dennises, there being no long term plan to retain the Straker Squires in service. Certain vehicles were merely given bodies which were in a better condition than their own in order to prolong their active lives by a few months. The majority of the replacement bodies came from Cambrian Straker Squires which had broken-down in 1925 and had never been mobilised since. Three rebodied Strakers never operated in service with their second body, apparently because of an abrupt change of policy which decreed the early scrapping of all those that remained.

Those concerned were Redburn's MF 3574/3084 and Tottenham Hotspur MF 4166.

Body No.	Stock No.		Body No.	Stock No.	

A1

XO8668	9265	D39	XP4051	9187	T101

Body replaced by 9260 (ex Western)
3/27
9265 to XW8641 (Redburn's, ex
Grafton) 3/27

			XP9081	9188	T111
			XP6421	9189	T108
			XP9080	9190	T110
			XP4705	9191	T102

ALBERTA

XX7606	9773(a)	D45	XP5449	9192	T104
XX8731	9774(b)	D46	XP5450	9193	T105
XX9344	9775(c)	D44	XP5984	9194	T106
XU6822	9776(d)	D42	XP5985	9195	T107
XU6823	9777(e)	D43	XO8225	9196	S53
XT5386	9778	L39	XO8591	9197	S59
XT8752	9779	L2	XO8224	9198(b)	S52

(a) Body replaced by 9775 (Alberta)
1/27 9773 to XR7778
(Redburn's, ex Fleet) 2/27
(b) Body replaced by 9776 (Alberta)
12/26 9774 to XU6823
(Alberta) 12/26
(c) Body replaced by 9777 (Alberta)
12/26 9775 to XX7606
(Alberta) 1/27
(d) Body replaced by 9357 (Ex
Dominion) 12/26 9776 to
XX8731 (Alberta) 12/26
(d) Body replaced by 9774 (Alberta)
12/26 9777 to XX9344
(Alberta) 12/26

			XT956	9199(c)	S66
			XT3342	9200(d)	S67
			XO8593	9201	S56
			XT7053	9202	S71
			ME9689	9203	S74
			XP4427	9204	S64
			ME7351	9205(e)	S78
			XO7779	9206	S51
			MF180	9207	S73
			XP4428	9208	S62
			XO8590	9209	S60
			XT3344	9210	S69
			XW341	9211	S75
			XO8226	9212	S54

ATLAS

HM4604	9808	L10	XW3680	9213	D4
HM4690	9809	L22	XW2273	9214	D1
XN7748	9810	L15	XW3679	9215	D3
HM3766	9811	L21	XW2505	9216	D2
HM4605	9812	L12	MH9006	9217	D6
HM4757	9813	L7	MH9005	9218	D5
HM4392	9814	L13	MH9421	9219	D7
HM4606	9815	L14	XY3470	9220	D8
HM4393	9816	L11	XP4426	9221(l)	S63
HM4195	9817	L19	XT3343	9222(m)	S68
HM3827	9818	L16	XO8589	9223	S57
XO5617	9819	L20	XT955	9224(f)	S65
HM4756	9820	L8	BA2851	9225(g)	S50
HM4755	9821	L9	XT7051	9226(h)	S72
HM4627	9822	L17	XW342	9227(i)	S76
HM4498	9825	L18	XW547	9228(j)	S77
XO4835	9472	L6	XP4425	9229	S61

BRITANNIA

			XO8592	9230(m)	S55
HM4745	9828	L26	XT7052	9231	S70
HM4746	9829	L23	XP6422	9232	T109
HM4695	9830	L25	XP9325	9233	T112
HM4698	9831	L24	ME8598	9234(k)	S79
HM3519	9832	L27			

(a) Body replaced by 9251 (ex EP)
3/26. 9183 scrapped
(b) 9198 to X0939 (Western) 10/26
(c) 9199 to X02107 (Western) 10/26
(d) 9200 to XN513 (EP) 10/26
(e) 9205 to MF1020 (EP) 12/26
(f) 9224 to MF6405 (Redburn's)
11/26
(g) 9225 to XO8747 (EP) 3/26

CAMBRIAN

XO8588	9183(a)	S58
XP9831	9184	T113
XP4706	9185	T103
XU2191	9186	T114

(h) 9226 to XR3507 (EP) 3/26
(i) 9227 to MF4401 (Redburn's)
    11/26
(j) 9228 to MF3084 (Redburn's)
    11/26
(k) 9234 to XX8837 (Redburn's, ex
    Dominion) 11/26
(l) Body sold to C. & P. Sales,
    Ipswich 4/27
(m) Bodies sold to H. Sabey,
    Paddington, 10/27

CAMBRIAN LANDRAY

IT413	8709	—
IT414	8710	—
IT418	8711	—
XB9888	8712	—
XH2265	8713	—
LX8984	8714	—
IT303	8715	—
IT292	9846	—
IT293	9847	—
IT301	9848	—
IT302	9849	—
XM2992	9850	—

CELTIC

| XR1195 | 9359 | — |

CENTRAL

XN7891	9235(a)	—
XN7386	9236(a)	—
YM6649	9237	—
XN8771	9238(b)	—
XP849	9239(b)	—

(a) Bodies sold to Silver Queen,
    Clacton 4/26
(b) Bodies sold to W. N. Anstey,
    Cranfield, Berks. 10/26

CLARENCE

| XU3027 | 9173(a) | D28 |
| XX772 | 9174 | D24 |

(a) Body replaced by 9356 (ex
    Dominion) 1/27
    9173 to MH 2594 (Redburn's, ex
    Criterion) 1/27

COSGROVE

| XT2864 | 9842 | L35 |

Body originally numbered 9181 on
    Royal Blue

CRITERION

| MH2594 | 9358 | D29 |

Body replaced by 9173 (ex Clarence)
    1/27
    9358 to XT110 (Redburn's, ex
    Western) 2/27

DIRECT

| MH5193 | 9325 | D27 |

DISTRICT

| XT5917 | 9927 | D60 |
| XU1748 | 9928 | D61 |

DOMINION

| XX8837 | 9356(a) | D21 |
| XX9591 | 9357(b) | D22 |

(a) Body replaced by 9234 (ex
    Cambrian) 11/26
    9356 to XU3027 (Redburn's, ex
    Clarence) 1/27
(b) Body replaced by 9262 (ex
    Western) 11/26
    9357 to XU6822 (Alberta) 12/26

EMPRESS

MF9159	9805	D47
XN4477	9806	L5
MH2516	9807	—

E.P.

XR5274	9244	—
XN6182	9245	—
XN6183	9246	—
XN513	9247(a)	—
MF1020	9248(b)	—
MF9171	9249	—
XM9888	9250	—
XR3507	9251(c)	—
XO8747	9252(d)	—
XR3506	9253	—
XM9995	9254	—
YL8115	9255	—
YM6664	9256	—
MH295	9757(e)	—
MH1095	9758(e)	—

(a) Body replaced by 9200 (ex
    Cambrian) 10/26
    9247 scrapped
(b) Body replaced by 9205 (ex
    Cambrian) 12/26
    9248 scrapped
(c) Body replaced by 9226 (ex
    Cambrian) 3/26
    9251 scrapped
(d) Body replaced by 9225 (ex
    Cambrian) 3/26
    9252 to MF4166 (Tottenham
    Hotspur) 1/27
(e) Body numbers allocated upon
    acquisition from Tottenham
    Hotspur 10/26

FLEET

XN5243	9240	—
XR7776	9241	D23
XN5244	9242	—
XR7778	9243(a)	D33

(a) Body replaced by 9773 (ex
    Alberta) 2/27
    9243 to MH846 (Redburn's 2/27)

FLORENCE

| XR888 | 9463(a) | D34 |
| XT6628 | 9464 | D35 |

(a) Body replaced by 9855 (ex The
    P.C.) 2/27. 9463 scrapped

GRAFTON

| XW8641 | 9473 | D38 |

Body replaced by 9265 (ex A1) 2/27
    9473 to XT8982 (Redburn's, ex
    Western) 3/27

GRANGEWOOD

YN3800	9833	L28

Body originally number 9270 when
   new to Horseshoe

HORSESHOE

MF7349	9268	—
MH1261	9269	—
YN3800	9270	—

IMPERIAL

MH1693	9361	D36

Body exchanged with 9759 (Lea
   Valley) 1/27

INVICTA

HM4482	9823	L38
HM4481	9824	L37
HM4820	9826	L40
HM2996	9827	—

JOCKEY, THE

XT4857	9475	L1

LEA RIG, THE

XW4774	9851	—

LEA VALLEY

XX1259	9759	D48

Body exchanged with 9361
   (Redburn's, ex Imperial) 1/27

LEGION

MF6914	9474	—

LONSDALE

XT946	9328	—
XW9413	9329	—

LOVELAND

XN6976	9844	L36

MARATHON

XO1942	9471	L29
XO4835	9472	L6

OLYMPIC

XR4559	9271	—

ORANGE SERVICE, THE

XU8727	9914	D50
XW473	9915	D51
YR4778	9916	D52
YM5154	9917	D53
YM5155	9918	D54
YM9971	9919	D55
YM9972	9920	D56
YM6965	9921	D57
YM6966	9922	D58
XP4355	9923	L41
XR4129	9924	L42
YK3657	9925	L43

P.C., THE

PU3549	9855(a)	D40
PU7282	9856(b)	D41

(a) Body replaced by 9462 (ex
   Superbus) 1/27
   9855 to XR888 (Redburn's, ex
   Florence) 2/27
(b) 9856 to XU4371 (Redburn's, ex
   Superbus) 1/27

PRIMROSE

XT4176	9266	D26
XM3527	9267	—

PULLMAN

XX874	9979	D65

R.A.

XW2849	9264	—

REDBURN'S MOTOR SERVICE

AR9831	8686	—
MD8090	8687	—
ME9197	8688	—
MD6825	8689	—
ME9102	9476	—
MF6110	9477(g)	—
ME9670	9478	—
ME9671	9479	—
MF1182	9480	—
MF1181	9481	—
MF1940	9482	—
MF1941	9483	—
MF3003	9484	—
MF3002	9485	—
MF3084	9486(a)	—
MF3485	9487	—
MF3574	9488(b) (f)	—
MF4401	9489(c) (f)	—
MF4519	9490	—
MF5160	9491(f)	—
MF1298	9492(g)	—
MF5161	9493	—
MF7511	9494	—
MF8166	9495	—
MH608	9496	D15
MH846	9497(d)	D16
MH1655	9498	D17
MH1925	9499	D18
MH2845	9500	D19
MH7786	9501	D9
MH7787	9502	D10
MH8520	9503	D11
MH8521	9504	D12
MH8522	9505	D13
MH8523	9506	D14
MF6405	9507(e) (g)	—
ME9624	9508	

(a) Body replaced by 9228 (ex
   Cambrian) 11/26
   9486 to MF3574 (Redburn's)
   11/26
(b) Body replaced by 9486 (Redburn's)
   11/26
(c) Body replaced by 9227 (ex
   Cambrian) 11/26
(d) Body replaced by 9243 (ex Fleet)
   2/27. 9497 scrapped
(e) Body replaced by 9224 (ex
   Cambrian) 11/26
(f) Bodies sold to East Kent 2/27
(g) Bodies sold to C & P Sales,
   Ipswich 3/27

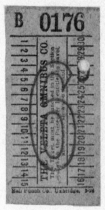

M5761   Bell Punch. Gleaner Omnibus Co. Ltd. 1d. Geographical layout with stage initials accent ated to assist correct punching. White.

OC7300   Bell Punch. Paterson Omnibus Co. Ltd. 1d. Fareboard, double sided, route 23 on both sides, and route 123D on back only. White.

Rb4505   Bell Punch. A. T. Bennett & Co. Ltd. Fareboard type. Special 1½d. fare for fare cutting against L.G.O.C. and trams. Route 538 on front and route 529 on back. Salmon.

A5782   Bell Punch. C.H.P. 8d. Geographical with special green etched overprinting on serial number to denote service 37B. Yellow.

Z0429   Bell Punch. Timpson's Omnibus Services. 6d. cheap day return, service 289. Grey.

A0173   Bell Punch. Express Omnibus Company. 4d. fare. Earliest numerical ticket used by Chocolate Express with stage numbers facing outwards and fare value sideways. Yellow.

P4489   Bell Punch. Omnibus Ticket. 1d. Standard stock ticket except for inclusion at foot of owner's initials, in this case CWB — Charles William Batten. White.

B0176   Bell Punch. The Veleta Omnibus Co. 6d. Numerical with stage numbers facing outwards. Buff.

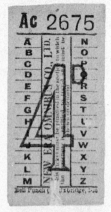

A8257   Bell Punch. X Service Bus. 1/-. Numerical type. Slogan on back reads "We helped you — Will you help us?" This enterprise is run by a small group of ex-Service officers and men who ALL, conductors, drivers, mechanics, etc., will participate in the profits." Salmon.

Ac2675   Bell Punch. New Era Omnibus Co. Ltd. 4d. Numerical type but with stage letters instead of numbers. Green.

J6207   Henry Booth. The Premier Omnibus Co. Ltd. 1/1d. Geographical with Routes 233 and part 73 on front, route 60 and remainder of 73 on back. Buff.

AE0402   Henry Booth. Premier Omnibus Co. Ltd. 4d. numerical. Advert on back for Premier Line Coach Services A and B. Green.

A5975   Williamson. Birch Bros. Ltd. 6d. fareboard type for route 536. Inscription on back reads "Five-Three-Six. Gets You There Quickest Way, Cheapest Fare." Primrose.

Ri2513   Williamson. City Motor Omnibus Co. Ltd. 5d. day return, route 536. White with pink edges.

Bl9961   Williamson. "The Primrose." 1d. Numerical. White.

B9006   Williamson. Dangerfield, Ltd. 8d. Numerical. Primrose.

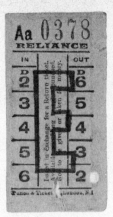
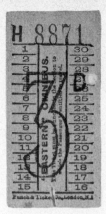

Sa9850   Punch & Ticket. The "Havelock" 1d. fareboard ticket for route 263. White.

P2613   Punch & Ticket. Nelson Omnibus Co. Ltd. ½d. Numerical, used only in conjunction with other values to make up odd fares. Light green.

Aa0378   Punch & Ticket. Reliance. Exchange ticket with inscription on back "Available on all buses on 511." Buff.

H8871   Punch & Ticket. "Eastern" Omnibus. 3d. Later numerical ticket with thinner stage numbers. Pink.

Nb7227   Punch & Ticket. Premier Omnibus Co. Ltd. Insert-type Setright. Buff.

Gb1487   Knight. "Clarendon" Omnibus. 1d. Geographical for route 29. White.

Ja0453   Knight. Meteor buses. 3d. Numerical. Pink.

Photo No. 97 (*above*)

Finding suitable garage accommodation was always a problem. Few independents could afford premises as spacious as the Admiral garage at Willow Walk, West Green. The Straker Squire looks lost in the corner of an otherwise empty building. This later became London Transport's WG garage and was used by them until 1962.

Photo No. 98 (*below*)

St. George's long-vanished garage in Peckham was old and cramped, but at least it was their own. Two buses were accommodated inside and a third in the yard. Seen in this view are the firm's last surviving open-topper, XX 9806, and their Leyland TD2 JJ 1269, which was the last but one Dodson-bodied Titan to be built.

Photo No. 99 (*upper right*)

Joseph Ryan rented a small portion of a large garage. The whole fleet is seen on parade outside the premises in Colin Road, Willesden. The old Dennis on the left now sports white-walled tyres and is kept as a spare for the Titan. Both are in immaculate condition.

Photo No. 100 (*centre right*)

Railway arches proved useful for housing buses, and here City's G10, a Guy FCX, is seen squeezing into one of the arches at Astbury Road, Peckham. A large conventional garage building is out of sight to the right of the picture, and from it has just emerged the Leyland petrol tanker which was once bus A16.

Photo No. 101 (*lower right*)

The allied BBP and Chadwell buses shared accommodation with a fleet of removal lorries in Gooch's simple but substantial garage in Chadwell Heath. The left hand bus is PU 292, the original Roberts-rebuilt Daimler operated by BBP. The other is Chadwell's Dennis PU 6034.

Photos No. 102, 103 & 104
In its search for mechanica[l] perfection City was the mo[st] advanced of all the inde[-]pendents, and in its later day[s] the fleet has a character all [of] its own. The development [of] the fleet over the years [is] shown in these two pages an[d] began with Leyland LB's suc[h] as A12 (fig. 102), a Wilto[n-]bodied example seen with th[e] Astbury Road garage in th[e] background. Dodson-bodie[d] A34, ex St. George, is seen [in] closing years (fig. 103) com[-]plete with pneumatic tyre[s.] Fig. 104 shows C1, the 192[ ] rebuild by City, from Leyla[nd] LB A18.

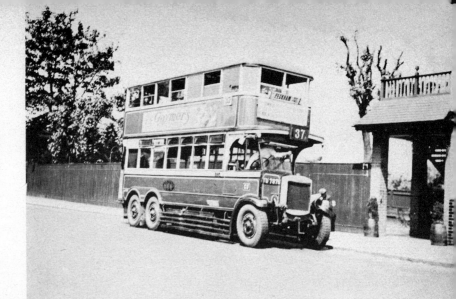

Photos No. 105, 106 & 107

City six-wheelers. 53 (fig. 105) is an ex-Public and later Amersham & District Guy FCX. CS4 (fig. 106) is one of the Ransomes-bodied 62-seaters on three axle chassis constructed by City themselves but incorporating a few parts from old Leyland LB's. TS1 (fig. 107) is a diesel-engined Leyland Titanic carrying the out-dated style of bodywork favoured by City as late as 1933.

Photo No. 108
The end draws nigh! One of City's special-type Leyland Titans is seen at Victoria already repainted in LPTB red in preparation for the takeover which lies ahead.

Photo No. 109
A picture that needs no caption. Three generations of the Birch family bid farewell to their London bus fleet.

Body No.	Stock No.			Body No.	Stock No.	

ROYAL BLUE

XR4596	9175(a)	—
XP1193	9176	—
XN3980	9177	—
XO3124	9178	—
XX9877	9179(b)	—
XU5778	9180	—
XT2864	9181	—
XU5779	9182	—
XX670	9324	—

(a) Body sold to C & P Sales, Ipswich 2/27

(b) Body sold to C & P Sales, Ipswich 3/27

SILVER STAR

ML611	9926	D59

SUPERBUS

XU4371	9462	D30

Body replaced by 9856 (ex The P.C.) 1/27

9462 to PU3549 (The P.C.) 1/27

T & W

XX1756	9355	D20

Body replaced by 9263 (ex Western) 11/26. 9355 scrapped

TIMPSON'S

XO3947	9858	—
XO3951	9859	—
XO3949	9860	—
XN2557	9861	—
XO3948	9862	—

Body numbers allocated upon disposal

TOTTENHAM HOTSPUR

AN6120	9835(a)	L30
XU5778	9836(b)	L31
XU5779	9837(c)	L32
YM6664	9838(d)	L34
YL8115	9839(e)	L33
MF7044	9840(f)	—
MF4463	9841(g)	—
MF4166	— (h)	—

(a) Body originally numbered 9327 on Ubique

(b) Body originally numbered 9180 on Royal Blue

(c) Body originally numbered 9182 on Royal Blue

(d) Body originally numbered 9255 on EP

(e) Body originally numbered 9256 on EP

(f) Body sold to C & P Sales, Ipswich 3/27

(g) Body sold to C & P Sales, Ipswich 6/27

(h) MF4166 taken over as a chassis only

Body 9252 (ex EP) fitted 1/27

TOWER

XT3717	9784	T1
XU2148	9785	T2
XU3280	9786	T3

UBIQUE

AN6452	9326	—
AN6120	9327	—

UNEEDUS

MK2245	9933	G1
MK2246	9934	G2
MF8953	9935	D62
MH1353	9936	D63
ML1169	9937	D64

VICTORIA ROAD CAR

XR555	9854	—

VIVID

XP7425	9834	—

WELLINGTON

XR2730	9782	L3
XX5413	9783	L4

WESTERN

YM8237	9257	D25
XT4731	9258	D32
XT110	9259(a)	D31
XT8982	9260(b)	D37
XN6661	9261	—
XO939	9262(c)	—
XO2107	9263(d)	—

(a) Body replaced by 9358 (ex Criterion) 1/27

9259 sold to C & P Sales, Ipswich 4/27

(b) Body replaced by 9473 (ex Grafton) 3/27

9260 to XO8668 (Redburn's, ex A1) 3/27

(c) Body replaced by 9198 (ex Cambrian) 10/26

9262 to XX9591 (Redburn's ex Dominion) 11/26

(d) Body replaced by 9199 (ex Cambrian) 10/26

9263 to XX1756 (Redburn's, ex T & W) 11/26

WHITE STAR

XX2024	9845

WW

MH2239	9843	D49

Fleets are listed in alphabetical order. In cases where operators super-seded one fleet name with another, their vehicles are listed under the name first used with cross-references to later names where appropriate. Vehicles are listed in order of their date of purchase.

In most cases where independent bus operators also ran coaches these are shown for completeness, with a small number of exceptions. The coach fleets of Gordon, Premier, Prince, Red Rover and Victory are omitted as they will appear in a future volume dealing with London area short distance express services. Two further omissions are the Julius & Lockwood and Samuelson coach fleets, records of which are too incomplete to justify inclusion.

The body classifications shown (column 5) are the same as those standardised by the Omnibus Society, P.S.V. Circle, etc. The letters preceding the seating capacity denote the body type viz:

- B – single-deck saloon bus
- C – single-deck saloon coach
- Ch – single deck charabanc
- H – highbridge type, covered-top double-decker
- OT – open top double-decker

The letters following the seating capacity denote the entrance position viz:

- C – centre entrance
- D – dual entrance; front – rear
- F – front entrance
- R – rear entrance (combined with enclosed staircase in the case of double-deckers)
- RO – rear entrance with open staircase (double-deckers)

In the case of double-deckers the seating capacity is shown by decks, the first figure relating to the upper deck and the second to the lower.

In several cases the body maker's name (column 6) has been abbreviated for space reasons. The body builders whose names appear in this volume are as follows: —

Abbott – E. D. Abbott Ltd., Farnham, Surrey.
Beadle – J. C. Beadle Ltd., Dartford, Kent.
Bell – Bell's Motor Body Works, Ltd., Scunthorpe, Lincs.
Birch – Birch Bros. Ltd., Kentish Town, London, N.W.5.
Clark – Clark, Scunthorpe.
Dodson – Christopher Dodson Ltd., Willesden, London, N.W.10.
Duple – Duple Bodies & Motors Ltd., Hendon, London, N.W.9.
Harr. – Thomas Harrington Ltd., Hove, Sussex.
H. Lewis – Hall Lewis & Co. Ltd., Park Royal, London, N.W.10.
Hickman – Hickman Bodybuilding Co. Ltd., Balham, London, S.W.12.
Holbrook – Samuel Holbrook Ltd., Wolverhampton, Staffs.
Leyland – Leyland Motors, Leyland, Lancs.
LGOC – London General Omnibus Co. Ltd., Chiswick, London, W.4.

LL	–	London Lorries Ltd., Kentish Town, London, N.W.5.
Metclf	–	Metcalfe's (London) Ltd., Romford, Essex.
Phoenix	–	Phoenix Coach Works Ltd., Farnham, Surrey.
P. R. V.	–	Park Royal Vehicles Ltd., London, N.W.10.
Redhead	–	Redhead's Motors Ltd., Lewisham, London.
R. S. J.	–	Ransomes, Sims & Jefferies Ltd., Ipswich, Suffolk.
S & B	–	Strachan & Brown Ltd., North Acton, London, W.3.
Straker	–	Straker Squire Ltd., Edmonton, London, N.9.
Thurgood	–	W. L. Thurgood, Ware, Herts.
Tilling	–	Thomas Tilling Ltd., Lewisham & elsewhere.
Tiverton	–	Tiverton Coachworks, Tiverton, Devon.
United	–	United Automobile Services Ltd., Lowestoft, Suffolk.
Wilton	–	Wilton Carriage Co. Ltd., Thornton Heath, Surrey.

It has not proved possible to establish the make of body fitted to any of the K-type double-deckers drafted into the formerly independent companies in 1926/7. These vehicles received a different body on each annual overhaul, and records do not exist to show these body exchanges in detail. K-type bodies were supplied by Brush, Dodson, Short and Strachan & Brown in addition to many built by the LGOC or by Ransomes, Sims & Jefferies.

Withdrawal dates from service are shown where known (column 10). These normally differ from the date of sale, sometimes by several months. The withdrawal date quoted refers to the first day that the vehicle concerned is non-operational, it having last been available for service on the previous day.

Disposals, where known, are noted at the end of each operator's fleet list. These do not include subsequent disposals of vehicles which went initially to General, Metropolitan, Public, Tilling and LPTB as these will be listed in a subsequent volume. The same applies to vehicles which remained in service with Overground from 1st January 1928 onwards.

London Transport stock numbers quoted for vehicles taken over before January 17th 1934 were officially allocated but in most cases were not carried. On this date most were renumbered, Leyland Titans becoming TD class, Leyland Lions LN class, Dennis H family becoming DH class, the gaps thus created within the D and L classes being filled by a consequent renumbering of the vehicles remaining within these classes.

A & W

Fleet No.	Regn. No.	Chassis Make & Type	Chassis No.	Body Type & Seating Capacity	Body Make	Colour Scheme	Date of First Regn.	Date Bought 2nd-hand	Date Withdrawn (if known)	Date Sold	Note
Buses											
	ME 4953	Crossley 25 h.p.	8358	B12F	?	Brown & Cream	16-8-22	New		24-3-26	
	ME 9478	"	7159	B14F	?	"	10-5-23	"		31-12-25	
	MH 1852	"	9412	B14F	S & B	"	4-11-24	"		?	
	OE 5780	"	13153		?	"	26-3-21	App 6-25		?	(1)
	MK 6400	Guy BB	22044	B32R	Hickman	Red & White	13-7-26	New		2-6-30	
	MH 1326	Daimler Y	6073	OT22/20RO	?	"	9-10-24	9-26		1929	
	MP 5344	Guy FBB	22882	B32R	"	"	2-7-28	New		2-6-30	
	MY 8142	"	23238	"	Duple	"	21-11-29	"		2-6-30	
Coaches (known fleet up to June 1930)											
	MY 7417	Guy FC	23284	C32F	?	Cream & Red	24-3-30	New		2-37	(2)
	MY 6072	Gilford 1680T	11351	"	?	"	15-4-30	"		7-40	

(1) Later B30R
(2) Rebodied Duple C32F 1936

Former Owner
OE 5780 New as a 4-seat car to W. Pagett, Dudley passing to
Stour Valley Motor Co Stourbridge 5-25
MH 1326 HFB

Disposal
ME 4953/9478 G. Warren, Watford
MH 1852/OE 5780 Filkins & Ainsworth, Harefield, Middx.
MK 6400/MP 5344/MY 8142 General
MH 1326 J. Bennett, London, SW15 (Lorry)
MY 7417 Pilgrim Coaches, Edgware, Middx., later to H. Day, Ipswich.
 Withdrawn 1-7-48
MY 6072 Garners Coaches, London, W5; Latham, Kenton, Middx. 11-40.
 Allison Doran Ltd., Thetford, Norfolk, 1942; Coach Services (Thetford)
 Ltd., 8-48; Rebodied Waveney C33F and withdrawn 13-7-54.
 Sold to a showman

A1

Fleet No.	Regn. No.	Chassis Make & Type	Chassis No.	Body Type & Seating Capacity	Body Make	Colour Scheme	Date of First Regn.	Date Bought 2nd-hand	Date Withdrawn (if known)	Date Sold	Note
K993	XO 8668	Dennis 4 ton	40049	OT26/22RO	Dodson	Maroon & Cream	3-8-23	New	5-2-27	8-3-27	
	XF 8010	AEC K	21259	OT24/22RO	?	"	4-21	4-2-27		1-1-28	

Former Owner
XF 8010 General

Disposal
XO 8668 Redburn No. D39; XF8010 General K993

AB—see BROWN

ADELAIDE SERVICE, THE/ADELAIDE

Fleet No.	Regn. No.	Chassis Make & Type	Chassis No.	Body Type & Seating Capacity	Body Make	Colour Scheme	Date of First Regn.	Date Bought 2nd-hand	Date Withdrawn (if known)	Date Sold	Note
	XW 2210	Dennis 4 ton	40227	OT26/22RO	Dodson	Red & Cream	4-11-24	New		1-11-33	(1)
	GC 3354	Leyland TD1	70965	H28/24RO	"	"	30-1-30	"		1-11-33	

(1) Later fitted with pneumatic tyres

Disposal
XW 2210/GC 3354 LPTB No. D177/L48

ADMIRAL (also NEWSTEAD)

No.	Reg.	S. Squire A	Chassis No.	Body	Builder	Livery	Date	New	Date	Note
1	ME 6185		A6219	OT22/22RO	Straker	Blue & White	4-12-22	New	5-23	
2	ME 6186		A6217	"	"	"	6-12-22	"	5-23	
3	ME 7240		A6214	"	"	"	21-2-23	"	3-26	
4	ME 7364		A6228	"	"	"	28-2-23	"	8-26	
5	ME 7351		A6206	"	"	"	17-3-23	"	7-23	
6	ME 7886		A6211	"	"	"	12-4-23	"	1-26	
7	ME 8598		A6210	"	"	"	23-4-23	"	7-23	
8	ME 8829		A6232	"	"	"	17-5-23	"	2-27	
1	ME 9689		A6239	OT24/22RO	Dodson	"	17-5-23	"	22-9-24	(1)
9	ME 9690		A6245	"	Straker	"	31-5-23	"	7-27	
2	MF 180		A6251	"	"	"	22-6-23	"	22-9-24	(1)
10	MF 691		A6255	"	"	"	4-7-23	"	1-26	
7	MF 1020		A6280	"	"	"	10-3-24	"	1-25	
11	MF 5397		A6373	"	"	"	9-4-24	"	17-8-27	
12	MF 6432		A6374	"	"	"	24-5-24	"	17-8-27	
14	MF 6881		A6375	"	"	"	4-7-24	"	17-8-27	
15	MF 9171		A6390	OT26/22RO	Dodson	"	25-8-24	"	1-25	
16	MH 473	Dennis 4 ton	40196	"	"	"	20-2-25	"	17-8-27	
12	MH 3883		40263	"	"	"	3-4-25	"	17-8-27	
14	MH 5256		40259	"	"	"	7-4-25	"	17-8-27	
15	MH 5449		40260	"	"	"	7-4-25	"	17-8-27	
16	MH 5450		40261	"	"	"	9-4-25	"	17-8-27	
17	MH 5555		40262	"	"	"	7-5-25	"	17-8-27	
18	MH 6323	Dennis 2¼ ton	45071	B26R	"	"	7-5-25	"	17-8-27	
19	MH 6325		45065	"	"	"	12-5-25	"	17-8-27	
20	MH 6324		45072	"	"	"	12-5-25	"	17-8-27	
21	MH 6470		45075	"	"	"	12-5-25	"	17-8-27	
22	MH 6468		45076	"	"	"	23-6-25	"	17-8-27	
23	MH 6469		45077	B25R	"	"	23-6-25	"	17-8-27	
24	MH 7957		45109	"	"	"	23-6-25	"	17-8-27	
25	MH 7958		45111	"	"	"	29-6-25	"	17-8-27	
26	MH 7956		45113	"	"	"	29-6-25	"	17-8-27	
27	MH 8182		45114	"	"	"	29-6-25	"	17-8-27	
28	MH 8184		45110	"	"	"		"	17-8-27	
29	MH 8183		45112	"	"	"		"	17-8-27	
7	MK 1572	Dennis 4 ton	40377	OT26/22RO	"	"	3-12-25	31-12-25	1-27	
30	NK 8877	Dennis 2¼ ton	30731	B20R	"	?	10-24	New	17-8-27	
3	MK 2236	Dennis 4 ton	40242	OT26/22RO	"	"	25-1-26	"	17-8-27	
1	MK 3072	Dennis 2¼ ton	40387	B25R	"	"	12-3-26	"	17-8-27	
31	MK 3401		45243	"	"	"	24-3-26	"	17-8-27	
32	MK 3700		45244	"	"	"	31-3-26	"	17-8-27	
33	MK 3701		45253	"	"	"	31-3-26	"	17-8-27	
2	MK 6959	Dennis 4 ton	40421	OT24/22RO	Straker	"	7-8-26	"	17-8-27	
34	MK 7066	Dennis 2¼ ton	45435	B25R	Dodson	"	16-8-26	"	17-8-27	(2)

409

Fleet	Reg	Make	Chassis	Body	Body builder	Colour	New	Acquired	Disposed
35	ML 539	Dennis E	17067	B30R	Dodson	Blue & White	20-10-26	New	17-8-27
36	ML 1582	"	17097	"	"	"	11-1-27	"	17-8-27
37	ML 1583	"	17093	"	"	"	11-1-27	"	17-8-27
38	ML 1584	"	17100	"	"	"	11-1-27	"	17-8-27
39	ML 1812	"	17115	"	"	"	26-1-27	"	17-8-27
40	ML 1813	"	17113	"	"	"	26-1-27	"	17-8-27
41	ML 1924	"	17114	"	"	"	2-2-27	"	17-8-27
4	ML 2140	Dennis 4 ton	40433	OT24/22RO	Straker	Blue	16-2-27	"	17-8-27
	MK 4777	Morris 30 cwt	153351	Van	?		14-5-26		

Fleet Nos 3/4/7-12/14/16 renumbered 1-5/7-11, approx 2-25
(1) Renamed Newstead and repainted red & white 12-23
(2) Body ex ME 7364, 8-26 (3) Body ex ME 8829, 2-27

Former Owner
NK 8877 Barnet Motor Services

Disposal
ME 6185/6186 Hertford & District, Ware No. 21/20
ME 7240 H. Fisher, Birkenhead (Lorry); withdrawn 1-7-31
ME 7364 Brooks Bros., Wrexham (Lorry); withdrawn 1-10-33
ME 7351/8598 CWP
ME 7886 J. Roberts, Chester (Lorry); withdrawn 1-1-32
ME 8829 Jones & Co., Oswestry (Lorry); withdrawn 1-7-28
ME 9689/MF 180 Cambrian No. S74/73
ME 9690 H. W. Scholes, London, E1 (Lorry)
MF 691 Ball, Birkenhead (Lorry); withdrawn 25-3-32
MF 1020/9171 EP No. 20/21
MF 5397/6432/7881/MH 473/3883/5256/5449/5450/5555/6323-5
6468-70/7956-8/8182-4/MK 1572/2236/3072/3401/3700/3701
6959/7066/ML 539/1582-4/1812/1813/1924/2140/MK 4777
Public No. —/—/D20/29/38/7/3/46/DS32/38/6/23/29/37/31
36/30/11/7/12/D35/45/53/DS3/2/1/D63/DS17/DE2/4/5/6/8/7/9/D54/—
NK 8877 Waltham Motor Services

AGS—see OXFORD

Fleet	Reg	Make	Chassis	Body	Body builder	Colour	New	Acquired	Disposed
AJM	MH 5067	Leyland LB5	13230	OT26/22RO	Dodson	Red & Grey	28-3-25	New	26-10-27

Disposal
MH 5067 Public No. L28

ALBERTA

Fleet	Reg	Make	Chassis	Body	Body builder	Colour	New	Acquired	Disposed
L1	XT 5386	Leyland LB4	12720	OT26/22RO	Dodson	Red & White	30-5-24	New	3-3-27
L2	XT 8752	"	12719	"	"	"	19-6-24	"	25-7-27
D3	XU 6822	Dennis 4 ton	40186	"	"	"	29-8-24	"	1-1-28
D4	XU 6823	"	40187	"	"	"	29-8-24	"	1-1-28
D5	XX 7606	"	40329	"	"	"	1-4-25	"	1-1-28
D6	XX 8731	"	40330	"	"	"	6-4-25	"	1-1-28
D7	XX 9344	"	40331	"	"	"	8-4-25	"	1-1-28
K308	XF 8082	AEC K	20308	OT24/22RO	?	?	1920	9-2-27	1-1-28
K334	LU 8478	"	20334	"	?	?	1920	22-7-27	1-1-28

(3)

ALEXANDRA

Former Owner: XF 8082/LU 8478 General

Reg	Chassis	Chassis No	Body	Builder	Colour	New			Withdrawn	Notes
XW 9375	Leyland LB5	13148	OT26/22RO	S & B	Red & White	30-1-25	New	5-25	11-7-25	(1)

Disposal
XT 5386 Invicta No. L39
XT 8752 National, Watford No. L2
XU 6822/6823/XX 7606/8731/9344/XF 8082/LU 8478 General No. D42/43/45/46/44/K308/334

Disposal
XW 9375 Lee & Beaulah, Elloughton, Yorks; East Yorkshire Motor Services, Hull No. 16, 5-10-26; to lorry 1933

ALLITT, G. H. & SONS LTD.

Buses

No.	Reg	Chassis	Chassis No	Body	Builder	Colour	New	Other	Withdrawn	Notes
	XU 3915	Leyland LB5	12917	OT26/22RO	Wilton	Red & White	25-7-24	New	1-31	
	XW 3199	"	12938	B30R	Abbott	"	14-11-24	"	19-2-31	
2	UL 4686	Karrier JKL	10661	"	Dodson	"	2-2-29	"	5-12-33	
	GU 2533	"	10665	"	"	"	25-3-29	"	5-12-33	
6	UC 3013	Dennis E	17322	B32R	"	Chocolate & White	1-2-28	7-29	5-12-33	
	MT 2992	Leyland PLSC3	47647	B30R	"	Yellow	28-3-29	7-29	5-12-33	
5	UW 1417	Dennis ES	17675	H30/26RO	"	Red & Cream	28-9-29	New	5-12-33	
	GK 6337	Leyland TD1	71727	B30R	Birch	"	28-11-30		5-12-33	
	GN 3185	Dennis ES	71728	"	"	"	21-1-31		5-12-33	
	UU 1907	"	17714	"	"	"	16-5-29	30-6-32	5-12-33	

Coaches

No.	Reg	Chassis	Chassis No	Body	Builder	Colour	New	Other	Withdrawn	Notes
7	MC 9718	AEC Y	8625	Ch 28	?	Grey	1920	New	1-1-31	1931
	YE 5869	Vulcan 3X	?	C30	?	Red	25-3-27	"		1-34
	YF 2594	Karrier WL6	42013	C39	?	"	25-3-27	"		29-8-29	(2)
	YF 2595	"	42012	"	?	"	25-3-27	"		29-8-29	(2)
5	YV 2466	Karrier JKL	10638	C32	?	"	27-3-28	"		1-34	
6	YV 2467	"	10639	"	?	"	27-3-28	"		12-33	
4	GU 2531	"	10662	"	?	"	25-3-29	"		1933	
1	GU 2532	"	10663	"	?	"	25-3-29	"		7-33	(1)
	GU 2534	"	10664	"	?	"	25-3-29	"		6-33	
3	GF 5096	Commer Inv	28013	C20F	?	"	25-3-30	"		7-33	(3)

(1) Colour later red & cream (2) 6-wheeler (3) To Allitt lorry 3-29

Former Owner
UC 3013/MT 2992 Newlands District
UU 1907 Eagle

Disposal
XU 3915/XW 3199 Chandlers Motors London SE8 (Lorry)
UL 4686/GU 2533/UC 3013/MT 2992/UW 1417/GK 6337/GN 3185/ UU 1907 LPTB No. KR1/2/DE27/L94/DE26/L92/93/DE25
MC 9718/YV 2466 scrapped
YE 5869 J. J. Maynard, London, SE16
YF 2594/2595 Karrier Motors and scrapped
YV 2467 Elephant & Castle Motor Repository (dealer); E. A. Matthews, London, W14, 12-33; G. Edwards, Wandsworth 12-33
GU 2531 to Lorry
GU 2532/2534/GF 5096 Grey Coaches (Wiggs), Peckham

ALMA

1	XR 999	Thornycroft J	10485	OT26/24RO	Dodson	Red & White	31-1-24	New	21-10-26
2	XX 8697	Leyland LB5	13305	OT26/22RO	"	"	6-4-25	"	3-8-27
1	YP 5156	"	13589	"	"	"	22-7-26	"	3-8-27

Disposal
XR 999 Thames Valley No. 138
XX 8697/YP 5156 Public No. L12/26

AMBASSADOR (see also EMPRESS (Crabb & Clarke))

XP 7183	Dennis 4 ton	40062	OT26/22RO	Dodson	Red & White	4-12-23	New	4-6-31
XX 6678	"	40264	H28/26RO	"	"	26-3-25	"	12-30
XV 3453	Dennis H	90051	H30/26R	Birch	"	6-11-28	"	29-8-34
GK 7167	Dennis Lance	125012	H28/26R	Dodson	"	2-12-30	"	29-8-34
GX 143	"	126050	"	"	"	23-3-32	"	29-8-34

Disposal
XP 7183 Eastwoods Ltd., London, SE1 (Lorry)
XX 6678 ?
XV 3453/GK 7167/GX 143 LPTB No. DH17/DL29/30

ARCHWAY/BIRCH

Buses

B1	XW 6188	Leyland LB5	13134	OT26/22RO	Birch	Red & White	22-12-24	New	21-2-34
B2	XW 6189	"	13133	"	"	"	22-12-24	"	29-5-31
B3	XX 5044	"	13226	"	"	Brown & Cream	23-3-25	"	18-12-30
B4	XX 5043	"	13228	"	"	"	23-3-25	"	5-3-31
B5	XX 7447	"	13306	"	"	"	31-3-25	"	21-4-31
B6	YL 2136	"	13309	"	"	Red & White	13-8-25	"	21-4-31
B7	YH 6292	"	13809	"	"	Brown & Cream	4-6-27	"	21-2-34
B8	YT 6958	Dennis E	17221	B30R	"	Red & White	11-8-27	"	21-2-34
B9	YU 1015	"	17224	"	"	"	3-10-27	"	21-2-34
B10	YU 1016	"	17229	"	"	"	3-10-27	"	21-2-34
B11	YU 1017	"	17230	"	"	"	3-10-27	"	21-2-34
B12	YU 1018	"	17231	"	"	Maroon & Cream	3-10-27	"	21-2-34
B13	YU 8159	"	17234	"	"	Red & White	20-12-27	"	21-2-34
B14	UC 1945	"	17349	"	"	Brown & Cream	1-2-28	"	21-2-34
B15	UC 1946	"	17356	"	"	"	1-2-28	"	21-2-34
B16	UC 8332	"	17386	"	"	"	8-3-28	"	21-2-34
B17	YV 1227	"	17401	B32R	"	"	26-3-28	"	21-2-34
B19	YX 4400	Leyland PLSC3	47196	B30R	"	"	3-8-28	"	19-4-35
B23	UL 1966	Dennis E	17584	"	"	"	19-1-29	"	21-2-34
B24	UL 4420	"	17606	"	"	"	1-2-29	"	21-2-34
B18	XX 1514	Daimler Y	6080	OT22/20RO	Hickman	Red & White	17-2-25	1-2-29	14-8-29	(1)
B20	XV 1153	Leyland PLSC3	47152	B32R	Birch	Brown & Cream	18-10-28	1-2-29	3-35	(2)

Fleet	Reg.	Chassis	Chassis No.	Body	Builder	Colour					Note
B21	XP 435	Leyland LB2	12641	OT26/22RO	Dodson	Red & White	1-9-23	1-2-29		5-3-31	
B22	XT 4608	Leyland LB4	12716	H28/26RO	"	"	20-5-24	1-2-29	1-2-31	3-2-31	(3)
B25	GU 977	Dennis H	90061	"	Birch	Brown & Cream	19-3-29	New		21-2-34	
B26	GU 6436	"	90064	"	"	"	18-4-29			21-2-34	
B27	UC 1817	Maudslay ML3	4219	B30R	H. Lewis	Dark Red & White	20-1-28	7-6-29	1-1-31	9-1-31	(3)
B28	UC 1816	"	4030	"	Birch	Brown & Cream	20-1-28	7-6-29	26-1-31	2-31	
B29	GK 6431	Leyland TD1	71492	H30/26RO	"	"	28-11-30	New		21-2-34	
B30	GK 8660	"	71764	"	"	"	11-12-30	"		21-2-34	
B31	GK 9718	"	71765	"	"	"	30-12-30	"		21-2-34	
B32	GN 4380	"	71768	"	"	"	31-1-31	"		21-2-34	
B33	GN 4381	"	71873	"	"	"	31-1-31	"		21-2-34	
B34	GN 5880	"	71791	"	"	"	28-2-31	"		21-2-34	
B35	GN 5881	"	71769	"	"	"	28-2-31	"		21-2-34	
B36	GO 1525	"	71770	"	"	"	30-4-31	"		21-2-34	
B37	GO 1526	"	71771	"	"	"	25-3-31	"		21-2-34	
B38	GP 7289	"	72214	"	"	"	31-7-31	"		21-2-34	
B39	GX 131	"	868	H30/26R	"	"	22-3-32	"		21-2-34	(4)
B40	GX 132	"	869	"	"	"	29-4-32	"		21-2-34	(5)

Coach fleet up to February 1934

Fleet	Reg.	Chassis	Chassis No.	Body	Builder	Colour					Note
K1	IT 253	TSM TS3A	1088	Ch 28	Birch	Maroon & Black	5-19	New		?	
K2	IT 254	"	1080	"	"	"	5-19			3-26	
K3	IT 255	"	1089	"	"	"	5-19			?	
K7	IT 268	Leyland S5	10141	Ch 23	"	Lead "	7-19	"		8-4-32	(6)
K4	IT 288	TSM TS3A	1666	"	"	Maroon & Black	15-5-20	"		14-5-29	(7)
K5	IT 289	"	1674	"	"	"	5-20	"		14-5-29	(7)
K6	IT 290	"	1675	"	"	"	5-20	"		19-2-32	(7)
K8	LX 8658	Leyland S5	10126	C28	"	Cream & Crimson	8-19	"		19-2-32	(8)
K9	LX 8659	"	10142	"	"	"	8-19	"		6-3-33	(8)
K10	YV 1228	Leyland PLSC3	46382	C30F	"	"	26-3-28	"	1-10-33	10-34	
K11	YV 5499	"	46384	"	"	"	5-5-28	"		3-35	
K12	YW 2793	"	46383	"	"	"	5-28	"		1934	
K13	YV 5210	Albion PJ26	5062K	C26D	?	"	4-28	"		1934	
K14	YV 5211	"	5062L	"	?	"	4-28	"		3-35	
K15	UL 1964	Leyland PLC1	47618	C24F	"	"	19-1-29	"	1-10-33	3-35	
K16	UL 1965	"	47619	"	"	"	19-1-29	"	1-10-33	5-37	
K17	UL 4418	"	47621	"	"	"	1-2-29	"		By 6-41	
K18	UL 4419	"	47620	"	"	"	1-2-29	"		3-40	
K19	GU 2972	Gilford 1660T	10675	C30D	?	"	5-29	"		12-45	
K20	GU 2973	"	10641	"	?	"	5-29	"		3-40	(9)
K21	UU 1463	"	10713	"	?	"	5-29	"		12-36	(9)
K22	UU 1464	"	10773	"	?	"	5-29	"		2-45	(9)
K23	UU 1465	"	10828	"	?	"	6-29	"		2-36	(9)
K24	UU 1466	"	10835	"	?	"	6-29	"		3-35	(9)
K28	YW 6778	Leyland PLSC3	47195	C32F	Birch	"	6-28	12-3-32			

K33	MT 5714	Gilford 1660T	10681	C32F	?	Cream & Crimson	9-5-29	30-11-32	5-35
K34	MY 9115	"	11003	C31F	?	"	30-11-29	30-11-32	1937
K35	MY 7225	"	11221	"	?	"	8-7-30	30-11-32	By 12-41

Vehicles renumbered: K10-14 to K25-27/31/32 in 3.32.   B1/2/6/9-13/21/22/27/28 Colour to brown & cream 1928/1928/ 6-25/1-29/8-28/1928/1928/
11-28/3-29/3-29/2-30/1-30.   B1-7/21/22 fitted with pneumatic tyres 9-29/1929/1929/1929/12-29/9-29/3-30/1929.
(1) Converted to C32R & rend. K29 Colour cream & crimson 9-3-32   (2) Converted to C32R & rend. K30 colour cream & crimson 25-3-32; repainted
cream & green 3-34.   (3) Re-seated to H30/26RO 3-30   (4) Leyland oil engine fitted and re-seated to H29/25R 9-6-33   (5) Re-seated to H29/25R
6-5-33   (6) Colour to maroon & black 23-9-19, converted to lorry 10-8-20, converted to Ch28 with pneumatic tyres 24-3-26
(7) Re-seated to Ch28 4-25   (8) New as lorries No. L1 & L2. Coach bodies and pneumatic tyres fitted 5-27   (9) Repainted cream & green
3-34/3-34/3-34/3-34/3-34/3-34/4-34 respectively

Former Owners
B18/20 I & B
B21/22 Drake
B27/28 AB
K28   St Albans & District
K33-35 Beaumont-Safeway, Enfield

Disposal
B1/7-17/23/24/25/26/29-40 LPTB No. L54/55/DE29-40/DH10/11/
    TD74-83/85/84
B2-6/21/22/27/28 Leyland Motors (dealer) SE1. B2 to Lorry 6-31.
B3 to Carjax Ltd., N1 (Van) 7-31; Challen Bros., EC3 1-35;
    Albury Motors, London, 9-35; A. McCann (dealer), Brixton 9-35.
B4/22 to Vale Bros., Beckenham (Lorry) 1931. B5 to L. Benjamin,
    Stockton-on-Tees (Lorry) 5-31; Woodhouse Bros., Preston, and scrap
    5-33. B6 to E. A. Shadrock, London, E6 (Lorry) 4-31. B21 to Barnards
    Ltd., London, SE8 (Lorry) 1931; withdrawn 1-1-37. B27/28 to
    J. Rothwell, Holt, Wrexham, as B32R, 6-31; Crosville M.S. No. 978/977,
    1-1-34; scrapped 7-35
B19/20 City Coaches, London, NW5, No. L22/21. B19 to W. L. Williams,
    Rhymney, 6-37; Praills Ltd. (dealer), Hereford and scrapped 11-49
B18 A. Speechley (dealer), London, W3; J. Bennett, London, SW15, (Lorry) 9-29
K1-3/31/32 ?
K2 Converted to Birch lorry; sold 4-32
K7 Reconverted to Birch lorry
K4-6 W. & S. Freeman (dealer), London, EC1
K8/9 Leyland Motors (dealer), London, SE1
K25 E. H. Green, London, NW2; Horne Products (dealer), Colnbrook, 7-38
K26 Taylor, Ryde, IOW; Newbury & District No. 45, 11-40; scrapped 11-43
K27 Deerness M.S. (Kelly & Briggs), Bear Park, Co. Durham; United Auto
    Services (not used) 10-38; Smith (dealer), Middlesbrough, 10-38
K15 Nightingale, Spalding, Lincs.; scrapped 9-37
K16 Alma Queen, Brynmawr, Mon.; Margaret Coaches, Liverpool 6-37;
    scrapped 1-39
K17 Kemp, Woodcote, Berks; sold 7-39
K18 to Lorry
K19/21 Ipswich Corporation (ARP); Mulley, Ixworth No. 18/17, 8-45;
    scrapped 3-47
K20/23 to Showman
K22 E. H. Green, London. NW5; Paddington Transport, London, W9 5-38;
    withdrawn 9-38

414

K24 Killick Dallington, Sussex; H. G. Goodman, Plumpton, as C32LD, 3-4/; withdrawn 10-49
K28 Hicks Bros., Braintree, Essex; W. A. Richardson, Braintree, (Lorry) 11-36; War Department 3-40
K33 Fountain Coaches (Susan's), Twickenham; Streatham Vale Coaches, London, SW16, 6-36; Ministry of Supply, 1940; withdrawn 31-12-42
K34 Skylark Express, London, W5; sold 7-39
K35 Arlington (dealer), Sudbury, and scrapped

ARO

No	Reg	Chassis	Chassis No	Body	Maker	Colour			
1	HM 6446	Dennis 2½ ton	45401	B25R	Dodson	Chocolate & Cream	1-6-26	New	3-8-27
2	HM 6445	"	45402	"	"	"	1-6-26	"	3-8-27
3	HM 6447	"	45403	"	"	"	1-6-26	"	3-8-27
4	HM 6749	"	45428	"	"	"	1-8-26	"	3-8-27
5	HM 6750	"	45431	"	"	"	1-8-26	"	3-8-27
6	HM 6751	"	45427	"	"	"	1-8-26	"	3-8-27
7	HM 7040	"	45457	"	"	"	2-12-26	"	

Disposal
1-7 Public No. DS16/4/10/39/5/14/25

ASTORIA

Reg	Chassis	Chassis No	Body	Maker	Colour			
YX 9732	Leyland PLSC3	47428	B32R	Birch	Crimson & Cream	29-9-28	New	13-6-34

Disposal
YX 9732 LPTB No. LN5

ATLAS

No	Reg	Chassis	Chassis No	Body	Maker	Colour				
1	XN 7748	Leyland LB2	12456	OT26/22RO	Dodson	Chocolate & Cream	7-5-23	New	13-10-27	1-1-28
2	XO 5617	"	12577	"	"	"	11-7-23	"	14-10-27	1-1-28
3	HM 3766	Leyland LB4	12737	"	"	"	25-3-24	"	15-10-27	22-12-27
4	HM 3827	"	12748	"	"	"	24-3-24	"	15-7-27	16-7-27
5	HM 4195	Leyland LB5	12718	"	"	"	6-24	"	17-10-27	1-1-28
6	HM 4392	"	12915	"	"	"	8-24	"	21-10-27	1-1-28
7	HM 4393	"	12921	"	"	"	1-9-24	"	25-10-27	1-1-28
8	HM 4498	"	12925	"	"	"	9-24	"	15-7-27	18-7-27
9	HM 4604	"	13130	"	"	"	1-12-24	"	13-10-27	1-1-28
10	HM 4605	"	13127	"	"	"	1-12-24	"	6-10-27	1-1-28
11	HM 4606	"	13129	"	"	"	1-12-24	"	6-10-27	17-12-27
12	HM 4627	"	13132	"	"	"	12-24	"	20-10-27	1-1-28
13	HM 4690	"	13135	"	"	"	2-25	"	17-10-27	1-1-28
14	HM 4755	"	13147	"	"	"	1-3-25	"	14-10-27	1-1-28
15	HM 4756	"	13222	"	"	"	1-3-25	"	17-10-27	1-1-28
16	HM 4757	"	13224	"	"	"	1-3-25	"	17-10-27	1-1-28
L6	XO 4835	Leyland LB2	12583	"	"	Red & White	4-7-23	11-4-27	20-10-27	21-12-27

K519	XC 8143	AEC K	20769	OT24/22RO	?	Red & White	1921	14-7-27	1-1-28
K561	XC 8194	"	20811	"	?	"	1921	14-7-27	1-1-28
K707	XC 8264	"	20957	"	?	"	1921	6-10-27	1-1-28
K729	XC 9742	"	20979	"	?	"	1921	6-10-27	1-1-28
K724	XC 8290	"	20974	"	?	"	1921	13-10-27	1-1-28
K908	XC 9739	"	21174	"	?	"	1920	13-10-27	1-1-28
K436	XC 8064	"	20436	"	?	"	1920	14-10-27	1-1-28
K522	XC 8129	"	20772	"	?	"	1921	14-10-27	1-1-28
K802	XC 8465	"	21068	"	?	"	1920	15-10-27	1-1-28
K435	XC 8041	"	20435	"	?	"	1921	17-10-27	1-1-28
K537	XC 8150	"	20787	"	?	"	1921	17-10-27	1-1-28
K688	XC 8248	"	20938	"	?	"		17-10-27	1-1-28
K1124	YR 3807	"	20677	"	?	"	11-11-26	20-10-27	1-1-28
K786	XC 9783	"	21052	"	?	"	1921	20-10-27	1-1-28
K910	XC 9722	"	21176	"	?	"	1921	21-10-27	1-1-28
K832	XC 8418	"	21098	"	?	"	1921	25-10-27	1-1-28
K663	XC 8240	"	20913	"	?	"	1921		1-1-28

Former Owner
L6 Marathon
All K-type General

Disposal
1/2/5-7/9/10/12-16 General No. L15/20/19/13/11/10/12/17/22/9/8/7
All K-Type, General
3/11/L6 C & P Sales (dealer), Ipswich
4/8 National, Watford, No. L16/18

BARNET MOTOR SERVICES

Buses

NK 5070	Fiat	205056	B12F	?	Brown	1-23	New	By 3-26
NK 5752	"	205186	"	?	"	6-23	"	By 3-26
NK 8696	"	?	B14F	?	"	26-7-24	"	By 3-26
NK 8877	Dennis 2¼ ton	30731	B20F	Dodson	Brown & White	10-24	"	31-12-25

Coach

NK 1885	Fiat	526	C12	?	Khaki	5-21	1922	?

Former Owner
NK 1885 Lees Coaches, Barnet

Disposal
NK 5070/5752/8696 Waltham Motor Services, Waltham Cross
NK 8877 Admiral No. 30
NK 1885 ?

BAYSWATER

2	XU 1368	Dennis 4 ton	40167	OT26/22RO	S & B	Red & White	7-7-24	New	17-8-27

Disposal
2 Public No. D17

BB

No	Reg	Chassis	Chassis No	Body	Builder	Colour	Date		Date out	Note
1	PU 1124	S. Squire A	A6349	OT24/22RO	Straker	Chocolate & Cream	30-11-23	New	3-8-27	(1)
2	PU 1125	"	A6348	OT26/22RO	S & B	"	30-11-23	"	3-8-27	(1)
3	PU 1998	Dennis 4 ton	40084	"	"	Dark Red & White	1-3-24	"	3-8-27	
4	PU 2667	"	40100	"	"	"	8-4-24	"	3-8-27	
5	PU 3225	"	40123	"	"	"	12-5-24	"	3-8-27	
6	NK 8082	"	40156	"	"	"	6-24	"	3-8-27	
7	NK 8605	"	40174	"	"	"	7-24	"	3-8-27	
8	NK 8606	"	40173	"	"	"	7-24	"	3-8-27	
9	NK 9295	"	40289	"	"	"	1-25	"	3-8-27	
10	RO 1471	Dennis 2½ ton	45144	B26R	"	"	8-25	"	3-8-27	(2)
11	RO 1596	"	45147	"	"	"	8-25	"	3-8-27	(2)
12	RO 5230	Dennis E	17101	B30R	"	"	12-26	"	3-8-27	
13	RO 7186	"	17210	"	"	"	6-27	"	3-8-27	

Coach

NO 9328	Buick	?		C14	?	?	1-6-23	New	?	

Disposal
1-13 Public No. —/—/D14/52/57/49/25/47/89/DS33/34/DE3/11
NO 9328 ?

(1) Colour to dark red & white 6-24
(2) Fitted with opening roofs

BBP

	Reg	Chassis	Chassis No	Body	Builder	Colour	Date		Date out	Note
	PU 292	Daimler Y	5477	OT22/20RO	Hickman	Violet & Grey	9-8-23	New	1928	(1)
	MF 8001	"	6063	"	"	Red & White	29-5-24	1928	15-12-33	
	VX 7702	Dennis HV	95009	H30/26RO	Birch	"	25-9-30	New	15-12-33	

(1) Colour to red & white 9-24

Former Owner
MF 8001 Capt. A. Morgan, Cork via Roberts (dealer)

Disposal
PU 292 ?
MF 8001/VX 7702 LPTB No. —/D190

BC (Edmonton Omnibus Co)

	Reg	Chassis	Chassis No	Body	Builder	Colour	Date		Date out	Note
	MF 1297	S. Squire	A6271	OT24/22RO	Straker	Chocolate & Yellow	16-7-23	New	14-1-26	(1)
	MF 1298	"	A6272	"	"	Red & White	16-7-23	"	12-23	
	MF 4511	"	A6338	"	"	"	31-1-24	"	7-24	
	MF 9160	Dennis 4 ton	40163	OT26/22RO	Dodson	"	4-7-24	"	5-25	

(1) Colour to red & white 7-24

Disposal
MF 1297 Earl
MF 1298 Redburns No. 13
MF 4511 R. Wilson, Birmingham (Lorry); withdrawn 1-1-45
MF 9160 Cosgrove

BEATTIE B & B

	Reg	Chassis	Chassis No	Body	Builder	Colour	Date		Date out
	XX 3458	Dennis 4 ton	40328	OT26/22RO	Wilton	Red & White	6-3-25	New	19-7-27

Disposal
XX 3458 Public No. D37

BELGRAVIA

Reg	Chassis	Chassis No	Body type	Builder	Colour	Date			
XU 8984	Leyland LB5	12928	OT26/22RO	Dodson	Scarlet & White	29-9-24	New		23-11-27

Disposal
XU 8984 Westminster

BIRCH—see ARCHWAY

BLUEBELL/INVICTA

Fleet	Reg	Chassis	Chassis No	Body	Builder	Colour	Date				
	HM 2996	S. Squire A	A6205	OT22/22RO	Straker	Peacock Blue & White	26-2-23	New	3-3-27	26-3-27	(1)
	HM 4481	Leyland LB5	12918	OT26/22RO	Dodson	Red & Grey	9-24	New	16-7-27	19-7-27	
	HM 4482	"	12924	"	"	"	9-24	"	18-7-27	20-7-27	
	HM 4820	"	13225	"	"	"	3-25	"	20-7-27	22-7-27	
	XT 5386	Leyland LB4	12720	"	"	Red & White	1-6-24	3-3-27	15-7-27	21-7-27	
L39	LU 8469	AEC K	20196	OT24/22RO	?	"	1920	15-7-27		1-1-28	
K196	XC 8079	"	20473	"	?	"	1920	16-7-27		1-1-28	
K473	XC 8090	"	20478	"	?	"	1920	17-7-27		1-1-28	
K478	XC 8267	"	20963	"	?	"	1921	19-7-27		1-1-28	
K713											

(1) Colour to red & grey 3-24

Former Owner
L39 Alberta
K196/473/478/713 General

Disposal
HM 2996 C. & P. Sales (dealer), Ipswich
HM 4481/2/4820/XT 5386 National, Watford, No. L37/38/40/39
K196/473/478/713 General

BRITISH LION

Reg	Chassis	Chassis No	Body	Builder	Colour	Date			
XT 2645	Leyland LB4	12711	OT26/22RO	Dodson	Red & Cream	5-5-24	New	13-10-27	2-9-27
XU 7545	Dennis 4 ton	40192	"	"	"	3-9-24	"	19-10-27	2-9-27

Disposal
XT 2645/XU 7545 Public No. L23/D58

BRITANNIA

Fleet	Reg	Chassis	Chassis No	Body	Builder	Colour	Date			
1	HM 3519	Leyland LB2	12640	OT26/22RO	Dodson	Chocolate & White	24-8-23	New	13-10-27	1-1-28
2	HM 4695	Leyland LB5	13150	"	"	"	2-25	"	19-10-27	1-1-28
3	HM 4698	"	13136	"	"	"	2-25	"	20-10-27	18-12-27
4	HM 4745	"	13146	"	"	"	2-25	"	6-10-27	12-12-27
5	HM 4746	"	13221	"	"	"	2-25	"	20-10-27	1-1-28
K622	XC 8296	AEC K	20872	OT24/22RO	?	"	1921	6-10-27	1-1-28	
K488	XC 8104	"	20488	"	?	"	1920	13-10-27	1-1-28	
K502	XC 8117	"	20502	"	?	"	1920	19-10-27	1-1-28	
K727	XC 8282	"	20977	"	?	"	1921	20-10-27	1-1-28	
K897	XC 9757	"	21163	"	?	"	1921	20-10-27	1-1-28	

Former Owner
K488/502/622/727/897 General

Disposal
1/2/5/K488/502/622/727/897 General No, L27/25/23/K488/502/622/727/897
3/4 C & P Sales (dealer), Ipswich

BROWN/AB

	Reg	Chassis	Chassis No	Body	Builder	Livery	Date	Source	Disposal	
	UC 1816	Maudslay ML3	4030	B32R	H. Lewis	Red & White	20-1-28	New	7-6-29	(1)
	UC 1817	"	4219	"	"	"	20-1-28	"	7-6-29	(1)

(1) Re-seated to B30R 1-29

Disposal
UC 1816/1817 Birch No. B28/27

BUCK—see GENIAL

BURLINGTON

	Reg	Chassis	Chassis No	Body	Builder	Livery	Date	Source	Disposal
1	MH 550	Dennis 4 ton	40189	OT24/22RO	Dodson	Chocolate & White	29-8-24	New	14-10-27
2	MH 551	"	40190	OT26/22RO	"	"	29-8-24	"	14-10-27

Coaches

	Reg	Chassis	Chassis No	Body	Builder	Livery	Date	Source	Disposal
	ML 4158	Morris	2996Z	C20	?	?	6-5-27	New	1930
	MP 3704	GMC T40E	403220	C26	?	?	4-28	"	1930
	MT 1143	Gilford 166SD	10532	"	?	?	12-28	"	1930
	MT 1664	"	10567	"	?	?	1-29	"	1930

Disposal
MH 550/551 Public No. D102/101
ML 4158 Pioneer (Gault), Felixstowe
MP 3704 Paddington Transport, London W9
MT 1143 Southend Express, Southend; Horne Products (dealer) Colnbrook, and scrapped 1935
MT 1664 Manny, London SW9; Marks, Worcester, 1939

B & V—see CLARENCE

CAMBRIAN

Buses

	Reg	Chassis	Chassis No	Body	Builder	Livery	Date	Source	Disposal	Disposal	
S50	BA 2851	S. Squire A	?	OT24/22RO	Straker	Green & White	24-9-20	4-23	1925	25-1-27	(1)
S51	XO 7779	"	A6257	OT26/22RO	"	"	27-7-23	New	22-3-27	31-3-27	
S52	XO 8224	"	A6263	"	"	"	31-7-23	"	17-9-26	29-3-27	
S53	XO 8225	"	A6269	"	"	"	31-7-23	"	13-4-27	25-4-27	
S54	XO 8226	"	A6262	"	"	"	31-7-23	"	23-4-27	5-5-27	
S55	XO 8592	"	A6273	"	"	"	3-8-23	"	5-3-26	3-27	
S56	XO 8593	"	A6268	"	"	"	3-8-23	"	26-4-27	11-5-27	
S57	XO 8589	"	A6270	"	"	"	3-8-23	"	1925	18-1-27	
S58	XO 8588	"	A6275	"	"	"	3-8-23	"	26-4-27	13-5-27	
S59	XO 8591	"	A6274	"	"	"	3-8-23	"	13-4-27	25-4-27	
S60	XO 8590	"	A6278	"	"	"	3-8-23	"	27-4-27	17-5-27	
T101	XP 4051	Thornycroft J	10432	OT26/24RO	Dodson	"	23-10-23	"		15-4-26	
S61	XP 4425	S. Squire A	A6331	OT24/22RO	Straker	"	27-10-23	"	4-10-26	3-27	
S62	XP 4428	"	A6334	"	"	"	27-10-23	"	13-4-27	27-4-27	
S63	XP 4426	"	A6332	"	"	"	27-10-23	"	1925	14-1-27	
S64	XP 4427	"	A6333	"	"	"	27-10-23	"	27-4-27	13-5-27	

(2)
(2)

T102	XP 4705	Thornycroft J	10437	OT26/24RO	Dodson	Green & White	31-10-23	New		19-4-26
T103	XP 4706	"	10436	"	"	"	31-10-23	"		13-4-26
T104	XP 5449	"	10438	"	"	"	10-11-23	"		19-4-26
T105	XP 5450	"	10439	"	"	"	10-11-23	"		19-4-26
T106	XP 5984	"	10435	"	"	"	16-11-23	"		19-4-26
T107	XP 5985	"	10440	"	"	"	16-11-23	"		19-4-26
T108	XP 6421	"	10447	"	"	"	23-11-23	"		16-4-26
T109	XP 6422	"	10444	"	"	"	23-11-23	"		29-4-26
T110	XP 9080	"	10446	"	"	"	3-1-24	"		16-4-26
T111	XP 9081	"	10443	"	"	"	3-1-24	"		15-4-26
T112	XP 9325	"	10434	"	"	"	7-1-24	"		29-4-26
T113	XP 9831	"	10463	"	"	"	12-1-24	"		13-4-26
S65	XT 955	S. Squire A	A6360	OT24/22RO	Straker	"	17-4-24		17-2-26	20-1-27
S66	XT 956	"	A6361	"	"	"	17-4-24		17-9-26	3-27
S67	XT 3342	"	A6364	"	"	"	9-5-24		1925	11-1-27
S68	XT 3343	"	A6363	"	"	"	9-5-24		1925	18-1-27
S69	XT 3344	"	A6362	"	"	"	9-5-24		25-4-27	30-4-27
S70	XT 7052	"	A6366	"	"	"	3-6-24		1925	11-1-27
S71	XT 7053	"	A6367	"	"	"	3-6-24		22-4-27	29-4-27
S72	XT 7051	"	A6365	"	"	"	3-6-24		17-2-26	2-3-27
S73	MF 180	"	A6251	"	Dodson	Red & White	31-5-23	22-9-24	26-4-27	5-5-27
S74	ME 9689	"	A6239	"	"	"	17-5-23	22-9-24	27-4-27	11-5-27
S75	XW 341	"	A6426	"	Straker	Green & White	10-10-24	New	27-4-27	17-5-27
S76	XW 342	"	A6427	"	"	"	10-10-24	"	1925	2-3-27
S77	XW 547	"	A6428	"	"	"	14-10-24	"	1925	2-3-27
S78	ME 7351	"	A6206	OT22/22RO	S & B	"	28-2-23	10-24	16-12-26	1927
S79	ME 8598	"	A6210	OT26/22RO	"	"	12-4-23	10-24	1-10-25	1926
D1	XW 2273	Dennis 4 ton	40233	"	"	"	4-11-24	New	18-4-28	1-5-28
D2	XW 2505	"	40235	"	"	"	7-11-24	"	19-4-28	1-5-28
D3	XW 3679	"	40239	"	"	"	21-11-24	"	18-2-28	1-5-28
D4	XW 3680	"	40226	"	"	"	21-11-24	"	18-2-28	1-5-28
T114	XU 2191	Thornycroft J	10552	OT26/24RO	Dodson	"	12-7-24	27-4-25		14-4-26
D5	MH 9005	Dennis 4 ton	40360	OT26/22RO	S & B	"	17-7-25	New		1-5-28
D6	MH 9006	"	40371	"	"	"	17-7-25	"		1-5-28
D7	MH 9421	"	40349	"	"	"	31-7-25	"	16-4-28	1-5-28
D8	XY 3470	S. Squire A	40338	OT22/22RO	Straker	"	4-5-25	21-8-25	17-4-28	1-5-28
	XN 7386	"	A6241	OT24/22RO	"	"	4-5-25	21-2-26		21-4-26
	XN 7891	"	A6243	"	"	"	8-5-23	21-2-26		15-3-26
	XN 8771	"	A6242	"	"	"	10-5-23	21-2-26		21-4-26
	XP 849	"	A6279	"	"	"	1-9-23	21 2-26		15-3-26
K296	LU 8555	AEC K	20296	OT24/22RO	?	"	1920	14-4-26		21-1-28
K329	LU 8586	"	20329	"	?	"	1920	14-4-26		16-2-28
K163	LU 8414	"	20163	"	?	"	1920	15-4-26		20-2-28
K95	LU 8314	"	20095	"	?	"	1920	16-4-26		1-5-28
K80	LU 8305	"	20080	"	?	"	1920	17-4-26		1-5-28

Fleet	Reg	No.	Chassis	Body No.	Builder	Body	Colour	Date	Date	Date	Date
K118	LU	8337	"	20118	?	"		1920	17-4-26		1-5-28
K325	LU	8599	"	20325	?	"		1920	17-4-26		1-5-28
K447	XC	8065	"	20447	?	"		1920	17-4-26		1-5-28
KB37	XC	8391	"	21103	?	"		1921	16-9-26		1-5-28
K610	XC	8225	"	21110	?	"		1921	17-9-26		1-5-28
K844	XC	8415	"	20860	?	"		1921	2-10-26		1-5-28
K672	XC	8243	"	20922	?	"		1921	21-12-26		1-5-28
K148	LU	8329	"	20148	?	"	Red & White	1920	21-3-27		1-5-28
K290	LU	8503	"	20290	?	"	"	1920	12-4-27		1-5-28
K307	LU	8517	"	20307	?	"	"	1920	12-4-27		1-5-28
K324	LU	8584	"	20324	?	"	"	1920	21-4-27		1-5-28
K413	XD	8311	"	20413	?	"	"	1920	21-4-27		1-5-28
K129	LU	8338	"	20129	?	"	"	1920	22-4-27		1-5-28
K109	LU	8347	"	20109	?	"	"	1920	23-4-27		1-5-28
K172	LU	8403	"	20172	?	"	"	1920	25-4-27		1-5-28
K209	LU	8432	"	20209	?	"	"	1920	25-4-27		1-5-28
K401	LU	8570	"	20401	?	"	"	1920	25-4-27		1-5-28
K81	LU	8303	"	20081	?	"	"	1920	26-4-27		1-5-28
K212	LU	8370	"	20212	?	"	"	1920	26-4-27		1-5-28
K465	XC	8070	"	20465	?	"	"	1920	26-4-27		1-5-28
K531	LU	8141	"	20781	?	"	"	1920	26-4-27		1-5-28
D40	PU	3549	Dennis 4 ton	40142	S & B	OT26/22RO		6-24	19-1-28	18-2-28	1-5-28
K85	XB	8394	AEC K	20085	?	OT24/22RO		1920	16-2-28		1-5-28
D48	XX	1259	Dennis 4 ton	40310	S & B	OT26/22RO		13-2-25	23-2-28		1-5-28
D49	MH	2239	"	40258	Dodson			29-11-24	6-3-28		1-5-28
K149	LU	8344	AEC K	20149	?	OT24/22RO		1920	16-4-28		1-5-28
K84	LU	8376	"	20084	?	"		1920	18-4-28		1-5-28
K88	LU	8295	"	20088	?	"		1920	18-4-28		1-5-28
K108	LU	8317	"	20108	?	"		1920	19-4-28		1-5-28

Coaches (excluding Kent based subsidiary companies)

Fleet	Reg	No.	Chassis	Body No.	Builder	Body	Colour	Date	Date	Date	Date
D501	MC	9823	S. Squire A	A6009	Straker	Ch 32	Green	1920	New		By 1-22
D502	XB	9777	Daimler Y	11642	?	Ch 28	"	5-20	"		1923
C306	XB	9778	"	10248	?	"	Grey	5-20	"		14-8-22
G208	XD	9949	Commer 3P	10034	?	Ch 24	Green	9-5-20	"	1-10-25	?
G212	XD	8110	Guy B	1110	?	"	"	9-5-20	"		?
A603	XD	8111	"	1035	?		"	10-6-20	"		?
A601	XD	8250	AEC YC	10436	?	Ch 28	"	10-6-20	"		?
D505	XD	8251	"	10584	?	"	"	6-20	"		?
D503	XD	8278	Daimler Y	10236	?	"	"	6-20	"		5-8-22
A602	XD	8279	"	11642	?	"	"	6-20	"		9-8-22
G204	XD	8280	AEC YC	10572	?	Ch 23	"	8-7-20	"		12-11-29
G202	XC	8820	Guy	10076	?	"	"	8-7-20	"		12-11-29
G203	XC	8821	"	10250	?	"	"	8-7-20	"		12-11-29
C307	XC	8822	"	10371	?		"	8-7-20	"		12-11-29
	XC	8823	Commer 3P	10046	?	Ch 28	"				

421

Fleet No.	Reg.	Chassis	Body No.	Seating	Body builder	Livery		In service	Acquired	Withdrawn	Notes
V405	XC 8826	Vulcan VSC	2362	Ch 14	?	Green	?	9-7-20	New	12-11-29	
V402	XC 8827	Commer 3P	2408	" 28	?	"	?	9-7-20	"	?	
C305	XC 8828	"	10047		?	"	?	9-7-20	"	?	
C315	XC 9274	"	10038		?	"	?	15-7-20	"	?	
C308	XC 9275	"	10059		?	"	?	15-7-20	"	?	
V408	XC 9277	Vulcan VSC	2380	Ch 14	?	Grey	?	15-7-20	"	12-11-29	
C303	XD 9231	Commer 3P	10045	" 28	?	Green	?	8-20	"	12-11-29	
C304	XD 9232	"	10057		?	"	?	8-20	"	?	
G207	XC 9897	Guy B	1118	" 29	?	"	?	4-21	"	?	
G213	XC 9898	"	1119	" 28	?	"	?	4-21	"	?	
G209	XH 4905	"	1084		?	"	?	1-7-21	"	12-11-29	
G210	XH 4906	"	1085		?	"	?	1-7-21	"	12-11-29	
G211	XH 4907	"	1086	Ch 14	?	Red	?	1-7-21	"	20-8-26	
V401	XH 4908	Vulcan VSC	2325		?	Green	?	1-7-21	"	12-11-29	
V406	XH 4909	"	2364		?	"	?	1-7-21	"	12-11-29	
V404	XH 4910	"	2216		?	"	?	1-7-21	"	?	
V407	XH 4911	"	1852	" 28	?	"	?	1-7-21	"	?	
C313	XH 4912	Commer 3P	10021		?	"	?	1-7-21	"	?	
C302	XH 4913	"	10022		?	"	?	1-7-21	"	?	
C312	XH 4914	"	10029		?	"	?	1-7-21	"	?	
C310	XH 4915	"	10044		?	"	?	1-7-21	"	?	
C314	XH 4916	"	10048		?	"	?	1-7-21	"	?	
G201	XH 1960	Guy B	1111	" 16	?	"	?	2-7-21	"	?	
G205	XH 1961	"	1042	" 22	?	"	?	5-7-21	"	?	
G206	XH 1962	"	1114		?	"	?	5-7-21	"	?	
V403	XH 1963	Vulcan VSC	2341	" 14	?	"	?	5-7-21	"	14-8-22	
C309	XH 2168	Commer 3P	10802	" 27	?	"	?	7-7-21	"	?	
C316	XH 2169	"	10650		?	"	?	7-7-21	"	22-6-26	
C301	XH 2170	"	10050		?	"	?	7-7-21	"	12-11-29	
C311	XH 2034	"	10038	" 28	?	"	?	8-7-21	"	?	
D504	XH 2035	Daimler Y	6376		?	"	?	8-7-21	New	14-8-22	(3)
C317	EL 2108	Commer	?		?	"	?	4-14	24-1-22	?	
C318	XA 9620	Commer WP1	1091	" 29	?	"	?	4-20	24-1-22	?	
C319	XB 9919	Commer 3P	10025		?	"	?	5-20	24-1-22	8-26	
C320	XB 9920	"	10033	" 28	?	"	?	31-5-20	24-1-22	8-1-27	
C321	XD 8189	"	10005		?	"	?	8-20	24-1-22	1-29	
C322	XD 9952	"	10058		?	"	?	8-20	24-1-22	1-29	
C323	XD 9953	"	10055	" 27	?	"	?	2-6-22	New	20-8-26	
C324	XL 2078	"	10063		?	"	?	2-6-22	"	1-29	
C325	XL 2079	"	10062		?	"	?	2-6-22	"	14-9-27	
C326	XL 2080	"	10061	" 28	?	"	?	20-6-20	6-6-24	14-9-27	
L701	XD 8867	Leyland S5	22086	C32R	S & B	"	?	30-4-27	New	12-11-29	
	YF 5236	Guy BB	22342		"	"	?	14-5-27	"	12-11-29	(3)
	YF 5237	"	22354		"	"	?	14-5-27	"	12-11-29	
	YF 5238	"	22359		"	"	?	14-5-27	"	12-11-29	

422

Reg	Fleet No	Chassis	Body	Former Owner	Colour	Date		Disposal
YF 5239	22368	"	"	"	"	28-5-27	"	12-11-29
YF 5240	22374	"	"	"	"	28-5-27	"	12-11-29
YF 5241	22358	"	"	"	"	7-8-27	"	12-11-29
YH 5090	22360	"	"	"	"	31-5-27	"	12-11-29
YT 1324	22421		C28R			1-7-27	29-11-27	12-11-29
YU 9471	18333	Chevrolet LM	C14F	?		12-27	29-11-27	12-11-29
UC 4854	40096	Chevrolet LO		?	Green & Grey	2-28	New	12-11-29
UC 4855	40136		C20F	?		2-28		12-11-29
UC 8759	40284		C26	?	"	3-28	"	1929
YV 7398	5053C	Albion PKA26		?		20-4-28	"	12-11-29
YV 7397	10339	Gilford 1660T	C24	?		26-4-28	"	12-11-29
YV 9601	10371	Gilford 166SD	C28	?		10-5-28	"	12-11-29
YW 375	10364	Gilford 1660T		?		14-5-28	"	12-11-29
YW 376	10362		C26	?	"	14-5-28	"	12-11-29
YW 2125	10375			?		18-5-28	"	12-11-29
YW 2938	10377			?		23-5-28	"	12-11-29
YW 3433	416935	ADC 416	C32	Clarke		25-5-28	"	12-11-29
YW 3432	416933		"	"		31-5-28	"	12-11-29
YW 3434	416937					31-5-28	"	12-11-29
YW 3435	10309	Gilford 1660T	C26	?		31-5-28	"	12-11-29
YW 3436	10383		"	?		31-5-28	"	12-11-29
YW 3437	10381		"	?		31-5-28	"	12-11-29
YW 3438	10389			?		31-5-28	"	12-11-29
YW 6379	846484	Safeway 64	C36	?		8-6-28	"	12-11-29 (4)
YW 6380	416936	ADC 416	C32	Clarke		8-6-28	"	12-11-29
YW 6381	416934			"		8-6-28	"	12-11-29
YW 9528	10412	Gilford 1660T	C30	?		6-28	"	12-11-29
YW 7559	416932	ADC 416	C32	Clarke		13-7-28	"	12-11-29
YX 1848	10445	Gilford 1660T	C26	?		21-7-28	"	12-11-29
YX 4439	417095	ADC 417		H. Lewis		3-8-28	"	12-11-29
YX 4440	417094		"	"		3-8-28	"	12-11-29
YX 4441	417093		"	"		3-8-28	"	12-11-29
YX 4442	417115		"	"		3-8-28	"	12-11-29
YX 4443	417096		"	"		3-8-28	"	12-11-29
YX 4444	417087		"	United		3-8-28	"	12-11-29
XV 6861	7016S	Daimler CF6	C32	Bell		4-12-28	"	3-10-29

(1) New as Ch 28; double-deck body fitted 10-24 and entered service 29-11-24
(2) Colour later green & white   (3) Rebodied Waveney C26/C26/C24 and
pneumatics fitted, colour to green, 7-28/7-28/10-28   (4) Six-wheeler
built in Philadelphia, USA

Former Owner
S50 The Motor Service Co, Eccles, Lancs
S73/74 Newstead No. 2/1

Disposal
S50/57/63/65/67/68/76/77 C & P Sales (dealer), Ipswich (chassis only).
S50 to Lorry in Essex, 8-27. S57 Harvey, Chelmsford (Lorry) 1927.
S65 J. Chandler, Feltwell, Norfolk (Lorry) 1927; withdrawn 25-3-32.
S67 C. Cornwall, Harleston, Norfolk (Lorry) 1927; withdrawn 25-3-34 and
scrapped. S68 Child & Sons, Ipswich (Lorry) 1927; withdrawn 1-1-39
S51/53/54/56/58-60/62/64/69/70/73/75 C & P Sales (dealer), Ipswich.

S78/79 CWP
T114 Shamrock
D8 LPOC
XN 7386/7891/8771/XP 849 Central no. A/B/C/D
K329 EP
K163 Fleet
All K-type except K163/329 General
D40/48/49 Metropolitan No. D40/48/49
C317 New to H. Whitelock, Bournemouth; to the Admiralty 1-17 then to London & South Coast Transport, N1, 1920
C318-21 London & South Coast Transport, London, N1
C322/23 New to E. S. Clifford, London, W6, then to London & South Coast Transport, London, N1, date ?
L701 C. White, London, SW1
YH 5090/YT 1324 A. J. Smith, London, N7

S51 S. Green, Birmingham (Lorry), 10-27; sold 1932.
S54 W. Hatcher, Framlingham (Lorry), 8-27.
S59/62 White Rose M.S (Brookes Bros), Rhyl, 6-27.
S60 Hicks Bros, Braintree, Essex 8-27.
S69 D. W. Doughton, Kelvedon, Essex (Lorry) 1927; withdrawn 3-29 and scrapped. S70 A. Garner, Colchester (Lorry), 1927; withdrawn 1-1-32.
S73 M. Hunter, Eccles, Lancs (Lorry) 1927; withdrawn 25-3-30.
S75 A. Church & Sons, Nutfield, Surrey (Lorry) 1927.
S52/61/66/78/79/XN 7386/7891/8771/XP 849 Body off and chassis scrapped.
S71/72/74 C & P Sales, Ipswich (Lorry). S71/72 withdrawn 1-1-36.
T101-114 Thames Valley T. Co no. 118/122/115/123-126/120/127/121/117/128/116/119. T101 Maidstone & District (NPSV) 10-31. T104/107 Star Haulage Co, London (Lorry)1931. T114 G. F. Jones, Maidstone (Lorry), 11-31.
D1-8/40/48/49 General no. D1-8/40/48/49
K163/296/327 Metropolitan
All K-type except K163/296/327 General
MC 9823 East London Motors, London E2
D501 Julius & Lockwood, Lewisham, London; withdrawn 7-27
D502/503/504/A602/V403 Brighton Motor Conveyances, Hove, Sussex.
  D503 converted to lorry 10-23; S. W. Howes Birmingham, 12-25;
  C. A. Steepley, Birmingham, 5-28; T. W. Annable, Loughborough, 2-34; sold 6-38
A601/603/C305/306/308/309/311/314/315/317-319/324/D505/G201/205-207/209/210/212/213/V401/402/404/406/408 ?
C301/303/304/307/310/312/313/G202-204/211/YF 5236-5241/YH5090/YT 1324/
YU 9471/UC 4554/4855/YV 7397/7398/9601/YW375/376/2125/2938/
3435-3438/6379/9528/YX 1848 East Kent. YF 5236/5238 London & South Coast MS, Folkestone 2-30; East Kent 12-33; Allen, Sandgate 3-35.
YF 5237/5240/5241/YH 5090/YT 1324 London & South Coast MS, 2-30;
East Kent, 12-33; body scrapped 1934, chassis to G. J. Dawson (dealer)
Clapham, 11-34 and scrapped 1-35. YF 5239 London & South Coast MS 2-30;
scrapped 5-32. UC 4854/4855 Not used by East Kent. YV 7397 G. C. Cook
(dealer), London SW9 10-35. YV 7398 G. J. Dawson (dealer), Clapham, 31-3-36.
YV 9601 G. C. Cook (dealer), SW9, 10-35; Taylor, Ryde, IOW, 3-36; W. Ball
& Sons, Ryde, 6-40. YW 375 Sayers Ltd, Margate, 5-34; J. Pascall, Dagenham,
Essex (van) by 10-41. YW 376 Sayers Ltd, Margate as C32 5-34. YW 2125/2938/
3437/3438 G. C. Cook (dealer), SW9; 10-35; Horne Products (dealer), Colnbrook,
4-36 and scrapped. YW 3435 G. C. Cook (dealer) SW9, 10-35. YW 3436
G. C. Cook (dealer) SW9, 10-35; F. G. Jones, Errwood, Brecon, 3-36.
YW 6379 Solent Coaches, Portsmouth. 9-30; AEC (dealer) Southall, 3-32;
E. Harrington, London SE16, 6-32; W. McCann (dealer) London W2, 8-32.
YW 9528 Elms Coaches. London, N17, 6-35; sold 6-37. YX 1848 T. Bowles,
Temple Guiting, Cheltenham 1933.
V405/407/YW 3432-3434/6380/6381/7559/YX 4439-4444 Maidstone & District.
YW 3432 Romilly Motor Co (dealer), Cardiff, 6-30; Enterprise Motor Service,
Gorseinon, 7-30. YW 3433 Tillotson (dealer) Burnley, 6-3-30; Hemingway Bros

Wakefield, 2-31; Advance Motor Service, Scunthorpe, 5-31; Enterprise & Silver Dawn M.S no. 69, 1-34; YW 3434 Tillotson (dealer) Burnley, 3-30; S. Holland, Chesterfield, 1-31; G. H. Burnham, Clifton-on-Teme, Worcs, 6-33. YW 6380 Leyland Motors (dealer), 1-30; F. Lockey, West Auckland, Co. Durham, 10-31. YW 6381 Leyland Motors (dealer) 1-30; Gala Motor Co, Lanark, 12-31; Stewart & McDonald, Carluke, Lanark, 5-32; Tocia Motor Co, Pwllheli, Caerns, 7-32; Crosville, 17-2-34; scrapped 7-35. YW 7559/YX 4439 Enterprise & Silver Dawn M.S no. 43/44, Scunthorpe, 7-30; scrapped 1-39. YX 4440/4444 Blue Motor Service, Boarhunt, Wickham, Hants. 7-30; withdrawn 1-1-37. YX 4441 Used Units (dealer), Burnley, 7-30. YX 4442 H. Cooke, Glasgow, 7-30; withdrawn 3-35. YX 4443 J. Jones, Pont-y-Berem, Carms, 12-31

C302 South Wales Comm. Motors, Cardiff (Lorry)
C316 J. Phipps, London E10; South Wales Comm. Motors, Cardiff, 8-26; Western Welsh 1926.
C320/325 South Wales Comm. Motors (dealer); Cardiff; Western Welsh, 1926; scrapped 12-31
C322/323/326 Constable Hart (contractors), London, SW1 (Lorry)
L701 J. Cartwright, London, SW8.
UC 8759 Miles, Sherston; withdrawn 12-33
XV 6861 Daimler Motor Co. (demo); Carlisle & Dist M.S, Carlisle, 4-31; Ribble No. 1294 1-9-31; Caledonian no. 76, Dumfries 10-31; Robinson & Davidson, Lockerbie, Dumfriesshire 1-35; scrapped 1938

CAMBRIAN LANDRAY

Buses and Coaches

Fleet No	Reg	Chassis	Chassis No	Body		New	Livery				Notes
	LX 8984	Leyland S5	10216	Ch 32	?	9-19	Olive Green	New		29-3-27	
	XB 9888	TSM TS3A	2277	Ch 28	?	5-20	"	"		14-2-27	
	IT 292	"	?	"	?	5-20	Red	"	21-1-27	11-2-27	(1)
	IT 293	"	?	"	?	6-20	"	"	21-1-27	15-2-27	(1)
	IT 301	"	?	"	?	6-20	"	"	21-1-27	11-2-27	(1)
	IT 302	De Dion	?	Ch 30	?	6-20	"	"		13-5-27	
	IT 303	TSM TS4A	?	Ch 19	?	12-20	"	"		14-2-27	
	IT 413	"	?	Ch 30	?	12-20	"	"		14-2-27	
	IT 414	"	?	Ch 14	?	12-20	"	"		22-4-27	
	IT 418	"	20810	Ch 28	?	8-7-21	"	"		24-3-27	(2)
	XH 2265	Unic M1A2	2237	OT24/22RO	?	2-11-22	"	"	21-1-27	11-2-27	(1)
	XM 2992	TSM TS3A	20119	"	?	1920	Red & White	21-1-27		21-10-27	
K119	LU 8340	AEC K	20124	"	?	1920	"	21-1-27		21-10-27	
K124	LU 8367	"	21099	"	?	1921	"	21-1-27		21-10-27	
K833	XC 8444	"	21117	"	?	1921	"	21-1-27		21-10-27	
K851	XC 8497	"	21170	"	?	1921	"	21-1-27		21-10-27	
K904	XC 9721	"		"	?		"				

(1) Rebodied Hickman OT26/22RO 7-24 to 2-25 colour red and white
(2) colour later to olive green

Former Owner
K119/124/833/851/904 General

CAPITOL

No	Reg	Chassis	No	Body	Bodybuilder	Livery			
1	VX 869	Chevrolet LQ	53298	B14F	Metcalf	Red & Grey	13-6-29	New	1-31
2	VX 870	"	54602	"	"	"	13-6-29	"	1-31
3	VX 2078	TSM B10A2	6527	B32F	"	"	24-8-29	"	21-9-31
4	VX 2079	"	6528	"	"	"	24-8-29	"	12-7-31
5	KX 3854	TSM B10A	5977	B26F	?	"	12-12-29	1-31	21-9-31
6	KX 3852	"	5982	"	?	"	12-12-29	1-31	12-7-31
S384	XL 3792	AEC S	21638	B30R	?	Red & White	4-9-22	18-8-31	25-11-31
S866	XO 7611	"	22120	"	?	"	8-23	18-8-31	25-11-31
S873	XO 4088	"	22127	"	?	"	8-23	18-8-31	25-11-31
S884	XO 4089	"	22138	"	?	"	4-23	18-8-31	25-11-31

Former Owner
5/6 Wendrome M.S. (Smith & Neight) Wendover, Bucks.
S384/866/873/884 Loan from General

Disposal
LX 8984 T. Murrell (dealer), London, N1; Morning Star Coaches Bristol, 1927
XB 9888/IT 292/293/301/302/XM 2992 Timpson no. 56/51-55
IT 303/418 A. J. Smith (dealer) London, SW1
IT 413 T. Tilling
IT 414 C & P Sales (dealer) Ipswich
XH 2265 H. Lane (dealer), London, SW10; C. J. Newman, Hythe, Kent, 6-27
K119/124/833/851/904 General

Disposal
1 ?
2 to lorry
3/5 General
4 destroyed by fire
6 body destroyed by fire, chassis to Rover Bus Service (G. Scott), Aberdeen, 1931
and rebodied by Walker, B26F Aberdeen; to Aberdeen Corpn No. 4
14-11-35; Greig, Inverness 1937; Clark, Southerness, Kirkcudbrightshire date ?
S384/866/873/884 General ex loan

CARDINAL

	Reg	Chassis	No	Body	Bodybuilder	Livery			
MF 9904		Dennis 4 ton	40179	OT26/22RO	Dodson	Red & White	30-7-24	New	1-27

Disposal
MF 9904 Claremont

CARLTON ASSOCIATION

Reg	Chassis	No	Body	Bodybuilder	Livery			
XN 912	S. Squire A	A6223	OT22/22RO	Dodson	Chocolate & White	10-3-23	New	21-6-26
YM 1060	Dennis 4 ton	40378	OT26/22RO	"	Red & White	24-11-25	"	26-11-26
YR 4523	"	40432	"	"		7-11-26	"	8-7-27

Disposal
XN 912 Hull & District M.S., Hull; East Yorkshire M.S., Hull: No. 39 5-10-26
YM 1060 Overington No. 5
YR 4523 Public No. D73

CARLTON/OVERGROUND (up to 31-12-27)

No.	Reg.	Chassis	Type				In service	New	Disposal
				OT26/22RO	Dodson	Brown & White			
21	XN 3091	12525	Leyland LB2	OT26/22RO	Dodson	Brown & White	27-3-23	New	
22	XN 9227	12540	"	"	"	"	17-5-23	"	
23	XO 2525	12569	"	"	"	"	14-6-23	"	
24	XO 3160	12532	"	"	"	"	21-6-23	"	
25	XO 3813	12570	"	"	"	"	29-6-23	"	
26	XO 8490	12565	"	"	"	"	2-8-23	"	
27	XP 3798	12702	Leyland LB4	"	"	"	23-10-23	"	
28	XP 7746	12705	Leyland LB2	"	"	"	13-12-23	"	
1	XT 3927	40124	Dennis 4 ton	"	"	Red & White	14-5-24	"	
2	XT 5507	40128	"	"	"	"	27-5-24	"	
3	XT 5517	40133	"	"	"	"	27-5-24	"	
4	XT 6847	40129	"	"	"	"	3-6-24	"	
5	XT 6837	40132	"	"	"	"	3-6-24	"	
6	XT 8294	12919	Leyland LB5	"	"	"	14-6-24	"	
29	XU 7889	40200	Dennis 4 ton	"	"	"	9-9-24	"	
7	XU 8830	40201	"	"	"	"	29-9-24	"	
8	XU 8829	40199	"	"	"	"	29-9-24	"	
9	XU 8831	40205	"	"	"	"	29-9-24	"	
30	XU 9857	40206	"	"	"	"	7-10-24	"	
31	XU 9867	40229	"	"	"	"	7-10-24	"	
32	XW 1867	40204	"	"	"	"	31-10-24	"	
10	XW 3177	40241	"	"	"	"	14-11-24	"	
11	XW 3167	40244	"	"	"	"	14-11-24	"	
12	XW 3697	40246	"	"	"	"	21-11-24	"	
13	XW 4407	40251	"	"	"	"	1-12-24	"	
14	XW 4897	40250	"	"	"	"	5-12-24	"	
15	XW 5377	40254	"	"	"	"	12-12-24	"	
16	XW 5378	40253	"	"	"	"	13-12-24	"	
17	XW 5379	40252	"	"	"	"	13-12-24	"	
18	XW 7614	40245	"	"	"	"	7-1-25	"	
19	XW 7615	40267	"	"	"	"	7-1-25	"	
20	XW 8817		"	"	"	"	21-1-25	"	
33	XM 9591	A6224	S. Squire A	OT24/22RO	"	"	20-2-23	3-7-25	
34	YM 527	13523	Leyland LB5	OT26/22RO	"	"	17-11-25	New	
35	YK 8897	13531	"	"	"	"	17-12-25	"	22-7-26
33	YP 5287	13588	"	"	"	"	23-7-26	"	
36	YE 6045	40436	Dennis 4 ton	"	"	"	9-2-27	"	

No. 21-28 repainted red & white between March and November 1925

Former Owner
XM 9591 X Service

Disposal
XM 9591 F. Arnott, London, SW1 (Lorry)

CARSWOOL

Reg	Chassis	Chassis No	Body	Builder	Livery	Date	In service		Withdrawn	Note
XR 2120	Leyland LB4	12743	OT26/22RO	S & B	Red	7-2-24	New		24-11-33	

Later repainted red & white

Disposal
XR 2120 LPTB L91

CBC—see CERTAINTY

CC—see DAISY

CELTIC

Reg	Chassis	Chassis No	Body	Builder	Livery	Date	In service		Withdrawn	Note
XR 1195	Daimler Y	6054	OT22/20RO	S & B	Red & Grey	29-1-24	New	4-4-27	11-4-27	
XR 9918	AEC K	20563	OT24/22RO	?	Red & White	2-5-24	2-4-27		1-1-28	(1)

(1) Later repainted red & white

Disposal
XR 1195 C & P Sales (dealer), Ipswich

Former Owner
K1069 General

CENTRAL (Omnibus Co Ltd)

	Reg	Chassis	Chassis No	Body	Builder	Livery	Date	In service		Withdrawn	Note
A	XN 7386	S. Squire A	A6241	OT22/22RO	Straker	Khaki & White	4-5-23	New		21-2-26	(1)
B	XN 7891	"	A6243	"	"	"	8-5-23	"		21-2-26	(1)
C	XN 8771	"	A6242	"	"	"	14-5-23	"		21-2-26	(1)
D	XP 849	"	A6279	"	"	"	1-9-23	"		21-2-26	(1)
	YM 6649	Leyland LB5	13533	OT26/22RO	Dodson	Red & White	29-1-26			1-3-26	(2)
K11	XF 8014	AEC K	20011	OT24/22RO	?	"	1920	20-2-26	1-2-26	1-1-28	
K42	LU 8251	"	20042	"	?	"	1920	20-2-26		1-1-28	
K70	LU 8287	"	20070	"	?	"	1920	20-2-26		1-1-28	
K980	XC 9800	"	21246	"	?	"	1921	20-2-26		1-1-28	

(1) Repainted red & white 3-24 to 8-24
(2) Delivered direct to LGOC Chiswick Works and never operated in London

Former Owner
K11/42/70/980 General

Disposal
XN 7386/7891/8771/XP 849 Cambrian
YM 6649 Lee & Beaulah, Elloughton, Yorks; East Yorkshire
M.S., Hull, 10-26; EYMS breakdown lorry, 12-35; withdrawn 6-42
K11/42/70/980 General

CENTRAL (London & Southend Central Motor Services Ltd)

Reg	Chassis	Chassis No	Body	Builder	Livery	Date	In service	Withdrawn
XW 5644	Daimler Y	6079	OT22/20RO	Hickman	Blue & White	17-12-24	New	1926
HJ 4671	"	6083	"	"	"	30-5-25	"	1926

Disposal
XW 5644/HJ 4671 Royal Blue Car Co., Southend; Westcliff-on-Sea
Motor Services date ?

CERTAINTY/CBC

Reg	Chassis	Chassis No	Body	Builder	Livery	Date	In service	Withdrawn
XU 5469	Dennis 4 ton	40169	OT26/22RO	S & B	Red & White	11-8-24	New	3-8-27

Disposal
XU 5469 Public No. D51

CHADWELL

Reg	Chassis	Chassis No	Body	Builder	Date	Colour	Acquired	Disposal	Notes
PU 6034	Dennis 4 ton	40285	OT26/22RO	Dodson	23-1-25	Red & White	New	15-12-33	
VW 5500	Leyland PLSC3	47121	B32R	"	27-6-28	Red & Grey	"	15-12-33	

Disposal
PU 6034/VW 5500 LPTB D189/L111

CHARIOT

Reg	Chassis	Chassis No	Body	Builder	Date	Colour	Acquired	Disposal	Notes
MH 1595	Dennis 4 ton	40230	OT26/22RO	S & B	17-10-24	Red & White	New	1-11-33	(1)
GJ 8501	AEC Regent	661362	H30/26RO	Birch	16-6-30	"	"	1-11-33	
BM 9201	Albion	9601	Van	?	3-1-21	Green & Cream	?	1-11-33	

(1) Rebuilt by Birch with enclosed staircase 7-32

Disposal
MH 1595/GJ 8501/BM 9201 LPTB No. D176/ST1028/—

CHP/PICKUP

Buses

No	Reg	Chassis	Chassis No	Body	Builder	Date	Colour	Acquired	Disposal	Notes
1	XN 2799	Leyland LB2	12442	OT26/22RO	Dodson	26-3-23	Light Blue & White	New	1-32	(1)
2	XN 4194	"	12443	"	"	6-4-23	"	"	30-4-32	(1)
3	XP 4668	"	12701	"	"	31-10-23	Light Brown & White	"	14-6-32	(2)
4	XR 8753	Leyland LB4	12745	"	"	5-4-24	Red & Straw	"	3-32	(2)
5	XU 9118	Leyland LB5	12922	"	"	29-9-24	Red & White	"	10-11-33	(2)
6	XX 9738	"	13303	"	"	9-4-25	"	"	5-4-32	(3)
7	YM 4735	"	13532	"	"	4-1-26	"	"	6-1-33	(3)
8	PD 5976	Leyland LB2	12533	"	"	20-6-23	"	3-28	1932	(3)
9	YW 7829	Guy FCX	22515	OT34/28RO	"	18-6-28	"	New	10-11-33	(4)
10	UW 1478	Leyland TD1	70724	OT30/26RO	"	30-9-29	"	"	10-11-33	
11	GO 4367	"	72058	H30/26RO	"	9-4-31	"	"	10-11-33	
12	GO 5424	"	72059	"	"	22-4-31	"	"	10-11-33	
1	GW 1224	AEC Regent	6611801	OT30/26R	PRV	5-1-32	Red & Green	"	10-11-33	
2	GW 1785	"	6611803	"	"	22-1-32	"	"	10-11-33	
3	GW 1744	"	6611802	"	"	1-2-32	"	"	10-11-33	
4	GX 167	"	6611804	"	"	23-3-32	"	"	10-11-33	
7	GY 839	"	6611846	"	"	1-7-32	Red & White	"	10-11-33	

Coaches

Reg	Chassis	Chassis No	Body	Builder	Date	Colour	Acquired	Disposal	Notes
XF 7268	Unic M1A2	20783	Ch 14	?	1-6-21	Grey	New	20-4-25	(5)
XH 4004	"	20717	"	?	21-6-21	"	"	11-11-25	(5)

(1) Colour to light brown & white 3-24, red & white 3-25, pneumatic tyres fitted 1930   (2) Colour to red & white 11-24/4-25/12-24, pneumatic tyres fitted 1930   (4) Six-wheeler
(3) Pneumatic tyres fitted 1930
(5) Colour to royal blue 5-22/3-23

Disposal
XN 2799 A. J. Freeman, Peterborough (Lorry); withdrawn 1934
XN 4194 R. J. Hillier, London, E7 (Lorry)
XP 4668 E. A. Dean, Marlow, Bucks, (Lorry)
XR 8753/PD 5976 ?
XU 9118/YW 7829/ UW 1478/ GO 4367/5424/GW 1224/1785/1744/
GX 167/GY 839 LPTB No. L79/GS 15/L80-82/STL 554/555/553/
556/557

Former Owner
PD 5976 Swift

XX 9738 AEC (dealer) Southall
YM 4735 F. Pettifer, London E12 (Lorry)
XF 7268 J. Healy, London, SE5; Ansell's Coaches, Camberwell, 6-30
XH 4004 J. Williams, Hove, Sussex; Southdown M.S. 10-27;
Dickinson, Hove 10-28; sold 3-32

CITY

No.	Reg.	Chassis	No.	Body	Builder	Livery	Date	Acq.	W/d	Sold	
A1	XN 732	Leyland LB2	12449	OT26/22RO	Dodson	Brown & Cream	6-3-23	New	14-8-32	8-32	(1)
A2	XN 964	"	12452	"	"	"	9-3-23	"	21-6-32	6-32	(1)
A3	XN 1231	"	12450	"	"	"	12-3-23	"	?	7-32	
A4	XN 1425	"	12451	"	"	"	14-3-23	"	17-5-31	3-32	(1)
A5	XN 2142	"	12453	"	"	"	15-3-23	"	17-3-32	3-32	
A6	XN 3001	"	12454	"	"	"	27-3-23	"	25-1-31	29-1-31	
A7	XN 3374	"	12510	"	"	"	28-3-23	"	27-9-32	9-32	
A8	XN 3373	"	12455	"	"	"	28-3-23	"	29-2-32	28-7-32	(1)
A9	XO 756	"	12534	"	"	"	1-6-23	"	21-6-31	6-31	(1)
A10	XP 9335	"	12541	"	"	"	18-5-23	"	7-6-31	?	(1)
A11	XP 7734	Leyland LB4	12730	"	Wilton	"	13-12-23	"	2-8-32	By 11-33	(1)
A12	XP 8309	"	12729	"	"	"	21-12-23	"	24-3-33	4-33	(1)
D1	XR 9753	Dennis 4 ton	40114	"	Dodson	"	12-4-24	"	24-3-33	12-2-26	
A13	XT 996	Leyland LB4	12715	"	Wilton	"	17-4-24	"	24-3-31	3-31	
A14	XT 1609	"	12942	"	"	"	30-4-24	"	19-3-33	?	
A15	XU 9104	Leyland LB5	12943	"	"	"	29-9-24	"	25-3-32	6-32	(1)
A16	XU 9106	"	12944	"	"	"	29-9-24	"	?	7-11-34	(2)
A17	XU 9105	"	13233	"	Dodson	"	29-9-24	"	29-11-32	1-33	(1)
A18	XX 6193	"	13234	"	"	"	25-3-25	"	?	7-10-28	
A19	XX 8457	"	13235	"	"	"	4-4-25	"	6-3-32	6-32	(1)
A20	XX 8456	"	13237	"	"	"	4-4-25	"	24-3-33	10-10-33	(1)
A21	XX 9061	"	13238	"	"	"	7-4-25	"	22-3-31	?	
A22	XX 9060	"	13304	"	"	"	7-4-25	"	30-3-30	5-30	(1)
A23	YL 417	"	12463	"	"	"	1-8-25	"	28-6-31	7-31	
A24	XN 1344	Leyland LB2	12926	"	"	"	13-3-23	12-2-26	6-3-32	3-32	(1)
A25	PU 5052	Leyland LB5	12797	"	"	"	1-10-24	2-4-26	?	7-11-34	(1)
A26	YF 2532	"	13790	"	"	"	25-3-27	New	15-3-31	3-31	(1)
A27	YF 2531	"	13794	"	"	"	25-3-27	"	24-3-31	?	
A28	YF 9649	"	13795	"	"	"	1-5-27	"	30-4-32	?	
A29	YF 8893	"	13796	"	"	"	1-5-27	"	29-4-32	10-33	
A30	YH 4135	"	13808	"	"	"	23-5-27	"	29-5-32	?	
A31	YT 7380	"	13149	"	"	"	30-8-27	"	?	7-11-34	(1)
A32	XW 9346	Leyland LB4	12744	"	"	"	27-1-25	11-11-27	?	7-11-34	(1)
A33	XR 6498	"	12731	"	Wilton	"	24-3-24	11-11-27	?	7-11-34	(1)
A34	XP 8535	"	?	"	"	"	31-12-23	10-27	?	7-11-34	(3)
G1	UC 3213	Guy FCX	22514	H34/28RO	Dodson	"	2-2-28	New	?	7-11-34	(4)
A35	MH 2484	Leyland LB5	13128	OT26/22RO	"	"	1-1-25	2-3-28	?	7-11-34	(1)

C1	XX 6193	Leyland/City	13233	OT29/26RO		"	7-10-28	Rebuilt	7-11-34	(5)
A36	PU 8660	Dennis 4 ton	40350	OT26/22RO		"	15-6-25	31-1-29	4-29	(6)
A36	GU 6062	Leyland LB5	13809			"	12-4-29	New	7-11-34	(7)
CS1	XX 9060	Leyland/City	13238	H34/28RO		"	5-30	Rebuilt	7-11-34	(8)
CS2	GN 5819		CS2		R. S. J.	"	5-3-31	"	7-11-34	
T1	GN 7571	Leyland TD Sp	61749	H30/26RO	Dodson	"	13-3-31	New	7-11-34	(8)
CS3	GN 1559	Leyland/City	CS3	H34/28RO	R. S. J.	"	24-3-31	Rebuilt	7-11-34	
T2	GO 1348	Leyland TD Sp	61748	H30/26RO	Dodson	"	26-3-31	New	7-11-34	
T3	GO 1933	"	61750	"	"	"	31-3-31	"	7-11-34	
T4	GO 1932	"	61751	"	"	"	31-3-31	"	7-11-34	
T5	GO 1346	"	61752	"	"	"	26-3-31	"	7-11-34	
T6	GO 1930	"	61753	"	"	"	31-3-31	"	7-11-34	
CS4	GP 127	Leyland/City	CS4	H34/28RO	R. S. J.	"	16-5-31	Rebuilt	7-11-34	(8)
CS5	GP 4336		CS5	"	"	"	18-6-31	"	7-11-34	(8)
CS6	GP 93		CS6	"	Dodson	"	1-8-31	"	7-11-34	(8)
T7	GW 2758	Leyland TD Sp	404	H30/26RO	"	"	27-2-32	New	7-11-34	(4)
T8	GW 2759	"	405	"	"	"	27-2-32	"	7-11-34	(4)
T9	GW 2760	"	406	"	"	"	27-2-32	"	7-11-34	(4)
T10	GW 2761	"	407	"	"	"	27-2-32	"	7-11-34	(4)
T11	GW 2762	"	408	H34/28RO	"	"	16-7-28	2-3-32	7-11-34	(4)
G2	YX 1833	Guy FCX	22853	H34/28RO		"	16-7-28	2-3-32	7-11-34	(4)
G3	YU 7375	"	22512	"		"	8-12-27	3-3-32	7-11-34	(4)
G4	YU 4431	"	22511	"		"	10-11-27	3-32	7-11-34	(4)
G5	YX 4101	"	22900	"		"	1-8-28	3-32	7-11-34	(4)
G6	YT 8954	"	22510	"		"	6-9-27	10-3-32	7-11-34	(4)
G7	YW 7838	"	22874	"		"	20-6-28	4-4-32	7-11-34	(4)
G8	YX 1834	"	22875	"		"	21-7-28	4-4-32	7-11-34	(4)
G9	YX 4098	"	22899	"		"	1-8-28	4-4-32	7-11-34	(4)
G10	YX 4100	"	22924	"		"	1-8-28	4-4-32	7-11-34	(4)
T12	GX 1839	Leyland TD Sp	409	H30/26RO		"	29-4-32	New	7-11-34	(9)
M2	YR 8860	Maudslay ML3	3999	C30R	H. Lewis	"	10-12-26	New	12-32	
L1	XV 7551	Leyland PLSC3	47725	C32R	Leyland	"	12-28	25-11-32	31-3-34	
L2	XV 9053	"	47724			"	19-12-28	25-11-32	31-3-34	
L3	GU 1815	"	47815	"		"	3-29	25-11-32	31-3-34	
L4	GU 1814	"	47955	"		"	3-29	25-11-32	31-3-34	
L5	UU 1065	"	47954	"		"	9-5-29	25-11-32	31-3-34	
L6	UU 1063	"	47956	"		"	9-5-29	25-11-32	31-3-34	
L7	UU 1064	"	47957	C32		"	9-5-29	25-11-32	31-3-34	
L8	UL 6583	"	47785	"	?	"	3-29	25-11-32	31-3-34	
L9	UL 6580	"	47675	"	?	"	3-29	25-11-32	31-3-34	
L10	UL 6594	"	47929	"	?	"	3-29	25-11-32	31-3-34	
L11	UL 6569	"	47639	C29	?	"	3-29	25-11-32	31-3-34	
L12	YE 9645	Leyland PLSC1	45510		Beadle	"	3-27	25-11-32	31-3-34	
L13	YE 9650	"	45515	"	"	"	3-27	25-11-32	31-3-34	
L14	YE 9646	"	45511	"	"	"	3-27	25-11-32	31-3-34	

						Brown & Cream				
L15	YE 9649	Leyland PLSC1	45514	C29	Beadle	Brown & Cream	3-27	25-11-32	31-3-34	(10)
L16	YE 9644	"	45509	"	"	"	3-27	25-11-32	31-3-34	(10)
L17	YE 9648	"	45513	"	"	"	3-27	25-11-32	31-3-34	(10)
TS1	AGH 149	Leyland TT1	2288	H34/28RO	Dodson	"	24-3-33	New	7-11-34	
TS2	AGH 150	"	2289	"	"	"	24-3-33	"	7-11-34	
TS3	AGH 151	"	2290	"	"	"	24-3-33	"	7-11-34	
MC1	GU 9017	Morris 1 ton	18055	Van	?	"	22-3-29			

Note: The coaches listed above are only those legally owned by City. Coaches owned by their subsidiary, New Empress Saloons Ltd, are not included

(1) Pneumatic tyres fitted 1-30 A20; 1930 A1-3/5/7-9/11/12/14/15/17/19/23-26/28-31/33/35; 12-33 A32. (2) Converted to petrol tanker on pneumatic tyres 9-32. (3) Rebodied Dodson OT26/22RO 10-27 and pneumatic tyres fitted 1930. (4) Six-wheeler. (5) Rebuilt from A18. (6) Chassis built from spare parts by City. (7) Six-wheeler rebuilt from A22. (8) Six-wheeler rebuilt from Leyland LB's. (9) Fitted with Leyland 6-cyl oil engine from new. (10) Six-wheeler fitted with Leyland 6-cyl oil engine

Former Owner
A24 Liberty
A25 Dispatch
A32 FW
A33 Veleta
A34 St George
A35 Empires Best
A36 (PU 8660) Fairhop
G2-10 New to Public, to General 11-12-29. G2/3 Later Amersham & District No. 7/1. G4/5? G6 Premier (Hewitt) Watford.
G7-10 Canvey & District, Canvey Island
M2 New to F & K; to Public 28-7-27; New Empress Saloons 25-10-28
L1-7 New to New Empress Saloons
L8-17 New to United Service Transport, Tooting; to New Empress Saloons 4-32

Disposal
A1/2/9/13/20 Smith & Blackwell, London, N1 (Lorry); E. Wells, London, SE16, 11-33. A1/2/9 withdrawn 1-38, A13 withdrawn 1-6-36. A20 to Smith & Blackwell, N1, 6-37 and scrapped
A3 Power Petrol (Tanker); B. J. Palmer, Peterborough, 1933; withdrawn 1-12-33
A4/10/12/14/21/27/28/30/36 (PU 8660) ?
A5/24 Effra Spares (dealer) Brixton, London
A6/26/29 scrapped by City
A7 Ford Bros, London, N1 (Lorry), withdrawn 29-8-39
A8/15/19 Medway Oil Co, Isle of Grain, Kent (Tanker)
A11 Mann, Crossman & Paulin, Whitechapel, London (Lorry)
D1 Liberty
A16/25/31-35/36 (GU 6062)/G1-10/C1/CS1-6/T1-12/TS1-3/ MC1 LPTB No. L66/58-64/GS16-25/L65/LM1-6/TD110-121/ TC1-3/M49
A17 E. Weller, Rotherhithe (Lorry)
A18/22 Rebuilt to C1 & CS1 by City
A23 Triumph (chassis only)
M2 H. T. Butters, London, NW10 (Lorry)
L1-17 New Empress Saloons, NW5. L1 sold 3-37, L2/12 scrapped 9-36. L3/6/7 G. C. Cook (dealer), London, SW8, 7-37 L4/5 scrapped, 3-37, L8 Flater, Barking, Essex, 5-36 L9 Pretty, Diss, Norfolk 1936; withdrawn 12-36 L10 Hugh Coaches, —?—, 7-36; scrapped 3-38 L11 to Lorry 1936, L13/14/17 to Lorry 10-36. L15/16 scrapped 4-36

CLAREMONT

Buses

1	XW 3890	Dennis 4 ton	40248	OT26/22RO	Dodson	Red & White	28-11-24	New	1-11-33	(1)
2	XW 3891	"	40275	"	S & B	"	28-11-24	"	30-9-27	
3	XW 5110	"	40279	"	Dodson	"	9-12-24	"	30-9-27	
4	XW 5716	"	40276	"	"	"	18-12-24	"	30-9-27	
5	XW 5717	"	40278	"	"	"	18-12-24	"	30-9-27	
3	MF 9904	"	40179	"	"	"	30-7-24	1-27		12-30

(continued)

No.	Reg.	Chassis	Chassis No.	Body	Builder	Livery	Date		Source	Withdrawn
5	UW 6734	Leyland TD1	70763	H28/24R⊙	"		29-11-29		New	1-11-33
7	GK 8667	Dennis Lance	125014		"		11-12-30		"	1-11-33

Coaches

No.	Reg.	Chassis	Chassis No.	Body	Builder	Livery	Date		Source	Withdrawn
	UL 7590	Dennis F	80096	C20F	Dodson	Tan, Green & Black	9-3-29		New	11-6-29
	UL 7692	"	80095	"	"		9-3-29		"	11-6-29

UL 7590
(1) Later fitted with pneumatic tyres

Former Owner
MF 9904 Cardinal

Disposal
XW 3890/UW 6734/GK 8667 LPTB No. D175/L45/DL26
XW 3891/5110/5716/5717 Public No. D90/95/91/94
MF 9904 A. Smith, Hessle (Lorry), withdrawn 7-32
UL 7590/7692 Westminster Coaching Services, London, N1;
Eastern Counties, Norwich No. DE4/— 7-33; UL 7590
G. A. Wheatley, London, E15 date ?, withdrawn 1-10-38.
UL 7692 Eastern National No. 3496, 11-33; C. H. Ballard,
Bradfield, Berks, 7-34; Newbury & Dist No. 85, Newbury
10-35; H. Lane (dealer), London, SW10, 1-37

CLARENCE/B & V

No.	Reg.	Chassis	Chassis No.	Body	Builder	Livery	Date		Source	Withdrawn
1	XU 3027	Dennis 4 ton	40166	OT26/22RO	S & B	Dark Red & Cream	20-7-24	8-12-26	New	6-1-27
2	XX 772		40295	OT24/22RO	"	Red & White	10-2-25	29-11-26	"	24-12-26
K754	XC 8365	AEC K	21020		?	"	1921		26-11-26	1-1-28
K200	XF 8080	"	20200		?	"	1920		7-12-26	1-1-28

Former Owner
K200/754 General

Disposal
XU 3027/XX 772 Redburn's No. D28/24
K200/754 General

CLARENDON

No.	Reg.	Chassis	Chassis No.	Body	Builder	Livery	Date	Source	Withdrawn
1	XP 440	Leyland LB2	12643	OT26/22RO	Dodson	Chocolate & White	30-8-23	New	11-8-27
2	XR 4807	Leyland LB4	12740	"	"	"	7-3-24	"	11-8-27
	XU 6691	Dennis 4 ton	40181	B26R	"	"	29-8-24	"	11-8-27
	YL 965	Dennis 2½ ton	45128	"	"	"	1-8-25	"	11-8-27
	YL 966	"	45129	"	"	"	1-8-25	"	11-8-27

Disposal
XP 440/XR 4807/XU 6691/YL 965/966 Public No. L5/1/D23/DS18/15

CLEVELAND—see MATCHLESS, THE

COMMONWEALTH

No.	Reg.	Chassis	Chassis No.	Body	Builder	Livery	Date	Source	Withdrawn
3	XO 6328	Leyland LB2	12571	OT26/22RO	Dodson	Red & White	16-7-23	New	8-11-27
1	MF 6321	Leyland LB4	12746	"	"	"	5-4-24	"	8-11-27
2	MH 1264	Leyland LB5	12929	"	"	"	7-10-24	"	8-11-27
4	YR 172	"	13640	"	"	"	6-9-26	1-3-27	8-11-27

Former Owner
YR 172 Rapid no. 8

Disposal
XO 6328/MF 6321/MH 1264/YR 172 Public No. L29-32

(1)

CORNWALL

No.	Reg	Chassis No	Chassis	Body	Builder	Colour	In	Ex	Out
1	XT 2093	40118	Dennis 4 ton	OT26/22RO	S & B	Red & White	1-5-24	New	17-8-27
3	XX 979	40292	"	"	"	"	10-2-25	"	17-8-27
4	XX 1478	40299	"	"	"	"	17-2-25	"	17-8-27
5	XX 1479	40294	"	"	"	"	17-2-25	"	17-8-27
6	XX 8833	40300	"	"	"	"	7-4-25	"	17-8-27
7	XX 8832	40301	"	"	"	"	7-4-25	"	17-8-27
8	YR 143	40426	"	"	"	"	6-9-26	"	17-8-27

Disposal
No. 1/3-8 Public No. D40/50/56/62/27/2/19

COSGROVE

No.	Reg	Chassis No	Chassis	Body	Builder	Colour	In	Ex		Out
	MF 2143	A6286	S. Squire A	OT24/22RO	Straker	Chocolate & Cream	29-8-23	New		5-25
	MF 9160	40163	Dennis 4 ton	OT26/22RO	Dodson	Red & White	4-7-24	5-25		9-26
	XT 2864	12708	Leyland LB4		"	"	6-5-24	31-8-26		1-1-28
K568	XC 8199	20878	AEC K	OT24/22RO	?	"	1921	26-10-27	26-10-27	1-1-28

Former Owner
MF 9160 BC
XT 2864 Royal Blue no. 4
K568 General

Disposal
MF 2143 T. Shaw, Birkenhead (Lorry), withdrawn 1-1-39
MF 9160 Hull & Dist M.S., Hull; East Yorkshire M.S.
No. 45 5-10-26; J. Howells, Eastville, Yorks (Lorry)
date ?, withdrawn 9-9-33
XT 2864/K568 General No. L35/K568

COSMOPOLITAN/RYAN

Reg	Chassis No	Chassis	Body	Builder	Colour	In	Ex	Out
MF 8159	6064	Daimler Y	OT22/20RO	Hickman	Red & White	2-6-24	New	7-25
MK 403	40372	Dennis 4 ton	OT26/22RO	Dodson	"	2-9-25	"	1-11-33
MY 4650	71168	Leyland TD1	H28/24RO	"	"	15-5-30	"	1-11-33

(1) Later fitted with pneumatic tyres

Disposal
MF 8159 Roberts (dealer) London, W12
MK 403/MY 4650 LPTB No. D179/L58

CRESCENT

Reg	Chassis No	Chassis	Body	Builder	Colour	In	Ex	Out
MF 7694	A6370	S. Squire A	OT24/22RO	Straker	Blue & White	19-5-24	New	8-7-27

Colour to red & white 10-24

Disposal
MF 7694 Public No. S3

CREST

Reg	Chassis No	Chassis	Body	Builder	Colour	In	Ex	Out
MF 9629	40184	Dennis 4 ton	OT26/22RO	Dodson	Red & White	18-7-24	New	5-8-27

Disposal
MF 9629 Public D39

CRITERION

Reg	Chassis	Chassis No.	Body	Body maker	Livery				
MH 2594	Dennis 4 ton	40291	OT26/22RO	S & B	Red & White	22-12-24	New	7-12-26	3-1-27
XC 8406	AEC K	21075	OT24/22RO	?	"	1921	13-12-26		1-1-28

Former Owner
K809 General

Disposal
MH 2594 Redburn's No. D29
K809 General

CWP

Buses

Reg	Chassis	Chassis No.	Body	Body maker	Livery				
ME 7351	S. Squire A	A6206	OT22/20RO	Straker	Blue & White	28-2-23	New	9-24	10-24
ME 8598	"	A6210	"	"	"	12-4-23	7-23	9-24	10-24

Coaches

AN 3857	S. Squire 20 hp	?	Ch ?	?	?	13-4-20	New		
AN 4143	Swiss Berna	?	Ch ?	?	?	6-5-20	"		
AN 5161	Daimler 35 hp	?	Ch ?	?	?	1-7-21	"		
AN 5425	Napier	?	Ch ?	?	?	1-4-22	"		
AN 6404	S. Squire A	?	Ch 28	?	Red	31-5-24	"		
AN 6520	"	?	Ch 28	?	"	8-24	"		

Former Owner
ME 7351/8598 Admiral No. 5/7

Disposal
ME 7351/8598 Cambrian No. S78/79
AN 3857/4143/5161/5425/6404/6520 ?

DAISY/CC

MF 7640	Daimler Y	6059	OT22/20RO	Hickman	Red & Cream	16-5-24	New		1-25
MH 3380	Dennis 4 ton	40286	OT26/22RO	Dodson	"	29-1-25	2-25		10-11-33
HX 2171	Dennis Lance	125013	H30/24RO	"	"	9-12-30	New		10-11-33

(1) Later fitted with pneumatic tyres

Former Owner
MH 3380 Stanmore

DAUNTLESS/RELIABLE

2	XW 2566	Dennis 4 ton	40243	OT26/22RO	Dodson	Red & White	7-11-24	New		30-9-27
1	XW 4334	"	40249	OT24/22RO	"	"	29-11-24	"		30-9-27
	XR 8763	S. Squire A	A6357	"	"	"	5-4-24	8-7-25		8-27
3	YM 6966	Dennis 2¼ ton	45209	B25R	"	"	1-2-26	New		25-3-26

Former Owner
XR 8763 X Service

Disposal
XW 2566/4334 Public No. D92/93
XR 8763 Claremont (F. J. Wood), Burnley, Lancs
YM 6966 Orange No. 10

DIAMOND/OLYMPIC

| K89 | XR 4559 | Thornycroft J | 10517 | OT26/24RO | Dodson | Red & White | 5-3-24 | 27-4-26 | | 14-5-26 |
| | LU 8293 | AEC K | 20089 | OT24/22RO | ? | " | 1920 | 27-4-26 | | 1-1-28 |

Former Owner
K89 General

DIRECT

	Fleet No.	Chassis	Reg.	Body code	Body	Colour	In service	New		
K756	MH 5193	Dennis 4 ton	40304	OT26/22RO	S & B	Red & White	1-4-25	New	7-12-26	31-12-26
	XC 8320	AEC K	21022	OT24/22RO	?	"	1921	6-12-26		1-1-28

Former Owner
K756 General

Disposal
XR 4559 Thames Valley No 129; Dock & General Transport Co,
London, EC1 (Lorry) 6-32
K89 General

Disposal
MH 5193 Redburn's No. D27
K756 General

DISPATCH

	Reg.	Chassis	Fleet No.	Body code	Body	Colour	In service	New	
	PU 5052	Leyland LB5	12926	OT26/22RO	Dodson	Red & White	1-10-24	New	2-4-26

Disposal
PU 5052 City No. A25

DISTRICT

	Reg.	Chassis	Fleet No.	Body code	Body	Colour	In service	New	
	XT 5917	Dennis 4 ton	40127	OT26/22RO	Dodson	Red & Cream	30-5-24	New	1-1-28
	XU 1748	"	40176	"	"	"	10-7-24	"	1-1-28

Disposal
XT 5917/XU 1748 General No. D60/61

DM

	Reg.	Chassis	Fleet No.	Body code	Body	Colour	In service	New		
	XU 2699	Thornycroft J	10556	OT26/24RO	Dodson	Red & White	17-7-24	New	2-27	1927
	YE 6365	Dennis 4 ton	40438	OT26/22RO	Birch	"	15-2-27	"		11-11-27

Disposal
XU 2699 to Lorry
YE 6365 Public No. D55

DOLPHIN

	Reg.	Chassis	Fleet No.	Body code	Body	Colour	In service	New	
4	XW 633	Dennis 4 ton	40222	OT26/22RO	S & B	Red & White	15-10-24	New	29-9-27

Repainted brown & cream 10-25

Disposal
XW 633 Public No. D96

DOMINION

	Reg.	Chassis	Fleet No.	Body code	Body	Colour	In service	New			
	XX 8837	Dennis 4 ton	40346	OT26/22RO	Dodson	Red	7-4-25	New	29-3-26	25-11-26	(1)
	XX 9591	"	40347	"	"	"	9-4-25	"	29-3-26	25-11-26	(1)

(1) Colour to red & white 1925

Disposal
XX 8837/9591 Redburn's No. D21/22

DRAKE & McCOWEN/DRAKE/W. R. DRAKE

XP 435	Leyland LB2	12641	OT26/22RO	Dodson	Cream & Black	31-8-23	New		1-2-29	(1)
XT 4608	Leyland LB4	12716	"	"	Red & White	20-5-24	"		1-2-29	(1)
XP 4355	"	12703	"	"	"	1-11-23	3-28			

(1) Colour to red & white 6-28

Disposal
XP 435/XT 4608 Birch Bo. B21/22
XP 4355 Acquired for spares only, chassis cannibalised
Body to a shed

Former Owner
XP 4355 New to The Orange Service, C & P Sales (deaier)
Ipswich 14-12-27

EAGLE—see KBB

EARL

MF 1297	S. Squire A	A6271	OT24/22RO	Straker	Red & White	16-7-23	14-1-26	25-3-27	By 2-30
ML 1800	Leyland LB5	13654	OT26/22RO	Dodson	"	25-1-27	New		24-11-33
MY 2806	Leyland TD1	71192	H28/24RO	"	"	3-2-30			24-11-33

(1) Later fitted with pneumatic tyres

Disposal
MF 1297 L. Wickin, London, N17 (Lorry)
ML 1800/MY 2806 LPTB No. L86/85

Former Owner
MF 1297 BC

EASTERN

XP 4850	Leyland LB2	12707	OT26/22RO	Dodson	Red & White	2-11-23	New	30-8-27
XT 9535	Dennis 4 ton	40149	"	"	"	28-6-24	"	30-8-27

Disposal
XP 4850/XT 9535 Public No. L22/D31

ECLIPSE

XN 8049	Leyland LB2	12538	OT26/22RO	Dodson	Carmine & Cream	9-5-23	New	8-7-27
XW 1620	Leyland LB5	12935	"	S & B	Red & White	30-10-24	"	8-7-27
PU 4769	Daimler Y	6069	OT22/20RO	Hickman	Carmine & White	2-9-24	1925	8-7-27
YE 7373	Dennis E	17123	B30R	Dodson		1-3-27	New	8-7-27

Former Owner
PU 4769 Fairlop

Disposal
XN 8049/XW 1620/PU 4769/YE 7373 Public No. L14/24/—/DE1

ELMS

XU 8238	Leyland LB5	12923	OT26/22RO	Dodson	Red	15-9-24	New	3-8-27

Colour to red & white 9-25

Disposal
XU 8238 Public No. L9

EMBASSY—see M & E

EMPIRE (F. C Kirk)

1	XU 5639	Dennis 4 ton	40183	OT26/22RO	Dodson	Red & White	13-8-24	New	11-32
2	VX 7487	AEC Regent	6611009	H30/24RO	"	"	4-9-30	"	1-11-33

EMPIRE (L. M. Newstead)

3	MH 1705	Leyland LB5	12940	OT26/22RO	S & B	Chocolate & White	28-10-24	New		21-11-27

Disposal
XU 5639 W. R. Davey, London, E6 (Lorry)
VX 7487 LPTB No. ST1029

EMPIRES BEST

	MH 2484	Leyland LB5	13128	OT26/22RO	Dodson	Red & White	1-1-25	New		2-3-28

Disposal
MH 1705 Public No. L33
Disposal
MH 2484 City No. A35

EMPRESS (Empress Omnibus Co Ltd)

	XN 4477	Leyland LB2	12473	OT26/22RO	Dodson	Chocolate & Cream	10-4-23	New	14-7-27	16-7-27
	MF 9159	Dennis 4 ton	40150	"	"	"	4-7-24	"	1-7-27	4-7-27
	MH 2516	Thornycroft J	10565	OT26/24RO	"	"	17-12-24	"	18-1-27	8-2-27
	YR 5805	Leyland LB5	13641	OT26/22RO	"	"	12-11-26	"		3-2-27
K1003	XF 8030	AEC K	21269	OT24/22RO	?	Red & White	4-21	18-1-27		1-1-28
K210	LU 8457	"	20210	"	?	"	1920	1-7-27		1-1-28
K195	LU 8170	"	20195	"	?	"	1920	13-7-27		1-1-28

Former Owner
K195/210/1003 General
XN 4477 National, Watford No. L5
MF 9159 Northern
MH 2516 C & P Sales (dealer), Ipswich; Pilkington Bros..
Colchester (Lorry), 1927; withdrawn 1-1-31
YR 5805 Peraeque No. 3
K195/210/1003 General

EMPRESS (Crabb & Clarke)/SPHERE/AMBASSADOR (see also AMBASSADOR for associated fleet)

1	MF 9241	Daimler Y	6066	OT22/20RO	Hickman	Chocolate & White	8-7-24	New		10-26	(1)
3	YR 3672	Dennis 4 ton	40431	OT26/22RO	Dodson	Red & White	26-10-26	"		29-8-34	
5	GK 7166	Dennis Lance	125015	H30/26R	"	"	2-12-30	"		29-8-34	

(1) Fitted with pneumatic tyres by 3-29

Disposal
MF 9241 Roberts (dealer), London W12; Capt. A. Morgan, Cork,
Eire, and re-registered TI 1802 10-26; withdrawn 1-1-27
YR 3672/GK 7166 LPTB No. D198/DL31

EMPRESS (F. F. Downes)/F.F.D./HORSESHOE

	MF 7349	Daimler Y	6060	OT22/20RO	Hickman	Chocolate & White	7-5-24	New	23-4-26	5-26	(1)
	MH 1261	"	6072	OT26/22RO	Dodson	Red & White	7-10-24	"	1-4-27	8-4-27	
	YN 3800	Leyland LB5	13585	"	"	"	29-4-26	"	20-8-26	31-8-26	

438

K206	LU 8473	AEC K	20206	OT24/22RO		Chocolate & White	1920	17-8-26	2-27	1-1-28	(1)
K171	LU 8415	"	20171	"	?	Red & White	1920	31-3-27		1-1-28	(2)

(1) Colour to red & white 5-25

Former Owner
K171/206 General

Disposal
MF 7349 Scrapped
MH 1261 C & P Sales (dealer) Ipswich; Roberts (dealer) London, W12, 5-27; Low Loaders Ltd, London, W12 (Lorry) 1927; withdrawn 1-1-28
YN 3800 Grangewood
K171/206 General

EMPRESS (Empress Motors Ltd)

Buses

1	XN 3270	S. Squire A	A6212	OT22/22RO	Straker	Brown & White	28-3-23	New		11-8-27
2	XT 2588	"	A6369	OT24/22RO	"	Red & White	5-5-24	"		5-29
3	YP 9564	Dennis 4 ton	40423	OT26/22RO	Dodson	"	30-8-26	"	1-6-32	10-10-32
1	YE 8274	"	40443	OT24/22RO	Straker	"	1-3-27	"	1-7-32	8-32
4	YX 7335	Leyland PLSC3	47437	B32R	Dodson	"	30-8-28	"		1-2-34
2	UU 1056	Dennis H	90091	H30/26RO	"	"	8-5-29	"		1-2-34
3	GX 2692	Leyland TD2	1532	H28/26R	"	"	2-6-32	"		1-2-34
1	GX 2693	"	1533	"	?	"	30-6-32	"		1-2-34
	MM 9288	Morris 15 cwt	309428	Van		Red & Black	14-9-29	"		1-2-34

Coach fleet up to February 1934

3	YV 7154	Dennis F	80050	C28D	S & B	Maroon & Black	18-4-28	New		9-35
1	YV 7155	"	80057	"	"	"	18-4-28	"		5-40
2	YV 7156	"	80048	"	"	"	18-4-28	"		9-36
5	GU 9791	Dennis G	70506	C20D	?	"	2-5-29	"		25-2-32
7	GN 7203	Morris Comm Dictator	032H	C32	L. L.	"	2-3-31	"		5-40
6	GO 1187	Morris Comm	031H	C20D	?	"	27-3-31	"	1-11-37	?
5	GW 9396	Viceroy	187	"	"	"	15-3-32	"		14-4-49

(1) Colour to red & white 3-24, body to YE 8274 2-27
(2) Body ex XN 3270

Disposal
XN 3270 Armstrong, Plaistow, London (Lorry)
XT 2588 Sommerfield & Thomas, Kings Lynn (Lorry); withdrawn 1-1-34
YP 9564 G. A. Head, London, N1 (Lorry)
YE 8274 to lorry
YX 7335/UU 1056/GX 2692/2693/MM 9288 LPTB No. LN4/DH9 TD72/73/M45
YV 7154/7156 scrapped
YV 7155 Ministry of Supply; scrapped 1944
GU 9791 W. C. Bell, Dunoon
GN 7203 Ministry of Supply
GO 1187 ?
GW 9396 F. W. Figg, South Fambridge, Essex

ENTERPRISE

Buses

No.	Reg	Chassis	Chassis No	Body	Builder	Colour		Date	Withdrawn
1	XN 4292	Leyland LB2	12524	OT26/22RO	Dodson	Choc & Prim	New	9-4-23	7-1-31
	XT 2173	Dennis 4 ton	40108	"	"	"	"	1-5-24	7-30
	XT 4825	"	40115	"	"	"	"	21-5-24	7-30
2	YE 1753	Leyland LB5	13656	"	"	"	"	4-1-27	5-31
3	XV 1354	Leyland PLSC3	47438	B32R	"	Red & White	"	16-10-28	By 1933
1	GJ 3435	Leyland TD1	71317	H28/24RO	"	"	"	30-5-30	5-12-33
2	GH 1100	"	71320	"	"	"	"	28-6-30	5-12-33
3	GH 1101	"	71321	"	"	"	"	31-7-30	5-12-33
4	GK 8925	"	71767	"	"	"	"	22-12-30	5-12-33
5	GO 8472	"	72042	"	"	"	"	8-5-31	5-12-33
	GJ 4572	Morris 15 cwt	333578	Van	?	Blue	7-12-31	30-5-30	5-12-33

Coaches

	Reg	Chassis	Chassis No	Body	Builder	Colour		Date	Withdrawn
	GU 6714	Maudslay ML3B	4460	C24D	Dodson	Chocolate & Black	New	20-4-29	25-10-29
	UU 820	"	4463	"	"	"	"	6-5-29	25-10-29
	UU 821	"	4472	"	"	"	"	6-5-29	25-10-29

Former Owner

GJ 4572 New to Harris & Co, London, E7

Disposal

XN 4292 A. Smith, Strathaven (Lorry)
XT 2173/4825 A. E. Prior, London, E1 (Lorry), withdrawn 28-3-36/25-3-35
YE 1753 T. Stuart, Lanark (Lorry), withdrawn 25-3-35
XV 1354 W. Alexander No. L80, Falkirk, to Lorry by 10-37
GJ 3435/GH 1100/1101/GK 8925/GO 8472/GJ 4572 LPTB No. L102-106/M42
GU 6714/UU 820/821 Bucks Expresses, Watford

EP

Buses

No.	Reg	Chassis	Chassis No	Body	Builder	Colour		Date	Withdrawn
1	XN 6182	S. Squire A	A6235	OT22/22RO	Straker	Crimson & Grey	New	30-4-23	16-3-27
2	XN 6183	"	A6238	"	"	"	"	30-4-23	16-3-27
3	XO 8747	"	A6284	OT24/22RO	"	"	"	3-8-23	16-3-27
8	XR 3507	"	A6337	"	"	"	"	29-2-24	16-3-27
9	XR 3506	"	A6341	"	"	"	"	29-2-24	16-3-27
10	XR 5274	"	A6359	"	"	"	"	12-3-24	16-3-27
14	XN 513	"	A6225	"	Dodson	"	10-24	3-3-23	16-3-27
15	XM 9995	"	A6227	"	"	"	3-11-24	1-3-23	29-10-26
16	XM 9888	"	A6226	"	"	"	3-11-24	3-3-23	29-10-26
20	MF 1020	"	A6280	"	Straker	"	1-25	4-7-23	16-3-27
21	MF 9171	"	A6390	"	"	"	1-25	4-7-24	24-2-27
22	YL 8115	Leyland LB5	13520	OT26/22RO	Dodson	"	New	23-10-25	22-3-27
	YM 6664	"	13534	"	"	"	18-8-26	27-1-26	22-10-26
23	XN 5243	S. Squire A	A6234	OT22/22RO	Straker	Red & White	18-8-26	17-4-23	22-10-26
	XN 5244	"	A6237	"	"	"		17-4-23	16-3-27 / 24-3-27

440

Fleet	Reg	Body No	Builder	Seating	Livery	New	To fleet	Withdrawn
	MH 295	A6379	"	OT24/22RO	"	15-8-24	22-10-26	16-3-27
	MH 1095	A6396	"	"	"	30-9-24	22-10-26	16-3-27
K329	LU 8586	20329	AEC K	?	Green & White	1920	20-3-26	14-4-26
K1037	XF 8072	20544		?	Red & White	1921	7-3-27	1-1-28
K18	LU 8276	20018	"	?	"	1920	8-3-27	1-1-28
K901	XC 8487	21167	"	?	"	1921	8-3-27	1-1-28
K20	LU 8248	20020	"	?	"	1920	10-3-27	1-1-28
K65	LU 8357	20065	"	?	"	1920	10-3-27	1-1-28
K459	XC 8056	20459	"	?	"	1920	10-3-27	1-1-28
K67	LU 8379	20067	"	?	"	1920	11-3-27	1-1-28
K92	LU 8397	20092	"	?	"	1920	11-3-27	1-1-28
K174	LU 8416	20174	"	?	"	1920	11-3-27	1-1-28
K516	XC 8137	20766	"	?	"	1921	11-3-27	1-1-28
K715	XC 9713	20965	"	?	"	1921	15-3-27	1-1-28
K598	XC 9744	20848	"	?	"	1921	15-3-27	1-1-28
K1008	XF 8040	20515	"	?	"	4-21	15-3-27	1-1-28

Coaches (known fleet up to December 1927)

Fleet	Reg	No	Builder	Seating	Livery	In	Cond		Out
IT	415	1817	TSM TS4	Ch 29	Grey & Lake	21-12-20	New	1-1-34	1934
YP	602	36403	Leyland C5	C35	Crimson Lake	6-26	"	"	7-34
8	YF 9204	5294	TSM B9A	C32	"	1-5-27	"	"	4-31
9	YF 9205	5295	"	"	"	1-5-27	"	"	4-31
10	YF 9203	5293	"	"	"	1-5-27	"	"	4-31

(1) Original body scrapped and ex-Cambrian body fitted (see appendix 5) 10-26

Former Owner
XN 513 Regent
XM 9995/9888 Premier nos. 3/2
MF 1020/9171 Admiral nos. 7/15
XN 5243/5244 Fleet nos. 2/4
MH 295/1095 Tottenham Hotspur nos. 20/22
All K-Type General

Disposal
XN 6182/XO 8747/XR 3506/3507/5274/XN 513/XM 9995/9888/
MF 1020/9171/XN 5244/MH 295/1095 C & P Sales (dealer)
Ipswich. XO 8747 to L. B. Clarke, Teddington, Middx,
(Lorry). XO 8747 to J. Hicks, Feltwell, Norfolk
(Lorry), 1927; withdrawn 1-1-33. MF 1020 Sommerfield
& Thomas, Kings Lynn (Lorry), 1927; withdrawn 1-1-33.
MF 9171 A. Fleming, Chester (Lorry), 1927; withdrawn
11-8-38. XN 5244 Johnson & Brown, Salford, (Lorry),
1927. MH 295 J & G. Matthews, Harold Wood, Essex
(Lorry), 1927; withdrawn 1-1-32
XN 6183/5243 C & P Sales, Ipswich (Lorry); withdrawn
25-3-34/1-1-36 respectively
YL 8115/YM 6664 Tottenham Hotspur
K329 Cambrian
All K-Type except K329 General
IT 415 R. Barley (Showman), Dartford, Kent
YP 602 to Lorry
YF 9204 F. T. Brook, Shoreham, Sussex; withdrawn 1-10-32
YF 9205 Bromley Coaches, Bromley, Kent
YF 9203 ?

ESSENTIAL—see LEWIS

ESSEX

Buses

Reg	Chassis	No	Body	Builder	Livery	In service	Body	Disposal	
HM 4662	Leyland LB5	13142	OT26/22RO	Dodson	Red & White	2-2-25	New	10-11-33	
HV 190	Leyland TD1	70872	H28/24RO	"	"	10-12-29	"	10-11-33	(1)

Coach

Reg	Chassis	No	Body	Builder	Livery	In service	Body	Disposal	
YF 1030	Maudslay ML4	4084	C26	?	Blue & Cream	23-3-27	2-29	10-11-33	

Disposal

HM 4662/HV 190/YF 1030 LPTB No. L83/84/—

(1) Later fitted with pneumatic tyres

Former Owner

YF 1030 Grey Green Coaches (Ewer), Stamford Hill

EWER, ALBERT

Buses

Reg	Chassis	No	Body	Builder	Livery	In service	Body	Disposal	
XW 478	Leyland LB5	12939	OT26/22RO	Dodson	Red & White	13-10-24	New	30-9-29	
XW 1634	"	12931	"	"	"	30-10-24	"	30-9-29	
XW 2993	"	12936	"	"	"	12-11-24	"	30-9-29	
XW 5572	"	13126	"	"	"	16-12-24	"	30-9-29	
XX 488	"	13131	"	"	"	6-2-25	"	30-9-29	
YL 5450	"	13512	B32R	"	"	1-10-25	"	30-9-29	
1A 6573	Maudslay ML3	?	"	"	"	1926	?	30-9-29	
YX 7083	Leyland PLSC3	47429	"	"	"	20-8-28	New	30-9-29	
YX 7084	"	47456	"	"	"	20-8-28	"	30-9-29	

Coach fleet up to September 1929

Reg	Chassis	No	Body	Builder	Livery	In service	Body	Disposal	
XB 9722	Dennis 2 ton	20029	Ch 31	?	?	5-20	New	6-28	
XB 9981	"	20071	Ch 27	?	?	5-20	17-4-24	?	
YM 8131	Maudslay ML4	3775	C24	?	Blue & Yellow	13-2-26	New	3-31	
YN 7781	Maudslay ML2	3836	"	?	"	4-26	"	3-31	
YE 5851	Maudslay ML3	3998	C38	?	"	4-27	"	3-31	
YE 5906	Maudslay ML3A	4019	"	?	"	4-27	"	3-31	
YE 5907	Maudslay ML4	3959	C24	?	"	4-27	"	3-31	
YE 5908	Maudslay ML3	3997	C38	?	"	4-27	"	3-31	
YE 5909	Maudslay ML3A	4020	C32	?	"	7-4-28	"	3-31	
MP 3521	Gilford 1660T	10306	"	H. Lewis	"	1-3-29	"	3-31	
UL 7079	Maudslay ML4B	4315	"	"	"	1-3-29	"	3-31	
UL 7080	"	4442	"	"	"	20-6-29	"	3-31	
MY 57	Gilford 166SD	10816	C26	?	"	"	"	1931	(1)

(1) Seats altered to C32 3-29

Former Owner

XB 9981 Samuelson, London, W1

Disposal

XW 478/1634/2993/5572/XX 488/YL 5450/1A 6573/YX 7083/
7084 General
XB 9722 G. J. Dawson (dealer) Clapham
XB 9981 ?
YM 8131/YN 7781/YE 5851/5906-5909/MP 3521/UL 7079/
7080 Eva's Motor Coaches, London, EC1
YM 8131/YN 7781/YE 5851/UL 7079/7080 to Grey Green
Coaches, Stamford Hill, 5-34. YM 8131 to Lorry, 4-36.

YN 7781/UL 7080 G. C. Cook (dealer), London, SW8, 1937.
YE 5851 to Lorry, 3-36. UL 7079 T. W. Goodman, Gosport, Hants, 1937
YE 5906/5909 to Showman, 3-34
YE 5908 Union Jack Coaches (Raymond), London. E2, 5-34
MP 3521 withdrawn, 1-10-31
MY 57 Universal Coaches, London, N9; withdrawn 1-10-31

EXPRESS

Fleet	Reg.	Chassis	Chassis No	Body	Builder	Colour	In service		New	Disposal	Ref
	XL 7513	Leyland LB1	12412	OT26/22RO	Dodson	Choc & Primrose	2-8-22	31-12-29	New	29-1-30	(1)
	XN 6774	Leyland LB2	12528	"	"	"	1-5-23	31-12-29	"	29-1-30	(2)
	XT 4951	Leyland LB4	12712	"	"	"	30-5-24		"	2-31	(3)
B6	XU 7498	Leyland LB5	12920	"	"	"	3-9-24		"	10-8-34	(4)
	UC 8658	"	12920A	"	"	"	25-3-28		"	31-10-29	
B1	UV 9097	Leyland TD1	70714	H28/24RO	"	"	30-7-29		"	10-8-34	(5)
B2	UW 6157	"	70815	"	"	"	21-11-29		"	10-8-34	
B3	UW 6987	"	70873	"	"	"	30-12-29		"	10-8-34	
B4	GC 6087	"	71193	"	"	"	10-2-30		"	10-8-34	
B5	GO 1636	"	72060	"	"	"	25-3-31		"	10-8-34	

(1) Chassis exchanged with UC 8658 10-29   (2) converted to Express lorry 3-30   (3) Pneumatic tyres fitted 3-30
(4) Chassis assembled from spare parts by Express and later exchanged with XL 7513 10-29   (5) Exhibited by Dodson at Olympia Motor Show 11-29

Disposal
XL 7513/XN 6774 Enterprise Bus Co., Clacton; Eastern National No. 3216/3215, 9-31 (pneumatics tyres fitted 3-30);
XL 7513 sold to a dealer, 7-33
XT 4951 ?
B1 to 6 LPTB TD 99-103/L56
UC 8658 Skinner, Hastings; AEC (dealer), Southall, 1-30

F & K

Buses

Reg.	Chassis	Chassis No	Body	Builder	Colour	In service	New	Disposal
YR 8860	Maudslay ML3	3999	B30R	H. Lewis	Red & Yellow	10-12-26	New	28-7-27
YR 8861	"	4000	"	"	"	10-12-26	"	28-7-27

Coaches (up to July 1927)

Reg.	Chassis	Chassis No	Body	Builder	Colour	In service	New	Disposal
YN 7201	Maudslay ML2	3854	C22	H. Lewis	Dark Red	30-3-26	New	11-4-28
YH 5553	Maudslay ML4A	4116	C26	"	"	1-6-27	"	20-1-30

Disposal
YR 8860/8861 Public No. M2/1
YN 7201 Prince Motor Coaches, Windsor, Berks
YH 5553 Eton Coaches, Balham, London; later to a Jersey operator

FAIRLOP

Reg.	Chassis	Chassis No	Body	Builder	Colour	In service	New	Disposal
PU 4769	Daimler Y	6069	OT22/20RO	Hickman	Red & White	2-9-24	New	6-25
PU 8660	Dennis 4 ton	40350	OT26/22RO	Dodson	"	15-6-25	"	31-1-29

Disposal
PU 4769 Roberts (dealer) London, W12; Eclipse 1925
PU 8660 City No. A36

FAR

Fleet No	Reg	Chassis	Chassis No	Body	Body builder	Livery	In	New	Into fleet	Disposal
	XU 8988	Daimler Y	6071	OT22/20RO	Hickman	Red & White	29-9-24	New		?
	MY 1689	Dennis HS	9011?	H28/26RO	Birch	Chocolate & Yellow	25-10-29	"	1-1-30	24-11-33

Disposal
XU 8988 ?
MY 1689 LPTB No. D185

FAVOURITE

Buses

Reg	Chassis	Chassis No	Body	Body builder	Livery	In	New	Disposal
XT 2643	Dennis 4 ton	40113	OT26/22RO	Wilton	Red & Cream	5-5-24	New	17-8-27
XT 9480	"	40151	"	"	"	25-6-24	"	17-8-27
XX 8348	"	40343	"	"	"	1-4-25	"	17-8-27

Coaches (up to August 1927)

Reg	Chassis	Chassis No	Body	Body builder	Livery	In	New	Disposal
XT 5427	Napier	B70	C14	?	Panhard Red	26-5-24	New	9-28
YO 4247	Maudslay ML4	3867	C28	?	Maroon	19-5-26	"	1-12-33
YF 6023	Maudslay ML4A	4054	"	?	"	3-27	"	4-38

Disposal
XT 2643/9480/XX 8348 Public No. D10/9/21
XT 5427 Clan Motor Works (dealer), Tooting, London
YO 4247 Maudslay Motor Co
YF 6023 Invincible Coaches (Cook), Westcliff-on-Sea;
Mountain Coaches, London, SW10, 5-41; withdrawn 7-42

FELIX/FLEUR DE LYS/REGAL

Reg	Chassis	Chassis No	Body	Body builder	Livery	In	New	Disposal
XU 4809	Dennis 4 ton	40195	OT26/22RO	Hickman	Red & Yellow	1-8-24	New	23-6-27

Disposal
XU 4809 Public No. D66

FFD—see EMPRESS (F. F. Downes)

FIELD MARSHAL

Fleet No	Reg	Chassis	Chassis No	Body	Body builder	Livery	In	New	Disposal
72	MH 866	Dennis 4 ton	40216	OT26/22RO	S & B	Red & White	16-9-24	New	17-2-28

Disposal
MH 866 Public No. D111

FLEET

Fleet No	Reg	Chassis	Chassis No	Body	Body builder	Livery	In	New/Acquired	Into fleet	Disposal	Notes
2	XN 5243	S. Squire A	A6234	OT22/22RO	Straker	Dark Green & White	17-4-23	New		18-8-26	(1)
4	XN 5244	"	A6237	OT26/22RO	"	"	17-4-23	"		18-8-26	(1)
6	XR 7776	Dennis 4 ton	40099	OT26/22RO	Dodson	"	31-3-24	"	12-11-26	20-12-26	(1)
8	XR 7778	"	40095	"	"	"	31-3-24	"	26-1-27	17-2-27	(1)
K163	LU 8414	AEC K	20163	OT24/22RO	?	"	1920	20-3-26		15-4-26	
K787	XC 8334	"	21053	"	?	Red & White	1921	18-8-26		1-1-28	
K712	XC 8270	"	20962	"	?	"	1921	18-8-26		1-1-28	

444

Fleet No	Reg	Chassis	No.	Body	Builder	Livery					Notes
K986	XC 9755	"	21252		"		1921	27-11-26		1-1-28	
K722	XC 8463	"	20972		"		1921	25-1-27		1-1-28	

(1) Colour to red & grey 2-24/2-24/3-25/3-25

Former Owner
All K-type General

FLEUR DE LYS—see FELIX & MAGNET

FLORENCE

Fleet No	Reg	Chassis	No.	Body	Builder	Livery					
	XR 888	Dennis 4 ton	40073	OT26/22RO	S & B	Red & Cream	26-1-24	New	26-1-27	11-2-27	
	XT 6628	"	40145	OT24/22RO	"	"	2-6-24	24-1-27	25-1-27	9-2-27	
K5	LU 8245	AEC K	20005	"	?	Red & White	1920	24-1-27		1-1-28	
K320	LU 8583	"	20320	"	?	"	1920	25-1-27		1-1-28	

Former Owner
K5/320 General

Disposal
XR 888/XT 6628 Redburn's No. D34/35
K5/320 General

FOUNTAIN THE

Fleet No	Reg	Chassis	No.	Body	Builder	Livery					
	XR 3546	Dennis 4 ton	40079	OT26/22RO	Dodson	Red	29-2-24	New		11-8-27	

Disposal
XR 3546 Public No. D42

FS PETROL ELECTRIC Frost Smith

Fleet No	Reg	No.	Body	Builder	Livery					Notes
3	XM 2056	FS 1-11	OT22/22RO	Dodson	Blue & Cream	30-10-22	New	1-12-24	3-25	(1)
4	XM 2057	FS 1-12	"	"		30-10-22	"	1-12-24	3-25	(1)
5	XM 3064	FS 1-13	"	"		3-11-22	"	1-12-24	3-25	(1)
1	XM 4568	FS 1-14	OT24/22RO	"		4-12-22	"	1-12-24	3-25	
6	XM 5302	FS 1-15	OT25/22RO	"		19-12-22	"	1-12-24	3-25	
2	XM 5761	FS 1-16	"	"		29-12-22	"	1-12-24	3-25	

(1) Seating altered to OT22/22RO 6-23

Disposal
XM 2056/2057/3064/4568/5302/5761 Timpson's No. —/50/—/—/—/49

FW

Fleet No	Reg	Chassis	No.	Body	Builder	Livery					
	XW 9346	Leyland LB5	13149	OT26/22RO	Dodson	Red & White	27-1-25	New		11-11-27	

Disposal
XW 9346 City No. A32

GENIAL/BUCK/ST GEORGE

Fleet No	Reg	Chassis	No.	Body	Builder	Livery					Notes
	XP 8535	Leyland LB4	12731	OT26/22RO	Wilton	Red & White	31-12-23	New		10-27	(1)
	XX 9806	Dennis 4 ton	40307	"	Dodson	"	9-4-25	"		18-7-34	(2)
	XW 910	"	40212	"	"	"	20-10-24	10-27		31-10-34	

Reg	Chassis	Chassis No	Body	Builder	Colour	Date	New	Date	
GO 5448	Leyland TD 1	71913	H30/26RO	Dodson	Red & White	5-5-31	New	18-7-34	
JJ 1269	Leyland TD 2	2010	Lorry	"	Green	6-1-33	"	18-7-34	
XX 7606	Dennis 4 ton	40329				1-4-25	28-9-28	30-6-33	(3)

(1) Pneumatic tyres fitted by 1930 and converted to a lorry 1-33   (2) Pneumatic tyres
fitted by 1930
(3) New as a bus to Alberta, purchased as a chassis only
for conversion to a lorry

Former Owner
XW 910 Veleta
XX 7606 C & P Sales (dealer) Ipswich

Disposal
XP 8535 City No. A34
XX 9806/GO 5448/JJ 1269 LPTB No. D197/TD 97/98
XW 910 Poole & Muddiman, London, E10; scrapped 3-35
XX 7606 B. Jarman, London, SE10; G. B. Hicks, Greenwich, 1-35;
J. Morris, London, E6, 6-36;

GLANDFIELD

	Reg	Chassis	Chassis No	Body	Builder	Colour	Date	New	Date
D1	XX 6558	Dennis 4 ton	40324	OT26/22RO	S & B	Red & White	26-3-25	New	19-8-27

Disposal
XX 6558 Public No. D1

GLEANER

	Reg	Chassis	Chassis No	Body	Builder	Colour	Date	New	Date
D1	MF 4499	Dennis 4 ton	40065	OT26/22RO	S & B	Red & White	30-1-24	New	12-8-27
D2	XU 9376	"	40209	"	"	"	1-10-24	"	12-8-27

Disposal
MF 4499/XU 9376 Public No. D26/24

GLEN

Reg	Chassis	Chassis No	Body	Builder	Colour	Date	New	Date	
XO 8835	S. Squire A	A6281	OT24/22RO	Straker	Peach & Brown	4-8-23	New	10-1-27	(1)
YR 2258	Leyland LB5	13642	OT26/22RO	Dodson	Red & White	4-10-26	"	1-11-33	(2)
GJ 8489	Leyland TD1	71319	H28/24RO	"	"	16-6-30	"	1-11-33	

(1) Colour to red & white 12-24
(2) Pneumatic tyres fitted later

Disposal
XO 8835 W. E. Hughes, Birkenhead (Lorry); withdrawn 3-29
YR 2258/GJ 8489 LPTB No. L47/46

GOLDEN ARROW—see SHANGHAI

GORDON/GOC

	Reg	Chassis	Chassis No	Body	Builder	Colour	Date	New	Date	
1	XU 8376	Dennis 4 ton	40202	OT26/22RO	Dodson	Red & White	29-9-24	New	15-12-33	(1)
2	XX 2572	"	40268	"	"	"	27-2-25	"	15-12-33	(2)
3	XX 7690	"	40333	B30R	"	"	1-4-25	"	15-12-33	(2)
4	TW 5863	Dennis E	17091	H28/24RO	"	"	21-10-26	"	15-12-33	
5	VX 2198	Leyland TD1	70717	"	"	"	5-9-29	"	15-12-33	
6	VX 5169	"	71166	H26/26R	"	"	4-4-30	"	15-12-33	
7	EV 3403	Maudslay ML7C2	4929		"	"	7-11-31	1-6-32	15-12-33	(3)

Disposal
No. 1-7 LPTB No. D194/192/191/193/L112/113/MY1

(1) Converted to pneumatic tyred lorry 6-32   (3) Fitted with
(2) Pneumatic tyres fitted —/1-29   opening "sunshine" roof and exhibited at Olympia 1931

446

GRAFTON

	Reg	Chassis	No.	Body	Builder	Livery				
K945	XW 8641	Dennis 4 ton	40282	OT26/22RO	Dodson	Red & White	19-1-25	New	3-2-27	5-3-27
	XC 9738	AEC K	21211	OT24/22RO	?	"	1921	2-2-27		1-1-28

Former Owner
K945 General

Disposal
XW 8641 Redburn's No. D38
K945 Metropolitan

GRANGEWOOD—see LEWIS

GRAY

Buses

	Reg	Chassis	No.	Body	Builder	Livery				
7	XP 9079	Leyland LB4	12738	OT26/22RO	Dodson	Red & White	2-1-24	New		21-2-30
6	XP 9776	"	12739	"	"	"	11-1-24	"		21-2-30
5	XR 481	"	12741	"	"	"	18-1-24	"		21-2-30
8	XR 658	"	12742	"	"	"	22-1-24	"		21-2-30
4	MF 9645	"	12910	"	"	"	18-7-24	"		21-2-30
3	MF 9846	"	12911	"	"	"	25-7-24	"		21-2-30
2	MH 304	"	12912	"	"	"	15-8-24	"		21-2-30
1	MH 402	"	12913	"	"	"	21-8-24	"		21-2-30
9	MH 7206	Leyland LB5	13307	"	"	"	28-5-25	"		21-2-30

Coaches

Reg	Chassis	No.	Body	Builder	Livery				
XA 8819	AEC Y	11232	Ch 28	?	Red & Black	3-20	New		31-5-27
MH 5498	Garford	?	C18	?	"	9-4-25	Rebuilt		3-26
MK 2249	Gilford WTU	?	"	?	"	25-1-26	Rebuilt		?
MK 4300	"	?	"	?	"	26-4-26	New		?
ML 3731	Gilford LL15	10161	C26	Redhead	"	14-4-27	New		?
ML 5155	"	10201	"	?	"	14-6-27	"		?
MP 3769	Gilford 166SD	10314	C28	?	"	20-4-28	"	1-10-29	?
MP 4466	"	10348	"	?	"	19-5-28	"		?
MP 4637	"	10358	"	?	"	26-5-28	"		?

(1)
(2)
(3)

(1) Rebuilt to MK 4300   (2) Formally a Garford origin
unknown   (3) Rebuilt from Garford MH 5498

Disposal
No. 1-9 General No. L40/42/39/41/37/44/38/36/43
XA 8819 Lewington, London, SE8 (Lorry)
MH 5498 E. B. Horne & Co (dealer), London, N7
MK 2249 Last owner A. Chambers, Islington, withdrawn 1-1-34
MK 4300 Last owner C. Holford London, SW17, withdrawn 3-36
ML 3731 Last owner A. Redburn, Ponders End, Middx, withdrawn 1-10-31
ML 5155 Scrapped
MP 3769/4637 Eva's Coaches, London, EC1. MP 3769 to J. M. Horne
& Co Ltd, London, N6; withdrawn 1-10-32. MP 4637 to Dorking
Coaches (E. R. Lipscombe), Dorking date ?; withdrawn 12-37
MP 4466 Blue Rambler Coaches, Margate, Kent by 1-42

GRETNA—see MTT

GWL

Reg	Chassis	Chassis No.	Body	Builder	Livery	Date	Source	Disposal
MH 4646	Thornycroft J	10651	OT26/24RO	Dodson	Red & White	24-3-25	New	8-7-27

Disposal
MH 4646 Public No. T1

H & B—see IMPERIAL

HAV-A-RIDE/HFB

Reg	Chassis	Chassis No.	Body	Builder	Livery	Date	Source	Disposal
MH 1326	Daimler Y	6073	OT22/20RO	Hickman	Red & White	9-10-24	New	9-26
MK 7335	Leyland LB5	13586	OT26/22RO	Dodson	,,	1-9-26	,,	7-10-27

Disposal
MH 1326 A & W, Harrow, Middx.
MK 7335 Public No. L27

HAVELOCK

Buses

No.	Reg	Chassis	Chassis No.	Body	Builder	Livery	Date	Source	Disposal	Note
1	XP 7888	Dennis 4 ton	40063	OT26/22RO	Dodson	Crimson & White	17-12-23	New	4-8-27	(1)
2	XW 3304	,,	40247	B25R	,,	Red & White	17-11-24	,,	4-8-27	
8	YO 8392	Dennis 2½ ton	45404	,,	,,	Chocolate & White	14-6-26	,,	4-8-27	
9	YO 8394	,,	45407	,,	,,	,,	14-6-26	,,	4-8-27	
10	YO 8393	,,	45405	,,	,,	,,	14-6-26	,,	4-8-27	
11	YR 8400	,,	45449	,,	,,	,,	6-12-26	,,	4-8-27	
12	YR 8601	,,	45450	,,	,,	,,	6-12-26	,,	4-8-27	

Coaches

Reg	Chassis	Chassis No.	Body	Builder	Livery	Date	Source	Disposal	Note
XB 8451	AEC B	?	Ch 23	?	Grey	16-8-20	New	4-8-27	
XH 9682	,,	?	Ch 28	?	Royal Blue	1-22	,,	4-8-27	(2)
XK 7608	,,	B3001	,,	?		5-22	,,	4-8-27	

Disposal
No. 1/2/8-12/XB 8451/XH 9682/XK 7608 Public No. D34/43/DS9/
8/13/24/22/—/—/—

(1) Colour to red & white 1-24
(2) Colour to royal blue 10-21

HAWK, THE

Bus

Reg	Chassis	Chassis No.	Body	Builder	Livery	Date	Source	Disposal
XW 6538	Daimler Y	6078	OT22/20RO	Hickman	Red & White	30-12-24	New	7-9-27

Coaches (fleet name Hawk Coaches)

No.	Reg	Chassis	Chassis No.	Body	Builder	Livery	Date	Source	Disposal
2	YF 6379	Daimler Y	CKR11	C26	?	Red	8-4-27	New	28-3-29
4	YV 2158	TSM B10A	5540	C30	?	,,	25-3-28	,,	16-9-37
6	UL 4084	TSM B10A2	6222	C32	?	,,	1-29	,,	By 10-46

Disposal
XW 6538 Public No. DA2
YF 6379 Kings Service Coaches, Clapham, London
YV 2158 Heatherley Motor Works (dealer), London, E8
UL 4084 Lorry

HAWKINS R/RH

Buses

Reg	Chassis	Chassis No	Body	Body Builder	Colour	Acquired	Source		Disposal	Note
XW 6925	Dennis 4 ton	40287	OT26/22RO	Wilton	Red & Cream	1-1-25	New	1-27	2-6-32	(1)
YE 3678	"	40434	"	Birch	"	28-1-27	"		20-2-31	(2)
GH 7079	Leyland TD1	71438	H30/26RO	"	"	29-8-30	"		12-5-32	(3)
GX 1955	"	1035	H30/26R	"	"	3-5-32	"		13-6-34	(4)

Coaches and Taxis

Reg	Chassis	Chassis No	Body	Body Builder	Colour	Acquired	Source	Disposal
LU 9931	Leyland	8473	Ch 27	?	Red	12-19	New	1927
YV 5864	Morris	6259	C14	?	"	9-5-28	"	44-36
XC 6901	Unic	12568	Taxi	?	Crimson Lake	2-2-21	"	13-6-34
XN 450	"	12104	"	?	Blue	2-3-23	"	13-6-34

(1) Body to YE 3678 1-27, 32-seat coach body and pneumatic tyres fitted 4-27   (2) Body ex XW 6925 1-27, pneumatic tyres fitted by 6-29   (3) Rebuilt to H30/26R by Birch 2-32, body to GX 1955 5-32 and new single deck body fitted (see Nil Desperandum)   (4) Body ex GH 7079

Disposal
XW 6925 S. J. Davis, Pen-y-Craig, Glam, as C28; W. J. Evans, Mumbles, Swansea (Lorry) 11-34
YE 3678 Arlington (dealer), London, SW1; Dunn, Taunton, Som, 3-31; to lorry 3-32
GH 7079 Nil Desperandum
GX 1955/XC 6901/XN 450 LPTB No. TD87/—/—
LU 9931 United Service Transport, Tooting, London
YV 5864 G. Ferguson, Murthly, Perth (Lorry)

HENSLOWE

No	Reg	Chassis	Chassis No	Body	Body Builder	Colour	Acquired	Source	Disposal	Note
1	XU 6730	Dennis 4 ton	40170	OT26/22RO	S & B	White & Green	26-8-24	New	17-2-28	(1)
2	XU 8234	"	40218	"	"	"	15-9-24	"	17-2-28	(1)
3	XW 3809	"	40231	"	"	"	24-11-24	"	17-2-28	(1)
4	XX 4194	"	40303	"	Wilton	"	12-3-25	"	17-2-28	(1)
5	XX 9918	"	40348	"	Dodson	"	14-4-25	"	12-2-27	(1)
	XN 5203	Leyland LB2	12526	"	S & B	Red & White	16-4-23	22-7-25	12-2-27	
	MH 2480	Dennis 4 ton	40274	"	"	"	15-12-24	Late -25	16-5-26	

(1) Colour to red & white 12-24/9-25/11-25/3-26/4-26

Former Owner
XN 5203 Waverley
MH 2480 The Leader

Disposal
No. 1-5 Public No. D106/107/109/108/110
XN 5203 Rapid No. 8
MH 2480 Varsity

HFB—see HAV-A-RIDE

HH

Reg	Chassis	Chassis No	Body	Body Builder	Colour	Acquired	Source	Disposal
NK 8710	Leyland LB5	12927	OT26/22RO	Dodson	Red & White	10-24	New	12-12-27

Disposal
NK 8710 Public No. L34

HHC

Reg	Chassis	Chassis No	Body	Body Builder	Colour	Acquired	Source	Disposal
YE 850	Dennis 2½ ton	45471	B24R	Dodson	Chocolate & White	1-1-27	New	5-8-27
YE 851	"	45473	"	"	"	1-1-27	"	5-8-27

No.	Reg	Chassis	Ch. No.	Body	Builder	Livery	In	Acq.	Wdn	Disposal	Notes
	YE 852	Dennis 2½ ton	45472	B24R	Dodson	Chocolate & White	1-1-27	New		5-8-27	

HL—see PIRATE THE

HORSESHOE—see EMPRESS (F. F. Downes)

I & B—see TALLY HO

IMPERIAL (A. E. Blane)

No.	Reg	Chassis	Ch. No.	Body	Builder	Livery	In	Acq.	Wdn	Disposal	Notes
1	TW 9013	Chevrolet LM	16224	B14F	Thgd	Green & Black	4-5-27	New		28-11-34	(1)
2	VW 543	"	17106	"	?	"	7-7-27	"		12-34	
3	VW 1212	"	17463	?	?	"	31-8-27	"	3-32	28-11-34	(2)
4	VW 3180	Dennis GL	70186	B18F	Metclf	"	5-4-28	"		28-11-34	
5	VW 7517	Chevrolet LP	47843	B14F	?	"	13-12-28	"		?	(3)
6	YU 9022	Chevrolet LM	17842	B25F	Thgd	"	15-10-27	17-9-29	3-34	28-11-34	(4)
7	VX 4253	AJS Pilot	175	B14F	Metclf	"	28-2-30	New		28-11-34	
8	VX 6739	Dennis 30 cwt	56009	"	Thgd	"	3-7-30	"		28-11-34	
9	VX 7334	"	56007	"	"	"	26-8-30	"		28-11-34	
10	VX 7401	"	56024	B26F	Metclf	"	1-10-30	"		28-11-34	
11	VX 9932	Morris Comm Dictator	035H	"	"	"	2-3-31	"		28-11-34	
12	EV 4760	Dennis Lancet	170014	B32F	"	"	11-2-32	"		28-11-34	
14	EV 6168	"	170021	"	"	"	12-5-32	"		28-11-34	
15	TR 8754	Gilford 1680T	11445	B26F	"	"	6-6-30	10-4-33		28-11-34	
16	TR 8755	"	11444	"	"	"	6-6-30	1-6-33		28-11-34	

(1) Fitted with van body ex YU 9022 9-29   (2) Rebodied   (3) Bus body ex
with new Metcalfe B18F Body 1931   (4) Seats altered to B26F later
TW 9013 fitted 9-29

Former Owner
YU 9022 Shifras Novelty Co, London, E1 (Van)
TR 8754/8755 Modern Travel Coaches, Southampton

Disposal
YE 850-852 Public No. DS28/27/26

Disposal
No. 1/4/6-12/14-16 LPTB No. CH6/DM5/CH5/AJS1/DM6/8/7/M50/
DL35/34/GD1/2
No. 2/3/5 ?

IMPERIAL (Holliday, Bangs & Dengate)/H & B

Buses

Reg	Chassis	Ch. No.	Body	Builder	Livery	In	Acq.	Wdn	Disposal
XU 5524	Daimler Y	6067	OT22/20RO	Hickman	Red	11-8-24	New	25-3-30	?
YU 4689	Dennis 4 ton	40465	OT26/22RO	Birch	"	26-11-27	"		5-12-33
GJ 5506	Dennis HS	90153	OT30/26RO	"	"	31-5-30	"		5-12-33

Coaches

Reg	Chassis	Ch. No.	Body	Builder	Livery	In	Acq.	Disposal
YX 4027	Reo Pullman	GB538	C24	?	Cream & Black	31-7-28	New	1934
XV 3023	Thornycroft A2Long	16413	C20	?	"	6-11-28	"	30-6-33
GK 9333	Dennis GL	70685	C18	Birch	Cream & Brown	31-10-30	New	?

GK 9334 .. 70686 31-10-30 .. 4-12-34
GK 9335 .. 70688 31-10-30 .. 4-12-34

Disposal
XU 5524 ?
YU 4689/GJ 5506 LPTB No. D187/186
YX 4027 Victory Coaches, Mortimer, Berks; withdrawn 5-47
XV 3023 John's Transport, Slough, Bucks (Lorry)
GK 9333 Ministry of Supply by 12-40
GK 9334/9335 Empress Coaches (Cooper), Stockbridge, Hants

IMPERIAL (Priest Bros)
2   MH 1693   Dennis 4 ton   S & B   OT26/22RO   40232   Red & White   1-11-24   New   29-1-27   26-2-27
K1041   XF 8076   AEC K   ?   OT24/22RO   20542   "   1921   28-1-27   1-1-28

Former Owner
K1041 General

Disposal
MH 1693 Redburn's No. D36
K1041 General

INDEPENDENT
XU 4662   Daimler Y   S & B   OT22/20RO   6061   Red & White   31-7-24   New   15-5-28
XT 5611   "   "   "   6062   "   27-5-24   1926   21-11-28   12-28

Former Owner
XT 5611   Peraeque

Disposal
XU 4662 Public
XT 5611 Cleveland

INVICTA—see TRINITY

JH—see BLUEBELL

JL
XP 4810   Daimler Y   Hickman   OT22/20RO   6050   Red & White   1-11-23   New   8-3-28
XR 8933   "   S & B   "   6058   "   8-4-24   5-24   10-24
XU 9098   Dennis 4 ton   "   OT26/22RO   40214   "   29-9-24   New   8-3-28
YR 1662   Leyland LB5   Birch   "   13643   "   29-9-26   8-3-28

Former Owner
XR 8933 JS & SR

Disposal
XP 4810/XU 9098/YR 1662 Public No. DA1/D125/L35
XR 8933 Venture

JOCKEY, THE
XT 4857   Leyland LB4   Dodson   OT26/22RO   12713   Red & White   21-5-24   New   23-9-27   8-12-27
K485   XC 8095   AEC K   "   OT24/22RO   20485   "   1920   30-9-27   1-1-28

Former Owner
K485 General

Disposal
XT 4857 C & P Sales (dealer) Ipswich; E. Hayes Ltd, London, SW1
(Lorry); 12-27; withdrawn 3-28
K485 Metropolitan

JS & SR

Reg	Chassis	No	Body	Builder	Livery	Date	Status	Disposed
XR 8933	Daimler Y	6058	OT22/20RO	S & B	Red	8-4-24	New	5-24

Disposal
XR 8933 JL

KATHLEEN

Reg	Chassis	No	Body	Builder	Livery	Date	Status	Disposed
MF 8001	Daimler Y	6063	OT22/20RO	Hickman	Red & White	29-5-24	New	By 3-25

Disposal
MF 8001 Roberts (dealer) London, W12; Peraeque by 3-25

KBB/EAGLE

Reg	Chassis	No	Body	Builder	Livery	Date	Status	Disposed	
XT 9231	Dennis 4 ton	40147	OT26/22RO	Dodson	Chocolate & Cream	23-6-24	New	3-30	(1)
UU 1907	Dennis ES	17714	B30R	Birch	Red & Cream	16-5-29	"	30-6-32	
GC 7388	Daimler CF6	7398S	H30/26RO	"	"	27-2-30	"	10-11-33	
MV 6306	Leyland TD2	352	H28/24R	Dodson	"	21-7-32	"	10-11-33	

(1) Colour later to red & cream
Disposal
XT 9231 ?
UU 1907 G. H. Allitt
GC 7388/MV 6306 LPTB No. DST4/L78

LANCASTRIAN

Reg	Chassis	No	Body	Builder	Livery	Date	Status	Disposed	
MF 9873	Daimler Y	6068	OT22/20RO	S & B	Chocolate & White	28-7-24	New	1-26	(1)
MK 2119	Dennis 4 ton	40382	OT26/22RO	Dodson	Red & White	15-1-26	"	5-8-27	

(1) Colour to red & white 1-25
Disposal
MF 9873 Roberts (dealer), London, W12; Low Loaders Ltd
London, W12 (Lorry) 6-26
MK 2119 Public No. D13

LCOC

Reg	Chassis	No	Body	Builder	Livery	Date	Status	Disposed
XN 5034	Leyland LB2	12511	OT26/22RO	Dodson	Maroon & Cream	15-4-23	New	5-24

Disposal
XN 5034 Dodson (dealer); to Omega 12-6-24

LEADER, THE

Reg	Chassis	No	Body	Builder	Livery	Date	Status	Disposed
MH 2480	Dennis 4 ton	40274	OT26/22RO	S & B	Red & White	15-12-24	New	1925

Disposal
MH 2480 Henslowe

LEA RIG, THE

Reg	Chassis	No	Body	Builder	Livery	Date	Status	Disposed
K160 XW 4774	Daimler Y	6076	OT22/20RO	Hickman	Red & White	4-12-24	New	1-4-27
LU 8325	AEC K	20160	OT24/22RO	?	"	1920	31-3-27	10-5-27

Former Owner
K160 General

Disposal
XW 4774 C & P Sales (dealer) Ipswich; Dunn, Taunton, Som, 6-27
K160 General

LEA VALLEY

Fleet No	Reg	Chassis	Chassis No	Body	Builder	Livery	Date 1	Source	Date 3	Date 4	Note
	XX 1259	Dennis 4 ton	40310	OT26/22RO	Dodson	Red & White	13-2-25	New		1-1-28	(1)

(1) Strachan & Brown body ex MH 1693 (Imperial) fitted 1-27

Disposal
XX 1259 Metropolitan No. D48

LEGION

Fleet No	Reg	Chassis	Chassis No	Body	Builder	Livery	Date 1	Source	Date 3	Date 4	Note
K903	MF 6914	Thornycroft J	10526	OT26/24RO	Dodson	Chocolate & White	23-4-24	New	6-11-26	10-11-26	(1)
	XC 9703	AEC K	21169	OT24/22RO	?	"	1921	6-11-26		1-1-28	

Former Owner
K903 General

Disposal
MF 6914 Thames Valley No. 135; G. Sullivan, London, SW2 (Lorry) 1931; withdrawn 1-8-37
K903 General

LEWIS/ESSENTIAL/GRANGEWOOD

Fleet No	Reg	Chassis	Chassis No	Body	Builder	Livery	Date 1	Source	Date 3	Date 4	Note
K686	XR 4694	Thornycroft J	10508	OT26/24RO	Dodson	Light Blue & White	6-3-24	New	14-9-26	15-10-26	(1)
	YN 3800	Leyland LB5	13585	OT26/22RO	"	Red & White	29-4-26	31-8-26	24-10-27	1-1-28	
	XC 8281	AEC K	20936	OT24/22RO	?	"	1921	24-10-27		1-1-28	

(1) Colour to dark red & white 1-25

Former Owner
YN 3800 Horseshoe
K686 General

Disposal
XR 4694 Thames Valley No. 137; Underhill Bros, Birmingham (Lorry) 3-31
YN 3800/K686 General No. L28/K686

LIBERTY

Fleet No	Reg	Chassis	Chassis No	Body	Builder	Livery	Date 1	Source	Date 3	Date 4	Note
	XN 1344	Leyland LB2	12463	OT26/22RO	Dodson	Blue & Primrose	13-3-23	New	12-2-26	12-2-26	(1)
	XR 9753	Dennis 4 ton	40114	"	"	Brown & Cream	12-4-24	12-2-26		29-9-27	

(1) Colour to red & white 5-26

Former Owner
XR 9753 City No D1

Disposal
XN 1344 City No. A24
XR 9753 Public No. D79

LONDON

Fleet No	Reg	Chassis	Chassis No	Body	Builder	Livery	Date 1	Source	Date 3	Date 4	Note
	XP 7425	Daimler Y	6051	OT22/20RO	Hickman	Red & White	26-12-23	New	6-24	6-24	
	XR 2651	"	6055	"	"		15-2-24		6-24	6-24	

Disposal
XP 7425/XR 2651 Roberts (dealer) London, W12. XP 7425 Vivid 12-24, XR 2651 White Star 4-7-24

LONSDALE

Fleet No	Reg	Chassis	Chassis No	Body	Builder	Livery	Date 1	Source	Date 3	Date 4	Note
K416	XT 946	Daimler Y	6057	OT22/20RO	S & B	Maroon & White	17-4-24	New	22-3-27	29-3-27	
	XW 9413	"	6075	"	"	Red & White	28-1-25	New	19-3-27	29-3-27	
K139	LU 8567	AEC K	20416	OT24/22RO	?	"	1920	18-3-27		1-1-28	
	XC 9710	"	20139	"	?	"	1921	21-3-27		1-1-28	

Former Owner
XT 946 New London

Disposal
XT 946/XW 9413 C & P Sales (dealer) Ipswich; Roberts (dealer)

London, W12, 5-27; XT 946 Low Loaders Ltd, London, W12
(Lorry) 8-27; withdrawn 1-1-28
K139/416 General

LOUMAX

	Reg	Chassis	Fleet No	Body	Body maker	Livery				Notes
	MY 1336	Guy OND	9201	B18R	Duple	Red & Cream	17-9-29	New	27-8-31	
	MY 3390	Guy ONDF	9443	B20F	United	"	18-3-30	"	16-9-32	
	MY 4117	"	9615	"	"	"	12-4-30	"	16-9-32	(1)

Disposal
MY 1336 Rainham Bus Service (Stephens), Rainham, Essex
MY 3390/4117 General No. G8/7

LOVELAND

	Reg	Chassis	Fleet No	Body	Body maker	Livery				
	XN 6976	Leyland LB2	12527	OT26/22RO	Dodson	Lake & White	2-5-23	11-10-24	25-10-27	1-1-28
K593	XC 8214	AEC K	20843	OT24/22RO	?	Red & White	1921	25-10-27		1-1-28

(1) Colour to red & white 6-27
Former Owner
XN 6976 New Times
K593 General
Disposal
XN 6976/K593 General No. L36/K593

LPOC

	Reg	Chassis	Fleet No	Body	Body maker	Livery				
	XY 3470	Dennis 4 ton	40338	OT26/22RO	S & B	Red & White	4-5-25	New	19-8-25	21-8-25

Disposal
XY 3470 Cambrian No. D8

MAGNET/FLEUR DE LYS

	Reg	Chassis	Fleet No	Body	Body maker	Livery				Notes
	XR 9847	Thornycroft J	10531	OT26/24RO	Dodson	Purple & Cream	14-4-24	New	25-6-26	(1)

(1) Colour to red & white 4-25
Disposal
XR 9847 Thames Valley No. 131

M & E/MORFAY/EMBASSY

	Reg	Chassis	Fleet No	Body	Body maker	Livery			
	XW 2324	Dennis 4 ton	40207	OT26/22RO	Dodson	Red & White	5-11-24	New	24-10-27
	XX 1007	"	40309	"	"	"	11-2-25	"	24-10-27

Disposal
XW 2324/XX 1007 Public No. D104/103

MAJESTIC

	Reg	Chassis	Fleet No	Body	Body maker	Livery				Notes
1	XO 7581	Leyland LB2	12585	OT26/22RO	Dodson	Chocolate & White	28-7-23	New	3-8-27	(1)
2	XT 3142	Leyland LB4	12709	"	"	"	8-5-24	"	3-8-27	(1)

(1) Colour to red & white 2-26/12-25
Disp3sal
XO 7581/XT 3142 Public No. L25/3

MARATHON

Fleet No	Reg	Chassis	Chassis No	Body	Builder	Livery	In Service	New/Acq	Withdrawn	Disposal
	XO 1942	Leyland LB2	12582	OT26/22RO	Dodson	Dk Green & Cream	8-6-23	New	17-3-27	5-4-27
	XO 4835	"	12583	OT24/22RO	"	Red & White	4-7-23	"	17-3-27	11-4-27
K104	LU 8310	AEC K	20104	"	?		1920	15-3-27		1-1-28
K167	LU 8389	"	20167	"	?		1920	15-3-27		1-1-28

Former Owner
K104/167 General

Disposal
XO 1942 Vivid No. L29
XO 4835 Atlas No. L6
K104/167 General

MARTIN

Fleet No	Reg	Chassis	Chassis No	Body	Builder	Livery	In Service	New/Acq	Withdrawn	Disposal	Notes
1	HM 5039	Leyland LB5	13229	OT26/22RO	S & B	Red & White	21-4-25	New	23-3-29	2-1-31	(1)
2	XX 1896	Daimler Y	6084	OT22/20RO	Hickman	"	28-2-25	11-26	1-10-30	13-6-34	(2)
3	HM 7507	Dennis 4 ton	40452	OT26/22RO	S & B	"	11-4-27	New		13-6-34	(2)
4	HM 7999	"	40459	"	"	"	30-7-27	"		13-6-34	(2)
5	HM 8092	"	40463	"	"	"	1-10-27	"		13-6-34	(2)
6	HM 8139	"	40464	"	Hickman	"	20-10-27	"		13-6-34	(2)
7	HM 9043	"	40471	OT22/20RO	S & B	"	27-8-28	"		13-6-34	
8	XR 1795	Daimler Y	6053	"	Hickman	"	4-2-24	1-4-29	24-7-30	?	
10	PU 5608	"	6077	H29/26R	"	"	11-12-24	1-4-29	1-4-30	?	
11	VW 9014	Dennis H	90093	"	"	"	23-3-29	New		13-6-34	
12	VX 97	"	90095	"	"	"	7-5-29	"		13-6-34	
13	VX 1361	"	90098	"	"	"	6-7-29	"		13-6-34	
14	VX 3074	"	90101	H30/26RO	Birch	"	12-29	"		22-2-33	
	VX 5533	"	95005	OT26/22RO	Dodson	"	30-4-30	New		13-6-34	
15	GH 5342	Dennis HV	5342			"	1-8-30	8-32		13-6-34	
16	HM 7855	Dennis 4 ton	40458			"	6-7-27	22-2-33		13-6-34	
	XC 7609	Buick	721992	Van	—	Yellow	17-5-21	?		?	

(1) AEC A110 engine fitted 1-27 fitted later
(2) Pneumatic tyres

Former Owner
XX 1896 Pat
XR 1795/PU 5608 Gretna
GH 5342 Red Rover
HM 7855 Miller

Disposal
HM 5039/XR 1795/PU 5608 ?
XX 1896 H. Wesley, London, NW10 (Lorry)
HM 7507/7999/8092/8139/9043/VW 9014/VX 97/1361/5533/
GH 5342/HM 7855/XC 7609 LPTB No. D190/191/193/192/
195/DH12/14/13/15/16/D194/—
VX 3074 Scrapped after accident

MATCHLESS, THE/CLEVELAND

Reg	Chassis	Chassis No	Body	Builder	Livery	In Service	New/Acq	Disposal
XU 2866	Daimler Y	6065	OT22/22RO	Hickman	Red & White	17-7-24	New	12-5-32
XT 5611	"	6062	"	S & B	"	27-5-24	12-28	7-30
GC 6664	Leyland TD1	70968	H28/24RO	Dodson	"	27-2-30	New	5-12-33

Former Owner
XT 5611 Independent

Disposal
XU 2866 Chiswick Motor Co (dealer) London, W4
XT 5611 ?
GC 6664 LPTB No. L110

MERCURY—see OXFORD

MERRY, H. M.

Reg	Chassis	Chassis No.	Body Type	Body	Livery			
XX 7200	Leyland LB5	13223	OT26/22RO	S & B	Dk Red & White	30-3-25	New	5-8-27
YL 5595	Dennis 2½ ton	45145	B26R	"	Maroon & White	1-10-25	"	5-8-27
YL 6476	"	45168	"	"	"	7-10-25	"	5-8-27

Disposal
XX 7200/YL 5595/6476 Public No. L16/DS20/19

METEOR

No.	Reg	Chassis	Chassis No.	Body Type	Body	Livery			
1	MF 3646	Leyland LB4	12733	OT26/22RO	Dodson	Red	19-12-23	New	18-8-27
2	MF 8611	"	40141	"	"	"	18-6-24	"	18-8-27
3	MH 1435	Leyland LB5	12932	"	"	"	17-10-24	"	18-8-27
4	MH 5536	Dennis 4 ton	40345	"	"	"	9-4-25	"	18-8-27
5	MH 5537	"	40344	"	"	"	9-4-25	"	18-8-27

Disposal
No. 1-5 Public No. L10/D18/L8/D33/22

MILLER

No.	Reg	Chassis	Chassis No.	Body Type	Body	Livery			
1	HM 4699	Leyland LB5	13144	OT26/22RO	Dodson	Red & White	2-25	New	1-31
2	HM 7254	"	13658	"	"	"	24-3-27	"	29-8-34
3	HM 7855	Dennis 4 ton	40458	"	"	"	6-7-27	"	22-2-33
4	HM 8661	Leyland PLSC3	46905	B32R	"	"	4-5-28	"	22-2-31
5	VX 4269	Leyland TD1	70967	H28/24RO	"	"	26-2-30	"	29-8-34
6	VX 5859	"	71171	"	"	"	13-5-30	"	29-8-34
7	VX 8831	"	71848	H30/26RO	"	"	3-1-31	"	29-8-34 (1)
8	VX 8835	"	71847	"	"	"	18-1-31	"	29-8-34 (1)
9	EV 7308	Leyland TD2	1792	H26/26R	"	"	1-9-32	"	29-8-34

(1) Pneumatic tyres fitted later

Disposal
No. 1 ?
No. 2/5-9 LPTB No. L57/TD104-108
No. 3 Martin No. 16
No. 4 Watford Co-op Mutual Transport Co, Watford, Herts

MONARCH/WHITE STAR

	Reg	Chassis	Chassis No.	Body Type	Body	Livery			
	XR 2651	Daimler Y	6055	OT22/20RO	Hickman	Red & White	15-2-24	4-7-24	17-2-26
	XX 2024	"	6081	"	"	"	27-2-25	New	8-4-27
K103	LU 8312	AEC K	20103	OT24/22RO	?	"	1920	1-4-27	1-1-28

Former Owner
K103 General

Disposal
XR 2651 A. R. Keeling, Blythe Bridge, Staffs (B26F);
J. M. Roberts, Hanley, 1927; Potteries M.T. 1927;
H. Brown, Sparkhill, Birmingham (Lorry) 1929;
withdrawn 3-33

XX 2024 C & P Sales (dealer) Ipswich; G. Robinson, Stepney, London (Lorry) 5-27; A. E. Brooks, London, E1. 10-27
K103   General

MORFAY—see M & E

MTT/GRETNA

Buses

9	XP 8185	Daimler Y	6052	OT24/20RO	S & B	Red & White	21-12-23	New	1-4-29	1-6-29	(1)
8	XR 1795	"	6053	"	"	"	4-2-24	"		1-4-29	(1)
10	PU 5608	"	6077	OT22/20RO	Hickman	"	11-12-24	6-26		1-4-29	(1)

Coaches (up to April 1929)

	HM 7707	Daimler CB	2906	C20	?	Red & Cream	25-4-27	New	4-4-31
	GU 2736	Daimler CMR	CMR8	C26	S & B	"	27-3-29	"	23-5-33

(1) Fleet numbers allocated under A. H. Martin's control 12-28

Former Owner
PU 5608 Victory

Disposal
XP 8185 Scrapped
XR 1795/PU 5608 Martin No. 8/10
HM 7707 ?
GU 2736 Rainham Bus Service (Stephens), Rainham, Essex

NELSON

1	XU 8538	Dennis 4 ton	40217	OT26/22RO	S & B	Red & Cream	19-9-24	New	4-30
2	XX 5499	"	40302	"	"	"	23-3-25	"	1-30
3	YV 2305	Leyland PLSC3	46733	B32R	Dodson	Red & White	26-3-28	"	14-7-32
4	GC 1804	Leyland TD1	70874	H28/24RO	"	"	3-1-30	"	1-11-33
5	GC 7493	"	71194	"	"	"	28-2-30	"	1-11-33
6	GX 1914	Leyland TD2	1299	H30/24R	"	"	7-5-32	"	1-11-33

Disposal
XU 8538 Dodson (dealer), Willesden. Rebodied as a van and sold to
     Sulston & Sons, Aylesbury, Bucks, 1930
XX 5499 Kent & Essex Farmers Ltd, Southend-on-Sea (Lorry);
     withdrawn 1-2-38
YV 2305 C. J. Dunn, Bridgwater, Som; Western National
     No. 3437, 6-33
GC 1804/7493/GX 1914 LPTB No. L51/50/49

NEW ERA

	XN 3322	Leyland LB2	12523	OT26/22RO	Dodson	Light Blue & White	28-3-23	New	11-7-27	(1)
	XW 2158	Leyland LB5	12941	"	"	Red & White	3-11-24	"	11-7-27

(1) Colour to red & white 4-24

Disposal
XN 3322/XW 2158 Public No. L20/4

NEWLANDS DISTRICT

B1	YX 7518	Bean	1569/11W	B20F	Holbrk	Brown & Cream	31-8-28	New	23-11-28	11-28	
B2	XV 5218	"	?	C30	Birch	Dark Yellow	26 10-28	"	23-11-28	11-28	(1)
	UC 4840	Dennis E	17324	B30R	Dodson	?	16-2-28	6-3-29	13-7-29	30-6-29	
	UC 3013	"	17322	B32R	"	"	1-2-28	3-29	13-7-29	7-29	
	MT 2992	Leyland PLSC3	47647	"	?	"	28-3-29	New		7-29	
	MT 3232	Dennis E	17639	"	?	"	11-4-29	"		30-6-29	
	MT 3233	"	17640	"	?	"	11-4-29	"		30-6-29	

(1) Seats altered to B18F" 10-28

Former Owner
UC 3013/4840 Red Line

Disposal
YX 7518 Darenth Bus Service (Hever), Eynsford, Kent
XV 5218 Highland Transport, Inverness, date unknown; withdrawn 6-33
UC 4840/MT 3232/3233 Arlington (dealer), Ponders End, Middx. UC 4840 to Lamb Bros, Luton 6-30; Union Jack, Dunstable, Beds, 4-33; scrapped 10-38
UC 3013/MT 2992 G. H. Allitt

NEW LONDON

	XT 946	Daimler Y	6057	OT22/20RO	S & B	Red & White	17-4-24	New	7-24

Disposal
XT 946 Roberts (dealer), London, W12; Lonsdale 7-24

NEWSTEAD—see ADMIRAL

NEW TIMES

	XN 6976	Leyland LB2	12527	OT26/22RO	Dodson	Grey	2-5-23	New	11-10-24	(1)
	XT 196	Leyland LB4	12747	"	"	Lake & White	15-4-24	"	3-28	

(1) Colour to lake & white 5-24

Disposal
XN 6976 Loveland
XT 196 Public No. L36

NIL DESPERANDUM

YX 7703	Leyland PLSC3	47442	B32R	Birch	Crimson & Cream	5-9-28	10-4-30	13-6-34	
GN 7512	Leyland LT2	51446	B30R	"	Maroon & Cream	6-3-31	New	13-6-34	
GH 7079	Leyland TD1	71438	"	"	Red & Cream	29-8-30	12-5-32	13-6-34	(1)

(1) Body new 5-32, This vehicle formerly operated as a double-decker (see RH)

Former Owner
YX 7703 Pembroke
GH 7079 RH

Disposal
YX 7703/GN 7512/GH 7079 LPTB No. LN6/7/TD86

NORTHERN

XP 2039	S. Squire A	A6328	OT24/22RO	Straker	Chocolate & White	24-9-23	New	4-7-27	27-7-27
MF 9159	Dennis 4 ton	40150	OT26/22RO	Dodson	Red & White	4-7-24	4-7-27		1-1-28

Former Owner
MF 9159 Empress Omnibus Co. Ltd.

NULLI SECUNDUS

Reg	Chassis	Chassis No	Body	Builder	Colour	New	Acquired	Disposal
XP 4908	Leyland LB4	12704	OT26/22RO	Dodson	Crimson & White	2-11-23	New	1-1-28
YM 6965	Dennis 2¼ ton	45210	B25R	"	Red & White	1-2-26	"	25-3-26

Disposal
XP 2039 C & P Sales (dealer), Ipswich
MF 9159 Overground No. 38

Disposal
XP 4908 Overground No. 36
YM 6965 Orange Service No. 11

OLYMPIC—see DIAMOND

OMEGA

Reg	Chassis	Chassis No	Body	Builder	Colour	New	Acquired	Disposal
XN 5034	Leyland LB2	12511	OT26/22RO	Dodson	Red & White	15-4-23	12-6-24	20-7-31
GP 3379	Leyland TD1	72160	H30/26RO	"	"	7-7-31	New	10-11-33

Former Owner
XN 5034 LCOC

Disposal
XN 5034 Arlington (dealer), London, SW1
GP 3379 LPTB No. L76

OPTIMIST—see WILSON

ORANGE SERVICE, THE

No.	Reg	Chassis	Chassis No	Body	Builder	Colour	New	Acquired	Transf.	Disposal
1	XP 4355	Leyland LB4	12703	OT26/22RO	Dodson	Orange & White	1-11-23	New	24-10-27	14-12-27
2	XR 4129	"	12749	"	"	"	1-3-24	"	22-10-27	1-1-28
3	XU 8727	Dennis 4 ton	40197	"	"	"	24-9-24	"		1-1-28
4	XW 473	"	40198	"	"	"	13-10-24	"	12-10-27	1-1-28
5	YK 3657	Leyland LB5	13308	B25R	"	"	29-6-25	"	4-10-27	11-11-27
6	YM 5154	Dennis 2¼ ton	45207	"	"	"	13-1-26	"	4-10-27	10-10-27
7	YM 5155	"	45208	"	"	"	13-1-26	"	4-10-27	18-11-27
8	YM 9971	"	45204	"	"	"	3-3-26	"	4-10-27	15-11-27
9	YM 9972	"	45103	"	"	"	3-3-26	"	4-10-27	9-11-27
10	YM 6966	"	45209	"	"	Red & White	1-2-26	25-3-26		11-10-27
11	YM 6965	"	45210	B30R	"	"	1-2-26	25-3-26		11-10-27
12	YR 4778	Dennis E	17095	Van	"	Orange & Black	9-11-26	New	3-9-27	25-10-27
	YE 1229	Morris 8 cwt	168642	OT24/22RO	"	Red & White	4-1-27	"		
K567	XC 8180	AEC K	20817	"	?	"	1921	13-9-27		1-1-28
K1129	TA 1006	"	20507	"	?	"	1921	13-9-27		1-1-28
K1130	TA 1168	"	20508	"	?	"	1921	14-9-27		1-1-28
K692	XC 8289	"	20942	"	?	"	1921	15-9-27		1-1-28
K730	XC 8283	"	20980	"	?	"	1921	15-9-27		1-1-28
K914	XF 8016	"	21180	"	?	"	1921	15-9-27		1-1-28
K923	XC 9762	"	21189	"	?	"	1921	15-9-27		1-1-28
K675	XC 8259	"	20925	"	?	"	1921	12-10-27		1-1-28

Fleet No	Reg	Chassis	Chassis No	Body code	Body	Colour	Date	Date	Date
K665	XC 8332	AEC K	20915	OT24/22RO	?	Red & White	1921	22-10-27	1-1-28
K666	XC 8472	"	20916	"	?	"	1921	24-10-27	1-1-28

(1) Colour to orange & black 3-27/-27/-27/-27/12-26/
1-27/1-27/3-27/3-27/4-27/12-26

Former Owners
No 10 Dauntless
No 11 Nulli Secundus
All K-type General

Disposal
No. 1 C & P Sales (dealer) Ipswich; W. R. Drake for spares 3-28
No. 2-5 General No. L42/D50/51/L43
No. 6/8-10 National, Watford No. D53/55-57
No. 7/11/12 Vectis Bus Co, Ryde IoW (on loan); to General 1-1-28
while still on loan to Vectis Bus Co
YE 1229 Overground
All K-type General

OUR BUS

Fleet No	Reg	Chassis	Body code	Body	Colour	Date	Date	Date
40089	XR 4395	Dennis 4 ton	OT26/22RO	S & B	Red & White	4-3-24	New	8-7-27
40236	XW 2996	"	"	"	"	12-11-24	"	8-7-27

Disposal
XR 4395/XW 2996 Public No. D28/36

OVERGROUND—see CARLTON

OVERINGTON

	Fleet No	Reg	Chassis	Body code	Body	Colour	Date	Date	Date
1	40180	XU 3752	Dennis 4 ton	OT26/22RO	S & B	Red & White	25-7-24	New	29-9-27
3	40215	XW 287	"	"	"	"	10-10-24	"	29-9-27
4	40221	XW 758	"	"	"	"	16-10-24	"	29-9-27
5	40378	YM 1060	"	"	Dodson	"	24-11-25	26-11-26	29-9-27

Former Owner
No 5 Carlton Association

Disposal
No. 1-3/5 Public No. D98/97/100/99

OVERLAND

Fleet No	Reg	Chassis	Body code	Body	Colour	Date	Date	Date
40160	XU 551	Dennis 4 ton	OT26/22RO	S & B	Red & White	2-7-24	New	31-8-27

Disposal
XU 551 Public No. D30

OXFORD/MERCURY/AGS

Fleet No	Reg	Chassis	Body code	Body	Colour	Date	Date	Date
40191	XU 5449	Dennis 4 ton	OT26/22RO	Dodson	Red & White	7-8-24	New	6-27
40210	XW 3474	"	"	"	"	19-11-24	"	2-30
40440	YE 6281	"	"	"	"	12-2-27	"	24-11-33
40467	YW 4483	"	"	"	"	4-6-28	"	24-11-33
71134	GC 5781	Leyland TD1	H30/26RO	Birch	"	1-2-30	"	24-11-33
498	GW 1285	Leyland TD2	"	"	"	16-2-32	"	24-11-33

(1) Pneumatic tyres fitted later

Disposal
XU 5449 F. Gilbert, London, SW4 (Lorry)
XW 3474 to Lorry
YE 6281/YW 4483/GC 5781/GW 1285 LPTB No. D182/183/L87/88

(1)

PARAGON

MF	419	S. Squire A	A6254	OT24/22RO	Straker	Dk Green & White	8-6-23	New	6-26
XW	8201	Dennis 4 ton	40266	OT26/22RO	Dodson	Red & White	13-1-25	"	26-8-27
YO	8528	"	40408	"	"	"	15-6-26	"	26-8-27 (1)

(1) Colour to red & white by 3-24

Disposal
MF 419 Malligan Bros, Birkenhead (Lorry); withdrawn 1-1-32
XW 8201/YO 8528 Public No. D61/60

PAT

| XX | 1896 | Daimler Y | 6084 | OT22/20RO | Hickman | Red & White | 28-2-25 | New | 11-26 |

Disposal
XX 1896 Martin No. 2

PC, THE

Buses

	PU 3549	Dennis 4 ton	40142	OT26/22RO	S & B	Red & Grey	6-24	New	1-1-28
	PU 7282	AEC K	40325	OT24/22RO	Dodson	Red & White	4-25	"	2-27
K60	LU 8265	"	20060	"	?	1920	15-12-27	23-12-26	1-1-28

Coach

| | NO 6211 | Ford T | 5824739 | Ch14 | ? | Red | 2-7-22 | New | ? |

Former Owner
K60 General

Disposal
PU 3549/K60 Metropolitan No. D40/K60
PU 7282 Chassis scrapped
NO 6211 ?

PEMBROKE

XU	7474	Dennis 4 ton	40175	OT26/22RO	S & B	Red & White	3-9-24	New	11-10-30
YX	7703	Leyland PLSC3	47442	B32R	Dodson	"	5-9-28	"	10-4-30
GJ	3020	AEC Regent	661771	H30/26RO	Birch	"	8-5-30	"	10-11-33

Disposal
XU 7474 H. F. Bond, Ipswich (Lorry)
YX 7703 Nil Desperandum
GJ 3020 LPTB No. ST1031

PERAEQUE

	XT 5611	Daimler Y	6062	OT22/20RO	S & B	Red & White	27-5-24	New	2-26
	MF 8001	"	6063	OT26/22RO	Hickman	"	29-5-24	3-25	2-26
1	YM 8086	Leyland LB5	13564	"	Dodson	"	12-2-26	New	10-2-31
2	YM 8087	"	13565	"	"	"	12-2-26	"	10-2-31
3	YR 5805	"	13641	"	"	"	12-11-26	3-2-27	29-8-32
4	YT 8381	Dennis 4 ton	40461	B32R	"	"	1-9-27	New	7-1-32
5	UC 4756	Leyland PLSC3	46552	H28/24RO	"	"	15-2-28	"	5-12-33
6	UV 7395	Leyland TD1	70716	"	"	"	21-8-29	"	5-12-33
7	UW 8539	"	70871	"	"	"	7-12-29	"	5-12-33

(1)
(1)

No	Registration	Chassis	Serial	Body	Builder	Livery				
8	GK 8779	Leyland TD1	71845	H30/26RO	Dodson	Red & White	16-12-30	New		5-12-33
9	GK 8780	"	71846	"	"	"	16-12-30	"		5-12-33
10	GK 9384	"	71844	"	"	"	2-1-31	"		5-12-33
11	GT 1083	"	72218	"	"	"	22-9-31	"		5-12-33

(1) Fitted with pneumatic tyres 3-30/?

Former Owner
MF 8001 Kathleen
YR 5805 Empress O.C. Ltd

Disposal
XT 5611/MF 8001 J. M. Roberts Motor Service, London, W12
No. 1/2 W. R. Wintour (dealer), London, W1
No. 3 E. Pinder, Glasgow (Lorry)
No. 4 H. F. Bond, Ipswich (Lorry)
No. 5-11 LPTB No. L95-101

PERKINS

Registration	Chassis	Serial	Body	Builder	Livery			
MH 2118	Dennis 4 ton	40272	OT26/22RO	S & B	Red & White	21-11-24	New	1-30
MY 2177	Leyland TD1	70870	H28/24RO	Dodson	"	12-12-29	"	29-8-34

(1) Fitted with pneumatic tyres 1928

Disposal
MH 2118 C. G. Leaphard, Thundersley, Essex. Purchased back by Perkins 10-30; to Eastwoods Ltd, London, SE1 (Lorry) date unknown; withdrawn 1-1-37
MY 2177 LPTB No. TD109

(1)

PHILLIPS H.F.

Registration	Chassis	Serial	Body	Builder	Livery				
RO 9162	Chevrolet LO	40568	C14F	?	Chocolate & Cream	2-28	10-31		11-32
DV 5364	Bean	H3263/8	B20F	Tivtn	"	30-5-30	1-7-32	20-11-33	14-12-33

Former Owner
RO 9162 New to B & B Services, Potten End, Herts; Reall (dealer) Ealing 1931; Maitland & Cubitt, Barnes, London 1931
DV 5364 W. A. Hart, Budleigh Salterton, Devon

Disposal
RO 9162 Reall (dealer), Ealing and scrapped
DV 5364 LPTB No. BN5

PHOENIX

Registration	Chassis	Serial	Body	Builder	Livery			
XL 5250	Thornycroft J	10484	OT26/24RO	Dodson	Red & White	31-1-24	New	9-11-27

(1) Seats altered to OT24/24RO 11-1-27 and altered back to original layout 18-1-27

Disposal
XL 5250 Public No. T2

(1)

PHRH

Registration	Chassis	Serial	Body	Builder	Livery			
XU 767	Dennis 4 ton	40146	OT26/22RO	Dodson	Red & White	3-7-24	New	29-9-27
XU 7430	"	40193	"	"	"	2-9-24	"	29-9-27
XU 9057	"	40194	"	"	"	29-9-24	"	29-9-27
YL 2999	Dennis 2½ ton	45135	B26R	"	"	26-8-25	"	29-9-27
YP 7106	"	45433	B25R	"	"	30-7-26	"	29-9-27
YE 5277	Dennis 4 ton	40435	OT26/22RO	"	"	3-2-27	"	29-9-27

Disposal
XU 767/7430/9057/YL 2999/YP 7106/YE 5277 Public No.
D76/75/77/DS40/41/D78

PICKUP—see CHP

PICKWICK

XX 195	Dennis 4 ton	40255	OT26/22RO	?	Red & White	9-2-25	New	By 12-29

Disposal
XX 195 Kingston-upon-Hull Corpn.; C. Digby, London, E12 (Lorry) date ?; withdrawn 1-1-43

PINNER BUS, THE

MY 3496	Bean	2147/11W	B18F	Birch	Red & White	22-3-30	New	11-9-30
DA2 GF 493	Dennis Dart	75707	"	LGOC	"	15-4-30	19-5-30	29-5-30

Former Owner
DA2 Loan from General
Disposal
MY 3496/DA2 General No. BN4/DA2

PIONEER

MF 1001	Thornycroft J	10377	OT26/24RO	Dodson	Crimson & White	3-7-23	New	6-28
MF 4173	Dennis 4 ton	40056	OT26/22RO	"	Lt Choc & Cream	17-1-24	"	9-29
ML 6105	"	40460	"	"		26-7-27	"	9-29
MP 5211	"	40470	"	"	"	28-6-28	"	1-31
1 MY 1140	Leyland TD1	70586	H28/24RO	"	Crimson & White	26-8-29	"	5-12-33
3 MY 1315	"	70585	"	"	"	13-9-29	"	5-12-33
2 HX 2492	"	71855	"	"	"	7-1-31	"	5-12-33

5 (1) Fitted with sprag gear

Disposal
MF 1001 J. R. Bradley London, NW10 (Lorry); withdrawn 10-30
MF 4173 Collins & Stevens, London, W4 (Lorry); withdrawn 1-10-33
ML 6105 to Lorry, MP 5211 ?
MY 1140/1315/HX 2492 LPTB No. L108/107/109

(1)

PIRATE, THE/HL

XP 7724	Thornycroft J	10476	OT26/24RO	Dodson	Red & White	13-12-23	New	2-3-28

Disposal
XP 7724 Public No. T3

POPPY

MF 7628	Leyland LB4	12717	OT26/22RO	Dodson	Dk Red & White	15-5-24	New	28-7-27

Disposal
MF 7628 Public No. L2

PREMIER

1 XN 513	S. Squire A	A6225	OT24/22RO	Dodson	Mauve & White	3-3-23	New	29-12-23
2 XM 9888	"	A6226	"	"	"	27-2-23	"	3-11-24
3 XM 9995	"	A6227	"	"	"	1-3-23	"	3-11-24
4 XN 1596	Leyland LB2	12441	OT26/22RO	"	"	16-3-23	"	11-30

5	XN 5018	12457	Leyland LB2	OT26/22RO	Dodson	Mauve & White	16-4-23	New	11-30	
6	XP 1957	12642	"	"	"	"	21-9-23	"	11-30	
7	XP 2347	40053	Dennis 4 ton	"	"	"	28-9-23	"	11-30	
8	XP 3760	40054	"	"	"	"	12-10-23	"	12-11-32	
9	XP 4208	40055	"	"	"	"	23-10-23	"	16-10-30	(1)
10	MF 3319	40058	"	"	"	"	27-11-23	"	1-31	
11	MF 5862	40105	"	"	"	"	26-3-24	"	2-30	
12	MF 6269	40109	"	"	"	"	4-4-24	"	1-31	
	MF 6399	40116	"	"	"	"	8-4-24	"	1-31	
2	MH 2138	40257	"	"	"	"	22 11-24	"	3-30	
3	MH 2215	40256	"	"	"	"	1-12-24	"	1-31	
13	YM 5524	40385	"	"	"	"	13-1-26	"	16-11-32	(1)
14	YR 2358	40427	"	"	"	"	5-10-26	"	20-12-33	(1)
	YE 3930	40437	"	"	"	"	1-2-27	"	15-11-32	(2)
	XT 8841	40157	"	"	"	Violet & White	20-6-24	17-1-28	1-31	
	UV 5096	70726	Leyland TD1	H28/24RO	S & B	Maroon & White	30-8-29	New	20-12-33	
	GC 1214	70915	"	"	Dodson	"	30-12-29	"	20-12-33	
	GJ 7536	71028	"	"	Duple	"	28-6-30	"	20-12-33	
	GJ 7537	71395	"	"	"	"	28-6-30	"	20-12-33	
	GJ 7538	71275	"	"	"	"	28-6-30	"	20-12-33	
	GH 889	71396	"	"	"	"	12-7-30	"	20-12-33	
	GH 890	71397	"	"	"	"	12-7-30	"	20-12-33	
	GH 2491	71375	"	"	"	"	12-7-30	"	20-12-33	
	GK 891	71739	"	"	"	"	28-11-30	"	20-12-33	
	GK 892	71740	"	"	"	"	28-11-30	"	20-12-33	
	GK 893	71741	"	"	"	"	28-11-30	"	20-12-33	
	GK 894	71742	"	"	"	"	28-11-30	"	20-12-33	
	GK 895	71743	"	"	"	"	28-11-30	"	20-12-33	
	GK 896	71744	"	"	"	"	28-11-30	"	20-12-33	
	XX 7176	79391	Morris 10 cwt	Van	—	Brown	30-3-25	27-8-26		
	EV 4507	363629	"	"	—	Grey	30-1-32	New		

(1) Pneumatic tyres fitted 1929   (2) Colour to Maroon & white 1928

Former Owner
XT 8841 Victor
XX 7176 Gardiners Stores, London, W12

Disposal
XN 513 Regent
XM 9888/9995 EP No. 16/15
XN 1596/5018 Willment Bros, London, SE1 (Lorry). XN 5018 withdrawn 1-1-39 and scrapped
XP 1957 T. Wright, Hayes, Middx (Lorry)
XP 2347 ?
XP 3760/YM 5524/YE 3930 Aylesbury Omnibus Co, Aylesbury, Bucks
XP 4208 E. V. Lissenden. London, W4 (Lorry)
MF 3319 F. J. Hyams, East Ham (Lorry); withdrawn 1-1-39
MF 5862 R. Weeks, London, E8 (Lorry); withdrawn 1-1-32
MF 6269/6399/MH 2215 H. Fox, London, E16 (Lorry); withdrawn 1-1-38/7-11-40/1-1-38 respectively

MH 2138 Welch, London, SE7 (Lorry); withdrawn 1-1-32
YR 2358/UV 5096/GC 1214/GJ 7536-7538/GH 889/890/2491/
GK 891-896/XX 7176/EV 4507 LPTB No. D195/L121/116/
114/115/118/117/119/120/123/124/122/127/126/125/M44/43
XT 8841 W. Board, London, SE15 (Lorry); withdrawn 1-1-37

(1)

PRIMROSE

Fleet	Reg	Chassis	Serial	Body	Body config	Colour				
1	XM 3527	S. Squire A	A6218	Straker	OT22/22RO	Primrose & White	14-11-22	New	28-2-27	12-3-27
2	XT 4176	Dennis 4 ton	40148	S & B	OT26/22RO	Red & Primrose	14-5-24	"	1-12-26	23-12-26
K805	XC 8405	AEC K	21071	?	OT24/22RO	Red & White	1921	30-11-26		1-1-28
K74	LU 8301	"	20074	"	"	Red & White	1920	7-3-27		1-1-28

(1) Colour to red & primrose 3-23

Disposal
XM 3527 C & P Sales (dealer) Ipswich; A. W. Berry, West Mersea.
XT 4176 Redburn's No. D26 Essex 10-27

Former Owner
K74/805 General K74/805 Metropolitan

PRINCE

Reg	Chassis	Serial	Body	Body config	Colour				
MF 399	Leyland LB2	12564	Dodson	OT26/22RO	Chocolate & Cream	8-6-23	New		3-32
MF 5214	Leyland LB4	12735	"	"	"	3-3-24	"		3-33
MH 3812	Dennis 4 ton	40271	"	B30R	Maroon & Cream	17-2-25	"		3-10-28
ML 754	Dennis E	17092	"	"	"	8-11-26	"		5-12-34
ML 2078		17124	"	B32R	Chocolate & Cream	11-2-27	"		5-12-34
MP 1844	Leyland PLSC3	46243	"	OT26/22RO	"	23-1-28	"		5-12-34
XU 8984	Leyland LB5	12928	"	H28/24RO	"	1-10-24	3-10-28	12-31	12-33
MY 2663	Leyland TD1	71195	"	"	"	21-1-30	New		5-12-34
MY 2917	"	71196	"	"	"	12-2-30			5-12-34
MY 4043	"	70970	"	B31R	"	10-4-30			5-12-34
MV 1019	Leyland TD2	393	Duple	"	"	17-12-31			5-12-34
MV 1376	Ford A	400	Dodson	B31R	Maroon & Black	26-1-32			5-12-34
HX 7298		4253056	"	Van		27-3-31			5-12-34

Former Owner
XU 8984 Westminster

Disposal
MF 399 Tinti, Matlock, Bath (Lorry)
MF 5214 Sturrock & McGregor, Kirkcaldy, Fife (Lorry)
MH 3812 Westminster
ML 754/2078/MP 1844/MY 2663/2917/4043/MV 1019/1376/
HX 7298 LPTB No. DE42/43/LN11/TD127-129/131/130/F6
XU 8984 Glass Cartage Co, Liverpool (Lorry)

PRO BONO PUBLICO

Buses

Reg	Chassis	Serial	Body	Body config	Colour			
MF 8186	Dennis 4 ton	40137	Dodson	OT26/22RO	Chocolate & White	2-6-24	New	5-32
VW 5135	Leyland-PLSC3	47070	"	B32R	Brown & Cream	8-6-28	"	5-30
VX 7553	AEC Regent	6611010	"	H30/23RO	"	11-9-30	"	10-11-33
EV 5860	Leyland TD2	1298	"	H27/26R	"	27-4-32	"	10-11-33

Coach

No	Reg	Chassis	Chassis No	Body	Body maker	Colour	In service	Acquired	Repainted	Withdrawn	Note
	VX 5149	Maudslay ML3B	4844	C30D	?	Brown & Cream	3-4-30		New	3-32	

Disposal

MF 8186 Eastwoods Ltd, London, SE1 (Lorry); withdrawn 12-37
VW 5135 R. Bamber (dealer), Southport, Lancs; Kitson, Sheffield 5-30;
Thomas, Maesteg, Glam, date ?; withdrawn 6-38
VX 7553/EV 5860 LPTB No. ST1030/L77
VX 5149 Ansells Coaches, London, SE5; Rutchley, London, E15
(Lorry) 1939

PULLMAN

No	Reg	Chassis	Chassis No	Body	Body maker	Colour	In service	Acquired	New	Withdrawn
XX 874		Dennis 4 ton	40280	OT26/22RO	S & B	Red & White	11-2-25		New	1-1-28

Disposal

XX 874 General No. D65

RA

No	Reg	Chassis	Chassis No	Body	Body maker	Colour	In service	Acquired	Withdrawn
K458	XW 2849	Daimler Y	6074	OT22/20RO	Hickman	Red & Grey	15-11-24	27-4-26	11-9-26
	XC 8068	AEC K	20458	OT24/22RO	?	Red & White	1920	27-4-26	1-1-28

Former Owner

K458 General

Disposal

XW 2849 Aylesbury Omnibus Co, Aylesbury, Bucks
K458 Metropolitan

RAPID

No	Reg	Chassis	Chassis No	Body	Body maker	Colour	In service	Acquired	Withdrawn	Note
1	XN 2910	Leyland LB2	12461	OT26/22RO	Dodson	Lt Green & Cream	27-3-23	New	29-7-27	(1)
2	XP 37	"	12584	"	"	"	22-8-23	"	29-7-27	(1)
3	XP 390	"	12605	"	"	"	28-8-23	"	29-7-27	(1)
4	XP 6211	Leyland LB4	12706	"	"	"	21-11-23	"	29-7-27	(1)
5	XP 7074	"	12728	"	"	"	3-12-23	"	29-7-27	(1)
6	XP 7075	"	12734	"	"	"	3-12-23	"	29-7-27	(1)
7	XW 2215	Leyland LB5	12933	"	"	"	4-11-24	"	29-7-27	
8	YR 172	"	13640	"	"	Red & White	6-9-26	"	1-3-27	
8	XN 5203	Leyland LB2	12526	"	"	"	16-4-23	12-2-27	29-7-27	

Coach

No	Reg	Chassis	Chassis No	Body	Body maker	Colour	In service	Acquired	Withdrawn
	XR 6475	Guy J	4246	Ch 14	?	Grey	21-3-24	New	17-3-25

(1) No 1-7 repainted red & white 3-26/8-25/9-25/11-25/
12-25/1-26/11-25 respectively

Former Owner

XN 5203 Henslowe

Disposal

No. 1-7/XN 5203 Public No. L15/7/6/13/21/17/11/18
YR 172 Commonwealth no. 4
XR 6475 Orange Luxury Coaches, London, SE11

REDBURN'S MOTOR SERVICE

Buses

No	Reg	Chassis	Chassis No	Body	Body maker	Colour	In service	Acquired	Repainted	Withdrawn
1	ME 9102	S. Squire A	A6240	OT22/22RO	Straker	Chocolate & White	3-5-23	New	26-11-26	14-3-27
2	ME 9624	"	A6246	"	"	"	15-5-23	"	18-2-27	2-3-27
3	ME 9670	"	A6253	"	"	"	17-5-23	"	10-2-27	26-3-27

No.	Reg.	Make	Chassis No.	Body	Builder	Colour				
4	ME 9671	"	A6247	OT24/22RO	"	"	17-5-23		12-2-27	25-3-27
5	MF 1182	"	A6276	"	"	"	10-7-23		28-2-27	29-3-27
6	MF 1181	"	A6277	"	"	"	10-7-23		17-2-27	2-3-27
7	MF 1940	"	A6282	"	"	"	15-8-23		30-12-26	7-1-27
8	MF 1941	"	A6283	"	"	"	15-8-23		1-3-27	14-3-27
9	MF 3003	"	A6343	"	"	"	31-10-23		9-3-27	18-3-27
10	MF 3002	"	A6330	"	"	"	31-10-23		7-3-27	21-3-27
11	MF 3084	"	A6344	"	"	"	8-11-23		8-11-26	8-3-27
12	MF 3485	"	A6345	"	"	Red & White	7-12-23	12-23	2-12-26	3-27
13	MF 1298	"	A6272	"	"	"	16-7-23	New		12-3-27
14	MF 3574	"	A6346	"	"	"	13-12-23		25-11-26	20-3-27
15	MF 4401	"	A6340	"	"	"	23-1-24		3-1-27	4-3-27
16	MF 4519	"	A6339	"	"	"	31-1-24		1-1-27	21-3-27
17	MF 5160	"	A6380	"	"	"	29-2-24		1-1-27	21-3-27
18	MF 5161	"	A6385	"	"	"	29-2-24			26-1-27
19	MF 6110	"	A6381	"	"	"	1-4-24		8-1-27	25-1-27
20	MF 6405	"	A6382	"	"	"	8-4-24		1-1-27	25-1-27
21	MF 7511	"	A6383	"	"	"	12-5-24		28-1-27	3-3-27
22	MF 8166	"	A6384	"	"	"	2-6-24		31-1-27	4-3-27
23	MH 608	Dennis 4 ton	40172	OT26/22RO	S & B	"	1-9-24			1-1-28
24	MH 846	"	40213	"	"	"	15-9-24			1-1-28
25	MH 1655	"	40225	"	"	"	23-10-24			1-1-28
26	MH 1925	"	40237	"	"	"	7-11-24			1-1-28
27	MH 2845	"	40293	"	"	"	31-12-24			1-1-28
28	MH 7786	Dennis 2½ ton	45106	B26R	"	"	16-6-25			1-1-28
29	MH 7787	"	45107	"	"	"	16-6-25			1-1-28
30	MH 8520	"	45119	"	"	"	4-7-25			1-1-28
31	MH 8521	"	45120	"	"	"	4-7-25			1-1-28
32	MH 8522	"	45121	"	"	"	4-7-25			1-1-28
33	MH 8523	"	45122	"	"	"	4-7-25			1-1-28
D20	XX 1756	Dennis 4 ton	40323	OT26/22RO	Dodson	"	19-2-25	25-11-26		1-1-28
D21	XX 8837	"	40346	"	Straker	"	7-4-25	25-11-26		1-1-28
D22	XX 9591	"	40347	"	Dodson	"	9-4-25	25-11-26		1-1-28
D23	XR 7776	"	40099	"	"	"	31-3-24	20-12-26		1-1-28
D24	XX 772	"	40295	"	S & B	"	9-2-25	24-12-26		1-1-28
D25	YM 8237	"	40383	"	Dodson	"	15-2-26	31-12-26		1-1-28
D26	XT 4176	"	40148	"	S & B	"	14-5-24	23-12-26		1-1-28
D27	MH 5193	"	40304	"	"	"	1-4-25	31-12-26		1-1-28
D28	XU 3027	"	40166	"	Dodson	"	20-7-24	6-1-27		1-1-28
D29	MH 2594	"	40291	"	S & B	"	22-12-24	3-1-27		1-1-28
D30	XU 4371	"	40185	"	Dodson	"	29-7-24	27-1-27		1-1-28
D31	XT 110	"	40107	"	S & B	"	14-4-24	7-2-27		1-1-28
D32	XT 4731	"	40121	"	Wilton	"	20-5-24	22-2-27		1-1-28
D33	XR 7778	"	40095	"	Dodson	"	31-3-24	17-2-27		1-1-28
D34	XR 888	"	40073	"	S & B	"	26-1-24	11-2-27		1-1-28

		Chassis	No.	Body	Maker				
D35	XT 6628	Dennis 4 ton	40145	OT26/22RO	S & B	2-6-24	9-2-27	1-1-28	
D36	MH 1693	"	40232	"	Dodson	27-10-24	26-2-27	1-1-28	
D37	XT 8982	"	40122	"	"	21-6-24	2-3-27	1-1-28	
D38	XW 8641	"	40282	"	"	19-1-25	5-3-27	1-1-28	
D39	XO 8668	"	40049	"	Wilton	3-8-23	8-3-27	1-1-28	(2)

Coaches

AR 9831	AEC YC	9704	Ch 32	?	1920	New	1-4-27
MD 6825	Daimler CC	427	Ch 27	?	13-5-21	"	19-5-27
MD 8090	Dennis 2 ton	20213	Ch 28	?	8-7-21	"	13-5-27
ME 9197	Daimler CC	707	Ch 32	?	7-5-23	"	18-5-27

(1) Dodson OT26/22RO body fitted 2-27
(2) Seats later to Ch 27

Former Owner

No 13 BC
D20 T & W
D21/22 Dominion
D23/33 Fleet
D24/28 B & V
D25/31/32/37 Western
D26 Primrose
D27 Direct
D29 Criterion
D30 Superbus
D34/35 Florence
D36 Imperial
D38 Grafton
D39 A1

Disposal

No. 1-12/14-22 C & P Sales (dealer), Ipswich, No. 1 to G. L. Holmes, Lincoln (Lorry) 1927; withdrawn 1-10-30. No. 2/6 White Rose M.S. (Brookes Bros), Rhyl, 1927. No. 2 then to L. Beaumont, Liverpool (Lorry) date ?; withdrawn 1-1-33. No. 6 then to British Leather Co, Birkenhead (Lorry) date ?; withdrawn 1-1-34. No. 3 C. K. Squirrell, Bildeston, Suffolk (Lorry) 1927; C & P Sales (dealer), Ipswich 1-33. No. 4/21 S. Green, Birmingham (Lorry) 1927, withdrawn 1-1-36. No. 5/11 Sommerfield & Thomas, Kings Lynn (Lorry) 1927; withdrawn 2-33. No. 8 Evans & Jones, Carmarthen (Lorry) 1927; withdrawn 1-28. No. 9 H. C. Chambers, Bures, Suffolk, 1927; withdrawn 1-10-29. No. 14 S. Daniels, Diss, Norfolk (Lorry) 1927; withdrawn 1-3-30. No. 15/19 W. E. Hughes, Birkenhead (Lorry) 1927. No. 16 P. C. Hounsfield, Stowmarket (Lorry) 1927; withdrawn 23-1-34. No. 17 L. Fletcher, Cambridge (Lorry) 1927; withdrawn 25-3-36. No. 22 Green Bros, Brandon, Suffolk (Lorry) 1927; withdrawn 9-11-31
No. 13 Chassis scrapped
No. 23-33/D20-39 General No. D15-19/9-14/20-39
AR 9831/MD 6825/8090/ME 9197 A. J. Smith (dealer) London, SW1. AR 9831 to Sussex Motors, Hove, 1927; converted to Lorry 1929. ME 9197 to H. Williams, London, SW4, 1927; withdrawn 1-10-29 and scrapped

RED LINE

Buses

		Chassis	No.	Body	Maker					
XP 7023	Thornycroft J	10462	OT26/24RO	S & B	1-12-23	New		2-11-28	
XT 6131	"	10553	"	"	30-5-24	"		6-29	
UC 3013	Dennis E	17322	B30R	Dodson	1-2-28	"		3-29	
UL 7670	Dennis H	90065	H30/26RO	"	9-3-29	"		2-31	
UU 4830	"	90097	"	"	30-5-29	"		5-12-33	
GC 1684	Daimler CF6	7392S	H28/24R	Birch	7-1-30	"	1-32	27-10-32	
GO 5538	Daimler CH6	9061	"	"	30-4-31	"		5-12-33	(1)
GW 2294	AEC Regent	6611810	H26/25R	"	8-3-32	"		5-12-33	(2)

Coaches (up to December 1933)

LX 8521	Daimler Y	?	Ch 32		Red	8-19	New	?
LX 8996	"	?	Ch ?		"	9-19	"	?
HJ 585	"	?	Ch 27		"	7-5-20	"	?
XD 9942	"	3024	Ch 28		"	8-21	"	?
XM 7952	"	5872	Ch 27		"	2-23	"	3-5-25
XB 9888	"	7129	C30		"	7-7-20	18-7-23	?
UC 4840	Dennis E	17324	C28	Duple	"	16-2-28	New	11-1-29
YV 1635	TSM B10B	5539	C28		"	23-3-28	"	5-5-32
YW 1641	Dennis E	17466	C30		"	16-5-28	"	31-3-30
UU 7958	Gilford 1660T	10888	C32		"	1-6-29	"	?
GJ 9149	Gilford 1680T	11426	"		"	30-6-30	1-7-34	24-3-33

(1) Body to GW 2294 1-32   (2) Body ex GC 1684, rebuilt
by Birch with enclosed stairs, new drivers cab,
extended wheelbase, blind indicators and revised seating
(3) Reg'n No originally issued 24-4-19 to a Straker Squire
Torpedo Chara of Southend Motor Co, Southend-on-Sea,
and body transferred to the Daimler chassis 5-20.
(4) Colour to blue & black 11-30.

Former Owner

XB 9888 Samuelson, London, SW1

Disposal

XP 7023 Issac Kahn, London, E2 (Lorry)
XT 6131 Motor Wreckers (dealer), Leeds
UC 3013/4840 Arlington (dealer), London, SW1; Newlands District
3-29/1-29 respectively
UL 7670 Birch Bros (dealer), London, NW5; Earlswood Bus Co,
Westgate-on-Sea, Kent 22-3-31; East Kent 5-11-35;
G. J. Dawson (dealer), Clapham 4-36
UU 4830/GO 5538/GW 2294 LPTB No. D188/DST5/STL558
GC 1684 A. H. Grove Bristol (Lorry)
LX 8521/8996/HJ 585/XD 9942/XB 9888/UU 7958 ?
XM 7952 L. Arkwright, London, W10; Speechley (dealer), Willesden,
12-31 and scrapped
YV 1635 Liberty Motors, Cardiff; Red & White, Chepstow No. 140
5-36; scrapped 1-39
YW 1641 Arlington (dealer), London, SW1; Gwendraeth Traction
Co, Llanelly 7-30; South Wales Transport 6-35; E. Morgan.
Llanelly 9-35
GJ 9149 S. H. Young, London, N15

RED ROSE (see also SERVICE & TRINITY)

20	XR 4899	Dennis 4 ton	40098	OT26/22RO	S & B	Red & White	8-3-24	New	3-3-28
21	XR 4900	"	40097	"	"	"	8-3-24	"	3-3-28
22	XR 6675	"	40092	"	"	"	24-3-24	"	3-3-28
23	XR 6676	"	40090	"	"	"	24-3-24	"	3-3-28
24	XR 7152	"	40102	"	"	"	26-3-24	"	3-3-28
25	XR 7153	"	40096	"	"	"	26-3-24	"	3-3-28
26	XR 7518	"	40104	"	"	"	28-3-24	"	3-3-28
27	XR 7519	"	40103	"	"	"	28-3-24	"	3-3-28
	YM 3395	"	40379	"	Dodson	"	22-12-25	"	3-3-28

Disposal
No. 20-27/YM 3395 Public No. D123/122/113/121/120/119/
118/117/124

RED ROVER (London bus fleet only)

Reg	Make	Chassis No	Type	Body	Colour	Date	New	Date	Notes
XU 3346	Dennis 4 ton	40182	OT26/22RO	S & B	Red & Cream	22-7-24	New	9-30	
GH 5342	Dennis HV	95005	H30/26RO	Birch	Red & White	1-8-30	"	8-32	
GY 1961	Dennis Lance	126065	H29/25R	"	"	2-8-32	"	14-2-34	

Disposal
XU 3346 to Lorry
GH 5342 Birch (dealer), London, NW5; Martin No. 15, 8-32
GY 1961 LPTB No. DL28

REGAL

Reg	Make	Chassis No	Type	Body	Colour	Date	New	Date	Notes
RK 678	Dennis 4 ton	40064	OT26/22RO	Wilton	Yellow & White	12-23	New	23-6-27	(1)
RK 1004	"	40081	"	"	Chocolate & White	2-24	"	23-6-27	(1)
RK 1509	"	40111	"	"	Red & White	4-24	"	23-6-27	
RK 1510	"	40126	"	"	"	4-24	"	23-6-27	
XW 5626	"	40270	"	Dodson	"	17-12-24	7-4-25	23-6-27	
RK 7521	"	40422	"	"	"	8-26	New	23-6-27	
RK 8899	"	40450	"	Birch	"	3-27	"	23-6-27	

(1) Colour to red & white 12-24/2-25

Disposal
RK 678/1004/1509/1510/XW 5626/RK 7521/8899 Public No.
D67-70/65/71/72

Former Owner
XW 5626 Royal Toots

REGENT

Reg	Make	Chassis No	Type	Body	Colour	Date	New	Date	Notes
XN 513	S. Squire A	A6225	OT24/22RO	Dodson	Chocolate & Grey	3-3-23	12-23	10-24	(1)

(1) Colour to maroon & lemon 3-24

Former Owner
XN 513 Premier

Disposal
XN 513 EP No. 14

REGINA

Reg	Make	Chassis No	Type	Body	Colour	Date	New	Date	Notes
XU 50	Dennis 4 ton	40220	OT26/22RO	S & B	Red & White	8-10-24	New	27-7-27	

Disposal
XU 50 Public No. D16

RELIABLE—see DAUNTLESS

RELIANCE (C. Churchman)

Reg	Make	Chassis No	Type	Body	Colour	Date	New	Date	Notes
ME 8109	Leyland LB2	12521	OT26/22RO	Dodson	Chocolate & White	26-3-23	New	18-8-27	
MH 1862	Dennis 4 ton	40240	"	"	"	5-11-24	"	18-8-27	

Disposal
ME 8109/MH 1862 Public No. L19/D32

RELIANCE, THE (A. Cook)

No	Reg	Make	Chassis No	Type	Body	Colour	Date	New	Date	Notes
1	XR 7078	S. Squire A	A6353	OT24/22RO	Straker	Red & White	26-3-24	New	5-11-27	(1)
2	XW 6378	Dennis 4 ton	40283	OT26/22RO	Dodson	"	30-12-24	"	17-6-31	(1)
3	XW 6379	"	40284	"	"	"	30-12-24	"	1-30	(1)

No.	Reg. No.	Chassis No.	Chassis	Body	Body by	Date		Withdrawn
4	XX 5800	40305	"	"	"	24-3-25	"	7-11-34 [1]
5	XX 5801	40306	"	"	"	24-3-25	"	4-2-33 [1]
6	YM 2955	40380	"	"	"	1-1-26	"	7-11-34 [1]
1	YF 6913	40445	"	"	"	11-4-27	"	7-11-34
7	YX 7619	47440	Leyland PLSC3	B32R	"	4-9-28	"	7-11-34
8	YX 7620	47441	"	"	"	4-9-28	"	7-11-34
9	XV 3915	47557	"	"	"	15-11-28	"	7-11-34
10	XV 6848	90055	Dennis H	OT30/26RO	"	3-12-28	"	7-11-34
11	UW 4198	70760	Leyland TD1	H28/24RO	"	30-10-29	"	7-11-34
12	VX 8364	125005	Dennis Lance	H27/24R	"	7-11-30	"	7-11-34
13	VX 8363	125006	"	"	"	7-11-30	"	7-11-34
14	EV 6510	1524	Leyland TD2	H28/26R	"	9-6-32	"	7-11-34
15	EV 6692	1523	"	"	"	29-6-32	"	7-11-34
16	EV 8334	1875	Leyland TS4	B31R	"	25-10-32	"	7-11-34
17	EV 8335	1697	Leyland TD2	H27/26R	"	25-10-32	"	7-11-34

(1) Pneumatic tyres fitted 1928 to 1929

Disposal

XR. 7078 G. V. Paynter, London, E8 (Lorry).
No. 2 Tuck Bros, London, E17 (Lorry).
No. 3 ?
No. 4/6/YF 6913/No. 7-17 LPTB No. D200/201/199/LN8-10/DH18/TD122/DL33/32/TD123/124/TR1/TD125
No. 5 W. Ardley, London, SE11 (Van); Arlington (dealer), SW1 10-38; Snell, Seal, Kent (storeshed) 11-38;

RENOWN

No.	Reg. No.	Chassis No.	Chassis	Body	Body by	Ex	Date		Acq.	Withdrawn
1	XU 9891	12930	Leyland LB5	OT26/22RO	Dodson	Red & White	7-10-24	New	8-30	9-30 [1]
2	HM 4754	13145	"	"	"	"	1-3-25	"	4-31	1933 [1]
3	HM 7440	13775	"	B32R	"	"	5-4-27	"		10-11-33
4	HM 8065	40462	Dennis 4 ton	"	"	"	20-9-27	"	13-4-33	10-11-33
5	HM 8618	46975	Leyland PLSC3	B32R	"	"	27-4-28	"	16-5-31	10-11-33
6	HV 93	70725	Leyland TD1	H28/24RO	"	"	26-9-29	"		10-11-33
7	HV 453	71167	"	"	"	"	27-3-30	"		10-11-33
8	HV 702	71318	"	"	"	"	3-6-30	"		10-11-33
9	HV 898	71322	"	"	"	"	25-8-30	"		10-11-33
10	HV 1188	71857	"	"	"	"	13-2-31	"		10-11-33
11	HV 1540	72211	"	"	"	"	8-7-31	"		10-11-33
12	HV 2822	2184	Leyland TD2	H30/26RO	"	"	8-4-33	"		10-11-33
	TW 6952	12076	Trojan 5 cwt	Van	"	Brown	14-1-27	—		10-11-33

(1) Pneumatic tyres fitted later

Disposal

No. 1 L. H. Blake, London, E6 (Lorry). Returned to Renown 1931 (not used)
No. 2 Body scrapped 1932, chassis sold
No. 3/4/6-12/TW 6952 LPTB No. L67/D180/L68-74/TV30
No. 5 Body destroyed by fire 16-5-31, chassis to LPTB No. L75

ROBERTS, J. M. MOTOR SERVICE

Reg	Chassis	Ch.No	Body	Builder	Colour					Note
MF 7640	Daimler Y	6059	OT22/20RO	Hickman	?	16-5-24	1-25	1-10-26	1926	(1)
MF 8159	"	6064	"	"	?	2-6-24	7-25	1-1-27	1927	(1)
MF 9873	"	6068	"	S & B	?	28-7-24	1-26		6-26	
MF 8001	"	6063	"	Hickman	Green & White	29-5-24	2-26		10-26	
XT 5611	"	6062	"	S & B	?	27-5-24	2-26		1926	

(1) These two vehicles may not have operated for Roberts as buses although owned by him and licensed. The others definitely operated during the General Strike of May 1926. All had been acquired by Roberts in his capacity as a dealer

Former Owner
MF 7640 Daisy
MF 8159 Cosmopolitan
MF 9873 Lancastrian
MF 8001/XT 5611 Peraeque

Disposal
MF 7640/8159 Scrapped
MF 9873 Low Loaders Ltd, London, W12 (Lorry)
MF 8001 Capt. A. Morgan, Cork, Eire
XT 5611 Independent

ROGUE, THE

Reg	Chassis	Ch.No	Body	Builder	Colour			
XW 1157	Dennis 4 ton	40208	OT26/22RO	Dodson	Red & White	23-10-24	New	4-8-27

Disposal
XW 1157 Public No. D44

ROMFORD DISTRICT MOTOR SERVICES

No.	Reg	Chassis	Ch.No	Body	Builder	Colour				Note
1	HJ 4156	Ford T	8861	B14F	?	Red & White	15-1-25	?	1-9-28	
2	TW 3186	Chevrolet X	10053	"	Metclf	"	4-5-26	New	7-1-32	
3	TW 3969	"	10716	"	"	"	15-6-26	"	1-3-31	
4	TW 5627	"	15757	"	"	"	1-10-26	"	11-5-32	
5	TW 8532	Chevrolet LM	50127	B20F	S & B	"	11-4-27	"	1-8-33	(1)
6	VA 4584	Dennis 30 cwt	?	B14F	Metclf	"	1-12-25	29-8-27	11-7-34	
7	PH 1973	Chevrolet	70646	B19F	Duple	"	6-10-27	6-7-28	11-7-34	(2)
8	GJ 2307	Dennis GL	70706	B20F		"	15-5-30	New	11-7-34	
9	VX 9897	"	56560	B14F	Metclf	"	1-3-31	"	11-7-34	
10	EV 4010	Dennis 30 cwt	75772	B20F	"	"	7-1-32	"	1-12-31 / 11-7-34	(3)
11	EV 4011	Dennis Dart	75783	B14F	"	"	7-1-32	"	11-7-34	
12	EV 5909	"	75797	B20F	"	"	11-5-32	"	11-7-34	
13	ANO 794	"		"	"	"	1-8-33	"	11-7-34	

(1) Seating later B18F (2) Body to EV 4010 1-32
(3) Body ex PH 1973

Former Owner
VA 4584/PH 1973 ?

Disposal
No. 1-4/7 ?
No. 5/6/8-13 LPTB No. CH4/DM1/3/4/2/DA43-45

ROYAL, THE

No.	Reg	Chassis	Ch.No	Body	Builder	Colour				Note
1	XU 1487	Dennis 4 ton	40168	OT26/22RO	S & B	Dark Blue & White	8-7-24	New	17-8-27	(1)
2	XX 8445	"	40337	"	"	"	4-4-25	"	17-8-27	(1)

(1) Later repainted red & white

Disposal
XU 1487/XX 8445 Public No. D11/12

ROYAL BLUE

No.	Reg	Chassis	Chassis No.	Body	Body builder				
1	XO 3124	S. Squire A	A6252	OT24/22RO	Straker	21-6-23	New	1926	26-1-27
2	XP 1193	"	A6285	"	"	7-9-23	"	1926	12-3-27
3	XR 4596	"	A6342		"	5-3-24		1-6-26	9-26
4	XT 2864	Leyland LB4	12708	OT26/22RO	Dodson	6-5-24	15-7-24	17-8-26	31-8-26
5	XN 3980	S. Squire A	A6236	OT22/22RO	Straker	5-4-23	New	1926	19-1-27
6	XU 5778	Leyland LB5	12916	OT26/22RO	Dodson	29-8-24		3-6-26	7-7-26
7	XU 5779	"	12914	"	"	29-8-24		8-6-26	7-7-26
8	XX 670	Dennis 4 ton	40269			9-2-25		1-6-26	12-6-26
9	XX 9877	S. Squire A	A6376	OT24/22RO	Straker	14-4-25	"		23-4-26
K127	LU 8327	AEC K	20127	"	?	1920		1-6-26	1-1-28
K143	LU 8342	"	20143	"	?	1920		1-6-26	1-1-28
K204	LU 8436	"	20204	"	?	1920		1-6-26	1-1-28
K284	LU 8465	"	20284	"	?	1920		1-6-26	1-1-28
K155	LU 8350	"	20155	"	?	1920		3-6-26	1-1-28
K381	LU 8565	"	20381	"	?	1920		8-6-26	1-1-28
K311	XC 8021	"	20311	"	?	1920		17-8-26	1-1-28
K691	XC 8306	"	20941	"	?	1921		30-11-26	1-1-28
K924	XC 9725	"	21190	"	?	1921		30-11-26	1-1-28

Former Owner
No. 5 Unity
All K-type General

Disposal
No. 1/2/5 C & P Sales (dealer), Ipswich. No. 5 then to W. Norfolk, Nayland, Suffolk 2-27; to Lorry 1931
No. 3/9 Chassis scrapped
No. 4 Cosgrove
No. 6/7 Tottenham Hotspur
No. 8 Hull & District M.S., Hull; East Yorkshire M.S. No. 48 Hull 10-26; R. Paterson, Stamford Bridge (Lorry) 1-34; scrapped 11-38
All K-type General

ROYAL HIGHLANDER

Reg	Chassis	Chassis No.	Body	Builder				
UR 9195	Guy OND	9736	B20F	Duple	28-3-31	New	Red & Cream	16-9-32
UR 9196	"	9737	"	"	28-3-31	"	"	16-9-32
HX 3466	Bean	2443/11W	B14F	Birch	31-3-31	"	"	16-9-32
HX 3467	"	2444/11W	"	"	31-3-31	"	"	16-9-32
UR 9899	Guy OND	9820	B20F	Duple	20-6-31	"	"	16-9-32
UR 9900	"	9819	"	"	20-6-31	"	"	16-9-32
UR 9997	"	9821	"	"	1-7-31	"	"	16-9-32
UR 9998	"	9829	"	"	1-7-31	"	"	16-9-32
MV 933	Bean	2457/11W	B14F	Birch	4-12-31	"	"	16-9-32

Disposal
UR 9195/9196/HX 3466/3467/UR 9899/9900/9997/9998/MV 933
General No. G1/2/BN2/3/G6/3-5/BN1

ROYAL TOOTS

Reg	No	Chassis	Body	Builder	Colour	Date	Origin		Date	Notes
XW 5626	40270	Dennis 4 ton	OT24/22RO	Dodson	Yellow & Cream	17-12-24	New		7-4-25	

Disposal
XW 5626 **Regal**

RYAN—see COSMOPOLITAN

ST GEORGE—see GENIAL

SAMUELSONS (bus fleet only)

Reg	No	Chassis	Body	Builder	Colour	Date	Origin		Date	
XB 9972	6075	Daimler Y	OT18/16RO	Tilling	Brown	11-7-20	New	12-23	1-24	(1)
XB 9986	5629	"	"	"	"	29-6-20	"	12-23	1-24	(1)
XB 9984	20065	Dennis 2 ton	"	"	"	1-7-20	"	12-23	?	(1)

(1) New as Ch27, converted to double deck with body ex Thomas Tilling 9-22, converted back to Ch27 1-24 the Daimlers then being immediately sold

Disposal
XB 9972/9986 Arlington (dealer), London, SW1
XB 9984 ?

SB

Reg	No	Chassis	Body	Builder	Colour	Date	Origin	Date
MH 1257	40211	Dennis 4 ton	OT26/22RO	Dodson	Red & White	7-10-24	New	5-28
MK 4483	45257	Dennis 2½ ton	B24R	S & B	"	3-5-26	"	5-28
MK 4484	45256	"	"	"	"	3-5-26	"	5-28
ML 2421	17128	Dennis E	B30R	"	"	7-3-27	"	5-28

Disposal
MH 1257/MK 4483/4484/ML 2421 Public No. D134/DS51/52/DE17

SCARBOROUGH/VICTORIA

Fleet	Reg	No	Chassis	Body	Builder	Colour	Date	Origin	Date
30	XU 409	40159	Dennis 4 ton	OT26/22RO	S & B	Red & White	1-7-24	New	5-8-27

Disposal
XU 409 Public No. D74

SERVICE/RED ROSE

Reg	No	Chassis	Body	Builder	Colour	Date	Origin	Date	Notes
XO 479	12562	Leyland LB2	OT26/22RO	Dodson	Orange & Chrome	30-5-23	New	2-10-26	(1)
YP 8995	40424	Dennis 4 ton	"	"	Red & White	31-8-26	"	3-3-28	
YT 2578	40455	"	"	Straker		12-7-27	"	3-3-28	

(1) Colour to red & white 3-26

Disposal
XO 479 Rosemex Oil Fields Ltd, London, SW1 (Lorry);
A. Wallaker, London, SE5 11-29; Road Haulage Executive 4-50
YP 8995/YT 2578 Public No. D115/112

SHAMROCK

Reg	No	Chassis	Body	Builder	Colour	Date	Origin	Date	Notes
XU 2191	10552	Thornycroft J	OT26/24RO	Dodson	Lt Green & White	12-7-24	New	27-4-25	(1)
XU 2192	10551	"	"	"	"	12-7-24	"	19-2-26	(1)
XU 2193	10550	"	"	"	"	12-7-24	"	19-2-26	(1)

Reg		Chassis	Chassis No.	Body		Colour	New	Acquired	Withdrawn	
K650	XF 8012	AEC K	20900	OT24/22RO		Green & Cream	1921	22-2-26	1-1-28	
K947	XF 8021	"	21213	"		"	1921	22-2-26	1-1-28	
K1038	XF 8073	"	20545	"		"	1921	22-2-26	1-1-28	

(1) Colour to red & white 12-24

Former Owner
K650/947/1038 General

Disposal
XU 2191 Cambrian No. T114
XU 2192/2193H & C Motor Works, Hull. XU 2193 C. H.Mason
(Lorry), Leeds 12-30; Motor Wreckers (dealer), Leeds 6-31;
scrapped 9-32

SHANGHAI/GOLDEN ARROW

Buses

Reg	Chassis	Chassis No.	Body	Builder	Colour	New	Acquired	Withdrawn
XU 5585	Dennis 4 ton	40188	OT26/22RO	S & B	Red & White	12-8-24	New	3-31
UC 9525	Dennis E	17364	B30R	Phoenix	"	14-3-28	"	24-11-33
GN 5896	Dennis HV	95026	H30/26RO	Dodson	"	3-3-31	"	24-11-33

Coaches

Reg	Chassis	Chassis No.	Body	Builder	Colour	New	Acquired	Withdrawn
YX 7689	Dennis E	17595	C32D	S & B	Green & Black	5-9-28	New	31-3-33
UU 1950	"	17593	"	Duple	"	14-5-29	"	5-33
JJ 1836	Dennis Lancet	170266	C32R	"	"	13-1-33	"	24-11-33
JJ 1837	"	170267	"	"	"	13-1-33	"	24-11-33

Disposal
XU 5585 ?
UC 9525/GN 5896/JJ 1836/1837 LPTB No. DE24/D184/DL29/30
YX 7689 London Carriers Ltd, London, WC2 (Lorry); withdrawn 1-2-38
UU 1950 Merrick, Catford, London (Lorry)

SILVER STAR

Reg	Chassis	Chassis No.	Body	Builder	Colour	New	Acquired	Withdrawn
ML 611	Dennis 2½ ton	45447	B24R	S & B	Red & White	27-10-26	New	1-1-28

Disposal
ML 611 General No. D59

SKYLARK

Reg	Chassis	Chassis No.	Body	Builder	Colour	New	Acquired	Withdrawn	
XN 555	A. Squire A	A6209	OT22/22RO	Straker	Crimson & Yellow	5-3-23	New	3-26	
XR 4558	Dennis 4 ton	40088	OT26/22RO	S & B	Red & Yellow	5-3-24	"	8-7-27	
XU 319	"	40165	"	"	"	1-7-24	"	8-7-27	
YM 8144	"	40384	OT24/22RO	Straker	"	13-2-26	"	8-7-27	(1)
YO 6917	"	40405	OT26/22RO	"	"	5-6-26	"	8-7-27	
XP 2874	Thornycroft J	10425	OT26/24RO	Dodson	Red & White	2-10-23	27-10-26	13-4-27	(2)

(1) Colour to red & yellow 3-24, body to YM 8144 2-26
(2) Body ex XN 555

Former Owner
XP 2874 Universal

Disposal
XN 555 ?
XR 4558/XU 319/YM 8144/YO 6917 Public No. D41/48/64/15
XP 2874 Enterprise Bus Co (J. H. Wavell), Newport, IoW;
J. M. Roberts (dealer), London, W12 2-28; Chater-Lea Mfg Co,
London, EC1 (Lorry) 7-28; A. H. Barker, London, E3 3-29.

SOUTHALL & DISTRICT—to be included in volume on country area independents

SOUTH LONDON COACHES

Bus

Reg	Chassis	Chassis No	Body	Builder	Colour	Date	New	Withdrawn	Note
XU 7405	Dennis 4 ton	40171	OT26/22RO	S & B	Blue & White	2-9-24	New	12-12-27	(1)

Coaches

Reg	Chassis	Chassis No	Body	Builder	Colour	Date	New	Withdrawn	Note
BM 7190	Commer 3P	?	Ch27	?	Sea Green	22-4-19	New	?	
XB 8034	Commer WP1	1120	Ch28	?	"	6-20	New	By 1930	(2)
XD 8161	Commer 3P	10054	Ch27	?	"	8-20	"	1930	
XK 7380	Crossley	10909	C14	?	"	4-22	"	7-23	
XO 8058	Wolseley	?		?		30-7-23	8-4-25	1928	(3)
YK 2022	Dennis 2½ ton	45102	C28	?		6-25	New	By 3-34	
YT 3708	Maudslay ML4B	4163	C24	?	Light Blue	19-7-27	"	4-10-33	
YT 3709	"	4154	"	?	"	19-7-27	"	4-10-33	
YW 2450	"	4345	C26	?	"	19-5-28	"	4-10-33	
YW 3481	"	4352	"	?	"	29-5-28	"	4-10-33	
UU 7978	Maudslay ML3B	4652	C29	?	"	17-6-29	"	4-10-33	

(1) Colour to red & white 10-27   (2) Colour to brown 3-29
(3) New as a private car, coach body fitted 4-25

Former Owner
XO 8058 H. G. Eastwood, London, SW9

Disposal
XU 7405 Public No. D105
BM 7190/XD 8161/XO 8058 ?
XB 8034 J. A. Transport, Chelsea (Lorry)
XK 7380 M. T. Co, London; Stansfield, London, SE5 (Lorry) 6-29;
  Breeds, Erith, Kent 7-29
YK 2022 to lorry
YT 3708/3709/YW 2450/3481/UU 7978 British Motor Trust,
  London, SW1, YW 3481 to R. Goodall, Maidstone, Kent (Lorry)
  by 2-38. UU 7978 Danny Boy Coaches (Payne) Birmingham
  by 4-37

SPHERE—see EMPRESS (Crabb & Clarke)

STANDARD

	Reg	Chassis	Chassis No	Body	Builder	Colour	Date	New	Withdrawn
1	XN 5401	Leyland LB2	12458	OT26/22RO	Dodson	Brown & Cream	19-4-23	New	7-28
2	XT 2565	Leyland LB4	12710	"	"	"	5-5-24	"	12-29
3	XW 2012	Leyland LB5	12934	"	"	"	1-11-24	"	8-4-31
4	YR 9020	"	13653	"	"	"	30-11-26	"	9-1-32
	UW 6777	Leyland TD1	70869	H28/24RO	"	"	29-11-29	"	1-11-33
	GN 4832	"	71909	"	"	"	12-2-31	"	1-11-33
	GW 550	Leyland TD2	102	H27/26R	"	"	16-12-31	"	1-11-33
	GY 2042	"	1751	H26/26R	"	"	22-7-32	"	1-11-33

Disposal
XN 5401 to van
XT 2565 T. Smith, London, N1 (Lorry); withdrawn 3-38
XW 2012 Ivetons Ltd, Margate, Kent (Lorry)
YR 9020 J. Saunders, London, SE15 (Lorry)
UW 6777/GN 4832/GW 550/GY 2042 LPTB No. L54-57

STANMORE

MH 3380	Dennis 4 ton	40286	OT26/22RO	Dodson	Red & White	29-1-25	New	17-2-25	2-25	
					Disposal					
					MH 3380 CC					

STAR (G. D. Glen)

VW 1798	Garner AEO	75192	B32F	?	?	29-10-27	New		4-33	(1)

Note—An earlier bus was owned but details are not known
Disposal VW 1798 to Lorry
(1) Altered to B28F 4-32

SUNBEAM/SUPREME

1 MF 5720	S. Squire A	A6356	OT24/22RO	Straker	Red & White	24-3-24	New	25-3-31	1931	
2 MH 5040	Dennis 4 ton	40332	OT26/22RO	Dodson	"	30-3-25	"		1-11-33	
3 MY 2742	Leyland TD1	70966	H28/24RO	"	"	29-1-30	"		1-11-33	
4 HX 2643	"	71880	H30/26RO	"	"	26-1-31	"		1-11-33	

(1) Pneumatic tyres fitted later
Disposal
MF 5720 S. Marston, Bury St. Edmunds (Lorry); withdrawn 5-2-34
MH 5040/MY 2742/HX 2643 LPTB No. D178/L52/53

SUPER BUS

XU 4371	Dennis 4 ton	40185	OT26/22RO	S & B	Red & White	29-7-24	New	7-1-27	27-1-27	
K759 XC 8321	AEC K	21025	OT24/22RO	?	"	1921	4-1-27		1-1-28	

Former Owner
K759 General
Disposal
XU 4371 Redburn's No. D30
K759 General

SUPREME—see SUNBEAM

SWIFT

PD 5976	Leyland LB2	12533	OT26/22RO	Dodson	Chocolate & White	20-6-23	New		28-5-27	(1)

(1) Colour to red & white 1-27
Disposal PD 5976 Pickup No. 8

TALLY HO/ I&B

XX 1514	Daimler Y	6080	OT22/20RO	Hickman	Red & White	17-2-25	New		1-2-29	
XV 1153	Leyland PLSC3	47152	B32R	Birch	Brown & White	18-10-28	"		1-2-29	(1)

(1) Carried Birch livery and fleet name
Disposal XX 1514/XV 1153 Birch No. B18/20

T & W

XX 1756	Dennis 4 ton	40323	OT26/22RO	Dodson	Red & White	19-2-25	New	29-3-26	25-11-26	

Disposal XX 1756 Redburn's No. D20

THACKRAYS

5	XX 3882	Dennis 4 ton	40326	OT26/22RO	Dodson	Red & White	10-3-25	New	11-10-27

Disposal
XX 3882 Public No. D86

THACKRAY, ROBT

4	XW 5667	Dennis 4 ton	40273	OT26/22RO	Dodson	Red & White	30-12-24	New	6-10-27
1	XW 5668	"	40281	"	"	"	30-12-24	"	6-10-27
	XW 5669	"	40234	"	"	"	30-12-24	"	6-10-27
	XW 5670	"	40238	"	"	"	30-12-24	"	6-10-27
3	XX 68	"	40277	"	"	"	2-2-25	"	6-10-27
2	XX 906	"	40290	"	"	"	10-2-25	"	6-10-27
	YM 4719	"	40381	"	"	"	4-1-26	"	6-10-27
	YF 5623	"	40451	"	"	"	3-5-27	"	6-10-27

Disposal
XW 5667-70/68/XX 906/YM 4719/YF 5623 Public No. D85/81/82/80/83/87/88/84

TIMPSON'S (bus fleet only)

29	XK 6809	S. Squire A	A6140	OT24/22RO	Dodson	Silver & Maroon	4-22	New	3-27	(1)
30	MC 9827	"	A6024	"	"	"	1920	5-22	3-27	(1)
31	XN 2556	"	A6213	OT22/22RO	Straker	"	23-3-23	New	8-27	
32	XN 2558	"	A6215	"	"	"	26-3-23	"	17-8-27	
33	XN 2263	"	A6220	"	"	"	22-3-23	"	8-27	
34	XN 2557	"	A6221	"	"	"	23-3-23	21-4-27	30-4-27	
35	XN 2555	"	A6229	"	"	"	23-3-23		1927	
36	XN 2554	"	A6230	"	"	"	23-3-23		29-8-27	
37	XO 3947	"	A6258	OT24/22RO	"	"	29-6-23	14-3-27	24-3-27	
38	XO 3948	"	A6259	"	"	"	29-6-23	28-4-27	6-5-27	
39	XO 3946	"	A6260	"	"	"	29-6-23		8-27	
40	XO 3949	"	A6264	"	"	"	29-6-23	6-4-27	27-4-27	
41	XO 3951	"	A6266	"	"	"	29-6-23	14-3-27	24-3-27	
42	XO 3950	"	A6265	"	"	"	29-6-23		8-27	
43	XP 9696	"	A6351	"	"	"	10-1-24	"	13-10-27	
44	XP 9697	"	A6352	"	"	"	10-1-24	"	8-27	
45	XR 3516	"	A6386	"	"	"	25-2-24	"	9-27	
46	XR 5747	"	A6388	"	"	"	17-3-24	"	11-27	
47	XR 3517	"	A6387	"	"	"	25-2-24	"	12-4-27	
48	XR 9417	"	A6389	"	"	"	10-4-24	"	1-28	
49	XM 5761	Frost Smith	FS1-16	"	Dodson	"	29-12-22	3-25	7-7-26	
50	XM 2057	"	FS1-12	"	"	"	30-10-22	3-25	7-7-26	
	XM 2056	"	FS1-11	OT22/22RO	"	Blue & Cream	30-10-22	3-25	7-7-26	
	XM 3064	"	FS1-13	"	"	"	3-11-22	3-25	31-7-26	(2)
	XM 4568	"	FS1-14	OT24/22RO	"	"	4-12-22	3-25	7-7-26	(2)

No.	Reg	TSM TS3A	FSI-15	OT26/22RO	Hickman	Silver & Maroon				
51	XM 5302		FSI-15	OT26/22RO	Hickman	Silver & Maroon	19-12-22	3-25	5-7-26	(2)
52	IT 292	"	?	"	"	"	5-20	11-2-27	1-1-28	
53	IT 293	"	?	"	"	"	5-20	15-2-27	1-1-28	
54	IT 301	"	?	"	"	"	6-20	11-2-27	1-1-28	
55	IT 302	"	2237	"	Dodson	"	6-20	11-2-27	1-1-28	(3)
56	XM 2992	"	2277	"	"	"	2-11-22	14-2-27	1-1-28	(4)
59	XB 9888	"	2250	"	Straker	"	5-20	16-3-27	1-1-28	(5)
60	XE 7856	"	2249	"	"	"	11-2-21	20-7-27	1-1-28	(6)
61	XH 8144	"	2245	"	"	"	15-11-21	29-7-27	1-1-28	(7)
62	XC 9437	"	2321	"	"	"	31-1-21	8-8-27	1-1-28	(6)
63	XH 9758	"	2322	"	"	"	3-5-22	8-27	1-1-28	(6)
64	XH 9759	"	3271	"	"	"	3-5-22	19-8-27	1-1-28	(6)
65	YK 2739	"	3269	"	"	"	1-7-25	19-8-27	1-1-28	(6)
66	YK 2737	"	3266	"	"	"	29-6-25	26-8-27	1-1-28	(6)
67	YK 2734	"	3270	"	"	"	1-7-25	31-8-27	1-1-28	(6)
68	YK 2738	"	3268	"	"	"	29-6-25	6-9-27	1-1-28	
69	YK 2736	"	3267	"	"	"	29-6-25	9-9-27	1-1-28	
70	YK 2735	"	3244	"	"	"	11-12-24	16-9-27	1-1-28	(8)
71	XW 5321	"	3255	"	"	"	23-3-25	14-9-27	1-1-28	(8)
72	XX 5260	"	3250	"	"	"	27-2-25	23-9-27	1-1-28	(8)

(1) New as Ch32, converted to double-deck with bodies ex No. 50/49 7-26
(2) Converted to C22, colour silver & maroon 7-25
(3) Converted to double-deck 2-27
(4) New as a box van, converted to lorry 1-26 and to a bus 3-27
(5) New as B22R, double-deck body fitted 7-27
(6) No. 61/64-69 new as box vans, converted to C22/C29/C29/C28/C29/C28/C28 12-25/3-26/3-26/3-26/3-26/3-26, and to bus 7-27/8-27/8-27/8-27/9-27/9-27
(7) Seats to Ch29 29-3-25 and converted to double-deck 8-27
(8) New as petrol tanker, converted to double-deck 9-27

Note—The bodies from Nos. 29-33/35/36/39/42-48 were transferred to Nos. 56/59-72 upon the conversion of the latter to buses, but not necessarily in the same sequence

Former Owner
No. 30 Straker Squire (demonstrator)
No. 49/50/XM 2056/3064/4568/5302 F. S. Petrol Electric (XM 2056 not used by Timpson)
No. 51-56 Cambrian Landray
No. 59-61/64-72 Thos Tilling
No. 62/63 New to Pickfords, London, SE1 as Ch23; to T. Tilling 28-9-23

Disposal
No. 29/30/39/43/45/46 H. A. Harvey, Harston, Cambs (Lorry).
No. 30 withdrawn 3-28 and scrapped
No. 31/32/33/44 S. Green, Birmingham (Lorry). No. 31 withdrawn 1-1-35
No. 34/37/38/40/41 C & P Sales (dealer), Ipswich. No. 37 to H. C. Chambers, Bures, Suffolk 3-27; withdrawn 11-30
No. 35/42 to Lorry, owners unknown
No. 36 E. H. Jones, London, SW1 (Lorry)
No. 47 Chassis scrapped
No. 48 Farm & Son, Birkenhead (Lorry)
No. 49/50/XM 2056/3064/4568/5302 E. Ash (dealer), Deptford, London. No. 49/50/XM 2056 H. Northwood (dealer), Westminster 7-26 and scrapped
No. 51-56/59-72 T. Tilling No. 1213-1232

TOTTENHAM HOTSPUR

No.	Reg	Chassis	Chassis No	Body	Builder	Livery					
14	MF 4166	S. Squire A	A6335	OT24/22RO	Straker	Red & Grey	17-1-24	New	12-26	14-1-27	
16	MF 4463	"	A6336	"	"	"	28-1-24	"	10-26	10-3-27	
18	MF 7044	"	A6368	"	"	"	29-4-24	"	10-26	29-3-27	
20	MH 295	"	A6379	"	"	"	15-8-24	"		22-10-26	
22	MH 1095	"	A6396	"	"	"	30-9-24	"		22-10-26	
6	XU 5778	Leyland LB5	12916	OT26/22RO	Dodson	Maroon & Cream	29-8-24	7-7-26	21-10-27	1-1-28	(1)
8	XU 5779	"	12914	"	"	"	29-8-24	7-7-26	24-10-27	1-1-28	(1)
2	YL 8115	"	13520	"	"	"	23-10-25	22-10-26	7-10-27	1-1-28	
4	YM 6664	"	13534	"	"	"	27-1-26	22-10-26	11-10-27	1-1-28	
	AN 6120	Leyland LB2	12700	OT24/22RO	"	Brown & White	27-10-23	4-1-27	13-10-27	1-1-28	
K642	XC 8338	AEC K	20892	"	?	"	1921	7-10-27		1-1-28	
K654	XC 8239	"	20904	"	?	"	1921	11-10-27		1-1-28	
K629	XC 8237	"	20879	"	?	"	1921	13-10-27		1-1-28	
K566	XC 8202	"	20816	"	?	"	1921	21-10-27		1-1-28	
K928	XC 9709	"	21194	"	?	"	1921	24-10-27		1-1-28	

(1) Colour to red & white 6-27

Former Owner
XU 5778/5779 Royal Blue nos. 6/7
YL 8115/YM 6664 EP
AN 6120 Ubique
All K-type General

Disposal
MF 4166/4463/7044 C & P Sales (dealer), Ipswich. MF 4166 to
S. Furze, Essex (Lorry) 1927; withdrawn 7-28
MF 7044 to H. Ball, Cheshire (Lorry).; withdrawn 1-1-34
MH 295/1095 EP
XU 5778/5779/YL 8115/YM 6664/AN 6120 General No. L31-34/30
All K-type General

TOWER

No.	Reg	Chassis	Chassis No	Body	Builder	Livery					
1	XT 3717	Thornycroft J	10532	OT26/24RO	Dodson	Tangerine & Cream	14-5-24	New	1-3-27	10-3-27	(1)
2	XU 2148	"	10557	"	"	"	12-7-24	"	3-2-27	3-3-27	(1)
3	XU 3280	"	10554	"	"	"	21-7-24	"	8-3-27	14-3-27	
K967	XC 9786	AEC K	21233	OT24/22RO	?	Red & White	1921	3-2-27		1-1-28	
K211	LU 8353	"	20211	"	?	"	1920	1-3-27		1-1-28	
K185	LU 8406	"	20185	"	?	"	1920	7-3-27		1-1-28	

(1) Colour to red & white 5-25/7-25/7-25

Former Owner
K185/211/967 General

Disposal
No. 1-3 C&P Sales (dealer), Ipswich; County Motors, Lancaster
5-27; Ribble M.S. No. 658/657/656 1-29. No. 1 withdrawn
7-29 then to V. J. Fuller, Brixton, London (Lorry) by 6-30 and
withdrawn 3-32. No. 2 & 3 withdrawn 7-29/11-29
K185/211/967 General

TRINITY/JH/RED ROSE

Reg	Chassis	Chassis No	Body	Builder	Livery			
XU 9497	Dennis 4 ton	40224	OT26/22RO	Wilton	Red & White	2-10-24	New	3-3-28
YH 3745	"	40456	"	Straker	"	23-5-27	"	3-3-28

Disposal
XU 9497/YH 3745 Public No. D114/116

TRIUMPH

Reg	Chassis	Chassis No.	Body	Builder	Colour	Date new	Acquired	Disposal	
XN 8524	Leyland LB2	12531	OT26/22RO	Dodson	Violet & White	12-5-23	New	11-11-31	(1)
UV 5764	Leyland TD1	70715	H28/24RO	"	Red & White	30-7-29	7-31	24-11-33	(2)
YL 417	Leyland LB5	13304	OT26/22RO	"	"	1-8-25		24-11-33	

(1) Colour to red & white 5-24, body to YL 417 7-31
(2) Body ex XN 8524 fitted 7-31

Disposal
XN 8524 City (chassis only) for spares
UV 5764/YL 417 LPTB No. L89/90

Former Owner
YL 417 City No. A23 (Chassis only acquired)

TURNER

Reg	Chassis	Chassis No.	Body	Builder	Colour	Date new	Acquired	Disposal	
YN 4594	Bean Type 5	13505	B12F	Birch	Dark Green, Grey roof	6-26	10-28	12-30	(1)
UL 1771	Bean	1753/11W	B14F	"	Red & White	14-1-29	New	12-30	

(1) Body new 1-29

Former Owner
YN 4594 ?

Disposal
YN 4594/UL 1771 Birch (dealer). London, NW5. UL 1771 to F. E. Nutt. London, NW11 6-32; W. Church, New Southgate (private bus) 1932; Ellingworth, Potters Bar, Herts 1945; to garden shed at Wendover, Bucks 1946; acquired for preservation 1966

UBIQUE

Reg	Chassis	Chassis No.	Body	Builder	Colour	Date new	Acquired	Disposal	
AN 6120	Leyland LB2	12700	OT26/22RO	Dodson	Chocolate & Cream	27-10-23		4-1-27	(1)
AN 6452	Thornycroft J	10555	OT26/24RO	"	"	1-7-24		20-5-26	(2)
K412 XC 8006	AEC K	20412	OT24/22RO	?	Green & White	1920	26-4-26	1-1-28	
K572 XC 8172		20822	"	?	Red & White	1921	2-2-27	1-1-28	

(1) Colour to red & cream by 1926
(2) Colour later red & white

Former Owner
K412/572 General

Disposal
AN 6120 Tottenham Hotspur
AN 6452 Thames Valley. No. 130
K412/572 General

UNEEDUS

No.	Reg	Chassis	Chassis No.	Body	Builder	Colour	Date new	Acquired	Disposal
1	MF 8953	Dennis 4 ton	40158	OT26/22RO	S & B	Red & White	30-6-24	New	1-1-28
2	MH 1353	"	40219	B24R	"	"	10-10-24	"	1-1-28
3	MK 2245	Guy BB	1887	B30R	"	"	25-1-26	27-7-27	23-9-27
4	MK 2246	"	1888	B24R	"	"	25-1-26	26-7-27	8-9-27
5	ML 1169	Dennis E	17103		"	"	13-12-26	"	1-1-28
K927	XC 9727	AEC K	21193	"	LGOC	"	1921	30-7-27	1-1-28
K1098	RO 2070	"	20645	"	"	"	25-11-25	30-7-27	1-1-28

Former Owner
K927/1098 General

Disposal
No. 1/2/5 General No. D62/63/64
No. 3/4 National, Watford No. G1/2
K927/1098 General

UNITED

1	XO 1390	Leyland LB2	12539	OT26/22RO	Dodson	Brown & Cream	4-6-23	New	30-4-31	(1)
2	XO 2962	"	12530	"	Wilton	"	20-6-23	"	2-30	(1)
3	XP 8732	Leyland LB4	12732	"	Dodson	"	31-12-23	"	30-9-31	(1)
4	XW 4090	Leyland LB5	12937	"	"	"	28-11-24	"	7-31	(1)
5	XX 9059	"	13236	"	"	"	7-4-25	"	1-11-33	(1)
6	YL 6337	"	13513	"	"	"	6-10-25	"	16-1-32	(1)
7	YT 346	"	13807	"	"	"	29-6-27	"	2-3-32	(1)
1	GC 1679	Leyland TD1	71129	H28/24RO	"	"	7-1-30	"	1-11-33	(1)
2	GC 4321	"	71130	"	"	"	24-1-30	"	1-11-33	(1)
3	GK 607	"	71634	H30/26RO	"	"	7-10-30	"	1-11-33	(1)
4	GK 608	"	71633	"	"	"	7-10-30	"	1-11-33	(1)
5	GP 168	"	72103	"	"	"	16-5-31	"	1-11-33	(1)
6	GP 2512	"	72102	"	"	"	3-6-31	"	1-11-33	(1)
7	GW 738	"	72351	"	"	"	30-12-31	"	1-11-33	(1)

(1) Pneumatic tyres fitted 1-30/1930/1930/5-30/1930/1930

Disposal
XO 1390 A. F. Minn, Chertsey, Surrey (Lorry)
XO 2962 Scrapped
XP 8732 J. Saunders, Hayes Wharf, London, SE15 (Lorry)
XW 4090 to Lorry
XX 9059/GC 1679/4321/GK 607/608/GP 168/2512/GW 738
   LPTB No. L66/60/59/61-65
YL 6337/YT 346 J. Wallaker, London, SE5 (Lorry)

UNITY

XN 3980	S. Squire A	A6236	OT22/22RO	Straker	Grey	5-4-23	New	15-7-24

Disposal
XN 3980 Royal Blue

UNIVERSAL

XN 8444	S. Squire A	A6248	OT22/22RO	Straker	Light Blue & White	11-5-23	New	6-27
XP 2874	Thornycroft J	10425	OT26/24RO	Dodson	"	2-10-23	"	27-10-26
YP 9836	Dennis 4 ton	40425	OT26/22RO	S & B	"	2-9-26	"	8-7-27
YH 3707	Dennis E	17182	B30R	"	Chocolate & Cream	21-5-27	"	8-7-27	(1)

(1) Carried fleetname "SKYLARK"

Disposal
XN 8444 to Lorry
XP 2874 Skylark
YP 9836/YH 3707 Public No. D8/DE10

VARSITY

XT 9991	Dennis 4 ton	40155	OT26/22RO	Dodson	Blue & White	30-6-24	New	19-8-27
XX 5762	"	40308	"	S & B	"	24-3-25	"	19-8-27
MH 2480	"	40274	"	"	"	15-12-24	16-5-26	19-8-27

Former Owner
MH 2480 Henslowe

Disposal
XT 9991/XX 5762/MH 2480 Public No. D6/4/5

Fleet	Reg.	Chassis No.	Chassis	Body	Colour / Notes				

VELETA

| | XR 6498 | 12744 | Leyland LB5 | OT26/22RO | Dodson | Red & White | 24-3-24 | New | 11-12-27 |
| | XW 910 | 40212 | Dennis 4 ton | " | " | " | 20-10-24 | " | 10-27 |

Disposal
XR 6498 City No. A33
XW 910 St. George

VENTURE

| | XR 4058 | 6056 | Daimler Y | OT22/20RO | S & B | Red & White | 29-2-24 | New | 25-2-28 |
| | XR 8933 | 6058 | " | " | " | " | 8-4-24 | 10-24 | 25-2-28 |

Former Owner
XR 8933 JL
Disposal
XR 4058/8933 Public No. DA3/2

VICTOR

| | XT 8841 | 40157 | Dennis 4 ton | OT26/22RO | S & B | Red & White | 20-6-24 | New | 17-1-28 |

(1) Colour to violet & white 10-25

Disposal
XT 8841 Premier

(1)

VICTORIA—see SCARBOROUGH

VICTORIA ROAD CAR

| 551 | XR 555 | A6358 | S. Squire A | OT24/22RO | Straker | Blue & White | 18-1-24 | New | 16-3-27 | 24-3-27 |
| K227 | LU 8355 | 20227 | AEC K | " | ? | Red & White | 1920 | 14-3-27 | | 1-1-28 |

Former Owner
K227 General
Disposal
XR 555 C & P Sales (dealer), Ipswich; A. W. Berry, West Mersea, Essex. 3-27; to lorry 10-29
K227 General

VICTORY

	PU 5608	6077	Daimler Y	OT22/20RO	Hickman	Red & White	11-12-24	New	6-26
	TW 3167	13587	Leyland LB5	OT26/22RO	Dodson	"	3-5-26	"	7-11-34
	VW 5140	47071	Leyland PLSC3	B32R	"	"	4-6-28	"	8-30
	VX 4261	70969	Leyland TD1	H28/24RO	"	"	26-2-30	"	7-11-34

Disposal
PU 5608 Gretna
TW 3167/VX 4261 LPTB No. L67/TD126
VW 5140 W. E. Hasking, Ramsgate, Kent

VIVID

	XP 7425	6051	Daimler Y	OT22/20RO	Hickman	Red & White	26-12-23	12-24	5-4-27	14-4-27
	XO 1942	12582	Leyland LB2	OT26/22RO	Dodson	"	8-6-23	5-4-27	22-7-27	23-7-27
K335	LU 8424	20335	AEC K	OT24/22RO	?	"	1920	21-7-27		1-1-28

483

(1)
(1)

Former Owner
XP 7425 London
XO 1942 Marathon
K335 General

Disposal
XP 7425 C & P Sales (dealer), Ipswich
XO 1942 National, Watford, No. L29
K335 General

WA—see WILTON

WALTHAM

NK 5070	205056	Fiat	B14F		Buff	1-23	by 3-26		by 8-27
NK 5752	205186	"	"		"	6-23	by 3-26		by 8-27
NK 8696	?			?	?	26-7-24	by 3-26		?
NK 8877	30731	Dennis 2½ ton	B20R	Dodson	Blue & White	10-24	12-26		3-8-27
RO 5240	45458	"	B24R	"	Chocolate & White	12-26	New		3-8-27

Former Owner
NK 5070/5752/8696 Barnet M. S., Barnet
NK 8877 Admiral No 30

Disposal
NK 5070/5752 Central (W. Taylor), Exeter
NK 8696 ?
NK 8877/RO 5240 Public No. DS35/21

WAVERLEY

XN 5203	12526	Leyland LB2	OT26/22RO	Dodson	Violet & Putty	16-4-23	New		22-7-25

Disposal
XN 5203 Henslowe

WAYMAN (Known fleet)

XA 9201	B2697	AEC B	B26R	?	Red & White	1913	1-20		by 7-26
HK 9496	B1300	LGOC B	OT20/16RO	?	"	1912	25-11-20		by 7-26
NH 1805	?	S. Squire	?	?	"	?	3-24		by 7-26

Former Owner
NH 1805 ?
XA 9201/HK9496 War Department ex LGOC

Disposal
XA 9201/HK 9496/NH 1805 ?

WELLINGTON

1	XR 2730	12736	Leyland LB4	OT26/22RO	Dodson	Red & White	15-2-24	New	8-10-27	1-1-28
2	XX 5413	13227	Leyland LB5	"	"	"	24-3-25	"	12-10-27	1-1-28
K499	XC 8128	20499	AEC K	OT24/22RO	?	"	1920	8-10-27		1-1-28
K471	XC 8110	20471	"	"	?	"	1920	12-10-27		1-1-28

Former Owner
K471/499 General

Disposal
XR 2730/XX 5413 General No. L3/4
K471/499 Metropolitan

WESTERN

1	XN 6661	A6222	S. Squire A	OT24/22RO	Dodson	Chocolate & White	30-4-23	New	12-3-27	7-4-27
2	XO 939	A6249	"	"	"	"	1-6-23	"	22-4-27	3-5-27
3	XO 2107	A6244	"	"	"	"	11-6-23	"	1-4-27	6-4-27

No	Reg	Chassis	Body	Builder	Livery				
4	XT 110	Dennis 4 ton	OT26/22RO	Wilton	Chocolate & Cream	14-4-24	"	25-1-27	7-2-27
5	XT 4731	"	"	"	"	20-5-24	"	28-1-27	22-2-27
6	XT 8982	"	"	"	"	21-6-24	"	3-2-27	2-3-27
7	YM 8237	"	"	Dodson	"	15-2-26	"	6-12-26	31-12-26
K611	XC 8234	AEC K	OT24/22RO	?	"	1921	4-12-26		1-1-28
K569	XC 8189	"	"	?	"	1921	24-1-27		1-1-28
K450	XC 8052	"	"	?	"	1920	27-1-27		1-1-28
K975	XC 9798	"	"	?	"	1921	2-2-27		1-1-28
K344	XF 8081	"	"	?	"	1920	17-3-27		1-1-28
K188	LU 8425	"	"	?	"	1920	8-4-27		1-1-28
K142	LU 8400	"	"	?	"	1920	21-4-27		1-1-28

(1) Fitted with ex-Cambrian Straker body 10-26

Former Owner
All K-type General

Disposal
No. 1/3 C & P Sales (dealer) Ipswich
No. 2 C &P Sales, Ipswich (Lorry); withdrawn 1937
No. 4-7 Redburn's No. D31/32/37/25
All K-type General

WESTMINSTER

Buses

No	Reg	Chassis	Body	Builder	Livery			
WR2	XR 9000	Dennis 4 ton	OT26/22RO	S & B	Red & White	8-4-24	New	10-29
WR4	XU 8451	"	"	"	"	18-9-24	"	13-11-30
WR6	XX 1161	"	"	Dodson	"	12-2-25	"	18-2-30
WR8	XX 1162	"	"	"	"	12-2-25	"	18-2-30
WR10	XX 8326	"	"	"	"	3-4-25	"	19-2-30
WR12	XX 8327	"	"	"	"	3-4-25	"	2-33
WR14	YO 60	"	"	"	"	29-6-26	"	11-7-34
WR16	YF 6944	Dennis E	B30R	"	Dark Red & Cream	11-4-27	23-11-27	3-10-28
	XU 8984	Leyland LB5	OT26/22RO	"	Red & White	1-10-24	3-10-28	1-10-31
	MH 3812	Dennis 4 ton	H28/24RO	"	"	17-2-25	New	11-7-34
WR8	UW 2308	Leyland TD1	"	"	"	2-10-29	"	11-7-34
WR10	UW 2309	"	"	"	"	16-10-29	"	11-7-34
WR2	UW 2310	"	"	"	"	28-10-29	"	11-7-34
WR14	UW 2311	"	"	"	"	1-11-29	"	11-7-34
WR12	GC 3170	"	"	"	"	8-1-30	"	11-7-34
WR4	GC 3171	"	"	"	"	21-1-30	"	11-7-34
WR6	GC 3172	"	"	"	"	23-1-30	"	11-7-34
WR16	GN 184	"	H30/26RO	"	"	13-1-31	"	11-7-34
WR18	GX 2602	"	"	"	"	12-5-32	"	11-7-34
WR20	JJ 9215	SMC Sikh	H36/28R	?	"	17-2-33	"	11-7-34
	XB 9722	Dennis 2 ton	Lorry	—	?	-21	6-28	
	YL 5024	Morris	Van	—		13-10-25	30-3-31	

Coaches

No	Reg	Chassis	Body	Builder	Livery			
	YU 9391	Dennis F	C20	?	Biscuit & Black	3-12-27	New	13-2-28
	UC 5468	Gilford 166SD	C20D	Redhead	Biscuit & Black	1-28	"	13-2-28

(1) Six wheeler

Former Owner
XU 8984 Belgravia
MH 3812 Prince
XB 9722 New to A. E. Ewer, London EC1 as Ch 31. To G. J. Dawson (dealer), Clapham 6-28 and fitted with lorry body, crane and pneumatic tyres
YL 5024 G. R. and W. D. Valli, London, W4

Disposal
XR 9000 ?
XU 8451 J. Welch, London, SE7 (Lorry)
XX 1161/1162/8326/8327 W. Urquhart (dealer), Tooting, London. XX 1161/8326 to J. Welch, London, SE7 (Lorry) 4-30. XX 1162 to Franklin & Co, Erith, Kent (Lorry) 9-30. XX 8327 to S. Moody, Gt. Ayton, Yorks (Lorry) 4-30; Fleming Bros, Redcar, Yorks 9-31; R. S. Braithwaite, Thornaby-on-Tees 1932; J. W. Allick, Middlesbrough 1932; H. Simpson, Middlesbrough 2-33; G. Taylor, Middlesbrough 8-33; Scrapped 9-33
YO 60 J. H. Howell, Narberth, Pembs, (Lorry) withdrawn 3-35
YF 6944/UW 2308-2311/GC 3170-3172/GN 184/GX 2602/JJ 9215/XB 9722/YL 5024 LPTB No. DE41/TD88-96/SM1/D196/M48
XU 8984 Prince
MH 3812 Stayfield, Salisbury, Wilts (Lorry)
YU 9391/UC 5468 Westminster Coaching Services. YU 9391 to Arlington (dealer), London, SW1, 7-31; Victoria Safety Coaches, London, E3, 5-34. UC 5468 to Lorry 10-30

WHITE STAR—see MONARCH

WILSON/OPTIMIST

XU 9110	Daimler Y	6070	OT22/20RO	Hickman	Red	29-9-24	New	29-7-27

Disposal
XU 9110 Public No. DA1

WILTON/WA

XT 5708	Dennis 4 ton	40125	OT26/22RO	Wilton	Red & White	30-5-24	New	2-9-27

Disposal
XT 5708 Public No. D59

WW

MH 2239	Dennis 4 ton	40258	OT26/22RO	Dodson	Red & White	1-12-24	New	1-1-28

Disposal
MH 2239 Metropolitan No. D49

X SERVICE

XM 9591	S. Squire A	A6224	OT24/22RO	Dodson	Khaki & Red	20-2-23	New	3-7-25
XR 8763	"	A6357	"	"	"	5-4-24	"	8-7-25

Disposal
XM 9591 Overground No. 33
XR 8763 Dauntless

INDEX OF OPERATORS

Figures in italics refer to photographs and are plate numbers

488

HAV-A-RIDE, HFB   17 254 267 268 378 393 448
HAVELOCK   316 317 378 379 393 448 *28*
HAWKINS R.   see RH
HAWK The   280 281 380 393 448
H & B, IMPERIAL   90 97 100 106-108 381 394 450 *18*
HENSLOWE   9 49 76-80 87 201 221 265 381 393 449
HFB   see HAV-A-RIDE
HH   311 314 393 449
HHC   324 325 378 382 449
HL, PIRATE The   92 93 370 395 463 *38*
HORSESHOE, EMPRESS, FFD   10 253-255 259-261 278 338 404 438

I & B   see TALLY HO!
IMPERIAL (Holiday, Bangs & Dengate)   see H & B
IMPERIAL (Priest Bros.)   279 280 394 396 404 451
IMPERIAL (A. E. Blane)   34 358-361 399 450 *69 70*
INDEPENDENT   81 85 86 183 188 451 *23*
INVICTA, BLUE BELL   336-338 381 391 394 404 418

JH   see TRINITY
JL   43-46 48 57 98 377 394 406 451 *37*
J. M. ROBERTS' MOTOR SERVICE   25 188 355 472
JOCKEY The   136 317 323 380 394 404 451
JS & SR   44 45 98 394 452

KATHLEEN   205 355 394 452
KBB   see EAGLE

LANCASTRIAN   188 253 262 263 394 452
LCOC   71 121-123 170 375 394 452
LEADER The   78 253 262 265 379 452
LEA RIG The   97 101 171 377 404 452
LEA VALLEY   317-319 380 394 404 453
LEGION   182 183 394 404 453
LEWIS   see ESSENTIAL
LGOC   see GENERAL
LIBERTY   59 90 109 110 379 394 453
LONDON   9 179 186 187 337 394 453
LONDON TRANSPORT   14 34-39 44 54-57 69 70 82 84 86 88 89 95 97 102 108
        116 119-121 165 166 168-170 182 184 185 194 203-205 235 244 258 262 264
        280 290 296 298-300 302 303 305 316 318 320 321 324 327 328 343-346
        348-361 407
LONSDALE   26 171 185 187 378 381 404 453
LOUMAX   see ROYAL HIGHLANDER
LOVELAND W.J.   172 293 294 296-298 404 454
LPOC   201 202 367 394 454

MAGNET   see FELIX
MAJESTIC   141 143 249-251 329 330 378 379 394 454
MARATHON   135 136 338 339 379 394 404 455
MARTIN   30 33 40 148 340-342 345-351 355 378 379 381 394 395 455 *61*
MATCHLESS The   see CLEVELAND
M & E, MORFAY, EMBASSY   280 288 320 381 454
MERCURY   see AGS
MERRY H. M.   239 308 381 382 394
METEOR   283 285 286 381 394 456
METROBUS   9
METROPOLITAN   1 27 155 269 284 298 318 319 323 329 407
MILLER   327 340 342 345 350 378 379 394 457 *75*
MONARCH   327 340 342 344 345 350 378 394 456 *75*
MONARCH   171 173 296 380-382 456
MORFAY   see M & E
MTT   see GRETNA

NATIONAL (Omnibus & Transport Co.)   210 311 312 357-359
NELSON   317 323-325 380 387 394 395 457
NEW ERA   173 174 178 370 379 386 395 457
NEWLANDS DISTRICT   70-76 88 89 377 382 458 *66*
NEW LONDON   9 185-187 395 458
NEWSTEAD, EMPIRE   253 254 258 259 367 379 381 438
NEW TIMES   16 68 171-173 188 252 296 297 395 458 *41*
NIL DESPERANDUM   see ASTORIA
NORTHERN   143-145 248 274 379 395 458
NULLI SECUNDUS   141 143-145 218 248 379 382 395 459